Professional C++

Nicholas A. Solter
Scott J. Kleper

Wiley Publishing, Inc.

Professional C++

Published by
Wiley Publishing, Inc.
10475 Crosspoint Boulevard
Indianapolis, IN 46256
www.wiley.com

Solter, Nicholas, 1977-
  Professional C++ / Nicholas Solter, Scott Kleper.
    p. cm.
  Includes index.
  ISBN 0-7645-7484-1 (paper/website)
  1. C++ (Computer program language) I. Kleper, Scott, 1977- II. Title.
  QA76.73.C153S665 2005
  005.13'3--dc22
                                            2004027959

Dedications

To Sonja, for her unconditional love and support, and to my son Kai, whose frequent interruptions reminded me what's important in life.

—Nicholas A. Solter

To Marni, whose unpredictable cuteness brightens every day.

—Scott J. Kleper

Acknowledgments

We owe a debt of gratitude to the many people who have made this book possible. We'd like to thank David Fugate of Waterside Productions for all of his advice and guidance, and Robert Elliot at Wiley for giving two unknown authors the opportunity to tell the C++ story in a new way. This book would not have turned out nearly as well as it did without the assistance of our development editor, Adaobi Obi Tulton. Thanks also to Kathryn Malm Bourgoine for her editorial assistance. The photo on the cover, which artfully minimized our nerdiness, was taken by Adam Tow.

We also want to thank all of the coworkers and teachers who have encouraged us to code the right way over the years. In particular, thanks to Mike Hanson, Maggie Johnson, Adam Nash, Nick Parlante, Bob Plummer, Eric Roberts, Mehran Sahami, Bill Walker, Dan Walkowski, Patrick Young, and Julie Zelenski. Our eternal thanks to Jerry Cain, who not only taught us C++ originally, but also served as technical editor, religiously analyzing the code in this book as though it were one of our final exams.

Thanks also to the following people, who reviewed one or more chapters: Rob Baesman, Aaron Bradley, Elaine Cheung, Marni Kleper, Toli Kuznets, Akshay Rangnekar, Eltefaat Shokri, Aletha Solter, Ken Solter, and Sonja Solter. Any remaining errors are, of course, our own. We'd like to thank our families for their patience and support.

Finally, we'd like to thank you, our readers, for trying out our approach to professional C++ development.

Author Bios

Nicholas A. Solter studied computer science at Stanford University, where he earned bachelor of science and master of science degrees, with a concentration in systems. While a student, he worked as a teaching assistant for several classes ranging from introductory computer science for nonmajors to an upper-division course on group projects and software engineering.

Now a software engineer at Sun Microsystems, Nick programs primarily in C and C++ in his work on high-availability software. His previous work experience includes several stints in the computer game industry. At Digital Media International, he was the lead programmer on the multimedia educational game, The Land Before Time Math Adventure. During an internship at Electronic Arts, he helped develop the Course Architect 2000 golf course–editing tool for the Tiger Woods PGA Tour 2000 game.

In addition to his industry experience, Nick taught C++ for one year as an adjunct professor of computer science at Fullerton College. When not working, Nick enjoys reading, playing basketball, taking care of his son Kai, and spending time with his family.

Scott J. Kleper began his programming career in elementary school, writing adventure games in BASIC for the Tandy TRS-80. As the resident Mac geek at his high school, Scott moved to higher-level languages and released several award-winning shareware applications.

Scott attended Stanford University, where he obtained bachelor of science and master of science degrees in computer science, with a concentration in human-computer interaction. While in college, Scott served as a teaching assistant for classes involving introductory programming, object-oriented design, data structures, GUI frameworks, group projects, and Internet programming.

Since graduating, Scott has served as a lead engineer on the founding teams of several companies and is currently a senior software engineer at Reactivity, Inc. Outside of work, Scott is a compulsive online shopper, an avid reader, and an awful guitarist.

Credits

Vice President and Executive Group Publisher
Richard Swadley

Vice President and Publisher
Joseph B. Wikert

Executive Editor
Robert Elliott

Editorial Manager
Kathryn Malm Bourgoine

Senior Production Editor
Geraldine Fahey

Senior Development Editor
Adaobi Obi Tulton

Production Editor
Felicia Robinson

Media Development Specialist
Richard Graves

Technical Editor
Jerry Cain

Text Design & Composition
Wiley Composition Services

Cover Photographer
Adam Tow

Contents

Part I: Introduction to Professional C++

Contents

Contents

Contents

Contents

Part III: Mastering Advanced Features of C++

Chapter 13: Effective Memory Management   349

Contents

Part IV: Ensuring Bug-Free Code

Chapter 16: Overloading C++ Operators   431

Contents

Contents

Contents

Part V: Using Libraries and Patterns

Chapter 22: Mastering STL Algorithms and Function Objects   619

Contents

Contents

Introduction

For many years, C++ has served as the de facto language for writing fast, powerful, and enterprise-class object-oriented programs. As popular as C++ has become, the language is surprisingly difficult to grasp in full. There are simple, but powerful, techniques that professional C++ programmers use that don't show up in traditional texts, and there are useful parts of C++ that remain a mystery even to experienced C++ programmers.

Too often, programming books focus on the syntax of the language instead of its real-world use. The typical C++ text introduces a major part of the language in each chapter, explaining the syntax and providing an example. *Professional C++* does not follow this pattern. Instead of giving you just the nuts and bolts of the language with little real-world context, this book will teach you how to use C++ in the real world. It will show you the little-known features that will make your life easier and the reusable coding patterns that separate novice programmers from professional programmers.

Who This Book Is For

Even if you have used the language for years, you might still be unfamiliar with the more advanced features of C++ or might not be using the full capabilities of the language. Perhaps you write competent C++ code, but would like to learn more about design in C++ and good programming style. Or maybe you're relatively new to C++, but want to learn the "right" way to program from the start. This book will bring your C++ skills to the professional level.

Because this book focuses on advancing from basic or intermediate knowledge of C++ to becoming a professional C++ programmer, it assumes some knowledge of the language. Chapter 1 covers the basics of C++ as a refresher, but it is not a substitute for actual training and use of the language. If you are just starting with C++, but you have significant experience in C, you should be able to pick up most of what you need from Chapter 1. In any case, you should have a solid foundation in programming fundamentals. You should know about loops, functions, and variables. You should know how to structure a program, and you should be familiar with fundamental techniques like recursion. You should have some knowledge of common data structures like hash tables and queues, and useful algorithms such as sorting and searching. You don't need to know about object-oriented programming just yet—that is covered in Chapter 3.

You will also need to be familiar with the compiler you will be using to develop your code. This book does not provide directions for using individual compilers. Refer to the documentation that came with your compiler for a refresher.

What This Book Covers

Professional C++ is an approach to C++ programming that will both increase the quality of your code and improve your programming efficiency. *Professional C++* teaches more than just the syntax and language features of C++. It also emphasizes programming methodologies, reusable design patterns, and good programming style. The *Professional C++* methodology incorporates the entire software development process—from designing and writing code to testing, debugging, and working in groups. This approach will enable you to master the C++ language and its idiosyncrasies, as well as take advantage of its powerful capabilities for large-scale software development.

Imagine someone who has learned all of the syntax of C++ without seeing a single example of its use. He knows just enough to be dangerous! Without examples, he might assume that all code should go in the `main()` function of the program or that all variables should be global—practices that are generally not considered hallmarks of good programming.

Professional C++ programmers understand the correct way to use the language, in addition to the syntax. They recognize the importance of good design, the theories of object-oriented programming, and the best ways to use existing libraries. They have also developed an arsenal of useful code and reusable ideas.

By reading this book, you will become a professional C++ programmer. You will expand your knowledge of C++ to cover lesser-known and often misunderstood language features. You will gain an appreciation for object-oriented design and acquire top-notch debugging skills. Perhaps most importantly, you will finish this book armed with a wealth of reusable ideas that can be applied to your actual daily work.

There are many good reasons to make the effort to be a professional C++ programmer, as opposed to a programmer who knows C++. Understanding the true workings of the language will improve the quality of your code. Learning about different programming methodologies and processes will help you to work better with your team. Discovering reusable libraries and common design patterns will improve your daily efficiency and help you stop reinventing the wheel. All of these lessons will make you a better programmer and a more valuable employee. While this book can't guarantee you a promotion, it certainly won't hurt!

How This Book Is Structured

This book is made up of six parts.

Part I, "Introduction to Professional C++ Design," begins with a crash course in C++ basics to ensure a foundation of C++ knowledge. Following the crash course, Part I explores C++ design methodologies. You will read about the importance of design, the object-oriented methodology, the use of libraries and patterns, the importance of code reuse, and the engineering practices being used by programming organizations today.

Part II, "Coding C++ the Professional Way," provides a technical tour of C++ from the Professional point-of-view. You will read about how to write *readable* C++ code, how to create reusable classes, and how to leverage important language features like inheritance and templates.

Part III, "Mastering Advanced Features of C++," demonstrates how you can get the most out of C++. This part of the book exposes the mysteries of C++ and describes how to use some of its more advanced features. You will read about the unusual and quirky parts of the language, the best ways to manage memory in C++, techniques for input and output, professional-grade error handling, advanced operator overloading, how to write efficient C++ code, and how to write cross-language and cross-platform code.

Part IV, "Ensuring Bug-Free Code," focuses on writing enterprise-quality software. You'll read about software testing concepts, such as unit testing and regression testing. You'll also read about techniques used to debug C++ programs.

Part V, "Using Libraries and Patterns," covers the use of libraries and patterns, which enable you to write better code with less work. You'll read about the standard library included with C++, including advanced topics such as extending the Standard Library. You'll also read about distributed objects, reusable C++ design techniques, and conceptual object-oriented design patterns.

The book concludes with a useful chapter-by-chapter guide to succeeding in a C++ technical interview. You will also a find a practical reference guide to the C++ Standard Library on the supplemental Web site for this book at www.wrox.com.

What You Need to Use This Book

All you need to use this book is any computer with a C++ compiler. While compilers often differ in their interpretations of the language, this book focuses on the parts of C++ that have been standardized. The programs in this book have been tested on Windows, Solaris, and Linux platforms.

Conventions

To help you get the most from the text and keep track of what's happening, we've used a number of conventions throughout the book.

> **Boxes like this one hold important, not-to-be forgotten information that is directly relevant to the surrounding text.**

Tips, hints, tricks, and asides to the current discussion are offset and placed in italics like this.

As for styles in the text:

❑   We *highlight* important words when we introduce them

❑   We show keyboard strokes like this: Ctrl+A

❑   We show filenames, URLs, and code within the text like so: monkey.cpp.

❑   We present code in two different ways:

```
In code examples we highlight new and important code with a gray background.
```

```
The gray highlighting is not used for code that's less important in the present
context or that has been shown before.
```

Source Code

As you work through the examples in this book, you may choose either to type in all the code manually or to use the source code files that accompany the book. All of the source code used in this book is available for download at www.wrox.com. Once at the site, simply locate the book's title (either by using the Search box or by using one of the title lists), and click the Download Code link on the book's detail page to obtain all the source code for the book.

> *Because many books have similar titles, you may find it easiest to search by ISBN; for this book the ISBN is 0-7645-7484-1.*

Once you download the code, just decompress it with your favorite compression tool. Alternately, you can go to the main Wrox code download page at www.wrox.com/dynamic/books/download.aspx to see the code available for this book and all other Wrox books.

Errata

We make every effort to ensure that there are no errors in the text or in the code. However, no one is perfect, and mistakes do occur. If you find an error in one of our books, such as a spelling mistake or faulty piece of code, we would be very grateful for your feedback. By sending in errata you may save another reader hours of frustration, and at the same time you will be helping us provide even higher-quality information.

To find the errata page for this book, go to www.wrox.com and locate the title using the Search box or one of the title lists. Then, on the book details page, click the Book Errata link. On this page you can view all errata that has been submitted for this book and posted by Wrox editors. A complete book list including links to each's book's errata is also available at www.wrox.com/misc-pages/booklist.shtml.

If you don't spot "your" error on the Book Errata page, go to www.wrox.com/contact/techsupport .shtml and complete the form there to send us the error you have found. We'll check the information and, if appropriate, post a message to the book's errata page and fix the problem in subsequent editions of the book.

p2p.wrox.com

For author and peer discussion, join the P2P forums at p2p.wrox.com. The forums are a Web-based system for you to post messages relating to Wrox books and related technologies and interact with other readers and technology users. The forums offer a subscription feature to e-mail you topics of interest of your choosing when new posts are made to the forums. Wrox authors, editors, other industry experts, and your fellow readers are present on these forums.

At http://p2p.wrox.com you will find a number of different forums that will help you not only as you read this book, but also as you develop your own applications. To join the forums, just follow these steps:

1. Go to p2p.wrox.com and click the Register link.

2. Read the terms of use and click Agree.

3. Complete the required information to join as well as any optional information you wish to provide and click Submit.

4. You will receive an e-mail with information describing how to verify your account and complete the joining process.

You can read messages in the forums without joining P2P but in order to post your own messages, you must join.

Once you join, you can post new messages and respond to messages other users post. You can read messages at any time on the Web. If you would like to have new messages from a particular forum e-mailed to you, click the Subscribe to this Forum icon by the forum name in the forum listing.

For more information about how to use the Wrox P2P, be sure to read the P2P FAQs for answers to questions about how the forum software works as well as many common questions specific to P2P and Wrox books. To read the FAQs, click the FAQ link on any P2P page.

1

A Crash Course
in C++

The goal of this chapter is to cover briefly the most important parts of C++ so that you have a base of knowledge before embarking on the rest of the book. This chapter is not a comprehensive lesson in the C++ programming language. The very basic points (like what a program is and the difference between = and ==) are not covered. The very esoteric points (remember what a `union` is? how about the `volatile` keyword?) are also omitted. Certain parts of the C language that are less relevant in C++ are also left out, as are parts of C++ that get in-depth coverage in later chapters.

This chapter aims to cover the parts of C++ that programmers encounter on a daily basis. If you've been away from C++ for a while and you've forgotten the syntax for a `for` loop, you'll find that in this chapter. If you're fairly new to C++ and you don't understand what a reference variable is, you'll learn that here as well.

If you already have significant experience with C++, skim this chapter to make sure that there aren't any fundamental parts of the language on which you need to brush up. If you're new to C++, take the time to read this chapter carefully and make sure that you understand the examples. If you need additional introductory information, consult the titles listed in Appendix B.

The Basics of C++

The C++ language is often viewed as a "better C" or a "superset of C." Many of the annoyances or rough edges of the C language were addressed when C++ was designed. Because C++ is based on C, much of the syntax you'll see in this section will look familiar to you if are an experienced C programmer. The two languages certainly have their differences, though. As evidence, *The C++ Programming Language* by C++ creator Bjarne Stroustrup weighs in at 911 pages, while Kernighan and Ritchie's *The C Programming Language* is a scant 274 pages. So if you're a C programmer, be on the lookout for new or unfamiliar syntax!

The Obligatory Hello, World

In all its glory, the following code is the simplest C++ program you're likely to encounter.

```
// helloworld.cpp

#include <iostream>

int main(int argc, char** argv)
{
    std::cout << "Hello, World!" << std::endl;

    return 0;
}
```

This code, as you might expect, prints the message Hello, World! on the screen. It is a simple program and unlikely to win any awards, but it does exhibit several important concepts about the format of a C++ program.

Comments

The first line of the program is a *comment*, a message that exists for the programmer only and is ignored by the compiler. In C++, there are two ways to delineate a comment. In the preceding example, two slashes indicate that whatever follows on that line is a comment.

```
// helloworld.cpp
```

The same behavior (this is to say, none) would be achieved by using a *C-style comment*, which is also valid in C++. C-style comments start with /* and end with */. In this fashion, C-style comments are capable of spanning multiple lines. The code below shows a C-style comment in action (or, more appropriately, inaction).

```
/* this is a multiline
 * C-style comment. The
 * compiler will ignore
 * it.
 */
```

Comments are covered in detail in Chapter 7.

Preprocessor Directives

Building a C++ program is a three-step process. First, the code is run through a *preprocessor*, which recognizes metainformation about the code. Next, the code is *compiled*, or translated into machine-readable object files. Finally, the individual object files are *linked* together into a single application. Directives that are aimed at the preprocessor start with the # character, as in the line #include <iostream> in the previous example. In this case, an include directive tells the preprocessor to take everything from the iostream header file and make it available to the current file. The most common use of header files is to declare functions that will be defined elsewhere. Remember, a *declaration* tells the compiler how a function is called. A *definition* contains the actual code for the function. The iostream header declares the input and output mechanisms provided by C++. If the program did not include it, it would be unable to perform its only task of outputting text.

> In C, included files usually end in .h, such as <stdio.h>. In C++, the suffix is omitted for standard library headers, such as <iostream>. Your favorite standard headers from C still exist in C++, but with new names. For example, you can access the functionality from <stdio.h> by including <cstdio>.

The table below shows some of the most common preprocessor directives.

Preprocessor Directive	Functionality	Common Uses
`#include [file]`	The specified file is inserted into the code at the location of the directive.	Almost always used to include header files so that code can make use of functionality that is defined elsewhere.
`#define [key] [value]`	Every occurrence of the specified key is replaced with the specified value.	Often used in C to define a constant value or a macro. C++ provides a better mechanism for constants. Macros are often dangerous so `#define` is rarely used in C++. See Chapter 12 for details.
`#ifdef [key]` `#ifndef [key]` `#endif`	Code within the `ifdef` ("if defined") or `ifndef` ("if not defined") blocks are conditionally included or omitted based on whether the specified value has been defined with `#define`.	Used most frequently to protect against circular includes. Each included file defines a value initially and surrounds the rest of its code with a `#ifndef` and `#endif` so that it won't be included multiple times.
`#pragma`	Varies from compiler to compiler. Often allows the programmer to display a warning or error if the directive is reached during preprocessing.	Because usage of `#pragma` is not standard across compilers, we advocate not using it.

The main function

`main()` is, of course, where the program starts. An `int` is returned from `main()`, indicating the result status of the program. `main()` takes two parameters: `argc` gives the number of arguments passed to the program, and `argv` contains those arguments. Note that the first argument is always the name of the program itself.

I/O Streams

If you're new to C++ and coming from a C background, you're probably wondering what `std::cout` is and what has been done with trusty old `printf()`. While `printf()` can still be used in C++, a much better input/output facility is provided by the streams library.

I/O streams are covered in depth in Chapter 14, but the basics of output are very simple. Think of an output stream as a laundry chute for data. Anything you toss into it will be output appropriately. `std::cout` is the chute corresponding to the user console, or *standard out*. There are other chutes, including `std::cerr`, which outputs to the error console. The << operator tosses data down the chute. In the preceding example, a quoted string of text is sent to standard out. Output streams allow multiple data of varying types to be sent down the stream sequentially on a single line of code. The following code outputs text, followed by a number, followed by more text.

```
std::cout << "There are " << 219 << " ways I love you." << std::endl;
```

`std::endl` represents an end of line character. When the output stream encounters `std::endl`, it will output everything that has been sent down the chute so far and move to the next line. An alternate way of representing the end of a line is by using the '\n' character. The \n character is an *escape character*, which refers to a new-line character. Escape characters can be used within any quoted string of text. The list below shows the most common escape characters.

- ❑ **\n** new line
- ❑ **\r** carriage return
- ❑ **\t** tab
- ❑ **** the backslash character
- ❑ **\"** quotation mark

Streams can also be used to accept input from the user. The simplest way to do this is to use the >> operator with an input stream. The `std::cin` input stream accepts keyboard input from the user. User input can be tricky because you can never know what kind of data the user will enter. See Chapter 14 for a full explanation of how to use input streams.

Namespaces

Namespaces address the problem of naming conflicts between different pieces of code. For example, you might be writing some code that has a function called `foo()`. One day, you decide to start using a third-party library, which also has a `foo()` function. The compiler has no way of knowing which version of `foo()` you are referring to within your code. You can't change the library's function name, and it would be a big pain to change your own.

Namespaces come to the rescue in such scenarios because you can define the context in which names are defined. To place code in a namespace, simply enclose it within a namespace block:

```
// namespaces.h

namespace mycode {
    void foo();
}
```

The implementation of a method or function can also be handled in a namespace:

```
// namespaces.cpp

#include <iostream>
#include "namespaces.h"

namespace mycode {

    void foo() {
        std::cout << "foo() called in the mycode namespace" << std::endl;
    }
}
```

By placing your version of `foo()` in the namespace "mycode," it is isolated from the `foo()` function provided by the third-party library. To call the namespace-enabled version of `foo()`, prepend the namespace onto the function name as follows.

```
mycode::foo();    // Calls the "foo" function in the "mycode" namespace
```

Any code that falls within a "mycode" namespace block can call other code within the same namespace without explicitly prepending the namespace. This implicit namespace is useful in making the code more precise and readable. You can also avoid prepending of namespaces with the `using` directive. This directive tells the compiler that the subsequent code is making use of names in the specified namespace. The namespace is thus implied for the code that follows:

```
// usingnamespaces.cpp

#include "namespaces.h"

using namespace mycode;

int main(int argc, char** argv)
{
    foo();  // Implies mycode::foo();
}
```

A single source file can contain multiple `using` directives, but beware of overusing this shortcut. In the extreme case, if you declare that you're using every namespace known to humanity, you're effectively eliminating namespaces entirely! Name conflicts will again result if you are using two namespaces that contain the same names. It is also important to know in which namespace your code is operating so that you don't end up accidentally calling the wrong version of a function.

You've seen the namespace syntax before — we used it in the Hello, World program. `cout` and `endl` are actually names defined in the `std` namespace. We could have rewritten Hello, World with the `using` directive as shown here:

```
// helloworld.cpp

#include <iostream>

using namespace std;

int main(int argc, char** argv)
{
    cout << "Hello, World!" << endl;

    return 0;
}
```

The `using` directive can also be used to refer to a particular item within a namespace. For example, if the only part of the `std` namespace that you intend to use is `cout`, you can refer to it as follows:

```
using std::cout;
```

Subsequent code can refer to `cout` without prepending the namespace, but other items in the `std` namespace will still need to be explicit:

```
using std::cout;
```

```
cout << "Hello, World!" << std::endl;
```

Variables

In C++, *variables* can be declared just about anywhere in your code and can be used anywhere in the current block below the line where they are declared. In practice, your engineering group should decide whether variables will be declared at the start of each function or on an as-needed basis. Variables can be declared without being given a value. These undeclared variables generally end up with a semirandom value based on whatever is in memory at the time and are the source of countless bugs. Variables in C++ can alternatively be assigned an initial value when they are declared. The code that follows shows both flavors of variable declaration, both using `int`s, which represent integer values.

```
// hellovariables.cpp

#include <iostream>

using namespace std;

int main(int argc, char** argv)
{
  int uninitializedInt;
  int initializedInt = 7;

  cout << uninitializedInt << " is a random value" << endl;
  cout << initializedInt << " was assigned an initial value" << endl;

  return (0);
}
```

When run, this code will output a random value from memory for the first line and the number 7 for the second. This code also shows how variables can be used with output streams.

The table that follows shows the most common variable types used in C++.

Type	Description	Usage
int	Positive and negative integers (range depends on compiler settings)	`int i = 7;`
short	Short integer (usually 2 bytes)	`short s = 13;`
long	Long integer (usually 4 bytes)	`long l = -7;`

unsigned int
unsigned short
unsigned long
	Limits the preceding types to values >= 0	`unsigned int i =2;`
		`unsigned short s = 23;`
		`unsigned long l = 5400;`

float double	Floating-point and double precision numbers	`float f = 7.2;` `double d = 7.2`
char	A single character	`char ch = 'm';`
bool	true or false (same as non-0 or 0)	`bool b = true;`

> C++ does not provide a basic string type. However, a standard implementation of a string is provided as part of the standard library as described later in this chapter and in Chapter 13.

Variables can be converted to other types by *casting* them. For example, an `int` can be cast to a `bool`. C++ provides three ways of explicitly changing the type of a variable. The first method is a holdover from C, but is still the most commonly used. The second method seems more natural at first but is rarely seen. The third method is the most verbose, but often considered the cleanest.

```
bool someBool = (bool)someInt;          // method 1

bool someBool = bool(someInt);          // method 2

bool someBool = static_cast<bool>(someInt);     // method 3
```

The result will be `false` if the integer was 0 and `true` otherwise. In some contexts, variables can be automatically cast, or *coerced*. For example, a `short` can be automatically converted into a `long` because a `long` represents the same type of data with additional precision.

```
long someLong = someShort;          // no explicit cast needed
```

When automatically casting variables, you need to be aware of the potential loss of data. For example, casting a `float` to an `int` throws away information (the fractional part of the number). Many compilers will issue a warning if you assign a `float` to an `int` without an explicit cast. If you are certain that the left-hand-side type is fully compatible with the right-hand side type, it's okay to cast implicitly.

Operators

What good is a variable if you don't have a way to change it? The table below shows the most common *operators* used in C++ and sample code that makes use of them. Note that operators in C++ can be *binary* (operate on two variables), *unary* (operate on a single variable), or even *ternary* (operate on three variables). There is only one ternary operator in C++ and it is covered in the next section, "Conditionals."

Operator	Description	Usage

=	Binary operator to assign the value on the right to the variable on the left.	`int ;`
		`i = 3;`
		`int j;`
		`j = i;`

!	Unary operator to negate the true/false (non-0/0) status of a variable.	`bool b = !true;` `bool b2 = !b;`

+	Binary operator for addition.	`int i = 3 + 2;`
		`int j = i + 5;`
		`int k = i + j;`

−
*
/
	Binary operators for subtraction, multiplication, and division.	`int i = 5-1;`
		`int j = 5*2;`
		`int k = j / i;`

%	Binary operator for remainder of a division operation. Also referred to as the *mod* operator.	`int remainder = 5 % 2;`
++	Unary operator to increment a variable by 1. If the operator occurs before the variable, the result of the expression is the unincremented value. If the operator occurs after the variable, the result of the expression is the new value.	`i++;` `++i;`
--	Unary operator to decrement a variable by 1.	`i--;` `--i;`
+=	Shorthand syntax for `i = i + j`	`i += j;`

-=
*=
/=
%=
	Shorthand syntax for
	`i = i - j;`
	`i = i * j;`
	`i = i / j;`
	`i = i % j;`
		`i -= j;`
		`i *= j;`
		`i /= j;`
		`i %= j;`

& &=	Takes the raw bits of one variable and performs a bitwise "and" with the other variable.	`i = j & k;` `j &= k;`
|	Takes the raw bits of one variable and performs a bitwise "or" with the other variable.	`i = j | k;` `j |= k;`

Operator	Description	Usage

<<
 >>
 <<=
 >>=
	Takes the raw bits of a variable and "shifts" each bit left (<<) or right (>>) the specified number of places.	`i = i << 1;`
		 `i = i >> 4;`
		 `i <<= 1;`
		 `i >>= 4;`

^ ^=	Performs a bitwise "exclusive or" operation on the two arguments.	`i = i ^ j;` `i ^= j;`

The following program shows the most common variable types and operators in action. If you're unsure about how variables and operators work, try to figure out what the output of this program will be, and then run it to confirm your answer.

```cpp
// typetest.cpp

#include <iostream>

using namespace std;

int main(int argc, char** argv)
{
    int someInteger = 256;
    short someShort;
    long someLong;
    float someFloat;
    double someDouble;

    someInteger++;
    someInteger *= 2;
    someShort = (short)someInteger;
    someLong = someShort * 10000;
    someFloat = someLong + 0.785;
    someDouble = (double)someFloat / 100000;

    cout << someDouble << endl;
}
```

The C++ compiler has a recipe for the order in which expressions are evaluated. If you have a complicated line of code with many operators, the order of execution may not be obvious. For that reason, it's probably better to break up a complicated statement into several smaller statements or explicitly group expressions using parentheses. For example, the following line of code is confusing unless you happen to know the C++ operator precedence table by heart:

```cpp
int i = 34 + 8 * 2 + 21 / 7 % 2;
```

Adding parentheses makes it clear which operations are happening first:

```cpp
int i = 34 + (8 * 2) + ( (21 / 7) % 2 );
```

Breaking up the statement into separate lines makes it even clearer:

```
int i = 8 * 2;
int j = 21 / 7;
j %= 2;
i = 34 + i + j;
```

For those of you playing along at home, all three approaches are equivalent and end up with i equal to 51. If you assumed that C++ evaluated expressions from left to right, your answer would have been 1. In fact, C++ evaluates /, *, and % first (in left to right order), followed by addition and subtraction, then bitwise operators. Parenthesis let you explicitly tell the compiler that a certain operation should be evaluated separately.

Types

In C++, you can use the basic types (int, bool, etc.) to build more complex types of your own design. Once you are an experienced C++ programmer, you will rarely use the following techniques, which are features brought in from C, because classes are far more powerful. Still, it is important to know about the two most common ways of building types so that you will recognize the syntax.

Enumerated Types

An integer really represents a value within a sequence — the sequence of numbers. *Enumerated types* let you define your own sequences so that you can declare variables with values in that sequence. For example, in a chess program, you *could* represent each piece as an int, with constants for the piece types, as shown in the following code. The integers representing the types are marked const to indicate that they can never change.

```
const int kPieceTypeKing = 0;
const int kPieceTypeQueen = 1;
const int kPieceTypeRook = 2;
const int kPieceTypePawn = 3;
//etc.

int myPiece = kPieceTypeKing;
```

This representation is fine, but it can become dangerous. Since the piece is just an int, what would happen if another programmer added code to increment the value of the piece? By adding one, a king becomes a queen, which really makes no sense. Worse still, someone could come in and give a piece a value of -1, which has no corresponding constant.

Enumerated types resolve these problems by tightly defining the range of values for a variable. The following code declares a new type, PieceT, that has four possible values, representing four of the chess pieces.

```
typedef enum { kPieceTypeKing, kPieceTypeQueen, kPieceTypeRook,
               kPieceTypePawn
             } PieceT;
```

Behind the scenes, an enumerated type is just an integer value. The real value of `kPieceTypeKing` is zero. However, by defining the possible values for variables of type `PieceT`, your compiler can give you a warning or error if you attempt to perform arithmetic on `PieceT` variables or treat them as integers. The following code, which declares a `PieceT` variable then attempts to use it as an integer, results in a warning on most compilers.

```
PieceT myPiece;

myPiece = 0;
```

Structs

Structs let you encapsulate one or more existing types into a new type. The classic example of a struct is a database record. If you are building a personnel system to keep track of employee information, you will need to store the first initial, last initial, middle initial, employee number, and salary for each employee. A struct that contains all of this information is shown in the header file that follows.

```
// employeestruct.h

typedef struct {
    char    firstInitial;
    char    middleInitial;
    char    lastInitial;
    int     employeeNumber;
    int     salary;
} EmployeeT;
```

A variable declared with type `EmployeeT` will have all of these *fields* built-in. The individual fields of a struct can be accessed by using the "." character. The example that follows creates and then outputs the record for an employee.

```
// structtest.cpp

#include <iostream>
#include "employeestruct.h"

using namespace std;

int main(int argc, char** argv)
{
    // Create and populate an employee.
    EmployeeT anEmployee;

    anEmployee.firstInitial = 'M';
    anEmployee.middleInitial = 'R';
    anEmployee.lastInitial = 'G';
    anEmployee.employeeNumber = 42;
    anEmployee.salary = 80000;

    // Output the values of an employee.
```

```
        cout << "Employee: " << anEmployee.firstInitial <<
                                anEmployee.middleInitial <<
                                anEmployee.lastInitial << endl;
    cout << "Number: " << anEmployee.employeeNumber << endl;
    cout << "Salary: $" << anEmployee.salary << endl;

    return 0;
}
```

Conditionals

Conditionals let you execute code based on whether or not something is true. There are three main types of conditionals in C++.

If/Else Statements

The most common conditional is the `if` statement, which can be accompanied by `else`. If the condition given inside the `if` statement is true, the line or block of code is executed. If not, execution continues to the `else` case if present, or to the code following the conditional. The following pseudocode shows a *cascading if statement*, a fancy way of saying that the `if` statement has an `else` statement that in turn has another `if` statement, and so on.

```
if (i > 4) {
    // Do something.
} else if (i > 2) {
    // Do something else.
} else {
    // Do something else.
}
```

The expression between the parentheses of an `if` statement must be a Boolean value or evaluate to a Boolean value. Conditional operators, described below, provide ways of evaluating expressions to result in a `true` or `false` Boolean value.

Switch Statements

The `switch` statement is an alternate syntax for performing actions based on the value of a variable. In `switch` statements, the variable must be compared to a constant, so the greater-than `if` statements above could not be converted to switch statements. Each constant value represents a "case". If the variable matches the case, the subsequent lines of code are executed until the `break` statement is reached. You can also provide a `default` case, which is matched if none of the other cases match.

`switch` statements are generally used when you want to do something based on the specific value of a variable, as opposed to some test on the variable. The following pseudocode shows a common use of the `switch` statement.

```
switch (menuItem) {
    case kOpenMenuItem:
        // Code to open a file
        break;
```

```
        case kSaveMenuItem:
            // Code to save a file
            break;
        default:
            // Code to give an error message
            break;
    }
```

If you omit the break statement, the code for the subsequent case will be executed whether or not it matches. This is sometimes useful, but more frequently a source of bugs.

The Ternary Operator

C++ has one operator that takes three arguments, known as the *ternary operator*. It is used as a shorthand conditional expression of the form "if [*something*] then [*perform action*], otherwise [*perform some other action*]". The ternary operator is represented by a ? and a :. The following code will output "yes" if the variable i is greater than 2, and "no" otherwise.

```
    std::cout << ((i > 2) ? "yes" : "no");
```

The advantage of the ternary operator is that it can occur within almost any context. In the preceding example, the ternary operator is used within code that performs output. A convenient way to remember how the syntax is used is to treat the question mark as though the statement that comes before it really is a question. For example, "Is i greater than 2? If so, the result is 'yes': if not, the result is 'no.'"

Unlike an if statement or a switch statement, the ternary operator doesn't execute code based on the result. Instead, it is used *within* code, as shown in the preceding example. In this way, it really is an operator (like + and –) as opposed to a true conditional, such as if and switch.

Conditional Operators

You have already seen a *conditional operator* without a formal definition. The > operator compares two values. The result is "true" if the value on the left is greater than the value on the right. All conditional operators follow this pattern — they all result in a true or false.

The table below shows other common conditional operators.

Operator	Description	Usage

<
<=
>
>=
	Determines if the left-hand side is less than, less than or equal to, greater than, or greater than or equal to the right-hand side.	`if (i <= 0) {`
		`    std::cout << "i is negative";`
		`}`

==	Determines if the left-hand side equals the right-hand side. Don't confuse this with the = (assignment) operator!	`if (i == 3) {`
		`    std::cout << "i is 3";`
		`}`

Table continued on following page

13

Operator	Description	Usage
!=	Not equals. The result of the statement is true if the left-hand side does *not* equal the right-hand side.	```if (i != 3) { std::cout << "i is not 3"; }```
!	Logical not. Negates the true/false status of a Boolean expression. This is a unary operator.	```if (!someBoolean) { std::cout << "someBoolean is false"; }```
&&	Logical and. The result is true if both parts of the expression are true.	```if (someBoolean && someOtherBoolean) { std::cout << "both are true"; }```
||	Logical or. The result is true if either part of the expression is true.	```if (someBoolean || someOtherBoolean) { std::cout << "at least one is true"; }```

C++ uses *short-circuit logic* when evaluating an expression. That means that once the final result is certain, the rest of the expression won't be evaluated. For example, if you are doing a logical or of several Boolean expressions as shown below, the result is known to be true as soon as one of them is found to be true. The rest won't even be checked.

```
bool result = bool1 || bool2 || (i > 7) || (27 / 13 % i + 1) < 2;
```

In the example above, if `bool1` is found to be `true`, the entire expression must be true, so the other parts aren't evaluated. In this way, the language saves your code from doing unnecessary work. It can, however, be a source of hard-to-find bugs if the later expressions in some way influence the state of the program (for example, by calling a separate function). The following code shows a statement using `&&` that will short-circuit after the second term because 1 always evaluates to `true`.

```
bool result = bool1 && 1 && (i > 7) && !done;
```

Loops

Computers are great for doing the same thing over and over. C++ provides three types of looping structures.

The While Loop

while loops let you perform a block of code repeatedly as long as an expression evaluates to `true`. For example, the following completely silly code will output "This is silly." five times.

```
int i = 0;
while (i < 5) {
    std::cout << "This is silly." << std::endl;
    i++;
}
```

The keyword break can be used within a loop to immediately get out of the loop and continue execution of the program. The keyword continue can be used to return to the top of the loop and reevaluate the while expression. Both are often considered poor style because they cause the execution of a program to jump around somewhat haphazardly.

The Do/While Loop

C++ also has a variation on the while loop called do/while. It works similarly to the while loop, except that the code to be executed comes first, and the conditional check for whether or not to continue happens at the end. In this way, you can use a loop when you want a block of code to always be executed at least once and possibly additional times based on some condition. The example that follows will output "This is silly." once even though the condition will end up being false.

```
int i = 100;
do {
    std::cout << "This is silly." << std::endl;
    i++;
} while (i < 5);
```

The For Loop

The *for loop* provides another syntax for looping. Any for loop can be converted to a while loop and vice versa. However, the for loop syntax is often more convenient because it looks at a loop in terms of a starting expression, an ending condition, and a statement to execute at the end of every iteration. In the following code, i is initialized to 0, the loop will continue as long as i is less than 5, and at the end of every iteration, i is incremented by 1. This code does the same thing as the while loop example, but to some programmers, it is easier to read because the starting value, ending condition, and per-iteration statement are all visible on one line.

```
for (int i = 0; i < 5; i++) {
    std::cout << "This is silly." << std::endl;
}
```

Arrays

Arrays hold a series of values, all of the same type, each of which can be accessed by its position in the array. In C++, you must provide the size of the array when the array is declared. You cannot give a variable as the size — it must be a constant value. The code that follows shows the declaration of an array of 10 integers followed by a for loop that initializes each integer to zero.

```
int myArray[10];

for (int i = 0; i < 10; i++) {
    myArray[i] = 0;
}
```

The preceding example shows a one-dimensional array, which you can think of as a line of integers, each with its own numbered compartment. C++ allows multidimensional arrays. You might think of a two-dimensional array as a checkerboard, where each location has a position along the x-axis and a position along the y-axis. Three-dimensional and higher arrays are harder to picture and are rarely used. The code below shows the syntax for allocating a two-dimensional array of characters for a Tic-Tac-Toe board and then putting an "o" in the center square.

```
char ticTacToeBoard[3][3];

ticTacToeBoard[1][1] = 'o';
```

Figure 1-1 shows a visual representation of this board with the position of each square.

ticTacToeBoard[0][0]	ticTacToeBoard[0][1]	ticTacToeBoard[0][2]
ticTacToeBoard[1][0]	ticTacToeBoard[1][1]	ticTacToeBoard[1][2]
ticTacToeBoard[2][0]	ticTacToeBoard[2][1]	ticTacToeBoard[2][2]

Figure 1-1

> In C++, the first element of an array is always at position 0, not position 1! The last position of the array is always the size of the array minus 1!

Functions

For programs of any significant size, placing all the code inside of main() is unmanageable. To make programs easy to understand, you need to break up, or *decompose*, code into concise functions.

In C++, you first declare a function to make it available for other code to use. If the function is used inside a particular file of code, you generally declare and define the function in the source file. If the function is for use by other modules or files, you generally put the declaration in a header file and the definition in a source file.

Function declarations are often called "function prototypes" or "signatures" to emphasize that they represent how the function can be accessed, but not the code behind it.

A function declaration is shown below. This example has a return type of void, indicating that the function does not provide a result to the caller. The caller must provide two arguments for the function to work with — an integer and a character.

```
void myFunction(int i, char c);
```

Without an actual definition to match this function declaration, the link stage of the compilation process will fail because code that makes use of the function myFunction() will be calling nonexistent code. The following definition simply prints the values of the two parameters.

```
void myFunction(int i, char c)
{
    std::cout << "the value of i is " << i << std::endl;
    std::cout << "the value of c is " << c << std::endl;
}
```

Elsewhere in the program, you can make calls to myFunction() and pass in constants or variables for the two parameters. Some sample function calls are shown here:

```
myFunction(8, 'a');
myFunction(someInt, 'b');
myFunction(5, someChar);
```

In C++, unlike C, a function that takes no parameters just has an empty parameter list. It is not necessary to use "void" to indicate that no parameters are taken. However, you should still use "void" to indicate when no value is returned.

C++ functions can also *return* a value to the caller. The following function declaration and definition is for a function that adds two numbers and returns the result.

```
int addNumbers(int number1, int number2);

int addNumbers(int number1, int number2)
{
    int result = number1 + number2;
    return (result);
}
```

Those Are the Basics

At this point, you have reviewed the basic essentials of C++ programming. If this section was a breeze, skim the next section to make sure that you're up to speed on the more advanced material. If you struggled with this section, you may want to obtain one of the fine introductory C++ books mentioned in Appendix D before continuing.

Diving Deeper into C++

Loops, variables, and conditionals are terrific building blocks, but there is much more to learn. The topics covered next include many features that are designed to help C++ programmers with their code as well as a few features that are often more confusing than helpful. If you are a C programmer with little C++ experience, you should read this section carefully.

Pointers and Dynamic Memory

Dynamic memory allows you to build programs with data that is not of fixed size at compile time. Most nontrivial programs make use of dynamic memory in some form.

The Stack and the Heap

Memory in your C++ application is divided into two parts — the *stack* and the *heap*. One way to visualize the stack is as a deck of cards. The current top card represents the current scope of the program, usually the function that is currently being executed. All variables declared inside the current function will take up memory in the top stack frame, the top card of the deck. If the current function, which we'll call foo() calls another function bar(), a new card is put on the deck so that bar() has its own *stack frame* to work with. Any parameters passed from foo() to bar() are copied from the foo() stack frame into the bar() stack frame. The mechanics of parameter passing and stack frames are covered in Chapter 13. Figure 1-2 shows what the stack might look like during the execution of a hypothetical function foo() that has declared two integer values.

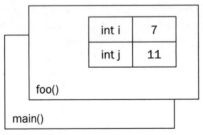

Figure 1-2

Stack frames are nice because they provide an isolated memory workspace for each function. If a variable is declared inside the foo() stack frame, calling the bar() function won't change it unless you specifically tell it to. Also, when the foo() function is done running, the stack frame goes away, and all of the variables declared within the function no longer take up memory.

The *heap* is an area of memory that is completely independent of the current function or stack frame. You can put variables on the heap if you want them to exist even when the function in which they were declared has completed. The heap is less structured than the stack. You can think of it as just a pile of bits. Your program can add new bits to the pile at any time or modify bits that are already in the pile.

Dynamically Allocated Arrays

Due to the way that the stack works, the compiler must be able to determine at compile time how big each stack frame will be. Since the stack frame size is predetermined, you cannot declare an array with a variable size. The following code will not compile because the arraySize is a variable, not a constant.

```
int arraySize = 8;
int myVariableSizedArray[arraySize];    // This won't compile!
```

Because the entire array must go on the stack, the compiler needs to know exactly what size it will be so variables aren't allowed. However, it is possible to specify the size of an array at run time by using *dynamic memory* and placing the array in the heap instead of the stack.

> Some C++ compilers actually do support the preceding declaration, but is not currently a part of the C++ specification. Most compilers offer a "strict" mode that will turn off these nonstandard extensions to the language.

To allocate an array dynamically, you first need to declare a *pointer*:

```
int* myVariableSizedArray;
```

The * after the int type indicates that the variable you are declaring refers to some integer memory in the heap. Think of the pointer as an arrow that points at the dynamically allocated heap memory. It does not yet point to anything specific because you haven't assigned it to anything; it is an uninitialized variable.

To initialize the pointer to new heap memory, you use the new command:

```
myVariableSizedArray = new int[arraySize];
```

This allocates memory for enough integers to satisfy the arraySize variable. Figure 1-3 shows what the stack and the heap both look like after this code is executed. As you can see, the pointer variable still resides on the stack, but the array that was dynamically created lives on the heap.

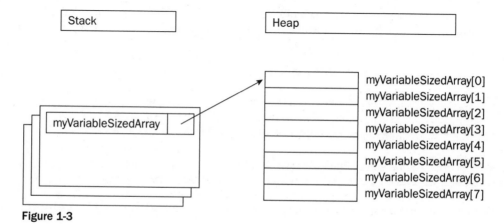

Figure 1-3

Now that the memory has been allocated, you can work with myVariableSizedArray as though it were a regular stack-based array:

```
myVariableSizedArray[3] = 2;
```

When your code is done with the array, it should remove it from the heap so that other variables can use the memory. In C++, you use the delete command to do this.

```
delete[] myVariableSizedArray;
```

The brackets after delete indicate that you are deleting an array.

> The C++ commands **new** and **delete** are similar to **malloc()** and **free()** from C. The syntax of **new** and **delete** is simpler because you don't need to know how many bytes of memory are required.

Working with Pointers

There are other reasons to use heap memory besides dynamically allocating arrays. You can put any variable in the heap by using a similar syntax:

```
int* myIntegerPointer = new int;
```

In this case, the pointer points to just a single integer value. To access this value, you need to *dereference* the pointer. Think of dereferencing as following the pointer's arrow to the actual value in the heap. To set the value of the newly allocated heap integer, you would use code like the following:

```
*myIntegerPointer = 8;
```

Notice that this is not the same as setting myIntegerPointer to the value 8. You are not changing the pointer, you are changing the memory that it points to. If you were to reassign the pointer value, it would point to the memory address 8, which is probably random garbage that will eventually make your program crash.

Pointers don't always point to heap memory. You can declare a pointer that points to a variable on the stack, even another pointer. To get a pointer to a variable, you use the & "address of" operator:

```
int i = 8;
int* myIntegerPointer = &i;   // Points to the variable with the value 8
```

C++ has a special syntax for dealing with pointers to structures. Technically, if you have a pointer to a structure, you can access its fields by first dereferencing it with *, then using the normal . syntax, as in the code that follows, which assumes the existence of a function called getEmployee().

```
EmployeeT* anEmployee = getEmployee();

cout << (*anEmployee).salary << endl;
```

This syntax is a little messy. The -> (arrow) operator lets you perform both the dereference and the field access in one step. The following code is equivalent to the preceding code, but is easier to read.

```
EmployeeT* anEmployee = getEmployee();
```

```
cout << anEmployee->salary << endl;
```

Normally, when you pass a variable into a function, you are *passing by value.* If a function takes an integer parameter, it is really a copy of the integer that you pass in. Pointers to stack variables are often used in C to allow functions to modify variables in other stack frames, essentially *passing by reference.* By dereferencing the pointer, the function can change the memory that represents the variable even though that variable isn't in the current stack frame. This is less common in C++ because C++ has a better mechanism, called *references,* which is covered below.

Strings in C++

There are three ways to work with strings of text in C++. There is the C-style, which represents strings as arrays of characters; the C++ style, which wraps that representation in an easier-to-use string type; and the general class of nonstandard approaches.

C-Style Strings

A string of text like "Hello, World" is internally represented as an array of characters with the character '\0' representing the end of the string. As you've seen, arrays and pointers are sometimes related. You could use either one to represent a string, as shown here:

```
char arrayString[20] = "Hello, World";
char* pointerString = "Hello, World";
```

For the `arrayString`, the compiler allocates space for 20 characters on the stack. The first 13 characters in the array are filled in with 'H', 'e', etc., ending with the character '\0'. The characters in positions 13 to 19 contain whatever random values happen to be in memory. The '\0' character tells code that uses the string where the content of the string ends. Even though the array has a length of 20, functions that process or output the string should ignore everything after the '\0' character.

For the `pointerString`, the compiler allocates enough memory on the stack just to hold the pointer. The pointer points to an area of memory that the compiler has set aside to hold the constant string "Hello, World." In this string, there is also a '\0' character after the 'd' character.

The C language provides a number of standard functions for working with strings, which are described in the <cstring> header file. The details of the standard library are not covered here because C++ provides a much cleaner and simpler way of working with strings.

C++ Strings

C-style strings are important to understand because they are still frequently used by C++ programmers. However, C++ includes a much more flexible string type. The string type, described by the <string> header file, acts just like a basic type. Just like I/O streams, the string type lives in the "std" package. The example that follows shows how strings can be used just like character arrays.

```
// stringtest.cpp

#include <string>
#include <iostream>

using namespace std;

int main(int argc, char** argv)
{
    string myString = "Hello, World";

    cout << "The value of myString is " << myString << endl;

    return 0;
}
```

The magic of C++ strings is that you can use standard operators to work with them. Instead of using a function, like strcat() in C to concatenate two strings, you can simply use +. If you've ever tried to use the == operator to compare two C-style strings, you've discovered that it doesn't work. == when used on C-style strings is actually comparing the address of the character arrays, not their contents. With C++ strings, == actually compares two strings. The example that follows shows some of the standard operators in use with C++ strings.

```
// stringtest2.cpp

#include <string>
#include <iostream>

using namespace std;

int main(int argc, char** argv)
{
    string str1 = "Hello";
    string str2 = "World";
    string str3 = str1 + " " + str2;

    cout << "str1 is " << str1 << endl;
    cout << "str2 is " << str2 << endl;
    cout << "str3 is " << str3 << endl;

    if (str3 == "Hello World") {
        cout << "str3 is what it should be." << endl;
    } else {
        cout << "Hmmm . . . str3 isn't what it should be." << endl;
    }

    return (0);
}
```

The preceding examples show just a few of the many features of C++ strings. Chapter 13 goes into further detail.

Nonstandard Strings

There are several reasons why many C++ programmers don't use C++-style strings. Some programmers simply aren't aware of the string type because it was not always part of the C++ specification. Others have discovered over the years that the C++ string doesn't provide the behavior they need and have developed their own string type. Perhaps the most common reason is that development frameworks and operating systems tend to have their own way of representing strings, such as the CString class in Microsoft's MFC. Often, this is for backward compatibility or legacy issues. When starting a project in C++, it is very important to decide ahead of time how your group will represent strings.

References

The pattern for most functions is that they take in zero or more parameters, do some calculations, and return a single result. Sometimes, however, that pattern is broken. You may be tempted to return two values or you may want the function to be able to change the value of one of the variables that were passed in.

In C, the primary way to accomplish such behavior is to pass in a pointer to the variable instead of the variable itself. The only problem with this approach is that it brings the messiness of pointer syntax into what is really a simple task. In C++, there is an explicit mechanism for "pass-by-reference." Attaching & to a type indicates that the variable is a reference. It is still used as though it was a normal variable, but behind the scenes, it is really a pointer to the original variable. Below are two implementations of an addOne() function. The first will have no effect on the variable that is passed in because it is passed by value. The second uses a reference and thus changes the original variable.

```
void addOne(int i)
{
    i++;  // Has no real effect because this is a copy of the original
}
```

```
void addOne(int& i)
{
    i++;  // Actually changes the original variable
}
```

The syntax for the call to the addOne() function with an integer reference is no different than if the function just took an integer.

```
int myInt = 7;
addOne(myInt);
```

Exceptions

C++ is a very flexible language, but not a particularly safe one. The compiler will let you write code that scribbles on random memory addresses or tries to divide by zero (computers don't deal well with infinity). One of the language features that attempts to add a degree of safety back to the language is *exceptions*.

An exception is an unexpected situation. For example, if you are writing a function that retrieves a Web page, several things could go wrong. The Internet host that contains the page might be down, the page might come back blank, or the connection could be lost. In many programming languages, you would handle this situation by returning a special value from the function, such as the NULL pointer. Exceptions provide a much better mechanism for dealing with problems.

Exceptions come with some new terminology. When a piece of code detects an exceptional situation, it *throws* an exception. Another piece of code *catches* the exception and takes appropriate action. The following example shows a function, divideNumbers(), that throws an exception if the caller passes in a denominator of zero.

```
#include <stdexcept>

double divideNumbers(double inNumerator, double inDenominator)
{
    if (inDenominator == 0) {
        throw std::exception();
    }

    return (inNumerator / inDenominator);
}
```

When the throw line is executed, the function will immediately end without returning a value. If the caller surrounds the function call with a try-catch block, as shown in the following code, it will receive the exception and be able to handle it.

```
#include <iostream>
#include <stdexcept>

int main(int argc, char** argv)
{
    try {
        std::cout << divideNumbers(2.5, 0.5) << std::endl;
        std::cout << divideNumbers(2.3, 0) << std::endl;
    } catch (std::exception exception) {
        std::cout << "An exception was caught!" << std::endl;
    }
}
```

The first call to divideNumbers() executes successfully, and the result is output to the user. The second call throws an exception. No value is returned, and the only output is the error message that is printed when the exception is caught. The output for the preceding block of code is:

```
5
An exception was caught!
```

Exceptions can get tricky in C++. To use exceptions properly, you need to understand what happens to the stack variables when an exception is thrown, and you have to be careful to properly catch and handle the necessary exceptions. The preceding example used the built-in std::exception exception type, but it is preferable to write your own exception types that are more specific to the error being thrown. Unlike the Java language, the C++ compiler doesn't force you to catch every exception that might occur.

If your code never catches any exceptions but an exception is thrown, it will be caught by the program itself, which will be terminated. These trickier aspects of exceptions are covered in much more detail in Chapter 15

The Many Uses of const

The keyword `const` can be used in several different ways in C++. All of its uses are related, but there are subtle differences. One of the authors has discovered that the subtleties of `const` make for excellent interview questions! In Chapter 12, you will learn all of the ways that `const` can be used. The following sections outline the most frequent uses.

Const Constants

If you assumed that the keyword `const` has something to do with constants, you have correctly uncovered one of its uses. In the C language, programmers often use the preprocessor #define mechanism to declare symbolic names for values that won't change during the execution of the program, such as the version number. In C++, programmers are encouraged to avoid #define in favor of using `const` to define constants. Defining a constant with `const` is just like defining a variable, except that the compiler guarantees that code cannot change the value.

```
const float kVersionNumber = "2.0";
const string kProductName = "Super Hyper Net Modulator";
```

Const to Protect Variables

In C++, you can cast a `non-const` variable to a `const` variable. Why would you want to do this? It offers some degree of protection from other code changing the variable. If you are calling a function that a coworker of yours is writing, and you want to ensure that the function doesn't change the value of a parameter you pass in, you can tell your coworker to have the function take a `const` parameter. If the function attempts to change the value of the parameter, it will not compile.

In the following code, a `char*` is automatically cast to a `const char*` in the call to `mysteryFunction()`. If the author of `mysteryFunction()` attempts to change the values within the character array, the code will not compile. There are actually ways around this restriction, but using them requires conscious effort. C++ only protects against accidentally changing `const` variables.

```
// consttest.cpp
void mysteryFunction(const char* myString);

int main(int argc, char** argv)
{
    char* myString = new char[2];
    myString[0] = 'a';
    myString[1] = '\0';

    mysteryFunction(myString);

    return (0);
}
```

Const References

You will often find code that uses `const` reference parameters. At first, that seems like a contradiction. Reference parameters allow you to change the value of a variable from within another context. `const` seems to prevent such changes.

The main value in `const` reference parameters is efficiency. When you pass a variable into a function, an entire copy is made. When you pass a reference, you are really just passing a pointer to the original so the computer doesn't need to make the copy. By passing a `const` reference, you get the best of both worlds — no copy is made but the original variable cannot be changed.

`const` references become more important when you are dealing with objects because they can be large and making copies of them can have unwanted side effects. Subtle issues like this are covered in Chapter 12.

C++ as an Object-Oriented Language

If you are a C programmer, you may have viewed the features covered so far in this chapter as convenient additions to the C language. As the name C++ implies, in many ways the language is just a "better C." There is one major point that this view overlooks. Unlike C, C++ is an object-oriented language.

Object-oriented programming (OOP) is a very different, arguably more natural, way to write code. If you are used to procedural languages such as C or Pascal, don't worry. Chapter 3 covers all the background information you need to know to shift your mindset to the object-oriented paradigm. If you already know the theory of OOP, the rest of this section will get you up to speed (or refresh your memory) on basic C++ object syntax.

Declaring a Class

A *class* defines the characteristics of an object. It is somewhat analogous to a struct except a class defines behaviors in addition to properties. In C++, classes are usually declared in a header file and fully defined in a corresponding source file.

A basic class definition for an airline ticket class is shown below. The class can calculate the price of the ticket based on the number of miles in the flight and whether or not the customer is a member of the "Elite Super Rewards Program." The definition begins by declaring the class name. Inside a set of curly braces, the *data members* (properties) of the class and its *methods* (behaviors) are declared. Each data member and method is associated with a particular access level: `public`, `protected`, or `private`. These labels can occur in any order and can be repeated.

```
// AirlineTicket.h

#include <string>

class AirlineTicket
{
    public:
        AirlineTicket();
```

```
        ~AirlineTicket();

        int     calculatePriceInDollars();

        std::string getPassengerName();
        void        setPassengerName(std::string inName);
        int         getNumberOfMiles();
        void        setNumberOfMiles(int inMiles);
        bool        getHasEliteSuperRewardsStatus();
        void        setHasEliteSuperRewardsStatus(bool inStatus);

    private:
        std::string mPassengerName;
        int         mNumberOfMiles;
        bool        fHasEliteSuperRewardsStatus;
};
```

The method that has the same name of the class with no return type is a *constructor*. It is automatically called when an object of the class is created. The method with a tilde (~) character followed by the class name is a *destructor*. It is automatically called when the object is destroyed.

The sample program that follows makes use of the class declared in the previous example. This example shows the creation of a stack-based `AirlineTicket` object as well as a heap-based object.

```
// AirlineTicketTest.cpp

#include <iostream>
#include "AirlineTicket.h"

using namespace std;

int main(int argc, char** argv)
{
    AirlineTicket myTicket;  // Stack-based AirlineTicket

    myTicket.setPassengerName("Sherman T. Socketwrench");
    myTicket.setNumberOfMiles(700);
    int cost = myTicket.calculatePriceInDollars();
    cout << "This ticket will cost $" << cost << endl;

    AirlineTicket* myTicket2; // Heap-based AirlineTicket

    myTicket2 = new AirlineTicket(); // Allocate a new object
    myTicket2->setPassengerName("Laudimore M. Hallidue");
    myTicket2->setNumberOfMiles(2000);
    myTicket2->setHasEliteSuperRewardsStatus(true);
    int cost2 = myTicket2->calculatePriceInDollars();
    cout << "This other ticket will cost $" << cost2 << endl;
    delete myTicket2;

    return 0;
}
```

The definitions of the AirlineTicket class methods are shown below.

```cpp
// AirlineTicket.cpp

#include <iostream>
#include "AirlineTicket.h"

using namespace std;

AirlineTicket::AirlineTicket()
{
    // Initialize data members
    fHasEliteSuperRewardsStatus = false;
    mPassengerName = "Unknown Passenger";
    mNumberOfMiles = 0;
}

AirlineTicket::~AirlineTicket()
{
    // Nothing much to do in terms of cleanup
}

int AirlineTicket::calculatePriceInDollars()
{
    if (getHasEliteSuperRewardsStatus()) {
        // Elite Super Rewards customers fly for free!
        return 0;
    }

    // The cost of the ticket is the number of miles times
    // 0.1. Real airlines probably have a more complicated formula!
    return static_cast<int>((getNumberOfMiles() * 0.1));
}

string AirlineTicket::getPassengerName()
{
    return mPassengerName;
}

void AirlineTicket::setPassengerName(string inName)
{
    mPassengerName = inName;
}

int AirlineTicket::getNumberOfMiles()
{
    return mNumberOfMiles;
}

void AirlineTicket::setNumberOfMiles(int inMiles)
{
    mNumberOfMiles = inMiles;
}
```

```
bool AirlineTicket::getHasEliteSuperRewardsStatus()
{
    return (fHasEliteSuperRewardsStatus);
}

void AirlineTicket::setHasEliteSuperRewardsStatus(bool inStatus)
{
    fHasEliteSuperRewardsStatus = inStatus;
}
```

The preceding example exposes you to the general syntax for creating and using classes. Of course, there is much more to learn. Chapters 8 and 9 go into more depth about the specific C++ mechanisms for defining classes.

Your First Useful C++ Program

The following program builds on the employee database example used earlier when discussing structs. This time, you will end up with a fully functional C++ program that uses many of the features discussed in this chapter. This real-world example includes the use of classes, exceptions, streams, arrays, namespaces, references, and other language features.

An Employee Records System

A program to manage a company's employee records needs to be flexible and have useful features. The feature set for this program includes the following.

❑   The ability to add an employee

❑   The ability to fire an employee

❑   The ability to promote an employee

❑   The ability to view all employees, past and present

❑   The ability to view all current employees

❑   The ability to view all former employees

The design for this program divides the code into three parts. The Employee class encapsulates the information describing a single employee. The Database class manages all the employees of the company. A separate UserInterface file provides the interactivity of the program.

The Employee Class

The Employee class maintains all the information about an employee. Its methods provide a way to query and change that information. Employees also know how to display themselves on the console. Methods also exist to adjust the employee's salary and employment status.

Employee.h

The `Employee.h` file declares the behavior of the `Employee` class. The sections of this file are described individually in the material that follows.

```
// Employee.h

#include <iostream>

namespace Records {
```

The first few lines of the file include a comment indicating the name of the file and the inclusion of the stream functionality.

This code also declares that the subsequent code, contained within the curly braces, will live in the Records namespace. Records is the namespace that is used throughout this program for application-specific code.

```
const int kDefaultStartingSalary = 30000;
```

This constant, representing the default starting salary for new employees, lives in the Records namespace. Other code that lives in Records can access this constant simply as `kDefaultStartingSalary`. Elsewhere, it must be referenced as `Records::kDefaultStartingSalary`.

```
class Employee
{
    public:

        Employee();

        void     promote(int inRaiseAmount = 1000);
        void     demote(int inDemeritAmount = 1000);
        void     hire();      // Hires or rehires the employee
        void     fire();      // Dismisses the employee
        void     display();   // Outputs employee info to the console

        // Accessors and setters
        void        setFirstName(std::string inFirstName);
        std::string getFirstName();
        void        setLastName(std::string inLastName);
        std::string getLastName();
        void        setEmployeeNumber(int inEmployeeNumber);
        int         getEmployeeNumber();
        void        setSalary(int inNewSalary);
        int         getSalary();
        bool        getIsHired();
```

The `Employee` class is declared, along with its public methods. The `promote()` and `demote()` methods both have integer parameters that are specified with a default value. In this way, other code can omit the integer parameters and the default will automatically be used.

A number of accessors provide mechanisms to change the information about an employee or query the current information about an employee:

```
        private:
            std::string    mFirstName;
            std::string    mLastName;
            int            mEmployeeNumber;
            int            mSalary;
            bool           fHired;
    };
}
```

Finally, the data members are declared as `private` so that other parts of the code cannot modify them directly. The accessors provide the only public way of modifying or querying these values.

Employee.cpp

The implementations for the `Employee` class methods are shown here:

```
// Employee.cpp

#include <iostream>

#include "Employee.h"

using namespace std;

namespace Records {

    Employee::Employee()
    {
        mFirstName = "";
        mLastName = "";
        mEmployeeNumber = -1;
        mSalary = kDefaultStartingSalary;
        fHired = false;
    }
```

The `Employee` constructor sets the initial values for the `Employee`'s data members. By default, new employees have no name, an employee number of -1, the default starting salary, and a status of not hired.

```
    void Employee::promote(int inRaiseAmount)
    {
        setSalary(getSalary() + inRaiseAmount);
    }

    void Employee::demote(int inDemeritAmount)
    {
        setSalary(getSalary() - inDemeritAmount);
    }
```

The `promote()` and `demote()` methods simply call the `setSalary()` method with a new value. Note that the default values for the integer parameters do not appear in the source file. They only need to exist in the header.

```
void Employee::hire()
{
    fHired = true;
}

void Employee::fire()
{
    fHired = false;
}
```

The `hire()` and `fire()` methods just set the `fHired` data member appropriately.

```
void Employee::display()
{
    cout << "Employee: " << getLastName() << ", " << getFirstName() << endl;
    cout << "-----------------------" << endl;
    cout << (fHired ? "Current Employee" : "Former Employee") << endl;
    cout << "Employee Number: " << getEmployeeNumber() << endl;
    cout << "Salary: $" << getSalary() << endl;
    cout << endl;
}
```

The `display()` method uses the console output stream to display information about the current employee. Because this code is part of the Employee class, it *could* access data members, such as `mSalary`, directly instead of using the `getSalary()` accessor. However, it is considered good style to make use of accessors when they exist, even within the class.

```
// Accessors and setters

void Employee::setFirstName(string inFirstName)
{
    mFirstName = inFirstName;
}

string Employee::getFirstName()
{
    return mFirstName;
}

void Employee::setLastName(string inLastName)
{
    mLastName = inLastName;
}

string Employee::getLastName()
{
    return mLastName;
}
```

```
        void Employee::setEmployeeNumber(int inEmployeeNumber)
        {
            mEmployeeNumber = inEmployeeNumber;
        }

        int Employee::getEmployeeNumber()
        {
            return mEmployeeNumber;
        }

        void Employee::setSalary(int inSalary)
        {
            mSalary = inSalary;
        }

        int Employee::getSalary()
        {
            return mSalary;
        }

        bool Employee::getIsHired()
        {
            return fHired;
        }

    }
```

A number of accessors and setters perform the simple task of getting and setting values. Even though these methods seem trivial, it's better to have trivial accessors and setters than to make your data members public. In the future, you may want to perform bounds checking in the setSalary() method, for example.

EmployeeTest.cpp

As you write individual classes, it is often useful to test them in isolation. The following code includes a main() function that performs some simple operations using the Employee class. Once you are confident that the Employee class works, you should remove or comment-out this file so that you don't attempt to compile your code with multiple main() functions.

```
// EmployeeTest.cpp

#include <iostream>

#include "Employee.h"

using namespace std;
using namespace Records;

int main (int argc, char** argv)
{
    cout << "Testing the Employee class." << endl;
```

```
        Employee emp;

        emp.setFirstName("Marni");
        emp.setLastName("Kleper");
        emp.setEmployeeNumber(71);
        emp.setSalary(50000);
        emp.promote();
        emp.promote(50);
        emp.hire();
        emp.display();

        return 0;
}
```

The Database Class

The `Database` class uses an array to store `Employee` objects. An integer called `mNextSlot` is used as a marker to keep track of the next unused array slot. This method for storing objects is probably not ideal because the array is of a fixed size. In Chapters 4 and 21, you will learn about data structures in the C++ standard library that you can use instead

Database.h

```
// Database.h

#include <iostream>
#include "Employee.h"

namespace Records {

    const int kMaxEmployees = 100;
    const int kFirstEmployeeNumber = 1000;
```

Two constants are associated with the database. The maximum number of employees is a constant because the records are kept in a fixed-size array. Because the database will also take care of automatically assigning an employee number to a new employee, a constant defines where the numbering begins.

```
    class Database
    {
        public:
            Database();
            ~Database();

            Employee& addEmployee(std::string inFirstName, std::string inLastName);
            Employee& getEmployee(int inEmployeeNumber);
            Employee& getEmployee(std::string inFirstName, std::string inLastName);
```

The database provides an easy way to add a new employee by providing a first and last name. For convenience, this method will return a reference to the new employee. External code can also get an employee reference by calling the `getEmployee()` method. Two versions of this method are declared. One allows retrieval by employee number. The other requires a first and last name.

```
        void        displayAll();
        void        displayCurrent();
        void        displayFormer();
```

Because the database is the central repository for all employee records, it has methods that will output all employees, the employees who are currently hired, and the employees who are no longer hired.

```
    protected:
        Employee    mEmployees[kMaxEmployees];
        int         mNextSlot;
        int         mNextEmployeeNumber;
    };
}
```

The `mEmployees` array is a fixed-size array that contains the `Employee` objects. When the database is created, this array will be filled with nameless employees, all with an employee number of -1. When the `addEmployee()` method is called, one of these blank employees will be populated with real data. The `mNextSlot` data member keeps track of which blank employee is next in line to be populated. The `mNextEmployeeNumber` data member keeps track of what employee number will be assigned to the new employee.

Database.cpp

```
// Database.cpp

#include <iostream>
#include <stdexcept>

#include "Database.h"

using namespace std;

namespace Records {

    Database::Database()
    {
        mNextSlot = 0;
        mNextEmployeeNumber = kFirstEmployeeNumber;
    }

    Database::~Database()
    {
    }
```

The Database constructor takes care of initializing the next slot and next employee number members to their starting values. `mNextSlot` is initialized to zero so that when the first employee is added, it will go into slot 0 of the `mEmployees` array.

```
Employee& Database::addEmployee(string inFirstName, string inLastName)
{
    if (mNextSlot >= kMaxEmployees) {
        cerr << "There is no more room to add the new employee!" << endl;
        throw exception();
    }

    Employee& theEmployee = mEmployees[mNextSlot++];
    theEmployee.setFirstName(inFirstName);
    theEmployee.setLastName(inLastName);
    theEmployee.setEmployeeNumber(mNextEmployeeNumber++);
    theEmployee.hire();

    return theEmployee;
}
```

The addEmployee() method fills in the next "blank" employee with actual information. An initial check makes sure that the mEmployees array is not full and throws an exception if it is. Note that after their use, the mNextSlot and mNextEmployeeNumber data members are incremented so that the next employee will get a new slot and number.

```
Employee& Database::getEmployee(int inEmployeeNumber)
{
    for (int i = 0; i < mNextSlot; i++) {
        if (mEmployees[i].getEmployeeNumber() == inEmployeeNumber) {
            return mEmployees[i];
        }
    }

    cerr << "No employee with employee number " << inEmployeeNumber << endl;
    throw exception();
}

Employee& Database::getEmployee(string inFirstName, string inLastName)
{
    for (int i = 0; i < mNextSlot; i++) {
        if (mEmployees[i].getFirstName() == inFirstName &&
            mEmployees[i].getLastName() == inLastName) {
            return mEmployees[i];
        }
    }

    cerr << "No match with name " << inFirstName << " " << inLastName << endl;
    throw exception();
}
```

Both versions of getEmployee() work in similar ways. The methods loop over all nonblank employees in the mEmployees array and check to see if each Employee is a match for the information passed to the method. If no match is found, an error is output and an exception is thrown.

```
    void Database::displayAll()
    {
        for (int i = 0; i < mNextSlot; i++) {
            mEmployees[i].display();
        }
    }

    void Database::displayCurrent()
    {
        for (int i = 0; i < mNextSlot; i++) {
            if (mEmployees[i].getIsHired()) {
                mEmployees[i].display();
            }
        }
    }

    void Database::displayFormer()
    {
        for (int i = 0; i < mNextSlot; i++) {
            if (!mEmployees[i].getIsHired()) {
                mEmployees[i].display();
            }
        }
    }
}
```

The display methods all use a similar algorithm. They loop through all nonblank employees and tell each employee to display itself to the console if the criterion for display matches.

DatabaseTest.cpp

A simple test for the basic functionality of the database follows:

```
    // DatabaseTest.cpp

#include <iostream>

#include "Database.h"

using namespace std;
using namespace Records;

int main(int argc, char** argv)
{
    Database myDB;

    Employee& emp1 = myDB.addEmployee("Greg", "Wallis");
    emp1.fire();

    Employee& emp2 = myDB.addEmployee("Scott", "Kleper");
    emp2.setSalary(100000);
```

```
        Employee& emp3 = myDB.addEmployee("Nick", "Solter");
        emp3.setSalary(10000);
        emp3.promote();

        cout << "all employees: " << endl;
        cout << endl;
        myDB.displayAll();

        cout << endl;
        cout << "current employees: " << endl;
        cout << endl;
        myDB.displayCurrent();

        cout << endl;
        cout << "former employees: " << endl;
        cout << endl;
        myDB.displayFormer();
}
```

The User Interface

The final part of the program is a menu-based user interface that makes it easy for users to work with the employee database.

UserInterface.cpp

```
// UserInterface.cpp

#include <iOstream>
#include <stdexcept>

#include "Database.h"

using namespace std;
using namespace Records;

int displayMenu();
void doHire(Database& inDB);
void doFire(Database& inDB);
void doPromote(Database& inDB);
void doDemote(Database& inDB);


int main(int argc, char** argv)
{
  Database employeeDB;
  bool done = false;

  while (!done) {
    int selection = displayMenu();

    switch (selection) {
```

```
    case 1:
      doHire(employeeDB);
      break;
    case 2:
      doFire(employeeDB);
      break;
    case 3:
      doPromote(employeeDB);
      break;
    case 4:
      employeeDB.displayAll();
      break;
    case 5:
      employeeDB.displayCurrent();
      break;
    case 6:
      employeeDB.displayFormer();
      break;
    case 0:
      done = true;
      break;
    default:
      cerr << "Unknown command." << endl;
    }
  }

  return 0;
}
```

The main() function is a loop that displays the menu, performs the selected action, then does it all again. For most actions, separate functions are defined. For simpler actions, like displaying employees, the actual code is put in the appropriate case.

```
int displayMenu()
{
    int selection;

    cout << endl;
    cout << "Employee Database" << endl;
    cout << "-----------------" << endl;
    cout << "1) Hire a new employee" << endl;
    cout << "2) Fire an employee" << endl;
    cout << "3) Promote an employee" << endl;
    cout << "4) List all employees" << endl;
    cout << "5) List all current employees" << endl;
    cout << "6) List all previous employees" << endl;
    cout << "0) Quit" << endl;
    cout << endl;
    cout << "---> ";

    cin >> selection;

    return selection;
}
```

Chapter 1

The `displayMenu()` function simply outputs the menu and gets input from the user. One important note is that this code assumes that the user will "play nice" and type a number when a number is requested. When you read about I/O in Chapter 14, you will learn how to protect against bad input

```cpp
void doHire(Database& inDB)
{
    string firstName;
    string lastName;

    cout << "First name? ";
    cin >> firstName;
    cout << "Last name? ";
    cin >> lastName;

    try {
        inDB.addEmployee(firstName, lastName);
    } catch (std::exception ex) {
        cerr << "Unable to add new employee!" << endl;
    }
}
```

The `doHire()` function simply gets the new employee's name from the user and tells the database to add the employee. It handles errors somewhat gracefully by outputting a message and continuing.

```cpp
void doFire(Database& inDB)
{
    int employeeNumber;

    cout << "Employee number? ";
    cin >> employeeNumber;

    try {
        Employee& emp = inDB.getEmployee(employeeNumber);
        emp.fire();
        cout << "Employee " << employeeNumber << " has been terminated." << endl;
    } catch (std::exception ex)
        cerr << "Unable to terminate employee!" << endl;
    }
}

void doPromote(Database& inDB)
{
    int employeeNumber;
    int raiseAmount;

    cout << "Employee number? ";
    cin >> employeeNumber;

    cout << "How much of a raise? ";
    cin >> raiseAmount;
```

```
    try {
        Employee& emp = inDB.getEmployee(employeeNumber);
        emp.promote(raiseAmount);
    } catch (std::exception ex) {
        cerr << "Unable to promote employee!" << endl;
    }
}
```

`doFire()` and `doPromote()` both ask the database for an employee by their employee number and then use the public methods of the `Employee` object to make changes.

Evaluating the Program

The preceding program covers a number of topics from the very simple to the more obscure. There are a number of ways that you could extend this program. For example, the user interface does not expose all of the functionality of the `Database` or `Employee` classes. You could modify the UI to include those features. You could also change the `Database` class to remove fired employees from the `mEmployees` array, potentially saving space.

If there are parts of this program that don't make sense, consult the preceding sections to review those topics. If something is still unclear, the best way to learn is to play with the code and try things out. For example, if you're not sure how to use the ternary operator, write a short `main()` function that tries it out.

Summary

Now that you know the fundamentals of C++, you are ready to become a professional C++ programmer. The next five chapters will introduce you to several important design concepts. By covering design at a high-level without getting into too much actual code, you will gain an appreciation for good program design without getting bogged down in the syntax.

When you start getting deeper into the C++ language later in the book, refer back to this chapter to brush up on parts of the language that you may need to review. Going back to some of the sample code in this chapter may be all you need to see to bring a forgotten concept back to the forefront of your mind.

2

Designing Professional C++ Programs

Before writing a single line of code in your application, you should design your program. What data structures will you use? What classes will you write? This plan is especially important when you program in groups. Imagine sitting down to write a program with no idea what your coworker, who is working on the same program, is planning! In this chapter, we'll teach you how to use the Professional C++ approach to C++ design.

Despite the importance of design, it is probably the most misunderstood and underused aspect of the software-engineering process. Too often programmers jump into applications without a clear plan: they design as they code. This approach inevitably leads to convoluted and overly complicated designs. It also makes the development, debugging, and maintenance tasks more difficult. Although counterintuitive, investing extra time at the beginning of a project to design it properly actually saves time over the life of the project.

Chapter 1 gave you a refresher course in the C++ syntax and feature set. Chapter 7 returns to the details of C++ syntax, but the remainder of Part I focuses on programming design.

After finishing this chapter, you will understand:

- ❏ The definition of programming design
- ❏ The importance of programming design
- ❏ The aspects of design that are unique to C++
- ❏ The two fundamental themes for effective C++ design: abstraction and reuse
- ❏ The specific components that make up a program design in C++

What Is Programming Design?

Your *program design*, or *software design*, is the specification of the architecture that you will implement to fulfill the functional and performance requirements of the program. Informally, the design is simply how you plan to write the program. You should generally write your design in the form of a design document. Although every company or project has its own variation of a desired design document format, most design documents share the same general layout, including two main parts:

1.   The gross subdivision of the program into subsystems, including interfaces and dependencies between the subsystems, data flow between the subsystems, input and output to and from each subsystem, and general threading model.

2.   The details of each subsystem, including subdivision into classes, class hierarchies, data structures, algorithms, specific threading model, and error-handling specifics.

The design documents usually include diagrams and tables showing subsystem interactions and class hierarchies. The exact format of the design document is less important than the process of thinking about your design.

> **The point of designing is to think about your program before you write it.**

You should generally complete your design before you begin coding. The design should provide a map of the program that any reasonable programmer could follow in order to implement the application. Of course, it is inevitable that the design will need to be modified once you begin coding and you encounter issues that you didn't think of earlier. Your software-engineering process should provide you the flexibility to make these changes. Chapter 6 describes various software-engineering process models in more detail.

The Importance of Programming Design

It's tempting to skip the design step, or to perform it only cursorily, in order to begin programming as soon as possible. There's nothing like seeing code compiling and running to give you the impression that you have made progress. It seems like a waste of time to formalize a design when you already know, more or less, how you want to structure your program. Besides, writing a design document just isn't as much fun as coding. If you wanted to write papers all day, you wouldn't be a computer programmer! As programmers ourselves, we understand this temptation to begin coding immediately, and have certainly succumbed to it on occasion. However, it invariably leads to problems on all but the simplest projects.

To understand the importance of programming design it helps to examine a real-world analogy. Imagine that you own a plot of land on which you want to build a house. When the builder shows up to begin construction you ask to see the blueprints. "What blueprints?" he responds, "I know what I'm doing. I don't need to plan every little detail ahead of time. Two-story house? No problem — I did a one-story house a few months ago — I'll just start with that model and work from there."

Suppose that you suspend your disbelief and allow the builder to proceed with the project. A few months later you notice that the plumbing appears to run outside the house instead of inside the walls.

When you query the builder about this anomaly he says, "Oh. Well, I forgot to leave space in the walls for the plumbing. I was so excited about this new drywall technology it just slipped my mind. But it works just as well outside, and functionality is the most important thing." You're starting to have your doubts about his approach, but, against your better judgment, you allow him to continue his work.

When you take your first tour of the completed building, you notice that the kitchen lacks a sink. The builder excuses himself by saying, "We were already 2/3 done with the kitchen by the time we realized there wasn't space for the sink. Instead of starting over we just added on a separate sink room next door. It works, right?"

> **Writing a program without a design is like building a house without blueprints.**

Do any of the builder's excuses sound familiar if you translate them to the software domain? Have you ever found yourself implementing an "ugly" solution to a problem like putting plumbing outside the house? For example, maybe you forgot to include locking in your queue data structure that is shared between multiple threads. By the time you realized the problem, it seemed easier to require all the threads to remember to do their own locking. Sure, it's ugly, but it works, you said. That is, until someone new joins the project who assumes that the locking is built into the data structure, fails to ensure mutual exclusion in her access to the shared data, and causes a race condition bug that takes three weeks to track down.

Formalizing a design before you code helps you determine how everything fits together. Just as blueprints for a house show how the rooms relate to each other and work together to fulfill the requirements of the house, the design for a program shows how the subsystems of the program relate to each other and work together to fulfill the software requirements. Without a design plan, you are likely to miss connections between subsystems, possibilities for reuse or shared information, and the simplest ways to accomplish tasks. Without the "big picture" that the design gives, you might become so bogged down in individual implementation details that you lose track of the overarching architecture and goals. Furthermore, the design provides written documentation to which all members of the project can refer.

If the above analogy still hasn't convinced you to design before you code, here is an example where jumping directly into coding fails to lead to an optimal design. Suppose that you want to write a chess program. Instead of designing the entire program before you begin programming, you decide to jump in with the easiest parts and move slowly to the more difficult parts. Following the object-oriented perspective introduced in Chapter 1 and covered in more detail in Chapter 3, you decide to model your chess pieces with classes. The pawn is the simplest chess piece, so you opt to start there. After considering the features and behaviors of a pawn, you write a class with the properties and behaviors shown in the following table:

Class	Properties	Behaviors
Pawn	Location on Board Color (Black or White) Captured	Move Check Move Legality Draw Promote (Upon Reaching Opposing Side of the Board)

Of course, you didn't actually write the table. You went straight to the implementation. Happy with that class you move on to the next easiest piece: the bishop. After considering its attributes and functionality, you write a class with the properties and behaviors shown in the next table:

Class	Properties	Behaviors
Bishop	Location on Board Color (Black or White) Captured	Move Check Move Legality Draw

Again, you didn't generate a table, because you jumped straight to the coding phase. However, at this point you begin to suspect that you might be doing something wrong. The bishop and the pawn look similar. In fact, their properties are identical and they share many behaviors. Although the implementations of the move behavior might differ between the pawn and the bishop, both pieces need the ability to move. If you had designed your program before jumping into coding, you would have realized that the various pieces are actually quite similar, and that you should find some way to write the common functionality only once. Chapter 3 explains the object-oriented design techniques for doing that.

Furthermore, several aspects of the chess pieces depend on other subsystems of your program. For example, you cannot accurately represent the location on the board in a chess piece class without knowing how you will model the board. On the other hand, perhaps you will design your program so that the board manages pieces in a way that doesn't require them to know their own locations. In either case, encoding the location in the piece classes before designing the board leads to problems. To take another example, how can you write a draw method for a piece without first deciding your program's user interface? Will it be graphical or text-based? What will the board look like? The problem is that subsystems of a program do not exist in isolation — they interrelate with other subsystems. Most of the design work determines and defines these relationships.

What's Different about C++ Design?

There are several aspects of the C++ language that make designing for C++ different, and more complicated, than designing for other languages.

❑   First, C++ has an immense feature set. It is almost a complete superset of the C language, plus classes and objects, operator overloading, exceptions, templates, and many other features. The sheer size of the language makes design a daunting task.

❑   Second, C++ is an object-oriented language. This means that your designs should include class hierarchies, class interfaces, and object interactions. This type of design is quite different from "traditional" design in C or other procedural languages. Chapter 3 focuses on object-oriented design in C++.

❑   Another unique aspect of C++ is its numerous facilities for designing generic and reusable code. In addition to basic classes and inheritance, you can use other language facilities such as templates and operator overloading for effective design. Chapter 5 covers design techniques for reusable code.

❑   Additionally, C++ provides a useful standard library, including a string class, I/O facilities, and many common data structures and algorithms. Also, many *design patterns*, or common ways to solve problems, are applicable to C++. Chapter 4 covers design with the standard library and introduces design patterns.

Because of all of these issues, tackling a design for a C++ program can be overwhelming. One of the authors has spent entire days scribbling design ideas on paper, crossing them out, writing more ideas, crossing those out, and repeating the process. Sometimes this process is helpful, and, at the end of those days (or weeks), leads to a clean, efficient design. Other times it can be frustrating, and leads nowhere. It's important to remain cognizant of whether or not you are making real progress. If you find that you are stuck, you can take one of the following actions:

❑   **Ask for help.** Consult a coworker, mentor, book, newsgroup, or Web page.

❑   **Work on something else for a while.** Come back to this design choice later.

❑   **Make a decision and move on.** Even if it's not an ideal solution, decide on something and try to work with it. An incorrect choice will soon become apparent. However, it may turn out to be an acceptable method. Perhaps there is no clean way to accomplish what you want to accomplish with this design. Sometimes you have to accept an "ugly" solution if it's the only realistic strategy to fulfill your requirements.

> **Keep in mind that good design is hard, and getting it right takes practice. Don't expect to become an expert overnight, and don't be surprised if you find it more difficult to master C++ design than C++ coding.**

Two Rules for C++ Design

There are two fundamental design rules in C++: *abstraction* and *reuse*. These guidelines are so important that they can be considered themes of this book. They come up repeatedly throughout the text, and throughout effective C++ program designs in all domains.

Abstraction

The principle of *abstraction* is easiest to understand through a real-world analogy. A television is a simple piece of technology that can be found in most homes. You are probably familiar with its features: you can turn it on and off, change the channel, adjust the volume, and add external components such as speakers, VCRs, and DVD players. However, can you explain how it works inside the black box? That is, do you know how it receives signals over the air or through a cable, translates them, and displays them on the screen? We certainly can't explain how a television works, yet we are quite capable of using it. That is because the television clearly separates its internal *implementation* from its external *interface*. We interact with the television through its interface: the power button, channel changer, and volume control. We don't know, nor do we care, how the television works; we don't care whether it uses a cathode ray tube or some sort of alien technology to generate the image on our screen. It doesn't matter because it doesn't affect the interface.

Chapter 2

Benefiting from Abstraction

The abstraction principle is similar in software. You can use code without knowing the underlying implementation. As a trivial example, your program can make a call to the `sqrt()` function declared in the header file `<cmath>` without knowing what algorithm the function actually uses to calculate the square root. In fact, the underlying implementation of the square root calculation could change between releases of the library, and as long as the interface stays the same, your function call will still work. The principle of abstraction extends to classes as well. As introduced in Chapter 1, you can use the `cout` object of class `ostream` to stream data to standard output like this:

```
cout << "This call will display this line of text\n";
```

In this line, you use the documented interface of the `cout` insertion operator with a character array. However, you don't need to understand how `cout` manages to display that text on the user's screen. You need only know the public interface. The underlying implementation of `cout` is free to change as long as the exposed behavior and interface remain the same. Chapter 14 covers I/O streams in more detail.

Incorporating Abstraction in Your Design

You should design functions and classes so that you and other programmers can use them without knowing, or relying on, the underlying implementations. To see the difference between a design that exposes the implementation and one that hides it behind an interface, consider the chess program again. You might want to implement the chess board with a two-dimensional array of pointers to ChessPiece objects. You could declare and use the board like this:

```
ChessPiece* chessBoard[10][10];
...
ChessBoard[0][0] = new Rook();
```

However, that approach fails to use the concept of abstraction. Every programmer who uses the chess board knows that it is implemented as a two-dimensional array. Changing that implementation to something else, such as an array of vectors, would be difficult, because you would need to change every use of the board in the entire program. There is no separation of interface from implementation.

A better approach is to model the chess board as a class. You could then expose an interface that hides the underlying implementation details. Here is an example of the ChessBoard class:

```
Class ChessBoard {
public:
    // This example omits constructors, destructors, and the assignment operator.
    void setPieceAt(ChessPiece* piece, int x, int y);
    ChessPiece& getPieceAt(int x, int y);
    bool isEmpty(int x, int y);
protected:
    // This example omits data members.
};
```

Note that this interface makes no commitment to any underlying implementation. The ChessBoard could easily be a two-dimensional array, but the interface does not require it. Changing the implementation does not require changing the interface. Furthermore, the implementation can provide additional functionality, such as bounds checking, that you were unable to do with the first approach.

Hopefully this example convinced you that abstraction is an important technique in C++ programming. Chapters 3 and 5 cover abstraction and object-oriented design in more detail, and Chapters 8 and 9 provide all the details about writing your own classes.

Reuse

The second fundamental rule of design in C++ is *reuse*. Again, it is helpful to examine a real-world analogy to understand this concept. Suppose that you give up your programming career in favor of work as a baker. On your first day of work, the head baker tells you to bake cookies. In order to fulfill his orders you find the recipe for chocolate-chip cookies in the cookbook, mix the ingredients, form cookies on the cookie sheet, and place the cookie sheet in the oven to bake. The head baker is pleased with the result.

Now, we are going to point out something so obvious that it will surprise you: you didn't build your own oven in which to bake the cookies. Nor did you churn your own butter, mill your own flour, or form your own chocolate chips. I can hear you think, "That goes without saying." That's true if you're a real cook, but what if you're a programmer writing a baking simulation game? In that case, you would think nothing of writing every component of the program, from the chocolate chips to the oven. However, you could save yourself time by looking around for code to reuse. Perhaps your office-mate wrote a cooking simulation game and has some nice oven code lying around. Maybe it doesn't do everything you need, but you might be able to modify it and add the necessary functionality.

To point out something else that you took for granted, you followed a recipe for the cookies instead of making up your own. Again, that goes without saying. However, in C++ programming, it does not go without saying. Although there are standard ways of approaching problems that arise over and over in C++, many programmers persist in reinventing these strategies in each design.

Reusing Code

The idea of using existing code is not new to you. You've been reusing code from the first day you printed something with `cout`. You didn't write the code to actually print your data to the screen. You used the existing `ostream` implementation to do the work.

Unfortunately, programmers generally do not take advantage of all the available code. Your designs should take into account existing code and reuse it when appropriate.

For example, suppose that you want to write an operating system scheduler. The scheduler is the component of the operating system that is responsible for deciding which processes run, and for how long. Since you want to implement priority-based scheduling, you realize that you need a priority queue on which to store the processes waiting to run. A naïve approach to this design is to write your own priority queue. However, you should know that the C++ *standard template library* (STL) provides a `priority_queue` container that you can use to store objects of any type. Thus, you should incorporate this `priority_queue` from the STL into your design for the scheduler instead of rewriting your own priority queue. Chapter 4 covers code reuse in more detail, and introduces the standard template library.

Writing Reusable Code

The design theme of reuse applies to code you write as well as to code that you use. You should design your programs so that you can reuse your classes, algorithms, and data structures. You and your coworkers should be able to utilize these components in both the current project and in future projects. In general, you should avoid designing overly specific code that is applicable only to the case at hand.

One language technique for writing general-purpose code in C++ is the template. The following example shows a templatized data structure. If you've never seen this syntax before, don't worry! Chapter 11 explains the syntax in depth.

Instead of writing a specific `ChessBoard` class that stores `ChessPieces`, as shown earlier, consider writing a generic `GameBoard` template that can be used for any type of two-dimensional board game such as chess or checkers. You would need only to change the class declaration so that it takes the piece to store as a template parameter instead of hard-coding it in the interface. The template could look something like this:

```
template <typename PieceType>
Class GameBoard {
public:
    // This example omits constructors, destructors, and the assignment operator.
    void setPieceAt(PieceType* piece, int x, int y);
    PieceType& getPieceAt(int x, int y);
    bool isEmpty(int x, int y);
protected:
    // This example omits data members.
};
```

With this simple change in the interface, you now have a generic game board class that you can use for any two-dimensional board game. Although the code change is simple, it is important to make these decisions in the design phase, so that you are able to implement the code effectively and efficiently.

Reusing Ideas

As the baker example illustrates, it would be ludicrous to reinvent recipes for every dish that you make. However, programmers often make an equivalent mistake in their designs. Instead of utilizing existing "recipes," or *patterns*, for designing programs, they reinvent these techniques every time they design a program. However, many *design patterns* appear in myriad different C++ applications. As a C++ programmer, you should familiarize yourself with these patterns so that you can incorporate them effectively into your program designs.

For example, you might want to design your chess program so that you have a single `ErrorLogger` object that serializes all errors from different components to a log file. When you try to design your `ErrorLogger` class, you realize that it would be disastrous to have more than one object instantiated from the `ErrorLogger` class in a single program. You also want to be able to access this `ErrorLogger` object from anywhere in your program. These requirements of a single, globally accessible, instance of a class arise frequently in C++ programs, and there is a standard strategy to implement them, called the *singleton*. Thus, a good design at this point would specify that you want to use the singleton pattern. Chapters 5, 25, and 26 cover design patterns and techniques in much more detail.

Designing a Chess Program

This section introduces a systematic approach to designing a C++ program in the context of a simple chess game application. In order to provide a complete example, some of the steps refer to concepts covered in later chapters. You should read this example now, in order to obtain an overview of the design process, but you might also consider rereading it after you have finished reading Part I.

Requirements

Before embarking on the design, it is important to possess clear requirements for the program's functionality and efficiency. Ideally, these requirements would be documented in the form of a requirements specification. The requirements for the chess program would contain the following types of specifications, although in more detail and number:

❑ The program will support the standard rules of chess.

❑ The program will support two human players. The program will not provide an artificially intelligent computer player.

❑ The program will provide a text-based interface:

    ❑ The program will render the game board and pieces in ASCII text.

    ❑ Players will express their moves by entering numbers representing locations on the chessboard.

The requirements ensure that you design your program so that it performs as its users expect. You would not want to waste time designing and coding a graphical user interface for the chess game if the users desire only a text-based interface. Conversely, it would be important to be aware of a user preference for a graphical user interface, so that you don't design the program in a way that precludes that possibility.

Design Steps

You should take a systematic approach to designing your program, working from the general to the specific. The following steps do not always apply to all programs, but they provide a general guideline. Your design should include diagrams and tables as appropriate. This example includes sample diagrams and tables. Feel free to follow the format used here or to invent your own.

There is no "right" way to draw software design diagrams as long as they are clear and meaningful to yourself and your colleagues.

Divide the Program into Subsystems

Your first step is to divide your program into its general functional subsystems and to specify the interfaces and interactions between the subsystems. At this point, you should not worry about specifics of data structures and algorithms, or even classes. You are trying only to obtain a general feel for the various parts of the program and their interactions. You can list the subsystems in a table that expresses the high-level behaviors or functionality of the subsystem, the interfaces exported from the subsystem to other subsystems, and the interfaces consumed, or used, by this subsystem on other subsystems. A table for the chess game subsystems could look like this:

Subsystem Name	Number	Functionality	Interfaces Exported	Interfaces Consumed
GamePlay	1	Starts game Controls game flow Controls drawing Declares winner Ends game	Game Over	Take Turn (on Player) Draw (on Chess Board)
Chess Board	1	Stores chess pieces Checks for draws and checkmates Draws itself	Get Piece At Set Piece At Draw	Game Over (on Game-Play) Draw (on Chess Piece)
Chess Piece	32	Draws itself Moves itself Checks for legal moves	Draw Move Check Move	Get Piece At (on Game Board) Set Piece At (on Game Board)
Player	2	Interacts with user: prompts user for move, obtains user's move Moves pieces	Take Turn	Get Piece At (on Game Board) Move (on Chess Piece) Check Move (on Chess Piece)
ErrorLogger	1	Writes error messages to log file	Log Error	None

As this table shows, the functional subsystems of this chess game include a GamePlay subsystem, a ChessBoard, 32 ChessPieces, two Players, and one ErrorLogger. However, that is not the only reasonable approach to a Chess Game. In software design, as in programming itself, there are often many different ways to accomplish the same goal. Not all ways are equal: some are certainly better than others. However, there are often several equally valid methods.

A good division into subsystems separates the program into its basic functional parts. For example, in the Chess Game, a Player is a subsystem distinct from the Board, Chess Pieces, or GamePlay. It wouldn't make sense to lump the players into the GamePlay object because they are logically separate subsystems. Other choices are not as obvious. Would it be reasonable to add a separate User Interface subsystem? If you intend to provide different kinds of user interfaces, or want to easily modify your interfaces later, you might want to separate out this aspect into a separate subsystem. To make these kinds of choices, you need to consider not only the current goals of the program, but future goals as well.

Because it is often difficult to visualize subsystem relationships from tables, it is usually helpful to show the subsystems of a program in a diagram, such as Figure 2-1. In this figure, arrows represent calls from one subsystem to another (for simplicity, the Error Logger subsystem is omitted).

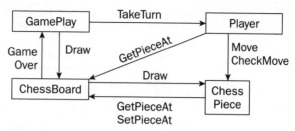

Figure 2-1

Choose Threading Models

In this step, you choose the number of threads in your program and specify their interactions. You should also specify any locking for shared data. If you are unfamiliar with multithreaded programs, or your platform does not support multithreading, then you should make your programs single-threaded. However, if your program has several distinct tasks, each of which should work in parallel, it might be a good candidate for multiple threads. For example, graphical user interface applications often have one thread performing the main application work and another thread waiting for the user to press buttons or select menu items.

Because threading is platform specific, this book does not cover multithreaded programming. See Chapter 18 for a discussion of platform considerations with C++.

The chess program needs only one thread to control the game flow.

Specify Class Hierarchies for Each Subsystem

In this step, you determine the class hierarchies that you intend to write in your program. The chess program needs only one class hierarchy, to represent the chess pieces. The hierarchy could work as shown in Figure 2-2.

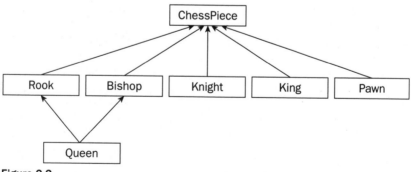

Figure 2-2

In this hierarchy, a generic `ChessPiece` class serves as the superclass. The hierarchy uses multiple inheritance to show that the queen piece is a combination of a rook and a bishop.

Chapter 3 explains the details of designing classes and class hierarchies.

Specify Classes, Data Structures, Algorithms, and Patterns for Each Subsystem

In this step, you consider a greater level of detail, and specify the particulars of each subsystem, including the specific classes that you write for each subsystem. It may well turn out that you model each subsystem itself as a class. This information can again be summarized in a table:

Subsystem	Classes	Data Structures	Algorithms	Patterns
GamePlay	GamePlay class	GamePlay object includes one ChessBoard and two Player objects	Simple loop giving each player a turn object to play	None
ChessBoard	ChessBoard class	ChessBoard object is a two-dimensional array of ChessPieces ChessBoard stores 32 ChessPieces	Checks for win or draw after each move	None
ChessPiece	ChessPiece abstract superclass Rook, Bishop, Knight, King, Pawn, and Queen classes	Each piece stores its location in the chess board	Piece checks for legal move by querying chess board for pieces at various locations	None
Player	One Player class	Two player objects (black and white)	Take Turn algorithm: loop to prompt user for move, check if move is legal, and move piece	None
ErrorLogger	One ErrorLogger class	A queue of messages to log	Buffers messages and writes them to a log file periodically	Singleton pattern to ensure only one ErrorLogger object

This section of the design document would normally present the actual interfaces for each class, but this example will forgo that level of detail.

Designing classes and choosing data structures, algorithms, and patterns can be tricky. You should always keep in mind the rules of abstraction and reuse discussed earlier in this chapter. For abstraction, the key is to consider the interface and the implementation separately. First, specify the interface from the perspective of the user. Decide *what* you want the component to do. Then decide *how* the component will do it by choosing data structures and algorithms. For reuse, familiarize yourself with standard data structures, algorithms, and patterns. Also, make sure you are aware of the standard library code in C++, as well as any proprietary code available in your workplace.

Chapters 3, 4, and 5 discuss these issues in more detail.

Specify Error Handling for Each Subsystem

In this design step, you delineate the error handling in each subsystem. The error handling should include both system errors, such as memory allocation failures, and user errors, such as invalid entries. You should specify whether each subsystem uses exceptions. You can again summarize this information in a table:

Subsystem	Handling System Errors	Handling User Errors
GamePlay	Logs an error with the ErrorLogger and terminates program if unable to allocate memory for ChessBoard or Players	Not applicable (no direct user interface)
ChessBoard	Logs an error with the ErrorLogger and throws an exception if unable to allocate memory for itself or for its ChessPieces	Not applicable (no direct user interface)
ChessPiece	Logs an error with the ErrorLogger and throws an exception if unable to allocate memory	Not applicable (no direct user interface)
Player	Logs an error with the ErrorLogger and throws an exception if unable to allocate memory.	Sanity-checks user move entry to ensure that it is not off the board; prompts user for another entry Checks each move legality before moving the piece; if illegal, prompts user for another move
ErrorLogger	Attempts to log an error and terminates the program if unable to allocate memory	Not applicable (no direct user interface)

The general rule for error handling is to handle everything. Think hard about all possible error conditions. If you forget one possibility, it will show up as a bug in your program! Don't treat anything as an "unexpected" error. Expect all possibilities: memory allocation failures, invalid user entries, disk failures, and network failures, to name a few. However, as the table for the chess game shows, you should handle user errors differently from internal errors. For example, a user entering an invalid move should not cause your chess program to terminate.

Chapter 15 discusses error handling in more depth.

Summary

In this chapter, you learned about the professional C++ approach to design. Hopefully, it convinced you that software design is an important first step in any programming project. You also learned about some of the aspects of C++ that make design difficult, including its object-oriented focus, its large feature set and standard library, and its facilities for writing generic code. With this information, you are better prepared to tackle C++ design.

This chapter introduced two design themes. The concept of abstraction, or separating interface from implementation, permeates this book and should be a guideline for all your design work. The notion of reuse, both of code and ideas, also arises frequently in real-world projects, and in this text. You should reuse existing code and ideas, and write your code to be as reusable as possible.

Now that you understand the importance of design and the basic design themes, you are ready for the rest of Part I. Chapter 3 describes strategies for utilizing the object-oriented aspects of C++ in your design. Chapters 4 and 5 present guidelines both for reusing preexisting code and ideas and for writing reusable code. Chapter 6 closes Part I with a discussion of software-engineering models and processes.

3

Designing with Objects

Now that you have developed an appreciation for good software design from Chapter 2, it's time to pair the notion of objects with the concept of good design. The difference between programmers who use objects in their code and those who truly grasp object-oriented programming comes down to the way their objects relate to each other and to the overall design of the program.

This chapter begins with the transition from procedural programming to object-oriented programming. Even if you've been using objects for years, you will want to read this chapter for some new ideas regarding how to think about objects. A discussion of the different kinds of relationships between objects includes pitfalls programmers often succumb to when building an object-oriented program. You will also learn how the principal of abstraction relates to objects.

An Object-Oriented View of the World

When making the transition from procedural (C-style) coding to object-oriented coding, the most important point to remember is that object-oriented programming (OOP) is just a different way to think about what's going on in your program. Too often, programmers get bogged down in the new syntax and jargon of OOP before they adequately understand what an object is. This chapter is light on code and heavy on concepts and ideas. For specifics on C++ object syntax, see Chapters 8, 9, and 10.

Am I Thinking Procedurally?

A procedural language, such as C, divides code into small pieces that each (ideally) accomplish a single task. Without procedures in C, all your code would be lumped together inside `main()`. Your code would be difficult to read, and your coworkers would be annoyed, to say the least.

The computer doesn't care if all your code is in `main()` or if it's split into bite-sized pieces with descriptive names and comments. Procedures are an abstraction that exists to help you, the programmer, as well as those who read and maintain your code. The concept is built around a fundamental question about your program — *What does this program do?* By answering that question in English, you are thinking procedurally. For example, you might begin designing a stock selection program by answering as follows: First, the program obtains stock quotes from the Internet. Then, it sorts this data by specific metrics. Next, it performs analysis on the sorted data. Finally, it outputs a list of buy and sell recommendations. When you start coding, you might directly turn this mental model into C functions: `retrieveQuotes()`, `sortQuotes()`, `analyzeQuotes()`, and `outputRecommendations()`.

> **Even though C refers to procedures as "functions," C is *not* a functional language. The term *functional* is very different from *procedural* and refers to languages like Lisp, which use an entirely different abstraction.**

The procedural approach tends to work well when your program follows a specific list of steps. In large modern applications, however, there is rarely a linear sequence of events. Often a user is able to perform any command at any time. Procedural thinking also says nothing about data representation. In the previous example, there was no discussion of what a stock quote actually is.

If the procedural mode of thought sounds like the way you approach a program, don't worry. Once you realize that OOP is simply an alternative, more flexible, way of thinking about software, it'll come naturally.

The Object-Oriented Philosophy

Unlike the procedural approach, which is based on the question *What does this program do?*, the object-oriented approach asks another question: *What real-world objects am I modeling?* OOP is based on the notion that you should divide your program not into tasks, but into models of physical objects. While this seems abstract at first, it becomes clearer when you consider physical objects in terms of their *classes*, *components*, *properties*, and *behaviors*.

Classes

A class helps distinguish an object from its definition. Consider the orange (the Florida Department of Citrus certainly hopes you will). There's a difference between talking about oranges in general as tasty fruit that grows on trees and talking about a specific orange, such as the one that's currently dripping juice on my keyboard.

When answering the question *What are oranges?* you are talking about the *class* of things known as oranges. All oranges are fruit. All oranges grow on trees. All oranges are some shade of orange. All oranges have some particular flavor. A class is simply the encapsulation of what defines a classification of objects.

When describing a specific orange, you are talking about an object. All objects belong to a particular class. Because the object on my desk is an orange, I know that it belongs to the orange class. Thus, I know that it is a fruit that grows on trees. I can further say that it is a medium shade of orange and ranks "mighty tasty" in flavor. An object is an *instance* of a class — a particular item with characteristics that distinguish it from other instances of the same class.

As a more concrete example, reconsider the stock selection application from above. In OOP, "stock quote" is a class because it defines the abstract notion of what makes up a quote. A specific quote, such as "current Microsoft stock quote," would be an object because it is a particular instance of the class.

From a C background, think of classes and objects as analogous to types and variables. In fact, in Chapter 8, you'll see the syntax for classes is similar to the syntax for C structs. Objects are syntactically very similar to C-style variables.

Components

If you consider a complex real-world object, such as an airplane, it should be fairly easy to see that it is made up of smaller components. There's the fuselage, the controls, the landing gear, the engines, and numerous other parts. The ability to think of objects in terms of their smaller components is essential to OOP, just as the breaking up of complicated tasks into smaller procedures is fundamental to procedural programming.

A component is essentially the same thing as a class, just smaller and more specific. A good object-oriented program might have an `Airplane` class, but this class would be huge if it fully described an airplane. Instead, the `Airplane` class deals with many smaller, more manageable, components. Each of these components might have further subcomponents. For example, the landing gear is a component of an airplane, and the wheel is a component of the landing gear.

Properties

Properties are what distinguish one object from another. Going back to the `Orange` class, recall that all oranges are defined as having some shade of orange and a particular flavor. These two characteristics are properties. All oranges have the same properties, just with different values. My orange has a "mighty tasty" flavor, but yours may have a "terribly unpleasant" flavor.

You can also think about properties on the class level. As recognized above, all oranges are fruit and grow on trees. These are properties of the fruit class whereas the specific shade of orange is determined by the particular fruit object. Class properties are shared by all members of a class, while object properties are present in all objects of the class, but with different values.

In the stock selection example, a stock quote has several object properties, including the name of the company, its ticker symbol, the current price, and other statistics.

Properties are the characteristics that describe an object. They answer the question *What makes this object different?*

Behaviors

Behaviors answer either of two questions: *What does this object do?* or *What can I do to this object?* In the case of an orange, it doesn't do a whole lot, but we can do things to it. One behavior is that it can be eaten. Like properties, you can think of behaviors on the class level or the object level. All oranges can pretty much be eaten in the same way. However, they might differ in some other behavior, such as being rolled down an incline, where the behavior of a perfectly round orange would differ from that of a more oblate one.

The stock selection example provides some more practical behaviors. As you recall, when thinking procedurally, we determined that our program needs to analyze stock quotes as one of its functions.

Thinking in OOP, we might decide that a stock quote object can analyze itself! Analysis becomes a behavior of the stock quote object.

In object-oriented programming, the bulk of functional code is moved out of procedures and into objects. By building objects that have certain behaviors and defining how they interact, OOP offers a much richer mechanism for attaching code to the data on which it operates.

Bringing It All Together

With these concepts, you could take another look at the stock selection program and redesign it in an object-oriented manner.

As discussed above, "stock quote" would be a fine class to start with. To obtain the list of quotes, the program needs the notion of a group of stock quotes, which is often called a *collection*. So a better design might be to have a class that represents a "collection of stock quotes," which is made up of smaller components that represent a single "stock quote."

Moving on to properties, the collection class would have at least one property — the actual list of quotes received. It might also have additional properties, such as the exact date and time of the most recent retrieval and the number of quotes obtained. As for behaviors, the "collection of stock quotes" would be able to talk to a server to get the quotes and provide a sorted list of quotes. This is the "retrieve quotes" behavior.

The stock quote class would have the properties discussed earlier — name, symbol, current price, and so on. Also as indicated above, it would have an analyze behavior. You might consider other behaviors, such as buying and selling the stock.

It is often useful to jot down diagrams showing the relationship between components. Figure 3-1 uses multiple lines to indicate that one "collection of stock quotes" contains many "stock quote" objects.

Figure 3-1

Another useful way of visualizing classes is to list properties and behaviors (as shown in the following two tables) when brainstorming the object representation of a program.

Class	Associated Components	Properties	Behaviors
Orange	None	Color Flavor	Eat Roll Toss

Class	Associated Components	Properties	Behaviors
Collection of Stock Quotes	Made up of individual Stock Quote objects	Individual Quotes Timestamp Number of Quotes	Retrieve quotes Sort quotes by various criteria
Stock Quote	None (yet)	Company Name Ticker Symbol Current Price and so on	Analyze Buy shares Sell shares

Living in a World of Objects

When programmers make the transition from thinking procedurally to the object-oriented paradigm, they often experience an epiphany about the combination of properties and behaviors into objects. Some programmers find themselves revisiting the design of programs they're working on and rewriting certain pieces as objects. Others might be tempted to throw all the code away and restart the project as a fully object-oriented application.

There are two major approaches to developing software with objects. To some people, objects simply represent a nice encapsulation of data and functionality. These programmers sprinkle objects throughout their programs to make the code more readable and easier to maintain. Programmers taking this approach slice out isolated pieces of code and replace them with objects like a surgeon implanting a pacemaker. There is nothing inherently wrong with this approach. These people see objects as a tool that is beneficial in many situations. Certain parts of a program just "feel like an object," like the stock quote. These are the parts that can be isolated and described in real-world terms.

Other programmers adopt the OOP paradigm fully and turn everything into an object. In their minds, some objects correspond to real-world things, such as an orange or a stock quote, while others encapsulate more abstract concepts, such as a sorter or an undo object. The ideal approach is probably somewhere in between these extremes. Your first object-oriented program may really have been a traditional procedural program with a few objects sprinkled in. Or perhaps you went whole hog and made everything an object, from a class representing an int to a class representing the main application. Over time, you will find a happy medium.

Overobjectification

There is often a fine line between designing a creative object-oriented system and annoying everybody else on your team by turning every little thing into an object. As Freud used to say, sometimes a variable is just a variable. Okay, that's a paraphrase of what he said.

Perhaps you're designing the next bestselling Tic-Tac-Toe game. You're going all-out OOP on this one, so you sit down with a cup of coffee and a notepad to sketch out your classes and objects. In games like this, there's often an object that oversees game play and is able to detect the winner. To represent the game board, you might envision a Grid object that will keep track of the markers and their locations. In fact, a component of the grid could be the Piece object that represents an X or an O.

Wait, back up! This design proposes to have a class that represents an X or an O. That is perhaps object overkill. After all, can't a `char` represent an X or an O just as well? Better yet, why can't the `Grid` just use a two-dimensional array of an enumerated type? Does a `Piece` object just complicate the code? Take a look at the table below representing the proposed piece class:

Class	Associated Components	Properties	Behaviors
Piece	None	X or O	None

The table is a bit sparse, strongly hinting that what we have here may be too granular to be a full-fledged object.

On the other hand, a forward-thinking programmer might argue that while `Piece` is a pretty meager class as it currently stands, making it into an object allows future expansion without any real penalty. Perhaps down the road, this will be a graphical application and it might be useful to have the `Piece` class support drawing behavior. Additional properties could be the color of the `Piece` or whether the `Piece` was the most recently moved.

Obviously, there is no right answer. The important point is that these are issues that you should consider when designing your application. Remember that objects exist to help programmers manage their code. If objects are being used for no reason other than to make the code "more object-oriented," something is wrong.

Overly General Objects

Perhaps a worse annoyance than objects that shouldn't be objects is objects that are too general. All OOP students start with examples like "orange" — things that are objects, no question about it. In real life coding, objects can get pretty abstract. Many OOP programs have an "application object," despite the fact that an application isn't really something you can envision in the real world. Yet it may be useful to represent the application as an object because the application itself has certain properties and behaviors.

An overly general object is an object that doesn't represent a particular thing at all. The programmer may be attempting to make an object that is flexible or reusable, but ends up with one that is confusing. For example, imagine a program that organizes and displays media. It can catalog your photos, organize your digital music collection, and serve as a personal journal. The overly general approach is to think of all these things as "media" objects and build a single class that can accommodate all of the formats. It might have a property called "data" that contains the raw bits of the image, song, or journal entry, depending on the type of media. It might have a behavior called "perform" that appropriately draws the image, plays the song, or brings up the journal entry for editing.

The clues that this class is too general are in the names of the properties and behaviors. The word "data" has little meaning by itself — we had to use a general term because this class has been overextended to three very different uses. Similarly, "perform" will do very different things in the three different cases. Finally, this design is too general because "media" isn't a particular object. Not in the user interface, not in real life, and not even in the programmer's mind. A major clue that a class is too general is when many ideas in the programmers mind all unite as a single object, as shown in Figure 3-2.

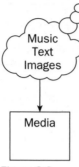

Figure 3-2

Object Relationships

As a programmer, you will certainly encounter cases where different classes have characteristics in common, or at least seem somehow related to each other. For example, although creating a "media" object to represent images, music, and text in a digital catalog program is too general, these objects do share characteristics. You may want all of them to keep track of the date and time that they were last modified, or you might want them all to support a delete behavior.

Object-oriented languages provide a number of mechanisms for dealing with such relationships between objects. The tricky part is to understand what the relationship actually is. There are two main types of object relationships — a *has-a* relationship and an *is-a* relationship.

The Has-A Relationship

Objects engaged in a has-a, or *aggregation,* relationship follow the pattern A has a B, or A contains a B. In this type of relationship, you can envision one object as part of another. Components, as defined earlier, generally represent a has-a relationship because they describe objects that are made up of other objects.

A real-world example of this might be the relationship between a zoo and a monkey. You could say that a zoo has a monkey or a zoo contains a monkey. A simulation of a zoo in code would have a zoo object, which has a monkey component.

Often, thinking about user interface scenarios is helpful in understanding object relationships. This is so because even though not all UIs are implemented in OOP (though these days, most are), the visual elements on the screen translate well into objects. One UI analogy for a has-a relationship is a window that contains a button. The button and the window are clearly two separate objects but they are obviously related in some way. Since the button is inside the window, we say that the window has a button.

Figure 3-3 shows various real-world and user interface has-a relationships.

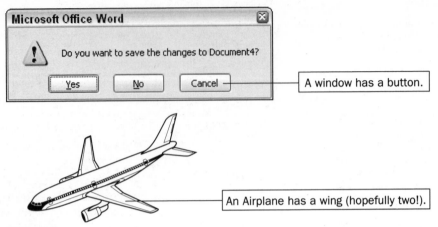

Figure 3-3

The Is-A Relationship (Inheritance)

The is-a relationship is such a fundamental concept of object-oriented programming that it has many names, including *subclassing, extending,* and *inheriting*. Classes model the fact that the real world contains objects with properties and behaviors. Inheritance models the fact that these objects tend to be organized in hierarchies. These hierarchies indicate is-a relationships.

Fundamentally, inheritance follows the pattern A is a B or A is really quite a bit like B — it can get tricky. To stick with the simple case, revisit the zoo, but assume that there are other animals besides monkeys. That statement alone has already constructed the relationship — a monkey is an animal. Similarly, a giraffe is an animal, a kangaroo is an animal, and a penguin is an animal. So what? Well, the magic of inheritance comes when you realize that monkeys, giraffes, kangaroos, and penguins have certain things in common. These commonalities are characteristics of animals in general.

What this means for the programmer is that you can define an `Animal` class that encapsulates all of the properties (size, location, diet, etc.) and behaviors (move, eat, sleep) that pertain to every animal. The specific animals, such as monkeys, become subclasses of `Animal` because a monkey contains all the characteristics of an animal (remember, a monkey is an animal plus some additional characteristics that make it distinct. Figure 3-4 shows an inheritance diagram for animals. The arrows indicate the direction of the is-a relationship.

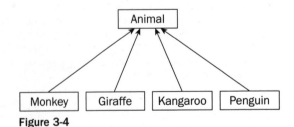

Figure 3-4

Just as monkeys and giraffes are different types of animals, a user interface often has different types of buttons. A checkbox, for example, is a button. Assuming that a button is simply a UI element that can be clicked and performs an action, a Checkbox extends the Button class by adding state — whether the box is checked or unchecked.

When relating classes in an is-a relationship, one goal is to factor common functionality into the *superclass*, the class that other classes extend. If you find that all of your subclasses have code that is similar or exactly the same consider how you could move some or all of the code into the superclass. That way, any changes that need to be made only happen in one place and future subclasses get the shared functionality "for free."

Inheritance Techniques

The preceding examples cover a few of the techniques used in inheritance without formalizing them. When subclassing, there are several ways tthat he programmer can distinguish an object from its *parent object* or *superclass*. A subclass may use one or more of these techniques and they are recognized by completing the sentence *A is a B that* . . . .

Adding Functionality

A subclass can augment its parent by adding additional functionality. For example, a monkey is an animal that can swing from trees. In addition to having all of the behaviors of Animal, the Monkey class also has a swing from trees behavior.

Replacing Functionality

A subclass can replace or *override* a behavior of its parent entirely. For example, most animals move by walking, so you might give the Animal class a move behavior that simulates walking. If that's the case, a kangaroo is an animal that moves by hopping instead of walking. All the other properties and behaviors of the Animal superclass still apply, but the Kangaroo subclass simply changes the way that the move behavior works. Of course, if you find yourself replacing *all* of the functionality of your superclass, it may be an indication that subclassing was not the correct thing to do after all.

Adding Properties

A subclass can also add new properties to the ones that were inherited from the superclass. A penguin has all the properties of an animal but also has a beak size property.

Replacing Properties

C++ provides a way of overriding properties similar to the way you can override behaviors. However, doing so is rarely appropriate. It's important not to get the notion of replacing a property confused with the notion of subclasses having different values for properties. For example, all animals have a diet property that indicates what they eat. Monkeys eat bananas and penguins eat fish, but neither of these is replacing the diet property — they simply differ in the value assigned to the property.

Polymorphism versus Code Reuse

Polymorphism is the notion that objects that adhere to a standard set of properties and behaviors can be used interchangeably. A class definition is like a contract between objects and the code that interacts with them. By definition, any monkey object must support the properties and behaviors of the monkey class.

This notion extends to superclasses as well. Since all monkeys are animals, all Monkey objects support the properties and behaviors of the Animal class as well.

Polymorphism is a beautiful part of object-oriented programming because it truly takes advantage of what inheritance offers. In a zoo simulation, we could programmatically loop through all of the animals in the zoo and have each animal move once. Since all animals are members of the Animal class, they all know how to move. Some of the animals have overridden the move behavior, but that's the best part — our code simply tells each animal to move without knowing or caring what type of animal it is. Each one moves whichever way it knows how.

There is another reason to subclass besides polymorphism. Often, it's just a matter of leveraging existing code. For example, if you need a class that plays music with an echo effect, and your coworker has already written one that plays music without any effects, you might be able to extend the existing class and add in the new functionality. The is-a relationship still applies (an echo music player is a music player that adds an echo effect), but you didn't intend for these classes to be used interchangeably. What you end up with are two separate classes, used in completely different parts of the programs (or maybe even in different programs entirely) that happen to be related only to avoid reinventing the wheel.

The Fine Line between Has-A and Is-A

In the real world, it's pretty easy to classify has-a and is-a relationships between objects. Nobody would claim that an orange has a fruit — an orange *is a* fruit. In code, things sometimes aren't so clear.

Consider a hypothetical class that represents a hash table. A hash table is a data structure that efficiently maps a key to a value. For example, an insurance company could use a Hashtable class to map member IDs to names so that given an ID, it's easy to find the corresponding member name. The member ID is the *key* and the member name is the *value*.

In a standard hash table implementation, every key has a single value. If the ID 14534 maps to the member name "Kleper, Scott", it cannot also map to the member name "Kleper, Marni". In most implementations, if you tried to add a second value for a key that already has a value, the first value would go away. In other words, if the ID 14534 mapped to "Kleper, Scott" and you then assigned the ID 14534 to "Kleper, Marni", then Scott would effectively be uninsured, as shown in the following sequence, which shows two calls to a hypothetical hash table enter() behavior and the resulting contents of the hash table. The notation hash.enter jumps ahead a bit to C++ object syntax. Just think of it as saying "use the enter behavior of the hash object.".

```
hash.enter(14534, "Kleper, Scott");
```

Keys	Values
14534	"Kleper, Scott" [string]

```
hash.enter(14534, "Kleper, Marni");
```

Keys	Values
14534	"Kleper, Marni" [string]

It's not difficult to imagine uses for a data structure that's *like* a hash table, but allows multiple values for a given key. In the insurance example, a family might have several names that correspond to the same ID. Because such a data structure is very similar to a hash table, it would be nice to leverage that functionality somehow. A hash table can only have a single value as a key, but that value can be anything. Instead of a string, the value could be a collection (such as an array or a list) containing the multiple values for the key. Every time you add a new member for an existing ID, simply add the name to the collection. This would work as shown in the following sequence.

```
Collection collection;                    // Make a new collection.
collection.insert("Kleper, Scott"); // Add a new element to the collection.
hash.enter(14534, collection);            // Enter the collection into the table.
```

Keys	Values
14534	{"Kleper, Scott"} [collection]

```
Collection collection = hash.get(14534);// Retrieve the existing collection.
collection.insert("Kleper, Marni");      // Add a new element to the collection.
hash.enter(14534, collection);           // Replace the collection with the updated one.
```

Keys	Values
14534	{"Kleper, Scott", "Kleper, Marni"} [collection]

Messing around with a collection instead of a string is tedious and requires a lot of repetitive code. It would be preferable to wrap up this multiple value functionality in a separate class, perhaps called a MultiHash. The MultiHash class would work just like Hashtable except that behind the scenes, it would store each value as a collection of strings instead of a single string. Clearly, MultiHash is somehow related to Hashtable because it is still using a hash table to store the data. What is unclear is whether that constitutes an is-a or a has-a relationship.

To start with the is-a relationship, imagine that MultiHash is a subclass of Hashtable. It would have to override the behavior that adds an entry into the table so that it would either create a collection and add the new element or retrieve the existing collection and add the new element. It would also override the behavior that retrieves a value. It could, for example, append all the values for a given key together into one string. This seems like a perfectly reasonable design. Even though it overrides all the behaviors of the superclass, it will still make use of the superclass's behaviors by using the original behaviors within the subclass. This approach is shown in Figure 3-5.

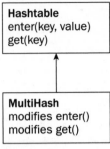

Figure 3-5

Now consider it as a has-a relationship. `MultiHash` is its own class, but it *contains* a `Hashtable` object. It probably has an interface very similar to `Hashtable`, but it need not be the same. Behind the scenes, when a user adds something to the `MultiHash`, it is really wrapped in a collection and put in a `Hashtable` object. This also seems perfectly reasonable and is shown in Figure 3-6.

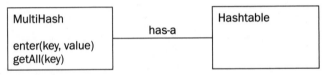

Figure 3-6

So, which solution is right? There's no clear answer, though one of the authors, who has written a MultiHash class for production use, viewed it as a has-a relationship. The main reason was to allow modifications to the exposed interface without worrying about maintaining hash table functionality. For example, in Figure 3-6, the `get` behavior was changed to `getAll`, making it clear that this would get all the values for a particular key in a `MultiHash`. Additionally, with a has-a relationship, you don't have to worry about any hash table functionality bleeding through. For example, if the hash table class supported a behavior that would get the total number of values, it would report the number of collections unless `MultiHash` knew to override it.

That said, one could make a convincing argument that a `MultiHash` actually is a `Hashtable` with some new functionality, and it should have been an is-a relationship. The point is that there is sometimes a fine line between the two relationships, and you will need to consider how the class is going to be used and whether what you are building just leverages some functionality from another class or really is that class with modified or new functionality.

The following table represents the arguments for and against taking either approach for the `MultiHash` class.

	Is-A	Has-A
Reasons For	• Fundamentally, it's the same abstraction with different characteristics. • It provides (almost) the same behaviors as `Hashtable`.	• `MultiHash` can have whatever behaviors are useful without needing to worry about what behaviors hash table has. The implementation could change to something other than a `Hashtable` without changing the exposed behaviors.
Reasons Against	• A hash table by definition hasone value per key. To say `MultiHash` is a hash table is blasphemy! `MultiHash` overrides both behaviors of `Hashtable`, a strong sign that something about the design is wrong. • Unknown or inappropriate properties or behaviors of `Hashtable` could "bleed through" to `MultiHash`.	• In a sense, `MultiHash` reinvents the wheel by coming up with new behaviors. • Some additional properties and behaviors of `Hashtable` might have been useful.

The Not-A Relationship

As you consider what type of relationship classes have, consider whether or not they actually have a relationship at all. Don't let your zeal for object-oriented design turn into a lot of needless class/subclass relationships.

One pitfall occurs when things are obviously related in the real world but have no actual relationship in code. Just because a Mustang is a Ford in real life doesn't mean that when you write a car simulator, `Mustang` should necessarily be a subclass of `Ford`. OO hierarchies need to model *functional* relationships, not artificial ones. Figure 3-7 shows relationships that are meaningful as ontologies or hierarchies, but are unlikely to represent a meaningful relationship in code.

The best way to avoid needless subclassing is to sketch out your design first. For every class and subclass, write down what properties and behaviors you're planning on putting there. If you find that a class has no particular properties or behaviors of its own, or if all of those properties and behaviors are completely overridden by its subclasses, you should rethink your design.

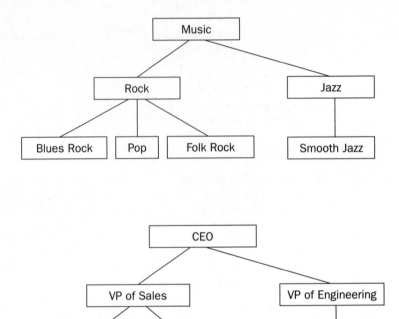

Figure 3-7

Hierarchies

Just as a class A can be a superclass of B, B can also be a superclass of C. Object-oriented hierarchies can model multilevel relationships like this. A zoo simulation with more animals might be designed with every animal as a subclass of a common Animal class as shown in Figure 3-8:

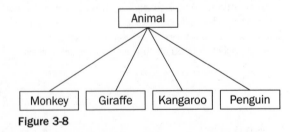

Figure 3-8

As you code each of these subclasses, you might find that a lot of them are similar. When this occurs, you should consider putting in a common parent. Realizing that Lion and Panther both move the same way and have the same diet might indicate a possible BigCat class. You could further subdivide the

`Animal` class to include `WaterAnimals`, and `Marsupials`. A more hierarchical design that leverages this commonality is shown in Figure 3-9.

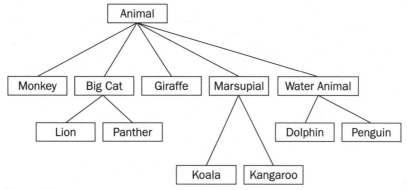

Figure 3-9

A biologist looking at this hierarchy may be disappointed — a penguin isn't really in the same family as a dolphin. However, it underlines a good point — in code, you need to balance real-world relationships with shared functionality relationships. Even though two things might be very closely related in the real world, they might have a not-a relationship in code because they really don't share functionality. You could just as easily divide animals into mammals and fish, but that wouldn't factor any commonality to the superclass.

Another important point is that there could be other ways of organizing the hierarchy. The preceding design is organized mostly by how the animals move. If it were instead organized by the animals' diet or height, the hierarchy could be very different. In the end, what matters is how the classes will be used. The needs will dictate the design of the object hierarchy.

A good object-oriented hierarchy accomplishes the following:

❑   Organizes classes into meaningful functional relationships

❑   Supports code reuse by factoring common functionality to superclasses

❑   Avoids having subclasses that override much of the parent's functionality

Multiple Inheritance

Every example so far has had a single inheritance chain. In other words, a given class has, at most, one immediate parent class. This does not have to be the case. Through multiple inheritance, a class can have more than one superclass.

> If you decide that there is no good animal object hierarchy because animals differ on too many axes, multiple inheritance may be just what you're looking for. With multiple inheritance, you could create three separate hierarchies — a size hierarchy, a diet hierarchy, and a movement hierarchy. Each animal would then choose one of each.

Figure 3-10 shows a multiple inheritance design. There is still a superclass called Animal, which is further divided by size. A separate hierarchy categorizes by diet, and a third takes care of movement. Each type of animal is then a subclass of all three of these classes, as shown by different-colored lines.

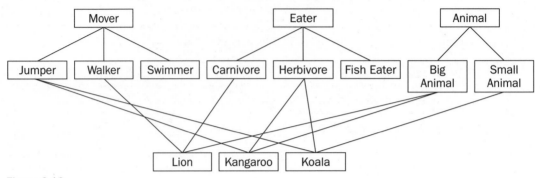

Figure 3-10

In a user interface context, imagine an image that the user can click on. This object seems to be both a button and an image so the implementation might involve subclassing both the Image class and the Button class, as shown in Figure 3-11:

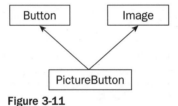

Figure 3-11

What's Bad about Multiple Inheritance?

Many programmers dislike multiple inheritance. C++ has explicit support for such relationships, though the Java language does away with them altogether. There are several reasons to which multiple inheritance critics point.

First, visualizing multiple inheritance is complicated. As Figure 3-10 shows, even a simple class diagram can become very complicated when there are multiple hierarchies and crossing lines. Class hierarchies are supposed to make it easier for the programmer to understand the relationships between code. With multiple inheritance, a class could have several parents that are in no way related to each other. With so many classes contributing code to your object, can you really keep track of what's going on? In the real world, we tend not to think of objects as having multiple is-a relationships.

Second, multiple inheritance can destroy otherwise clean hierarchies. In the animal example, switching to a multiple inheritance approach means that the Animal superclass is less meaningful because the code that describes animals is now separated into three separate hierarchies. While the design illustrated in Figure 3-10 shows three clean hierarchies, it's not difficult to imagine how they could get messy. For example, what if you realize that not only do all Jumpers move in the same way, they also eat the same things? Because there are separate hierarchies, there is no way to join the concepts of movement and diet without adding yet another subclass.

Third, implementation of multiple inheritance is complicated. What if two of your superclasses implement the same behavior in different ways? Can you have two superclasses that are themselves a subclass of a common superclass? These possibilities complicate the implementation because structuring such intricate relationships in code is difficult both for the author and a reader.

The reason that other languages can leave out multiple inheritance is that it is usually avoidable. By rethinking your hierarchy or using some of the *design patterns* covered in Chapter 26, you can avoid introducing multiple inheritance when you have control over the design of a project.

Mix-in Classes

Mix-in classes represent another type of relationship between classes. In C++, a mix-in class is implemented syntactically just like multiple inheritance, but the semantics are refreshingly different! A mix-in class answers the question "What *else* is this class able to do?" and the answer often ends with "-able." Mix-in classes are a way that you can add functionality to a class without committing to a full is-a relationship.

Going back to the zoo example, you might want to introduce the notion that some animals are "pettable." That is, there are some animals that visitors to the zoo can pet, presumably without being bitten or mauled. You might want all pettable animals to support the behavior "be pet." Since pettable animals don't have anything else in common and you don't want to break the existing hierarchy you've designed, `Pettable` makes a great mix-in class.

Mix-in classes are used frequently in user interfaces. Instead of saying that a `PictureButton` class is both an `Image` and a `Button`, you might say that it's an `Image` that is `Clickable`. A folder icon on your desktop could be an `Image` that is `Draggable`. In software development, we make up lots of fun adjectives.

The difference between a mix-in class and a superclass has more to do with how you think about the class than any code difference. In general, mix-in classes are easier to digest than multiple inheritance because they are very limited in scope. The `Pettable` mix-in class just adds one behavior to any existing class. The `Clickable` mix-in class might just add "mouse down" and "mouse up" behaviors. Also, mix-in classes rarely have a large hierarchy so there's no cross-contamination of functionality.

Abstraction

In Chapter 2, you learned about the concept of abstraction — the notion of separating implementation from the means used to access it. Abstraction is a good idea for many reasons explored earlier. It's also a fundamental part of object-oriented design.

Interface versus Implementation

The key to abstraction is effectively separating the *interface* from the *implementation*. Implementation is the code you're writing to accomplish the task you set out to accomplish. Interface is the way that other people use your code. In C, the header file that describes the functions in a library you've written is an interface. In object-oriented programming, the interface to a class is the collection of publicly accessible properties and behaviors.

Deciding on an Exposed Interface

The question of how other programmers will interact with your objects comes into play when designing a class. In C++, a class's properties and behaviors can each be `public`, `protected`, or `private`. `public` means that other code can access the property or behavior. `protected` means that other code cannot. `private` is a stricter control, which means that not only are the properties or behaviors locked for other code, but even subclasses can't access them.

Designing the exposed interface is all about choosing what to make `public`. When working on a large project with other programmers, you should view the exposed interface design as a process.

Consider the Audience

The first step in designing an exposed interface is to consider for whom you are designing it. Is your audience another member of your team? Is this an interface that you will personally be using? Is it something that a programmer external to your company will use? Perhaps a customer or an off-shore contractor? In addition to determining who will be coming to you for help with the interface, this should shed some light on some of your design goals.

If the interface is for your own use, you probably have more freedom to iterate on the design. As you're making use of the interface, you can change it to suit your own needs. However, you should keep in mind that roles on an engineering team change and it is quite likely that, some day, others will be using this interface as well.

Designing an interface for other internal programmers to use is slightly different. In a way, your interface becomes a contract with them. For example, if you are implementing the data store component of a program, others are depending on that interface to support certain operations. You will need to find out all of the things that the rest of the team will be using your class to do. Do they need versioning? What types of data can they store? As a contract, you should view the interface as slightly less flexible. If the interface is agreed upon before coding begins, you'll receive some groans from other programmers if you decide to change it after code has been written.

If the client is an external customer, you will be designing with a very different set of requirements. Ideally, the target customer will be involved in specifying what functionality your interface exposes. You'll need to consider both the specific features they want as well as what customers might want in the future. The terminology used in the interface will have to correspond to the terms that the customer is familiar with, and the documentation will have to be written with that audience in mind. Inside jokes, codenames, and programmer slang should probably be left out of your design.

Consider the Purpose

There are many reasons for writing an interface. Before putting any code on paper or even deciding on what functionality you're going to expose, you need to understand the purpose of the interface.

Application Programming Interface (API)

An *API* is an externally visible mechanism to extend a product or use its functionality within another context. If an internal interface is a contract, an API is closer to a set-in-stone law. Once people who don't even work for your company are using your API, they don't want it to change unless you're adding new features that will help them. So, care should be given to planning the API and discussing it with customers before making it available to them.

The main tradeoff in designing an API is usually ease of use versus flexibility. Because the target audience for the interface is not familiar with the internal working of your product, the learning curve to use the API should be gradual. After all, your company is exposing this API to customers because the company wants it to be used. If it's too difficult to use, the API is a failure. Flexibility often works against this. Your product may have a lot of different uses, and you want the customer to be able to leverage all the functionality you have to offer. However, an API that lets the customer do anything that your product can do may be too complicated.

As a common programming adage goes, "A good API makes the easy case easy and the hard case *possible*." That is, APIs should have a simple learning curve. The things that most programmers will want to do should be accessible. However, the API should allow for more advanced usage, and it's acceptable to trade off complexity of the rare case for simplicity of the common case.

Utility Class or Library

Often, your task is to develop some particular functionality for general use elsewhere in the application. It could be a random number library or a logging class. In these cases, the interface is somewhat easier to decide on because you tend to expose most or all of the functionality, ideally without giving too much away about its implementation. Generality is an important issue to consider. Since the class or library is general purpose, you'll need to take the possible set of use cases into account in your design.

Subsystem Interface

You may be designing the interface between two major subsystems of the application, such as the mechanism for accessing a database. In these cases, separating the interface from the implementation is paramount because other programmers are likely to start implementing against your interface before your implementation is complete. When working on a subsystem, first think about what its one main purpose is. Once you have identified the main task your subsystem is charged with, think about specific uses and how it should be presented to other parts of the code. Try to put yourself in their shoes and not get bogged down in implementation details.

Component Interface

Most of the interfaces you define will probably be smaller than a subsystem interface or an API. These will be objects that you use within other code that you've written. In these cases, the main pitfall is when your interface evolves gradually and becomes unruly. Even though these interfaces are for your own use, think of them as though they weren't. As with a subsystem interface, consider the one main purpose of each class and be cautious of exposing functionality that doesn't contribute to that purpose.

Consider the Future

As you are designing your interface, keep in mind what the future holds. Is this a design you will be locked into for years? If so, you might need to leave room for expansion by coming up with a plug-in architecture. Do you have evidence that people will try to use your interface for purposes other than what it was designed for? Talk to them and get a better understanding of their use case. The alternative is rewriting it later, or worse, attaching new functionality haphazardly and ending up with a messy interface. Be careful though! Speculative generality is yet another pitfall. Don't design the be-all end-all logging class if the future uses are unclear.

Designing a Successful Abstraction

Experience and iteration are essential to good abstractions. Truly well-designed interfaces come from years of writing and using other abstractions. As you encounter other abstractions, try to remember what worked and didn't work. What did you find lacking in the Windows file system API you used last week? What would you have done differently if you had written the network wrapper, instead of your coworker? The best interface is rarely the first one you put on paper, so keep iterating. Bring your design to your peers and ask for feedback. Don't be afraid to change the abstraction once coding has begun, even it means forcing other programmers to adapt. Hopefully, they'll realize that a good abstraction is beneficial to everyone in the long term.

Sometimes you need to evangelize a bit when communicating your design to other programmers. Perhaps the rest of the team didn't see a problem with the previous design or feels that your approach requires too much work on their part. In those situations, be prepared both to defend your work and to incorporate their ideas when appropriate. If you're still getting pushback, good documentation and sample code should help win them over.

Beware of single-class abstractions. If there is significant depth to the code you're writing, consider what other companion classes might accompany the main interface. For example, if you're exposing an interface to do some data processing, consider also writing a result object that provides an easy way to view and interpret the results.

When possible, turn properties into behaviors. In other words, don't allow external code to manipulate the data behind your class directly. You don't want some careless or nefarious programmer to set the height of a bunny object to a negative number. Instead, have a "set height" behavior that does the necessary bounds checking.

Iteration is worth mentioning again because it is the most important point. Seek and respond to feedback on your design, change it when necessary, and learn from mistakes.

Chapter 5 covers more guidelines for designing interfaces and reusable code.

Summary

In this chapter, you've gained an appreciation for the design of object-oriented programs without a lot of code getting in the way. The concepts you've learned are applicable in almost any object-oriented language. Some of it may have been a review to you, or it may be a new way of formalizing a familiar concept. Perhaps you picked up some new approaches to old problems or new arguments in favor of the concepts you've been preaching to your team all along. Even if you've never used objects in your code, or have only used them sparingly, you now know more about how to design object-oriented programs than many experienced C++ programmers.

The relationships between objects are important to study, not just because well-linked objects contribute to code reuse and reduce clutter, but because you will be working in a team. Objects that relate in meaningful ways are easier to read and maintain. You may decide to use the "Object Relationships" section as a reference when you design you programs.

Finally, you learned about creating successful abstractions and the two most important design considerations — audience and purpose. Chapter 4 will expand on the development of abstractions, including topics such as code reuse, idea reuse, and some of the libraries that are available to you.

Designing with Libraries and Patterns

Experienced C++ programmers never start a project from scratch. They incorporate code from a wide variety of sources, such as the standard template library, open-source libraries, proprietary code bases in their workplace, and their own code from previous projects. In addition, good C++ programmers reuse approaches or strategies to address various common design issues. These strategies can range from a technique that worked for a past project to a formal *design pattern*. This chapter explains how to take into account existing code and strategies when designing your programs.

Chapter 2 introduced the theme of reuse, explaining that it can apply both to code reuse and to idea reuse. This chapter expands on that theme by giving specific details and strategies that you can use in your program designs. After finishing this chapter, you will understand:

❑ The different types of code available for reuse

❑ The advantages and disadvantages of code reuse

❑ General strategies and guidelines for reusing code

❑ Open-source libraries

❑ The C++ standard library

❑ Design techniques and patterns

Reusing Code

You should reuse code liberally in your designs. In order to make the most of this rule, you need to understand the types of code that you can reuse and the tradeoffs involved in code reuse.

A Note on Terminology

Before analyzing the advantages and disadvantages of code reuse, it is helpful to specify the terminology involved and to categorize the types of reused code. There are three categories of code available for reuse:

❑   Code you wrote yourself in the past

❑   Code written by a coworker

❑   Code written by a third party outside your current organization or company

There are also several ways that the code you use can be structured:

❑   **Stand-alone functions or classes.** When you reuse your own code or coworkers' code, you will generally encounter this variety.

❑   **Libraries.** A *library* is a collection of code used to accomplish a specific task, such as parsing XML, or to handle a specific domain, such as cryptography. When you use third-party code, it will generally come in the form of a library. You should already be familiar with libraries from using simple ones like the math library in C or C++. Other examples of functionality usually found in libraries include threads and synchronization support, networking, and graphics.

❑   **Frameworks.** A *framework* is a collection of code around which you design a program. For example, the Microsoft Foundation Classes (MFC) provide a framework for creating graphical user interface applications for Microsoft Windows. Frameworks usually dictate the structure of your program. Chapter 25 provides more information on frameworks.

> A program *uses* a library but *fits into* a framework. Libraries provide specific functionality, while frameworks are fundamental to your program design and structure.

Another term that arises frequently is *application programming interface*, or *API*. An API is an interface to a library or body of code for a specific purpose. For example, programmers often refer to the sockets API, meaning the exposed interface to the sockets networking library, instead of the library itself.

> *Although people use the terms API and library interchangeably, they are not equivalent. The library refers to the implementation, while the API refers to the published interface to the library.*

For the sake of brevity, the rest of this chapter uses the term library to refer to any reused code, whether it is really a library, framework, or random collection of functions from your office-mate.

Deciding Whether or Not to Reuse Code

The rule to reuse code is easy to understand in the abstract. However, it's somewhat vague when it comes to the details. How do you know when it's appropriate to reuse code, and which code to reuse? There is always a tradeoff, and the decision depends on the specific situation. However, there are some general advantages and disadvantages to reusing code.

Advantages to Reusing Code

Reusing code can provide tremendous advantages to you and to your project.

- ❏ First of all, you might not be capable of, or willing to, write the code that you reuse. Would you really want to write code to handle formatted input and output? Of course not: that's why you use the standard C++ I/O streams.

- ❏ Reusing code saves time. Any code that you reuse is code you don't need to write yourself. Also, your designs will be simpler because you will not need to design those components of the application that you reuse.

- ❏ The code that you reuse will theoretically require less debugging than code you write yourself. You should expect bugs in any code you write yourself, but can often assume that the library code is bug-free because it has already been tested and used extensively. There are exceptions, of course; the library you choose to use could be poorly written and buggy.

- ❏ Libraries probably also handle more error conditions than would your first attempt at the code. You might forget obscure errors or edge cases at the beginning of the project, and would waste time fixing these problems later. Or worse, they would show up as bugs to your users. Library code that you reuse has generally been tested extensively and used by many programmers before you, so you can assume that it handles most errors properly.

- ❏ Reusing code written by domain experts is safer than writing your own code for that area. For example, you should not attempt to write your own security code unless you are a security expert. If you need security or cryptography in your programs, use a library. Many seemingly minor details in code of that nature could compromise the security of the entire program if you got them wrong.

- ❏ Finally, library code is constantly improving. If you reuse the code, you receive the benefits of these improvements without doing the work yourself! In fact, if the library writers properly separated the interface from the implementation, you can obtain these benefits by upgrading your library version without changing your interaction with the library. A good upgrade modifies the underlying implementation without changing the interface.

Disadvantages to Reusing Code

Unfortunately, there are also some disadvantages to reusing code.

- ❏ When you use only code that you wrote yourself, you understand exactly how it works. When you use libraries that you didn't write yourself, you must spend time understanding the interface and correct usage before you can jump in and use it. This extra time at the beginning of your project will slow your initial design and coding.

- ❏ When you write your own code, it does exactly what you want. Library code might not provide the exact functionality that you require. For example, one of the authors once made the mistake of failing to notice a glaring deficiency in an eXtensible Markup Language (XML) parsing library before he started using it. The library appeared great at first glance: it supported both Document Object Model (DOM) and Simple API for XML (SAX) parsing models, ran efficiently, and didn't have a licensing fee. It wasn't until he was well into his coding that he realized that the library didn't support validation against a Document Type Definition.

❑ Even if the library code provides the exact functionality you need, it might not give you the performance that you desire. The performance might be bad in general, poor for your specific use case, or completely undocumented. Additionally, the person who wrote the library or documentation might not have the same standards as you do of good and bad performance.

❑ Using library code introduces a Pandora's box of support issues. If you discover a bug in the library, what do you do? Often you don't have access to the source code, so you couldn't fix it even if you wanted to. If you have already invested significant time learning the library interface and using the library, you probably don't want to give it up, but you might find it difficult to convince the library developers to fix the bug on your time schedule. Also, if you are using a third-party library, what do you do if the library authors drop support for the library before you stop supporting the product that depends on it?

❑ In addition to support problems, libraries present licensing issues. Using an open-source library often requires you to make your own code open source. Libraries also sometimes require license fees, in which case it might be cheaper to redo the work and develop your own code.

❑ Another consideration with reusing code is cross-platform portability. Most libraries and frameworks are platform specific. For example, the MFC framework is, unsurprisingly, available primarily on Microsoft Windows. Even code that claims to be cross-platform will probably exhibit subtle differences between platforms. If you want to write a cross-platform application, you may need to use different libraries on different platforms.

❑ Open-source software presents its own issue: security. Some programmers are wary of using open-source code for security reasons. By reading the source code for a program, *crackers* (malicious hackers) can spot and exploit bugs that might otherwise go undetected.

❑ Finally, reusing code requires a trust factor. You must trust whoever wrote the code by assuming that he or she did a good job. Some people like to have control over all aspects of their project, including every line of source code. One of the authors certainly finds it difficult at times to trust library code that he didn't write himself. However, that is generally not a helpful or realistic attitude in software development.

Putting It Together to Make a Decision

Now that you are familiar with the terminology, advantages, and disadvantages of reusing code, you are better prepared to make the decision about whether or not to reuse code. Often, the decision is obvious. For example, if you want to write a graphical user interface (GUI) in C++ for Microsoft Windows, you should use a framework such as MFC. You probably don't know how to write the underlying code to create a GUI in Windows, and more importantly, you don't want to waste the time to learn it. You can probably save person-years of effort by using a framework in this case.

However, other times the choice is less obvious. For example, if you are unfamiliar with a library or framework, and need only a simple data structure, it might not be worth the time to learn the entire framework to reuse only one component that you could write in a few days.

Ultimately, the decision is a subjective choice that you need to make for your own particular needs. It often comes down to a tradeoff between the time it would take to write it yourself and the time required to find and learn how to use a library to solve the problem. Carefully consider how the advantages and disadvantages listed previously apply to your specific case, and decide which factors are most important to you. Finally, remember that you can always change your mind!

Strategies for Reusing Code

When you use libraries, frameworks, coworkers' code, or your own code, there are several guidelines you should keep in mind.

Understand the Capabilities and Limitations

Take the time to familiarize yourself with the code. It is important to understand both its capabilities and its limitations. Start with the documentation and the published interfaces or APIs. Ideally, that will be sufficient to understand how to use the code. However, if the library doesn't provide a clear separation between interface and implementation, you may need to explore the source code itself. Also, talk to other programmers who have used the code and who might be able to explain its intricacies. You should begin by learning the basic functionality. If it's a library, what behaviors does it provide? If it's a framework, how does your code fit in? What classes should you subclass? What code do you need to write yourself? You should also consider specific issues depending on the type of code.

Here are some points to keep in mind for any library or framework:

❏ Is the code safe for multithreaded programs?

❏ What initialization calls does the library or framework need? What cleanup does it need?

❏ On what other libraries does the library or framework depend?

Here are some points to keep in mind for any library call you use:

❏ If a call returns memory pointers, who is responsible for freeing the memory: the caller or the library? If the library is responsible, when is the memory freed?

❏ What error conditions does the library call check for, and what does it assume? How does it handle errors?

❏ What are all the return values (by value or reference) from a call? What are all the possible exceptions thrown?

Here are some points to keep in mind for a framework:

❏ If you inherit from a class, which constructor should you call on it? Which virtual methods should you override?

❏ What memory are you responsible for freeing, and what memory is the framework responsible for freeing?

Understand the Performance

It is important to know the performance guarantees that the library or other code provides. Even if your particular program is not performance sensitive, you should make sure that the code you use doesn't have awful performance for your particular use. For example, a library for XML parsing might claim to be fast even though it actually stores temporary information in a file, incurring disk I/O that decreases performance considerably.

Big-O Notation

Programmers generally discuss and document algorithm and library performance using *big-O notation*. This section explains the general concepts of algorithm complexity analysis and big-O notation without a lot of unnecessary mathematics. If you are already familiar with these concepts, you may skip this section.

Big-O notation specifies *relative*, rather than *absolute*, performance. For example, instead of saying that an algorithm runs in a specific amount of time, such as 300 milliseconds, big-O notation specifies how an algorithm performs as its input size increases. Examples of input sizes include the number of items to be sorted by a sorting algorithm, the number of elements in a hash table during a key lookup, and the size of a file to be copied between disks.

Note that big-O notation applies only to algorithms whose speed depends on their inputs. It does not apply to algorithms that take no input or whose running time is random. In practice, you will find that the running times of most algorithms of interest depend on their input, so this limitation is not significant.

To be more formal: big-O notation specifies algorithm run time as a function of its input size, also known as the *complexity* of the algorithm. However, that's not as complicated as it sounds. For example, suppose that a sorting algorithm takes 50 milliseconds to sort 500 elements and 100 milliseconds to sort 1,000 elements. Because it takes twice as long to sort twice as many elements, its performance is *linear* as a function of its input. That is, you could graph the performance versus input size as a straight line. Big-O notation summarizes the sorting algorithm performance like this: $O(n)$. The O just means that you're using big-O notation, while the n represents the input size. $O(n)$ specifies that the sorting algorithm speed is a direct linear function of the input size.

Unfortunately, not all algorithms have performance that is linear with respect to the input size. Computer programs would run a lot faster if that were true! The following table summarizes the common categories of functions, in order of their performance from best to worst:

Algorithm Complexity	Big-O Notation	Explanation	Example Algorithms
Constant	$O(1)$	Running time is independent of input size.	Accessing a single element in an array
Logarithmic	$O(\log n)$	The running time is a function of the logarithm base 2 of the input size.	Finding an element in a sorted list using binary search
Linear	$O(n)$	The running time is directly proportional to the input size.	Finding an element in an unsorted list
Linear Logarithmic	$O(n \log n)$	The running time is a function of the linear times the logarithmic functions of the input size.	Merge sort
Quadratic	$O(n^2)$	The running time is a function of the square of the input size.	A slower sorting algorithm like selection sort

There are two advantages to specifying performance as a function of the input size instead of in absolute numbers:

1. It is platform independent. Specifying that a piece of code runs in 200 milliseconds on one computer says nothing about its speed on a second computer. It is also difficult to compare two different algorithms without running them on the same computer with the exact same load. On the other hand, performance specified as a function of the input size is applicable to any platform.

2. Performance as a function of input size covers all possible inputs to the algorithm with one specification. The specific time in seconds that an algorithm takes to run covers only one specific input, and says nothing about any other input.

Tips for Understanding Performance

Now that you are familiar with big-O notation, you are prepared to understand most performance documentation. The C++ standard template library in particular describes its algorithm and data structure performance using big-O notation. However, big-O notation is sometimes insufficient or misleading. Consider the following issues whenever you think about big-O performance specifications:

❑ If an algorithm takes twice as long to work on twice as much data, that says nothing about how long it took in the first place! If the algorithm is written badly but scales well, it's still not something you want to use. For example, suppose the algorithm makes unnecessary disk accesses. That probably wouldn't affect the big-O time but would be very bad for performance.

❑ Along those lines, it's difficult to compare two algorithms with the same big-O running time. For example, if two different sorting algorithms both claim to be $O(n \log n)$, it's hard to tell which is really faster without running your own tests.

❑ For small inputs, big-O time can be very misleading. An $O(n2)$ algorithm might actually perform better than an $O(\log n)$ algorithm on small input sizes. Consider your likely input sizes before making a decision.

In addition to considering big-O characteristics, you should look at other facets of the algorithm performance. Here are some guidelines to keep in mind:

❑ You should consider how often you intend to use a particular piece of library code. Some people find the "90/10" rule helpful: 90 percent of the running time of most programs is spent in only 10 percent of the code (Hennessy and Patterson, 2002) If the library code you intend to use falls in the oft-exercised 10 percent category of your code, you should make sure to analyze its performance characteristics carefully. On the other hand, if it falls into the oft-ignored 90 percent of the code, you should not spend much time analyzing its performance because it will not benefit your overall program performance very much.

❑ Don't trust the documentation. Always run performance tests to determine if library code provides acceptable performance characteristics.

Understand Platform Limitations

Before you start using library code, make sure that you understand on which platforms it runs. That might sound obvious. Of course, you wouldn't try to use the MFC in an application that should also run on Linux. However, even libraries that claim to be cross-platform might contain subtle differences on the different platforms.

Also, platforms include not only different operating systems but different versions of the same operating system. If you write an application that should run on Solaris 8, Solaris 9, and Solaris 10, ensure that any libraries you use also support all those releases. You cannot assume either forward or backward compatibility across operating system versions. That is, just because a library runs on Solaris 9 doesn't mean that it will run on Solaris 10 and vice versa. The library on Solaris 10 might use operating system features or other libraries that are new to that release. On the other hand, the library on Solaris 9 might use features that have been removed in Solaris 10, or might use an old binary format.

Understand Licensing and Support

Using third-party libraries often introduces complicated licensing issues. You must sometimes pay license fees to third-party vendors for the use of their libraries. There may also be other licensing restrictions, including export restrictions. Additionally, open-source libraries are often distributed under licenses that require any code that links with them to be open source as well.

> **Make sure that you understand the license restrictions of any third-party libraries you use if you plan to distribute or sell the code you develop. When in doubt, consult a legal expert.**

Using third-party libraries also introduces support issues. Before you use a library, make sure that you understand the process for submitting bugs, and that you realize how long it will take for bugs to be fixed. If possible, determine how long the library will continue to be supported so that you can plan accordingly.

Interestingly, even using libraries from within your own organization can introduce support issues. You may find it just as difficult to convince a coworker in another part of your company to fix a bug in his or her library as you would to convince a stranger in another company to do the equivalent. In fact, you may even find it harder, because you're not a paying customer. Make sure that you understand the politics and organizational issues within your own organization before using internal libraries.

Know Where to Find Help

Using libraries and frameworks can sometimes be daunting at first. Fortunately, there are many avenues of support available. First of all, consult the documentation that accompanies the library. If the library is widely used, such as the standard template library (STL), or the MFC, you should be able to find a good book on the topic. In fact, for help with the STL, consult Chapters 21 to 23 of this book! If you have specific questions that are not addressed by the books and product documentation, try searching the Web. Type your question into a search engine like Google (at www.google.com) to find Web pages that discuss the library. For example, when I google for the phrase "introduction to C++ STL" I find several hundred Web sites about C++ and the STL.

> **A note of caution: don't believe everything you read on the Web! Web pages do not necessarily undergo the same review process as printed books and documentation, and may contain inaccuracies.**

Also consider browsing newsgroups and signing up for mailing lists. You can search the Usenet news-groups at http://groups.google.com for information about your library or framework. For example, suppose that you didn't know that the C++ standard omits a hash table from the STL. Searching for the phrase "hashtable in C++ STL" in the google groups reveals several postings explaining that there is no hash table in the standard, but that many vendors supply implementations anyway.

> **Newsgroups are often unmoderated. The postings can be rude and offensive. Browse and post at your own discretion.**

Finally, many Web sites contain their own private newsgroups on specific topics for which you can register.

Prototype

When you first sit down with a new library or framework, it is often a good idea to write a quick proto-type. Trying out the code is the best way to familiarize yourself with the library's capabilities. You should consider experimenting with the library even before you tackle your program design so that you are intimately familiar with the library's capabilities and limitations before inserting it into your design. This empirical testing will allow you to determine the performance characteristics of the library as well.

Even if your prototype application looks nothing like your final application, time spent prototyping is not a waste. Don't feel compelled to write a prototype of your actual application. Write a dummy pro-gram that just tests the library capabilities you want to use. The point is only to familiarize yourself with the library.

> **Due to time constraints, programmers sometimes find their prototypes morphing into the final product. If you have hacked together a prototype that is insufficient as the basis for the final product, make sure that it doesn't get used that way.**

Bundling Third-Party Applications

Your project might include multiple applications. Perhaps you need a Web server front end to support your new e-commerce infrastructure. It is possible to bundle third-party applications, such as a Web server, with your software. This approach takes code reuse to the extreme in that you reuse entire appli-cations! However, most of the caveats and guidelines for using libraries apply to bundling third-party applications as well. Specifically, make sure that you understand the legality and licensing ramifications of your decision.

Consult a legal expert before bundling third-party applications with your software distributions.

Also, the support issue becomes more complex. If customers encounter a problem with your bundled Web server, should they contact you or the Web server vendor? Make sure that you resolve this issue *before* you release the software.

Open-Source Libraries

Open-source libraries are an increasingly popular class of reusable code. The general meaning of *open-source* is that the source code is available for anyone to look at. There are formal definitions and legal rules about including source with all your distributions, but the important thing to remember about open-source software is that anyone (including you) can look at the source code. Note that open-source applies to more than just libraries. In fact, the most famous open-source product is probably the Linux operating system.

The Open-Source Movements

Unfortunately, there is some confusion in terminology in the open-source community. First of all, there are two competing names for the movement (some would say two separate, but similar, movements). Richard Stallman and the GNU project use the term *free software*. Note that the term free does not imply that the finished product must be available without cost. Developers are welcome to charge as much or as little as they want for a free software product. Instead, the term free refers to the freedom for people to examine the source code, modify the source code, and redistribute the software. Think of the free in free speech rather than the free in free beer. You can read more about Richard Stallman and the GNU project at www.gnu.org.

> Don't confuse *free software* with *freeware*. Freeware or *shareware* applications are available at no cost, but the source code can be private, or *proprietary*. Free software, on the other hand, can require payment to use, but the source code must be available.

The Open Source Initiative uses the term *open-source software* to describe software in which the source must be available. As with free software, open-source software does not require the product or library to be available for free. You can read more about the Open Source Initiative at www.opensource.org.

Because the name "open-source" is less ambiguous than "free software," this book uses "open-source" to refer to products and libraries with which the source code is available. The choice of name is not intended to imply endorsement of the open-source philosophy over the free software philosophy: it is only for ease of comprehension.

Finding and Using Open-Source Libraries

Regardless of the terminology, you can gain amazing benefits from using open-source software. The main benefit is functionality. There are a plethora of open-source C++ libraries available for varied tasks: from XML parsing to cross-platform error logging.

Although open-source libraries are not required to provide free distribution and licensing, many open-source libraries are available without monetary cost. You will generally be able to save money in licensing fees by using open-source libraries.

Finally, you are often free to modify open-source libraries to suit your exact needs.

Most open-source libraries are available on the Web. Try googling for what you need. For example, the first link in Google from the search string "open-source C++ library XML parsing" is a list of links to XML libraries in C and C++, including libxml and Xerces C++ Parser.

There are also a few open-source portals where you can start your search, including:

❑   www.opensource.org

❑   www.gnu.org

❑   www.sourceforge.net

Your own searches should quickly uncover many more resources on the Web.

Guidelines for Using Open-Source Code

Open-source libraries present several unique issues and require new strategies. First of all, open-source libraries are usually written by people in their "free" time. The source base is generally available for any programmer who wants to pitch in and contribute to development or bug fixing. As a good programming citizen, you should try to contribute to open-source projects if you find yourself reaping the benefits of open-source libraries. If you work for a company, you may find resistance to this idea from your management because it does not lead directly to revenue for your company. However, you might be able to convince management that indirect benefits, such as exposure of your company name, and perceived support from your company for the open-source movement, should allow you to pursue this activity.

Second, because of the distributed nature of their development, and lack of single ownership, open-source libraries often present support issues. If you desperately need a bug fixed in a library, it is often more efficient to make the fix yourself than to wait for someone else to do it. If you do fix bugs, you should make sure to put the fixes into the public source base for the library. Even if you don't fix any bugs, make sure to report problems that you find so that other programmers don't waste time encountering the same issues.

> **When using open-source libraries, respect the movement's philosophy of "freedom." Try not to abuse this freedom or to profit unnecessarily from work to which you do not contribute.**

The C++ Standard Library

The most important library that you will use as a C++ programmer is the C++ standard library. As its name implies, this library is part of the C++ standard, so any standards-conforming compiler should include it. The standard library is not monolithic: it includes several disparate components, some of which you have probably been using already. You may even have assumed they were part of the core language. This section introduces the various components of the standard library from a design perspective. You will learn what facilities are available for you to use, but you will not learn the coding details. Those details are covered in other chapters throughout the book.

Note that the following overview is not comprehensive. Some details are introduced later in the book where they are more appropriate, and some details are omitted entirely. The standard library is too extensive to cover in its entirety in a general C++ book; there are 800-page books that cover only the standard library!

C Standard Library

Because C++ is a superset of C, the entire C library is still available. Its functionality includes mathematical functions such as abs(), sqrt(), and pow(), random numbers with srand() and rand(), and error-handling helpers such as assert() and errno. Additionally, the C library facilities for manipulating character arrays as strings, such as strlen() and strcpy(), and the C-style I/O functions, such as printf() and scanf(), are all available in C++.

> *C++ provides better strings and I/O support than does C. Even though the C-style strings and I/O routines are available in C++, you should avoid them in favor of C++ strings and I/O streams.*

This book assumes that you are familiar with the C libraries. If not, consult one of the C reference books listed in Appendix B. Note also that the C header files have different names in C++ than in C. For details, see the Standard Library Reference resource on the Web site.

Strings

C++ provides a built-in string class. Although you may still use C-style strings of character arrays, the C++ string class is superior in almost every way. It handles the memory management; provides some bounds checking, assignment semantics, and comparisons; and supports manipulations such as concatenation, substring extraction, and substring or character replacement.

> Technically, the C++ **string** is actually a **typedef** name for a **char** instantiation of the **basic_string** template. However, you need not worry about these details; you can use **string** as if it were a bona fide nontemplate class.

In case you missed it, Chapter 1 reviewed the string class functionality. The Standard Library Reference resource on the Web site provides further details.

I/O Streams

C++ introduces a new model for input and output using *streams*. The C++ library provides routines for reading and writing built-in types from and to files, console/keyboard, and strings. C++ also provides the facilities for coding your own routines for reading and writing your own objects.

Chapter 1 reviewed the basics of I/O streams. Chapter 14 provides the details of streams.

Internationalization

C++ also provides support for *internationalization*. These features allow you to write programs that work with different languages, character formats, and number formats.

Chapter 14 discusses internationalization.

Smart Pointers

C++ provides a limited smart pointer template, called the auto_ptr. This templatized class allows you to wrap a pointer of any type such that delete is called on it automatically when it goes out of scope.

However, this class does not support reference counting, so the pointer can have only one owner at a time.

Chapters 13, 15, 16, and 25 discuss smart pointers in more detail.

Exceptions

The C++ language supports exceptions, which allow functions or methods to pass errors of various types up to calling functions or methods. The C++ standard library provides a class hierarchy of exceptions that you can use in your program as is, or that you can subclass to create your own exception types. Chapter 15 covers the details of exceptions and the standard exception classes.

Mathematical Utilities

The C++ library provides some mathematical utility classes. Although they are templatized, so that you can use them with any type, they are not generally considered part of the standard template library. Unless you are using C++ for numeric computation, you will probably not need to use these utilities.

The standard library provides a complex number class, called `complex`, which provides an abstraction for working with numbers that contain both real and imaginary components.

The standard library also contains a class called `valarray`, which is essentially a vector in the mathematical sense. The library provides several related classes to represent the concept of vector slices. From these building blocks, it is possible to build classes to perform matrix mathematics. However, there is no built-in matrix class.

C++ also provides a new way to obtain information about numeric limits, such as the maximum possible value for an integer on the current platform. In C, you could access #defines such as INT_MAX. While those are still available in C++, you can also use the new `numeric_limits` template class family.

The Standard Template Library

The heart of the C++ standard library is its generic containers and algorithms. This aspect of the library is often called the *standard template library*, or *STL* for short, because of its abundant use of templates. The beauty of the STL is that it provides generic containers and generic algorithms in such a way that most of the algorithms work on most of the containers, no matter what type of data the containers store. This section introduces the various containers and algorithms in the STL. Chapters 21 to 23 provide the code details for using them in your programs.

STL Containers

The STL provides implementations of most of the standard data structures. When you use C++, you should not need to write data structures such as a linked list or queue ever again. Data structures, or *containers*, store pieces of information, or *elements*, in a way that allows appropriate access. Different data structures have different insertion, deletion, and access behavior and performance characteristics. It is important to be familiar with the data structures available so that you can choose the most appropriate one for any given task.

All the containers in the STL are templates, so you can use them to store any type, from built-in types such as int and double to your own classes. Note that you must store elements of the same type in any given container. That is, you cannot store elements of both `int` and `double` in the same queue. However, you could create two separate queues: one for `int`s and one for `double`s.

> **The C++ STL containers are *homogenous*: they allow elements of only one type in each container.**

Note that the C++ standard specifies the interface, but not the implementation, of each container and algorithm. Thus, different vendors are free to provide different implementations. However, the standard also specifies performance requirements as part of the interface, which the implementations must meet.

This section provides an overview of the various containers available in the STL.

Vector

A *vector* stores a sequence of elements and provides random access to these elements. You can think of a vector as an array of elements that grows dynamically as you insert elements and provides some bounds checking. Like an array, the elements of a vector are stored in contiguous memory.

> *A vector in C++ is a synonym for a dynamic array: an array that grows and shrinks automatically in response to the number of elements it stores. The C++ **vector** does not refer to the mathematical concept of a vector. C++ models mathematical vectors by the **valarray** container.*

Vectors provide fast (constant time) element insertion and deletion at the end of the vector, but slow (linear time) insertion and deletion anywhere else. Insertion and deletion are slow because the operation must move all the elements "down" or "up" by one to make room for the new element or to fill the space left by the deleted element. Like arrays, vectors provide fast (constant time) access to any of their elements.

You should use a vector in your programs when you need fast access to the elements, but do not plan to add or remove elements often. A good rule of thumb is to use a vector whenever you would have used an array. For example, a system-monitoring tool might keep a list of computer systems that it monitors in a vector. Only rarely would new computers be added to the list, or current computers removed from the list. However, users would often want to look up information about a particular computer, so lookup times should be fast.

> **Use a vector instead of an array whenever possible.**

List

An STL list is a standard linked list structure. Like an array or vector, it stores a sequence of elements. However, unlike in an array or vector, the elements of a linked list are not necessarily in contiguous memory. Instead, each element in the list specifies where to find the next and previous elements in the list (usually via pointers). Note that a list in which elements point both to the next and to the previous elements is called a *doubly linked list*.

The performance characteristics of a list are the exact opposite of a vector. Lists provide slow (linear time) element lookup and access, but quick (constant time) insertion and deletion of elements once the relevant position has been found. Thus, you should use a list when you plan to insert and remove many elements, but do not require quick lookup. For example, in a chat room implementation you might keep track of all the current participants in the chat in a list. Participants in chat rooms tend to come and go frequently, so you need quick insertion and deletion. On the other hand, you rarely need to look up participants in the list, so you don't care about slow lookup times.

Deque

The name *deque* is an abbreviation for a *double-ended queue*. A deque is partway between a vector and a list, but closer to a vector. Like a vector, it provides quick (constant time) element access. Like a list, it provides fast (amortized constant time) insertion and deletion at both ends of the sequence. However, unlike a list, it provides slow (linear time) insertion and deletion in the middle of the sequence.

You should use a deque instead of a vector when you need to insert or remove elements from either end of the sequence but still need fast access time to all elements. However, this requirement does not apply to many programming problems; in most cases a vector or queue should suffice.

> The vector, list, and deque containers are called *sequential containers* because they store a sequence of elements.

Queue

The name *queue* comes directly from the definition of the English word queue, which means a line of people or objects. The queue container provides standard *first in, first out* (or *FIFO*) semantics. A queue is a container in which you insert elements at one end and take them out at the other end. Both insertion and removal of elements is quick (constant time).

You should use a queue structure when you want to model real-life "first come, first served" semantics. For example, consider a bank. As customers arrive at the bank, they get in line. As tellers become available, they serve the next customer in line, thus providing "first come, first served" behavior. You could implement a bank simulation by storing Customer objects in a queue. As each customer arrives at the bank, you add him or her to the end of the queue. As each teller is ready to serve a customer, he or she serves the customer at the front of the queue. That way, customers are served in the order in which they arrived.

Priority Queue

A priority queue provides queue functionality in which each element has a priority. Elements are removed from the queue in priority order. In the case of priority ties, the FIFO semantics hold so that the first element inserted is the first removed. Priority queue insertion and deletion are generally slower than simple queue insertion and deletion, because the elements must be reordered to support the priority ordering.

You can use priority queues to model "queues with exceptions." For example, in the bank simulation above, suppose that customers with business accounts take priority over regular customers. Many real-life banks implement this behavior with two separate lines: one for business customers and one for everyone else. Any customers in the business queue are taken before customers in the other line. However, banks could also provide this behavior with a single line in which business customers simply move to the front of the line ahead of any nonbusiness customers. In your program, you could use a priority queue in which customers have one of two priorities: business or regular. All business customers would be serviced before all regular customers, but each group would be serviced in first-come, first-served order.

Stack

The STL stack provides standard *first-in, last-out* (or *FILO*) semantics. Like a queue, elements are inserted and removed from the container. However, in a stack the most recent element inserted is the first one removed. The name *stack* derives from a visualization of this structure as a stack of objects in which only the top object is visible. When you add an object to the stack, you hide all the objects underneath it.

Stacks model the real-life "first-come, last served" behavior. As an example, think of a parking lot in a big city in which the first cars to arrive are boxed in by cars that arrive later. In this case, the last cars to arrive are the first cars that are able to leave.

The STL stack container provides fast (constant time) insertion and removal of elements. You should use the stack structure when you want FILO semantics. For example, an error-processing tool might want to store errors on a stack so that the most recent error is the first one available for a human administrator to read. It is often useful to process errors in a FILO order because newer errors sometimes obviate older ones.

> Technically, the queue, priority queue, and stack containers are *container adapters*. They are interfaces built on top of one of the three standard sequential containers (vector, deque, and list).

Set and Multiset

A set in STL is a collection of elements. Although the mathematical definition of a set implies an unordered collection, the STL set stores the elements in an ordered fashion so that it can provide reasonably fast lookup, insertion, and deletion. In fact, the set provides logarithmic insertion, deletion, and lookup, which are faster insertion and deletion than a vector provides, and faster lookup than a list provides. However, insertion and deletion are slower than a list, and lookup is slower than a vector. The underlying implementation is usually a balanced binary tree, so you should use a set when you would normally use a balanced binary tree structure. Specifically, you should use a set when you have equal amounts of insertion/deletion and lookups, and want to optimize both as much as possible. For example, an inventory-tracking program in a busy bookstore might want to use a set to store the books. The list of books in stock must be updated whenever books arrive or are sold, so insertion and deletion should be quick. Customers also need the ability to look for a specific book, so the program should provide fast lookup as well.

> Use a set instead of a vector or list if you want equal performance for insertion, deletion, and lookup.

Note that a set does not allow duplication of elements. That is, each element in the set must be unique. If you want to store duplicate elements, you must use a multiset.

> **A multiset is simply a set that allows duplication of elements.**

Map and Multimap

A map stores key/value pairs. The elements are sorted according to the keys. In all other respects, it is identical to a set. You should use a map when you want to associate keys and values. For example, in an online multiplayer game you might want to store some information about each player, such as his or her login name, real name, IP address, and other characteristics. You could store this information in a map, using the players' login names as keys.

A multimap has the same relation to a map as a multiset does to a set. Specifically, a multimap is a map that allows duplicate keys.

Note that you can use a map as an *associative array*. That is, you can use it as an array in which the index can be any type, such as a string.

> **The set and map containers are called *associative containers* because they associate keys and values. This term is confusing when applied to sets, because in sets the keys are themselves the values. Because these containers sort their elements, they are called *sorted* associative containers.**

Bitset

C and C++ programmers commonly store a set of flags in a single `int` or `long`, using one bit for each flag. They set and access these bits with the bitwise operators: `&`, `|`, `^`, `~`, `<<`, and `>>`. The C++ standard library provides a `bitset` class that abstracts this bitfield manipulation, so you shouldn't need to use the bit manipulation operators anymore.

The `bitset` container is not a container in the normal sense, in that it does not implement a specific data structure in which you insert and remove elements. However, you can think of it as a sequence of Boolean values that you can read and write.

Summary of STL Containers

The following table summarizes the containers provided by the STL. It uses big-O notation to present the performance characteristics on a container of *N* elements. An N/A entry in the table means that the operation is not part of the container semantics.

Container Class Name	Container Type	Insertion Performance	Deletion Performance	Lookup Performance	When to Use
vector	Sequential	$O(1)$ at end $O(N)$ anywhere else	$O(1)$ at end $O(N)$ anywhere else	$O(1)$	Need quick lookup Don't mind slow insertion/ deletion Whenever you would use an array
list	Sequential	$O(1)$	$O(1)$	$O(N)$	Need quick insertion/ deletion Don't mind slow lookup
deque	Sequential	$O(1)$ at beginning or end $O(N)$ anywhere else	$O(1)$ at beginning or end $O(N)$ anywhere else	$O(1)$	Not usually needed; use a vector or list instead
queue	Container Adapter	$O(1)$	$O(1)$	N/A	When you want a FIFO structure
priority_ queue	Container Adapter	$O(\log(N))$	$O(\log(N))$	N/A	When you want a FIFO structure with priority
stack	Container Adapter	$O(1)$	$O(1)$	N/A	When you want a FILO structure
set / multiset	Sorted Associative	$O(\log(N))$	$O(\log(N))$	$O(\log(N))$	When you want a collection of elements with equal lookup, insertion, and deletion times
map / multimap	Sorted Associative	$O(\log(N))$	$O(\log(N))$	$O(\log(N))$	When you want to associate keys and values
bitset	Special	N/A	N/A	$O(1)$	When you want a collection of flags

Note that `strings` are technically containers as well. They can be thought of as `vectors` of characters. Thus, some of the algorithms described in the material that follows work on `strings` also.

STL Algorithms

In addition to containers, the STL provides implementations of many generic algorithms. An *algorithm* is a strategy for performing a particular task, such as sorting or searching. These algorithms are also implemented as templates, so they work on most of the different container types. Note that the algorithms are not generally part of the containers. The STL takes the surprising approach of separating the data (containers) from the functionality (algorithms). Although this approach seems counter to the spirit of object-oriented programming, it is necessary in order to support generic programming in the STL. The guiding principle of *orthogonality* maintains that algorithms and containers are independent, with (almost) any algorithm working with (almost) any container.

> *Although the algorithms and containers are theoretically independent, some containers provide certain algorithms in the form of class methods because the generic algorithms do not perform well on those particular containers. For example, sets provide their own **find()** algorithm that is faster than the generic **find()** algorithm. You should use the method form of the algorithm, if provided, because it is generally more efficient or appropriate to the container at hand.*

Note that the generic algorithms do not work directly on the containers. They use an intermediary called an *iterator*. Each container in the STL provides an iterator that supports traversing the elements in the container in a sequence. Iterators temporarily convert elements in even sets and maps to a sequence. The different iterators for the various containers adhere to standard interfaces, so algorithms can perform their work using iterators without worrying about the underlying container implementation. Chapters 21 to 23 and the Web site material provide all the details about iterators, algorithms, and containers.

> *Iterators mediate between algorithms and containers. They provide a standard interface to traverse the elements of a container in sequence, so that any algorithm can work on any container. The iterator design pattern is discussed further below.*

There are approximately 60 algorithms in the STL (depending on how you count them), generally divided into several different categories. The categories tend to vary slightly from book to book. This book uses the following five categories: utility, nonmodifying, modifying, sorting, and set. Some of the categories can be subdivided further. Note that whenever the following algorithms are specified as working on a "sequence" of elements, that sequence is given to the algorithm as an iterator.

> When examining the list of algorithms, keep in mind that the STL was designed by a committee. To quote an old joke, "a zebra is a horse designed by a committee." In other words, committees often arrive at designs that contain extra or unneeded functionality, such as a zebra's stripes. You may find that some of the algorithms in the STL are equally strange or unnecessary. That's fine. You are not obligated to use every algorithm available. It is important only to be aware of what's available in case you ever find it useful.

Utility Algorithms

Unlike the other algorithms, the utility algorithms do not work on sequences of data. We consider them part of the STL only because they are templatized.

Algorithm Name	Algorithm Synopsis
`min()`, `max()`	Return the minimum or maximum of two values.
`swap()`	Swap two values.

Nonmodifying Algorithms

The nonmodifying algorithms are those that look at a sequence of elements and return some information about the elements, or execute some function on each element. As "nonmodifying" algorithms, they cannot change the values of elements or the order of elements within the sequence. This category contains four types of algorithms. The following tables list and provide brief summaries of the various nonmodifying algorithms. With these algorithms, you should rarely need to write a `for` loop to iterate over a sequence of values.

Search Algorithms

Algorithm Name	Algorithm Synopsis	Requires Sorted Sequence?
`find()`, `find_if()`	Finds the first element that matches a value or causes a predicate to return `true`	No
`find_first_of()`	Like find, except searches for one of several elements at the same time	No
`adjacent_find()`	Finds the first instance of two consecutive elements that are equal to each other	No
`search()`, `find_end()`	Finds the first (`search()`) or last (`find_end()`) subsequence in a sequence that matches another sequence	No
`search_n()`	Finds the first instance of n consecutive elements that are equal to a given value	No
`lower_bound()`, `upper_bound()`, `equal_range()`	Finds the beginning, (`lower_bound()`) end (`upper_bound()`), or both sides (`equal_range()`) of the range including a specified element	Yes
`binary_search()`	Finds a value in a sorted sequence	Yes
`min_element()`, `max_element()`	Finds the minimum or maximum element in a sequence	No

Numerical Processing Algorithms

Algorithm Name	Algorithm Synopsis
count(), count_if()	Counts the number of elements matching a value or that cause a predicate to return true.
accumulate()	"Accumulates" the values of all the elements in a sequence. The default behavior is to sum the elements, but the caller can supply a different binary function instead.
inner_product()	Similar to accumulate, but works on two sequences. Calls a binary function on parallel elements in the sequences, accumulating the result. The default binary function is multiplication. If the sequences represent mathematical vectors, the algorithm calculates the dot product of the vectors.
partial_sum()	Generates a new sequence in which each element is the sum (or other binary operation) of the parallel element, and all preceding elements, in the source sequence.
adjacent_difference()	Generates a new sequence in which each element is the difference (or other binary operation) of the parallel element, and its predecessor, in the source sequence.

Comparison Algorithms

Algorithm Name	Algorithm Synopsis
equal()	Determines if two sequences are equal by checking if they have the same order of elements.
mismatch()	Returns the first element in each sequence that does not match the element in the same location in the other sequence.
lexicographical_compare()	Compares two sequences to determine their "lexicographical" ordering. Compares each element of the first sequence with its equivalent element in the second. If one element is less than the other, that sequence is lexicographically first. If the elements are equal, compares the next elements in order.

Operational Algorithms

Algorithm Name	Algorithm Synopsis
for_each()	Executes a function on each element in the sequence. This algorithm is useful for printing out each element in a container.

Modifying Algorithms

The modifying algorithms modify some or all of the elements in a sequence. Some of them modify elements *in place*, so that the original sequence changes. Others copy the results to a different sequence so that the original sequence is unchanged. The following table summarizes the modifying algorithms:

Algorithm Name	Algorithm Synopsis
transform()	Calls a function on each element or each pair of elements.
copy(), copy_backward()	Copies elements from one sequence to another.
iter_swap(), swap_ranges()	Swap two elements or sequences of elements.
replace(), replace_if(), replace_copy(), replace_copy_if()	Replaces with a new element all elements matching a value or that cause a predicate to return true, either in place or by copying results to a new sequence.
fill(), fill_n()	Sets all elements in the sequence to a new value.
generate(), generate_n()	Like fill() and fill_n(), except calls a specified function to generate values to place in the sequence.
remove(), remove_if(), remove_copy(), remove_copy_if()	Removes from the sequence elements that match a given value or that cause a predicate to return true, either in place or by copying results to a different sequence.
unique(), unique_copy()	Removes consecutive duplicates from the sequence, either in place or by copying results to a different sequence.
reverse(), reverse_copy()	Reverses the order of the elements in the sequence, either in place or by copying the results to a different sequence.
rotate(), rotate_copy()	Swaps the first and second "halves"of the sequence, either in place or by copying the results to a different sequence. The two subsequences to be swapped need not be equal in size.
next_permutation(), prev_permutation()	Modifies the sequence by transforming it into its "next" or "previous" permutation. Successive calls to one or the other will permute the sequence into all possible permutations of elements.

Sorting Algorithms

Sorting algorithms are a special category of modifying algorithms that sort the elements of a sequence. The STL provides several different sorting algorithms with varying performance guarantees.

Algorithm Name	Algorithm Synopsis
sort(), stable_sort()	Sorts elements in place, either preserving the order of duplicate elements or not. The performance of sort() is similar to quicksort, and the performance of stable_sort() is similar to merge-sort (although the exact algorithms may differ).
partial_sort(), partial_sort_copy()	Partially sorts the sequence: the first *n* elements of a fully sorted sequence are sorted, the rest are not. Either in place or by copying them to a new sequence.
nth_element()	Relocates the *n*th element of the sequence as if the entire sequence were sorted.
merge(), inplace_merge()	Merges two sorted sequences, either in place or by copying them to a new sequence.
make_heap(), push_heap(), pop_heap(), sort_heap()	A heap is a standard data structure in which the elements of an array or sequence are ordered in a semi-sorted fashion so that finding the "top" element is quick. These four algorithms allow you to use heap-sort on sequences.
partition(), stable_partition()	Sorts the sequence such that all elements for which a predicate returns true are before all elements for which it returns false, either preserving the original order of the elements within each partition or not.
random_shuffle()	"Unsorts" the sequence by randomly reordering the elements.

Set Algorithms

Set algorithms are special modifying algorithms that perform set operations on sequences. They are most appropriate on sequences from set containers, but work on sorted sequences from most containers.

Algorithm Name	Algorithm Synopsis
includes()	Determines if one sequence is a subset of another.
set_union(), set_intersection(), set_difference(), set_symmetric_difference()	Perform the specified set operations on two sorted sequences, copying results to a third sorted sequence. See Chapter 22 for an explanation of the set operations.

Choosing an Algorithm

The number and capabilities of the algorithms might overwhelm you at first. It can also be difficult to see how to apply them at first glance. However, now that you are familiar with the options available, you are better able to tackle your program designs. Chapters 21 to 23 cover the details of how to use these algorithms in your code.

What's Missing from the STL

The STL is powerful, but it's not perfect. Here is a list of omissions and unsupported functionality:

❏ The STL does not provide synchronization for multithread safety. The STL standard does not provide for any multithreading synchronization support because threading is platform specific. Thus, if you have a multithreaded program, you must implement your own synchronization for the containers.

❏ The STL does not provide a hash table. More generally, it does not provide any *hashed associative containers*: associative containers in which the elements are not sorted, but are stored according to hashing. Note that many implementations of the STL provide a hash table or hashmap, but since it is not part of the standard, using it is not portable. Chapter 23 provides an example hashmap implementation.

❏ The STL does not provide any generic tree or graph structures. Although maps and sets are generally implemented as balanced binary trees, the STL does not expose this implementation in the interface. If you need a tree or graph structure for something like writing a parser, you will need to implement your own or find an implementation in another library.

❏ The STL does not provide any table abstractions. If you want to implement something like a chessboard, you will probably need to use a two-dimensional array.

However, it is important to keep in mind that the STL is *extensible*. You can write your own containers or algorithms that will work with existing algorithms or containers. So, if the STL doesn't provide exactly what you need, consider writing your desired code such that it works with the STL.

Deciding Whether or Not to Use the STL

The STL was designed with functionality, performance, and orthogonality as its priorities. It was not designed to be easy to use, so naturally it did not turn out to be easy to use. In fact, the introduction in this chapter barely scratched the surface of its complexity. Thus, there is a steep learning curve for using the STL. However, the benefits are substantial. Think about the number of times you've tracked down pointer errors in linked list or balanced binary tree implementations, or debugged a sorting algorithm that wasn't sorting properly. If you use the STL correctly, you will rarely, if ever, need to perform that kind of coding again.

If you decide to pursue the STL in your programs, consult Chapters 21 to 23. They provide an in-depth tutorial for using the containers and algorithms that the STL provides.

Designing with Patterns and Techniques

Learning the C++ language and becoming a good C++ programmer are two very different things. If you sat down and read the C++ standard, memorizing every fact, you would know C++ as well as anybody else. However, until you gain some experience by looking at code and writing your own programs, you wouldn't necessarily be a good programmer. The reason is that the C++ syntax defines what the language can do in its raw form, but doesn't say anything about how each feature should be used.

As they become more experienced in using the C++ language, C++ programmers develop their own individual ways of using the features of the language. The C++ community at large has also built some standard ways of leveraging the language, some formal and some informal. Throughout this book, the authors point out these reusable applications of the language, known as *design techniques* and *design patterns*. Additionally, Chapters 25 and 26 focus almost exclusively on design techniques and patterns. Some patterns and techniques will seem obvious to you because they are simply a formalization of the obvious solution. Others describe novel solutions to problems you've encountered in the past. Some present entirely new ways of thinking about your program organization.

It is important for you to familiarize yourself with these patterns and techniques so that you can recognize when a particular design problem calls for one of these solutions. There are obviously many more techniques and patterns applicable to C++ than those described in this book. Although the authors feel that the most useful ones are covered, you may want to consult a book on design patterns for more and different patterns and techniques. See Appendix B for suggestions.

Design Techniques

A *design technique* is simply a standard approach for solving a particular problem in C++. Often, a design technique aims to overcome an annoying feature or language deficiency of C++. Other times, a design technique is simply a piece of code that you use in many different programs to solve a common problem.

A Design Technique Example: Smart Pointers

Memory management in C++ is a perennial source of errors and bugs. Many of these bugs arise from the use of dynamic memory allocation and pointers. When you use extensive dynamic memory allocation in your program and pass many pointers between objects, it's difficult to remember to call `delete` on each pointer exactly once. The consequences of getting it wrong are severe: when you free dynamically allocated memory more than once you can cause memory corruption, and when you forget to free dynamically allocated memory you cause memory leaks.

Smart pointers help you manage your dynamically allocated memory. Conceptually, a smart pointer is a pointer to dynamically allocated memory that remembers to free the memory when it goes out of scope. In your programs, a smart pointer is generally an object that contains a regular, or *dumb*, pointer. This object is allocated on the stack. When it goes out of scope its destructor calls `delete` on the contained pointer.

Note that some language implementations provide *garbage collection* so that programmers are not responsible for freeing any memory. In these languages, all pointers can be thought of as smart pointers because you don't need to remember to free any of the memory to which they point. Although some languages, such as Java, provide garbage collection as a matter of course, it is very difficult to write a garbage collector for C++. Thus, smart pointers are simply a technique to make up for the fact that C++ exposes memory management without garbage collection.

Managing pointers presents more problems than just remembering to delete them when they go out of scope. Sometimes several objects or pieces of code contain copies of the same pointer. This problem is called *aliasing*. In order to free all memory properly, the last piece of code to use the memory should call `delete` on the pointer. However, it is often difficult to know which piece of code uses the memory last. It may even be impossible to determine the order when you code because it might depend on run-time inputs. Thus, a more sophisticated type of smart pointer implements *reference counting* to keep track of its owners. When all owners are finished using the pointer, the number of references drops to 0 and the smart pointer calls `delete` on its underlying dumb pointer. Many C++ frameworks, such as Microsoft's Object Linking and Embedding (OLE) and Component Object Model (COM) use reference counting extensively. Even if you don't intend to implement reference counting yourself, it is important to be familiar with the concept.

C++ provides several language features that make smart pointers attractive. First, you can write a type-safe smart pointer class for any pointer type using templates. Second, you can provide an interface to the smart pointer objects using operator overloading that allows code to use the smart pointer objects as if they were dumb pointers. Specifically, you can overload the * and -> operators such that the client code can dereference a smart pointer object the same way it dereferences a normal pointer. Chapter 25 provides an implementation of a reference counted smart pointer that you can plug directly into your program. The C++ standard library also provides a simple smart pointer called the `auto_ptr`, as described in the overview of the standard library.

Design Patterns

A *design pattern* is a standard approach to program organization that solves a general problem. C++ is an object-oriented language, so the design patterns of interest to C++ programmers are generally object-oriented patterns, which describe strategies for organizing objects and object relationships in your programs. These patterns are usually applicable to any object-oriented language, such as C++, Java, or Smalltalk. In fact, if you are familiar with Java programming, you will recognize many of these patterns.

Design patterns are less language specific than are techniques. The difference between a pattern and a technique is admittedly fuzzy, and different books employ different definitions. This book defines a technique as a strategy particular to the C++ language that overcomes a deficiency in the language itself, while a pattern is a more general strategy for object-oriented design applicable to any object-oriented language.

Note that many patterns have several different names. The distinctions between the patterns themselves can be somewhat vague, with different sources describing and categorizing them slightly differently. In fact, depending on the books or other sources you use, you may find the same name applied to different patterns. There is even disagreement as to which design approaches qualify as patterns. With a few exceptions, this book follows the terminology used in the seminal book *Design Patterns: Elements of Reusable Object-Oriented Software*, by Erich Gamma et al. However, other pattern names and variations are noted when appropriate.

Chapter 26 provides a catalog of several different design patterns, including sample implementations in C++.

A Design Pattern Example: Iterator

The iterator pattern provides a mechanism for separating algorithms or operations from the data on which they operate. At first glance, this pattern seems to contradict the fundamental principle in object-oriented programming of grouping together in objects data and the behaviors that operate on that data. While that argument is true on a certain level, this pattern does not advocate removing fundamental behaviors from objects. Instead, it solves two problems that commonly arise with tight coupling of data and behaviors.

The first problem with tightly coupling data and behaviors is that it precludes generic algorithms that work on a variety of objects, not all of which are in the same class hierarchy. In order to write generic algorithms, you need some standard mechanism to access the contents of the objects.

The second problem with tightly coupled data and behaviors is that it's sometimes difficult to add new behaviors. At the very least, you need access to the source code for the data objects. However, what if the object hierarchy of interest is part of a third-party framework or library that you cannot change? It would be nice to be able to add an algorithm or operation that works on the data without modifying the original object hierarchy of data.

You've already seen an example of the iterator pattern in the STL. Conceptually, *iterators* provide a mechanism for an operation or algorithm to access a container of elements in a sequence. The name comes from the English word *iterate*, which means "repeat." It applies to iterators because they repeat the action of moving forward in the sequence to reach each new element. In the STL, the generic algorithms use iterators to access the elements of the containers on which they operate. By defining a standard iterator interface, the STL allows you to write algorithms that can work on any container that supplies an iterator with the appropriate interface. Thus, iterators allow you to write generic algorithms without modifying the data. Figure 4-1 shows an iterator as an assembly line that sends the elements of a data object to an "operation."

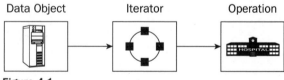

Figure 4-1

Summary

This chapter focused on the design theme of *reuse*. You learned that your C++ design should include both reuse of code, in the form of libraries and frameworks, and reuse of ideas, in the form of techniques and patterns.

Although code reuse is a general goal, there are both advantages and disadvantages associated with it. You learned about these tradeoffs and about specific guidelines for reusing code, including understanding the capabilities and limitations, the performance, licensing and support models, the platform limitations, prototyping, and where to find help. You also learned about performance analysis and big-O notation, as well as special issues and considerations involved in using open-source libraries.

This chapter also provided an overview of the C++ standard library, which is the most important library that you will use in your code. It subsumes the C library and includes additional facilities for strings, I/O, error handling, and other tasks. It also includes generic containers and algorithms, which are together referred to as the standard template library. Chapters 21 to 23 describe the standard template library in detail.

When you design your programs, reusing patterns and techniques is just as important as reusing code. You should avoid reinventing the wheel as well as rebuilding it! To that end, this chapter introduced the notion of design techniques and patterns. Chapters 25 to 26 provide additional examples, including code and sample applications of techniques and patterns.

However, *using* libraries and patterns is only half of the reuse strategy. You also need to *design* your own code so that you and others can reuse it as much as possible. Chapter 5 presents strategies for designing reusable code.

5

Designing for Reuse

Reusing libraries and other code in your programs is an important design strategy. However, it is only half of the *reuse* strategy. The other half is designing and writing the code that you can reuse in your programs. As you've probably discovered, there is a significant difference between well-designed and poorly designed libraries. Well-designed libraries are a pleasure to use, while poorly designed libraries can prod you to give up in disgust and write the code yourself. Whether you're writing a library explicitly designed for use by other programmers or merely deciding on a class hierarchy, you should design your code with reuse in mind. You never know when you'll need a similar piece of functionality in a subsequent project.

Chapter 2 introduced the design theme of reuse. Chapter 4 explained how to apply this theme by incorporating libraries and other code in your designs. This chapter discusses the other side of reuse: designing reusable code. It builds on the object-oriented design principles described in Chapter 3 and introduces some new strategies and guidelines.

After finishing this chapter, you will understand:

❑   The reuse philosophy: why you should design code for reuse

❑   How to design reusable code

    ❑   How to use abstraction

    ❑   Three strategies for structuring your code for reuse

    ❑   Six strategies for designing usable interfaces

❑   How to reconcile generality with ease of use

The Reuse Philosophy

You should design code that both you and other programmers can reuse. This rule applies not only to libraries and frameworks that you specifically intend for other programmers to use, but also to any class, subsystem, or component that you design for a program. You should always keep in mind the motto, "write once, use often." There are several reasons for this design approach:

❑ **Code is rarely used in only one program.** You may not intend your code to be reused when you write it, but you may find yourself or your colleagues incorporating components of the program in similar projects a few months or years later. You know that your code will probably be used again somehow, so design it correctly to begin with.

❑ **Designing for reuse saves time and money.** If you design your code in a way that precludes future use, you ensure that you or your partners will spend time reinventing the wheel later when you encounter a need for a similar piece of functionality. Even if you don't explicitly prevent reuse, if you provide a poor interface or omit functionality, it will require extra time and effort to use the code in the future.

❑ **Other programmers in your group must be able to use the code that you write.** Even in cases where your code is useful only for the specific program at hand, you are probably not working alone on a project. Your coworkers will appreciate your efforts to offer them well-designed, functionality-packed libraries and pieces of code to use. You know what it's like to use a bad interface or poorly thought-out class that someone else wrote. Designing for reuse can also be called *cooperative coding*. You should write code to benefit programmers in projects other than the current one.

❑ **You will be the primary beneficiary of your own work.** Experienced programmers never throw away code. Over time, they build a personal library of evolving tools. You never know when you will need a similar piece of functionality in the future. For example, when one of the authors took his first network programming course as an undergraduate, he wrote some generic networking routines for creating connections, sending messages, and receiving messages. He has consulted that code during every project that involves networking since then, and has reused pieces of it in several different programs.

> When you design or write code as an employee of a company, the company, not you, generally owns the intellectual property rights. It is often illegal to retain copies of your designs or code when you terminate your employment with the company.

How to Design Reusable Code

Reusable code fulfills two main goals. First, it is general enough to use for slightly different purposes or in different application domains. Program components with details of a specific application are difficult to reuse in other programs.

Reusable code is also easy to use. It doesn't require significant time to understand its interface or functionality. Programmers must be able to incorporate it readily into their applications.

> **Reusable code is general purpose and easy to use.**

A collection of reusable code that you provide does not need to be a formal library. It could be a class, a collection of functions, or a program subsystem. However, as in Chapter 4, this chapter uses the term "library" to refer generally to any collection of code that you write.

> *Note that this chapter uses the term "client" to refer to a programmer who uses your interfaces. Don't confuse clients with "users" who run your programs. The chapter also uses the phrase "client code" to refer to code that is written to use your interfaces.*

The most important strategy for designing reusable code is abstraction. Chapter 2 presented the real-world analogy of a television, which you can use through its interfaces without understanding how it works inside. Similarly, when you design code, you should clearly separate the interface from the implementation. This separation makes the code easier to use, primarily because clients do not need to understand the internal implementation details in order to use the functionality.

Abstraction separates code into interface and implementation, so designing reusable code focuses on these two main areas. First, you must structure the code appropriately. What class hierarchies will you use? Should you use templates? How should you divide the code into subsystems?

Second, you must design the *interfaces*, which are the "entries" into your library or code that programmers use to access the functionality you provide. Note that an interface does not need to be a formal API. The concept includes any border between the code you provide and the code that uses it. The public methods of a class or a header file of function prototypes are both perfectly valid interfaces.

> *The term "interface" can refer to a single access point, such as an individual function or method call, or to an entire collection such as an API, class declaration, or header file.*

Use Abstraction

You learned about the principle of abstraction in Chapter 2 and read more about its application to object-oriented design in Chapter 3. To follow the principle of abstraction, you should provide interfaces to your code that hide the underlying implementation details. There should be a clear distinction between the interface and the implementation.

Using abstraction benefits both you and the clients who use your code. Clients benefit because they don't need to worry about the implementation details; they can take advantage of the functionality you offer without understanding how the code really works. You benefit because you can modify the underlying code without changing the interface to the code. Thus, you can provide upgrades and fixes without requiring clients to change their use. With dynamically linked libraries, clients don't even need to rebuild their executables! Finally, you both benefit because you, as the library writer, can specify in the interface exactly what interactions you expect and functionality you support. A clear separation of interfaces and implementations will prevent clients from using the library in ways that you didn't intend, which can otherwise cause unexpected behaviors and bugs.

Suppose that you are designing a random number library and want to provide some way for the user to specify the range of the random numbers. A bad design would expose the global variables or class members that the random number generator implementation uses internally to affect the range. This badly designed library would require client code to set these variables directly. A good design would hide the variables used by the internal implementation and instead provide an implementation-independent function or method call to set the range. That way the client isn't required to understand the internal algorithm. In addition, because the implementation details are not exposed, you could change the algorithm without affecting the client code's interaction with the library.

Sometimes libraries require client code to keep information returned from one interface in order to pass it to another. This information is sometimes called a *handle* and is often used to keep track of specific instances that require state to be remembered between calls. If your library design requires a handle, don't expose its internals. Make that handle into an *opaque* class, in which the programmer can't access the internal data members. Don't require the client code to tweak variables inside this handle. As an example of a bad design, one of the authors actually used a library that required him to set a specific member of a structure in a supposedly opaque handle in order to turn on error logging.

> **C++ fails to provide mechanisms for good abstraction when writing classes. You must place the private data member and method declarations in the same header file as the public method declarations. Chapter 9 describes some techniques for working around this limitation in order to present clean interfaces.**

Abstraction is so important that it should guide your entire design. As part of every decision you make, ask yourself whether your choice fulfills the principle of abstraction. Put yourself in your clients' shoes and determine whether or not you're requiring knowledge of the internal implementation in the interface. You should rarely, if ever, make exceptions to this rule.

Structure Your Code for Optimal Reuse

You must consider reuse from the beginning of your design. The following strategies will help you organize your code properly. Note that all of these strategies focus on making your code general purpose. The second aspect of designing reusable code, providing ease of use, is more relevant to your interface design and is discussed later in this chapter.

Avoid Combining Unrelated or Logically Separate Concepts

When you design a library or framework, keep it focused on a single task or group of tasks. Don't combine unrelated concepts such as a random number generator and an XML parser.

Even when you are not designing code specifically for reuse, keep this strategy in mind. Entire programs are rarely reused on their own. Instead, pieces or subsystems of the programs are incorporated directly into other applications, or are adapted for slightly different uses. Thus, you should design your programs so that you divide logically separate functionality into distinct components that can be reused in different programs.

This program strategy models the real-world design principle of discrete, interchangeable parts. For example, you could take the tires off an old car and use them on a new car of a different model. Tires are separable components that are not tied to other aspects of the car. You don't need to bring the engine along with the tires!

You can employ the strategy of logical division in your program design on both the macro subsystem level and the micro class hierarchy level.

Divide Your Programs into Logical Subsystems

Design your subsystems as discrete components that can be reused independently. For example, if you are designing a networked game, keep the networking and graphical user interface aspects in separate subsystems. That way you can reuse either component without dragging in the other. For example, you might want to write a non-networked game, in which case you could reuse the graphical interface subsystem, but wouldn't need the networking aspect. Similarly, you could design a peer-to-peer file-sharing program, in which case you could reuse the networking subsystem but not the graphical user interface functionality.

Make sure to follow the principle of abstraction for each subsystem, clearly separating the interface in the subsystem from its underlying implementation. Think of each subsystem as a miniature library for which you must provide a coherent and easy-to-use interface. Even if you're the only programmer who ever uses these miniature libraries, you will benefit from well-designed interfaces and implementations that separate logically distinct functionality.

Use Class Hierarchies to Separate Logical Concepts

In addition to dividing your program into logical subsystems, you should avoid combining unrelated concepts at the class level. For example, suppose you want to write a balanced binary tree structure for a multithreaded program. You decide that the tree data structure should allow only one thread at a time to access or modify the structure, so you incorporate locking into the data structure itself. However, what if you want to use this binary tree in another program that happens to be single-threaded? In that case, the locking is a waste of time, and would require your program to link with libraries that it could otherwise avoid. Even worse, your tree structure might not compile on a different platform because the locking code is probably not cross-platform. The solution is to create a class hierarchy (introduced in Chapter 3) in which a thread-safe binary tree is a subclass of a generic binary tree. That way you can use the binary tree superclass in single-threaded programs without incurring the cost of locking unnecessarily, or on a different platform without rewriting the locking code. Figure 5-1 shows this hierarchy:

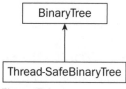

Figure 5-1

This strategy works well when there are two logical concepts, such as thread safety and binary trees. It becomes more complicated when there are three or more concepts. For example, suppose you want to provide both an *n*-ary tree and a binary tree, each of which could be thread-safe or not. Logically, the binary tree is a special-case of an *n*-ary tree, and so should be a subclass of an *n*-ary tree. Similarly, thread-safe structures should be subclasses of non-thread-safe structures. You can't provide these separations with a linear hierarchy. One possibility is to make the thread-safe aspect a mix-in class as shown in Figure 5-2:

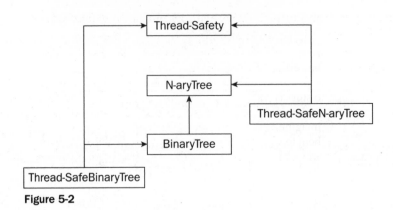

Figure 5-2

That hierarchy requires you to write five different classes, but the clear separation of functionality is worth the effort.

You can also use class hierarchies to separate generic functionality from more specific functionality. For example, suppose you are designing an operating system that supports user-level multithreading. You might be tempted to write a process class that includes multithreading support. However, what about those user processes that don't want to be multithreaded? A better design creates a generic process class, and makes a multithreaded process a subclass of it.

Use Aggregation to Separate Logical Concepts

Aggregation, discussed in Chapter 3, models the *has-a* relationship: objects contain other objects to perform some aspects of their functionality. You can use aggregation to separate unrelated or related but separate functionality when inheritance is not appropriate.

Continuing with the operating system example, you might want to store ready processes in a priority queue. Instead of integrating the priority queue structure with your ReadyQueue class, write a separate priority queue class. Then your ReadyQueue class can contain and use a priority queue. To use the object-oriented terminology, the ReadyQueue has-a priority queue. With this technique, the priority queue could be reused more easily in another program.

Use Templates for Generic Data Structures and Algorithms

Whenever possible, you should use a generic design for data structures and algorithms instead of encoding specifics of a particular program. Don't write a balanced binary tree structure that stores only book objects. Make it generic, so that it can store objects of any type. That way you could use it in a bookstore, a music store, an operating system, or anywhere that you need a balanced binary tree. This strategy underlies the standard template library (STL) discussed in Chapter 4. The STL provides generic data structures and algorithms that work on any types.

As the STL demonstrates, C++ provides an excellent language feature for this type of generic programming: templates. As described in Chapters 2 and 4, templates allow you to write both data structures and algorithms that work on any types. Chapter 11 provides the coding details of templates, but this section discusses some of their important design aspects.

Why Templates Are Better Than Other Generic Programming Techniques

Templates are not the only mechanism for writing generic data structures. You can write generic structures in C and C++ by storing `void*` pointers instead of a specific type. Clients can use this structure to store anything they want by casting it to a `void*`. However, the main problem with this approach is that it is not *type-safe*: the containers are unable to check or enforce the types of the stored elements. You can cast any type to a `void*` to store in the structure, and when you remove the pointers from the data structure, you must cast them back to what you think they are. Because there are no checks involved, the results can be disastrous. Imagine a scenario where one programmer stores pointers to `int` in a data structure by first casting them to `void*`, but another programmer thinks they are pointers to `Process` objects. The second programmer will blithely cast the `void*` pointers to `Process*` pointers and try to use them as `Process*`s. Needless to say, the program will not work as expected.

A second approach is to write the data structure for a specific class. Through polymorphism, any subclass of that class can be stored in the structure. Java takes this approach to an extreme: it specifies that every class derives directly or indirectly from the `Object` class. The Java containers store `Object`s, so they can store objects of any type. However, this approach is also not truly type-safe. When you remove an object from the container, you must remember what it really is and down-cast it to the appropriate type.

Templates, on the other hand, are type-safe when used correctly. Each instantiation of a template stores only one type. Your program will not compile if you try to store different types in the same template instantiation.

Problems with Templates

Templates are not perfect. First of all, their syntax is confusing, especially for someone who has not used them before. Second, the parsing is difficult, and not all compilers fully support the C++ standard.

Furthermore, templates require homogeneous data structures, in which you can store only objects of the same type in a single structure. That is, if you write a templatized balanced binary tree, you can create one tree object to store `Process` objects and another tree object to store `int`s. You can't store both `int`s and `Processes` in the same tree. This restriction is a direct result of the type-safe nature of templates. Although type-safety is important, some programmers consider the homogeneity requirement a significant restriction.

Another problem with templates is that they lead to *code bloat*. When you create a tree object to store `int`s, the compiler actually "expands" the template to generate code as if you had written a tree structure just for `int`s. Similarly, if you create a tree object to store `Processes`, the compiler generates code as if you had written a tree structure just for `Processes`. If you instantiate templates for many different types, you end up with huge executable files because of all the different code that is generated.

Templates versus Inheritance

Programmers sometimes find it tricky to decide whether to use templates or inheritance. Here are some tips to help you make the decision.

Use templates when you want to provide identical functionality for different types. For example, if you want to write a generic sorting algorithm that works on any type, use templates. If you want to create a container that can store any type, use templates. The key concept is that the templatized structure or algorithm treats all types the same.

When you want to provide different behaviors for related types, use inheritance. For example, use inheritance if you want to provide two different, but similar, containers such as a queue and a priority queue.

Note that you can combine inheritance and templates. You could write a templatized queue that stores any type, with a subclass that is a templatized priority queue. Chapter 11 covers the details of the template syntax.

Provide Appropriate Checks and Safeguards

You should always design your programs to be as safe as possible for use by other programmers. The most important aspect of this guideline is to perform error checking in your code. For example, if your random number generator requires a non-negative integer for a seed, don't just trust the user to correctly pass a non-negative integer. Check the value that is passed in, and reject the call if it is invalid.

As an analogy, consider an accountant who prepares income tax returns. When you hire an accountant, you provide him or her with all your financial information for the year. The accountant uses this information to fill out forms from the Internal Revenue Service. However, the accountant does not blindly fill out your information on the form, but instead makes sure the information makes sense. For example, if you own a house, but forget to specify the property tax you paid, the accountant will remind you to supply that information. Similarly, if you say that you paid $12,000 in mortgage interest, but made only $15,000 gross income, the accountant might gently ask you if you provided the correct numbers (or at least recommend more affordable housing).

You can think of the accountant as a "program" where the input is your financial information and the output is an income tax return. However, the value added by an accountant is not just that he or she fills out the forms. You choose to employ an accountant also because of the checks and safeguards that he or she provides. Similarly in programming, you should provide as many checks and safeguards as possible in your implementations.

There are several techniques and language features that help you incorporate checks and safeguards in your programs. First, use exceptions to notify the client code of errors. Chapter 15 covers exceptions in detail. Second, use smart pointers (discussed in Chapter 4) and other safe memory techniques discussed in Chapter 13.

Design Usable Interfaces

In addition to abstracting and structuring your code appropriately, designing for reuse requires you to focus on the *interface* with which programmers interact. If you hide an ugly implementation behind a pretty interface, no one needs to know. However, if you provide a beautiful implementation behind a wretched interface, your library won't be much good.

Note that every subsystem and class in your program should have good interfaces, even if you don't intend them to be used in multiple programs. First of all, you never know when something will be reused. Second, a good interface is important even for the first use, especially if you are programming in a group and other programmers must use the code you design and write.

The main purpose of interfaces is to make the code easy to use, but some interface techniques can help you follow the principle of generality as well.

Design Interfaces That Are Easy to Use

Your interfaces should be easy to use. That doesn't mean that they must be trivial, but they should be as simple and intuitive as the functionality allows. You shouldn't require consumers of your library to wade through pages of source code in order to use a simple data structure, or go through contortions in their code to obtain the functionality they need. This section provides four specific strategies for designing interfaces that are easy to use.

Develop Intuitive Interfaces

Computer programmers use the term *intuitive* to describe interfaces that people can figure out easily and without much instruction. The use of the word intuitive is similar to its meaning in the phrase "intuitively obvious," which means apparent without much reasoning or examination. Intuitive interfaces are, almost by definition, easy to use.

The best strategy for developing intuitive interfaces is to follow standard and familiar ways of doing things. When people encounter an interface similar to something they have used in the past, they will understand it better, adopt it more readily, and be less likely to use it improperly.

For example, suppose that you are designing the steering mechanism of a car. There are a number of possibilities: a joystick, two buttons for moving left or right, a sliding horizontal lever, or a good-old steering wheel. Which interface do you think would be easiest to use? Which interface do you think would sell the most cars? Consumers are familiar with steering wheels, so the answer to both questions is, of course, the steering wheel. Even if you developed another mechanism that provided superior performance and safety, you would have a tough time selling your product, let alone teaching people how to use it. When you have a choice between following standard interface models and branching out in a new direction, it's usually better to stick to the interface to which people are accustomed.

Innovation is important, of course, but you should focus on innovation in the underlying implementation, not in the interface. For example, consumers are excited about the innovative hybrid gasoline-electric engine in some car models. These cars are selling well in part because the interface to use them is identical to cars with standard engines.

Applied to C++, this strategy implies that you should develop interfaces that follow standards to which C++ programmers are accustomed. For example, C++ programmers expect the constructor and destructor of a class to initialize and clean up an object, respectively. When you design your classes, you should follow this standard. If you require programmers to call `initialize()` and `cleanup()` methods for initialization and cleanup instead of placing that functionality in the constructor and destructor, you will confuse everyone who tries to use your class. Because your class behaves differently from other C++ classes, programmers will take longer to learn how to use it and will be more likely to use it incorrectly by forgetting to call `initialize()` or `cleanup()`.

> *Always think about your interfaces from the perspective of someone using them. Do they make sense? Are they what you would expect?*

C++ provides a language feature called *operator overloading* that can help you develop intuitive interfaces for your objects. Operator overloading allows you to write classes such that the standard operators work on them just as they work on built-in types like `int` and `double`. For example, you can write a `Fraction` class that allows you to add, subtract, and stream fractions like this:

```
Fraction f1(3,4), f2(1,2), sum, diff;
sum = f1 + f2;
diff = f1 - f2;
cout << f1 << " " << f2 << endl;
```

Contrast that with the same behavior using method calls:

```
Fraction f1(3,4), f2(1,2), sum, diff;
sum = f1.add(f2);
diff = f1.subtract(f2);
f1.print(cout);
cout << " ";
f2.print(cout);
cout << endl;
```

As you can see, operator overloading allows you to provide intuitive interfaces for your classes. However, be careful not to abuse operator overloading. It's possible to overload the + operator so that it implements subtraction and the – operator so that it implements multiplication. Those implementations would be counterintuitive. Always follow the expected meaning of the operators. See Chapters 9 and 16 for details on operator overloading.

Don't Omit Required Functionality

This strategy is twofold. First, include interfaces for all behaviors that clients could need. That might sound obvious at first. Returning to the car analogy, you would never build a car without a speedometer for the driver to view his or her speed! Similarly, you would never design a Fraction class without a mechanism for the client code to access the actual value of the fraction.

However, other possible behaviors might be more obscure. This strategy requires you to anticipate all the uses to which clients might put your code. If you are thinking about the interface in one particular way, you might miss functionality that could be needed when clients use it differently. For example, suppose that you want to design a game board class. You might consider only the typical games, such as chess and checkers, and decide to support a maximum of one game piece per spot on the board. However, what if you later decide to write a backgammon game, which allows multiple pieces in one spot on the board? By precluding that possibility, you have ruled out the use of your game board as a backgammon board.

Obviously, anticipating every possible use for your library is difficult, if not impossible. Don't feel compelled to agonize over potential future uses in order to design the perfect interface. Just give it some thought and do the best you can.

The second part of this strategy is to include as much functionality in the implementation as possible. Don't require client code to specify information that you already know in the implementation, or could know if you designed it differently. For example, if your XML parser library requires a temporary file in which to store results, don't make the clients of your library specify that path. They don't care what file you use; find some other way to determine an appropriate file path.

Furthermore, don't require library users to perform unnecessary work to amalgamate results. If your random number library uses a random number algorithm that calculates the low-order and high-order bits of a random number separately, combine the numbers before giving them to the user.

> **Don't require library users to perform tasks that you could do for them.**

Present Uncluttered Interfaces

In order to avoid omitting functionality in their interfaces, some programmers go to the opposite extreme: they include every possible piece of functionality imaginable. Programmers who use the interfaces are never left without the means to accomplish a task. Unfortunately, the interface might be so cluttered that they never figure out how to do it!

Don't provide unnecessary functionality in your interfaces; keep them clean and simple. It might appear at first that this guideline directly contradicts the previous strategy of avoiding omitting necessary functionality. Although one strategy to avoid omitting functionality would be to include every imaginable interface, that is not a sound strategy. You should include *necessary* functionality and omit useless or counterproductive interfaces.

Consider cars again. You drive a car by interacting with only a few components: the steering wheel, the brake and accelerator pedals, the gearshift, the mirrors, the speedometer, and a few other dials on your dashboard. Now, imagine a car dashboard that looked like an airplane cockpit, with hundreds of dials, levers, monitors, and buttons. It would be unusable! Driving a car is so much easier than flying an airplane that the interface can be much simpler: you don't need to view your altitude, communicate with control towers, or control the myriad components in an airplane such as the wings, engines, and landing gear.

Additionally, from the library development perspective, smaller libraries are easier to maintain. If you try to make everyone happy, then you have more room to make mistakes, and if your implementation is complicated enough so that everything is intertwined, even one mistake can render the library useless.

Unfortunately, the idea of designing uncluttered interfaces looks good on paper, but is remarkably hard to put into practice. The rule is ultimately subjective: you decide what's necessary and what's not. Of course, your clients will be sure to tell you when you get it wrong! Here are a few tips to keep in mind:

- ❑ **Eliminate duplicate interfaces.** If you have one method to return a result in feet and another to return a result in meters, combine them into a method that returns an object than can provide a result in either feet or meters.

- ❑ **Determine the simplest way to provide the functionality you need.** Eliminate unnecessary parameters and methods and combine multiple methods into single methods when appropriate. For example, combine a library initialization routine with a method that sets initial user-specified parameters.

- ❑ **Limit the library's uses when appropriate.** It's impossible to cater to everyone's whims and desires. Inevitably, someone will try to use the library in ways that you didn't intend. For example, if you provide a library for XML parsing, someone might try to use it to parse SGML. That wasn't your intention, so you shouldn't feel compelled to include the functionality to support it.

Provide Documentation and Comments

Regardless of how easy to use and intuitive you make your interfaces, you should supply documentation for their use. You can't expect programmers to use your library properly unless you tell them how to do it. Think of your library or code as a product for other programmers to consume. Any tangible product that you purchase, such as a DVD player, comes with a set of instructions explaining its interface, functionality, limitations, and troubleshooting. Even simple products such as chairs usually provide instructions for proper use, even if it's only something like, "Sit here. If you use this product in any other manner, death or serious injury could result." Similarly, your product should have documentation explaining its proper use.

There are two ways to provide documentation for your interfaces: comments in the interfaces themselves and external documentation. You should strive to provide both. Most public APIs provide only external documentation: comments are a scarce commodity in many of the standard Unix and Windows header files. In Unix, the documentation usually comes in the form of online manuals called *man pages*. In Windows, the documentation usually accompanies the integrated development environment.

Despite the fact that most APIs and libraries omit comments in the interfaces themselves, we actually consider this form of documentation the most important. You should never give out a "naked" header file that contains only code. Even if your comments repeat exactly what's in the external documentation, it is less intimidating to look at a header file with friendly comments than one with only code. Even the best programmers still like to see written language every so often!

Some programmers use tools to create documentation automatically from comments. These tools parse comments with specific keywords and formatting to generate documentation, often in Hypertext Markup Language (HTML) form. The Java programming language popularized this technique with the JavaDoc tool, but there are many similar tools available for C++. Chapter 7 discusses this technique in more detail.

Whether you provide comments, external documentation, or both, the documentation should describe the *behavior* of the library, not the *implementation*. The behavior includes the inputs, outputs, error conditions and handling, intended uses, and performance guarantees. For example, documentation describing a call to generate a single random number should specify that it takes no parameters, returns an integer in a previously specified range, and throws an "out of memory" exception if it can't allocate memory. This documentation should not explain the details of the linear congruence algorithm for actually generating the number. The client of the interface doesn't care about the algorithm as long as the numbers appear random! Providing too much implementation detail in interface comments is probably the single most common mistake in interface development. We've seen many perfectly good separations of interface and implementation ruined by comments in the interface that are more appropriate for library maintainers than clients.

> **Public documentation should specify behaviors, not underlying implementations.**

Of course you should still document your internal implementation, just don't make it publicly available as part of your interface. Chapter 7 provides details on the appropriate use of comments in your code.

Design General-Purpose Interfaces

The interfaces should be general purpose enough that they can be adapted to a variety of tasks. If you encode specifics of one application in a supposedly general interface, it will be unusable for any other purpose. Here are some guidelines to keep in mind.

Provide Multiple Ways to Perform the Same Functionality

In order to satisfy all your "customers," it is sometimes helpful to provide multiple ways to perform the same functionality. Use this technique judiciously, however, because overapplication can easily lead to cluttered interfaces.

Consider cars again. Most new cars these days provide remote keyless entry systems, with which you can unlock your car by pressing a button on a key fob. However, these cars always provide a standard key that you can use to physically unlock the car. Although these two methods are redundant, most customers appreciate having both options.

Sometimes there are similar situations in program interface design. For example, suppose that one of your methods takes a string. You might want to provide two interfaces: one that takes a C++ `string` object and one that takes a C-style character pointer. Although it's possible to convert between the two, different programmers prefer different types of strings, so it's helpful to cater to both approaches.

Note that this strategy should be considered an exception to the "uncluttered" rule in interface design. There are a few situations where the exception is appropriate, but you should most often follow the "uncluttered" rule.

Provide Customizability

In order to increase the flexibility of your interfaces, provide customizability. People generally appreciate customizability the most when it's absent. For example, one of the authors recently purchased a new car with an antitheft device. This alarm automatically deactivates when the doors are unlocked using the remote keyless entry. Unfortunately, if the doors are not opened within 30 seconds after they are unlocked, the alarm reactivates. This feature becomes quite annoying when trying to use the trunk of the car. It's inconvenient to open a car door just to access something in the trunk. However, if the alarm is not deactivated, slamming the trunk lid triggers it. The most annoying aspect of this problem is that there is no way to permanently deactivate the antitheft device! The car designers must have assumed that everyone would want the same functionality in their antitheft devices, and didn't provide a mechanism to customize it.

Customizability can be as simple as allowing a client to turn on or off error logging. The basic premise of customizability is that it allows you to provide the same basic functionality to every client, but gives clients the ability to tweak it slightly.

You can allow greater customizability through function pointers and template parameters. For example, you could allow clients to set their own error-handling routines. This technique is an application of the decorator pattern described in Chapter 26.

The STL takes this customizability strategy to the extreme and actually allows clients to specify their own memory allocators for containers. If you want to use this feature, you must write a memory allocator object that follows the STL guidelines and adheres to the required interfaces. Each container in the STL takes an allocator as one of its template parameters. Chapter 23 provides the details.

Reconciling Generality and Ease of Use

The two goals of ease of use and generality sometimes appear to conflict. Often, introducing generality increases the complexity of the interfaces. For example, suppose that you need a graph structure in a map program to store cities. In the interest of generality, you might use templates to write a generic map structure for any type, not just cities. That way, if you need to write a network simulator in your next program, you could employ the same graph structure to store routers in the network. Unfortunately, by using templates, you made the interface a little clumsier and harder to use, especially if the potential client is not familiar with templates.

However, generality and ease of use are not mutually exclusive. Although in some cases increased generality may decrease ease of use, it is possible to design interfaces that are both general purpose and straightforward to use. Here are two guidelines you can follow.

Supply Multiple Interfaces

In order to reduce complexity in your interfaces while still providing enough functionality, you can provide two separate interfaces. For example, you could write a generic networking library with two separate facets: one presents the networking interfaces useful for games, and one presents the networking interfaces useful for the Hypertext Transport Protocol (HTTP) Web browsing protocol.

The STL takes this approach with its `string` class. As noted in Chapter 4, the `string` class is actually a `char` instantiation of the `basic_stream` template. You can think of the `string` class as an interface that hides the full complexity of the `basic_stream` template.

Optimize the Common Functionality

When you provide a general-purpose interface, some functionality will be used more often than other functionality. You should make the commonly used functionality easy to use, while still providing the option for the more advanced functionality. Returning to the map program, you might want to provide an option for clients of the map to specify names of cities in different languages. English is so predominant that you could make that the default but provide an extra option to change languages. That way most clients will not need to worry about setting the language, but those who want to will be able to do so.

This strategy is similar to the performance principle discussed in Chapter 4 of optimizing the parts of the code that are executed most often. Focus on optimizing those aspects of your design that provide the most benefit for the most people.

Summary

By reading this chapter, you learned *why* you should design reusable code and *how* you should do it. You read about the philosophy of reuse, summarized as "write once, use often," and learned that reusable code should be both general purpose and easy to use. You also discovered that designing reusable code requires you to use abstraction, to structure your code appropriately, and to design good interfaces.

This chapter presented three specific tips for structuring your code: avoid combining unrelated or logically separate concepts, use templates for generic data structures and algorithms, and provide appropriate checks and safeguards.

The chapter also presented six strategies for designing interfaces: develop intuitive interfaces, don't omit required functionality, present uncluttered interfaces, provide documentation and comments, provide multiple ways to perform the same functionality, and provide customizability. It concluded with two tips for reconciling the often-conflicting demands of generality and ease of use: supply multiple interfaces and optimize common functionality.

This chapter concludes the discussion of design themes that began in Chapter 2. Chapter 6 finishes the design section of this book with a discussion of software-engineering methodologies. Chapters 7 through 11 delve into the implementation phase of the software engineering process with details of C++ coding.

6

Maximizing Software-Engineering Methods

When you first learned how to program, you were probably on your own schedule. You were free to do everything at the last minute if you wanted to, and you could radically change your design during implementation. When coding in the professional world, however, programmers rarely have such flexibility. Even the most liberal engineering managers admit that some amount of process is necessary. Knowing the software-engineering process is as important these days as knowing how to code.

This chapter surveys various approaches to software engineering. It does not go into great depth on any one approach — there are plenty of excellent books on software-engineering processes. The idea is to cover the different types of processes in broad strokes so you can compare and contrast them. We try not to advocate or discourage any particular methodology. Rather, we hope that by learning about the tradeoffs of several different approaches, you'll be able to construct a process that works for you and the rest of your team.

Whether you're a contractor working alone on projects or your team consists of hundreds of engineers on several continents, understanding the different approaches to software development will help your job on a daily basis.

The Need for Process

The history of software development is filled with tales of failed projects. From over-budget and poorly marketed consumer applications to grandiose mega-hyped operating systems, it seems that no area of software development is free from this trend.

Even when software successfully reaches users, bugs have become so commonplace that end users are forced to endure constant updates and patches. Sometimes the software does not accomplish the tasks it is supposed to or doesn't work the way the user would expect. These issues all point to a common truism of software — writing software is hard.

One wonders why software engineering seems to differ from other forms of engineering in its frequency of failures. While cars do have their share of bugs, you rarely see them stop suddenly and demand a reboot due to a buffer overflow (though as more auto components become software-driven, you just may!) Your TV may not be perfect, but you don't have to upgrade to version 2.3 to get Channel 6 to work.

Is it the case that other engineering disciplines are just more advanced than software? Is a civil engineer able to construct a working bridge by drawing upon the long history of bridge building? Are chemical engineers able to build a compound successfully because most of the bugs were worked out in earlier generations?

> **Is software simply too new, or is it really a different type of discipline with inherent qualities contributing to the occurrence of bugs, unusable results, and doomed projects?**

It certainly seems as if there's something different about software. For one thing, technology changes rapidly in software, creating uncertainty in the software development process. Even if an earth-shattering breakthrough does not occur during your project, the pace of the industry leads to paranoia. Software often needs to be developed quickly because competition is fierce.

Software development can also be unpredictable. Accurate scheduling is nearly impossible when a single gnarly bug can take days or even weeks to fix. Even when things seem to be going according to schedule, the widespread tendency of product definition changes (feature creep) can throw a wrench in the process.

Software is complex. There is no easy and accurate way to prove that a program is bug-free. Buggy or messy code can have an impact on software for years if it is maintained through several versions. Software systems are often so complex that when staff turnover occurs, nobody wants to get anywhere near the messy code that forgotten engineers have left behind. This leads to a cycle of endless patching, hacks, and workarounds.

Of course, standard business risks apply to software as well. Marketing pressures and miscommunication get in the way. Many programmers try to steer clear of corporate politics, but it's not uncommon to have adversity between the development and product marketing groups.

All of these factors working against software-engineering products indicate the need for some sort of process. Software projects are big, complicated, and fast-paced. To avoid failure, engineering groups need to adopt a system to control this unwieldy process.

Software Life-Cycle Models

Complexity in software isn't new. The need for formalized process was recognized decades ago. Several approaches to modeling the *software life cycle* have attempted to bring some order to the chaos of software development by defining the software process in terms of steps from the initial idea to the final product. These models, refined over the years, guide much of software development today.

The Stagewise and Waterfall Models

The classic life cycle model for software is often referred to as the *Stagewise Model*. This model is based on the idea that software can be built almost like following a recipe. There is a set of steps that, if followed correctly, will yield a mighty fine chocolate cake, or program as the case may be. Each stage must be completed before the next stage can begin, as shown in Figure 6-1.

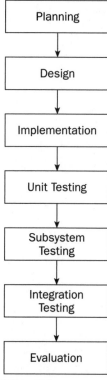

Figure 6-1

The process starts with formal planning, including gathering an exhaustive list of requirements. This list defines feature completeness for the product. The more specific the requirements are, the more likely that the project will succeed. Next, the software is designed and fully specified. The design step, like the requirements step, needs to be as specific as possible to maximize the chance of success. All design decisions are made at this time, often including pseudocode and the definition of specific subsystems that will need to be written. Subsystem owners work out how their code will interact, and the team agrees on the specifics of the architecture. Implementation of the design occurs next. Because the design has been fully specified, the code needs to adhere strongly to the design or else the pieces won't fit together. The final four stages are reserved for unit testing, subsystem testing, integration testing, and evaluation.

The main problem with the Stagewise Model is that, in practice, it is nearly impossible to complete one stage without at least exploring the next stage. A design cannot be set in stone without at least writing *some* code. Furthermore, what is the point of testing if the model doesn't provide a way to go back to the coding phase?

A number of refinements to the Stagewise Model were formalized as the *Waterfall Model* in the early 1970s. This model continues to be highly influential, if not downright dominant, in modern software-engineering organizations. The main advancement that the Waterfall Model brought was a notion of feedback between stages. While it still stresses a rigorous process of planning, designing, coding, and testing, successive stages can overlap in part. Figure 6-2 shows an example of the Waterfall Model, illustrating the feedback and overlap refinements. Feedback allows lessons learned in one phase to result in changes to the previous phase. Overlap permits activity in two phases to occur simultaneously.

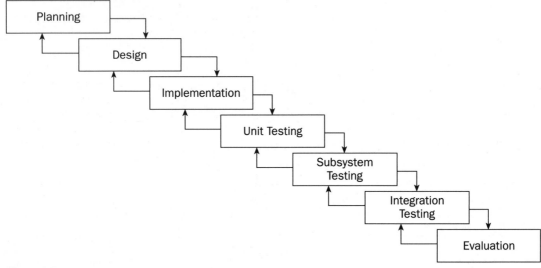

Figure 6-2

Various incarnations of the waterfall method have refined the process in different ways. For example, some plans include a "feasibility" step where experiments are performed before formal requirements are even gathered.

Benefits of the Waterfall Model

The value of the Waterfall Model lies in its simplicity. You, or your manager, may have followed this approach in past projects without formalizing it or recognizing it by name. The underlying assumption behind the Stepwise and Waterfall Models is that as long as each step is accomplished as completely and accurately as possible, subsequent steps will go smoothly. As long as all of the requirements are carefully specified in the first step, and all the design decisions and problems are hashed out in the second step, implementation in the third step should be a simple matter of translating the designs into code.

The simplicity of the Waterfall Model makes project plans based on this system organized and easy to manage. Every project is started the same way: by exhaustively listing all the features that are necessary. Managers using this approach can require that by the end of the design phase, for example, all engineers in charge of a subsystem submit their design as a formal design document or a functional subsystem specification. The benefit for the manager is that by having engineers specify and design upfront, risks are, hopefully, minimized.

From the engineer's point of view, the Waterfall Method forces resolution of major issues upfront. All engineers will need to understand their project and design their subsystem before writing a significant amount of code. Ideally, this means that code can be written once instead of hacked together or rewritten when the pieces don't fit.

For small projects with very specific requirements, the Waterfall Method can work quite well. Particularly for consulting arrangements, it has the advantage of specifying specific metrics for success at the start of the project. Formalizing requirements helps the consultant to produce exactly what the client wants and forces the client to be specific about the goals for the project.

Drawbacks of the Waterfall Model

In many organizations, and almost all modern software-engineering texts, the Waterfall Method has fallen out of favor. Critics disparage its fundamental premise that software development tasks happen in discrete linear steps. While the Waterfall Method allows for the overlapping of phases, it does not allow backward movement to a large degree. In many projects today, requirements come in throughout the development of the product. Often, a potential customer will request a feature that is necessary for the sale or a competitor's product will have a new feature that requires parity.

> **The upfront specification of all requirements makes the Waterfall Method unusable for many organizations because it simply is not dynamic enough.**

Another drawback is that in an effort to minimize risk by making decisions as formally and early as possible, the Waterfall Model may actually be hiding risk. For example, a major design issue might be undiscovered, glossed over, forgotten, or purposely avoided in the design phase. By the time integration testing reveals the mismatch, it may be too late to save the project. A major design flaw has arisen but, according to the Waterfall Model, the product is one step away from shipping! A mistake anywhere in the waterfall process will likely lead to failure at the end of the process. Early detection is difficult and rare.

While the Waterfall Model is still quite common and can be an effective way of visualizing the process, it is often necessary to make it more flexible by taking cues from other approaches.

The Spiral Method

The *Spiral Method* was proposed by Barry W. Boehm in 1988 in recognition of the occurrence of unexpected problems and changing requirements in the software development process. This method is part of a family of techniques known as *iterative processes*. The fundamental idea is that it's okay if something goes wrong because you'll fix it the next time around. A single spin through the spiral method is shown in Figure 6-3.

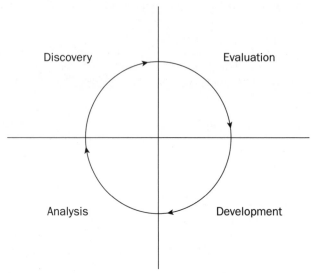

Figure 6-3

The phases of the Spiral Method are similar to the steps of the Waterfall Method. The discovery phase involves building requirements and determining objectives. During the evaluation phase, implementation alternatives are considered and prototypes may be built. In the Spiral Method, particular attention is paid to evaluating and resolving risks in the evaluation phase. The tasks deemed most risky are the ones that are implemented in the current cycle of the spiral. The tasks in the development phase are determined by the risks identified in the evaluation phase. For example, if evaluation reveals a risky algorithm that may be impossible to implement, the main task for development in the current cycle will be modeling, building, and testing that algorithm. The fourth phase is reserved for analysis and planning. Based on the results of the current cycle, the plan for the subsequent cycle is formed. Each iteration is expected to be fairly short in duration, taking only a few key features and risks into consideration.

Figure 6-4 shows an example of three cycles through the spiral in the development of an operating system. The first cycle yields a plan containing the major requirements for the product. The second cycle results in a prototype showing the user experience. The third cycle builds a component that is determined to be a high risk.

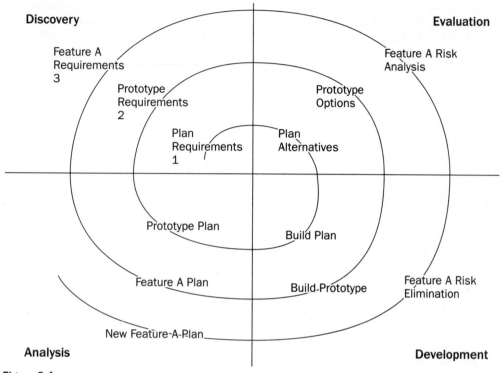

Figure 6-4

Benefits of the Spiral Method

The Spiral Method can be viewed as the application of an iterative approach to the best that the Waterfall Method has to offer. Figure 6-5 shows the Spiral Method as a waterfall process that has been modified to allow iteration. Hidden risks and a linear development path, the main drawbacks of the Waterfall Method, are resolved through short iterative cycles.

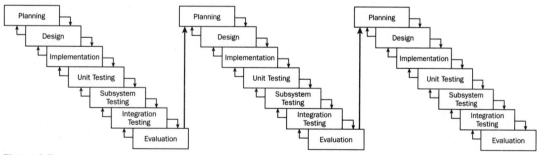

Figure 6-5

Performing the riskiest tasks first is another benefit. By bringing risk to the forefront and acknowledging that new conditions can arise at any time, the Spiral Method avoids the hidden time bombs that can occur in the Waterfall Model. When unexpected problems arise, they can be dealt with using the same four-stage approach that works for the rest of the process.

Finally, by repeatedly analyzing after each cycle and building new designs, the practical difficulties with the design-then-implement approach are virtually eliminated. With each cycle, there is more knowledge of the system that can influence the design.

Drawbacks of the Spiral Method

The main drawback of the Spiral Method is that it can be difficult to scope each iteration small enough to gain real benefit. In a worst-case scenario, the Spiral Method can degenerate into the Waterfall Model because the iterations are too long. Unfortunately, the Spiral Model only *models* the software life cycle. It cannot prescribe a specific way to break down a project into single-cycle iterations because that division varies from project to project.

Other possible drawbacks are the overhead of repeating all four phases for each cycle and the difficulty of coordinating cycles. Logistically, it may be difficult to assemble all the group members for design discussions at the right time. If different teams are working on different parts of the product simultaneously, they are probably operating in parallel cycles, which can get out of synch. For example, the user interface group could be ready to start the discovery phase of the Window Manager cycle, but the core OS group is still in the development phase of the memory subsystem.

The Rational Unified Process

The *Rational Unified Process (RUP)* is a disciplined and formal approach to managing the software development process. The most important characteristic of the RUP is that, unlike the Spiral Method or the Waterfall Model, RUP is more than just a theoretical process model. RUP is actually a software product, marketed and sold by Rational Software, a division of IBM. Treating the process as software is compelling for a number of reasons:

❑   The process itself can be updated and refined, just as software products periodically have updates.

❑   Rather than simply suggesting a development framework, RUP includes a set of software tools for working with that framework.

❑   As a product, RUP can be rolled out to the entire engineering team so that all members are using the exact same processes and tools.

❑   Like many software products, RUP can be customized to the needs of the users.

RUP as a Product

As a product, the RUP takes the form of a suite of software applications that guides developers through the software development process. The product also offers specific guidance for other Rational products, such as the Rational Rose visual modeling tool and the Rational ClearCase configuration management tool. Extensive groupware communication tools are included as part of the "marketplace of ideas" that allow developers to share knowledge.

One of the basic principles behind RUP is that each iteration on a development cycle should have a tangible result. During the Rational Unified Process, users will create numerous designs, requirement documents, reports, and plans. The RUP software provides visualization and development tools for the creation of these artifacts.

RUP as a Process

Defining an accurate model is the central principle of RUP. Models, according to RUP, help explain the complicated structures and relationships in the software development process. In RUP, models are often expressed in Unified Modeling Language (UML) format.

RUP defines each part of the process as an individual *workflow*. Workflows represent each step of a process in terms of who is responsible for it, what tasks are being performed, the artifacts or results of these tasks, and the sequence of events that drives the tasks. Almost everything about RUP is customizable, but several *core process workflows* are defined "out of the box" by RUP.

The core process workflows bear some resemblance to the stages of the Waterfall Model, but each one is iterative and more specific in definition. The *business modeling workflow* models business processes, usually with the goal of driving software requirements forward. The *requirements workflow* creates the requirements definition by analyzing the problems in the system and iterating on its assumptions. The *analysis and design workflow* deals with system architecture and subsystem design. The *implementation workflow* covers the modeling, coding, and integration of software subsystems. The *test workflow* models the planning, implementation and evaluation of software quality tests. The *deployment workflow* is a high-level view on overall planning, releasing, supporting, and testing workflows. The *configuration management workflow* goes from new project conception to iteration and end-of-product scenarios. Finally, the *environment workflow* supports the engineering organization through the creation and maintenance of development tools.

RUP in Practice

RUP is aimed mainly at larger organizations and offers several advantages over the adoption of traditional life-cycle models. Once the team has gotten over the learning curve to use the software, all members will be using a common platform for designing, communicating, and implementing their ideas. The process can be customized to the needs of the team and each stage reveals a wealth of valuable artifacts that document each phase of development.

A product like RUP can be too heavyweight for some organizations. Teams with diverse development environments or tight engineering budgets might not want or be able to standardize on a software-based development system. The learning curve can also be a factor — new engineers that aren't familiar with the process software will have to learn how to use it while getting up to speed on the product and the existing code base.

Software-Engineering Methodologies

Software life-cycle models provide a formal way of answering the question "What do we do next?" but they are rarely (with the exception of formalized systems like RUP) able to contribute an answer to the logical follow-up question, "How do we do it?" To provide some answers to the "how" question, a number of methodologies have developed that provide practical rules of thumb for professional software development. Books and articles on software methodologies abound, but two recent innovations, *Extreme Programming* and *Software Triage*, deserve particular attention.

Extreme Programming (XP)

When one of the authors arrived home from work a few years ago and told his wife that his company had adopted some of the principles of Extreme Programming, she joked, "I hope you wear a safety harness for that." Despite the somewhat hokey name, Extreme Programming effectively bundles up the best of existing software development guidelines and new material into a novel and increasingly popular methodology.

XP, popularized by Kent Beck in *eXtreme Programming eXplained* (Addison-Wesley, 1999), claims to take the best practices of good software development and turn them up a notch. For example, most programmers would agree that testing is a good thing. In XP, testing is deemed so good that you're supposed to write the tests before you write the code!

XP in Theory

The Extreme Programming methodology is made up of 12 main guiding principles. These principles are manifested throughout all phases of the software development process and have a direct impact on the daily tasks of engineers.

Plan as You Go

In the Waterfall Model, planning happened once, at the beginning of the process. Under the Spiral Method, planning was the first phase of each iteration. In RUP, planning is an integral step in most of the workflows. Under XP, planning is more than just a step — it's a never-ending task. XP teams start with a rough plan that captures the major points of the product being developed. Throughout the development process, the plan is refined and modified as necessary. The theory is that conditions are constantly changing and new information is obtained all the time.

Under XP, estimates for a given feature are always made by the person who will be implementing that particular feature. This helps to avoid situations where the implementer is forced to adhere to an unrealistic and artificial schedule. Initially, estimates are very rough, perhaps on the order of weeks for a feature. As the time horizon shortens, the estimates get more granular. Features are broken out into tasks taking no more than five days.

Build Small Releases

One of the theories of XP is that software projects grow risky and unwieldy when they try to accomplish too much at one time. Instead of massive software releases that involve core changes and several pages of release notes, XP advocates smaller releases with a timeframe closer to two months than eighteen months. With such a short release cycle, only the most important features can make it into the product. This forces engineering and marketing to agree on what features are truly important.

Share a Common Metaphor

XP uses the term *metaphor* as other methodologies might use *architecture*. The idea is that all members of the team should share a common high-level view of the system. This isn't necessarily the specifics of how objects will communicate or the exact APIs that will be written. Rather, the metaphor is the mental model for the components of the system. Team members should use the metaphor to drive shared terminology when discussing the project.

Simplify Your Designs

A mantra frequently sung by XP-savvy engineers is "avoid speculative generality." This goes against the natural inclinations of many programmers. If you are given the task of designing a file-based object store, you may start down the path of creating the be-all, end-all solution to all file-based storage problems. Your design might quickly evolve to cover multiple languages and any type of object. XP says you should lean towards the other end of the generality continuum. Instead of making the ideal object store that will win awards and be celebrated by your peers, design the simplest possible object store that gets the job done. You should understand the current requirements and write your code to those specifications to avoid overly complex code.

It may be hard to get used to simplicity in design. Depending on the type of work you do, your code may need to exist for years and be used by other parts of the code that you haven't even dreamed of. As discussed in Chapter 5, the problem with building in functionality that *may* be useful in the future is that you don't know what those hypothetical use cases are and there is no way to craft a good design that is purely speculative. Instead, XP says you should build something that is useful today and leave open the opportunity to modify it later.

Test Constantly

According to *eXtreme Programming eXplained*, "Any program feature without an automated test simply doesn't exist." Extreme Programming is zealous about testing. Part of your responsibility as an XP engineer is to write the unit tests that accompany your code. A unit test is generally a small piece of code that makes sure that an individual piece of functionality works. For example, individual unit tests for a file-based object store may include `testSaveObject`, `testLoadObject`, and `testDeleteObject`.

XP takes unit testing one step further by suggesting that unit tests should be written before the actual code is written! Of course, the tests won't pass because the code hasn't been written yet. In theory, if your tests are thorough, you should know when your code is done because all the tests will complete successfully. We told you it was "extreme."

Refactor When Necessary

Most programmers *refactor* their code from time to time. Refactoring is the process of redesigning existing working code to take into account new knowledge or alternate uses that have been discovered since the code was written. Refactoring is difficult to build into a traditional software-engineering schedule because its results are not as tangible as implementing a new feature. Good managers, however, recognize its importance for long-term code maintainability.

The extreme way of refactoring is to recognize situations during development when refactoring is useful and to do the refactoring at that time. Instead of deciding at the start of a release which existing parts of the product need design work, XP programmers learn to recognize the signs of code that is ready to be refactored. While this practice will almost certainly result in unexpected and unscheduled tasks, restructuring the code when appropriate should make feature development easier.

Code in Pairs

The notion of *pair programming* contributes to the stigma of Extreme Programming as some sort of touchy-feely software process for hippies. In fact, the motivation for pair programming is much more practical than you might think. XP suggests that all production code should be written by two people working side by side simultaneously. Obviously, only one person can actually be in control of the keyboard. The other person takes a high-level approach, thinking about issues such as testing, necessary refactoring, and the overall model of the project.

As an example, if you are in charge of writing the user interface for a particular feature of your application, you might want to ask the original author of the feature to sit down with you. She can advise you about the correct use of the feature, warn you about any "gotchas" you should watch out for, and help oversee your efforts at a high level. Even if you can't acquire the help of the original author, just grabbing another member of the team can help. The theory is that working in pairs builds shared knowledge, ensures proper design, and puts an informal system of checks and balances in place.

Share the Code

In many traditional development environments, code ownership is strongly defined and often enforced. One of the authors worked previously in an environment where the manager explicitly forbid checking in changes to code written by any other member of the team! XP takes the extreme opposite approach by declaring that the code is collectively owned by everybody. This is another XP facet that initially evokes images of programmers holding hands and swaying gently to a Grateful Dead album. In fact, it's not so touchy-feely.

Collective ownership is practical for a number of reasons. From a management point of view, it is less detrimental when a single engineer leaves suddenly because there are others who understand that part of the code. From an engineer's point of view, collective ownership builds a common view of how the system works. This helps design tasks and frees the individual programmer to make any change that will add value to the overall project.

One important note about collective ownership is that it is not necessary for every programmer to be familiar with every single line of code. It is more of a mindset that the project is a team effort, and there is no reason for any one person to hoard knowledge.

Integrate Continuously

All programmers are familiar with the dreaded chore of integrating code. This is the task when you discover that your view of the object store is a complete mismatch with the way it was actually written. When subsystems come together, problems are exposed. XP recognizes this phenomenon and advocates integrating code into the project frequently as it is being developed.

XP suggests a specific method for integration. Two programmers (the pair that developed the code) sit down at a designated "integration station" and merge the code in together. The code is not checked in until it passes 100 percent of the tests. By having a single station, conflicts are avoided and integration is clearly defined as a step that must occur before a check-in.

The authors have found that a similar approach can still work on an individual level. Engineers run tests individually or in pairs before checking code into the repository. A designated machine continually runs automated tests. When the automated tests fail, the team receives an email indicating the problem and listing the most recent check-ins.

Work Sane Hours

XP has a thing or two to say about the hours you've been putting in. The claim is that a well-rested programmer is a happy and productive programmer. XP advocates a work week of approximately 40 hours and warns against putting in overtime for more than two consecutive weeks.

Of course, different people need different amounts of rest. The main idea, though, is that if you sit down to write code without a clear head, you're going to write poor code and abandon many of the XP principles.

Have a Customer on Site

Since an XP-savvy engineering group constantly refines its product plan and builds only what is currently necessary, having a customer contribute to the process is very valuable. Although it is not always possible to convince a customer to be physically present during development, the idea that there should be communication between engineering and the end user is clearly a valuable notion. In addition to assisting with the design of individual features, a customer can help prioritize tasks by conveying his or her individual needs.

Share Common Coding Standards

Due to the collective ownership guideline and the practice of pair programming, coding in an extreme environment can be difficult if each engineer has her own naming and indenting conventions. XP doesn't advocate any particular style, but supplies the guideline that if you can look at a piece of code and immediately identify the author, your group probably needs better definition of its coding standards.

For additional information on various approaches to coding style, see Chapter 7.

XP in Practice

XP purists claim that the 12 tenets of Extreme Programming are so intertwined that adopting some of them without others would largely ruin the methodology. For example, pair programming is vital to testing because if you can't determine how to test a particular piece of code, your partner can help. Also, if you're tired one day and decide to skip the testing, your partner will be there to evoke feelings of guilt.

Some of the XP guidelines, however, can prove difficult to implement. To some engineers, the idea of writing tests before code is too abstract. For those engineers, it may be sufficient to *design* the tests without actually writing them until there is code to test. Many of the XP principles are rigidly definedm, but if you understand the theory behind it, you may be able to find ways to adapt the guidelines to the needs of your project.

The collaborative aspects of XP can be challenging as well. Pair programming has measurable benefits, but it may be difficult for a manager to rationalize having half as many people actually writing code each day. Some members of the team may even feel uncomfortable with such close collaboration, perhaps finding it difficult to type while others are watching. Pair programming also has obvious challenges if the team is physically spread out or if members tend to telecommute regularly.

For some organizations, Extreme Programming may be too radical. Large established companies with formal policies in place for engineering may be slow to adopt new approaches like XP. However, even if your company is resistant to the implementation of XP, you can still improve your own productivity by understanding the theory behind it.

Software Triage

In the fatalistically-named book *Death March* (Prentice Hall, 2003) Edward Yourdon describes the frequent and scary condition of software that is behind schedule, short on staff, over budget, or poorly designed. Yourdon's theory is that when software projects get into this state, even the best modern software development methodologies will no longer apply. As you have learned in this chapter, many approaches to software development are built around formalized documents or taking a user-centered approach to design. In a project that's already in "death march" mode, there simply isn't time for these approaches.

The idea behind software triage is that when a project is already in a bad state, resources are scarce. Time is scarce, engineers are scarce, and money may be scarce. The main mental obstacle that managers and developers need to overcome when a project is way behind schedule is that it will be impossible to satisfy the original requirements in the allotted time. The task then becomes organizing remaining functionality into "must-have," "should-have," and "nice-to-have" lists.

Software triage is a daunting and delicate process. It often requires the leadership of a seasoned veteran of "death march" projects to make the tough decisions. For the engineer, the most important point is that in certain conditions, it may be necessary to throw familiar processes out the window (along with some existing code, unfortunately) to finish a project on time.

Building Your Own Process and Methodology

There is one software development methodology that we wholeheartedly endorse, and it's not necessarily any of the above. It's unlikely that any book or engineering theory will perfectly match the needs of your project or organization. We recommend that you learn from as many approaches as you can and design your own process. Combining concepts from different approaches may be easier than you think. For example, RUP optionally supports an XP-like approach. Here are some tips for building the software-engineering process of your dreams.

Be Open to New Ideas

Some engineering techniques seem crazy at first or unlikely to work. Look at new innovations in software-engineering methodologies as a way to refine your existing process. Try things out when you can. If XP sounds intriguing, but you're not sure if it will work in your organization, see if you can work it in slowly, taking a few of the principles at a time or trying it out with a smaller pilot project.

Bring New Ideas to the Table

Most likely, your engineering team is made up of people from varying backgrounds. You may have people who are veterans of startups, long-time consultants, recent graduates, and PhDs on your team. You all have a different set of experiences and your own ideas of how a software project should be run. Sometimes the best processes turn out to be a combination of the way things are typically done in these very different environments.

Recognize What Works and What Doesn't Work

At the end of a project (or better yet, during), get the team together to evaluate the process. Sometimes there's a major problem that nobody notices until the whole team stops to think about it. Perhaps there's a problem that *everybody* knows about but nobody has discussed! Consider what isn't working and see how those parts can be fixed. Some organizations require formal code reviews prior to any source code check-in. If code reviews are so long and boring that nobody does a good job, discuss code-reviewing techniques as a group. Also consider what is going well and see how those parts can be extended. For example, if maintaining the feature tasks as a group-editable Web site is working, maybe devote some time to making the Web site better.

Don't Be a Renegade

Whether a process is mandated by your manager or custom-built by the team, it's there for a reason. If your process involves writing formal design documents, make sure you write them. If you think that the process is broken or too complex, see if you can talk to your manager about it. Don't just avoid the process — it will come back to haunt you.

Summary

This chapter has introduced you to several models and methodologies for the software process. There are certainly many other ways of building software, both formalized and informal. There probably isn't a single correct method for developing software except the method that works for your team. The best way to find this method is to do your own research, learn what you can from various methods, talk to your peers about their experiences, and iterate on your process. Remember, the only metric that matters when examining a process methodology is how much it helps your team write code.

This chapter concludes the first part of the book, which has surveyed the landscape of software design. You have learned how to design a program, how to organize object relationships, how to make use of existing patterns and libraries, how to code effectively with others, and how to manage the process of developing software. Throughout the rest of the book, the design principles you have learned will be tied directly to C++. The next part of the book gets into the nitty-gritty details of writing professional-quality code in C++. Try not to forget the design lessons from the last few chapters as you get deep into the coding portion of the book — we put the design chapters first because we wanted to highlight their importance.

7

Coding with Style

If you're going to spend several hours each day in front of a keyboard writing code, you should take some pride in all that work. Writing code that gets the job done is only part of a programmer's work. After all, anybody can learn the fundamentals of coding. It takes a true master to code with style.

This chapter explores the question of what makes good code. Along the way, you'll see several approaches to C++ style. As you will discover, simply changing the style of code can make it appear very different. For example, C++ code written by Windows programmers often has its own style, using Windows conventions. It almost looks like a completely different language than C++ code written by Mac OS programmers. Exposure to several different styles will help you avoid that sinking feeling you get opening up a C++ source file that barely resembles the C++ you thought you knew.

The Importance of Looking Good

Writing code that is stylistically "good" takes time. You could probably whip together a program to parse an XML file into a plain text file in a couple of hours. Writing the same program with functional decomposition, adequate comments, and a clean structure would probably take days. Is it really worth it?

Thinking Ahead

How confident would you be in your code if a new programmer had to work with it a year from now? One of the authors, faced with a growing mess of Web application code, encouraged his team to think about a hypothetical intern who would be starting in a year. How would this poor intern ever get up to speed on the code base when there was no documentation and scary multiple-page functions? When you're writing code, imagine that somebody new will have to maintain it in the future. Will you even remember how it works? What if you're not available to help? Well-written code avoids these problems because it is easy to read and understand.

Keeping It Clear

Present concerns are another reason to write good code. Unless you're working alone on a project and always will be, other programmers are going to look at, and possibly modify, your code. By writing code that your team can actually read and understand, you free yourself from constant questions and complaints.

Elements of Good Style

It is difficult to enumerate the characteristics of code that make it "stylistically good." Over time, you'll find styles that you like and notice useful techniques in code that others wrote. Perhaps more importantly, you'll encounter horrible code that teaches you what to avoid. However, good code shares several universal tenets that will be explored in this chapter.

- ❑ Documentation
- ❑ Decomposition
- ❑ Naming
- ❑ Use of the Language
- ❑ Formatting

Documenting Your Code

In the programming context, documentation usually refers to comments that are contained in the source files. Comments are your opportunity to tell the world what was going through your head when you wrote the accompanying code. They are a place to say anything that isn't obvious from looking at the code itself.

Reasons to Write Comments

It may seem obvious that writing comments is a good idea, but have you ever stopped to think about why you need to comment your code? Sometimes programmers recognize the importance of commenting without fully understanding why comments are important. There are several reasons, explored next.

Commenting to Explain Usage

One reason to use comments is to explain how clients should interact with the code. As you read in Chapter 5, each publicly accessible function or method in a header file should have a comment explaining what it does. Some organizations prefer to formalize these comments by explicitly listing the purpose of each method, what each of its arguments are, what values it returns, and possible exceptions it can throw.

Providing a comment with public methods accomplishes two things. First, you are given the opportunity to state, in English, anything that you can't state in code. For example, there's really no way in C++ code to indicate that the `adjustVolume()` method of a media player object can only be called after the `initialize()` method is called. A comment, however, can be the perfect place to note this restriction, as follows.

```
/*
 * adjustVolume()
 *
 * Sets the player volume based on the user's
 * preferences
 *
 * This method will throw an "UninitializedPlayerException"
 * if the initialize() method has not yet been called.
 */
```

The second effect of a comment on a public method can be to state usage information. The C++ language forces you to specify the return type of a method, but it does not provide a way for you to say what the returned value actually represents. For example, the declaration of the `adjustVolume()` method may indicate that it returns an `int`, but the client reading that declaration wouldn't know what the `int` means. Other ancillary data can be included in a comment as well, as shown here:

```
/*
 * adjustVolume()
 *
 * Sets the player volume based on the user's
 * preferences
 *
 * Parameters:
 *     none
 * Returns:
 *     an int, which represents the new volume setting.
 *
 * Throws:
 *     UninitializedPlayerException if the initialize() method has not
 *     yet been called.
 *
```

Commenting to Explain Complicated Code

Good comments are also important inside the actual source code. In a simple program that processes input from the user and writes a result to the console, it is probably easy to read through and understand all of the code. In the professional world, however, you will often need to write code that is algorithmically complex or too esoteric to understand simply by inspection.

Consider the code that follows. It is well written, but it may not be immediately apparent what it is doing. You might recognize the algorithm if you have seen it before, but a newcomer probably wouldn't understand the way the code works.

```
void sort(int inArray[], int inSize)
{
    for (int i = 1; i < inSize; i++) {
        int element = inArray[i];

        int j = i - 1;
        while (j >= 0 && inArray[j] > element) {
            inArray[j+1] = inArray[j];
            j--;
        }
        inArray[j+1] = element;
    }
}
```

A better approach would be to include comments that describe the algorithm that is being used. In the modified function that follows, a thorough comment at the top explains the algorithm at a high level, and inline comments explain specific lines that may be confusing.

```
/*
 * Implements the "insertion sort" algorithm. The algorithm separates the array
 * into two parts--the sorted part and the unsorted part. Each element, starting
 * at position 1, is examined. Everything earlier in the array is in the sorted
 * part, so the algorithm shifts each element over until the correct position is
 * found for the current element. When the algorithm finishes with the last
 * element, the entire array is sorted.
 */
void sort(int inArray[], int inSize)
{
    // Start at position 1 and examine each element.
    for (int i = 1; i < inSize; i++) {
        int element = inArray[i];

        // j marks the position in the sorted part of the array.
        int j = i - 1;
        // As long as the current slot in the sorted array is higher than
        // the element, shift the slot over and move backwards.
        while (j >= 0 && inArray[j] > element) {
            inArray[j+1] = inArray[j];
            j--;
        }
        // At this point the current position in the sorted array
        // is *not* greater than the element, so this is its new position.
        inArray[j+1] = element;
    }
}
```

The new code is certainly more verbose, but a reader unfamiliar with sorting algorithms would be much more likely to understand it with the comments included. In some organizations, inline comments are frowned upon. In such cases, writing clean code and having good comments at the top of the function becomes vital.

Commenting to Convey Metainformation

Another reason to use comments is to provide information at a higher level than the code itself. This *metainformation* provides details about the creation of the code without addressing the specifics of its behavior. For example, your organization may want to keep track of the original author of each method. You can also use metainformation to cite external documents or refer to other code.

The example below shows several instances of metainformation, including the author of the file, the date it was created, and the specific feature it addresses. It also includes inline comments expressing meta-data, such as the bug number that corresponds to a line of code and a reminder to revisit a possible problem in the code later.

```
/*
 * Author:  klep
 * Date:    040324
 * Feature: PRD version 3, Feature 5.10
 */
int adjustVolume()
{
    if (fUninitialized) {
        throw UninitializedPlayerException();
    }

    int newVol = getPlayer()->getOwner()->getPreferredVolume();

    if (newVol == -1) return -1;  // Added to address bug #142 - jsmith 040330

    setVolume(newVol);

    // TODO: What if setVolume() throws an exception? - akshayr 040401

    return newVol;
}
```

It's easy to go overboard with comments. A good approach is to discuss which types of comments are most useful with your group and form a policy. For example, if one member of the group uses a "TODO" comment to indicate code that still needs work, but nobody else knows about this convention, the code in need could be overlooked.

> **If your group decides to use metainformation comments, make sure that you all include the same information or your files will be inconsistent!**

Commenting Styles

Every organization has a different approach to commenting code. In some environments, a particular style is mandated to give the code a common standard for documentation. Other times, the quantity and style of commenting is left up to the programmer. The following examples depict several approaches to commenting code.

Commenting Every Line

One way to avoid lack of documentation is to force yourself to overdocument by including a comment for every line. Commenting every line of code should ensure that there's a specific reason for everything you write. In reality, such heavy commenting on a large-scale basis is unscalable, messy, and tedious. For example, consider the following useless comments.

```
int result;                  // Declare an integer to hold the result.

result = doodad.getResult(); // Get the doodad's result.

if (result % 2 ==  0) {      // If the result mod 2 is 0 . . .
   logError();               // then log an error,
} else {                     // otherwise . . .
   logSuccess();             // log success.
}                            // End if/else

return (result);              // Return the result
```

The comments in this code express each line as part of an easily readable English story. This is entirely useless if you assume that the reader has at least basic C++ skills. These comments don't add any additional information to code. Specifically, look at this line:

```
if (result % 2 == 0) {       // If the result mod 2 is 0 . . .
```

The comment is just an English translation of the code. It doesn't say *why* the programmer has used the mod operator on the result with the value 2. A better comment would be:

```
if (result % 2 == 0) {       // If the result is even . . .
```

The modified comment, while still fairly obvious to most programmers, gives additional information about the code. The result is "modded" by 2 because the code needs to check if the result is even.

Despite its tendency to be verbose and superfluous, heavy commenting can be useful in cases where the code would otherwise be difficult to comprehend. The following code also comments every line, but these comments are actually helpful.

140

```
// Call the calculate method with the default values.
result = doodad.calculate(getDefaultStart(), getDefaultEnd(), getDefaultOffset());

// To determine success or failure, we need to bitwise AND the result with the
// processor-specific mask (see docs, page 201).
result = result & getProcessorMask();

// Set the user field value based on the "Marigold Formula."
setUserField( (result + kMarigoldOffset) / MarigoldConstant) + MarigoldConstant );
```

This code above is taken out of context, but the comments give you a good idea of what each line does. Without them, the calculations involving & and the mysterious "Marigold Formula" would be difficult to decipher.

> **Commenting every line of code is usually untenable, but if the code is complicated enough to require it, don't just translate the code to English: explain what's really going on.**

Prefix Comments

Your group may decide to begin all of your source files with a standard comment. This is an excellent opportunity to document important information about the program and specific file. Examples of information that you might want to document at the top of every file include:

- ❑ The file/class name
- ❑ The last-modified date
- ❑ The original author
- ❑ The feature ID addressed by the file
- ❑ Copyright information
- ❑ A brief description of the file/class
- ❑ Incomplete features
- ❑ Known bugs

Your development environment may allow you to create a template that automatically starts new files with your prefix comment. Some source control systems such as Concurrent Versions System (CVS) can even assist by filling in metadata. For example, if your comment contains the string `$Id$`, CVS will automatically expand the comment to include the author, filename, revision, and date.

An example of a prefix comment is shown here:

```
/*
 * Watermelon.cpp
 *
 * $Id: Watermelon.cpp,v 1.6 2004/03/10 12:52:33 klep Exp $
 *
 * Implements the basic functionality of a watermelon. All units are expressed
 * in terms of seeds per cubic centimeter. Watermelon theory is based on the
 * white paper "Algorithms for Watermelon Processing."
 *
 * The following code is (c)opyright 2004, FruitSoft, Inc. ALL RIGHTS RESERVED
```

Fixed-Format Comments

Writing comments in a standard format that can be parsed by external document builders is an increasingly popular programming practice. In the Java language, programmers can write comments in a standard format that allows a tool called JavaDoc to create hyperlinked documentation for the project automatically. For C++, a free tool called Doxygen (available at www.doxygen.org) parses comments to automatically build HTML documentation, class diagrams, UNIX man pages, and other useful documents. Doxygen even recognizes and parses JavaDoc-style comments in C++ programs. The code that follows shows JavaDoc-style comments that are recognized by Doxygen.

```
/**
 * Implements the basic functionality of a watermelon
 *
 * TODO: Implement updated algorithms!
 */
class Watermelon
{
    public:
    /**
     * @param initialSeeds The starting number of seeds
     */
    Watermelon(int initialSeeds);

    /**
     * Computes the seed ratio, using the Marigold
     * algorithm.
     *
     * @param slowCalc Whether or not to use long (slow) calculations
     * @return The marigold ratio
     */
    double calcSeedRatio(bool slowCalc);
};
```

Doxygen recognizes the C++ syntax and special comment directives such as @param and @return to generate customizable output. An example of a Doxygen-generated HTML class reference is shown in Figure 7-1.

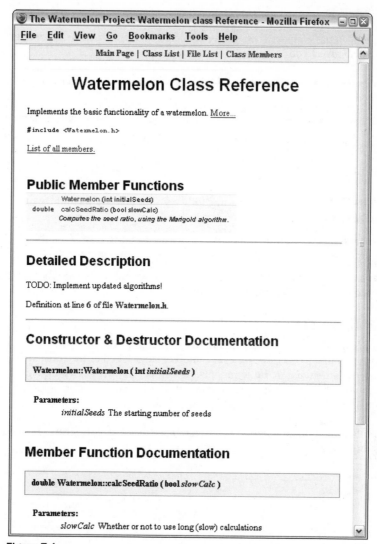

Figure 7-1

Automatically generated documentation like the file shown in Figure 7-1 can be helpful during development because it allows developers to browse through a high-level description of classes and their relationships. Your group can easily customize a tool like Doxygen to work with the style of comments that you have adopted. Ideally, your group would set up a machine that builds documentation on a daily basis.

Ad Hoc Comments

Most of the time, you use comments on an as-needed basis. Here are some guidelines for comments that appear within the body of your code.

❑   Do your best to avoid offensive or derogatory language. You never know who might look at your code some day.

❑   Liberal use of inside jokes is generally considered okay. Check with your manager.

❑   Reference bug numbers or feature IDs when possible.

❑   Include your initials and the date if you think somebody might want to follow up on the comment with you in the future.

❑   Resist the temptation to include somebody *else's* initials and the date to avoid having to take responsibility for the code.

❑   Remember to update your comments when you update the code. Nothing is more confusing than code that is fully documented with incorrect information!

❑   If you use comments to separate a function into sections, consider whether the function might be broken into multiple, smaller functions.

Self-Documenting Code

Well-written code doesn't always need abundant commenting. The best code is written to be readable. If you find yourself adding a comment for every line, consider whether the code could be rewritten to better match what you are saying in the comments. Remember that C++ is a language. Its main purpose is to tell the computer what to do, but the semantics of the language can also be used to explain its meaning to a reader.

A classic example is the implementation of a function to copy a C-style string. The code that follows has no comments, but doesn't need any.

```
void copyString(const char* inSource, char *outDest)
    int position = 0;

    while (inSource[position] != '\0') {
        outDest[position] = inSource[position];
        position++;
    }

    outDest[position] = '\0';
}
```

The following implementation works the same way, but it is too concise to make sense immediately to the reader. There's nothing wrong with the implementation, but it would require some comments to provide an explanation.

```
void copyString(const char* inSource, char* outDest)
{
    int i = 0;
    while (outDest[i] = inSource[i++]);
    outDest[i] = '\0';
}
```

Another way of writing self-documenting code is to break up, or *decompose*, your code into smaller pieces. Decomposition is covered in detail in the matierial that follows.

> **Good code is naturally readable and only requires comments to provide useful additional information.**

Comments in This Book

The code examples you will see in this book often use comments to explain complicated code or to point things out to you that may not be evident. We usually omit any prefix comments and fixed-format comments to save space, but we wholeheartedly advocate their inclusion in professional C++ projects.

Decomposition

Decomposition is the practice of breaking up code into smaller pieces. There is nothing more daunting in the world of coding than opening up a file of source code to find 300-line functions and massive nested blocks of code. Ideally, each function or method should accomplish a single task. Any subtasks of significant complexity should be decomposed into separate functions or methods. For example, if somebody asks you what a method does and you answer "First it does A, then it does B; then, if C, it does D; otherwise, it does E," you should probably have separate helper methods for A, B, C, D, and E.

Decomposition is not an exact science. Some programmers will say that no function should be longer than a page of printed code. That may be a good rule of thumb, but you could certainly find a quarter-page of code that is desperately in need of decomposition. Another rule of thumb is, whether the code is long or short, if you squint your eyes and look at the format of the code without reading the actual content, it shouldn't appear too dense in any one area. For example, Figures 7-2 and 7-3 show code that has been purposely blurred so that you can't read the content. It should be obvious that the code in Figure 7-3 has better decomposition than the code in Figure 7-2.

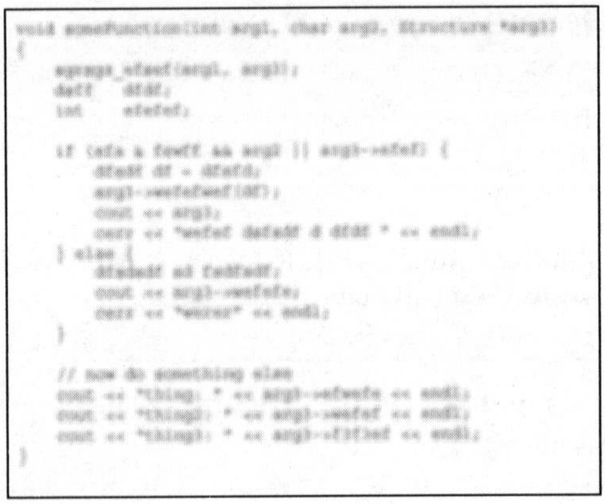

Figure 7-2

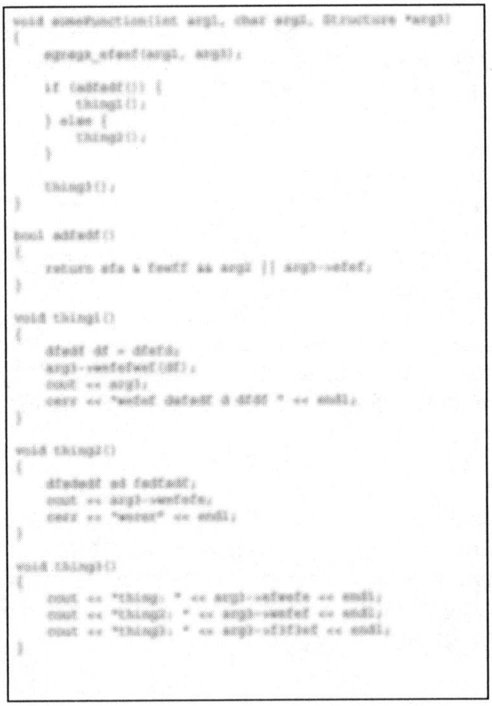

Figure 7-3

Decomposition through Refactoring

Sometimes when you've had a few sodas and you're really in the programming zone, you start coding so fast that you end up with code that does exactly what it's supposed to do, but is far from pretty. All programmers do this from time to time. Short periods of vigorous coding are sometimes the most productive times in the course of a project.

Dense code also arises over the course of time as code is modified. As new requirements and bug fixes emerge, existing code is amended with small modifications. The computing term *cruft* refers to the gradual accumulation of small amounts of code that eventually turns a once-elegant piece of code into a mess of patches and special cases.

Whether your code starts its life as a dense block of unreadable cruft or it just evolves that way, *refactoring* is necessary to periodically purge the code of accumulated hacks. Through refactoring, you revisit existing code and rewrite it to make it more readable and maintainable. Refactoring is an opportunity to revisit the decomposition of code. If the purpose of the code has changed or if it was never decomposed in the first place, when you refactor the code, squint at it and determine if it needs to be broken down into smaller parts.

Decomposition by Design

Decomposition is a boon for procrastinators. If you write your code using decomposition from the beginning, you can put off the hard parts until later. This style of coding, often called *top-down design*, takes a high-level view of the program and subsequently moves into more specific pieces.

For example, using top-down design, you could immediately get the main body of code down for a program that simulates a hurricane. The following code shows a possible implementation of main() for such a program.

```
int main(int argc, char** argv)
{
    cout << "Welcome to the Hurricane Simulator" << endl;

    getUserInputs();
    performCalculations();
    outputResults();
}
```

By taking a top-down approach, you accomplish two things. First, you can start coding immediately. Even if the program doesn't turn out the way you initially viewed it at a high level, writing some code might help you organize your thoughts. Second, the program will evolve naturally in a well-decomposed way. If you approach every method or function by considering what pieces of it you can put off until later, your programs will generally be less dense and more organized than if you implemented every feature in its entirety as you coded.

Of course, we still advocate that you do some design of your program *before* jumping into the code. However, a top-down approach can be helpful when deciding on the specific implementation of a part of your program or when working on small projects.

Decomposition in This Book

You will see decomposition in many of the examples in this book. In many cases, we have referred to methods for which we don't show the implementations because they are not relevant to the example and would take up too much space.

Naming

Your computer doesn't care what you name your variables and functions as long as the name doesn't result in a conflict with another variable or function. Names exist only to help you and your fellow programmers work with the individual elements of your program. Given this purpose, it is surprising how often programmers use unspecific or inappropriate names in their programs.

Choosing a Good Name

The best name for a variable, method, function, or class accurately describes the purpose of the item. Names can also imply additional information, such as the type or specific usage. Of course, the real test is whether other programmers understand what you are trying to convey with a particular name.

There are no set-in-stone rules for naming other than the rules that work for your organization. However, there are some names that are rarely appropriate. The table below shows some names at the two extreme ends of the naming continuum.

Good Names	Bad Names
srcName, dstName Distinguishes two objects	thing1, thing2 Too general
gSettings Conveys global status	globalUserSpecificSettingsAndPreferences Too long
mNameCounter Conveys data member status	mNC Too obscure, concise
performCalculations() Simple, accurate	doAction() Too general, imprecise
mTypeString Easy on the eyes	_typeSTR256 A name only a computer could love
mWelshRarebit Good use of inside joke	mIHateLarry Inappropriate inside joke

Naming Conventions

Selecting a name doesn't always require a lot of thought and creativity. In many cases, you'll want to use standard techniques for naming. Following are some of the types of data for which you can make use of standard names.

Counters

Early in your programming career, you probably saw code that used the variable "i" as a counter. It is customary to use i and j as counters and inner-loop counters, respectively. Be careful with nested loops, however. It's a common mistake to refer to the "ith" element when you really mean the "jth" element. Some programmers prefer using counters like outerLoopIndex and innerLoopIndex instead.

Getters and Setters

If your class contains a data member, such as mStatus, it is customary to provide access to the member via a getter called getStatus() and a setter called setStatus(). The C++ language has no prescribed naming for these methods, but your organization will probably want to adopt this or a similar naming scheme.

Prefixes

Many programmers begin their variable names with a letter that provides some information about the variable's type or usage. The table below shows some common prefixes.

Prefix	Example Name	Literal Prefix Meaning	Usage
m _	mData _data	"member"	Data member within a class. Some programmers use _ as a prefix to indicate a data member. Others consider m to be more readable.
s	sLookupTable	"static"	Static variable or data member. Used for variables that exist on a per-class basis.
k	kMaximumLength	"konstant" (German for "constant" or a horrible misspelling? You decide.)	Indicates a constant value. Some programmers use all uppercase names to indicate constants as well.
f	fCompleted	"flag"	Designates a Boolean value. Used especially to indicate a yes/no property of a class that modifies the object's behavior based on its value.
n mNum	nLines mNumLines	"number"	A data member that is also a counter. Since an "n" looks similar to an "m," some programmers instead use mNum as a prefix, as in mNumLines.
tmp	tmpName	"temporary"	Indicates that a variable is only used to hold a value temporarily. Implies that subsequent code should not rely on its value.

Capitalization

There are many different ways of capitalizing names in your code. As with most elements of coding style, the most important thing is that your group standardizes on an approach and that all members adopt that approach. One way to get messy code is to have some programmers naming classes in all lowercase with underscores representing spaces (`priority_queue`) and others using capitals with each subsequent word capitalized (`PriorityQueue`). Variables and data members almost always start with a lowercase letter and either use underscores (`my_queue`) or capitals (`myQueue`) to indicate word breaks. Functions and methods are traditionally capitalized in C++, but, as you've seen, in this book we have adopted the style of lowercase functions and methods to distinguish them from class names. We adopt a similar style of capitalizing letters to indicate word boundaries for class and data member names.

Smart Constants

Imagine that you are writing a program with a graphical user interface. The program has several menus, including File, Edit, and Help. To represent the ID of each menu, you may decide to use a constant. A perfectly reasonable name for a constant referring to the Help menu ID is `kHelp`.

The name `kHelp` will work fine until one day you add a Help button to the main window. You also need a constant to refer to the ID of the button, but `kHelp` is already taken.

There are a few ways to resolve this problem. One way is to put the two constants in different namespaces, which were discussed in Chapter 1. However, namespaces may seem like too large a hammer for the small problem of a single name conflict between constants. You could easily resolve the name conflict by renaming the constants to `kHelpMenu` and `kHelpButton`. However, a smarter way of naming the constants may be to reverse that into `kMenuHelp` and `kButtonHelp`.

The reversed names initially seem not to roll off the tongue very well. However, they provide several benefits. First, an alphabetized list of all of your constants will show all of the menu constants together. If your development environment has an autocomplete or a pop-up menu that shows up as you type your code, this can work to your advantage. Second, it provides a weak, but easy naming hierarchy. Instead of using namespaces, which can become cumbersome, the namespace is effectively part of the name. You can even extend the hierarchy when referring to individual menu items within the help menu, such as `kMenuFileSave`.

Hungarian Notation

Hungarian Notation is a variable and data member naming convention that is popular with Microsoft Windows programmers. The basic idea is that instead of using single-letter prefixes such m, you should use more verbose prefixes to indicate additional information. The following line of code displays the use of Hungarian Notation:

```
char* pszName; // psz means "pointer to a null-terminated string"
```

The term Hungarian Notion arose from the fact that its inventor, Charles Simonyi, is Hungarian. Some also say that it accurately reflects the fact that programs using Hungarian notation end up looking as if they were written in a foreign language. For this latter reason, some programmers tend to dislike Hungarian Notation. In this book, we use prefixes, but not Hungarian Notation. We feel that adequately named variables don't need much additional context information besides the prefix. We think that a data member named `mName` says it all.

> Good names convey information about their purpose without making the code unreadable.

Using Language Features with Style

The C++ language lets you do all sorts of terribly unreadable things. Take a look at this wacky code:

```
i++ + ++i;
```

With all the power that the C++ language offers, it is important to consider how the language features can be used towards stylistic good instead of evil.

Use Constants

Bad code is often littered with "magic numbers." In some function, the code is dividing by 24. Why 24? Is it because there are 24 hours in a day? Or because the average price of cheese in New Brunswick is $24? The language offers constants to give a symbolic name to a value that doesn't change, such as 24.

```
const int kAveragePriceOfCheeseInNewBrunswick = 24;
```

Take Advantage of const Variables

The const keyword in C++ is basically *syntactic sugar* (a techie term for syntax that helps the programmer more than the program) for "don't change this variable." Proper use of const is more about style than about programming correctness. There are certainly experienced C++ programmers who have never found a reason to use const and feel that it has not had a negative impact on their careers. Like many parts of C++, const exists to help the programmer more than the program. It is your responsibility to use const and to use it correctly. The ins and outs of const are covered in Chapter 12. Below is the prototype for a function that tells the caller that it will not change the content of the C-style string that is passed in.

```
void wontChangeString(const char* inString);
```

Use References Instead of Pointers

Traditionally, C++ programmers learn C first. If you have taken this path, you probably recognize that references don't really add any new functionality to the language. They merely introduce a new syntax for functionality that pointers could already provide. In C, pointers were the only pass-by-reference mechanism, and they certainly worked just fine for many years. Pointers are still required in some cases, but in many situations you can switch to references.

There are several advantages to using references rather than pointers. First, references are safer than pointers because they don't deal directly with memory addresses and cannot be NULL. Second, references are more stylistically pleasing than pointers because they use the same syntax as stack variables, avoiding symbols such as * and &. They're also easy to use, so you should have no problem adopting references into your style palette.

Another benefit of references is that they clarify ownership of memory. If you are writing a method and another programmer passes you a reference to an object, it is clear that you can read and modify the object, but you have no easy way of freeing its memory. If you are passed a pointer, this is less clear. Do you need to delete the object to clean up memory? Or will the caller do that? Your group should determine how variable passing techniques imply memory ownership. One simple way is to agree that, if your code is given a pointer, it owns the memory and should do any necessary cleanup. All other variables are passed as references or copies.

The function prototype that follows makes it clear that the parameter will be changed, but, because it is a reference, the memory will not be freed.

```
void changeMe(ChessBoard& outBoard);
```

Use Custom Exceptions

C++ makes it easy to ignore exceptions. Nothing about the language syntax forces you to deal with exceptions, and you could easily write error-tolerant programs with traditional mechanisms such as returning NULL or setting an error flag.

Exceptions provide a much richer mechanism for error handling, and custom exceptions allow you to tailor this mechanism to your needs. For example, a custom exception type for a Web browser could include fields that specify the Web page that contained the error, the network state when the error occurred, and additional context information.

Chapter 15 contains a wealth of information about exceptions in C++.

> **Language features exist to help the programmer. Understand and make use of features that contribute to good programming style.**

Formatting

Many programming groups have been torn apart and friendships ruined over code-formatting arguments. In college, one of the authors got into such a heated debate with a peer over the use of spaces in an if statement that people were stopping by to make sure that everything was okay.

If your organization has standards in place for code formatting, consider yourself lucky. You may not like the standards they have in place, but at least you won't have to argue about it. If everybody on your team is writing code their own way, try to be as tolerant as you can. As you'll see, some practices are just a matter of taste, while others actually make it difficult to work in teams.

The Curly Brace Alignment Debate

Perhaps the most frequently argued-about point is where to put the curly braces that demark a block of code. There are several styles of curly brace use. In this book, we put the curly brace on the same line as the leading statement, except in the case of a function, class, or method name. This style is shown in the code that follows (and throughout the book).

```
void someFunction()
{
    if (condition()) {
        cout << "condition was true" << endl;
    } else {
        cout << "condition was false" << endl;
    }
}
```

This style conserves vertical space while still showing blocks of code by their indentation. Some programmers would argue that preservation of vertical space isn't relevant in real-world coding (especially if you're getting paid by the line of code!) A more verbose style is shown below.

```
void someFunction()
{
    if (condition())
    {
        cout << "condition was true" << endl;
    }
    else
    {
        cout << "condition was false" << endl;
    }
}
```

Some programmers are even liberal with use of horizontal space, yielding code like that in the following example.

```
void someFunction()
{
    if (condition())
        {
            cout << "condition was true" << endl;
        }
    else
        {
            cout << "condition was false" << endl;
        }
}
```

Of course, we won't recommend any particular style because we don't want hate mail.

> When selecting a style for denoting blocks of code, the important consideration is how well you can see which block falls under which condition simply by looking at the code.

Coming to Blows over Spaces and Parentheses

The formatting of individual lines of code can also be a source of disagreement. Again, we won't advocate a particular approach, but we will show you a few styles that you are likely to encounter.

In this book, we use a space after any keyword and use parentheses to clarify the order of operations, as follows:

```
if (i == 2) {
    j = i + (k / m);
}
```

The alternative, shown next, treats `if` stylistically like a function, with no space between the keyword and the left parenthesis. Also, the parentheses used above to clarify the order of operations inside of the `if` statement are omitted because they have no semantic relevance.

```
if( i == 2 ) {
    j = i + k / m;
}
```

The difference is subtle, and the determination of which is better is left to the reader, yet we can't move on from the issue without pointing out that `if` is not a function!

Spaces and Tabs

The use of spaces and tabs is not merely a stylistic preference. If your group does not agree on a convention for spaces and tabs, there are going to be major problems when programmers work jointly. The most obvious problem occurs when Alice uses four spaces to indent code and Bob uses five space tabs; neither will be able to display code properly when working on the same file. An even worse problem arises when Bob reformats the code to use tabs at the same time that Alice edits the same code; many source code control systems won't be able to merge in Alice's changes.

Most, but not all, editors have configurable settings for spaces and tabs. Some environments even adapt to the formatting of the code as it is read in, or always save using spaces even if the tab key is used for authoring. If you have a flexible environment, you have a better chance of being able to work with other people's code. Just remember that tabs and spaces are different because tabs can be any length and a space is always a space. For this reason, we recommend that you use an editor that always translates tabs into four spaces.

Stylistic Challenges

Many programmers begin a new project by pledging that, this time, they will do everything right. Any time a variable or parameter shouldn't be changed, it'll be marked `const`. All variables will have clear, concise, readable names. Every developer will put the left curly brace on the subsequent line and will adopt the standard text editor and its conventions for tabs and spaces.

For a number of reasons, it is difficult to sustain this level of stylistic consistency. In the case of `const`, sometimes programmers just aren't educated about how to use it. You will eventually come across old code or a library function that isn't const-savvy. A good programmer will use `const_cast` to temporarily suspend the `const` property of a variable but an inexperienced programmer will start to unwind the `const` property back from the calling function, once again ending up with a program that never uses `const`.

Other times, standardization of style comes up against programmers' own individual tastes and biases. Perhaps the culture of your team makes it impractical to enforce strict style guidelines. In such situations, you may have to decide which elements you really need to standardize (such as variable names and tabs) and which ones are safe to leave up to individuals (perhaps spacing and commenting style). You can even obtain or write scripts that will automatically correct style "bugs" or flag stylistic problems along with code errors.

Summary

The C++ language provides a number of stylistic tools without any formal guidelines for how to use them. Ultimately, any style convention is measured by how widely it is adopted and how much it benefits the readability of the code. When coding as part of a team, you should raise issues of style early in the process as part of the discussion of what language and tools to use.

The most important point about style is to appreciate that it is an important aspect of programming. Teach yourself to check over the style of your code before you make it available to others. Recognize good style in the code you interact with and adopt the conventions that you and your organization find useful.

8

Gaining Proficiency with Classes and Objects

As an object-oriented language, C++ provides facilities for using *objects* and for writing object definitions, called *classes.* You can certainly write programs in C++ without classes and objects, but by doing so, you do not take advantage of the most fundamental and useful aspect of the language; writing a C++ program without classes is like traveling to Paris and eating at McDonald's! In order to use classes and objects effectively, you must understand their syntax and capabilities.

Chapter 1 reviewed the basic syntax of class definitions. Chapter 3 introduced the object-oriented approach to programming in C++ and presented specific design strategies for classes and objects. This chapter describes the fundamental concepts involved in using classes and objects, including writing class definitions, defining methods, using objects on the stack and the heap, writing constructors, default constructors, compiler-generated constructors, initializer lists in constructors, copy constructors, destructors, and assignment operators. Even if you are already comfortable with classes and objects, you should skim this chapter because it contains various tidbits of information with which you might not yet be familiar.

Introducing the Spreadsheet Example

This chapter and the next present a running example of a simple spreadsheet application. A spreadsheet is a two-dimensional grid of "cells," and each cell contains a number or string. Professional spreadsheets such as Microsoft Excel provide the ability to perform mathematical operations such as calculating the sum of the values of a set of cells. The spreadsheet example in these chapters does not attempt to challenge Microsoft in the marketplace, but is useful for illustrating the issues of classes and objects.

The spreadsheet application uses two basic classes: `Spreadsheet` and `SpreadsheetCell`. Each `Spreadsheet` object contains `SpreadsheetCell` objects. In addition, a `SpreadsheetApplication` class manages the various `Spreadsheet`s. This chapter focuses on the `SpreadsheetCell`. Chapter 9 develops the `Spreadsheet` and `SpreadsheetApplication` classes.

This chapter shows several different versions of the **SpreadsheetCell** *class in order to introduce concepts gradually. Thus, the various attempts at the class throughout the chapter do not always illustrate the "best" way to do every aspect of class writing. In particular, the early examples omit important features that would normally be included, but have not yet been introduced. You can download the final version of the class as described in the Introduction.*

Writing Classes

When you write a class you specify the behaviors, or *methods*, that will apply to objects of that class and the properties, or *data members*, that each object will contain.

There are two elements to writing classes: defining the classes themselves and defining their methods.

Class Definitions

Here is a first attempt at a simple SpreadsheetCell class, in which each cell can store only a single number:

```
// SpreadsheetCell.h
class SpreadsheetCell
{
    public:
        void setValue(double inValue);
        double getValue();

    protected:
        double mValue;
};
```

As described in Chapter 1, every class definition begins with the keyword class and the name of the class. A class definition is a *statement* in C++, so it must end with a semicolon. If you fail to terminate your class definition with a semicolon, your compiler will probably give you several errors, most of which will appear to be completely unrelated.

Class definitions usually go in a file with the name ClassName.h.

Methods and Members

The two lines that look like function prototypes declare the methods that this class supports:

```
void setValue(double inValue);
double getValue();
```

The line that looks like a variable declaration declares the data member for this class:

```
double mValue;
```

Each object will contain its own mValue variable. However, the implementation of the methods is shared across all objects. Classes can contain any number of methods and members. You cannot give a member the same name as a method.

Access Control

Every method and member in a class is subject to one of three *access specifiers*: `public`, `protected`, or `private`. An access specifier applies to all method and member declarations that follow it, until the next access specifier. In the `SpreadsheetCell` class, the `setValue()` and `getValue()` methods have `public` access, while the `mValue` member has `protected` access:

```
public:
    void setValue(double inValue);
    double getValue();
protected:
    double mValue;
```

The default access specifier for classes is `private`: all method and member declarations before the first access specifier have the `private` access specification. For example, moving the `public` access specifier below the `setValue()` method declaration gives `setValue()` private access instead of `public`:

```
class SpreadsheetCell
{
        void setValue(double inValue); // now has private access
    public:
        double getValue();

    protected:
        double mValue;
};
```

> In C++, structs can have methods just like classes. In fact, the only difference between a struct and a class is that the default access specifier for a struct is **public** and the default for a class is **private**.

The following table summarizes the meanings of the three access specifiers:

Access Specification	Meaning	When to Use
public	Any code can call a `public` method or access a `public` member of an object.	Behaviors (methods) that you want clients to use. Access methods for `private` and `protected` data members.
protected	Any method of the class can call a `protected` method and access a `protected` member. Methods of a *subclass* (see Chapter 10) can call a `protected` method or access a `protected` member of an object.	"Helper" methods that you do not want clients to use. Most data members.

Table continued on following page

Access Specification	Meaning	When to Use
private	Only methods of the class can call a private method and access a private member. Methods in subclasses *cannot* access private methods or members.	Only if you want to restrict access from subclasses.

> Access specifiers are at the class level, not the object level, so methods of a class can access protected or private methods and members on any object of that class.

Order of Declarations

You can declare your methods, members, and access control specifiers in any order: C++ does not impose any restrictions such as methods before members or public before private. Additionally, you can repeat access specifiers. For example, the SpreadsheetCell definition could look like this:

```
class SpreadsheetCell
{
    public:
        void setValue(double inValue);

    protected:
        double mValue;

    public:
        double getValue();
};
```

However, for clarity it is a good idea to group public, protected, and private declarations, and to group methods and members within those declarations. In this book, we order the definitions and access specifiers in our classes as follows:

```
class ClassName
{
    public:
        // Method declarations
        // Member declarations

    protected:
        // Method declarations
        // Member declarations

    private:
        // Method declarations
        // Member declarations
};
```

Defining Methods

The preceding definition for the `SpreadsheetCell` class is enough for you to create objects of the class. However, if you try to call the `setValue()` or `getValue()` methods, your linker will complain that those methods are not defined. That's because the class definition specifies the prototypes for the methods, but does not define their implementations. Just as you write both a prototype and a definition for a stand-alone function, you must write a prototype and a definition for a method. Note that the class definition must precede the method definitions. Usually the class definition goes in a header file, and the method definitions go in a source file that `includes` that header. Here are the definitions for the two methods of the `SpreadsheetCell` class:

```
// SpreadsheetCell.cpp
#include "SpreadsheetCell.h"

void SpreadsheetCell::setValue(double inValue)
{
    mValue = inValue;
}

double SpreadsheetCell::getValue()
{
    return (mValue);
}
```

Note that the name of the class followed by two colons precedes each method name:

```
void SpreadsheetCell::setValue(double value)
```

The `::` is called the *scope resolution operator*. In this context, the syntax tells the compiler that the coming definition of the `setValue()` method is part of the `SpreadsheetCell` class. Note also that you do not repeat the access specification when you define the method.

Accessing Data Members

Most methods of a class, such as `setValue()` and `getValue()`, are always executed on behalf of a specific object of that class (the exceptions are *static* methods, which are discussed below). Inside the method body, you have access to all the data members of the class *for that object.* In the previous definition for `setValue()`, the following line changes the `mValue` variable inside whatever object calls the method:

```
mValue = inValue;
```

If `setValue()` is called for two different objects, the same line of code (executed once for each object) changes the variable in two different objects.

Calling Other Methods

You can call methods of a class from inside another method. For example, consider an extension to the `SpreadsheetCell` class. Real spreadsheet applications allow text data as well as numbers in the cells. When you try to interpret a text cell as a number, the spreadsheet tries to convert the text to a number. If the text does not represent a valid number, the cell value is ignored. In this program, strings that are not numbers will generate a cell value of 0. Here is a first stab at a class definition for a `SpreadsheetCell` that supports text data:

```
#include <string>
using std::string;

class SpreadsheetCell
{
    public:
        void setValue(double inValue);
        double getValue();
        void setString(string inString);
        string getString();

    protected:
        string doubleToString(double inValue);
        double stringToDouble(string inString);

        double mValue;
        string mString;
};
```

This version of the class stores both text and numerical representations of the data. If the client sets the data as a `string`, it is converted to a `double`, and a `double` is converted to a `string`. If the text is not a valid number, the `double` value is 0. This class definition shows two new methods to set and retrieve the text representation of the cell and two new protected *helper methods* to convert a `double` to a `string` and vice versa. These helper methods use string streams, which are covered in detail in Chapter 14. Here are the implementations of all the methods:

```
#include "SpreadsheetCell.h"

#include <iostream>
#include <sstream>
using namespace std;

void SpreadsheetCell::setValue(double inValue)
{
    mValue = inValue;
    mString = doubleToString(mValue);
}

double SpreadsheetCell::getValue()
{
    return (mValue);
}

void SpreadsheetCell::setString(string inString)
{
    mString = inString;
    mValue = stringToDouble(mString);
}

string SpreadsheetCell::getString()
{
```

```
        return (mString);
    }

    string SpreadsheetCell::doubleToString(double inValue)
    {
        ostringstream ostr;

        ostr << inValue;
        return (ostr.str());
    }

    double SpreadsheetCell::stringToDouble(string inString)
    {
        double temp;

        istringstream istr(inString);

        istr >> temp;
        if (istr.fail() || !istr.eof()) {
            return (0);
        }
        return (temp);
    }
```

Note that each of the set methods calls a helper method to perform a conversion. With this technique, both mValue and mString are always valid.

The this Pointer

Every normal method call passes a pointer to the object for which it is called as a "hidden" first parameter with the name this. You can use this pointer to access data members or call methods, and can pass it to other methods or functions. It is also sometimes useful for disambiguating names. For example, you could have defined the SpreadsheetCell class such that the setValue() method took a parameter named mValue instead of inValue. In that case, setValue() would look like this:

```
    void SpreadsheetCell::setValue(double mValue)
    {
        mValue = mValue; // Ambiguous!
        mString = doubleToString(mValue);
    }
```

That line is confusing. Which mValue do you mean: the mValue that was passed as a parameter, or the mValue that is a member of the object? In order to disambiguate the names you can use the this pointer:

```
    void SpreadsheetCell::setValue(double mValue)
    {
        this->mValue = mValue;
        mString = doubleToString(this->mValue);
    }
```

However, if you use the naming conventions described in Chapter 7, you will never encounter this type of name collision.

You can also use the `this` pointer to call a function or method that takes a pointer to an object from within a method of that object. For example, suppose you write a `printCell()` stand-alone function (not method) like this:

```
void printCell(SpreadsheetCell* inCellp)
{
    cout << inCellp->getString() << endl;
}
```

If you want to call `printCell()` from the `setValue()` method, you must pass `this` as the argument to give `printCell()` a pointer to the `SpreadsheetCell` on which `setValue()` operates:

```
void SpreadsheetCell::setValue(double mValue)
{
    this->mValue = mValue;
    mString = doubleToString(this->mValue);
    printCell(this);
}
```

Using Objects

The previous class definition says that a `SpreadsheetCell` consists of two member variables, four public methods, and two protected methods. However, the class definition does not actually create any `SpreadsheetCells`; it just specifies their format. In that sense, a class is similar to architectural blueprints. The blueprints specify what a house should look like, but drawing the blueprints doesn't build any houses. Houses must be constructed later based on the blueprints.

Similarly, in C++ you can construct a `SpreadsheetCell` "object" from the `SpreadsheetCell` class definition by declaring a variable of type `SpreadsheetCell`. Just as a builder can build more than one house based on a given blueprints, a programmer can create more than one `SpreadsheetCell` object from a `SpreadsheetCell` class. There are two ways to create and use objects: on the stack and on the heap.

Objects on the Stack

Here is some code that creates and uses `SpreadsheetCell` objects on the stack:

```
SpreadsheetCell myCell, anotherCell;
myCell.setValue(6);
anotherCell.setValue(myCell.getValue());

cout << "cell 1: " << myCell.getValue() << endl;
cout << "cell 2: " << anotherCell.getValue() << endl;
```

You create objects just as you declare simple variables, except that the variable type is the class name. The `.` in lines like `myCell.setValue(6);` is called the "dot" operator; it allows you to call methods on the object. If there were any public data members in the object, you could access them with the dot operator as well.

The output of the program is:

```
cell 1: 6
cell 2: 6
```

Objects on the Heap

You can also dynamically allocate objects using `new`:

```
SpreadsheetCell* myCellp = new SpreadsheetCell();

myCellp->setValue(3.7);
cout << "cell 1: " << myCellp->getValue() <<
    " " << myCellp->getString() << endl;
delete myCellp;
```

When you create an object on the heap, you call its methods and access its members through the "arrow" operator: `->`. The arrow combines dereferencing (`*`) and method or member access (`.`). You could use those two operators instead, but doing so would be stylistically awkward:

```
SpreadsheetCell* myCellp = new SpreadsheetCell();

(*myCellp).setValue(3.7);
cout << "cell 1: " << (*myCellp).getValue() <<
    " " << (*myCellp).getString() << endl;
delete myCellp;
```

Just as you must free other memory that you allocate on the heap, you must free the memory for objects that you allocate on the heap by calling `delete` on the objects.

> If you allocate an object with `new`, free it with `delete` when you are finished with it.

Object Life Cycles

The object life cycle involves three activities: creation, destruction, and assignment. Every object is created, but not every object encounters the other two "life events." It is important to understand how and when objects are created, destroyed, and assigned, and how you can customize these behaviors.

Object Creation

Objects are created at the point you declare them (if they're on the stack) or when you explicitly allocate space for them with `new` or `new[]`.

It is often helpful to give variables initial values as you declare them. For example, you should usually initialize integer variables to `0` like this:

```
int x = 0, y = 0;
```

Similarly, you should give initial values to objects. You can provide this functionality by declaring and writing a special method called a *constructor*, in which you can perform initialization work for the object. Whenever an object is created, one of its constructers is executed.

> C++ programmers often call a constructor a "ctor."

Writing Constructors

Here is a first attempt at adding a constructor to the `SpreadsheetCell` class:

```
class SpreadsheetCell
{
    public:
        SpreadsheetCell(double initialValue);
        void setValue(double inValue);
        double getValue();
        void setString(string inString);
        string getString();

    protected:
        string doubleToString(double inValue);
        double stringToDouble(string inString);

        double mValue;
        string mString;
};
```

Note that the constructor has the same name as the name of the class and does not have a return type. These facts are always true about constructors. Just as you must provide implementations for normal methods, you must provide an implementation for the constructor:

```
SpreadsheetCell::SpreadsheetCell(double initialValue)
{
    setValue(initialValue);
}
```

The `SpreadsheetCell` constructor is a method of the `SpreadsheetCell` class, so C++ requires the normal `SpreadsheetCell::` scope resolution phrase before the method name. The method name itself is also `SpreadsheetCell`, so the code ends up with the funny looking `SpreadsheetCell::SpreadsheetCell`. The implementation simply makes a call to `setValue()` in order to set both the numeric and text representations.

Using Constructors

Using the constructor creates an object and initializes its values. You can use constructors with both stack-based and heap-based allocation.

Constructors on the Stack

When you allocate a `SpreadsheetCell` object on the stack, you use the constructor like this:

```
SpreadsheetCell myCell(5), anotherCell(4);

cout << "cell 1: " << myCell.getValue() << endl;
cout << "cell 2: " << anotherCell.getValue() << endl;
```

Note that you do NOT call the `SpreadsheetCell` constructor explicitly. For example, do not use something like the following:

```
SpreadsheetCell myCell.SpreadsheetCell(5); // WILL NOT COMPILE!
```

Similarly, you cannot call the constructor later. The following is also incorrect:

```
SpreadsheetCell myCell;
myCell.SpreadsheetCell(5); // WILL NOT COMPILE!
```

Again, the only correct way to use the constructor on the stack is like this:

```
SpreadsheetCell myCell(5);
```

Constructors on the Heap

When you dynamically allocate a `SpreadsheetCell` object, you use the constructor like this:

```
SpreadsheetCell *myCellp = new SpreadsheetCell(5);
SpreadsheetCell *anotherCellp;
anotherCellp = new SpreadsheetCell(4);
delete anotherCellp;
```

Note that you can declare a pointer to a `SpreadsheetCell` object without calling the constructor immediately, which is different from objects on the stack, where the constructor is called at the point of declaration.

As usual, remember to call `delete` on the objects that you dynamically allocate with `new`!

Providing Multiple Constructors

You can provide more than one constructor in a class. All constructors have the same name (the name of the class), but different constructors must take a different number of arguments or different argument types.

In the `SpreadsheetCell` class, it is helpful to have two constructors: one to take an initial `double` value and one to take an initial `string` value. Here is the class definition with the second constructor:

```
class SpreadsheetCell
{
    public:
        SpreadsheetCell(double initialValue);
        SpreadsheetCell(string initialValue);
        void setValue(double inValue);
        double getValue();
        void setString(string inString);
        string getString();

    protected:
        string doubleToString(double inValue);
        double stringToDouble(string inString);

        double mValue;
        string mString;
};
```

Here is the implementation of the second constructor:

```
SpreadsheetCell::SpreadsheetCell(string initialValue)
{
    setString(initialValue);
}
```

And here is some code that uses the two different constructors:

```
SpreadsheetCell aThirdCell("test"); // Uses string-arg ctor
SpreadsheetCell aFourthCell(4.4);    // Uses double-arg ctor
SpreadsheetCell* aThirdCellp = new SpreadsheetCell("4.4"); // string-arg ctor
cout << "aThirdCell: " << aThirdCell.getValue() << endl;
cout << "aFourthCell: " << aFourthCell.getValue() << endl;
cout << "aThirdCellp: " << aThirdCellp->getValue() << endl;
delete aThirdCellp;
```

When you have multiple constructors, it is tempting to attempt to implement one constructor in terms of another. For example, you might want to call the double constructor from the string constructor as follows:

```
SpreadsheetCell::SpreadsheetCell(string initialValue)
{
    SpreadsheetCell(stringToDouble(initialValue));
}
```

That seems to make sense. After all, you can call normal class methods from within other methods. The code will compile, link, and run, but will not do what you expect. The explicit call to the SpreadsheetCell constructor actually creates a new temporary unnamed object of type SpreadsheetCell. It does not call the constructor for the object that you are supposed to be initializing.

Don't attempt to call one constructor of a class from another.

Default Constructors

A *default constructor* is a constructor that takes no arguments. It is also called a *0-argument constructor*. With a default constructor, you can give reasonable initial values to data members even though the client did not specify them.

Here is part of the SpreadsheetCell class definition with a default constructor:

```
class SpreadsheetCell
{
    public:
        SpreadsheetCell();
        SpreadsheetCell(double initialValue);
        SpreadsheetCell(string initialValue);
        // Remainder of the class definition omitted for brevity
};
```

Here is a first crack at an implementation of the default constructor:

```
SpreadsheetCell::SpreadsheetCell()
{
    mValue = 0;
    mString = "";
}
```

You use the default constructor on the stack like this:

```
SpreadsheetCell myCell;
myCell.setValue(6);

cout << "cell 1: " << myCell.getValue() << endl;
```

The preceding code creates a new `SpreadsheetCell` called `myCell`, sets its value, and prints out its value. Unlike other constructors for stack-based objects, you do not call the default constructor with function-call syntax. Based on the syntax for other constructors, you might be tempted to call the default constructor like this:

```
SpreadsheetCell myCell(); // WRONG, but will compile.
myCell.setValue(6);       // However, this line will not compile.

cout << "cell 1: " << myCell.getValue() << endl;
```

Unfortunately, the line attempting to call the default constructor will compile. The line following it will not compile. The problem is that your compiler thinks the first line is actually a function declaration for a function with the name `myCell` that takes zero arguments and returns a `SpreadsheetCell` object. When it gets to the second line, it thinks that you're trying to use a function name as an object!

> **When creating an object on the stack, omit parenthesis for the default constructor.**

However, when you use the default constructor with a heap-based object allocation, you are required to use function-call syntax:

```
SpreadsheetCell* myCellp = new SpreadsheetCell(); // Note the function-call syntax
```

Don't waste a lot of time pondering why C++ requires different syntax for heap-based versus stack-based object allocation with a default constructor. It's just one of those things that makes C++ such an exciting language to learn.

Compiler-Generated Default Constructor

If your class doesn't provide a default constructor, you cannot create objects of that class without specifying arguments. For example, suppose that you have the following `SpreadsheetCell` class definition:

```
class SpreadsheetCell
{
    public:
```

```
        SpreadsheetCell(double initialValue); // No default constructor
        SpreadsheetCell(string initialValue);
        void setValue(double inValue);
        double getValue();
        void setString(string inString);
        string getString();

    protected:
        string doubleToString(double inValue);
        double stringToDouble(string inString);

        double mValue;
        string mString;
};
```

With the preceding definition, the following code will not compile:

```
SpreadsheetCell myCell;
myCell.setValue(6);
```

But that code used to work! What's wrong here? Nothing is wrong. Since you didn't declare a default constructor, you can't construct an object without specifying arguments.

The real question is why the code used to work. The reason is that if you don't specify *any* constructors, the compiler will write one for you that doesn't take any arguments. This compiler-generated default constructor calls the default constructor on all object members of the class, but does not initialize the language primitives such as int and double. Nonetheless, it allows you to create objects of that class. However, if you declare a default constructor, or any other constructor, the compiler no longer generates a default constructor for you.

> A default constructor is the same thing as a 0-argument constructor. The term "default constructor" does not refer only to the constructor that is automatically generated if you fail to declare any constructors.

When You Need a Default Constructor

Consider arrays of objects. The act of creating an array of objects accomplishes two tasks: it allocates contiguous memory space for all the objects and it calls the default constructor on each object. C++ fails to provide any syntax to tell the array creation code directly to call a different constructor. For example, if you do not define a default constructor for the SpreadsheetCell class, the following code does not compile:

```
SpreadsheetCell cells[3]; // FAILS compilation without a default constructor
SpreadsheetCell* myCellp = new SpreadsheetCell[10]; // Also FAILS
```

You can circumvent this restriction for stack-based arrays by using *initializers* like this:

```
SpreadsheetCell cells[3] = {SpreadsheetCell(0), SpreadsheetCell(23),
    SpreadsheetCell(41)};
```

However, it is usually easier to ensure that your class has a default constructor if you intend to create arrays of objects of that class.

Default constructors are also useful when you want to create objects of that class inside other classes, which is shown in the following section, *Initializer Lists*.

Finally, default constructors are convenient when the class serves as a base class of an inheritance hierarchy. In that case, it's convenient for subclasses to initialize superclasses via their default constructors. Chapter 10 covers this issue in more detail.

Initializer Lists

C++ provides an alternative method for initializing data members in the constructor, called the *initializer list*. Here is the 0-argument `SpreadsheetCell` constructor rewritten to use the initializer list syntax:

```
SpreadsheetCell::SpreadsheetCell() : mValue(0), mString("")
{
}
```

As you can see, the initializer list lies between the constructor argument list and the opening brace for the body of the constructor. The list starts with a colon and is separated by commas. Each element in the list is an initialization of a data member using function notation or a call to a superclass constructor (see Chapter 10).

Initializing data members with an initializer list provides different behavior than does initializing data members inside the constructor body itself. When C++ creates an object, it must create all the data members of the object before calling the constructor. As part of creating these data members, it must call a constructor on any of them that are themselves objects. By the time you assign a value to an object inside your constructor body, you are not actually constructing that object. You are only modifying its value. An initializer list allows you to provide initial values for data members as they are created, which is more efficient than assigning values to them later. Interestingly, the default initialization for `strings` gives them the empty string; so explicitly initializing `mString` to the empty string as shown in the preceding example is superfluous.

> **Initializer lists allow initialization of data members at the time of their creation.**

Even if you don't care about efficiency, you might want to use initializer lists if you find that they look "cleaner." Some programmers prefer the more common syntax of assigning initial values in the body of the constructor. However, several data types must be initialized in an initializer list. The following table summarizes them:

Data Type	Explanation
`const` data members	You cannot legally assign a value to a `const` variable after it is created. Any value must be supplied at the time of creation.
Reference data members	References cannot exist without referring to *something*.

Table continued on following page

Data Type	Explanation
Object data members for which there is no default constructor	C++ attempts to initialize member objects using a default constructor. If no default constructor exists, it cannot initialize the object.
Superclasses without default constructors	[Covered in Chapter 10]

There is one important caveat with initializer lists: they initialize data members in the order that they appear in the class definition, not their order in the initializer list. For example, suppose you rewrite your `SpreadsheetCell` string constructor to use initializer lists like this:

```
SpreadsheetCell::SpreadsheetCell(string initialValue) :
    mString(initialValue), mValue(stringToDouble(mString))    // INCORRECT ORDER!
{
}
```

The code will compile (although some compilers issue a warning), but the program does not work correctly. You might assume that `mString` will be initialized before `mValue` because `mString` is listed first in the initialier list. But C++ doesn't work that way. The `SpreadsheetCell` class declares `mValue` before `mString`:

```
class SpreadsheetCell
{
    public:
        // Code omitted for brevity
    protected:
        // Code omitted for brevity
        double mValue;
        string mString;
};
```

Thus, the initializer list tried to initialize `mValue` before `mString`. However, the code to initialize `mValue` tries to use the value of `mString`, which is not yet initialized! The solution in this case is to use the `initialValue` argument instead of `mString` when initializing `mValue`. You should also swap their order in the initializer list to avoid confusion:

```
SpreadsheetCell::SpreadsheetCell(string initialValue) :
    mValue(stringToDouble(initialValue)), mString(initialValue)
{
}
```

> **Initializer lists initialize data members in their declared order in the class definition, not their order in the list.**

Copy Constructors

There is a special constructor in C++ called a *copy constructor* that allows you to create an object that is an exact copy of another object. If you don't write a copy constructor yourself, C++ generates one for you that initializes each data member in the new object from its equivalent data member in the source object. For object data members, this initialization means that their copy constructors are called.

Here is the declaration for a copy constructor in the `SpreadsheetCell` class:

```
class SpreadsheetCell
{
    public:
        SpreadsheetCell();
        SpreadsheetCell(double initialValue);
        SpreadsheetCell(string initialValue);
        SpreadsheetCell(const SpreadsheetCell& src);
        void setValue(double inValue);
        double getValue();
        void setString(string inString);
        string getString();

    protected:
        string doubleToString(double inValue);
        double stringToDouble(string inString);

        double mValue;
        string mString;
};
```

The copy constructor takes a `const` reference to the source object. Like other constructors, it does not return a value. Inside the constructor, you should copy all the data fields from the source object. Technically, of course, you can do whatever you want in the constructor, but it's generally a good idea to follow expected behavior and initialize the new object to be a copy of the old one. Here is a sample implementation of the `SpreadsheetCell` copy constructor:

```
SpreadsheetCell::SpreadsheetCell(const SpreadsheetCell& src) :
    mValue(src.mValue), mString(src.mString)
{
}
```

Note the use of the initializer list. The difference between setting values in the initializer list and in the copy constructor body is examined below in the section on assignment.

> The compiler-generated SpreadsheetCell copy constructor is identical to the one shown above. Thus, for simplicity, you could omit the explicit copy constructor and rely on the compiler-generated one. Chapter 10 describes some types of classes for which a compiler-generated copy constructor is insufficient.

When the Copy Constructor Is Called

The default semantics for passing arguments to functions in C++ is pass-by-value. That means that the function or method receives a copy of the variable, not the variable itself. Thus, whenever you pass an object to a function or method the compiler calls the copy constructor of the new object to initialize it.

For example, recall that the definition of the setString() method in the SpreadsheetCell class looks like this:

```
void SpreadsheetCell::setString(string inString)
{
    mString = inString;
    mValue = stringToDouble(mString);
}
```

Recall, also, that the C++ string is actually a class, not a built-in type. When your code makes a call to setString() passing a string argument, the string parameter inString is initialized with a call to its copy constructor. The argument to the copy construction is the string you passed to setString(). In the following example, the string copy constructor is executed for the inString object in setString() with name as its parameter.

```
SpreadsheetCell myCell;
string name = "heading one";

myCell.setString(name); // Copies name
```

When the setString() method finishes, inString is destroyed. Because it was only a copy of name, name remains intact.

The copy constructor is also called whenever you return an object from a function or method. In this case, the compiler creates a temporary, unnamed, object through its copy constructor. Chaper 17 explores the impact of temporary objects in more detail.

Calling the Copy Constructor Explicitly

You can use the copy constructor explicitly as well. It is often useful to be able to construct one object as an exact copy of another. For example, you might want to create a copy of a SpreadsheetCell object like this:

```
SpreadsheetCell myCell2(4);
SpreadsheetCell anotherCell(myCell2);   // anotherCell now has the values of myCell2
```

Passing Objects by Reference

In order to avoid copying objects when you pass them to functions and methods you can declare that the function or method takes a reference to the object. Passing objects by reference is usually more efficient than passing them by value, because only the address of the object is copied, not the entire contents of the object. Additionally, pass-by-reference avoids problems with dynamic memory allocation in objects, which we will discuss in Chapter 9.

> **Pass objects by const reference instead of by value.**

When you pass an object by reference, the function or method using the object reference could change the original object. When you're only using pass-by-reference for efficiency, you should preclude this possibility by declaring the object const as well. Here is the SpreadsheetCell class definition in which string objects are passed const reference:

```
class SpreadsheetCell
{
    public:
        SpreadsheetCell();
        SpreadsheetCell(double initialValue);
        SpreadsheetCell(const string& initialValue);
        SpreadsheetCell(const SpreadsheetCell& src);
        void setValue(double inValue);
        double getValue();
        void setString(const string& inString);
        string getString();

    protected:
        string doubleToString(double inValue);
        double stringToDouble(const string& inString);

        double mValue;
        string mString;
};
```

Here is the implementation for setString(). Note that the method body remains the same; only the parameter type is different.

```
void SpreadsheetCell::setString(const string& inString)
{
    mString = inString;
    mValue = stringToDouble(mString);
}
```

The SpreadsheetCell methods that return a string still return it by value. Returning a reference to a data member is risky because the reference is valid only as long as the object is "alive." Once the object is destroyed, the reference is invalid. However, there are sometimes legitimate reasons to return references to data members, as you will see later in this chapter and in subsequent chapters.

Summary of Compiler-Generated Constructors

The compiler will automatically generate a 0-argument constructor and a copy constructor for every class. However, the constructors you define yourself replace these constructors according to the following rules:

If you define . . .	. . . then the compiler generates . . .	. . . and you can create an object . . .	Example
[no constructors]	A 0-argument constructor A copy constructor	With no arguments. As a copy of another object.	`SpreadsheetCell cell;` `SpreadsheetCell myCell(cell);`
A 0-argument constructor only	A copy constructor	With no arguments. As a copy of another object.	`SpreadsheetCell cell;` `SpreadsheetCell myCell(cell);`

Table continued on following page

If you define . . .	. . . then the compiler generates . . .	. . . and you can create an object . . .	Example
A copy constructor only	No constructors	Theoretically, as a copy of another object. Practically, you can't create any objects.	No example.
A single-argument (noncopy constructor) or multiargument constructor only	A copy constructor	With arguments. As a copy of another object.	`SpreadsheetCell cell(6);` `SpreadsheetCell myCell(cell);`
A 0-argument constructor as well as a single-argument (noncopy constructor) or multiargument constructor	A copy constructor	With no arguments. With arguments. As a copy of another object.	`SpreadsheetCell cell;` `SpreadsheetCell myCell(5);` `SpreadsheetCell anotherCell(cell);`

Note the lack of symmetry between the default constructor and the copy constructor. As long as you don't define a copy constructor explicitly, the compiler creates one for you. On the other hand, as soon as you define *any* constructor, the compiler stops generating a default constructor.

Object Destruction

When an object is destroyed, two events occur: the object's *destructor* method is called, and the memory it was taking up is freed. The destructor is your chance to perform any cleanup work for the object, such as freeing dynamically allocated memory or closing file handles. If you don't declare a destructor, the compiler will write one for you that does recursive memberwise destruction and allows the object to be deleted. The section on dynamic memory allocation in Chapter 9 shows you how to write a destructor.

Objects on the stack are destroyed when they go *out of scope*, which means whenever the current function, method, or other execution *block* ends. In other words, whenever the code encounters an ending curly brace, any objects created on the stack within those curly braces are destroyed. The following program shows this behavior:

```
int main(int argc, char** argv)
{
    SpreadsheetCell myCell(5);

    if (myCell.getValue() == 5) {
        SpreadsheetCell anotherCell(6);
    } // anotherCell is destroyed as this block ends.

    cout << "myCell: " << myCell.getValue() << endl;

    return (0);
} // myCell is destroyed as this block ends.
```

Objects on the stack are destroyed in the reverse order of their declaration (and construction). For example, in the following code fragment, `myCell2` is allocated before `anotherCell2`, so `anotherCell2` is destroyed before `myCell2` (note that you can start a new code block at any point in your program with an opening curly brace):

```
{
    SpreadsheetCell myCell2(4);
    SpreadsheetCell anotherCell2(5); // myCell2 constructed before anotherCell2
} // anotherCell2 destroyed before myCell2
```

This ordering applies to objects that are data members of other objects. Recall that data members are initialized in the order of their declaration in the class. Thus, following the rule that objects are destroyed in the reverse order of their construction, data member objects are destroyed in the reverse order of their declaration in the class.

Objects allocated on the heap are not destroyed automatically. You must call delete on the object pointer to call its destructor and free the memory. The following program shows this behavior:

```
int main(int argc, char** argv)
{
    SpreadsheetCell* cellPtr1 = new SpreadsheetCell(5);
    SpreadsheetCell* cellPtr2 = new SpreadsheetCell(6);

    cout << "cellPtr1: " << cellPtr1->getValue() << endl;

    delete cellPtr1; // Destroys cellPtr1

    return (0);
} // cellPtr2 is NOT destroyed because delete was not called on it.
```

Assigning to Objects

Just as you can assign the value of one int to another in C++, you can assign the value of one object to another. For example, the following code assigns the value of `myCell` to `anotherCell`:

```
SpreadsheetCell myCell(5), anotherCell;
```

```
anotherCell = myCell;
```

You might be tempted to say that `myCell` is "copied" to `anotherCell`. However, in the world of C++, "copying" only occurs when an object is being initialized. If an object already has a value that is being overwritten, the more accurate term is "assigned" to. Note that the facility that C++ provides for copying is the copy constructor. Since it is a constructor, it can only be used for object creation, not for later assignments to the object.

Therefore, C++ provides another method in every class to perform assignment. This method is called the *assignment operator*. Its name is `operator=` because it is actually an overloading of the = operator for that class. In the above example, the assignment operator for `anotherCell` is called, with `myCell` as the argument.

As usual, if you don't write your own assignment operator, C++ writes one for you to allow objects to be assigned to one another. The default C++ assignment behavior is almost identical to its default copying behavior: it recursively assigns each data member from the source to the destination object. The syntax is slightly tricky, though.

Declaring an Assignment Operator

Here is another attempt at the `SpreadsheetCell` class definition, this time including an assignment operator:

```
class SpreadsheetCell
{
    public:
        SpreadsheetCell();
        SpreadsheetCell(double initialValue);
        SpreadsheetCell(const string& initialValue);
        SpreadsheetCell(const SpreadsheetCell &src);
        SpreadsheetCell& operator=(const SpreadsheetCell& rhs);
        void setValue(double inValue);
        double getValue();
        void setString(const string& inString);
        string getString();

    protected:
        string doubleToString(double inValue);
        double stringToDouble(const string& inString);

        double mValue;
        string mString;
};
```

The assignment operator, like the copy constructor, takes a `const` reference to the source object. In this case, we call the source object `rhs`, which stands for "right-hand side" of the equals sign. The object on which the assignment operator is called is the left-hand side of the equals sign.

Unlike a copy constructor, the assignment operator returns a reference to a `SpreadsheetCell` object. The reason is that assignments can be chained, as in the following example:

```
myCell = anotherCell = aThirdCell;
```

When that line is executed, the first thing that happens is that the assignment operator for `anotherCell` is called with `aThirdCell` as its "right-hand side" parameter. Next, the assignment operator for `myCell` is called. However, its parameter is not `anotherCell`. Its right-hand side is the *result* of the assignment of `aThirdCell` to `anotherCell`. If that assignment fails to return a result, there is nothing to pass to `myCell`!

You might be wondering why the assignment operator for `myCell` can't just take `anotherCell`. The reason is that using the equals sign is actually just shorthand for what is really a method call. When you look at the line in its full functional syntax, you can see the problem:

```
myCell.operator=(anotherCell.operator=(aThirdCell));
```

Now, you can see that the `operator=` call from `anotherCell` must return a value, which is passed to the `operator=` call for `myCell`. The correct value to return is `anotherCell` itself, so it can serve as the source for the assignment to `myCell`. However, returning `anotherCell` directly would be inefficient, so you can return a reference to `anotherCell`.

> **You could actually declare the assignment operator to return whatever type you wanted, including `void`. However, you should always return a reference to the object on which it is called because that's what clients expect.**

Defining an Assignment Operator

The implementation of the assignment operator is similar to that of a copy constructor, with several important differences. First, a copy constructor is called only for initialization, so the destination object does not yet have valid values. An assignment operator can overwrite the current values in an object. This consideration doesn't really come into play until you have dynamically allocated memory in your objects. See Chapter 10 for details.

Second, it's legal in C++ to assign an object to itself. For example, the following code compiles and runs:

```
SpreadsheetCell cell(4);
cell = cell; // Self-assignment
```

Your assignment operator shouldn't prohibit self-assignment, but also shouldn't perform a full assignment if it happens. Thus, assignment operators should check for self-assignment at the beginning of the method and return immediately.

Here is the definition of the assignment operator for the `SpreadsheetCell` class:

```
SpreadsheetCell& SpreadsheetCell::operator=(const SpreadsheetCell& rhs)
{
    if (this == &rhs) {
```

The previous line checks for self-assignment, but is a bit cryptic. Self-assignment occurs when the left-hand side and the right-hand side of the equals sign are the same. One way to tell if two objects are the same is if they occupy the same memory location — more explicitly, if pointers to them are equal. Recall that `this` is a pointer to an object accessible from any method called on the object. Thus, `this` is a pointer to the left-hand side object. Similarly, `&rhs` is a pointer to the right-hand-side object. If these pointers are equal, the assignment must be self-assignment.

```
        return (*this);
    }
```

`this` is a pointer to the object on which the method executes, so `*this` is the object itself. The compiler will return a reference to the object to match the declared return value.

```
    mValue = rhs.mValue;
    mString = rhs.mString;
```

Here the method copies the values:

```
        return (*this);
    }
```

Finally it returns *this, as explained previously.

The syntax for overriding operator= may seem a strange at first. You probably felt the same way when you first learned about some other C or C++ syntax, such as switch statements — the syntax just doesn't feel right. With operator=, you're getting into some deep language features. You are actually changing the meaning of the = operator. This powerful capability unfortunately requires some unusual syntax. Don't worry, you'll get used to it!

Distinguishing Copying from Assignment

It is sometimes difficult to tell when objects are initialized with a copy constructor rather than assigned to with the assignment operator. Consider the following code:

```
    SpreadsheetCell myCell(5);
    SpreadsheetCell anotherCell(myCell);
```

AnotherCell is constructed with the copy constructer.

```
    SpreadsheetCell aThirdCell = myCell;
```

aThirdCell is also constructed with the copy constructer. This line does not call operator=! This syntax is just another way to write: SpreadsheetCell aThirdCell(myCell);

```
    anotherCell = myCell; // Calls operator= for anotherCell.
```

Here anotherCell has already been constructed, so the compiler calls operator=:

= does not always mean assignment! It can also be shorthand for copy construction when used on the same line as the variable declaration.

Objects as Return Values

When you return objects from functions or methods, it is sometimes difficult to see exactly what copying and assignment is happening. Recall that the code for getString() looks like this:

```
    string SpreadsheetCell::getString()
    {
        return (mString);
    }
```

Now consider the following code:

```
SpreadsheetCell myCell2(5);
string s1;
s1 = myCell2.getString();
```

When `getString()` returns `mString`, the compiler actually creates an unnamed temporary `string` object by calling a `string` copy constructor. When you assign this result to `s1`, the assignment operator is called for `s1` with the temporary `string` as a parameter. Then, the temporary `string` object is destroyed. Thus, the single line of code invokes the copy constructor and the assignment operator (for two different objects).

In case you're not confused enough, consider this code:

```
SpreadsheetCell myCell3(5);
string s2 = myCell3.getString();
```

In this case, `getString()` still creates a temporary unnamed `string` object when it returns `mString`. But now `s1` gets its copy constructor called, not its assignment operator.

If you ever forget the order in which these things happen or which constructor or operator is called, you can easily figure it out by temporarily including helpful output in your code or by stepping through it with a debugger.

Copy Constructors and Object Members

You should also note the difference between assignment and copy constructor calls in constructors. If an object contains other objects, the compiler-generated copy constructor calls the copy constructors of each of the contained objects recursively. When you write your own copy constructor, you can provide the same semantics by using an initializer list, as shown previously. If you omit a data member from the initializer list, the compiler performs default initialization on it (a call to the 0-argument constructor for objects) before executing your code in the body of the constructor. Thus, by the time the body of the constructor executes, all object data members have already been initialized.

You could write your copy constructor without using an initialization list, like this:

```
SpreadsheetCell::SpreadsheetCell(const SpreadsheetCell& src)
{
    mValue = src.mValue;
    mString = src.mString;
}
```

However, when you assign values to data members in the body of the copy constructor, you are using the assignment operator on them, not the copy constructor, because they have already been initialized, as described previously.

Summary

This chapter covered the fundamental aspects of C++'s facilities for object-oriented programming: classes and objects. It first reviewed the basic syntax for writing classes and using objects, including access control. Then, it covered object life cycles: when objects are constructed, destructed, and assigned, and what methods those actions invoke. The chapter included details of the constructor syntax, including initializer lists. It also specified exactly which constructors the compiler writes for you, and under what circumstances, and explained that default constructors take no arguments.

For some of you, this chapter was mostly review. For others, it hopefully opened your eyes to the world of object-oriented programming in C++. In any case, now that you are proficient with objects and classes you can learn, read Chapter 9 to learn more about their tricks and subtleties.

Mastering Classes and Objects

Chapter 8 helped you gain proficiency with classes and objects. Now it's time to master their subtleties so you can use them to their full potential. By reading this chapter, you will learn how to manipulate and exploit some of the most complicated aspects of the C++ language in order to write safe, effective, and useful classes.

This chapter provides a detailed tutorial of advanced topics, including dynamic memory allocation in objects, `static` methods and members, `const` methods and members, reference and `const` reference members, method overloading and default parameters, `inline` methods, nested classes, friends, operator overloading, pointers to methods and members, and separate interface and implementation classes.

Many of the concepts in this chapter arise in advanced C++ programming, especially in the standard template library.

Dynamic Memory Allocation in Objects

Sometimes you don't know how much memory you will need before your program actually runs. As you know, the solution is to dynamically allocate as much space as you need during program execution. Classes are no exception. Sometimes you don't know how much memory an object will need when you write the class. In that case, the object should dynamically allocate memory.

Dynamically allocated memory in objects provides several challenges, including freeing the memory, handling object copying, and handling object assignment.

The Spreadsheet Class

Chapter 8 introduced the `SpreadsheetCell` class. This chapter moves on to write the `Spreadsheet` class. As with the SpreadsheetCell class, the Spreadsheet class will evolve throughout this chapter. Thus, the various attempts do not always illustrate the best way to do every aspect of class writing. To start, a `Spreadsheet` is simply a two-dimensional array of `SpreadsheetCells`, with methods to set and retrieve cells at specific locations in the `Spreadsheet`. Although most spreadsheet applications use letters in one direction and numbers in the other to refer to cells, this `Spreadsheet` uses numbers in both directions. Here is a first attempt at a class definition for a simple `Spreadsheet` class:

```
// Spreadsheet.h
#include "SpreadsheetCell.h"

class Spreadsheet
{
    public:
        Spreadsheet(int inWidth, int inHeight);

        void setCellAt(int x, int y, const SpreadsheetCell& cell);
        SpreadsheetCell getCellAt(int x, int y);

    protected:
        bool inRange(int val, int upper);

        int mWidth, mHeight;
        SpreadsheetCell** mCells;
};
```

Note that the `Spreadsheet` class does not contain a standard two-dimensional array of `SpreadsheetCells`. Instead, it contains a `SpreadsheetCell**`. The reason is that each `Spreadsheet` object might have different dimensions, so the constructor of the class must dynamically allocate the two-dimensional array based on the client-specified height and width. In order to allocate dynamically a two-dimensional array you need to write the following code:

```
#include "Spreadsheet.h"

Spreadsheet::Spreadsheet(int inWidth, int inHeight) :
    mWidth(inWidth), mHeight(inHeight)
{
    mCells = new SpreadsheetCell* [mWidth];
    for (int i = 0; i < mWidth; i++) {
        mCells[i] = new SpreadsheetCell[mHeight];
    }
}
```

The resultant memory for a `Spreadsheet` called `s1` on the stack with width four and height three is shown in Figure 9-1.

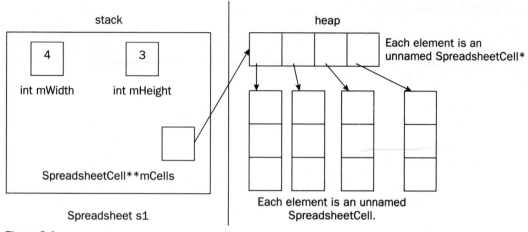

Figure 9-1

If this code confuses you, consult Chapter 13 for details on memory management.

The implementations of the set and retrieval methods are straightforward:

```
void Spreadsheet::setCellAt(int x, int y, const SpreadsheetCell& cell)
{
    if (!inRange(x, mWidth) || !inRange(y, mHeight)) {
        return;
    }

    mCells[x][y] = cell;
}

SpreadsheetCell Spreadsheet::getCellAt(int x, int y)
{
    SpreadsheetCell empty;

    if (!inRange(x, mWidth) || !inRange(y, mHeight)) {
        return (empty);
    }

    return (mCells[x][y]);
}
```

Note that these two methods use a helper method `inRange()` to check that x and y represent valid coordinates in the spreadsheet. Attempting to access an invalid field in the array will cause the program to malfunction. A production application would probably use exceptions to report error conditions, as described in Chapter 15.

Freeing Memory with Destructors

Whenever you are finished with dynamically allocated memory, you should free it. If you dynamically allocate memory in an object, the place to free that memory is in the destructor. The compiler guarantees that the destructor will be called when the object is destroyed. Here is the `Spreadsheet` class definition from earlier with a destructor:

```
class Spreadsheet
{
    public:
        Spreadsheet(int inWidth, int inHeight);
        ~Spreadsheet();

        void setCellAt(int x, int y, const SpreadsheetCell& inCell);
        SpreadsheetCell getCellAt(int x, int y);

    protected:
        bool inRange(int val, int upper);

        int mWidth, mHeight;
        SpreadsheetCell** mCells;
};
```

The destructor has the same name as the name of the class (and of the constructors), preceded by a tilde (~). The destructor takes no arguments, and there can only be one of them.

Here is the implementation of the `Spreadsheet class` destructor:

```
Spreadsheet::~Spreadsheet()
{
    for (int i = 0; i < mWidth; i++) {
        delete[] mCells[i];
    }

    delete[] mCells;
}
```

This destructor frees the memory that was allocated in the constructor. However, no dictate requires you only to free memory in the destructor. You can write whatever code you want in the destructor, but it is a good idea to use it only for freeing memory or disposing of other resources.

Handling Copying and Assignment

Recall from Chapter 8 that, if you don't write a copy constructor and an assignment operator yourself, C++ writes them for you. These compiler-generated methods recursively call the copy constructor or assignment operator, respectively, on object data members. However, for primitives, such as `int`, `double`, and pointers, they provide *shallow* or *bitwise* copying or assignment: they just copy or assign the data members from the source object directly to the destination object. That presents problems when you dynamically allocate memory in your object. For example, the following code copies the spreadsheet `s1` to initialize `s` when `s1` is passed to the `printSpreadsheet()` function.

```
#include "Spreadsheet.h"

void printSpreadsheet(Spreadsheet s)
{
    // Code omitted for brevity.
}

int main(int argc, char** argv)
{
    Spreadsheet s1(4, 3);
    printSpreadsheet(s1);

    return (0);
}
```

The Spreadsheet contains one pointer variable: mCells. A shallow copy of a spreadsheet gives the destination object a copy of the mCells pointer, but not a copy of the underlying data. Thus, you end up with a situation where both s and s1 have a pointer to the same data, as shown in Figure 9-2.

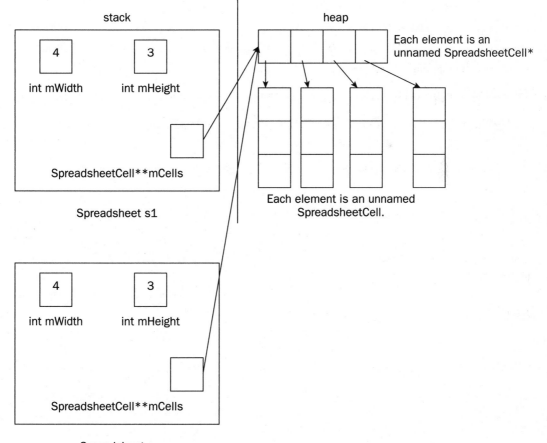

Figure 9-2

If s were to change something to which mCells points, that change would show up in s1 too. Even worse, when the printSpreadsheet() function exits, s's destructor is called, which frees the memory pointed to by mCells. That leaves the situation shown in Figure 9-3.

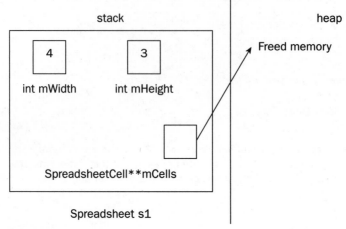

Figure 9-3

Now s1 has a dangling pointer!

Unbelievably, the problem is even worse with assignment. Suppose that you had the following code:

```
Spreadsheet s1(2, 2), s2(4, 3);
s1 = s2;
```

After both objects are constructed, you would have the memory layout shown in Figure 9-4.

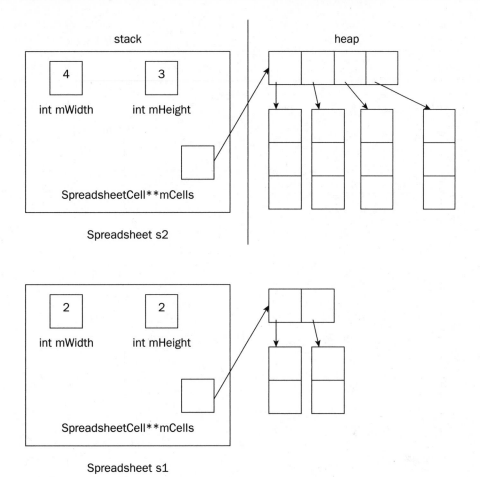

stack

4

int mWidth

3

int mHeight

SpreadsheetCell**mCells

Spreadsheet s2

heap

2

int mWidth

2

int mHeight

SpreadsheetCell**mCells

Spreadsheet s1

Figure 9-4

After the assignment statement, you would have the layout shown in Figure 9-5.

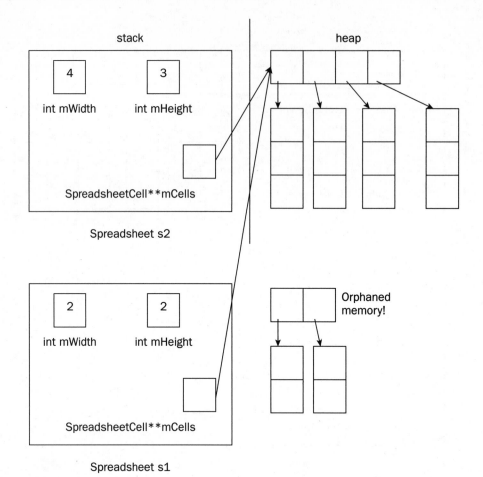

Figure 9-5

Now, not only do the mCells pointers in s1 and s2 point to the same memory, but you have orphaned the memory to which mCells in s1 previously pointed. That is why in assignment operators you must first free the old memory, and then do a deep copy.

As you can see, relying on C++'s default copy constructor or assignment operator is not always a good idea. Whenever you have dynamically allocated memory in a class, you should write your own copy constructor to provide a *deep* copy of the memory.

The Spreadsheet Copy Constructor

Here is a declaration for a copy constructor in the Spreadsheet class:

```
class Spreadsheet
{
    public:
        Spreadsheet(int inWidth, int inHeight);
        Spreadsheet(const Spreadsheet& src);
```

```
        ~Spreadsheet();

        void setCellAt(int x, int y, const SpreadsheetCell& cell);
        SpreadsheetCell getCellAt(int x, int y);

    protected:
        bool inRange(int val, int upper);

        int mWidth, mHeight;
        SpreadsheetCell** mCells;
};
```

Here is the definition of the copy constructor:

```
Spreadsheet::Spreadsheet(const Spreadsheet& src)
{
    int i, j;

    mWidth = src.mWidth;
    mHeight = src.mHeight;

    mCells = new SpreadsheetCell* [mWidth];
    for (i = 0; i < mWidth; i++) {
        mCells[i] = new SpreadsheetCell[mHeight];
    }

    for (i = 0; i < mWidth; i++) {
        for (j = 0; j < mHeight; j++) {
            mCells[i][j] = src.mCells[i][j];
        }
    }
}
```

Note that the copy constructor copies all data members, including `mWidth` and `mHeight`, not just the pointer data members. The rest of the code in the copy constructor provides a deep copy of the `mCells` dynamically allocated two-dimensional array.

> **Copy all data members in a copy constructor, not just pointer members.**

The Spreadsheet Assignment Operator

Here is the definition for the `Spreadsheet` class with an assignment operator:

```
class Spreadsheet
{
    public:
        Spreadsheet(int inWidth, int inHeight);
        Spreadsheet(const Spreadsheet& src);
        ~Spreadsheet();

        Spreadsheet& operator=(const Spreadsheet& rhs);

        void setCellAt(int x, int y, const SpreadsheetCell& cell);
        SpreadsheetCell getCellAt(int x, int y);
```

```
    protected:
        bool inRange(int val, int upper);

        int mWidth, mHeight;
        SpreadsheetCell** mCells;
};
```

Here is the implementation of the assignment operator for the Spreadsheet class, with explanations interspersed. Note that when an object is assigned to, it already has been initialized. Thus, you must free any dynamically allocated memory before allocating new memory. You can think of an assignment operator as a combination of a destructor and a copy constructor. You are essentially "reincarnating" the object with new life (or data) when you assign to it.

```
Spreadsheet& Spreadsheet::operator=(const Spreadsheet& rhs)
{
    int i, j;

    // Check for self-assignment.
    if (this == &rhs) {
        return (*this);
    }
```

The above code checks for self-assignment.

```
    // Free the old memory.
    for (i = 0; i < mWidth; i++) {
        delete[] mCells[i];
    }

    delete[] mCells;
```

This chunk of code is identical to the destructor. You must free all the memory before reallocating it, or you will create a memory leak.

```
    // Copy the new memory.
    mWidth = rhs.mWidth;
    mHeight = rhs.mHeight;

    mCells = new SpreadsheetCell* [mWidth];
    for (i = 0; i < mWidth; i++) {
        mCells[i] = new SpreadsheetCell[mHeight];
    }

    for (i = 0; i < mWidth; i++) {
        for (j = 0; j < mHeight; j++) {
            mCells[i][j] = rhs.mCells[i][j];
        }
    }
```

This chunk of code is identical to the copy constructor.

```
    return (*this);
}
```

The assignment operator completes the "big 3" routines for managing dynamically allocated memory in an object: the destructor, the copy constructor, and the assignment operator. Whenever you find yourself writing one of those methods you should write all of them.

> Whenever a class dynamically allocates memory, write a destructor, copy constructor, and assignment operator.

Common Helper Routines for Copy Constructor and Assignment Operator

The copy constructor and the assignment operator are quite similar. Thus, it's usually convenient to factor the common tasks into a helper method. For example, you could add a copyFrom() method to the Spreadsheet class, and rewrite the copy constructor and assignment operator to use it like this:

```
void Spreadsheet::copyFrom(const Spreadsheet& src)
{
    int i, j;

    mWidth = src.mWidth;
    mHeight = src.mHeight;

    mCells = new SpreadsheetCell* [mWidth];
    for (i = 0; i < mWidth; i++) {
        mCells[i] = new SpreadsheetCell[mHeight];
    }

    for (i = 0; i < mWidht; i++) {
        for (j = 0; j < mHeight; j++) {
            mCells[i][j] = src.mCells[i][j];
        }
    }
}

Spreadsheet::Spreadsheet(const Spreadsheet &src)
{
    copyFrom(src);
}

Spreadsheet& Spreadsheet::operator=(const Spreadsheet& rhs)
{
    int i;

    // Check for self-assignment.
    if (this == &rhs) {
        return (*this);
    }
    // Free the old memory.
    for (i = 0; i < mWidth; i++) {
        delete[] mCells[i];
    }
```

```
        delete[] mCells;

        // Copy the new memory.
        copyFrom(rhs);

        return (*this);
    }
```

Disallowing Assignment and Pass-By-Value

Sometimes when you dynamically allocate memory in your class, it's easiest just to prevent anyone from copying or assigning to your objects. You can do this by marking your copy constructor and operator= private. That way, if anyone tries to pass the object by value, return it from a function or method, or assign to it, the compiler will complain. Here is a Spreadsheet class definition that prevents assignment and pass-by-value:

```
class Spreadsheet
{
    public:
        Spreadsheet(int inWidth, int inHeight);
        ~Spreadsheet();

        void setCellAt(int x, int y, const SpreadsheetCell& cell);
        SpreadsheetCell getCellAt(int x, int y);

    protected:
        bool inRange(int val, int upper);

        int mWidth, mHeight;
        SpreadsheetCell** mCells;

    private:
        Spreadsheet(const Spreadsheet& src);
        Spreadsheet& operator=(const Spreadsheet& rhs);
};
```

When you write code to copy or assign to a Spreadsheet object, the compiler will complain with a message like '=' : cannot access private member declared in class 'Spreadsheet'.

> You don't need to provide implementations for private copy constructors and assignment operators. The linker will never look for them because the compiler won't allow code to call them.

Different Kinds of Data Members

C++ gives you many choices for data members. In addition to declaring simple data members in your classes, you can create data members that all objects of the class share, const members, reference members, const reference members, and more. This section explains the intricacies of these different kinds of data members.

Static Data Members

Sometimes giving each object of a class a copy of a variable is overkill or won't work. The data member might be specific to the class, but not appropriate for each object to have its own copy. For example, you might want to give each spreadsheet a unique numerical identifier. You would need a counter that starts at 0 from which each new object could obtain its ID. This spreadsheet counter really belongs to the Spreadsheet class, but it doesn't make sense for each Spreadsheet object to have a copy of it because you would have to keep all the counters synchronized somehow. C++ provides a solution with *static data members*. A static data member is a data member associated with a class instead of an object. You can think of static data members as global variables specific to a class. Here is the Spreadsheet class definition, including the new static counter data member:

```
class Spreadsheet
{
    public:
        // Omitted for brevity
    protected:
        bool inRange(int val, int upper);
        void copyFrom(const Spreadsheet& src);

        int mWidth, mHeight;
        SpreadsheetCell** mCells;

        static int sCounter;
};
```

In addition to listing static class members in the class definition, you must allocate them space in a source file, usually the source file in which you place your class method definitions. You can initialize them at the same time, but note that unlike normal variables and data members, they are initialized to 0 by default. Here is the code to allocate space for and initialize the sCounter member:

```
int Spreadsheet::sCounter = 0;
```

This code appears outside of any function or method bodies. It's almost like declaring a global variable, except that the Spreadsheet:: scope resolution specifies that it's part of the Spreadsheet class.

Accessing Static Data Members within Class Methods

You can use static data members as if they were regular data members from within class methods. For example, you might want to create an mId member of the Spreadsheet class and initialize it from the sCounter member in the Spreadsheet constructor. Here is the Spreadsheet class definition with an mId member:

```
class Spreadsheet
{
    public:
        Spreadsheet(int inWidth, int inHeight);
        Spreadsheet(const Spreadsheet& src);
        ~Spreadsheet();
        Spreadsheet& operator=(const Spreadsheet& rhs);

        void setCellAt(int x, int y, const SpreadsheetCell& cell);
        SpreadsheetCell getCellAt(int x, int y);
```

```
            int getId();

    protected:
            bool inRange(int val, int upper);
            void copyFrom(const Spreadsheet& src);

            int mWidth, mHeight;
            int mId;
            SpreadsheetCell** mCells;

            static int sCounter;
};
```

Here is an implementation of the Spreadsheet constructor that assigns the initial ID:

```
Spreadsheet::Spreadsheet(int inWidth, int inHeight) :
    mWidth(inWidth), mHeight(inHeight)
{
    mId = sCounter++;
    mCells = new SpreadsheetCell* [mWidth];
    for (int i = 0; i < mWidth; i++) {
        mCells[i] = new SpreadsheetCell[mHeight];
    }
}
```

As you can see, the constructor can access sCounter as if it were a normal member. Remember to assign an ID in the copy constructor as well:

```
Spreadsheet::Spreadsheet(const Spreadsheet& src)
{
    mId = sCounter++;
    copyFrom(src);
}
```

You should not copy the ID in the assignment operator. Once an ID is assigned to an object it should never change.

Accessing Static Data Members Outside Methods

Access control specifiers apply to static data members: sCounter is protected, so it cannot be accessed from outside class methods.

However, even though it is protected, you are allowed to assign it a value when you declare space for it in the source file, despite the fact that the code is not inside any Spreadsheet class method. Here is that line of code again:

```
int Spreadsheet::sCounter = 0;
```

Const Data Members

Data members in your class can be declared const, meaning they can't be changed after they are created and initialized. Constants almost never make sense at the object level, so const data members are usually static as well. You should use static const data members in place of global constants when the constants apply only to the class. For example, you might want to specify a maximum height and width for spreadsheets. If the user tries to construct a spreadsheet with a greater height or width than the maximum, the maximum is used instead. You can make the max height and width static const members of the Spreadsheet class:

```
class Spreadsheet
{
    public:
        // Omitted for brevity

        static const int kMaxHeight;
        static const int kMaxWidth;

    protected:
        // Omitted for brevity
};
```

Because these members are static, you must declare space for them in the source file. Because they are const, this is your last chance to give them a value:

```
const int Spreadsheet::kMaxHeight = 100;
const int Spreadsheet::kMaxWidth = 100;
```

The C++ standard actually permits you to assign static const member variables a value as you declare them in the class file if they are of integral type (such as int or char).

```
class Spreadsheet
{
    public:
        // Omitted for brevity

        static const int kMaxHeight = 100;
        static const int kMaxWidth = 100;

    protected:
        // Omitted for brevity
};
```

This capability is useful if you want to use the constant later in your class definition. Although some older compilers fail to support this syntax, most now accept it. In fact, many compilers allow you to omit the extra definition of the static const member in a source file if you initialize it in the class definition, and if you don't perform any operations on it that require actual storage, such as taking its address.

You can use these new constants in your constructor as shown in the following section of code (note the use of the ternary operator):

```
Spreadsheet::Spreadsheet(int inWidth, int inHeight) :
    mWidth(inWidth < kMaxWidth ? inWidth : kMaxWidth),
    mHeight(inHeight < kMaxHeight ? inHeight : kMaxHeight)
{
    mId = sCounter++;
```

```
        mCells = new SpreadsheetCell* [mWidth];
        for (int i = 0; i < mWidth; i++) {
            mCells[i] = new SpreadsheetCell[mHeight];
        }
    }
```

kMaxHeight and kMaxWidth are public, so you can access them from anywhere in your program as if they were global variables, but with slightly different syntax: you must specify that the variable is part of the Spreadsheet class with the scope resolution operator, ::.

```
cout << "Maximum height is: " << Spreadsheet::kMaxHeight << endl;
```

Reference Data Members

Spreadsheets and SpreadsheetCells are great, but they don't make a very useful application by themselves. You need code to control the whole spreadsheet program, which you could package into a SpreadsheetApplication class.

The implementation of this class is unimportant at the moment. For now, consider this architecture problem: how can spreadsheets communicate with the application? The application stores a list of spreadsheets, so it can communicate with the spreadsheets. Similarly, each spreadsheet should store a reference to the application object. The Spreadsheet class must know about the SpreadsheetApplication class, but instead of using a full #include, you can just use a *forward reference* to the class name (see Chapter 12 for details). Here is the new Spreadsheet class definition:

```
class SpreadsheetApplication; // forward declaration

class Spreadsheet
{
    public:
        Spreadsheet(int inWidth, int inHeight,
            SpreadsheetApplication& theApp);
        // Code omitted for brevity.

    protected:
        // Code omitted for brevity.
        SpreadsheetApplication& mTheApp;

        static int sCounter;
};
```

Note that the application reference is given to each Spreadsheet in its constructor. A reference cannot exist without referring to something, so mTheApp must be given a value in the initializer list of the constructor:

```
Spreadsheet::Spreadsheet(int inWidth, int inHeight,
    SpreadsheetApplication& theApp)
    : mWidth(inWidth < kMaxWidth ? inWidth : kMaxWidth),
      mHeight(inHeight < kMaxHeight ? inHeight : kMaxHeight), mTheApp(theApp)
{
    // Code omitted for brevity.
}
```

You must also initialize the reference member in the copy constructor:

```
Spreadsheet::Spreadsheet(const Spreadsheet& src) :
    mTheApp(src.mTheApp)
{
    mId = sCounter++;
    copyFrom(src);
}
```

Remember that after you have initialized a reference you cannot change the object to which it refers. Thus, you do not need to attempt to assign to references in the assignment operator.

Const Reference Data Members

Your reference members can refer to const objects just as normal references can refer to const objects. For example, you might decide that Spreadsheets should only have a const reference to the application object. You can simply change the class definition to declare mTheApp as a const reference:

```
class Spreadsheet
{
    public:
        Spreadsheet(int inWidth, int inHeight,
            const SpreadsheetApplication& theApp);
        // Code omitted for brevity.

    protected:
        // Code omitted for brevity.
        const SpreadsheetApplication& mTheApp;

        static int sCounter;
};
```

It's also possible to have a static reference member or a static const reference member, but you will rarely find the need for something like that.

More about Methods

C++ also provides myriad choices for methods. This section explains all the tricky details.

Static Methods

Methods, like members, sometimes apply to the class as a whole, not to each object. You can write static methods as well as members. As an example, consider the SpreadsheetCell class from Chapter 8. It has two helper methods: stringToDouble() and doubleToString(). These methods don't access information about specific objects, so they could be static. Here is the class definition with these methods static:

```
class SpreadsheetCell
{
    public:
```

```
         // Omitted for brevity

    protected:
        static string doubleToString(double val);
        static double stringToDouble(const string& str);

        // Omitted for brevity
};
```

The implementations of these two methods are identical to the previous implementations! You don't even need to repeat the `static` keyword in front of the method definitions. However, note that `static` methods are not called on a specific object, so they have no `this` pointer, and are not executing for a specific object with access to its non-`static` members. In fact, a `static` method is just like a regular function. The only difference is that it can access `private` and `protected` `static` data members of the class and `private` and `protected` non-`static` data members on other objects of the same type.

You cannot access non-static data members inside a static method.

You call a `static` method just like a regular function from within any method of the class. Thus, the implementation of all methods in `SpreadsheetCell` can stay the same. Outside of the class, you need to qualify the method name with the class name using the scope resolution operator (as for `static` members). Access control applies as usual.

You might want to make `stringToDouble()` and `doubleToString()` `public` so that other code outside the class could make use of them. If so, you could call them from anywhere like this:

```
string str = SpreadsheetCell::doubleToString(5);
```

Const Methods

A `const` object is an object whose value cannot be changed. If you have a `const` or reference to `const` object, the compiler will not let you call any methods on that object unless those methods guarantee that they won't change any data members. The way you guarantee that a method won't change data members is to mark the method itself with the `const` keyword. Here is a modified `SpreadsheetCell` class with the methods that don't change any data member marked `const`:

```
class SpreadsheetCell
{
    public:
        SpreadsheetCell();
        SpreadsheetCell(double initialValue);
        SpreadsheetCell(const string& initialValue);
        SpreadsheetCell(const SpreadsheetCell& src);
        SpreadsheetCell& operator=(const SpreadsheetCell& rhs);
        void setValue(double inValue);
        double getValue() const;
        void setString(const string& inString);
        string getString() const;
```

```
    static string doubleToString(double inValue);
    static double stringToDouble(const string& inString);

protected:

    double mValue;
    string mString;
};
```

The const specification is part of the method prototype and must accompany its definition as well:

```
double SpreadsheetCell::getValue() const
{
    return (mValue);
}
string SpreadsheetCell::getString() const
{
    return (mString);
}
```

Marking a method as const signs a contract with client code guaranteeing that you will not try to change the internal values of the object within the method. If you try to declare a method const that actually modifies a data member, the compiler will complain. You also cannot declare a static method const because it is redundant. Static methods do not have an instance of the class so it would be impossible for them to change internal values. const works by making it appear inside the method that you have a const reference to each data member. Thus, if you try to change the data member the compiler will flag an error.

A non-const object can call const and non-const methods. However, a const object can only call const methods. Here are some examples:

```
SpreadsheetCell myCell(5);

cout << myCell.getValue() << endl; // OK
myCell.setString("6"); // OK

const SpreadsheetCell& anotherCell = myCell;

cout << anotherCell.getValue() << endl; // OK
anotherCell.setString("6"); // Compilation Error!
```

You should get into the habit of declaring const all methods that don't modify the object so that you can use references to const objects in your program.

Note that const objects can still be destroyed, and their destructor can be called. You shouldn't try to mark the destructor const.

Mutable Data Members

Sometimes you write a method that is "logically" const but happens to change a data member of the object. This modification has no effect on any user-visible data, but is technically a change, so the compiler won't let you declare the method const. For example, suppose that you want to profile your spreadsheet application to obtain info about how often data is being read. A crude way to do this would be to add a counter to the `SpreadsheetCell` class that counts each call to `getValue()` or `getString()`. Unfortunately, that makes those methods non-const in the compiler's eyes, which is not what you intended. The solution is to make your new counter variable `mutable`, which tells the compiler that it's okay to change it in a const method. Here is the new `SpreadsheetCell` class definition:

```
class SpreadsheetCell
{
    public:
        SpreadsheetCell();
        SpreadsheetCell(double initialValue);
        SpreadsheetCell(const string& initialValue);
        SpreadsheetCell(const SpreadsheetCell& src);
        SpreadsheetCell& operator=(const SpreadsheetCell& rhs);
        void setValue(double inValue);
        double getValue() const;
        void setString(const string& inString);
        string getString() const;

        static string doubleToString(double inValue);
        static double stringToDouble(const string& inString);

    protected:
        double mValue;
        string mString;

        mutable int mNumAccesses;
};
```

Here are the definitions for `getValue()` and `getString()`:

```
double SpreadsheetCell::getValue() const
{
    mNumAccesses++;
    return (mValue);
}

string SpreadsheetCell::getString() const
{
    mNumAccesses++;
    return (mString);
}
```

Remember to initialize `mNumAccesses` in all your constructors!

Method Overloading

You've already noticed that you can write multiple constructors in a class, all of which have the same name. These constructors differ only in the number of types of their parameters. You can do the same thing for any method or function in C++. Specifically, you can *overload* the function or method name by using it for multiple functions, as long as the number or types of the parameters differ. For example, in the `SpreadsheetCell` class you could rename both `setString()` and `setValue()` to `set()`. The class definition now looks like this:

```
class SpreadsheetCell
{
    public:
        SpreadsheetCell();
        SpreadsheetCell(double initialValue);
        SpreadsheetCell(const string& initialValue);
        SpreadsheetCell(const SpreadsheetCell& src);
        SpreadsheetCell& operator=(const SpreadsheetCell& rhs);
        void set(double inValue);
        void set(const string& inString);
        double getValue() const;
        string getString() const;

        // Remainder of the class omitted for brevity
};
```

The implementations of the set() methods stay the same. Note that the double constructor that previously called setValue() must now call set(). When you write code to call set(), the compiler determines which version to call based on the parameter you pass: if you pass a string the compiler calls the string version, if you pass a double the compiler calls the double version.

You might be tempted to do the same thing for getValue() and getString(): rename each of them to get(). However, that does not compile. C++ does not allow you to overload a method name based only on the return type of the method because in many cases it would be impossible for the compiler to determine which version of the method to call. For example, if the return value of the method is not captured anywhere, the compiler has no way to tell which version of the method you wanted.

Note also that you can overload a method based on const. That is, you can write two methods with the same name and same parameters, one of which is declared const and one of which is not. The compiler will call the const method if you have a const object and the non-const method if you have a non-const object.

Default Parameters

A feature similar to method overloading in C++ is *default parameters*. You can specify defaults for function and method parameters in the prototype. If the user specifies those arguments, the defaults are ignored. If the user omits those arguments, the default values are used. There is a limitation, though: you can only provide defaults for a continuous list of parameters starting from the *rightmost parameter*. Otherwise, the compiler would not be able to match missing arguments to default parameters. Default parameters are most useful in constructors. For example, you can assign default values to the width and height in your Spreadsheet constructor:

```
class Spreadsheet
{
    public:
        Spreadsheet(const SpreadsheetApplication& theApp, int inWidth = kMaxWidth,
            int inHeight = kMaxHeight);
        Spreadsheet(const Spreadsheet& src);
        ~Spreadsheet();
        Spreadsheet& operator=(const Spreadsheet& rhs);
```

```
        void setCellAt(int x, int y, const SpreadsheetCell& inCell);
        SpreadsheetCell getCellAt(int x, int y);

        int getId();

        static const int kMaxHeight = 100;
        static const int kMaxWidth = 100;

    protected:
        // Omitted for brevity
};
```

The implementation of the `Spreadsheet` constructor stays the same. Note that you specify the default parameters only in the method declaration, but not in the definition.

Now you can call the `Spreadsheet` constructor with one, two, or three arguments even though there is only one noncopy constructor:

```
SpreadsheetApplication theApp;
Spreadsheet s1(theApp);
Spreadsheet s2(theApp, 5);
Spreadsheet s3(theApp, 5, 6);
```

A constructor with defaults for all its parameters can function as a default constructor. That is, you can construct an object of that class without specifying any arguments. If you try to declare both a default constructor and a multiargument constructor with defaults for all its parameters, the compiler will complain because it won't know which constructor to call if you don't specify any arguments.

Note that anything you can do with default parameters you can do with method overloading. You could write three different constructors, each of which takes a different number of parameters. However, default parameters allow you to write only one constructor to take three different numbers of arguments. You should use the mechanism with which you are most comfortable.

Inline Methods

C++ gives you the ability to recommend that a call to a method or function should not actually be a method or function call. Instead, the compiler should insert the method or function body directly into the code where the method or function call is made. This process is called *inlining*, and methods or functions that want this behavior are called `inline` methods or functions. The process is just a safer version of #define macros.

You can specify an `inline` method or function by placing the `inline` keyword in front of its name in the function or method definition. For example, you might want to make the setter and accessor methods of the `SpreadsheetCell` class `inline`, in which case you would define them like this:

```
inline double SpreadsheetCell::getValue() const
{
    mNumAccesses++;
    return (mValue);
}
```

```
inline string SpreadsheetCell::getString() const
{
    mNumAccesses++;
    return (mString);
}
```

Now, the compiler has to option to replace calls to `getValue()` and `getString()` with the actual method body instead of generating code to make a function call.

There is one major caveat: definitions of `inline` methods and functions must be available in every source file in which they are called. That makes sense if you think about it: how can the compiler substitute the function body if it can't see the function definition? Thus, if you write `inline` functions or methods you should place the definitions in a header file along with their prototypes. For methods, this means placing the definitions in the `.h` file that includes the class definition. This placement is perfectly safe: the linker doesn't complain about multiple definitions of the same method. It's just like a `#define` macro in this sense.

C++ provides an alternate syntax for declaring `inline` methods that doesn't use the `inline` keyword at all. Instead, you place the method definition directly in the class definition. Here is a `SpreadsheetCell` class definition with this syntax:

```
class SpreadsheetCell
{
    public:
        SpreadsheetCell();
        SpreadsheetCell(double initialValue);
        SpreadsheetCell(const string& initialValue);
        SpreadsheetCell(const SpreadsheetCell& src);
        SpreadsheetCell& operator=(const SpreadsheetCell& rhs);
        void set(double inValue);
        void set(const string& inString);

        double getValue() const {mNumAccesses++; return (mValue); }
        string getString() const {mNumAccesses++; return (mString); }

        static string doubleToString(double inValue);
        static double stringToDouble(const string& inString);

    protected:
        double mValue;
        string mString;

        mutable int mNumAccesses;
};
```

Many C++ programmers discover the `inline` method syntax and employ it without understanding the ramifications of making a method `inline`. First, there are many restrictions on which methods can be `inline`. Compilers will only `inline` the simplest methods and functions. If you define an `inline` method that the compiler doesn't want to `inline`, it may silently ignore the directive. Second, `inline` methods can lead to code bloat. The body of the methods are reproduced everywhere they are called, increasing the size of your program executable. Thus, you should use `inline` methods and functions sparingly.

Nested Classes

Class definitions can contain more than just methods and members. You can also write nested classes and structs, declare typedefs, or create enumerated types. Anything declared inside a class is in the scope of that class. If it is public, you can access it outside the class by scoping it with the ClassName:: scope resolution syntax.

You can provide a class definition inside another class definition. For example, you might decide that the SpreadsheetCell class is really part of the Spreadsheet class. You could define both of them like this:

```
class Spreadsheet
{
    public:

        class SpreadsheetCell
        {
            public:
                SpreadsheetCell();
                SpreadsheetCell(double initialValue);
                SpreadsheetCell(const string& initialValue);
                SpreadsheetCell(const SpreadsheetCell& src);
                SpreadsheetCell& operator=(const SpreadsheetCell& rhs);
                void set(double inValue);
                void set(const string& inString);

                double getValue() const {mNumAccesses++; return (mValue); }
                string getString() const {mNumAccesses++; return (mString); }

                static string doubleToString(double inValue);
                static double stringToDouble(const string& inString);

            protected:
                double mValue;
                string mString;

                mutable int mNumAccesses;
        };

        Spreadsheet(const SpreadsheetApplication& theApp, int inWdith = kMaxWidth,
            int inHeight = kMaxHeight);
        Spreadsheet(const Spreadsheet& src);
        ~Spreadsheet();
        Spreadsheet& operator=(const Spreadsheet& rhs);

        // Remainder of Spreadsheet declarations omitted for brevity
};
```

Now, the SpreadsheetCell class is defined inside the Spreadsheet class, so anywhere you refer to a SpreadsheetCell outside of the Spreadsheet class you must qualify the name with the Spreadsheet:: scope. This applies even to the method definitions. For example, the default constructor now looks like this:

```
Spreadsheet::SpreadsheetCell::SpreadsheetCell() : mValue(0), mNumAccesses(0)
{
}
```

This syntax can quickly become clumsy. For example, the definition of the `SpreadsheetCell` assignment operator now looks like this:

```
Spreadsheet::SpreadsheetCell& Spreadsheet::SpreadsheetCell::operator=(
    const SpreadsheetCell& rhs)
{
    if (this == &rhs) {
        return (*this);
    }
    mValue = rhs.mValue;
    mString = rhs.mString;
    mNumAccesses = rhs.mNumAccesses;
    return (*this);
}
```

In fact, you must even use the syntax for return types (but not parameters) of methods in the `Spreadsheet` class itself:

```
Spreadsheet::SpreadsheetCell Spreadsheet::getCellAt(int x, int y)
{
    SpreadsheetCell empty;

    if (!inRange(x, mWidth) || !inRange(y, mHeight)) {
        return (empty);
    }
    return (mCells[x][y]);
}
```

You can avoid the clumsy syntax by using a `typedef` to rename `Spreadsheet::SpreadsheetCell` to something more manageable like `SCell`:

```
typedef Spreadsheet::SpreadsheetCell SCell;
```

This `typedef` should go outside the `Spreadsheet class` definition, or else you will have to qualify the `typedef` name itself with `Spreadsheet::` to get `Spreadsheet::SCell`. That wouldn't do you much good!

Now you can write your constructor like this:

```
SCell::SpreadsheetCell() : mValue(0), mNumAccesses(0)
{
}
```

Normal access control applies to nested class definitions. If you declare a `private` or `protected` nested class, you can only use it inside the outer class.

You should generally use nested class definitions only for trivial classes. It is really too clumsy for something like the `SpreadsheetCell` class.

Friends

C++ allows classes to declare that other classes or nonmember functions are *friends*, and can access `protected` and `private` data members and methods. For example, the `SpreadsheetCell` class could specify that the `Spreadsheet` class is its "friend" like this:

```
class SpreadsheetCell
{
    public:
        friend class Spreadsheet;

        // Remainder of the class omitted for brevity
};
```

Now all the methods of the `Spreadsheet` class can access the `private` and `protected` data and members of the `SpreadsheetCell` class.

Similarly, you can specify that one or more functions or members of another class are `friends`. For example, you might want to write a function to verify that the value and the string of a `SpreadsheetCell` object are really in synch. You might want this verification routine to be outside the `SpreadsheetCell` class to model an external audit, but the function should be able to access the internal data members of the object in order to check it properly. Here is the `SpreadsheetCell` class definition with a `friend checkSpreadsheetCell()` function:

```
class SpreadsheetCell
{
    public:
        // Omitted for brevity

        friend bool checkSpreadsheetCell(const SpreadsheetCell &cell);

        // Omitted for brevity
};
```

The `friend` declaration in the class serves as the function's prototype. There's no need to write the prototype elsewhere (although it's harmless to do so).

Here is the function definition:

```
bool checkSpreadsheetCell(const SpreadsheetCell &cell)
{
    return (SpreadsheetCell::stringToDouble(cell.mString) == cell.mValue);
}
```

You write this function just like any other function, except that you can directly access `private` and `protected` data members of the `SpreadsheetCell` class. You don't repeat the `friend` keyword on the function definition.

`friend` classes and methods are easy to abuse; they allow you to violate the principle of abstraction by exposing internals of your class to other classes or functions. Thus, you should use them only in limited circumstances such as operator overloading.

Operator Overloading

You often want to perform operations on objects such as adding them, comparing them, or streaming them to or from files. For example, spreadsheets are really only useful when you can perform arithmetic actions on them such as summing an entire row of cells.

Implementing Addition

In true object-oriented fashion, SpreadsheetCell objects should be able to add themselves to other SpreadsheetCell objects. Adding a cell to another cell produces a third cell with the result. It doesn't change either of the original cells. The meaning of addition for SpreadsheetCells is the addition of the values of the cells. The string representations are ignored.

First Attempt: The add Method

You can declare and define an add method for your SpreadsheetCell class like this:

```
class SpreadsheetCell
{
    public:
        // Omitted for brevity

        const SpreadsheetCell add(const SpreadsheetCell& cell) const;

    // Omitted for brevity
};
```

This method adds two cells together, returning a new third cell whose value is the sum of the first two. It is declared const and takes a reference to a const SpreadsheetCell because add() does not change either of the source cells. It returns a const SpreadsheetCell because you don't want users to change the return value. They should just assign it to another object. add() is a method, so it is called on one object and passed another. Here is the implementation:

```
const SpreadsheetCell SpreadsheetCell::add(const SpreadsheetCell& cell) const
{
    SpreadsheetCell newCell;
    newCell.set(mValue + cell.mValue); // call set to update mValue and mString
    return (newCell);
}
```

Note that the implementation creates a new SpreadsheetCell called newCell and returns a *copy* of that cell. That only works because you wrote a copy constructor for this class. You might be tempted to return a reference to the cell instead. However, that will not work because as soon as the add() method ends and newCell goes out of scope it will be destroyed. The reference that you returned will then be a dangling reference.

You can use the add method like this:

```
SpreadsheetCell myCell(4), anotherCell(5);
SpreadsheetCell aThirdCell = myCell.add(anotherCell);
```

That works, but it's a bit clumsy. You can do better.

Second Attempt: Overloaded operator+ as a Method

It would be convenient to be able to add two cells with the plus sign the way that you add two ints or two doubles. Something like this:

```
SpreadsheetCell myCell(4), anotherCell(5);
SpreadsheetCell aThirdCell = myCell + anotherCell;
```

Luckily, C++ allows you to write your own version of the plus sign, called the addition operator, to work correctly with your classes. To do that you write a method with the name operator+ that looks like this:

```
class SpreadsheetCell
{
    public:
        // Omitted for brevity

        const SpreadsheetCell operator+(const SpreadsheetCell& cell) const;

    // Omitted for brevity

};
```

The definition of the method is identical to the implementation of the add() method:

```
const SpreadsheetCell SpreadsheetCell::operator+(const SpreadsheetCell& cell)
const
{
    SpreadsheetCell newCell;
    newCell.set(mValue + cell.mValue); // Call set to update mValue and mString.
    return (newCell);
}
```

Now you can add two cells together using the plus sign as shown previously!

This syntax takes a bit of getting used to. Try not to worry too much about the strange method name operator+ — it's just a name like foo or add. In order to understand the rest of the syntax, it helps to understand what's really going on. When your C++ compiler parses a program and encounters an operator, such as +, -, =, or <<, it tries to find a function or method with the name operator+, operator-, operator=, or operator<<, respectively, that takes the appropriate parameters. For example, when the compiler sees the following line, it tries to find either a method in the SpreadsheetCell class named operator+ that takes another SpreadsheetCell object or a global function named operator+ that takes two SpreadsheetCell objects:

```
SpreadsheetCell aThirdCell = myCell + anotherCell;
```

Note that there's no requirement that operator+ take as a parameter an object of the same type as the class for which it's written. You could write an operator+ for SpreadsheetCells that takes a Spreadsheet to add to the SpreadsheetCell. That wouldn't make sense to the programmer, but the compiler would allow it.

Note also that you can give operator+ any return value you want. Operator overloading is a form of function overloading, and recall that function overloading does not look at the return type of the function.

Implicit Conversions

Surprisingly, once you've written the `operator+` shown earlier, not only can you add two cells together, you can also add a cell to a `string`, a `double`, or an `int`!

```
SpreadsheetCell myCell(4), aThirdCell;
string str = "hello";

aThirdCell = myCell + str;
aThirdCell = myCell + 5.6;
aThirdCell = myCell + 4;
```

The reason this code works is that the compiler does more to try to find an appropriate `operator+` than just look for one with the exact types specified. The compiler also tries to find an appropriate conversion for the types so that an `operator+` can be found. Constructors that take the type in question are appropriate converters. In the preceding example, when the compiler sees a `SpreadsheetCell` trying to add itself to `double`, it finds the `SpreadsheetCell` constructor that takes a `double` and constructs a temporary `SpreadsheetCell` object to pass to `operator+`. Similarly, when the compiler sees the line trying to add a `SpreadsheetCell` to a `string`, it calls the `string SpreadsheetCell` constructor to create a temporary `SpreadsheetCell` to pass to `operator+`.

This implicit conversion behavior is usually convenient. However, in the preceding example, it doesn't really make sense to add a `SpreadsheetCell` to a `string`. You can prevent the implicit construction of a `SpreadsheetCell` from a `string` by marking that constructor with the `explicit` keyword:

```
class SpreadsheetCell
{
    public:
        SpreadsheetCell();
        SpreadsheetCell(double initialValue);
        explicit SpreadsheetCell(const string& initialValue);
        SpreadsheetCell(const SpreadsheetCell& src);
        SpreadsheetCell& operator=(const SpreadsheetCell& rhs);
    // Remainder omitted for brevity
};
```

The `explicit` keyword goes only in the `class` definition, and only makes sense when applied to constructors with exactly one argument.

Third Attempt: Global Operator+

Implicit conversions allow you to use an `operator+` method to add your `SpreadsheetCell` objects to `int`s and `double`s. However, the operator is not commutative, as shown in the following code:

```
aThirdCell = myCell + 4; // Works fine.
aThirdCell = myCell + 5.6; // Works fine.

aThirdCell = 4 + myCell; // FAILS TO COMPILE!
aThirdCell = 5.6 + myCell; // FAILS TO COMPILE!
```

The implicit conversion works fine when the `SpreadsheetCell` object is on the left of the operator, but doesn't work when it's on the right. Addition is supposed to be commutative, so something is wrong here. The problem is that the `operator+` method must be called on a `SpreadsheetCell` object, and that object must be on the left-hand side of the `operator+`. That's just the way the C++ language is defined. So, there's no way you can get the above code to work with an `operator+` method.

However, you can get it to work if you replace the in-class `operator+` with a global `operator+` function that is not tied to any particular object. The function looks like this:

```
const SpreadsheetCell operator+(const SpreadsheetCell& lhs,
    const SpreadsheetCell& rhs)
{
    SpreadsheetCell newCell;
    newCell.set(lhs.mValue + rhs.mValue); // Call set to update mValue and mString.
    return (newCell);
}
```

Now all four of the addition lines work as you expect:

```
aThirdCell = myCell + 4; // Works fine.
aThirdCell = myCell + 5.6; // Works fine.

aThirdCell = 4 + myCell; // Works fine.
aThirdCell = 5.6 + myCell; // Works fine.
```

Note that the implementation of the global `operator+` accesses `protected` data members of `SpreadsheetCell` objects. Therefore, it must be a `friend` function of the `SpreadsheetCell` class:

```
class SpreadsheetCell
{
    public:
        // Omitted for brevity

        friend const SpreadsheetCell operator+(const SpreadsheetCell& lhs,
            const SpreadsheetCell& rhs);

    //Omitted for brevity
};
```

You might be wondering what happens if you write the following code:

```
aThirdCell = 4.5 + 5.5;
```

It compiles and runs, but it's not calling the `operator+` you wrote. It does normal `double` addition of 4.5 and 5.5, and then constructs a temporary `SpreadsheetCell` object with the `double` constructor, which it assigns to `aThirdCell`.

Third time's the charm. A global `operator+` is the best you can do in C++.

Overloading Arithmetic Operators

Now that you understand how to write `operator+`, the rest of the basic arithmetic operators are straightforward. Here are declarations of `-`, `*`, and `/` (you can also overload `%`, but it doesn't make sense for the `double` values stored in `SpreadsheetCells`):

```
class SpreadsheetCell
{
    public:

        // Omitted for brevity

        friend const SpreadsheetCell operator+(const SpreadsheetCell& lhs,
            const SpreadsheetCell& rhs);
        friend const SpreadsheetCell operator-(const SpreadsheetCell& lhs,
            const SpreadsheetCell& rhs);
        friend const SpreadsheetCell operator*(const SpreadsheetCell& lhs,
            const SpreadsheetCell& rhs);
        friend const SpreadsheetCell operator/(const SpreadsheetCell& lhs,
            const SpreadsheetCell& rhs);

    // Omitted for brevity
};
```

Here are the implementations. The only tricky aspect is remembering to check for division by 0. Although not mathematically correct, this implementation sets the result to 0 if division by zero is detected:

```
const SpreadsheetCell operator-(const SpreadsheetCell& lhs,
    const SpreadsheetCell& rhs)
{
    SpreadsheetCell newCell;
    newCell.set(lhs.mValue - rhs.mValue); // Call set to update mValue and mString.
    return (newCell);
}

const SpreadsheetCell operator*(const SpreadsheetCell& lhs,
    const SpreadsheetCell& rhs)
{
    SpreadsheetCell newCell;
    newCell.set(lhs.mValue * rhs.mValue); // Call set to update mValue and mString.
    return (newCell);
}

const SpreadsheetCell operator/(const SpreadsheetCell& lhs,
    const SpreadsheetCell& rhs)
{
    SpreadsheetCell newCell;
    if (rhs.mValue == 0) {
        newCell.set(0); // Call set to update mValue and mString.
    } else {
        newCell.set(lhs.mValue / rhs.mValue); // Call set to update mValue
                                               // and mString.
    }
    return (newCell);
}
```

C++ does not require you to actually implement multiplication in operator*, division in operator/, and so on. You could implement multiplication in operator/, division in operator+, and so forth. However, that would be extremely confusing, and there is no good reason to do so except as a practical joke. Whenever possible, stick to the commonly used operator meanings in your implementations.

Overloading the Arithmetic Shorthand Operators

In addition to the basic arithmetic operators, C++ provides shorthand operators such as += and -=. You might assume that writing operator+ for your class provides operator+= also. No such luck. You have to overload the shorthand arithmetic operators explicitly. These operators differ from the basic arithmetic operators in that they change the object on the left-hand side of the operator instead of creating a new object. A second, subtler, difference is that, like the assignment operator, they generate a result that is a reference to the modified object.

The arithmetic operators always require an object on the left-hand side, so you should write them as methods, not as global functions. Here are the declarations for the SpreadsheetCell class:

```
class SpreadsheetCell
{
    public:
        // Omitted for brevity
        friend const SpreadsheetCell operator+(const SpreadsheetCell& lhs,
            const SpreadsheetCell& rhs);
        friend const SpreadsheetCell operator-(const SpreadsheetCell& lhs,
            const SpreadsheetCell& rhs);
        friend const SpreadsheetCell operator*(const SpreadsheetCell& lhs,
            const SpreadsheetCell& rhs);
        friend const SpreadsheetCell operator/(const SpreadsheetCell& lhs,
            const SpreadsheetCell& rhs);
        SpreadsheetCell& operator+=(const SpreadsheetCell& rhs);
        SpreadsheetCell& operator-=(const SpreadsheetCell& rhs);
        SpreadsheetCell& operator*=(const SpreadsheetCell& rhs);
        SpreadsheetCell& operator/=(const SpreadsheetCell& rhs);

        // Omitted for brevity
};
```

Here are the implementations:

```
SpreadsheetCell& SpreadsheetCell::operator+=(const SpreadsheetCell& rhs)
{
    set(mValue + rhs.mValue); // Call set to update mValue and mString.
    return (*this);
}

SpreadsheetCell& SpreadsheetCell::operator-=(const SpreadsheetCell& rhs)
{
    set(mValue - rhs.mValue); // Call set to update mValue and mString.
    return (*this);
}

SpreadsheetCell& SpreadsheetCell::operator*=(const SpreadsheetCell& rhs)
{
    set(mValue * rhs.mValue); // Call set to update mValue and mString.
    return (*this);
}

SpreadsheetCell& SpreadsheetCell::operator/=(const SpreadsheetCell& rhs)
{
```

```
        set(mValue / rhs.mValue); // Call set to update mValue and mString.
        return (*this);
    }
```

The shorthand arithmetic operators are combinations of the basic arithmetic and the assignment operators. With the above definitions, you can now write code like this:

```
SpreadsheetCell myCell(4), aThirdCell(2);
aThirdCell -= myCell;
aThirdCell += 5.4;
```

You cannot, however, write code like this (which is a good thing!):

```
5.4 += aThirdCell;
```

Overloading Comparison Operators

The comparison operators, such as >, <, and ==, are another useful set of operators to define for your classes. Like the basic arithmetic operators, they should be global `friend` functions so that you can use implicit conversion on both the left-hand side and right-hand side of the operator. The comparison operators all return a `bool`. Of course, you can change the return type, but we don't recommend it. Here are the declarations and definitions:

```
class SpreadsheetCell
{
    public:
        // Omitted for brevity

        friend const SpreadsheetCell operator+(const SpreadsheetCell& lhs,
            const SpreadsheetCell& rhs);
        friend const SpreadsheetCell operator-(const SpreadsheetCell& lhs,
            const SpreadsheetCell& rhs);
        friend const SpreadsheetCell operator*(const SpreadsheetCell& lhs,
            const SpreadsheetCell& rhs);
        friend const SpreadsheetCell operator/(const SpreadsheetCell& lhs,
            const SpreadsheetCell& rhs);
        SpreadsheetCell& operator+=(const SpreadsheetCell& rhs);
        SpreadsheetCell& operator-=(const SpreadsheetCell& rhs);
        SpreadsheetCell& operator*=(const SpreadsheetCell& rhs);
        SpreadsheetCell& operator/=(const SpreadsheetCell& rhs);
        friend bool operator==(const SpreadsheetCell& lhs,
            const SpreadsheetCell& rhs);
        friend bool operator<(const SpreadsheetCell& lhs,
            const SpreadsheetCell& rhs);
        friend bool operator>(const SpreadsheetCell& lhs,
            const SpreadsheetCell& rhs);
        friend bool operator!=(const SpreadsheetCell& lhs,
            const SpreadsheetCell& rhs);
        friend bool operator<=(const SpreadsheetCell& lhs,
            const SpreadsheetCell& rhs);
        friend bool operator>=(const SpreadsheetCell& lhs,
            const SpreadsheetCell& rhs);
```

```
    // Omitted for brevity
};
```

```
bool operator==(const SpreadsheetCell& lhs, const SpreadsheetCell& rhs)
{
    return (lhs.mValue == rhs.mValue);
}

bool operator<(const SpreadsheetCell& lhs, const SpreadsheetCell& rhs)
{
    return (lhs.mValue < rhs.mValue);
}

bool operator>(const SpreadsheetCell& lhs, const SpreadsheetCell& rhs)
{
    return (lhs.mValue > rhs.mValue);
}

bool operator!=(const SpreadsheetCell& lhs, const SpreadsheetCell& rhs)
{
    return (lhs.mValue != rhs.mValue);
}

bool operator<=(const SpreadsheetCell& lhs, const SpreadsheetCell& rhs)
{
    return (lhs.mValue <= rhs.mValue);
}

bool operator>=(const SpreadsheetCell& lhs, const SpreadsheetCell& rhs)
{
    return (lhs.mValue >= rhs.mValue);
}
```

In classes with more data members, it might be painful to compare each data member. However, once you've implemented == and <, you can write the rest of the comparison operators in terms of those two. For example, here is a definition of operator>= that uses operator<:

```
bool operator>=(const SpreadsheetCell& lhs, const SpreadsheetCell& rhs)
{
    return (!(lhs < rhs));
}
```

You can use these operators to compare SpreadsheetCells to other SpreadsheetCells, and to doubles and ints:

```
if (myCell > aThirdCell || myCell < 10) {
    cout << myCell.getValue() << endl;
}
```

Building Types with Operator Overloading

Many people find the syntax of operator overloading tricky and confusing, at least at first. The irony is that it's supposed to make things simpler. As you've discovered, that doesn't mean simpler for the person writing the class, but simpler for the person using the class. The point is to make your new classes as similar as possible to built-in types such as int and double: it's easier to add objects using + than to remember whether the method name you should call is add() or sum().

> **Provide operator overloading as a service to clients of your class.**

At this point, you might be wondering exactly which operators you can overload. The answer is "almost all of them — even some you've never heard of." You have actually just scratched the surface: you've seen the assignment operator in the section on object life cycles, the basic arithmetic operators, the short-hand arithmetic operators, and the comparison operators. Overloading the stream insertion and extraction operators is also useful. In addition, there are some tricky, but interesting, things you can do with operator overloading that you might not anticipate at first. The STL uses operator overloading extensively. Chapter 16 explains how and when to overload the rest of the operators. Chapters 21 to 23 cover the STL.

Pointers to Methods and Members

Recall that you can create and use pointers to both variables and functions (if you need a refresher on pointers or function pointers, consult Chapter 13). Now, consider pointers to class members and methods. It's perfectly legitimate in C++ to take the addresses of class members and methods in order to obtain pointers to them. However, remember that you can't access a non-static member or call a non-static method without an object. The whole point of class members and methods is that they exist on a per-object basis. Thus, when you want to call the method or access the member via the pointer, you must dereference the pointer in the context of an object. Here is an example:

```
SpreadsheetCell myCell;
double (SpreadsheetCell::*methodPtr) () const = &SpreadsheetCell::getValue;
    cout << (myCell.*methodPtr)() << endl;
```

Don't panic at the syntax. The second line declares a variable called methodPtr of type pointer to a const method that takes no arguments and returns a double. At the same time, it initializes this variable to point to the getValue() method of the SpreadsheetCell class. This syntax is quite similar to declaring a simple function pointer, except for the addition of SpreadsheetCell:: before the *methodPtr. That just means that this method pointer points to a method of the SpreadsheetCell class.

The second line calls the getValue() method (via the methodPtr pointer) on the myCell object. Note the use of parentheses surrounding cell.*methodPtr. They are needed because () has higher precedence than *.

Most of the time C++ programmers simplify the first line by using a typedef:

```
SpreadsheetCell myCell;
typedef double (SpreadsheetCell::*PtrToGet) () const;
PtrToGet methodPtr = &SpreadsheetCell::getValue;
    cout << (myCell.*methodPtr)() << endl;
```

Pointers to methods and members usually won't come up in your programs. However, it's important to keep in mind that you can't dereference a pointer to a non-static method or member without an object. Every so often, you'll find yourself wanting to try something like passing a pointer to a non-static method to a function such as qsort() that requires a function pointer, which simply won't work.

*Note that C++ permits you to dereference a pointer to a **static** member or method without an object.*

Chapter 22 discusses pointers to methods further in the context of the STL.

Building Abstract Classes

Now that you understand all the gory syntax of writing classes in C++, it helps to revisit the design principles from Chapters 3 and 5. Classes are the main unit of abstraction in C++. You should apply the principles of abstraction to your classes to separate the interface from the implementation as much as possible. Specifically, you should make all data members protected or private and provide getter and setter methods for them. This is how the SpreadsheetCell class is implemented. mValue and mString are protected, and set(), getValue(), and getString() retrieve those values. That way you can keep mValue and mString in synch internally without worrying about clients delving in and changing those values.

Using Interface and Implementation Classes

Even with the preceding measures and the best design principles, the C++ language is fundamentally unfriendly to the principle of abstraction. The syntax requires you to combine your public interfaces and private (or protected) data members and methods together in one class definition, thereby exposing some of the internal implementation details of the class to its clients.

The good news is that you can make your interfaces a lot cleaner and hide your implementation details. The bad news is that it takes a bit of hacking. The basic principle is to define two classes for every class you want to write: the interface class and the implementation class. The implementation class is identical to the class you would have written if you were not taking this approach. The interface class presents public methods identical to those of the implementation class, but it only has one data member: a pointer to an implementation class object. The interface class method implementations simply call the equivalent methods on the implementation class object. To use this approach with the Spreadsheet class, simply rename the old Spreadsheet class to SpreadsheetImpl. Here is the new SpreadsheetImpl class (which is identical to the old Spreadsheet class, but with a different name):

```
// SpreadsheetImpl.h
#include "SpreadsheetCell.h"

class SpreadsheetApplication; // Forward reference

class SpreadsheetImpl
{
    public:

        SpreadsheetImpl(const SpreadsheetApplication& theApp,
            int inWidth = kMaxWidth, int inHeight = kMaxHeight);
        SpreadsheetImpl(const SpreadsheetImpl& src);
```

```
        ~SpreadsheetImpl();
        SpreadsheetImpl &operator=(const SpreadsheetImpl& rhs);

        void setCellAt(int x, int y, const SpreadsheetCell& inCell);
        SpreadsheetCell getCellAt(int x, int y);

        int getId();

        static const int kMaxHeight = 100;
        static const int kMaxWidth = 100;

protected:
        bool inRange(int val, int upper);
        void copyFrom(const SpreadsheetImpl& src);

        int mWidth, mHeight;
        int mId;
        SpreadsheetCell** mCells;
        const SpreadsheetApplication& mTheApp;

        static int sCounter;
};
```

Then define a new `Spreadsheet` class that looks like this:

```
#include "SpreadsheetCell.h"

// Forward declarations
class SpreadsheetImpl;
class SpreadsheetApplication;

class Spreadsheet
{
    public:

        Spreadsheet(const SpreadsheetApplication& theApp, int inWidth,
            int inHeight);
        Spreadsheet(const SpreadsheetApplication& theApp);
        Spreadsheet(const Spreadsheet& src);
        ~Spreadsheet();
        Spreadsheet& operator=(const Spreadsheet& rhs);
        void setCellAt(int x, int y, const SpreadsheetCell& inCell);
        SpreadsheetCell getCellAt(int x, int y);
        int getId();

    protected:
        SpreadsheetImpl* mImpl;
};
```

This class now contains only one data member: a pointer to a `SpreadsheetImpl`. The `public` methods are identical to the old `Spreadsheet` with one exception: the `Spreadsheet` constructor with default arguments has been split into two constructors because the values for the default arguments were `const` members that are no longer in the `Spreadsheet` class. Instead, the `SpreadsheetImpl` class will provide the defaults.

The implementations of the `Spreadsheet` methods such as `setCellAt()` and `getCellAt()` just pass the request on to the underlying `SpreadsheetImpl` object:

```
void Spreadsheet::setCellAt(int x, int y, const SpreadsheetCell& inCell)
{
    mImpl->setCellAt(x, y, inCell);
}

SpreadsheetCell Spreadsheet::getCellAt(int x, int y)
{
    return (mImpl->getCellAt(x, y));
}

int Spreadsheet::getId()
{
    return (mImpl->getId());
}
```

The constructors for the `Spreadsheet` must construct a new `SpreadsheetImpl` to do its work, and the destructor must free the dynamically allocated memory. Note that the `SpreadsheetImpl` class has only one constructor with default arguments. Both normal constructors in the `Spreadsheet` class call that constructor on the `SpreadsheetImpl` class:

```
Spreadsheet::Spreadsheet(const SpreadsheetApplication &theApp, int inWidth,
    int inHeight)
{
    mImpl = new SpreadsheetImpl(theApp, inWidth, inHeight);
}

Spreadsheet::Spreadsheet(const SpreadsheetApplication& theApp)
{
    mImpl = new SpreadsheetImpl(theApp);
}

Spreadsheet::Spreadsheet(const Spreadsheet& src)
{
    mImpl = new SpreadsheetImpl(*(src.mImpl));
}

Spreadsheet::~Spreadsheet()
{
    delete (mImpl);
    mImpl = NULL;
}
```

The copy constructor looks a bit strange because it needs to copy the underlying `SpreadshetImpl` from the source spreadsheet. Because the copy constructor takes a reference to a `SpreadsheetImpl`, not a pointer, you must dereference the `mImpl` pointer to get to the object itself to the constructor call can take its reference.

The `Spreadsheet` assignment operator must similarly pass on the assignment to the underlying `SpreadsheetImpl`:

```
Spreadsheet& Spreadsheet::operator=(const Spreadsheet& rhs)
{
    *mImpl = *(rhs.mImpl);
    return (*this);
}
```

The first line in the assignment operator looks a little strange. You might be tempted to write this line instead:

```
mImpl = rhs.mImpl; // Incorrect assignment!
```

That code will compile and run, but it doesn't do what you want. It just copies pointers so that the left-hand side and right-hand side `Spreadsheet`s now both possess pointers to the same `SpreadsheetImpl`. If one of them changes it, the change will show up in the other. If one of them destroys it, the other will be left with a dangling pointer. Therefore, you can't just assign the pointers. You must force the `SpreadsheetImpl` assignment operator to run, which only happens when you copy direct objects. By dereferencing the `mImpl` pointers, you force direct object assignment, which causes the assignment operator to be called. Note that you can only do this because you already allocated memory for `mImpl` in the constructor.

This technique to truly separate interface from implementation is powerful. Although a bit clumsy at first, once you get used to it you will find it natural to work with. However, it's not common practice in most workplace environments, so you might find some resistance to trying it from your coworkers.

Summary

This chapter, along with Chapter 8, provided all the tools you need to write solid, well-designed classes, and to use objects effectively.

You discovered that dynamic memory allocation in objects presents new challenges: you must free the memory in the destructor, copy the memory in the copy constructor, and both free and copy memory in the assignment operator. You learned how to prevent assignment and pass-by-value by declaring a `private` copy constructor and assignment operator.

You learned more about different kinds of data members, including `static`, `const`, `const` reference, and mutable members. You also learned about `static`, `inline`, and `const` methods, and method overloading and default parameters. The chapter also described nested class definitions and `friend` classes and functions.

You encountered operator overloading, and learned how to overload the arithmetic and comparison operators, both as global `friend` functions and as class methods.

Finally, you learned how to take abstraction to an extreme by providing separate interface and implementation classes.

Now that you're fluent in the language of object-oriented programming, it's time to tackle inheritance and templates, which are covered in Chapters 10 and 11, respectively.

10

Discovering Inheritance Techniques

Without inheritance, classes would simply be data structures with associated behaviors. That alone would be a powerful improvement over procedural languages, but inheritance adds an entirely new dimension. Through inheritance, you can build new classes based on existing ones. In this way, your classes become reusable and extensible components. This chapter will teach you the different ways to leverage the power of inheritance. You will learn about the specific syntax of inheritance as well as sophisticated techniques for making the most of inheritance.

After finishing this chapter, you will understand:

- ❑ How to extend a class through inheritance
- ❑ How to employ inheritance to reuse code
- ❑ How to build interactions between superclasses and subclasses
- ❑ How to use inheritance to achieve polymorphism
- ❑ How to work with multiple inheritance
- ❑ How to deal with unusual problems in inheritance

The portion of this chapter relating to polymorphism draws heavily on the spreadsheet example discussed in Chapters 8 and 9. If you have not read Chapters 8 and 9, you may wish to skim the sample code in those chapters to get a background on this example. This chapter also refers to the object-oriented methodologies described in Chapter 3. If you have not read that chapter and are unfamiliar with the theories behind inheritance, you should review Chapter 3 before continuing.

Building Classes with Inheritance

In Chapter 3, you learned that an "is-a" relationship recognizes the pattern that real-world objects tend to exist in hierarchies. In programming, that pattern becomes relevant when you need to write a class that builds on, or slightly changes, another class. One way to accomplish this aim is to copy code from one class and paste it into the other. By changing the relevant parts or amending the code, you can achieve the goal of creating a new class that is slightly different from the original. This approach, however, leaves an OOP programmer feeling sullen and slightly annoyed for the following reasons:

❑ A bug fix to the original class will not be reflected in the new class because the two classes contain completely separate code.

❑ The compiler does not know about any relationship between the two classes, so they are not polymorphic — they are not just different variations on the same thing.

❑ This approach does not build a true is-a relationship. The new class is very similar to the original because it shares code, not because it really *is* the same type of object.

❑ The original code might not be obtainable. It may exist only in a precompiled binary format, so copying and pasting the code might be impossible.

Not surprisingly, C++ provides built-in support for defining a true is-a relationship. The characteristics of C++ is-a relationships are described in the following section.

Extending Classes

When you write a class definition in C++, you can tell the compiler that your class is *inheriting from,* or *extending,* an existing class. By doing so, your class will automatically contain the data members and methods of the original class, which is called the *parent class* or *superclass*. Extending an existing class gives your class (which is now called a *derived* class or a *subclass*) the ability to describe only the ways in which it is different from the parent class.

To extend a class in C++, you specify the class you are extending when you write the class definition. To show the syntax for inheritance, we use two classes called Super and Sub. Don't worry — more interesting examples are coming later. To begin, consider the following definition for the Super class.

```
class Super
{
    public:
        Super();

        void someMethod();

    protected:
        int mProtectedInt;

    private:
        int mPrivateInt;
};
```

If you wanted to build a new class, called Sub, which inherits from Super, you would tell the compiler that Sub derives from Super with the following syntax:

```
class Sub : public Super
{
    public:
        Sub();

        void someOtherMethod();
};
```

Sub itself is a full-fledged class that just happens to share the characteristics of the Super class. Don't worry about the word public for now — its meaning is explained later in this chapter. Figure10-1 shows the simple relationship between Sub and Super. You can declare objects of type Sub just like any other object. You could even define a third class that subclasses Sub, forming a chain of classes, as shown in Figure 10-2.

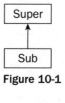

Figure 10-1

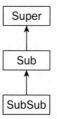

Figure 10-2

Sub doesn't have to be the only subclass of Super. Additional classes can also subclass Super, effectively becoming *siblings* to Sub, as shown in Figure 10-3.

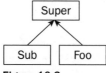

Figure 10-3

Clients' View of Inheritance

To a client, or another part of your code, an object of type Sub is also an object of type Super because Sub inherits from Super. This means that all the public methods and data members of Super *and* all the public methods and data members of Sub are available.

Code that uses the subclass does not need to know which class in your inheritance chain has defined a method in order to call it. For example, the following code calls two methods of a Sub object even though one of the methods was defined by the Super class.

```
Sub mySub;

mySub.someMethod();
mySub.someOtherMethod();
```

It is important to understand that inheritance only works in one direction. The Sub class has a very clearly defined relationship to the Super class, but the Super class, as written, doesn't know anything about the Sub class. That means that objects of type Super do not support public methods and data members of Sub because Super is *not* a Sub.

The following code will not compile because the Super class does not contain a public method called someOtherMethod().

```
Super mySuper;

mySuper.someOtherMethod();  // BUG! Super doesn't have a someOtherMethod().
```

> **From the perspective of other code, an object belongs to its defined class as well as to any superclasses.**

A pointer or reference to an object can refer to an object of the declared class or any of its subclasses. This tricky subject is explained in detail later in this chapter. The concept to understand at this point is that a pointer to a Super can actually be pointing a Sub object. The same is true for a reference. The client can still access only the methods and data members that exist in Super, but through this mechanism, any code that operates on a Super can also operate on a Sub.

For example, the following code compiles and works just fine even though it initially appears that there is a type mismatch:

```
Super* superPointer = new Sub();  // Create a sub, and store it in a super pointer.
```

Subclass's View of Inheritance

To the subclass itself, nothing much has changed in terms of how it is written or how it behaves. You can still define methods and data members on a subclass just as you would on a regular class. The previous definition of Sub declares a method called someOtherMethod(). Thus, the Sub class augments the Super class by adding an additional method.

A subclass can access public and protected methods and data members declared in its superclass as though they were its own, because technically, they are. For example, the implementation of someOtherMethod() on Sub could make use of the data member mProtectedInt, which was declared as part of Super. The following code shows this implementation. Accessing a superclass data member or method is no different than if the data member of method were declared as part of the subclass.

```
void Sub::someOtherMethod()
{
```

```
        cout << "I can access the superclass data member mProtectedInt." << endl;
        cout << "Its value is " << mProtectedInt << endl;
    }
```

When we introduced access specifiers (`public`, `private`, and `protected`) in Chapter 8, the difference between `private` and `protected` may have been confusing. Now that you understand subclasses, the difference should be clearer. If a class declares methods or data members as `protected`, subclasses have access to them. If they are declared as `private`, subclasses do not have access.

The following implementation of `someOtherMethod()` will not compile because the subclass attempts to access a `private` data member from the superclass.

```
void Sub::someOtherMethod()
{
    cout << "I can access the superclass data member mProtectedInt." << endl;
    cout << "Its value is " << mProtectedInt << endl;

    cout << "The value of mPrivateInt is " << mPrivateInt << endl;   // BUG!
}
```

The `private` access specifier gives you control over how a potential subclass could interact with your class. In practice, most data members are declared as `protected`, and most methods are either `public` or `protected`. The reason is that most of the time, you or someone you work with will be extending the class so you don't want to shut out any potential uses by making methods or members `private`. Occasionally, the `private` specifier is useful to block subclasses from accessing potentially dangerous methods. It is also useful when writing classes that external or unknown parties will extend because you can block access to prevent misuse.

> **From the perspective of a subclass, all `public` and `protected` data members and methods from the superclass are available for use.**

Overriding Methods

As you read in Chapter 3, the main reasons to inherit from a class are to add or replace functionality. The definition of `Sub` adds functionality to its parent class by providing an additional method, `someOtherMethod()`. The other method, `someMethod()`, is inherited from `Super` and behaves in the subclass exactly as it does in the superclass. In many cases, you will want to modify the behavior of a class by replacing, or *overriding*, a method.

How I Learned to Stop Worrying and Make Everything virtual

There is one small twist to overriding methods in C++ and it has to do with the keyword `virtual`. Only methods that are declared as `virtual` in the superclass can be overridden properly by subclasses. The keyword goes at the beginning of a method declaration as shown in the modified version of `Super` that follows.

```
class Super
{
    public:
        Super();
```

```
            virtual void someMethod();

    protected:
        int mProtectedInt;

    private:
        int mPrivateInt;
};
```

The virtual keyword has a few subtleties and is often cited as a poorly designed part of the language. A good rule of thumb is to just make all of your methods virtual. That way, you won't have to worry about whether or not overriding the method will work. The only drawback is a small performance hit. The subtleties of the virtual keyword are covered toward the end of this chapter, and performance is discussed further in Chapter 17.

Even though it is unlikely that the Sub class will be extended, it is a good idea to make its methods virtual as well, just in case.

```
class Sub : public Super
{
    public:
        Sub();

            virtual void someOtherMethod();
};
```

> As a rule of thumb, make all your methods virtual (including the destructor, but not constructors) to avoid problems associated with omission of the virtual keyword.

Syntax for Overriding a Method

To override a method, you simply redeclare it in the subclass class definition exactly as it was declared in the superclass. In the subclass's implementation file, you provide the new definition.

For example, the Super class contains a method called someMethod(). The definition of someMethod() is provided in Super.cpp and shown here:

```
void Super::someMethod()
{
    cout << "This is Super's version of someMethod()." << endl;
}
```

Note that you do not repeat the virtual keyword in front of the method definition.

If you wish to provide a new definition for someMethod() in the Sub class, you must first add it to the class definition for Sub, as follows:

```
class Sub : public Super
{
    public:
        Sub();
```

```
        virtual void someMethod();  // Overrides Super's someMethod()
        virtual void someOtherMethod();
};
```

The new definition of someMethod() is specified along with the rest of Sub's methods.

```
void Sub::someMethod()
{
    cout << "This is Sub's version of someMethod()." << endl;
}
```

Clients' View of Overridden Methods

With the preceding changes, other code would still call someMethod() the same way it did before. Just as before, the method could be called on an object of class Super or an object of class Sub. Now, however, the behavior of someMethod() will vary based on the class of the object.

For example, the following code works just as it did before, calling Super's version of someMethod():

```
Super mySuper;

mySuper.someMethod();  // Calls Super's version of someMethod().
```

The output of this code is:

```
This is Super's version of someMethod().
```

If the code declares an object of class Sub, the other version will automatically be called.

```
Sub mySub;

mySub.someMethod();    // Calls Sub's version of someMethod()
```

The output this time is:

```
This is Sub's version of someMethod().
```

Everything else about objects of class Sub remains the same. Other methods that might have been inherited from Super will still have the definition provided by Super unless they are explicitly overridden in Sub.

As you learned earlier, a pointer or reference can refer to an object of a class or any of its subclasses. The object itself "knows" the class of which it is actually a member, so the appropriate method is called as long as it was declared virtual. For example, if you have a Super reference that refers to an object that is really a Sub, calling someMethod() will actually call the subclass's version, as shown next. This aspect of overriding will *not* work properly if you omit the virtual keyword in the superclass.

```
Sub mySub;
Super& ref = mySub;

ref.someMethod();   // Calls Sub's version of someMethod()
```

Remember that even though a superclass reference or pointer knows that it is actually a subclass, you cannot access subclass methods or members that are not defined in the superclass. The following code will not compile because a `Super` reference does not have a method called `someOtherMethod()`.

```
Sub mySub;
Super& ref = mySub;

mySub.someOtherMethod();   // This is fine.
ref.someOtherMethod();     // BUG
```

The subclass knowledge characteristic is *not* true of nonpointer nonreference objects. You can cast or assign a `Sub` to a `Super` because a `Sub` is a `Super`. However, the object will lose any knowledge of the subclass at this point:

```
Sub mySub;
Super assignedObject = mySub;   // Assign Sub to a Super.

assignedObject.someMethod();    // Calls Super's version of someMethod()
```

One way to remember this seemingly strange behavior is to imagine what the objects look like in memory. Picture a `Super` object as a box taking up a certain amount of memory. A `Sub` object is a box that is a little bit bigger because it has everything a `Super` has plus a bit more. When you have a reference or pointer to a `Sub`, the box doesn't change — you just have a new way of accessing it. However, when you cast a `Sub` into a `Super`, you are throwing out all the "uniqueness" of the `Sub` class to fit it into a smaller box.

> Subclasses retain their overridden methods when referred to by superclass pointers or references. They lose their uniqueness when cast to a superclass object. The loss of overridden methods and subclass data is called *slicing*.

Inheritance for Reuse

Now that you are familiar with the basic syntax for inheritance, it's time to explore one of the main reasons that inheritance is an important feature of the C++ language. As you read in Chapter 3, inheritance is a vehicle that allows you to leverage existing code. This section presents a real-world application of inheritance for the purposes of code reuse.

The WeatherPrediction Class

Imagine that you are given the task of writing a program to issue simple weather predictions. Weather predictions may be a little out of your area of expertise as a programmer, so you obtain a third-party class library that was written to make weather predictions based on the current temperature and the present distance between Jupiter and Mars (hey, it's plausible). This third-party package is distributed as a compiled library to protect the intellectual property of the prediction algorithms, but you do get to see the class definition. The class definition for `WeatherPrediction` is shown here:

```
// WeatherPrediction.h

/**
 * Predicts the weather using proven new-age
 * techniques given the current temperature
 * and the distance from Jupiter to Mars. If
 * these values are not provided, a guess is
 * still given but it's only 99% accurate.
 */
class WeatherPrediction
{
    public:
        virtual void setCurrentTempFahrenheit(int inTemp);
        virtual void setPositionOfJupiter(int inDistanceFromMars);

    /**
     * Gets the prediction for tomorrow's temperature
     */
    virtual int getTomorrowTempFahrenheit();

    /**
     * Gets the probability of rain tomorrow. 1 means
     * definite rain. 0 means no chance of rain.
     */
    virtual double getChanceOfRain();

    /**
     * Displays the result to the user in this format:
     * Result: x.xx chance. Temp. xx
     */
    virtual void showResult();

    protected:
        int mCurrentTempFahrenheit;
        int mDistanceFromMars;
};
```

This class solves most of the problems for your program. However, as is usually the case, it's not *exactly* right for your needs. First, all the temperatures are given in Fahrenheit. Your program needs to operate in Celsius as well. Also, the showResult() method doesn't produce a very user-friendly result. It would be nice to give the user some friendlier information.

Adding Functionality in a Subclass

When you learned about inheritance in Chapter 3, adding functionality was the first technique described. Fundamentally, your program needs something just like the WeatherPrediction class but with a few extra bells and whistles. Sounds like a good case for inheritance to reuse code. To begin, define a new class, MyWeatherPrediction, that inherits from WeatherPrediction.

```
// MyWeatherPrediction.h

class MyWeatherPrediction : public WeatherPrediction
{
};
```

The class definition above will compile just fine. The `MyWeatherPrediction` class can already be used in place of `WeatherPrediction`. It will provide the same functionality, but nothing new yet.

For the first modification, you might want to add knowledge of the Celsius scale to the class. There is a bit of a quandary here because you don't know what the class is doing internally. If all of the internal calculations are made using Fahrenheit, how do you add support for Celsius? One way is to use the subclass to act as a go-between, interfacing between the user, who can use either scale, and the superclass, which only understands Fahrenheit.

The first step in supporting Celsius is to add new methods that allow clients to set the current temperature in Celsius instead of Fahrenheit and to get tomorrow's prediction in Celsius instead of Fahrenheit. You will also need protected helper methods that convert between Celsius and Fahrenheit. These methods can be `static` because they are the same for all instances of the class.

```
// MyWeatherPrediction.h

class MyWeatherPrediction : public WeatherPrediction
{
    public:
        virtual void setCurrentTempCelsius(int inTemp);

        virtual int getTomorrowTempCelsius();

    protected:
        static int convertCelsiusToFahrenheit(int inCelsius);
        static int convertFahrenheitToCelsius(int inFahrenheit);
};
```

The new method follows the same naming convention as the parent class. Remember that from the point of view of other code, a `MyWeatherPrediction` object will have all of the functionality defined in both `MyWeatherPrediction` and `WeatherPrediction`. Adopting the parent class's naming convention presents a consistent interface.

We will leave the implementation of the Celsius/Fahrenheit conversion methods as an exercise for the reader — and a fun one at that! The other two methods are more interesting. To set the current temperature in Celsius, you need to convert the temperature first and then present it to the parent class in units that it understands.

```
void MyWeatherPrediction::setCurrentTempCelsius(int inTemp)
{
    int fahrenheitTemp = convertCelsiusToFahrenheit(inTemp);
    setCurrentTempFahrenheit(fahrenheitTemp);
}
```

As you can see, once the temperature is converted, the method simply calls the existing functionality from the superclass. Similarly, the implementation of `getTomorrowTempCelsius()` uses the parent's existing functionality to get the temperature in Fahrenheit, but converts the result before returning it.

```
int MyWeatherPrediction::getTomorrowTempCelsius()
{
    int fahrenheitTemp = getTomorrowTempFahrenheit();
    return convertFahrenheitToCelsius(fahrenheitTemp);
}
```

The two new methods effectively reuse the parent class because they simply "wrap" the existing functionality in a way that provides a new interface for using it.

Of course, you can also add new functionality that is completely unrelated to existing functionality of the parent class. For example, you could add a method that will retrieve alternative forecasts from the Internet or a method that will suggest an activity based on the predicted weather.

Replacing Functionality in a Subclass

The other major technique for subclassing is replacing existing functionality. The showResult() method in the WeatherPrediction class is in dire need of a facelift. MyWeatherPrediction can override this method to replace the behavior with its own implementation.

The new class definition for MyWeatherPrediction is shown below.

```
// MyWeatherPrediction.h

class MyWeatherPrediction : public WeatherPrediction
{
  public:
    virtual void setCurrentTempCelsius(int inTemp);

    virtual int getTomorrowTempCelsius();

    virtual void showResult();

  protected:
    static int convertCelsiusToFahrenheit(int inCelsius);
    static int convertFahrenheitToCelsius(int inFahrenheit);
};
```

A possible new user-friendly implementation follows.

```
void MyWeatherPrediction::showResult()
{
    cout << "Tomorrow's temperature will be " <<
            getTomorrowTempCelsius() << " degrees Celsius (" <<
            getTomorrowTempFahrenheit() << " degrees Fahrenheit)" << endl;

    cout << "The chance of rain is " << (getChanceOfRain() * 100) << " percent"
         << endl;

    if (getChanceOfRain() > 0.5) {
        cout << "Bring an umbrella!" << endl;
    }
}
```

To clients making use of this class, it's like the old version of showResult() never existed. As long as the object is a MyWeatherPrediction object, the new version will be called.

As a result of these changes, MyWeatherPrediction has emerged as a new class with new functionality tailored to a more specific purpose. Yet, it did not require much code because it leveraged its superclass's existing functionality.

Respect Your Parents

When you write a subclass, you need to be aware of the interaction between parent classes and child classes. Issues such as order of creation, constructor chaining, and casting are all potential sources of bugs.

Parent Constructors

Objects don't spring to life all at once; they must be constructed along with their parents and any objects that are contained within them. C++ defines the creation order as follows:

1. The base class, if any, is constructed.

2. Non-static data members are constructed in the order in which they were declared.

3. The body of the constructor is executed.

These rules can apply recursively. If the class has a grandparent, the grandparent is initialized before the parent, and so on. The following code shows this creation order. As a reminder, we generally advise against inlining methods, as we've done in the code that follows. In the interest of readable and concise examples, we have broken our own rule. The proper execution will output the result 123.

```cpp
#include <iostream>
using namespace std;

class Something
{
    public:
        Something() { cout << "2"; }
};

class Parent
{
    public:
        Parent() { cout << "1"; }
};

class Child : public Parent
{
    public:
        Child() { cout << "3"; }

    protected:
        Something mDataMember;
};

int main(int argc, char** argv)
{
    Child myChild;
}
```

When the myChild object is created, the constructor for Parent is called first, outputting the string "1". Next, mDataMember is initialized, calling the Something constructor which outputs the string "2". Finally, the Child constructor is called, which outputs 3.

Note that the `Parent` constructor was called automatically. C++ will automatically call the default constructor for the parent class if one exists. If no default constructor exists in the parent class, or if one does exist but you wish to use an alternate constructor, you can *chain* the constructor just as when initializing data members in the initializer list.

The following code shows a version of `Super` that lacks a default constructor. The associated version of `Sub` must explicitly tell the compiler how to call the `Super` constructor or the code will not compile.

```
// Super.h
class Super
{
    public:
        Super(int i);
};

// Sub.h
class Sub : public Super
{
    public:
        Sub();
};

// Sub.cpp
Sub::Sub() : Super(7)
{
    // Do Sub's other initialization here.
}
```

In the preceding code, the `Sub` constructor passes a fixed value (7) to the `Super` constructor. `Sub` could also pass a variable if its constructor required an argument:

```
Sub::Sub(int i) : Super(i) {}
```

Passing constructor arguments from the subclass to the superclass is perfectly fine and quite normal. Passing data members, however, will not work. The code will compile, but remember that data members are not initialized until *after* the superclass is constructed. If you pass a data member as an argument to the parent constructor, it will be uninitialized.

Parent Destructors

Because destructors cannot take arguments, the language can automatically call the destructor for parent classes. The order of destruction is conveniently the reverse of the order of construction:

1. The body of the destructor is called.

2. Any data members are destroyed in the reverse order of their construction.

3. The parent class, if any, is destructed.

Again, these rules apply recursively. The lowest member of the chain is always destructed first. The following code adds destructors to the previous example. If executed, this code will output `"123321"`.

```cpp
#include <iostream>
using namespace std;

class Something
{
    public:
        Something() { cout << "2"; }
        virtual ~Something() { cout << "2"; }
};

class Parent
{
    public:
        Parent() { cout << "1"; }
        virtual ~Parent() { cout << "1"; }
};

class Child : public Parent
{
    public:
        Child() { cout << "3"; }
        virtual ~Child() { cout << "3"; }

    protected:
        Something mDataMember;
};

int main(int argc, char** argv)
{
    Child myChild;
}
```

Notice that the destructors are all `virtual`. As a rule of thumb, all destructors should be declared `virtual`. If the preceding destructors were not declared `virtual`, the code would continue to work fine. However, if code ever called delete on a superclass pointer that was really pointing to a subclass, the destruction chain would begin in the wrong place. For example, the following code is similar to the previous example but the destructors are not `virtual`. This becomes a problem when a `Child` object is accessed as a pointer to a `Parent` and deleted.

```cpp
class Something
{
    public:
        Something() { cout << "2"; }
        ~Something() { cout << "2"; }  // Should be virtual, but will work
};

class Parent
{
    public:
        Parent() { cout << "1"; }
        ~Parent() { cout << "1"; }  // BUG! Make this virtual!
};

class Child : public Parent
{
```

```
    public:
        Child() { cout << "3"; }
        ~Child() { cout << "3"; }    // Should be virtual, but will work

    protected:
        Something mDataMember;
};

int main(int argc, char** argv)
{
    Parent* ptr = new Child();
    delete ptr;
}
```

The output of this code is a shockingly terse "1231". When the ptr variable is deleted, only the Parent destructor is called because the Child destructor was not declared virtual. As a result, the Child destructor is not called and the destructors for its data members are not called.

Technically, you could fix the above problem by simply making the Parent destructor virtual. The "virtualness" would automatically be used by any children. However, we advocate making all destructors virtual so that you never have to worry about it.

Always make your destructors virtual!

Referring to Parent Data

Names can become ambiguous within a subclass, especially when multiple inheritance (see below) comes into play. C++ provides a mechanism to disambiguate names between classes: the scope resolution operator. The syntax (two colons) is the same as referencing static data in a class.

When you override a method in a subclass, you are effectively replacing the original as far as other code is concerned. However, that parent version of the method still exists and you may want to make use of it. If you simply called the method by name, however, the compiler would assume that you meant the subclass version. This could easily lead to an infinite loop, as in the example that follows;

```
Sub::doSomething()
{
    cout << "In Sub's version of doSomething()" << endl;
    doSomething();    // BUG! This will recursively call this method!
}
```

To call the parent's version of the method explicitly, simply prepend the parent's name and two colons:

```
Sub::doSomething()
{
    cout << "In Sub's version of doSomething()" << endl;
    Super::doSomething();  // call the parent version.
}
```

Calling the parent version of the current method is a commonly used pattern in C++. If you have a chain of subclasses, each might want to perform the operation already defined by the superclass but add their own additional functionality as well.

For example, imagine a class hierarchy of types of books. A diagram showing such a hierarchy is shown in Figure 10-4.

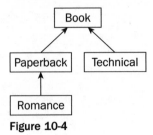

Figure 10-4

Since each lower class in the hierarchy further specifies the type of book, a method that gets the description of a book really needs to take all levels of the hierarchy into consideration. This can be accomplished by chaining to the parent method as above. The following code illustrates this pattern:

```
#include <iostream>
#include <string>

using namespace std;

class Book
{
    public:
        virtual string getDescription() { return "Book"; }
};

class Paperback : public Book
{
    public:
        virtual string getDescription() {
                        return "Paperback " + Book::getDescription();
                }
};

class Romance : public Paperback
{
    public:
        virtual string getDescription() {
                        return "Romance " + Paperback::getDescription();
                }
};

class Technical : public Book
{
    public:
        virtual string getDescription() {
                        return "Technical " + Book::getDescription();
                }
};

int main()
```

```
{
    Romance novel;
    Book book;
    cout << novel.getDescription() << endl; // Outputs "Romance Paperback Book"
    cout << book.getDescription() << endl;  // Outputs "Book"
}
```

Casting Up and Down

As you have already seen, an object can be cast or assigned to its parent class. If the cast or assignment is performed on a plain old object, this results in slicing:

```
Super mySuper = mySub;  // SLICE!
```

Slicing occurs in situations like this because the end result is a Super object, and Super objects lack the additional functionality defined in the Sub class. However, slicing does *not* occur if a subclass is assigned to a pointer or reference to its superclass:

```
Super& mySuper = mySub; // No slice!
```

This is generally the correct way to refer to a subclass in terms of its superclass, also called *upcasting*. This is always why it's a good idea to make your methods and functions take references to classes instead of directly using objects of those classes. By using references, subclasses can be passed in without slicing.

> **When upcasting, use a pointer or reference to the superclass to avoid slicing.**

Casting from a superclass to one of its subclasses, also called *downcasting*, is often frowned upon by professional C++ programmers. The reason is that there is no guarantee that the object really belongs to that subclass. For example, consider the following code.

```
void presumptuous(Super* inSuper)
{
    Sub* mySub = static_cast<Sub*>(inSuper);
    // Proceed to access Sub methods on mySub.
}
```

If the author of presumptuous() also wrote code that called presumptuous(), everything would probably be okay because the author knows that the function expects the argument to be of type Sub*. However, if another programmer were to call presumptuous(), they might pass in a Super*. There are no compile-time checks that can be done to enforce the type of the argument, and the function blindly assumes that inSuper is actually a pointer to a Sub.

Downcasting is sometimes necessary, and you can use it effectively in controlled circumstances. If you're going to downcast, however, you should use a dynamic_cast, which uses the object's built-in knowledge of its type to refuse a cast that doesn't make sense.

The previous example should have been written as follows.

```
void lessPresumptuous(Super* inSuper)
{
    Sub* mySub = dynamic_cast<Sub*>(inSuper);
    if (mySub != NULL) {
        // Proceed to access Sub methods on mySub.
    }
}
```

If a dynamic cast fails on a pointer, as above, the pointer's value will be NULL instead of pointing to non-sensical data. If a dynamic_cast fails on an object reference, a std::bad_cast exception will be thrown. For more on casts, see Chapter 12. For more on exceptions, see Chapter 15.

Use downcasting only when necessary and be sure to use a dynamic cast.

Inheritance for Polymorphism

Now that you understand the relationship between a subclass and its parent, you can use inheritance in its most powerful scenario — polymorphism. As you learned in Chapter 3, polymorphism allows you to use objects with a common parent class interchangeably, and to use objects in place of their parents.

Return of the Spreadsheet

Chapters 8 and 9 used a spreadsheet program as an example of an application that lends itself to an object-oriented design. As you may recall, a SpreadsheetCell represented a single element of data. That element could be either a double or a string. A simplified class definition for SpreadsheetCell follows. Note that a cell can be set either as a double or a string. The current value of the cell, however, is always returned as a string for this example.

```
class SpreadsheetCell
{
    public:
        SpreadsheetCell();

        virtual void set(double inDouble);
        virtual void set(const std::string& inString);
        virtual std::string getString();

    protected:
        static std::string doubleToString(double inValue);
        static double stringToDouble(const std::string& inString);

        double      mValue;
        std::string mString;
};
```

The preceding SpreadsheetCell class seems to be having an identity crisis — sometimes a cell represents a double, sometimes a string. Sometimes it has to convert between these formats. To achieve this duality, the class needs to store both values even though a given cell should only be able to contain a single value. Worse still, what if additional types of cells are needed, such as a formula cell or a date cell? The SpreadsheetCell class would grow dramatically to support all of these data types and the conversions between them.

Designing the Polymorphic Spreadsheet Cell

The SpreadsheetCell class is screaming out for a hierarchical makeover. A reasonable approach would be to narrow the scope of the SpreadsheetCell to cover only strings, perhaps renaming it StringSpreadsheetCell in the process. To handle doubles, a second class, DoubleSpreadsheetCell, would inherit from the StringSpreadsheetCell and provide functionality specific to its own format. Figure 10-5 illustrates such a design. This approach models inheritance for reuse since the DoubleSpreadsheetCell would only be subclassing StringSpreadsheetCell to make use of some of its built-in functionality.

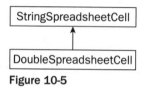

Figure 10-5

If you were to implement the design shown in Figure 10-5, you might discover that the subclass would override most, if not all, of the functionality of the base class. Since doubles are treated differently from strings in almost all cases, the relationship may not be quite as it was originally understood. Yet, there clearly is a relationship between a cell containing strings and a cell containing doubles. Rather than use the model in Figure 10-5, which implies that somehow a DoubleSpreadsheetCell "is-a" StringSpreadsheetCell, a better design would make these classes peers with a common parent, SpreadsheetCell. Such a design is shown in Figure 10-6.

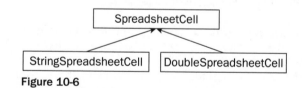

Figure 10-6

The design in Figure 10-6 shows a polymorphic approach to the SpreadsheetCell hierarchy. Since DoubleSpreadsheetCell and StringSpreadsheetCell both inherit from a common parent, SpreadsheetCell, they are interchangeable in the view of other code. In practical terms, that means:

❑ Both subclasses support the same interface (set of methods) defined by the base class

❑ Code that makes use of SpreadsheetCell objects can call any method in the interface without even knowing whether the cell is a DoubleSpreadsheetCell or a StringSpreadsheetCell

❑ Through the magic of virtual methods, the appropriate version of every method in the interface will be called depending on the class of the object

❑ Other data structures, such as the Spreadsheet class described in Chapter 9, can contain a collection of multityped cells by referring to the parent type

The Spreadsheet Cell Base Class

Since all spreadsheet cells are subclasses of the SpreadsheetCell base class, it is probably a good idea to write that class first. When designing a base class, you need to consider how the subclasses relate to each other. From this information, you can derive the commonality that will go inside the parent class. For example, string cells and double cells are similar in that they both contain a single piece of data. Since the data is coming from the user and will be displayed back to the user, the value is set as a string and retrieved as a string. These behaviors are the shared functionality that will make up the base class.

A First Attempt

The SpreadsheetCell base class is responsible for defining the behaviors that all SpreadsheetCell subclasses will support. In our simple example, all cells need to be able to set their value as a string. All cells also need to be able to return their current value as a string. The base class definition, therefore, declares these methods.

```
class SpreadsheetCell
{
    public:
        SpreadsheetCell();
        virtual ~SpreadsheetCell();

        virtual void set(const std::string& inString);

        virtual std::string getString() const;
};
```

When you start writing the .cpp file for this class, you very quickly run into a problem. Since the base class of spreadsheet cell contains neither a double nor a string, how can you implement it? More generally, how do you write a parent class that declares the behaviors that are supported by subclasses without actually defining the implementation of those behaviors?

One possible approach is to implement "do nothing" functionality for those behaviors. For example, calling the set() method on the SpreadsheetCell base class will have no effect because the base class has nothing to set. This approach still doesn't feel right, however. Ideally, there should never be an object that is an instance of the base class. Calling set() should always have an effect because it should always be called on either a DoubleSpreadsheetCell or a StringSpreadsheetCell. A good solution will enforce this constraint.

Pure Virtual Methods and Abstract Base Classes

Pure virtual methods are methods that are explicitly undefined in the class definition. By making a method pure virtual, you are telling the compiler that no definition for the method exists in the current class. Thus, the class is said to be *abstract* because no other code will be able to instantiate it. The compiler enforces the fact that if a class contains one or more pure virtual methods, it can never be used by itself to construct an object.

The syntax for a pure virtual method is shown below. Simply set the method equal to zero in the class definition. No code needs to be written in the .cpp file.

```
class SpreadsheetCell
{
    public:
        SpreadsheetCell();
        virtual ~SpreadsheetCell();

        virtual void set(const std::string& inString) = 0;

        virtual std::string getString() const = 0;
};
```

Now that the base class is an abstract class, it is impossible to create a `SpreadsheetCell` object. The following code will not compile, and will give an error such as `Cannot declare object of type 'SpreadsheetCell' because one or more virtual functions are abstract`.

```
int main(int argc, char** argv)
{
    SpreadsheetCell cell; // BUG! Attempts to create instance of an abstract class
}
```

> **An abstract class provides a way to prevent other code from instantiating an object directly, as opposed to one of its subclasses.**

Base Class Source Code

There is not much code required for `SpreadsheetCell.cpp`. As the class was defined, most of the methods are pure virtual — there is no definition to give. All that is left is the type conversion method and the constructor and destructor. For this example, the constructor and destructor are implemented just as a placeholder in case initialization and destruction tasks need to happen in the future.

```
SpreadsheetCell::SpreadsheetCell()
{
}

SpreadsheetCell::~SpreadsheetCell()
{
}
```

The Individual Subclasses

Writing the `StringSpreadsheetCell` and `DoubleSpreadsheetCell` classes is just a matter of implementing the functionality that is defined in the parent. Because we want clients to be able to instantiate and work with `string` cells and `double` cells, they can't be abstract — they *must* implement all of the pure virtual methods inherited from their parent.

String Spreadsheet Cell Class Definition

The first step in writing the class definition of `StringSpreadsheetCell` is to subclass `SpreadsheetCell`.

```
class StringSpreadsheetCell : public SpreadsheetCell
{
```

StringSpreadsheetCell declares its own constructor, giving it a chance to initialize its own data.

```
    public:
        StringSpreadsheetCell();
```

Next, the inherited pure virtual methods are overridden, this time without being set to zero.

```
        virtual void set(const std::string& inString);

        virtual std::string getString() const;
```

Finally, the string cell adds a protected data member, mValue, which stores the actual cell data.

```
        protected:
            std::string mValue;
};
```

String Spreadsheet Cell Implementation

The .cpp file for StringSpreadsheetCell is a bit more interesting than the base class. In the constructor, the value string is initialized to a string that indicates that no value has been set.

```
StringSpreadsheetCell::StringSpreadsheetCell() : mValue("#NOVALUE")
{
}
```

The set method is straightforward since the internal representation is already a string. Similarly, the getString() method simply returns the stored value.

```
void StringSpreadsheetCell::set(const string& inString)
{
    mValue = inString;
}

string StringSpreadsheetCell::getString() const
{
    return mValue;
}
```

Double Spreadsheet Cell Class Definition and Implementation

The double version follows a similar pattern, but with different logic. In addition to the set() method that takes a string, it also provides a new set() method that allows a client to set the value with a double. Two new protected methods are used to convert between a string and a double. Like StringSpreadsheetCell, it has a data member called mValue, this time a double. Because DoubleSpreadsheetCell and StringSpreadsheetCell are siblings, no hiding or naming conflicts occur as a result.

```
class DoubleSpreadsheetCell : public SpreadsheetCell
{
    public:

        DoubleSpreadsheetCell ();
        virtual void set(double inDouble);
        virtual void set(const std::string& inString);

        virtual std::string getString() const;

    protected:
        static std::string doubleToString(double inValue);
        static double stringToDouble(const std::string& inValue);
        double mValue;
};
```

The implementation of the `DoubleSpreadsheetCell` is shown here:

```
DoubleSpreadsheetCell::DoubleSpreadsheetCell() : mValue(-1)
}
}
```

The `set()` method that takes a `double` is straightforward. The `string` version makes use of the `protected static` method `stringToDouble()`. The `getString()` method converts the stored `double` value into a `string`:

```
void DoubleSpreadsheetCell::set(double inDouble)
{
    mValue = inDouble;
}

void DoubleSpreadsheetCell::set(const string& inString)
{
    mValue = stringToDouble(inString);
}

string DoubleSpreadsheetCell::getString() const
{
    return doubleToString(mValue);
}
```

You may already see one major advantage of implementing spreadsheet cells in a hierarchy — the code is much simpler. You don't need to worry about using two fields to represent the two types of data. Each object can be self-centered and only deal with its own functionality.

Note that the implementations of `doubleToString()` and `stringToDouble()` were omitted because they are the same as in Chapter 8.

Leveraging Polymorphism

Now that the `SpreadsheetCell` hierarchy is polymorphic, client code can take advantage of the many benefits that polymorphism has to offer. The following test program explores many of these features.

```
int main(int argc, char** argv)
{
```

First, an array of three `SpreadsheetCell` pointers is declared. Remember that since `SpreadsheetCell` is an abstract class, you can't create objects of that type. However, you can still have a pointer or reference to a `SpreadsheetCell` because it would actually be pointing to one of the subclasses. This array takes advantage of the common type between the two subclasses. Each of the elements of the array could be either a `StringSpreadsheetCell` or a `DoubleSpreadsheetCell`. Because they have a common parent, they can be stored together.

```
SpreadsheetCell* cellArray[3];
```

The 0th element of the array is set to point to a new `StringSpreadsheetCell`; the first is also set to a new `StringSpreadsheetCell`, and the second is a new `DoubleSpreadsheetCell`.

```
cellArray[0] = new StringSpreadsheetCell();
cellArray[1] = new StringSpreadsheetCell();
cellArray[2] = new DoubleSpreadsheetCell();
```

Now that the array contains multityped data, any of the methods declared by the base class can be applied to the objects in the array. The code just uses `SpreadsheetCell` pointers — the compiler has no idea at compile time what types the objects actually are. However, because they are subclasses of `SpreadsheetCell`, they must support the methods of `SpreadsheetCell`.

```
cellArray[0]->set("hello");
cellArray[1]->set("10");
cellArray[2]->set("18");
```

When the `getString()` method is called, each object properly returns a `string` representation of their value. The important, and somewhat amazing, thing to realize is that the different objects do this in different ways. A `StringSpreadsheetCell` will simply return its stored value. A `DoubleSpreadsheetCell` will first perform a conversion. As the programmer, you don't need to know how the object does it — you just need to know that because the object is a `SpreadsheetCell`, it *can* perform this behavior.

```
cout << "Array values are [" << cellArray[0]->getString() << "," <<
                                cellArray[1]->getString() << "," <<
                                cellArray[2]->getString() << "]" << endl;
}
```

Future Considerations

The new implementation of the `SpreadsheetCell` hierarchy is certainly an improvement from an object-oriented design point of view. Yet, it would probably not suffice as an actual class hierarchy for a real-world spreadsheet program for several reasons.

First, despite the improved design, one feature of the original is still missing: the ability to convert from one cell type to another. By dividing them into two classes, the cell objects become more loosely integrated. To provide the ability to convert from a `DoubleSpreadsheetCell` to a `StringSpreadsheetCell`, you could add a typed constructor. It would have a similar appearance to a copy constructor but instead of a reference to an object of the same class, it would take a reference to an object of a sibling class.

```
class StringSpreadsheetCell
{
    public:
        StringSpreadsheetCell();
        StringSpreadsheetCell(const DoubleSpreadsheetCell& inDoubleCell);
...
```

With a typed constructor, you can easily create a `StringSpreadsheetCell` given a `DoubleSpreadsheetCell`. Don't confuse this with casting, however. Casting from one sibling to another will not work, unless you overload the cast operator as described in Chapter 16.

> **You can always cast up the hierarchy, and you can sometimes cast down the hierarchy, but you can never cast across the hierarchy unless you have changed the behavior of the cast operator.**

The question of how to implement overloaded operators for cells is an interesting one, and there are several possible solutions. One approach is to implement a version of each operator for every combination of cells. With only two subclasses, this is manageable. There would be an operator+ function to add two double cells, to add two string cells, and to add a double cell to a string cell.Another approach is to decide on a common representation. The preceding implementation already standardizes on a `string` as a common representation of sorts. A single `operator+` function could cover all the cases by taking advantage of this common representation. One possible implementation, which assumes that the result of adding two cells is always a `string` cell, is shown here:

```
const StringSpreadsheetCell operator+(const StringSpreadsheetCell &lhs,
                          const StringSpreadsheetCell &rhs)
{
    StringSpreadsheetCell newCell;
    newCell.set(lhs.getString() + rhs.getString());
    return (newCell);
}
```

As long as the compiler has a way to turn a particular cell into a `StringSpreadsheetCell`, the operator will work. Given the previous example of having a `StringSpreadsheetCell` constructor that takes a `DoubleSpreadsheetCell` as an argument, the compiler will automatically perform the conversion if it is the only way to get the `operator+` to work. That means that the following code will work, even though `operator+` was explicitly written to work on `StringSpreadsheetCells`.

```
DoubleSpreadsheetCell myDbl;

myDbl.set(8.4);

StringSpreadsheetCell result = myDbl + myDbl;
```

Of course, the result of this addition won't really add the numbers together. It will convert the `double` cell into a `string` cell and add the `strings`, resulting in a `StringSpreadsheetCell` with a value of `8.48.4`.

If you are still feeling a little unsure about polymorphism, start with the code for this example and try things out. The main function in the preceding example is a great starting point for experimental code that simply exercises various aspects of the class.

Multiple Inheritance

As you read in Chapter 3, multiple inheritance is often perceived as a complicated and unnecessary part of object-oriented programming. We'll leave the decision of whether or not it is useful up to you and your coworkers. This section explains the mechanics of multiple inheritance in C++.

Inheriting from Multiple Classes

Defining a class to have multiple parent classes is very simple from a syntactic point of view. All you need to do is list the superclasses individually when declaring the class name.

```
class Baz : public Foo, public Bar
{
    // Etc.
};
```

By listing multiple parents, the Baz object will have the following characteristics:

- ❑ A Baz object will support the public methods and contain the data members of both Foo and Bar.

- ❑ The methods of the Baz class will have access to protected data and methods in both Foo and Bar.

- ❑ A Baz object can be upcast to either a Foo or a Bar.

- ❑ Creating a new Baz object will automatically call the Foo and Bar default constructors, in the order that the classes were listed in the class definition.

- ❑ Deleting a Baz object will automatically call the destructors for the Foo and Bar classes, in the reverse order that the classes were listed in the class definition.

The following simple example shows a class, DogBird, that has two parent classes — a Dog class and a Bird class. The fact that a dog-bird is a ridiculous example should not be viewed as a statement that multiple inheritance itself is ridiculous. Honestly, we leave that judgment up to you.

```
class Dog
{
    public:
        virtual void bark() { cout << "Woof!" << endl; }
};

class Bird
{
```

```
        public:
            virtual void chirp() { cout << "Chirp!" << endl; }
    };
    class DogBird : public Dog, public Bird
    {
    };
```

The class hierarchy for `DogBird` is shown in Figure 10-7.

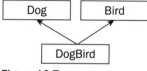

Figure 10-7

Using objects of classes with multiple parents is no different from using objects without multiple parents. In fact, the client code doesn't even have to know that the class has two parents. All that really matters are the properties and behaviors supported by the class. In this case, a `DogBird` object supports all of the `public` methods of `Dog` and `Bird`.

```
int main(int argc, char** argv)
{
    DogBird myConfusedAnimal;

    myConfusedAnimal.bark();
    myConfusedAnimal.chirp();
}
```

The output of this program is:

```
Woof!
Chirp!
```

Naming Collisions and Ambiguous Base Classes

It's not difficult to construct a scenario where multiple inheritance would seem to break down. The following examples show some of the edge cases that must be considered.

Name Ambiguity

What if the `Dog` class and the `Bird` class both had a method called `eat()`? Since `Dog` and `Bird` are not related in any way, one version of the method does not override the other — they both continue to exist in the `DogBird` subclass.

As long as client code never attempts to call the `eat()` method, that is not a problem. The `DogBird` class will compile correctly despite having two versions of `eat()`. However, if client code attempts to call the `eat()` method, the compiler will give an error indicating that the call to `eat()` is ambiguous. The compiler will not know which version to call. The following code provokes this ambiguity error.

```
class Dog
{
    public:
        virtual void bark() { cout << "Woof!" << endl; }
        virtual void eat() { cout << "The dog has eaten." << endl; }
};

class Bird
{
    public:
        virtual void chirp() { cout << "Chirp!" << endl; }
        virtual void eat() { cout << "The bird has eaten." << endl; }
};

class DogBird : public Dog, public Bird
{
};

int main(int argc, char** argv)
{
    DogBird myConfusedAnimal;

    myConfusedAnimal.eat();    // BUG! Ambiguous call to method eat()
}
```

The solution to the ambiguity is to either explicitly upcast the object, essentially hiding the undesired version of the method from the compiler, or to use a disambiguation syntax. For example, the following code shows two ways to invoke the Dog version of eat().

```
static_cast<Dog>(myConfusedAnimal).eat();    // Slices, calling Dog::eat()
myConfusedAnimal.Dog::eat();                 // Calls Dog::eat()
```

Methods of the subclass itself can also explicitly disambiguate between different methods of the same name by using the same syntax used to access parent methods, the :: operator. For example, the DogBird class could prevent ambiguity errors in other code by defining its own eat() method. Inside this method, it would determine which parent version to call.

```
void DogBird::eat()
{
    Dog::eat();    // Explicitly call Dog's version of eat()
}
```

Another way to provoke ambiguity is to inherit from the same class twice. For example, if the Bird class inherited from Dog for some reason, the code for DogBird would not compile because Dog becomes an ambiguous base class.

```
class Dog {};

class Bird : public Dog {};

class DogBird : public Bird, public Dog {};    // BUG! Dog is an ambiguous base
class.
```

Most occurrences of ambiguous base classes are either contrived "what-if" examples, like the one above, or arise from untidy class hierarchies. Figure 10-8 shows a class diagram for the preceding example, indicating the ambiguity.

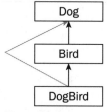

Figure 10-8

Ambiguity can also occur with data members. If Dog and Bird both had a data member with the same name, an ambiguity error would occur when client code attempted to access that member.

Ambiguous Base Classes

A more likely scenario is that multiple parents themselves have common parents. For example, perhaps both Bird and Dog are subclasses of an Animal class, as shown in Figure 10-9.

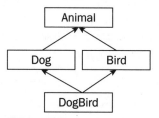

Figure 10-9

This type of class hierarchy is permitted in C++, though name ambiguity can still occur. For example, if the Animal class has a public method called sleep(), that method could not be called on a DogBird object because the compiler would not know whether to call the version inherited by Dog or by Bird.

The best way to use these "diamond-shaped" class hierarchies is to make the topmost class an abstract base class with all methods declared as pure virtual. Since the class only declares methods without providing definitions, there are no methods in the base class to call and thus there are no ambiguities at that level.

The following example implements a diamond-shaped class hierarchy with a pure virtual eat() method that must be defined by each subclass. The DogBird class still needs to be explicit about which parent's eat() method it uses, but any ambiguity would be caused by Dog and Bird having the same method, not because they inherit from the same class.

```
class Animal
{
    public:
        virtual void eat() = 0;
};

class Dog : public Animal
{
    public:
        virtual void bark() { cout << "Woof!" << endl; }
        virtual void eat() { cout << "The dog has eaten." << endl; }
};

class Bird : public Animal
{
    public:
        virtual void chirp() { cout << "Chirp!" << endl; }
        virtual void eat() { cout << "The bird has eaten." << endl; }
};

class DogBird : public Dog, public Bird
{
    public:
        virtual void eat() { Dog::eat(); }
};
```

A more refined mechanism for dealing with the top class in a diamond-shaped hierarchy, virtual base classes, is explained at the end of this chapter.

Uses for Multiple Inheritance

At this point, you're probably wondering why anyone would want to tackle multiple inheritance in her program. The most straightforward use case for multiple inheritance is to define a class of object that is-a something and also is-a something else. As we said in Chapter 3, any real-world objects you find that follow this pattern are unlikely to translate well into code.

One of the most compelling and simple uses of multiple inheritance is for the implementation of mix-in classes. Mix-in classes were explained in Chapter 3. An example implementation using multiple inheritance is shown in Chapter 25.

Another reason that people sometimes use multiple inheritance is to model a component-based class. Chapter 3 gave the example of an airplane simulator. The Airplane class had an engine, a fuselage, controls, and other components. While the typical implementation of an Airplane class would make each of these components a separate data member, you *could* use multiple inheritance. The airplane class would inherit from engine, fuselage, and controls, in effect getting the behaviors and properties of all of its components. We recommend you stay away from this type of code because it confuses a clear has-a relationship with inheritance, which should be used for is-a relationships.

Interesting and Obscure Inheritance Issues

Extending a class opens up a variety of issues. What characteristics of the class can and cannot be changed? What does the mysterious `virtual` keyword really do? These questions, and many more, are answered in the following sections.

Changing the Overridden Method's Characteristics

For the most part, the reason you override a method is to change its implementation. Sometimes, however, you may want to change other characteristics of the method.

Changing the Method Return Type

A good rule of thumb is to override a method with the exact method declaration, or *method signature*, that the superclass uses. The implementation can change, but the signature stays the same.

That does not have to be the case, however. In C++, an overriding method can change the return type as long as the original return type is a pointer or reference to a class, and the new return type is a pointer or reference to a descendent class. Such types are called *covariant returns types*. This feature sometimes comes in handy when the superclass and subclass work with objects in a *parallel hierarchy*. That is, another group of classes that is tangential, but related, to the first class hierarchy.

For example, consider a hypothetical cherry orchard simulator. You might have two hierarchies of classes that model different real-world objects but are obviously related. The first is the `Cherry` chain. The base class, `Cherry`, has a subclass called `BingCherry`. Similarly, there is another chain of classes with a base class called `CherryTree` and a subclass called `BingCherryTree`. Figure 10-10 shows the two class chains.

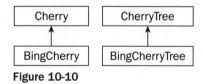

Figure 10-10

Now assume that the `CherryTree` class has a method called `pick()` that will retrieve a single cherry from the tree:

```
Cherry* CherryTree::pick()
{
    return new Cherry();
}
```

In the `BingCherryTree` subclass, you may want to override this method. Perhaps Bing Cherries need to be polished when they are picked (bear with us on this one). Because a `BingCherry` is a `Cherry`, you could leave the method signature as is and override the method as in the following example. The `BingCherry` pointer is automatically cast to a `Cherry` pointer.

```
Cherry* BingCherryTree::pick()
{
    BingCherry* theCherry = new BingCherry();

    theCherry->polish();

    return theCherry;
}
```

The implementation above is perfectly fine and is probably the way that the authors would write it. However, because you know that the `BingCherryTree` will always return `BingCherry` objects, you could indicate this fact to potential users of this class by changing the return type, as shown here:

```
BingCherry* BingCherryTree::pick()
{
    BingCherry* theCherry = new BingCherry();

    theCherry->polish();

    return theCherry;
}
```

A good way to figure out whether you can change the return type of an overridden method is to consider whether existing code would still work. In the preceding example, changing the return type was fine because any code that assumed that the `pick()` method would always return a `Cherry*` would still compile and work correctly. Because a `BingCherry` is a `Cherry`, any methods that were called on the result of `CherryTree`'s version of `pick()` could still be called on the result of `BingCherryTree`'s version of `pick()`.

You could *not*, for example, change the return type to something completely unrelated, such as `void*`. The following code will not compile because the compiler thinks that you are trying to overload `pick()`, but cannot distinguish `BingCherryTree`'s `pick()` method from `CherryTree`'s `pick()` method because return types are not used in method disambiguation.

```
void* BingCherryTree::pick()   // BUG!
{
    BingCherry* theCherry = new BingCherry();

    theCherry->polish();

    return theCherry;
}
```

Changing the Method Parameters

In general, if you try to change the parameters to an overridden method, you are no longer overriding it — you are creating a new method. Returning to the `Super` and `Sub` example from earlier in this chapter, you could *attempt* to override `someMethod()` in `Sub` with a new argument list, as shown here:

```
class Super
{
    public:
        Super();
        virtual void someMethod();
```

```
};

class Sub : public Super
{
    public:
        Sub();

        virtual void someMethod(int i);   // Compiles, but doesn't override
        virtual void someOtherMethod();
};
```

The implementation of this method is shown here:

```
void Sub::someMethod(int i)
{
    cout << "This is Sub's version of someMethod with argument " << i
        << "." << endl;
}
```

The preceding class definition will compile, but you have not overridden someMethod(). Because the arguments are different, you have created a new method that exists only on Sub. If you want a method called someMethod() that takes an int, and you want it to only work on objects of class Sub, the preceding code is correct. However, it is stylistically questionable to have a method that has the same name as a method in the superclass but no real relationship to that method.

In fact, the original method is now hidden as far as Sub is concerned. The following sample code will not compile because there is no longer a no-argument version of someMethod().

```
Sub mySub;

mySub.someMethod();     // BUG! Won't compile because the original method is hidden.
```

There is a case where you actually can change the argument list for an overridden method. The trick is that the new argument list must be compatible with the old one. If we modified the above example to give the i parameter a default value, then Sub's version of someMethod() would actually be overriding Super's version of someMethod():

```
class Sub : public Super
{
    public:
        Sub();

        virtual void someMethod(int i = 2);  // actually overrides
        virtual void someOtherMethod();
```

Why is this any different? The answer is that in order to override a method, other code needs to be able to call the method in the same way on either the superclass or the subclass. Just as in the earlier return type case, the acid test for changing method arguments is whether existing code would have to be modified. With a default argument, any code that called Super's someMethod() could call Sub's someMethod() without modification.

The following sample code shows that this time Sub has actually overridden Super's version of someMethod(). Even a Super reference will correctly call Sub's version.

```
Sub mySub;
Super& ref = mySub;

mySub.someMethod();        // Calls Sub's someMethod with default argument
mySub.someMethod(1);       // Calls Sub's someMethod
ref.someMethod();          // Calls Sub's someMethod with default argument
```

The output of this code is:

```
This is Sub's version of someMethod with argument 2.
This is Sub's version of someMethod with argument 1.
This is Sub's version of someMethod with argument 2.
```

There is also a somewhat obscure technique you can use to have your cake and eat it too. That is, you can use this technique to effectively override a method in the subclass with a new signature but continue to inherit the superclass version. This technique uses the `using` keyword to explicitly include the super-class definition of the method within the subclass, as shown here:

```
class Super
{
    public:
        Super();
        virtual void someMethod();
};

class Sub : public Super
{
    public:
        Sub();

        using Super::someMethod;    // Explicitly "inherits" the Super version
        virtual void someMethod(int i);  // Adds a new version of someMethod
        virtual void someOtherMethod();
};
```

> **It is rare to find an overridden method that changes the parameter list.**

Special Cases in Overriding Methods

Several edge cases require special attention when overriding a method. In this section, we have outlined the cases that are likely to encounter.

If the Superclass Method Is Static

In C++, you cannot override a `static` method. For the most part, that's all you need to know. There are, however, a few corollaries that you need to understand.

First of all, a method cannot be both `static` and `virtual`. This is the first clue that attempting to override a `static` method will not do what you intend for it to do. If you have a `static` method in your subclass with the same name as a `static` method in your superclass, you actually have two separate methods.

The following code shows two classes that both happen to have `static` methods called `beStatic()`. These two methods are in no way related.

```
class SuperStatic
{
    public:
        static void beStatic() { cout << "SuperStatic being static, yo." << endl;
};

class SubStatic
{
    public:
        static void beStatic() { cout << "SubStatic keepin' it static." << endl;
};
```

Because a `static` method belongs to its class, calling the identically named methods on the two different classes will call their respective methods:

```
SuperStatic::beStatic();
SubStatic::beStatic();
```

Will output:

```
SuperStatic being static, yo.
SubStatic keepin' it static.
```

Everything makes perfect sense as long as the methods are accessed by class. The behavior is less clear when objects are involved. In C++, you can call a `static` method on an object syntactically, but in reality, the method only exists on the class. Consider the following code:

```
SubStatic mySubStatic;
SuperStatic& ref = mySubStatic;

mySubStatic.beStatic();
ref.beStatic();
```

The first call to `beStatic()` will obviously call the `SubStatic` version because it is explicitly called on an object declared as a `SubStatic`. The second call is less clear. The object is a `SuperStatic` reference, but it refers to a `SubStatic` object. In this case, `SuperStatic`'s version of `beStatic()` will be called. The reason is that C++ doesn't care what the object actually is when calling a `static` method. It only cares about the compile-time type. In this case, the type is a reference to a `SuperStatic`.

The output of the previous example is:

```
SubStatic keepin' it static.
SuperStatic being static, yo.
```

> **static** methods are bound to the class in which they are defined, not to any object. A method in a class that calls a **static** method calls the version defined in that class, independent of the run-time type of the object on which the original method is called.

If the Superclass Method Is Overloaded

When you override a method, you are implicitly hiding any other versions of the method. It makes sense if you think about it — why would you want to change some versions of a method and not others? Consider the following subclass, which overrides a method without overriding its associated overloaded siblings:

```
class Foo
{
    public:
        virtual void overload() { cout << "Foo's overload()" << endl; }
        virtual void overload(int i) { cout << "Foo's overload(int i)" << endl; }
};

class Bar : public Foo
{
    public:
        virtual void overload() { cout << "Bar's overload()" << endl; }
};
```

If you attempt to call the version of overload() that takes an int parameter on a Bar object, your code will not compile because it was not explicitly overridden.

```
myBar.overload(2); // BUG! No matching method for overload(int).
```

It is possible, however, to access this version of the method from a Bar object. All you need is a pointer or a reference to a Foo object.

```
Bar myBar;
Foo* ptr = &myBar;

ptr->overload(7);
```

The hiding of unimplemented overloaded methods is only skin deep in C++. Objects that are explicitly declared as instances of the subtype will not make the method available, but a simple cast to the superclass will bring it right back.

The using keyword can be employed to save you the trouble of overloading all the versions when you really only want to change one. In the following code, the Bar class definition uses one version of overload() from Foo and explicitly overloads the other.

```
class Foo
{
    public:
        virtual void overload() { cout << "Foo's overload()" << endl; }
        virtual void overload(int i) { cout << "Foo's overload(int i)" << endl; }
};

class Bar : public Foo
{
    public:
        using Foo::overload;
        virtual void overload() { cout << "Bar's overload()" << endl; }
};
```

> To avoid obscure bugs, you should override all versions of an overloaded method, either explicitly or with the **using** keyword.

If the Superclass Method Is Private or Protected

There's absolutely nothing wrong with overriding a `private` or `protected` method. Remember that the access specifier for a method determines who is able to *call* the method. Just because a subclass can't call its parent's `private` methods doesn't mean it can't override them. In fact, overriding a `private` or `protected` method is a common pattern in object-oriented languages. It allows subclasses to define their own "uniqueness" that is referenced in the superclass.

For example, the following class is part of a car simulator that estimates the number of miles the car can travel based on its gas mileage and amount of fuel left.

```
class MilesEstimator
{
    public:
        virtual int getMilesLeft() {
                return (getMilesPerGallon() * getGallonsLeft());
        }

        virtual void setGallonsLeft(int inValue) { mGallonsLeft = inValue; }
        virtual int  getGallonsLeft() { return mGallonsLeft; }
    private:
        int mGallonsLeft;
        virtual int getMilesPerGallon() { return 20; }
}
```

The `getMilesLeft()` method performs a calculation based on the results of two of its own methods. The following code uses the `MilesEstimator` to calculate how many miles can be traveled with 2 gallons of gas.

```
MilesEstimator myMilesEstimator;

myMilesEstimator.setGallonsLeft(2);
cout << "I can go " << myMilesEstimator.getMilesLeft() << " more miles." << endl;
```

The output of this code is:

```
I can go 40 more miles.
```

To make the simulator more interesting, you may want to introduce different types of vehicles, perhaps a more efficient car. The existing `MilesEstimator` assumes that cars all get 20 miles per gallon, but this value is returned from a separate method specifically so that a subclass could override it. Such a subclass is shown here:

```
class EfficientCarMilesEstimator : public MilesEstimator
{
    private:
        virtual int getMilesPerGallon() { return 35; }
};
```

By overriding this one `private` method, the new class completely changes the behavior of existing, unmodified, `public` methods. The `getMilesLeft()` method in the superclass will automatically call the overridden version of the `private getMilesPerGallon()` method. An example using the new class is shown here:

```
EfficientCarMilesEstimator myEstimator;

myEstimator.setGallonsLeft(2);
cout << "I can go " << myEstimator.getMilesLeft() << " more miles." << endl;
```

This time, the output reflects the overridden functionality:

```
I can go 70 more miles.
```

> Overriding **private** and **protected** methods is a good way to change certain features of a class without a major overhaul.

If the Superclass Method Has Default Arguments

Subclasses and superclasses can each have different default arguments, but the argument that is used depends on the declared type of the variable, not the underlying object. Following is a simple example of a subclass that provides a different default argument in an overridden method:

```
class Foo
{
    public:
        virtual void go(int i = 2) { cout << "Foo's go with param " << i << endl; }
};

class Bar : public Foo
{
    public:
        virtual void go(int i = 7) { cout << "Bar's go with param " << i << endl; }
};
```

If `go()` is called on a `Bar` object, `Bar`'s version of `go()` will executed with the default argument of 7. If `go()` is called on a `Foo` object, `Foo`'s version of `go()` will be executed with the default argument of 2. However (this is the weird part), if `go()` is called on a `Foo` pointer or `Foo` reference that really points to a `Bar` object, `Bar`'s version of `go()` will be called it will use the default `Foo` argument of 2. This behavior is shown here:

```
Foo myFoo;
Bar myBar;
Foo& myFooReferenceToBar;

myFoo.go();
myBar.go();
myFooReferenceToBar.go();
```

The output of this code is:

```
Foo's go with param 2
Bar's go with param 7
Bar's go with param 2
```

Tricky, eh? The reason for this behavior is that C++ binds default arguments to the type of the variable denoting the object, not the object itself. For this same reason, default arguments are not "inherited" in C++. If the Bar class above failed to provide a default argument as its parent did, it would be overloading the go() method with a new zero-argument version.

> When overriding a method that has a default argument, you should provide a default argument as well, and it should probably be the same value.

If the Superclass Method Has a Different Access Level

There are two ways you may wish to change the access level of a method — you could try to make it more restrictive or less restrictive. Neither case makes much sense in C++, but there are a few legitimate reasons for attempting to do so.

To enforce tighter restriction on a method (or on a data member for that matter), there are two approaches you can take. One way is to change the access specifier for the entire base class. This approach is described at the end of this chapter. The other approach is simply to redefine the access in the subclass, as illustrated in the Shy class that follows:

```cpp
class Gregarious
{
    public:
        virtual void talk() { cout << "Gregarious says hi!" << endl; }
};

class Shy : public Gregarious
{
    protected:
        virtual void talk() { cout << "Shy reluctantly says hello." << endl; }
};
```

The protected version of talk() in the Shy class properly overrides the method. Any client code that attempts to call talk() on a Shy object will get a compile error:

```cpp
myShy.talk();  // BUG! Attempt to access protected method.
```

However, the method is not fully protected. One only has to obtain a Gregarious reference or pointer to access the method that you thought was protected:

```cpp
Shy myShy;
Gregarious& ref = myShy;

ref.talk();
```

The output of the preceding code is:

```
Shy reluctantly says hello.
```

This proves that making the method `protected` in the subclass did actually override the method (because the subclass version was correctly called), but it also proves that the `protected` access can't be fully enforced if the superclass makes it `public`.

> **There is no reasonable way (or good reason why) to restrict access to a `public` parent method.**

It's much easier (and makes a lot more sense) to lessen access restrictions in subclasses. The simplest way is simply to provide a `public` method that calls a `protected` method from the superclass, as shown here:

```cpp
class Secret
{
    protected:
        virtual void dontTell() { cout << "I'll never tell." << endl; }
};

class Blabber : public Secret
{
    public:
        virtual void tell() { dontTell(); }
};
```

A client calling the `public tell()` method of a `Blabber` object would effectively access the `protected` method of the `Secret` class. Of course, this doesn't *really* change the access level of `dontTell()`, it just provides a `public` way of accessing it.

You could also override `dontTell()` explicitly in the `Blabber` subclass and give it new behavior with `public` access. This makes a lot more sense than reducing the level of access because it is entirely clear what happens with a reference or pointer to the base class. For example, suppose that `Blabber` actually made the `dontTell()` method public:

```cpp
class Secret
{
    protected:
        virtual void dontTell() { cout << "I'll never tell." << endl; }
};

class Blabber : public Secret
{
    public:
        virtual void dontTell() { cout << "I'll tell all!" << endl; }
};
```

If the `dontTell()` method is called on a `Blabber` object, it will output `I'll tell all!`

```
myBlabber.dontTell(); // Outputs "I'll tell all!"
```

In this case, however, the `protected` method in the superclass stays `protected` because any attempts to call `Secret`'s `dontTell()` method through a pointer or reference will not compile.

```
Blabber myBlabber;
Secret& ref = myBlabber;
Secret* ptr = &myBlabber;

ref.dontTell();  // BUG! Attempt to access protected method.
ptr->dontTell(); // BUG! Attempt to access protected method.
```

> **The only truly useful way to change a method's access level is by providing a less restrictive accessor to a `protected` method.**

Copy Constructors and the Equals Operator

In Chapter 9, we said that providing a copy constructor and assignment operator is considered a good programming practice when you have dynamically allocated memory in the class. When defining a subclass, you need to be careful about copy constructors and `operator=`.

If your subclass does not have any special data (pointers, usually) that require a nondefault copy constructor or `operator=`, you don't need to have one, regardless of whether or not the superclass has one. If your subclass omits the copy constructor, the parent copy constructor will still be called when the object is copied. Similarly, if you don't provide an explicit `operator=`, the default one will be used, and `operator=` will still be called on the parent class.

On the other hand, if you *do* specify a copy constructor in the subclass, you need to explicitly chain to the parent copy constructor, as shown in the following code. If you do not do this, the default constructor (not the copy constructor!) will be used for the parent portion of the object.

```
class Super
{
    public:
        Super();
        Super(const Super& inSuper);
};

class Sub : public Super
{
    public:
        Sub();
        Sub(const Sub& inSub);
};

Sub::Sub(const Sub& inSub) : Super(inSub)
{
}
```

Similarly, if the subclass overrides `operator=`, it is almost always necessary to call the parent's version of `operator=` as well. The only case where you wouldn't do this is if there is some bizarre reason why you only want part of the object assigned when an assignment takes place. The following code shows how to call the parent's assignment operator from the subclass:

```
Sub& Sub::operator=(const Sub& inSub)
{
    if (&inSub == this) {
        return *this;
    }

    Super::operator=(inSub) // Call parent's operator=.

    // Do necessary assignments for subclass.


    return (*this);
}
```

> If your subclass does not specify its own copy constructor or `operator=`, the parent functionality continues to work. If the subclass does provide its own copy constructor or `operator=`, it needs to explicitly reference the parent versions.

The Truth about Virtual

When you first encountered method overriding above, we told you that only `virtual` methods can be properly overridden. The reason we had to add the qualifier *properly* is that if a method is not `virtual`, you can still attempt to override it but it will be wrong in subtle ways.

Hiding Instead of Overriding

The following code shows a superclass and a subclass, each with a single method. The subclass is attempting to override the method in the superclass, but it is not declared to be `virtual` in the superclass.

```
class Super
{
    public:
        void go() { cout << "go() called on Super" << endl; }
};

class Sub : public Super
{
    public:
        void go() { cout << "go() called on Sub" << endl; }
};
```

Attempting to call the `go()` method on a `Sub` object will initially appear to work.

```
Sub mySub;

mySub.go();
```

The output of this call is, as expected, `go() called on Sub`. However, since the method was not `virtual`, it was not actually overridden. Rather, the `Sub` class created a new method, also called `go()` that is completely unrelated to the `Super` class's method called `go()`. To prove this, simply call the method in the context of a `Super` pointer or reference.

```
Sub mySub;

Super& ref = mySub;

ref.go();
```

You would expect the output to be, `go() called on Sub`, but in fact, the output will be, `go() called on Super`. This is because the `ref` variable is a `Super` reference and because the `virtual` keyword was omitted. When the `go()` method is called, it simply executes `Super`'s `go()` method. Because it is not `virtual`, there is no need to consider whether a subclass has overridden it.

> **Attempting to override a non-`virtual` method will "hide" the superclass definition and will only be used in the context of the subclass.**

How virtual Is Implemented

To understand why method hiding occurs, you need to know a bit more about what the `virtual` keyword actually does. When a class is compiled in C++, a binary object is created that contains all of the data members and methods for the class. In the non-`virtual` case, the code to jump to the appropriate method is hard-coded directly where the method is called based on the compile-time type.

If the method is declared `virtual`, the implementation is looked up in a special area of memory called the *vtable*, for "virtual table." Each class that has one or more `virtual` methods has a vtable that contains pointers to the implementations of the `virtual` methods. In this way, when a method is called on an object, the pointer is followed into the vtable and the appropriate version of the method is executed based on the type of the object, not the type of the variable used to access it.

Figure 10-11 shows a high-level view of how the vtable makes the overriding of methods possible. The diagram shows two classes, `Super` and `Sub`. `Super` declares two virtual methods, `foo()` and `bar()`. As you can see by looking at `Super`'s vtable, each method has its own implementation defined by the `Super` class. The `Sub` class does not override `Super`'s version of `foo()`, so the `Sub` vtable points to the same implementation of `foo()`. `Sub` does, however, override `bar()`, so the vtable points to the new version.

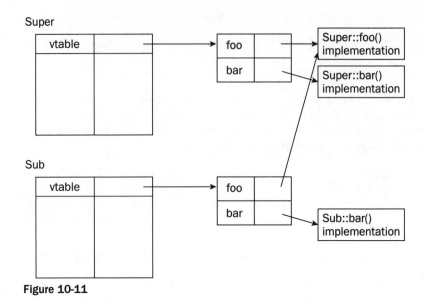

Figure 10-11

The Justification for virtual

Given the fact that you are advised to make all methods virtual, you might be wondering why the virtual keyword even exists. Can't the compiler automatically make all methods virtual? The answer is yes, it *could*. Many people think that the language *should* just make everything virtual. The Java language effectively does this.

The argument against making everything virtual, and the reason that the keyword was created in the first place, has to do with the overhead of the vtable. To call a virtual method, the program needs to perform an extra operation by dereferencing the pointer to the appropriate code to execute. This is a miniscule performance hit for most cases, but the designers of C++ thought that it was better, at least at the time, to let the programmer decide if the performance hit was necessary. If the method was never going to be overridden, there was no need to make it virtual and take the performance hit. There is also a small hit to code size. In addition to the implementation of the method, each object would also need a pointer, which takes up a small, but measurable, amount of space.

The Horror of Non-virtual Destructors

Even programmers who don't adopt the guideline of making all methods virtual still adhere to the rule when it comes to destructors. The reason is that making your destructors non-virtual can easily cause memory leaks.

For example, if a subclass uses memory that is dynamically allocated in the constructor and deleted in the destructor, it will never be freed if the destructor is never called. As the following code shows, it is easy to "trick" the compiler into skipping the call to the destructor if it is non-virtual.

```
class Super
{
    public:
        Super();
        ~Super();
};

class Sub : public Super
{
    public:
        Sub() { mString = new char[30]; }
        ~Sub() { delete[] mString; }

    protected:
        char* mString;
};

int main(int argc, char** argv)
{
    Super* ptr = new Sub();   // mString is allocated here.

    delete ptr;    // ~Super is called, but not ~Sub because the destructor
                   // is not virtual!
}
```

> **Unless you have a specific reason not to, we highly recommend making all methods (except constructors) `virtual`. Constructors cannot and need not be `virtual` because you always specify the exact class being constructed when creating an object.**

Runtime Type Facilities

Relative to other object-oriented languages, C++ is very compile-time oriented. Overriding methods, as you learned above, works because of a level of indirection between a method and its implementation, not because the object has built-in knowledge of its own class.

There are, however, features in C++ that provide a run-time view of an object. These features are commonly grouped together under a feature set called *Runtime Type Identification*, or *RTTI*. RTTI provides a number of useful features for working with information about an object's class membership.

dynamic_cast

Way back in Chapter 1, you read about `static_cast`, one of C++'s mechanisms for converting between types. The `static_cast` operator is so-named because the conversion is built into the compiled code. A `static` downcast will always succeed, regardless of the runtime type of the object.

As you read in the earlier section on downcasting, `dynamic_cast` provides a safer mechanism for converting between types within an OO hierarchy. To review, the syntax for dynamically casting an object is similar to a `static` cast. However, with a dynamic cast, an invalid cast will return NULL for a pointer or will throw an exception for a reference. The following example shows how to properly perform a dynamic cast to a reference.

```
SomeObject myObject = getSomeObject();

try {
    SomeOtherObject& myRef = dynamic_cast<SomeOtherObject&>(myObject);
} catch (std::bad_cast) {
    cerr << "Could not convert the object into the desired type." << endl;
}
```

typeid

The `typeid` operator lets you query an object at run time to find out its type. For the most part, you shouldn't ever need to use `typeid` because any code that is conditionally run based on the type of the object would be better handled with `virtual` methods.

The following code uses `typeid` to print a message based on the type of the object.

```
#include <typeinfo>

void speak(const Animal& inAnimal)
{
    if (typeid(inAnimal) == typeid(Dog&)) {
        cout << "Woof!" << endl;
    } else if (typeid(inAnimal) == typeid(Bird&)) {
        cout << "Chirp!" << endl;
    }
}
```

Anytime you see code like that shown above, you should immediately consider reimplementing the functionality as a `virtual` method. In this case, a better implementation would be to declare a `virtual` method called `speak()` in the `Animal` class. `Dog` would override the method to print `"Woof!"` and `Bird` would override the method to print `"Chirp!"`. This approach better fits object-oriented programming, where functionality related to objects is given to those objects.

The `typeid` functionality is sometimes handy in debugging, however. It is useful to print out the type of an object for logging and debugging purposes. The following code makes use of `typeid` for logging. The `logObject` function takes a "loggable" object as a parameter. The design is such that any object that can be logged subclasses the `Loggable` class and supports a method called `getLogMessage()`. In this way, `Loggable` is a mix-in class.

```
#include <typeinfo>

void logObject(Loggable& inLoggableObject)
{
    logfile << typeid(inLoggableObject).name() << " ";
    logfile << inLoggableObject.getLogMessage() << endl;
}
```

The `logObject()` function first writes the name of the object's class to the file, followed by its log message. This way, when you read the log later, you can see which object was responsible for every line of the file.

Non-Public Inheritance

In all of the examples above, parent classes were always listed using the `public` keyword. You may be wondering if a parent can be `private` or `protected`. In fact it can, though neither is as common as `public`.

Declaring the relationship with the parent to be `protected` means that all `public` and `protected` methods and data members from the superclass become `protected` in the context of the subclass. Similarly, specifying `private` access means that all `public`, `protected`, and `private` methods and data members of the superclass become `private` in the subclass.

There are a handful of reasons why you might want to uniformly degrade the access level of the parent in this way, but most reasons imply flaws in the design of the hierarchy. Some programmers abuse this language feature, often in combination with multiple inheritance, to implement "components" of a class. Instead of making an `Airplane` class that contains an engine data member and a fuselage data member, they make an `Airplane` class that is a `protected` engine and a `protected` fuselage. In this way, the `Airplane` doesn't look like an engine or a fuselage to client code (because everything is `protected`), but it is able to use all of that functionality internally.

> Non-`public` inheritance is rare and we recommend using it cautiously, if for no other reason than because of most programmers' unfamiliarity with it.

Virtual Base Classes

Earlier in this chapter, you learned about ambiguous base classes, a situation that arises when multiple parents each have a parent in common, as shown in Figure 10-9. The solution that we recommended was to make sure that the shared parent doesn't have any functionality of its own. That way, its methods can never be called and there is no ambiguity problem.

C++ has another mechanism for addressing this problem in the event that you do want the shared parent to have its own functionality. If the shared parent is a *virtual base class*, there will not be any ambiguity. The following code adds a `sleep()` method to the `Animal` base class and modifies the `Dog` and `Bird` classes to inherit from `Animal` as a virtual base class. Without the `virtual` keyword, a call to `sleep()` on a `DogBird` object would be ambiguous because both `Dog` and `Bird` would have inherited versions of `sleep()` from `Animal`. However, when `Animal` is inherited virtually, only one copy of each method or member exists in its descendents.

```
class Animal
{
    public:
        virtual void eat() = 0;
        virtual void sleep() { cout << "zzzzz...." << endl; }
};
```

```
class Dog : public virtual Animal
{
    public:
        virtual void bark() { cout << "Woof!" << endl; }
        virtual void eat() { cout << "The dog has eaten." << endl; }
};

class Bird : public virtual Animal
{
    public:
        virtual void chirp() { cout << "Chirp!" << endl; }
        virtual void eat() { cout << "The bird has eaten." << endl; }
};

class DogBird : public Dog, public Bird
{
    public:
        virtual void eat() { Dog::eat(); }
};

int main(int argc, char** argv)
{
    DogBird myConfusedAnimal;

    myConfusedAnimal.sleep();   // Not ambiguous because Animal is virtual
}
```

> **Virtual base classes are a great way to avoid ambiguity in class hierarchies. The only drawback is that many C++ programmers are unfamiliar with the concept.**

Summary

This chapter has taken you through the myriad points of inheritance. You have learned about its many applications, including code reuse and polymorphism. You have also learned about its many abuses, including poorly designed multiple inheritance schemes. Along the way, you've uncovered some of the less common edge cases that are unlikely to come up on a daily basis but make for some gnarly bugs (and interview questions!).

Inheritance is a powerful language feature that takes some time to get used to. After you have worked with the examples of this chapter and experimented on your own, we hope that inheritance will become your tool of choice for object-oriented design.

11

Writing Generic Code with Templates

C++ provides language support not only for object-oriented programming, but also for *generic programming*. As discussed in Chapter 5, the goal of generic programming is to write reusable code. The fundamental tools for generic programming in C++ are templates. Although not strictly an object-oriented feature, templates can be combined with object-oriented programming for powerful results. Unfortunately, many programmers consider templates to be the most difficult part of C++ and, for that reason, tend to avoid them. However, even if you never write your own templates, you need to understand their syntax and capabilities in order to use the C++ standard library.

This chapter provides the code details for fulfilling the design principle of generality discussed in Chapter 5 and prepares you to understand the standard template library, which is discussed further in Chapters 21 to 23. The chapter is divided into two halves. The first half presents the most commonly used template features, including:

- ❏ How to write template classes
- ❏ How the compiler processes templates
- ❏ How to organize template source code
- ❏ How to use nontype template parameters
- ❏ How to write templates of individual class methods
- ❏ How to write customizations of your class templates for specific types
- ❏ How to combine templates and inheritance
- ❏ How to write function templates
- ❏ How to make template functions friends of template classes

The second half of the chapter delves into some of the more obscure template features, including:

❏ The three kinds of template parameters and their subtleties

❏ Partial specialization

❏ Function template deduction

❏ How to exploit template recursion

Overview of Templates

The main programming unit in the procedural paradigm is the *procedure* or *function*. Functions are useful primarily because they allow you to write algorithms that are independent of specific values and can thus be reused for many different values. For example, the sqrt() function in C and C++ calculates the square root of a value supplied by the caller. A square root function that calculated only the square root of one number, like four, would not be particularly useful! The sqrt() function is written in terms of a *parameter*, which is a stand-in for whatever value the caller passes. Computer scientists say that functions *parameterize* values.

The object-oriented programming paradigm adds the concept of objects, which group related data and behaviors, but does not change the way functions and methods parameterize values.

Templates take the concept of parameterization a step further to allow you to parameterize on *types* as well as *values*. Recall that types in C++ include primitives such as int and double, as well as user-defined classes such as SpreadsheetCells and CherryTrees. With templates you can write code that is independent not only of the values it will be given, but of the types of those values as well! For example, instead of writing separate stack classes to store ints, Cars, and SpreadsheetCells, you can write one stack class definition that can be used for any of those types.

Although templates are an amazing language feature, templates in C++ are both conceptually and syntactically confusing, and many programmers overlook or avoid them. A committee designed template support in C++, and it sometimes seems as if the committee took an "everything but the kitchen sink" approach: the purpose of many template features might not be readily apparent. Even worse, compiler support for templates has historically been, and continues to be, spotty. Very few commercial compilers provide complete support for templates according to the C++ standard.

For these reasons, most C++ books only scratch the surface of templates. However, it is extremely important for you to understand C++ templates for one major reason: the C++ standard template library is, as its name suggests, built with templates. In order to take advantage of this library you must understand template fundamentals.

Thus, this chapter will teach you about template support in C++ with an emphasis on the aspects that arise in the standard template library. Along the way, you will learn about some nifty features that you can employ in your programs aside from using the standard library.

Class Templates

Class templates are useful primarily for containers, or data structures, that store objects. This section uses a running example of a `Grid` container. In order to keep the examples reasonable in length and simple enough to illustrate specific points, different sections of the chapter will add features to the `Grid` container that are not used in subsequent sections.

Writing a Class Template

Suppose that you want a generic game board class that you can use as a chessboard, checkers board, Tic-Tac-Toe board, or any other two-dimensional game board. In order to make it general-purpose, you should be able to store chess pieces, checkers pieces, Tic-Tac-Toe pieces, or any type of game piece.

Coding without Templates

Without templates, the best approach to build a generic game board is to employ polymorphism to store generic `GamePiece` objects. Then, you could subclass the pieces for each game from the `GamePiece` class. For example, in the chess game, the `ChessPiece` would be a subclass of `GamePiece`. Through polymorphism, the `GameBoard`, written to store `GamePieces`, can also store `ChessPieces`. Your class definition might look like similar to the `Spreadsheet` class from Chapter 9, which used a dynamically allocated two-dimensional array as the underlying grid structure:

```
// GameBoard.h

class GameBoard
{
    public:
        // The general-purpose GameBoard allows the user to specify its dimensions
        GameBoard(int inWidth = kDefaultWidth, int inHeight = kDefaultHeight);
        GameBoard(const GameBoard& src); // Copy constructor
        ~GameBoard();
        GameBoard &operator=(const GameBoard& rhs); // Assignment operator

        void setPieceAt(int x, int y, const GamePiece& inPiece);
        GamePiece& getPieceAt(int x, int y);
        const GamePiece& getPieceAt(int x, int y) const;

        int getHeight() const { return mHeight; }
        int getWidth() const { return mWidth; }
        static const int kDefaultWidth = 10;
        static const int kDefaultHeight = 10;

    protected:
        void copyFrom(const GameBoard& src);
        // Objects dynamically allocate space for the game pieces.
        GamePiece** mCells;
        int mWidth, mHeight;
};
```

`getPieceAt()` returns a reference to the piece at a specified spot instead of a copy of the piece. The `GameBoard` serves as an abstraction of a two-dimensional array, so it should provide array access semantics by giving the actual object at an index, not a copy of the object.

*This implementation of the class provides two versions of **getPieceAt()**, one of which returns a reference and one of which returns a const reference. Chapter 16 explains how this overload works.*

Here are the method and static member definitions. The implementation is almost identical to the Spreadsheet class from Chapter 9. Production code would, of course, perform bounds checking in setPieceAt() and getPieceAt(). That code is omitted because it is not the point of this chapter.

```cpp
// GameBoard.cpp
#include "GameBoard.h"

const int GameBoard::kDefaultWidth;
const int GameBoard::kDefaultHeight;

GameBoard::GameBoard(int inWidth, int inHeight) :
    mWidth(inWidth), mHeight(inHeight)
{
    mCells = new GamePiece* [mWidth];
    for (int i = 0; i < mWidth; i++) {
        mCells[i] = new GamePiece[mHeight];
    }
}

GameBoard::GameBoard(const GameBoard& src)
{
    copyFrom(src);
}

GameBoard::~GameBoard()
{
    // Free the old memory
    for (int i = 0; i < mWidth; i++) {
        delete[] mCells[i];
    }

    delete[] mCells;
}

void GameBoard::copyFrom(const GameBoard& src)
{
    int i, j;
    mWidth = src.mWidth;
    mHeight = src.mHeight;

    mCells = new GamePiece* [mWidth];
    for (i = 0; i < mWidth; i++) {
        mCells[i] = new GamePiece[mHeight];
    }
    for (i = 0; i < mWidth; i++) {
        for (j = 0; j < mHeight; j++) {
            mCells[i][j] = src.mCells[i][j];
        }
    }
}
```

```
GameBoard& GameBoard::operator=(const GameBoard& rhs)
{
    // Check for self-assignment
    if (this == &rhs) {
        return (*this);
    }
    // Free the old memory
    for (int i = 0; i < mWidth; i++) {
        delete[] mCells[i];
    }
    delete[] mCells;

    // Copy the new memory
    copyFrom(rhs);

    return (*this);
}

void GameBoard::setPieceAt(int x, int y, const GamePiece& inElem)
{
    mCells[x][y] = inElem;
}

GamePiece& GameBoard::getPieceAt(int x, int y)
{
    return (mCells[x][y]);
}

const GamePiece& GameBoard::getPieceAt(int x, int y) const
{
    return (mCells[x][y]);
}
```

This GameBoard class works pretty well. Assuming that you wrote a ChessPiece class, you can create GameBoard objects and use them like this:

```
GameBoard chessBoard(10, 10);
ChessPiece pawn;

chessBoard.setPieceAt(0, 0, pawn);
```

A Template Grid Class

The GameBoard class in the previous section is nice, but insufficient. For example, it's quite similar to the Spreadsheet class from chapter 9, but the only way you could use it as a spreadsheet would be to make the SpreadsheetCell class a subclass of GamePiece. That doesn't make sense because it doesn't fulfill the is-a principle of inheritance: a SpreadsheetCell is not a GamePiece. It would be nice if you could write a generic grid class that you could use for purposes as diverse as a Spreadsheet or a ChessBoard. In C++, you can do this by writing a class *template*, which allows you to write a class without specifying one or more types. Clients then *instantiate* the template by specifying the types they want to use.

The Grid Class Definition

In order to understand class templates, it is helpful to examine the syntax. The following example shows how you can tweak your GameBoard class slightly to make a templatized Grid class. Don't let the syntax scare you — it's all explained following the code. Note that the class name has changed from GameBoard to Grid, and setPieceAt() and getPieceAt() have changed to setElementAt() and getElementAt() to reflect the class' more generic nature.

```cpp
// Grid.h

template <typename T>
class Grid
{
    public:
        Grid(int inWidth = kDefaultWidth, int inHeight = kDefaultHeight);
        Grid(const Grid<T>& src);
        ~Grid();
        Grid<T>& operator=(const Grid<T>& rhs);

        void setElementAt(int x, int y, const T& inElem);
        T& getElementAt(int x, int y);
        const T& getElementAt(int x, int y) const;
        int getHeight() const { return mHeight; }
        int getWidth() const { return mWidth; }
        static const int kDefaultWidth = 10;
        static const int kDefaultHeight = 10;

    protected:
        void copyFrom(const Grid<T>& src);
        T** mCells;
        int mWidth, mHeight;
};
```

Now that you've seen the full class definition, take another look at it, one line at a time:

```cpp
template <typename T>
```

This first line says that the following class definition is a template on one type. Both `template` and `typename` are keywords in C++. As discussed earlier, templates "parameterize" types the same way that functions "parameterize" values. Just as you use parameter names in functions to represent the arguments that the caller will pass, you use type names (such as T) in templates to represent the types that the caller will specify. There's nothing special about the name T — you can use whatever name you want.

> For historical reasons, you can use the keyword **class** instead of **typename** to specify template type parameters. Thus, many books and existing programs use syntax like this: **template <class T>**. However, the use of the word "class" in this context is confusing because it implies that the type must be a class, which is not true. Thus, this book uses **typename** exclusively.

The template specifier holds for the entire statement, which in this case is the class definition.

Several lines further, the copy constructor looks like this:

```
Grid(const Grid<T>& src);
```

As you can see, the type of the `src` parameter is no longer a `const Grid&`, but a `const Grid<T>&`. When you write a class template, what you used to think of as the class name (`Grid`) is actually the template name. When you want to talk about actual `Grid` classes or types, you discuss them as instantiations of the `Grid` class template for a certain type, such as `int`, `SpreadsheetCell`, or `ChessPiece`. You haven't specified the real type yet, so you must use a stand-in template parameter, `T`, for whatever type might be used later. Thus, when you need to refer to a type for a `Grid` object as a parameter to, or return value from, a method you must use `Grid<T>`. You can see this change with the parameter to, and return value from, the assignment operator, and the parameter to the `copyFrom()` method.

Within a class definition, the compiler will interpret `Grid` as `Grid<T>` where needed. However, it's best to get in the habit of specifying `Grid<T>` explicitly because that's the syntax you use outside the class to refer to types generated from the template.

The final change to the class is that methods such as `setElementAt()` and `getElementAt()` now take and return parameters and values of type `T` instead of type `GamePiece`:

```
void setElementAt(int x, int y, const T& inElem);
T& getElementAt(int x, int y);
const T& getElementAt(int x, int y) const;
```

This type `T` is a placeholder for whatever type the user specifies. `mCells` is now a `T**` instead of a `GameBoard**` because it will point to a dynamically allocated two-dimensional array of `T`s, for whatever type `T` the user specifies.

Template classes can contain inline methods such as `getHeight()` and `getWidth()`.

The Grid Class Method Definitions

The `template <typename T>` specifier must precede each method definition for the `Grid` template. The constructor looks like this:

```
template <typename T>
Grid<T>::Grid(int inWidth, int inHeight) : mWidth(inWidth), mHeight(inHeight)
{
    mCells = new T* [mWidth];
    for (int i = 0; i < mWidth; i++) {
        mCells[i] = new T[mHeight];
    }
}
```

Note that the class name before the `::` is `Grid<T>`, not `Grid`. You must specify `Grid<T>` as the class name in all your methods and static data member definitions. The body of the constructor is identical to the `GameBoard` constructor except that the placeholder type `T` replaces the `GamePiece` type.

The rest of the method and static member definitions are also similar to their equivalents in the `GameBoard` class with the exception of the appropriate `template` and `Grid<T>` syntax changes:

```
template <typename T>
const int Grid<T>::kDefaultWidth;

template <typename T>
const int Grid<T>::kDefaultHeight;

template <typename T>
Grid<T>::Grid(const Grid<T>& src)
{
    copyFrom(src);
}

template <typename T>
Grid<T>::~Grid()
{
    // Free the old memory.
    for (int i = 0; i < mWidth; i++) {
        delete [] mCells[i];
    }
    delete [] mCells;
}

template <typename T>
void Grid<T>::copyFrom(const Grid<T>& src)
{
    int i, j;
    mWidth = src.mWidth;
    mHeight = src.mHeight;

    mCells = new T* [mWidth];
    for (i = 0; i < mWidth; i++) {
        mCells[i] = new T[mHeight];
    }

    for (i = 0; i < mWidth; i++) {
        for (j = 0; j < mHeight; j++) {
            mCells[i][j] = src.mCells[i][j];
        }
    }
}

template <typename T>
Grid<T>& Grid<T>::operator=(const Grid<T>& rhs)
{
    // Check for self-assignment.
    if (this == &rhs) {
        return (*this);
    }
    // Free the old memory.
    for (int i = 0; i < mWidth; i++) {
        delete [] mCells[i];
    }
    delete [] mCells;
```

```
    // Copy the new memory.
    copyFrom(rhs);

    return (*this);
}
```

```
template <typename T>
void Grid<T>::setElementAt(int x, int y, const T& inElem)
{
    mCells[x][y] = inElem;
}
```

```
template <typename T>
T& Grid<T>::getElementAt(int x, int y)
{
    return (mCells[x][y]);
}
```

```
template <typename T>
const T& Grid<T>::getElementAt(int x, int y) const
{
  return (mCells[x][y]);
}
```

Using the Grid Template

When you want to create grid objects, you cannot use Grid alone as a type; you must specify the type that will be stored in that Grid. Creating an object of a template class for a specific type is called instantiating the template. Here is an example:

```
#include "Grid.h"

int main(int argc, char** argv)
{
    Grid<int> myIntGrid; // Declares a grid that stores ints
    myIntGrid.setElementAt(0, 0, 10);
    int x = myIntGrid.getElementAt(0, 0);

    Grid<int> grid2(myIntGrid);
    Grid<int> anotherIntGrid = grid2;

    return (0);
}
```

Note that the type of mIntGrid, grid2, and anotherIntGrid is Grid<int>. You cannot store SpreadsheetCells or ChessPieces in these grids; the compiler will generate an error if you try to do so.

The type specification is important: neither of the following two lines compiles:

```
    Grid test; // WILL NOT COMPILE
    Grid<> test; // WILL NOT COMPILE
```

The first causes your compiler to complain with something like, "use of class template requires template argument list." The second causes it to say something like, "wrong number of template arguments."

If you want to declare a function or method that takes a Grid object, you must specify the type stored in that grid as part of the Grid type:

```
void processIntGrid(Grid<int>& inGrid)
{
    // Body omitted for brevity
}
```

The Grid template can store more than just ints. For example, you can instantiate a Grid that stores SpreadsheetCells:

```
Grid<SpreadsheetCell> mySpreadsheet;
SpreadsheetCell myCell;
mySpreadsheet.setElementAt(3, 4, myCell);
```

You can store pointer types as well:

```
Grid<char*> myStringGrid;
myStringGrid.setElementAt(2, 2, "hello");
```

The type specified can even be another template type. The following example uses the vector template from the standard template library (introduced in Chapter 4):

```
Grid<vector<int> > gridOfVectors; // Note the extra space!
vector<int> myVector;
gridOfVectors.setElementAt(5, 6, myVector);
```

You must leave a space between the two closing angle brackets when you have nested templates. C++ requires this syntax because compilers would interpret >> in the following example as the I/O streams extraction operator:

```
Grid<vector<int>> gridOfVectors; // INCORRECT SYNTAX
```

You can also dynamically allocate Grid template instantiations on the heap:

```
Grid<int>* myGridp = new Grid<int>();
myGridp->setElementAt(0, 0, 10);
int x = myGridp->getElementAt(0, 0);

delete myGridp;
```

How the Compiler Processes Templates

In order to understand the intricacies of templates, you need to learn how the compiler processes template code. When the compiler encounters template method definitions, it performs syntax checking, but doesn't actually compile the templates. It can't compile template definitions because it doesn't know for which types they will be used. It's impossible for a compiler to generate code for something like x = y without knowing the types of x and y.

When the compiler encounters an instantiation of the template, such as Grid<int> myIntGrid, it writes code for an int version of the Grid template by replacing each T in the template class definition with `int`. When the compiler encounters a different instantiation of the template, such as `Grid<SpreadsheetCell> mySpreadsheet`, it writes another version of the `Grid` class for `SpreadsheetCell`s. The compiler just writes the code that you would write if you didn't have template support in the language and had to write separate classes for each element type. There's no magic here; templates just automate an annoying process. If you don't instantiate a class template for any types in your program, then the class method definitions are never compiled.

This instantiation process explains why you need to use the `Grid<T>` syntax in various places in your definition. When the compiler instantiates the template for a particular type, such as `int`, it replaces `T` with `int`, so that `Grid<int>` is the type.

Selective Instantiation

Instantiating a template for many different types can lead to code bloat because the compiler generates copies of the template code for each type. You can end up with large executable files when you use templates.

However, the problem is ameliorated because the compiler only generates code for the class methods that you actually call for a particular type. For example, given the `Grid` template class above, suppose that you write this code (and only this code) in `main()`:

```
Grid<int> myIntGrid;
myIntGrid.setElementAt(0, 0, 10);
```

The compiler generates only the 0-argument constructor, the destructor, and the `setElementAt()` method for an `int` version of the `Grid`. It does not generate other methods like the copy constructor, the assignment operator, or `getHeight()`.

Template Requirements on Types

When you write code that is independent of types, you must assume certain things about those types. For example, in the `Grid` template, you assume that the element type (represented by `T`) will have an assignment operator because of this line: `mCells[x][y] = inElem`. Similarly, you assume it will have a default constructor to allow you to create an array of elements.

If you attempt to instantiate a template with a type that does not support all the operations used by the template in your particular program, the code will not compile. However, even if the type you want to use doesn't support the operations required by all the template code, you can exploit selective instantiation to use some methods but not others. For example, if you try to create a grid for an object that has no assignment operator, but you never call `setElementAt()` on that grid, your code will work fine. As soon as you try to call `setElementAt()`, however, you will receive a compilation error.

Distributing Template Code between Files

Normally you put class definitions in a header file and method definitions in a source file. Code that creates or uses objects of the class `#includes` the header file and obtains access to the method code via the linker. Templates don't work that way. Because they are "templates" for the compiler to generate the actual methods for the instantiated types, both template class definitions and method definitions must be available to the compiler in any source file that uses them. In this sense, methods of a template class are similar to inline methods. There are several mechanisms to obtain this inclusion.

Template Definitions in Header Files

You can place the method definitions directly in the same header file where you define the class itself. When you #include this file in a source file where you use the template, the compiler will have access to all the code it needs.

Alternatively, you can place the template method definitions in a separate header file that you #include in the header file with the class definitions. Make sure the #include for the method definitions follows the class definition; otherwise the code won't compile!

```
// Grid.h

template <typename T>
class Grid
{
    // Class definition omitted for brevity
};

#include "GridDefinitions.h"
```

This division helps keep the distinction between class definitions and method definitions.

Template Definitions in Source Files

Method implementations look strange in header files. If that syntax annoys you, there is a way that you can place the method definitions in a source file. However, you still need to make the definitions available to the code that uses the templates, which you can do by #includeing the method implementation *source* file in the template class definition header file. That sounds odd if you've never seen it before, but it's legal in C++. The header file looks like this:

```
// Grid.h

template <typename T>
class Grid
{
    // Class definition omitted for brevity
};

#include "Grid.cpp"
```

The C++ standard actually defines a way for template method definitions to exist in a source file, which does not need to be #included in a header file. You use the export keyword to specify that the template definitions should be available in all *translation units* (source files). Unfortunately, as of this writing, few commercial compilers support this feature, and many vendors seem disinclined to support it anytime soon.

Template Parameters

In the Grid example, the Grid template has one *template parameter*: the type that is stored in the grid. When you write the class template, you specify the parameter list inside the angle brackets, like this:

```
template <typename T>
```

This parameter list is similar to the parameter list in a function or method. As in functions and methods, you can write a class with as many template parameters as you want. Additionally, these parameters don't have to be types, and they can have default values.

Nontype Template Parameters

Nontype parameters are "normal" parameters such as ints and pointers: the kind of parameters with which you're familiar from functions and methods. However, templates allow nontype parameters to be values of only "simple" types: ints, enums, pointers, and references.

In the Grid template class, you could use nontype template parameters to specify the height and width of the grid instead of specifying them in the constructor. The principle advantage to specifying nontype parameters in the template list instead of in the constructor is that the values are known before the code is compiled. Recall that the compiler generates code for templatized methods by substituting in the template parameters before compiling. Thus, you can use a normal two-dimensional array in your implementation instead of dynamically allocating it. Here is the new class definition:

```
template <typename T, int WIDTH, int HEIGHT>
class Grid
{
    public:
        void setElementAt(int x, int y, const T& inElem);
        T& getElementAt(int x, int y);
        const T& getElementAt(int x, int y) const;
        int getHeight() const { return HEIGHT; }
        int getWidth() const { return WIDTH; }

    protected:
        T mCells[WIDTH][HEIGHT];
};
```

This class is significantly simpler than the old version. Note that the template parameter list requires three parameters: the type of object stored in the grid and the width and height of the grid. The width and height are used to create a two-dimensional array to store the objects. There is no dynamically allocated memory in the class, so it no longer needs a user-defined copy constructor, destructor, or assignment operator. In fact, you don't even need to write a default constructor; the compiler generated one is just fine. Here are the class method definitions:

```
template <typename T, int WIDTH, int HEIGHT>
void Grid<T, WIDTH, HEIGHT>::setElementAt(int x, int y, const T& inElem)
{
    mCells[x][y] = inElem;
}

template <typename T, int WIDTH, int HEIGHT>
T& Grid<T, WIDTH, HEIGHT>::getElementAt(int x, int y)
{
    return (mCells[x][y]);
}

template <typename T, int WIDTH, int HEIGHT>
const T& Grid<T, WIDTH, HEIGHT>::getElementAt(int x, int y) const
{
    return (mCells[x][y]);
}
```

Note that wherever you previously specified Grid<T> you must now specify Grid<T, WIDTH, HEIGHT> to represent the three template parameters.

You can instantiate this template and use it like this:

```
Grid<int, 10, 10> myGrid;
Grid<int, 10, 10> anotherGrid;

myGrid.setElementAt(2, 3, 45);
anotherGrid = myGrid;

cout << anotherGrid.getElementAt(2, 3);
```

This code seems great! Despite the slightly messy syntax for declaring a Grid, the actual Grid code is a lot simpler. Unfortunately, there are more restrictions than you might think at first. First, you can't use a nonconstant integer to specify the height or width. The following code doesn't compile:

```
int height = 10;
Grid<int, 10, height> testGrid; // DOES NOT COMPILE
```

However, if you make height const, it compiles:

```
const int height = 10;
Grid<int, 10, height> testGrid; // compiles and works
```

The second problem is much more significant. Now that the width and height are template parameters, they are part of the type of each grid. That means that Grid<int, 10, 10> and Grid<int, 10, 11> are two different types. You can't assign an object of one type to an object of the other, and variables of one type can't be passed to functions or methods that expect variables of another type.

> Nontype template parameters become part of the type specification of instantiated objects.

Default Values for Integer Nontype Parameters

If you continue the approach of making height and width template parameters, you might want to be able to provide defaults for the height and width just as you did previously in the constructor of the Grid<T> class. C++ allows you to provide defaults for template parameters with a similar syntax. Here is the class definition:

```
template <typename T, int WIDTH = 10, int HEIGHT = 10>
class Grid
{
    // Remainder of the implementation is identical to the previous version
};
```

You do not need to specify the default values for WIDTH and HEIGHT in the template specification for the method definitions. For example, here is the implementation of setElementAt():

```
template <typename T, int WIDTH, int HEIGHT>
void Grid<T, WIDTH, HEIGHT>::setElementAt(int x, int y, const T& inElem)
{
    mCells[x][y] = inElem;
}
```

Now, you can instantiate a Grid with only the element type, the element type and the width, or the element type, width, and height:

```
Grid<int> myGrid;
Grid<int, 10> anotherGrid;
Grid<int, 10, 10> aThirdGrid;
```

The rules for default parameters in template parameter lists are the same as for functions or methods: you can provide defaults for parameters in order starting from the right.

Method Templates

C++ allows you to templatize individual methods of a class. These methods can be inside a class template or in a nontemplatized class. When you write a templatized class method, you are actually writing many different versions of that method for many different types. Method templates come in useful for assignment operators and copy constructors in class templates.

> **Virtual methods and destructors cannot be templatized.**

Consider the original Grid template with only one parameter: the element type. You can instantiate grids of many different types, such as ints and doubles:

```
Grid<int> myIntGrid;
Grid<double> myDoubleGrid;
```

However, Grid<int> and Grid<double> are two different types. If you write a function that takes an object of type Grid<double>, you cannot pass a Grid<int>. Even though you know that an int grid could be copied to a double grid, because the ints could be coerced into doubles, you cannot assign an object of type Grid<int> to one of type Grid<double> or construct a Grid<double> from a Grid<int>. Neither of the following two lines compiles:

```
myDoubleGrid = myIntGrid; // DOES NOT COMPILE
Grid<double> newDoubleGrid(myIntGrid); // DOES NOT COMPILE
```

The problem is that the Grid template copy constructor and operator= signatures look like this:

```
Grid(const Grid<T>& src);
Grid<T>& operator=(const Grid<T>& rhs);
```

The `Grid` copy constructor and `operator=` both take a reference to a `const Grid<T>`. When you instantiate a `Grid<double>` and try to call the copy constructor and `operator=`, the compiler generates methods with these signatures:

```
Grid(const Grid<double>& src);
Grid<double>& operator=(const Grid<double>& rhs);
```

Note that there are no constructors or `operator=` that take a `Grid<int>` within the generated `Grid<double>` class. However, you can rectify this oversight by adding templatized versions of the copy constructor and `operator=` to the `Grid` class to generate routines that will convert from one grid type to another. Here is the new `Grid` class definition:

```cpp
template <typename T>
class Grid
{
    public:
        Grid(int inWidth = kDefaultWidth, int inHeight = kDefaultHeight);
        Grid(const Grid<T>& src);
        template <typename E>
        Grid(const Grid<E>& src);
        ~Grid();

        Grid<T>& operator=(const Grid<T>& rhs);
        template <typename E>
        Grid<T>& operator=(const Grid<E>& rhs);

        void setElementAt(int x, int y, const T& inElem);
        T& getElementAt(int x, int y);
        const T& getElementAt(int x, int y) const;

        int getHeight() const { return mHeight; }
        int getWidth() const { return mWidth; }

        static const int kDefaultWidth = 10;
        static const int kDefaultHeight = 10;

    protected:
        void copyFrom(const Grid<T>& src);
        template <typename E>
        void copyFrom(const Grid<E>& src);

        T** mCells;
        int mWidth, mHeight;
};
```

> Member templates do not replace nontemplate members with the same name. This rule leads to problems with the copy constructor and `operator=` because of the compiler-generated versions. If you write templatized versions of the copy constructor and `operator=` and omit nontemplatized versions, the compiler will not call these new templatized versions for assignments of grids with the same type. Instead, it will generate a copy constructor and `operator=` for creating and assigning two grids of the same type, which will not do what you want! Thus, you must keep the old nontemplatized copy constructor and `operator=` as well.

Examine the new templatized copy constructor signature first:

```
template <typename E>
Grid(const Grid<E>& src);
```

You can see that there is another template declaration with a different typename, E (short for "element"). The class is templatized on one type, T, and the new copy constructor is also templatized on a different type, E. This twofold templatization allows you to copy grids of one type to another.

Here is the definition of the new copy constructor:

```
template <typename T>
template <typename E>
Grid<T>::Grid(const Grid<E>& src)
{
    copyFrom(src);
}
```

As you can see, you must declare the class template line (with the T parameter) before the member template line (with the E parameter). You can't combine them like this:

```
template <typename T, typename E> // INCORRECT TEMPLATE PARAMETER LIST!
Grid<T>::Grid(const Grid<E>& src)
```

> Some compilers require that you provide method template definitions inline in the class definition, but the C++ standard permits method template definitions outside the class definition.

The copy constructor uses the protected copyFrom() method, so the class needs a templatized version of copyFrom() as well:

```
template <typename T>
template <typename E>
void Grid<T>::copyFrom(const Grid<E>& src)
{
    int i, j;
    mWidth = src.getWidth();
    mHeight = src.getHeight();

    mCells = new T* [mWidth];
    for (i = 0; i < mWidth; i++) {
        mCells[i] = new T[mHeight];
    }
    for (i = 0; i < mWidth; i++) {
        for (j = 0; j < mHeight; j++) {
            mCells[i][j] = src.getElementAt(i, j);
        }
    }
}
```

In addition to the extra template parameter line before the copyFrom() method definition, note that you must use public accessor methods getWidth(), getHeight(), and getElementAt() to access the elements of `src`. That's because the object you're copying to is of type `Grid<T>`, and the object you're copying from is of type `Grid<E>`. They will not be the same type, so you must resort to public methods.

The final templatized method is the assignment operator. Note that it takes a `const Grid<E>&` but returns a `Grid<T>&`.

```
template <typename T>
template <typename E>
Grid<T>& Grid<T>::operator=(const Grid<E>& rhs)
{
    // Free the old memory.
    for (int i = 0; i < mWidth; i++) {
        delete [] mCells[i];
    }
    delete [] mCells;

    // Copy the new memory.
    copyFrom(rhs);

    return (*this);
}
```

You do not need to check for self-assignment in the templatized assignment operator, because assignment of the same types still happens in the old, nontemplatized, version of `operator=`, so there's no way you can get self-assignment here.

In addition to the confusing syntax for method templates, there is another problem: some compilers don't implement full (or any) support for them. Try this example out on your compiler of choice to see if you can use these features.

Method Templates with Nontype Parameters

In the earlier example with integer template parameters for `HEIGHT` and `WIDTH`, we noted that a major problem is that the height and width become part of the types. This restriction prevents you from assigning a grid with one height and width to a grid with a different height and width. In some cases, however, it's desirable to assign or copy a grid of one size to a grid of a different size. Instead of making the destination object a perfect clone of the source object, you would copy only those elements from the source array that fit in the destination array, padding the destination array with default values if the source array is smaller in either dimention. With method templates for the assignment operator and copy constructor, you can do exactly that, thus allow assignment and copying of different sized grids. Here is the class definition:

```
template <typename T, int WIDTH = 10, int HEIGHT = 10>
class Grid
{
    public:
        Grid() {}

        template <typename E, int WIDTH2, int HEIGHT2>
        Grid(const Grid<E, WIDTH2, HEIGHT2>& src);

        template <typename E, int WIDTH2, int HEIGHT2>
        Grid<T, WIDTH, HEIGHT>& operator=(const Grid<E, WIDTH2, HEIGHT2>& rhs);
```

```
        void setElementAt(int x, int y, const T& inElem);
        T& getElementAt(int x, int y);
        const T& getElementAt(int x, int y) const;
        int getHeight() const { return HEIGHT; }
        int getWidth() const { return WIDTH; }

    protected:
        template <typename E, int WIDTH2, int HEIGHT2>
        void copyFrom(const Grid<E, WIDTH2, HEIGHT2>& src);

        T mCells[WIDTH][HEIGHT];
};
```

We have added method templates for the copy constructor and assignment operator, plus a helper method copyFrom(). Recall from Chapter 8 that when you write a copy constructor, the compiler stops generating a default constructor for you, so we had to add a default constructor as well. Note, however, that we do not need to write nontemplatized copy constructor and assignment operator methods because the compiler-generated ones continue to be generated. They simply copy or assign mCells from the source to the destination, which is exactly the semantics we want for two grids of the same size.

When you templatize the copy constructor, assignment operator, and copyFrom(), you must specify all three template parameters. Here is the templatized copy constructor:

```
template <typename T, int WIDTH, int HEIGHT>
template <typename E, int WIDTH2, int HEIGHT2>
Grid<T, WIDTH, HEIGHT>::Grid(const Grid<E, WIDTH2, HEIGHT2>& src)
{
    copyFrom(src);
}
```

Here are the implementations of copyFrom() and operator=. Note that copyFrom() copies only WIDTH and HEIGHT elements in the x and y dimensions, respectively, from src, even if src is bigger than that. If src is smaller in either dimension, copyFrom() pads the extra spots with zero-initialized values. T() calls the default constructor for the object if T is a class type, or generates 0 if T is a simple type. This syntax is called the *zero-initialization* syntax. It's a good way to provide a reasonable default value for a variable whose type you don't yet know.

```
template <typename T, int WIDTH, int HEIGHT>
template <typename E, int WIDTH2, int HEIGHT2>
void Grid<T, WIDTH, HEIGHT>::copyFrom(const Grid<E, WIDTH2, HEIGHT2>& src)
{
    int i, j;
    for (i = 0; i < WIDTH; i++) {
        for (j = 0; j < HEIGHT; j++) {
            if (i < WIDTH2 && j < HEIGHT2) {
                mCells[i][j] = src.getElementAt(i, j);
            } else {
                mCells[i][j] = T();
            }
        }
    }
}
```

```
template <typename T, int WIDTH, int HEIGHT>
template <typename E, int WIDTH2, int HEIGHT2>
Grid<T, WIDTH, HEIGHT>& Grid<T, WIDTH, HEIGHT>::operator=(
    const Grid<E, WIDTH2, HEIGHT2>& rhs)
{
    // No need to check for self-assignment because this version of
    // assignment is never called when T and E are the same

    // No need to free any memory first

    // Copy the new memory.
    copyFrom(rhs);
    return (*this);
}
```

Template Class Specialization

You can provide alternate implementations of class templates for specific types. For example, you might decide that the Grid behavior for char*s (C-style strings) doesn't make sense. The grid currently stores shallow copies of pointer types. For char*'s, it might make sense to do a deep copy of the string.

Alternate implementations of templates are called *template specializations*. Again, the syntax is a little weird. When you write a template class specialization, you must specify that it's a template, and that you are writing the version of the template for that particular type. Here is the syntax for specializing the original version of the Grid for char *s.

```
// #includes for working with the C-style strings.
#include <cstdlib>
#include <cstring>
using namespace std;

// When the template specialization is used, the original template must be visible
// too. #including it here ensures that it will always be visible when this
// specialization is visible.
#include "Grid.h"

template <>
class Grid<char*>
{
    public:
        Grid(int inWidth = kDefaultWidth, int inHeight = kDefaultHeight);
        Grid(const Grid<char*>& src);
        ~Grid();
        Grid<char*>& operator=(const Grid<char*>& rhs);

        void setElementAt(int x, int y, const char* inElem);
        char* getElementAt(int x, int y) const;

        int getHeight() const { return mHeight; }
        int getWidth() const { return mWidth; }
        static const int kDefaultWidth = 10;
        static const int kDefaultHeight = 10;
```

```
    protected:
        void copyFrom(const Grid<char*>& src);

        char*** mCells;
        int mWidth, mHeight;
};
```

Note that you don't refer to any type variable, such as T, in the specialization: you work directly with char*s. One obvious question at this point is why this class is still a template. That is, what good is this syntax?

```
template <>
class Grid<char *>
```

This syntax tells the compiler that this class is a char * specialization of the Grid class. Suppose that you didn't use that syntax and just tried to write this:

```
class Grid
```

The compiler wouldn't let you do that because there is already a class named Grid (the original template class). Only by specializing it can you reuse the name. The main benefit of specializations is that they can be invisible to the user. When a user creates a Grid of ints or SpreadsheetCells, the compiler generates code from the original Grid template. When the user creates a Grid of char*'s, the compiler uses the char* specialization. This can all be "behind the scenes."

```
Grid<int> myIntGrid; // Uses original Grid template
Grid<char*> stringGrid1(2, 2); // Uses char* specialization

char* dummy = new char[10];

strcpy(dummy, "dummy");

stringGrid1.setElementAt(0, 0, "hello");
stringGrid1.setElementAt(0, 1, dummy);
stringGrid1.setElementAt(1, 0, dummy);
stringGrid1.setElementAt(1, 1, "there");

delete[] dummy;

Grid<char*> stringGrid2(stringGrid1);
```

When you specialize a template, you don't "inherit" any code: specializations are not like subclasses. You must rewrite the entire implementation of the class. There is no requirement that you provide methods with the same names or behavior. In fact, you could write a completely different class with no relation to the original! Of course, that would abuse the template specialization ability, and you shouldn't do it without good reason. Here are the implementations for the methods of the char* specialization. Unlike in the original template definitions, you do not repeat the template<> syntax before each method or static member definition!

```
const int Grid<char*>::kDefaultWidth;
const int Grid<char*>::kDefaultHeight;

Grid<char*>::Grid(int inWidth, int inHeight) :
```

```
        mWidth(inWidth), mHeight(inHeight)
{
    mCells = new char** [mWidth];
    for (int i = 0; i < mWidth; i++) {
        mCells[i] = new char* [mHeight];
        for (int j = 0; j < mHeight; j++) {
            mCells[i][j] = NULL;
        }
    }
}
```

```
Grid<char*>::Grid(const Grid<char*>& src)
{
    copyFrom(src);
}
```

```
Grid<char*>::~Grid()
{
    // Free the old memory.
    for (int i = 0; i < mWidth; i++) {
        for (int j = 0; j < mHeight; j++) {
            delete[] mCells[i][j];
        }
        delete[] mCells[i];
    }
    delete[] mCells;
}
```

```
void Grid<char*>::copyFrom(const Grid<char*>& src)
{
    int i, j;
    mWidth = src.mWidth;
    mHeight = src.mHeight;

    mCells = new char** [mWidth];
    for (i = 0; i < mWidth; i++) {
        mCells[i] = new char* [mHeight];
    }

    for (i = 0; i < mWidth; i++) {
        for (j = 0; j < mHeight; j++) {
            if (src.mCells[i][j] == NULL) {
                mCells[i][j] = NULL;
            } else {
                mCells[i][j] = new char[strlen(src.mCells[i][j]) + 1];
                strcpy(mCells[i][j], src.mCells[i][j]);
            }
        }
    }
}
```

```
Grid<char*>& Grid<char*>::operator=(const Grid<char*>& rhs)
{
    int i, j;
```

```
    // Check for self-assignment.
    if (this == &rhs) {
        return (*this);
    }
    // Free the old memory.
    for (i = 0; i < mWidth; i++) {
        for (j = 0; j < mHeight; j++) {
            delete[] mCells[i][j];
        }
        delete[] mCells[i];
    }
    delete[] mCells;

    // Copy the new memory.
    copyFrom(rhs);

    return (*this);
}
```

```
void Grid<char*>::setElementAt(int x, int y, const char* inElem)
{
    delete[] mCells[x][y];
    if (inElem == NULL) {
        mCells[x][y] = NULL;
    } else {
        mCells[x][y] = new char[strlen(inElem) + 1];
        strcpy(mCells[x][y], inElem);
    }
}
```

```
char* Grid<char*>::getElementAt(int x, int y) const
{
    if (mCells[x][y] == NULL) {
        return (NULL);
    }
    char* ret = new char[strlen(mCells[x][y]) + 1];
    strcpy(ret, mCells[x][y]);

    return (ret);
}
```

getElementAt() returns a deep copy of the string, so you don't need an overload that returns a const char*.

Subclassing Template Classes

You can write subclasses of template classes. If the subclass inherits from the template itself, it must be a template as well. Alternatively, you can write a subclass to inherit from a specific instantiation of the template class, in which case your subclass does not need to be a template. As an example of the former, suppose you decide that the generic Grid class doesn't provide enough functionality to use as a game board. Specifically, you would like to add a move() method to the game board that moves a piece from one location on the board to another. Here is the class definition for the GameBoard template:

```
#include "Grid.h"

template <typename T>
class GameBoard : public Grid<T>
{
    public:
        GameBoard(int inWidth = Grid<T>::kDefaultWidth,
            int inHeight = Grid<T>::kDefaultHeight);
        void move(int xSrc, int ySrc, int xDest, int yDest);
};
```

This GameBoard template subclasses the Grid template, and thereby inherits all its functionality. You don't need to rewrite setElementAt(), getElementAt(), or any of the other methods. You also don't need to add a copy constructor, operator=, or destructor, because you don't have any dynamically allocated memory in the GameBoard. The dynamically allocated memory in the Grid superclass will be taken care of by the Grid copy constructor, operator=, and destructor.

The inheritance syntax looks normal, except that the superclass is Grid<T>, not Grid. The reason for this syntax is that the GameBoard template doesn't really subclass the generic Grid template. Rather, each instantiation of the GameBoard template for a specific type subclasses the Grid instantiation for that type. For example, if you instantiate a GameBoard with a ChessPiece type, then the compiler generates code for a Grid<ChessPiece> as well. The ": public Grid<T>" syntax says that this class subclasses from whatever Grid instantiation makes sense for the T type parameter. Note that the C++ name lookup rules for template inheritance require you to specify that kDefaultWidth and kDefaultHeight are declared in, and thus dependent on, the Grid<T> superclass.

Here are the implementations of the constructor and the move method. Again, note the use of Grid<T> in the call to the superclass constructor. Additionally, although many compilers don't enforce it, the name lookup rules require you to use the this pointer to refer to data members and methods in the superclass.

```
template <typename T>
GameBoard<T>::GameBoard(int inWidth, int inHeight) :
    Grid<T>(inWidth, inHeight)
{
}

template <typename T>
void GameBoard<T>::move(int xSrc, int ySrc, int xDest, int yDest)
{
    this->mCells[xDest][yDest] = this->mCells[xSrc][ySrc];
    this->mCells[xSrc][ySrc] = T(); // zero-initialize the src cell
}
```

As you can see, move() uses the zero-initializtion syntax T() described in the section on "Method Templates with Nontype Parameters."

You can use the GameBoard template like this:

```
GameBoard<ChessPiece> chessBoard;

ChessPiece pawn;
chessBoard.setElementAt(0, 0, pawn);
chessBoard.move(0, 0, 0, 1);
```

Inheritance versus Specialization

Some programmers find the distinction between template inheritance and template specialization confusing. The following table summarizes the differences.

	Inheritance	Specialization
Reuses code?	Yes: subclasses contain all superclass members and methods.	No: you must rewrite all code in the specialization.
Reuses name?	No: the subclass name must be different from the superclass name.	Yes: the specialization must have the same name as the original.
Supports polymorphism?	Yes: objects of the subclass can stand in for objects of the superclass.	No: each instantiation of a template for a type is a different type.

> **Use inheritance for extending implementations and for polymorphism. Use specialization for customizing implementations for particular types.**

Function Templates

You can also write templates for stand-alone functions. For example, you could write a generic function to find a value in an array and return its index:

```
template <typename T>
int Find(T& value, T* arr, int size)
{
    for (int i = 0; i < size; i++) {
        if (arr[i] == value) {
            // Found it; return the index
            return (i);
        }
    }
    // Failed to find it; return -1
    return (-1);
}
```

The `Find()` function template can work on arrays of any type. For example, you could use it to find the index of an `int` in an array of `ints` or a `SpreadsheetCell` in an array of `SpreadsheetCells`.

You can call the function in two ways: explicitly specifying the type with angle brackets or omitting the type and letting the compiler *deduce* it from the arguments. Here are some examples:

```cpp
int x = 3, intArr[4] = {1, 2, 3, 4};
double d1 = 5.6, dArr[4] = {1.2, 3.4, 5.7, 7.5};

int res;
res = Find(x, intArr, 4); // Calls Find<int> by deduction
res = Find<int>(x, intArr, 4); // call Find<int> explicitly.

res = Find(d1, dArr, 4); // Call Find<double> by deduction.
res = Find<double>(d1, dArr, 4); // Calls Find<double> explicitly.

res = Find(x, dArr, 4);  // DOES NOT COMPILE! Arguments are different types.

SpreadsheetCell c1(10), c2[2] = {SpreadsheetCell(4), SpreadsheetCell(10)};

res = Find(c1, c2, 2); // calls Find<SpreadsheetCell> by deduction
res = Find<SpreadsheetCell>(c1, c2, 2); // Calls Find<SpreadsheetCell>
                                        // explicitly.
```

Like class templates, function templates can take nontype parameters. For brevity, we only show an example of a type parameter for function templates.

> The C++ standard library provides a templatized find() function that is much more powerful than the one above. See Chapter 22 for details.

Function Template Specialization

Just as you can specialize class templates, you can specialize function templates. For example, you might want to write a Find() function for char* C-style strings that compares them with strcmp() instead of operator==. Here is a specialization of the Find() function to do this:

```cpp
template<>
int Find<char*>(char*& value, char** arr, int size)
{
    for (int i = 0; i < size; i++) {
        if (strcmp(arr[i], value) == 0) {
            // Found it; return the index
            return (i);
        }
    }
    // Failed to find it; return -1
    return (-1);
}
```

You can omit the <char*> in the function name when the parameter type can be deduced from the arguments, making your prototype look like this:

```cpp
template<>
int Find(char*& value, char** arr, int size)
```

However, the deduction rules are tricky when you involve overloading as well (see next section), so, in order to avoid mistakes, it's better to note the type explicitly.

Although the specialized find function could take just `char*` instead of `char*&` as its first parameter, it's best to keep the arguments parallel to the nonspecialized version of the function for the deduction rules to function properly.

You can use the specialization like this:

```
char* word = "two";
char* arr[4] = {"one", "two", "three", "four"};
int res;

res = Find<char*>(word, arr, 4); // Calls the char* specialization
res = Find(word, arr, 4); // Calls the char* specialization
```

Function Template Overloading

You can also overload template functions with nontemplate functions. For example, instead of writing a `Find()` template specialization for `char*`, you could write a nontemplate `Find()` function that works on `char*`s:

```
int Find(char*& value, char** arr, int size)
{
    for (int i = 0; i < size; i++) {
        if (strcmp(arr[i], value) == 0) {
            // Found it; return the index
            return (i);
        }
    }
    // Failed to find it; return -1
    return (-1);
}
```

This function is identical in behavior to the specialized version in the previous section. However, the rules for when it is called are different:

```
char* word = "two";
char* arr[4] = {"one", "two", "three", "four"};
int res;

res = Find<char*>(word, arr, 4); // Calls the Find template with T=char*
res = Find(word, arr, 4); // Calls the Find nontemplate function!
```

Thus, if you want your function to work both when `char*` is explicitly specified and via deduction when it is not, you should write a specialized template version instead of a nontemplate, overloaded version.

Like template class method definitions, function template definitions (not just the prototypes) must be available to all source files that use them. Thus, you should put the definitions in header files if more than one source file uses them.

Function Template Overloading and Specialization Together

It's possible to write both a specialized `Find()` template for `char*`s and a stand-alone `Find()` function for `char*`s. The compiler always prefers the nontemplate function to a templatized version. However, if you specify the template instantiation explicitly, the compiler will be forced to use the template version:

```
char* word = "two";
char* arr[4] = {"one", "two", "three", "four"};
int res;

res = Find<char *>(word, arr, 4); // Calls the char* specialization of the
                                  // template
res = Find(word, arr, 4); // Calls the Find nontemplate function.
```

Friend Function Templates of Class Templates

Function templates are useful when you want to overload operators in a class template. For example, you might want to overload the insertion operator for the `Grid` class template to stream a grid.

> *If you are unfamiliar with the mechanics for overloading **operator<<**, consult Chapter 16 for details.*

As discussed in Chapter 16, you can't make `operator<<` a member of the `Grid` class: it must be a stand-alone function template. The definition, which should go directly in `Grid.h`, looks like this:

```
template <typename T>
ostream& operator<<(ostream& ostr, const Grid<T>& grid)
{
    for (int i = 0; i < grid.mHeight; i++) {
        for (int j = 0; j < grid.mWidth; j++) {
            // Add a tab between each element of a row.
            ostr << grid.mCells[j][i] << "\t";
        }
        ostr << std::endl; // Add a newline between each row.
    }
    return (ostr);
}
```

This function template will work on any `Grid`, as long as there is an insertion operator for the elements of the grid. The only problem is that `operator<<` accesses `protected` members of the `Grid` class. Therefore, it must be a `friend` of the `Grid` class. However, both the `Grid` class and the `operator<<` are templates. What you really want is for each instantiation of `operator<<` for a particular type `T` to be a friend of the `Grid` template instantiation for that type. The syntax looks like this:

```
//Grid.h
#include <iostream>
using std::ostream;

// Forward declare Grid template.
template <typename T> class Grid;

// Prototype for templatized operator<<.
template<typename T>
ostream& operator<<(ostream& ostr, const Grid<T>& grid);
```

```
template <typename T>
class Grid
{
    public:
        // Omitted for brevity
        friend ostream& operator<< <T>(ostream& ostr, const Grid<T>& grid);
        // Omitted for brevity
};
```

This friend declaration is tricky: you're saying that, for an instance of the template with type T, the T instantiation of operator<< is a friend. In other words, there is a one-to-one mapping of friends between the class instantiations and the function instantiations. Note particularly the explicit template specification <T> on operator<< (the space after operator<< is optional). This syntax tells the compiler that operator<< is itself a template. Some compilers fail to support this syntax, but it's legal C++, and works on most new compilers.

Advanced Templates

The first half of this chapter covered the most widely used features of class and function templates. If you are interested in only a basic knowledge of templates so that you can use the STL or perhaps write your own simple classes, you can stop here. However, if templates interest you and you want to uncover their full power, read the second half of this chapter to learn about some of the more obscure, but fascinating, details.

More about Template Parameters

There are actually three kinds of template parameters: type, nontype and template template (no, you're not seeing double: that really is the name!) You've seen examples of type and nontype parameters above, but not template template parameters yet. There are also some tricky aspects to both template and nontype parameters that were not covered above.

More about Template Type Parameters

Type parameters to templates are the main purpose of templates. You can declare as many type parameters as you want. For example, you could add to the grid template a second type parameter specifying another templatized class container on which to build the grid. Recall from Chapter 4 that the standard template library defines several templatized container classes, including vector and deque. In your original grid class you might want to have an array of vectors or an array of deques instead of just an array of arrays. With another template type parameter, you can allow the user to specify whether she wants the underlying container to be a vector or a deque. Here is the class definition with the additional template parameter:

```
template <typename T, typename Container>
class Grid
{
    public:
        Grid(int inWidth = kDefaultWidth, int inHeight = kDefaultHeight);
        Grid(const Grid<T, Container>& src);
        ~Grid();
```

```
        Grid<T, Container>& operator=(const Grid<T, Container>& rhs);
        void setElementAt(int x, int y, const T& inElem);
        T& getElementAt(int x, int y);
        const T& getElementAt(int x, int y) const;
        int getHeight() const { return mHeight; }
        int getWidth() const { return mWidth; }
        static const int kDefaultWidth = 10;
        static const int kDefaultHeight = 10;
    protected:
        void copyFrom(const Grid<T, Container>& src);
        Container* mCells;
        int mWidth, mHeight;
};
```

This template now has two parameters: T and Container. Thus, wherever you previously referred to Grid<T> you must refer to Grid<T, Container> to specify both template parameters. The only other change is that mCells is now a pointer to a dynamically allocated array of Containers instead of a pointer to a dynamically allocated two-dimensional array of T elements.

Here is the constructor definition. It assumes that the Container type has a resize() method. If you try to instantiate this template by specifying a type that has no resize() method, the compiler will generate an error, as described below.

```
template <typename T, typename Container>
Grid<T, Container>::Grid(int inWidth, int inHeight) :
    mWidth(inWidth), mHeight(inHeight)
{
    // Dynamically allocate the array of mWidth containers
    mCells = new Container[mWidth];
    for (int i = 0; i < mWidth; i++) {
        // Resize each container so that it can hold mHeight elements.
        mCells[i].resize(mHeight);
    }
}
```

Here is the destructor definition. There's only one call to new in the constructor, so only one call to delete in the destructor.

```
template <typename T, typename Container>
Grid<T, Container>::~Grid()
{
    delete [] mCells;
}
```

The code in copyFrom() assumes that you can access elements in the container using array [] notation. Chapter 16 explains how to overload the [] operator to implement this feature in your own container classes, but for now, it's enough to know that the vector and deque from the STL both support this syntax.

```
template <typename T, typename Container>
void Grid<T, Container>::copyFrom(const Grid<T, Container>& src)
{
    int i, j;
    mWidth = src.mWidth;
    mHeight = src.mHeight;
```

```
        mCells = new Container[mWidth];
        for (i = 0; i < mWidth; i++) {
            // Resize each element, as in the constructor.
            mCells[i].resize(mHeight);
        }
        for (i = 0; i < mWidth; i++) {
            for (j = 0; j < mHeight; j++) {
                mCells[i][j] = src.mCells[i][j];
            }
        }
    }
```

Here are the implementations of the remaining methods.

```
template <typename T, typename Container>
Grid<T, Container>::Grid(const Grid<T, Container>& src)
{
    copyFrom(src);
}
```

```
template <typename T, typename Container>
Grid<T, Container>& Grid<T, Container>::operator=(const Grid<T, Container>& rhs)
{
    // Check for self-assignment.
    if (this == &rhs) {
        return (*this);
    }
    // Free the old memory.
    delete [] mCells;

    // Copy the new memory.
    copyFrom(rhs);

    return (*this);
}
```

```
template <typename T, typename Container>
void Grid<T, Container>::setElementAt(int x, int y, const T& inElem)
{
    mCells[x][y] = inElem;
}
```

```
template <typename T, typename Container>
T& Grid<T, Container>::getElementAt(int x, int y)
{
    return (mCells[x][y]);
}
```

```
template <typename T, typename Container>
const T& Grid<T, Container>::getElementAt(int x, int y) const
{
    return (mCells[x][y]);
}
```

Now you can instantiate and use grid objects like this:

```
Grid<int, vector<int> > myIntGrid;
Grid<int, deque<int> > myIntGrid2;

myIntGrid.setElementAt(3, 4, 5);
cout << myIntGrid.getElementAt(3, 4);

Grid<int, vector<int> > grid2(myIntGrid);
grid2 = myIntGrid;
```

The use of the word `Container` for the parameter name doesn't mean that the type really must be a container. You could try to instantiate the `Grid` class with an `int` instead:

```
Grid<int, int> test; // WILL NOT COMPILE
```

This line will not compile, but it might not give you the error you expect. It won't complain that the second type argument is an `int` instead of a container. Instead it will tell you that `left of '.resize'` `must have class/struct/union type`. That's because the compiler attempts to generate a `Grid` class with `int` as the `Container`. Everything works fine until it tries to compile this line:

```
mCells[i].resize(mHeight);
```

At that point, the compiler realizes that `mCells[i]` is an `int`, so you can't call the `resize()` method on it!

This approach may seem convoluted and useless to you. However, it arises in the standard template library. The `stack`, `queue`, and `priority_queue` class templates all take a template type parameter specifying the underlying container, which can be a `vector`, `deque`, or `list`.

Default Values for Template Type Parameters

You can give template parameters default values. For example, you might want to say that the default container for your `Grid` is a `vector`. The template class definition would look like this:

```
#include <vector>
using std::vector;

template <typename T, typename Container = vector<T> >
class Grid
{
    public:
        // Everything else is the same as before.
};
```

You can use the type `T` from the first template parameter as the argument to the `vector` template in the default value for the second template parameter. Note also that you must leave a space between the two closing angle brackets to avoid the parsing problem discussed earlier in the chapter.

C++ syntax requires that you do not repeat the default value in the template header line for method definitions.

With this default parameter, clients can now instantiate a grid with or without specifying an underlying container:

```
Grid<int, vector<int> > myIntGrid;
Grid<int> myIntGrid2;
```

Introducing Template Template Parameters

There is one problem with the `Container` parameter in the previous section. When you instantiate the class template, you write something like this:

```
Grid<int, vector<int> > myIntGrid;
```

Note the repetition of the `int` type. You must specify that it's the element type both of the `Grid` and of the `vector`. What if you wrote this instead?

```
Grid<int, vector<SpreadsheetCell> > myIntGrid;
```

That wouldn't work very well! It would be nice to be able to write the following, so that you couldn't make that mistake:

```
Grid<int, vector> myIntGrid;
```

The `Grid` class should be able to figure out that it wants a `vector` of `int`s. The compiler won't allow you to pass that argument to a normal type parameter, though, because `vector` by itself is not a type, but a template.

If you want to take a template as a template parameter, you must use a special kind of parameter called a *template template parameter*. The syntax is crazy, and some compilers don't yet support it. However, if you're still interested, read on.

Specifying a template template parameter is sort of like specifying a function pointer parameter in a normal function. Function pointer types include the return type and parameter types of a function. Similarly, when you specify a template template parameter, the full specification of the template template parameter includes the parameters to that template.

Containers in the STL have a template parameter list that looks something like this:

```
template <typename E, typename Allocator = allocator<E> >
class vector
{
    // Vector definition
};
```

The `E` parameter is simply the element type. Don't worry about the `Allocator` for now — it's covered in Chapter 21.

Given the above template specification, here is the template class definition for the `Grid` class that takes a container template as its second template parameter:

```
template <typename T, template <typename E, typename Allocator = allocator<E> >
    class Container = vector >
class Grid
{
    public:
        // Omitted code that is the same as before
        Container<T>* mCells;
        // Omitted code that is the same as before
};
```

What is going on here? The first template parameter is the same as before: the element type `T`. The second template parameter is now a template itself for a container such as `vector` or `deque`. As you saw earlier, this "template type" must take two parameters: an element type `E` and an allocator `Allocator`. Note the repetition of the word `class` after the nested template parameter list. The name of this parameter in the `Grid` template is `Container` (as before). The default value is now `vector`, instead of `vector<T>`, because the `Container` is a template instead of an actual type.

The syntax rule for a template template parameter more generically is this:

```
template <other params, ..., template <TemplateTypeParams> class ParameterName,
    other params, ...>
```

Now that you've suffered through the above syntax to declare the template, the rest is easy. Instead of using `Container` by itself in the code, you must specify `Container<T>` as the container type you use. For example, the constructor now looks like this (you don't repeat the default template template parameter argument in the template specification for the method definition):

```
template <typename T, template <typename E, typename Allocator = allocator<E> >
    class Container>
Grid<T, Container>::Grid(int inWidth, int inHeight) :
    mWidth(inWidth), mHeight(inHeight)
{
    mCells = new Container<T>[mWidth];
    for (int i = 0; i < mWidth; i++) {
        mCells[i].resize(mHeight);
    }
}
```

After implementing all the methods, you can use the template like this:

```
Grid<int, vector> myGrid;

myGrid.setElementAt(1, 2, 3);
myGrid.getElementAt(1,2);
Grid<int, vector> myGrid2(myGrid);
```

If you haven't skipped this section entirely, you're surely thinking at this point that C++ deserves every criticism that's ever been thrown at it. Try not to bog down in the syntax here, and keep the main concept in mind: you can pass templates as parameters to other templates.

More about Nontype Template Parameters

You might want to allow the user to specify an empty(not in the literal sense) element that is used to initialize each cell in the grid. Here is a perfectly reasonable approach to implement this goal:

```cpp
template <typename T, const T EMPTY>
class Grid
{
    public:
        Grid(int inWidth = kDefaultWidth, int inHeight = kDefaultHeight);
        Grid(const Grid<T, EMPTY>& src);
        ~Grid();
        Grid<T, EMPTY>& operator=(const Grid<T, EMPTY>& rhs);

        // Omitted for brevity

    protected:
        void copyFrom(const Grid<T, EMPTY>& src);
        T** mCells;
        int mWidth, mHeight;
};
```

This definition is legal. You can use the type T from the first parameter as the type for the second parameter and nontype parameters can be const just like function parameters. You can use this initial value for T to initialize each cell in the grid:

```cpp
template <typename T, const T EMPTY>
Grid<T, EMPTY>::Grid(int inWidth, int inHeight) :
    mWidth(inWidth), mHeight(inHeight)
{
    mCells = new T* [mWidth];
    for (int i = 0; i < mWidth; i++) {
        mCells[i] = new T[mHeight];
        for (int j = 0; j < mHeight; j++) {
            mCells[i][j] = EMPTY;
        }
    }
}
```

The other method definitions stay the same, except that you must add the second type parameter to the template lines, and all the instances of Grid<T> become Grid<T, EMPTY>. After making those changes, you can then instantiate an int Grid with an initial value for all the elements:

```cpp
Grid<int, 0> myIntGrid;
Grid<int, 10> myIntGrid2;
```

The initial value can be any integer you want. However, suppose that you try to create a SpreasheetCell Grid:

```cpp
SpreadsheetCell emptyCell;
Grid<SpreadsheetCell, emptyCell> mySpreadsheet; // WILL NOT COMPILE
```

That line leads to a compiler error because you cannot pass objects as arguments to nontype parameters.

> **Nontype parameters cannot be objects, or even doubles or floats. They are restricted only to ints, enums, pointers, and references.**

This example illustrates one of the vagaries of template classes: they can work correctly on one type but fail to compile for another type.

Reference and Pointer Nontype Template Parameters

A more comprehensive way of allowing the user to specify an initial empty element for the grid uses a reference to a T as the nontype template parameter. Here is the new class definition:

```
template <typename T, const T& EMPTY>
class Grid
{
    // Everything else is the same as the previous example, except the
    // template lines in the method definitions specify const T& EMPTY
    // instead of const T EMPTY.
};
```

Now you can instantiate this template class for any type. However, the reference you pass as the second template argument must refer to a global variable with *external linkage.* External linkage can be thought of as the opposite of *static* linkage, and just means that the variable is available in source files outside the one in which it is defined. See Chapter 12 for more details. For now, it suffices to know that you can declare that a variable has external linkage with the extern keyword:

```
extern const int x = 0;
```

Note that this line occurs outside of any function or method body. Here is a full program that declares int and SpreadsheetCell grids with initialization parameters:

```
#include "GridRefNonType.h"
#include "SpreadsheetCell.h"

extern const int emptyInt = 0;
extern const SpreadsheetCell emptyCell(0);

int main(int argc, char** argv)
{
    Grid<int, emptyInt> myIntGrid;
    Grid<SpreadsheetCell, emptyCell> mySpreadsheet;

    Grid<int, emptyInt> myIntGrid2(myIntGrid);

    return (0);
}
```

> **Reference and pointer template arguments must refer to global variables that are available from all translation units. The technical term for these types of variables is data with *external linkage*.**

Using Zero-Initialization of Template Types

Neither of the options presented so far for providing an initial empty value for the cells is very attractive. Instead, you may simply want to initialize each cell to a reasonable default value that you choose (instead of allowing the user to specify). Of course, the immediate question is: what's a reasonable value for any possible type? For objects, a reasonable value is an object created with the default constructor. In fact, that's exactly what you're already getting when you create an array of objects. However, for simple data types like int and double, and for pointers, a reasonable initial value is 0. Therefore, what you really want to be able to do is assign 0 to nonobjects and use the default constructor on objects. You actually saw the syntax for this behavior in the section on "Method Templates with Nontype Parameters." Here is the implementation of the Grid template constructor using the zero-initialization syntax:

```
template <typename T>
Grid<T>::Grid(int inWidth, int inHeight) : mWidth(inWidth), mHeight(inHeight)
{
    mCells = new T* [mWidth];
    for (int i = 0; i < mWidth; i++) {
        mCells[i] = new T[mHeight];
        for (int j = 0; j < mHeight; j++) {
            mCells[i][j] = T();
        }
    }
}
```

Given this ability, you can revert to the original Grid class (without an EMPTY nontype parameter) and just initialize each cell element to its zero-initialized "reasonable value."

Template Class Partial Specialization

The char* class specialization shown in the first part of this chapter is called *full class template specialization* because it specializes the Grid template for every template parameter. There are no template parameters left in the specialization. That's not the only way you can specialize a class; you can also write a *partial class specialization*, in which you specialize some template parameters but not others. For example, recall the basic version of the Grid template with width and height nontype parameters:

```
template <typename T, int WIDTH, int HEIGHT>
class Grid
{
    public:
        void setElementAt(int x, int y, const T& inElem);
        T& getElementAt(int x, int y);
        const T& getElementAt(int x, int y) const;
        int getHeight() const { return HEIGHT; }
        int getWidth() const { return WIDTH; }

    protected:
        T mCells[WIDTH][HEIGHT];
};
```

You could specialize this template class for `char*` C-style strings like this:

```
#include "Grid.h" // The file containing the Grid template definition shown above
#include <cstdlib>
#include <cstring>
using namespace std;

template <int WIDTH, int HEIGHT>
class Grid<char*, WIDTH, HEIGHT>
{
    public:
        Grid();
        Grid(const Grid<char*, WIDTH, HEIGHT>& src);
        ~Grid();

        Grid<char*, WIDTH, HEIGHT>& Grid<char*, WIDTH, HEIGHT>::operator=(
            const Grid<char*, WIDTH, HEIGHT>& rhs);
        void setElementAt(int x, int y, const char* inElem);
        char* getElementAt(int x, int y) const;
        int getHeight() const { return HEIGHT; }
        int getWidth() const { return WIDTH; }
    protected:
        void copyFrom(const Grid<char*, WIDTH, HEIGHT>& src);
        char* mCells[WIDTH][HEIGHT];
};
```

In this case, you are not specializing all the template parameters. Therefore, your template line looks like this:

```
template <int WIDTH, int HEIGHT>
class Grid<char*, WIDTH, HEIGHT>
```

Note that the template has only two parameters: `WIDTH` and `HEIGHT`. However, you're writing a `Grid` class for three arguments: `T`, `WIDTH`, and `HEIGHT`. Thus, your template parameter list contains two parameters, and the explicit `Grid<char *, WIDTH, HEIGHT>` contains three arguments. When you instantiate the template, you must still specify three parameters. You can't instantiate the template with only height and width:

```
Grid<int, 2, 2> myIntGrid; // Uses the original Grid
Grid<char*, 2, 2> myStringGrid; // Uses the partial specialization for char *s
Grid<2, 3> test; // DOES NOT COMPILE! No type specified.
```

Yes, the syntax is confusing. And it gets worse. In partial specializations, unlike in full specializations, you include the template line in front of every method definition:

```
template <int WIDTH, int HEIGHT>
Grid<char*, WIDTH, HEIGHT>::Grid()
{
    for (int i = 0; i < WIDTH; i++) {
        for (int j = 0; j < HEIGHT; j++) {
            // Initialize each element to NULL.
            mCells[i][j] = NULL;
        }
    }
}
```

You need this template line with two parameters to show that this method is parameterized on those two parameters. Note that wherever you refer to the full class name, you must use `Grid<char*, WIDTH, HEIGHT>`.

The rest of the method definitions follow:

```
template <int WIDTH, int HEIGHT>
Grid<char*, WIDTH, HEIGHT>::Grid(const Grid<char*, WIDTH, HEIGHT>& src)
{
    copyFrom(src);
}

template <int WIDTH, int HEIGHT>
Grid<char*, WIDTH, HEIGHT>::~Grid()
{
    for (int i = 0; i < WIDTH; i++) {
        for (int j = 0; j < HEIGHT; j++) {
            delete [] mCells[i][j];
        }
    }
}

template <int WIDTH, int HEIGHT>
void Grid<char*, WIDTH, HEIGHT>::copyFrom(
    const Grid<char*, WIDTH, HEIGHT>& src)
{
    int i, j;

    for (i = 0; i < WIDTH; i++) {
        for (j = 0; j < HEIGHT; j++) {
            if (src.mCells[i][j] == NULL) {
                mCells[i][j] = NULL;
            } else {
                mCells[i][j] = new char[strlen(src.mCells[i][j]) + 1];
                strcpy(mCells[i][j], src.mCells[i][j]);
            }
        }
    }
}

template <int WIDTH, int HEIGHT>
Grid<char*, WIDTH, HEIGHT>& Grid<char*, WIDTH, HEIGHT>::operator=(
    const Grid<char*, WIDTH, HEIGHT>& rhs)
{
    int i, j;

    // Check for self-assignment.
    if (this == &rhs) {
        return (*this);
    }
    // Free the old memory.
    for (i = 0; i < WIDTH; i++) {
        for (j = 0; j < HEIGHT; j++) {
            delete [] mCells[i][j];
        }
    }
```

```
        // Copy the new memory.
        copyFrom(rhs);
        return (*this);
}

template <int WIDTH, int HEIGHT>
void Grid<char*, WIDTH, HEIGHT>::setElementAt(
        int x, int y, const char* inElem)
{
        delete[] mCells[x][y];
        if (inElem == NULL) {
            mCells[x][y] = NULL;
        } else {
            mCells[x][y] = new char[strlen(inElem) + 1];
            strcpy(mCells[x][y], inElem);
        }
}

template <int WIDTH, int HEIGHT>
char* Grid<char*, WIDTH, HEIGHT>::getElementAt(int x, int y) const
{
        if (mCells[x][y] == NULL) {
            return (NULL);
        }
        char* ret = new char[strlen(mCells[x][y]) + 1];
        strcpy(ret, mCells[x][y]);

        return (ret);
}
```

Another Form of Partial Specialization

The previous example does not show the true power of partial specialization. You can write specialized implementations for a subset of possible types without specializing individual types. For example, you can write a specialization of the Grid class for all pointer types. This specialization might perform deep copies of objects to which pointers point instead of storing shallow copies of the pointers in the grid.

Here is the class definition, assuming that you're specializing the initial version of the Grid with only one parameter:

```
#include "Grid.h"

template <typename T>
class Grid<T*>
{
    public:
        Grid(int inWidth = kDefaultWidth, int inHeight = kDefaultHeight);
        Grid(const Grid<T*>& src);
        ~Grid();
        Grid<T*>& operator=(const Grid<T*>& rhs);

        void setElementAt(int x, int y, const T* inElem);
        T* getElementAt(int x, int y) const;
```

```
        int getHeight() const { return mHeight; }
        int getWidth() const { return mWidth; }
        static const int kDefaultWidth = 10;
        static const int kDefaultHeight = 10;
    protected:
        void copyFrom(const Grid<T*>& src);
        T** mCells;
        int mWidth, mHeight;
};
```

As usual, these two lines are the crux of the matter:

```
template <typename T>
class Grid<T*>
```

The syntax says that this class is a specialization of the Grid template for all pointer types. At least that's what it's telling the compiler. What it's telling you and me is that the C++ standards committee should have come up with a better syntax! Unless you've been working with it for a long time, it's quite jarring.

You are providing the implementation only in cases where T is a pointer type. Note that if you instantiate a grid like this: Grid<int*> myIntGrid, then T will actually be int, not int *. That's a bit unintuitive, but unfortunately, the way it works. Here is a code example:

```
Grid<int*> psGrid(2, 2); // Uses the partial specialization for pointer types

int x = 3, y = 4;
psGrid.setElementAt(0, 0, &x);
psGrid.setElementAt(0, 1, &y);
psGrid.setElementAt(1, 0, &y);
psGrid.setElementAt(1, 1, &x);

Grid<int> myIntGrid; // Uses the nonspecialized grid
```

At this point, you're probably wondering whether this really works. We sympathize with your skepticism. One of the authors was so surprised by this syntax when he first read about it that he didn't believe it actually worked until he was able to try it out. If you don't believe us, try it out yourself! Here are the method implementations. Pay close attention to the template line syntax before each method.

```
template <typename T>
const int Grid<T*>::kDefaultWidth;

template <typename T>
const int Grid<T*>::kDefaultHeight;

template <typename T>
Grid<T*>::Grid(int inWidth, int inHeight) : mWidth(inWidth), mHeight(inHeight)
{
    mCells = new T* [mWidth];
    for (int i = 0; i < mWidth; i++) {
        mCells[i] = new T[mHeight];
    }
}
```

```
template <typename T>
Grid<T*>::Grid(const Grid<T*>& src)
{
    copyFrom(src);
}

template <typename T>
Grid<T*>::~Grid()
{
    // Free the old memory.
    for (int i = 0; i < mWidth; i++) {
        delete [] mCells[i];
    }
    delete [] mCells;
}

template <typename T>
void Grid<T*>::copyFrom(const Grid<T*>& src)
{
    int i, j;
    mWidth = src.mWidth;
    mHeight = src.mHeight;

    mCells = new T* [mWidth];
    for (i = 0; i < mWidth; i++) {
        mCells[i] = new T[mHeight];
    }

    for (i = 0; i < mWidth; i++) {
        for (j = 0; j < mHeight; j++) {
            mCells[i][j] = src.mCells[i][j];
        }
    }
}

template <typename T>
Grid<T*>& Grid<T*>::operator=(const Grid<T*>& rhs)
{
    // Check for self-assignment.
    if (this == &rhs) {
        return (*this);
    }
    // Free the old memory.
    for (int i = 0; i < mWidth; i++) {
        delete [] mCells[i];
    }
    delete [] mCells;

    // Copy the new memory.
    copyFrom(rhs);
    return (*this);
}
```

```
template <typename T>
void Grid<T*>::setElementAt(int x, int y, const T* inElem)
{
    mCells[x][y] = *inElem;
}

template <typename T>
T* Grid<T*>::getElementAt(int x, int y) const
{
    T* newElem = new T(mCells[x][y]);
    return (newElem);
}
```

Emulating Function Partial Specialization with Overloading

The C++ standard does not permit partial template specialization of functions. Instead, you can over-load the function with another template. The difference is subtle. Suppose that you want to write a specialization of the Find() function, presented earlier in this chapter, that dereferences the pointers to use operator== directly on the objects pointed to. Following the syntax for class template partical specialization, you might be tempted to write this:

```
template <typename T>
int Find<T*>(T*& value, T** arr, int size)
{
    for (int i = 0; i < size; i++) {
        if (*arr[i] == *value) {
            // Found it; return the index
            return (i);
        }
    }
    // Failed to Find it; return -1
    return (-1);
}
```

However, that syntax declares a partial specialization of the function template, which the C++ standard does not allow (although some compilers support it). The standard way to implement the behavior you want is to write a new template for Find():

```
template <typename T>
int Find(T*& value, T** arr, int size)
{
    for (int i = 0; i < size; i++) {
        if (*arr[i] == *value) {
            // Found it; return the index
            return (i);
        }
    }
    // Failed to Find it; return -1
    return (-1);
}
```

The difference might seem trivial and academic, but it makes the difference between portable, standard, code and code that probably won't compile.

More on Deduction

You can define in one program the original Find() template, the overloaded Find() for partial specialization on pointer types, the complete specialization for char*s, and the overloaded Find() just for char*s. The compiler will choose the appropriate version to call based on its deduction rules.

> **The compiler always chooses the "most specific" version of the function, with non-template versions being preferred over template versions.**

The following code calls the specified versions of Find():

```
char* word = "two";
char* arr[4] = {"one", "two", "three", "four"};
int res;

int x = 3, intArr[4] = {1, 2, 3, 4};
double d1 = 5.6, dArr[4] = {1.2, 3.4, 5.7, 7.5};

res = Find(x, intArr, 4); // Calls Find<int> by deduction
res = Find<int>(x, intArr, 4); // Call Find<int> explicitly

res = Find(d1, dArr, 4); // Call Find<double> by deduction
res = Find<double>(d1, dArr, 4); // Calls Find<double> explicitly

res = Find<char *>(word, arr, 4); // Calls template specialization for char*s
res = Find(word, arr, 4); // Calls the overloaded Find for char *s

int *px = &x, *pArr[2] = {&x, &x};
res = Find(px, pArr, 2); // Calls the overloaded Find for pointers

SpreadsheetCell c1(10), c2[2] = {SpreadsheetCell(4), SpreadsheetCell(10)};

res = Find(c1, c2, 2); // Calls Find<SpreadsheetCell> by deduction
res = Find<SpreadsheetCell>(c1, c2, 2); // Calls Find<SpreadsheetCell>
                                        // explicitly
SpreadsheetCell *pc1 = &c1;
SpreadsheetCell *psa[2] = {&c1, &c1};

res = Find(pc1, psa, 2); // Calls the overloaded Find for pointers
```

Template Recursion

Templates in C++ provide capabilities that go far beyond the simple classes and functions you have seen so far in this chapter. One of these capabilities is *template recursion*. This section first provides a motivation for template recursion, and then shows how to implement it.

*This section employs some operator overloading features discussed in Chapter 16. If you are unfamiliar with the syntax for overloading **operator[]**, consult that chapter before continuing.*

An N-Dimensional Grid: First Attempt

The `Grid` template example earlier in this chapter supports only two dimensions, which limits its usefulness. What if you wanted to write a 3-D Tic-Tac-Toe game or write a math program with four-dimensional matrices? You could, of course, write a template or nontemplate class for each of those dimensions. However, that would repeat a lot of code. Another approach is to write only a single-dimensional grid. Then, you could create a `Grid` of any dimension by instantiating the `Grid` with another `Grid` as its element type. This `Grid` element type could itself be instantiated with a `Grid` as its element type, and so on. Here is the implementation of the `OneDGrid` class template. It's simply a one-dimensional version of the `Grid` template from the earlier examples, with the addition of a `resize()` method, and the substitution of `operator[]` for `setElementAt()` and `getElementAt()`. Production code, of course, would do bounds-checking on the array access, and would throw an exception if something were amiss.

```
template <typename T>
class OneDGrid
{
    public:
        OneDGrid(int inSize = kDefaultSize);
        OneDGrid(const OneDGrid<T>& src);
        ~OneDGrid();

        OneDGrid<T> &operator=(const OneDGrid<T>& rhs);
        void resize(int newSize);

        T& operator[](int x);
        const T& operator[](int x) const;
        int getSize() const { return mSize; }
        static const int kDefaultSize = 10;
    protected:
        void copyFrom(const OneDGrid<T>& src);
        T* mElems;
        int mSize;
};

template <typename T>
const int OneDGrid<T>::kDefaultSize;

template <typename T>
OneDGrid<T>::OneDGrid(int inSize) : mSize(inSize)
{
    mElems = new T[mSize];
}

template <typename T>
OneDGrid<T>::OneDGrid(const OneDGrid<T>& src)
{
    copyFrom(src);
}
```

```
template <typename T>
OneDGrid<T>::~OneDGrid()
{
    delete [] mElems;
}

template <typename T>
void OneDGrid<T>::copyFrom(const OneDGrid<T>& src)
{
    mSize = src.mSize;
    mElems = new T[mSize];

    for (int i = 0; i < mSize; i++) {
        mElems[i] = src.mElems[i];
    }
}

template <typename T>
OneDGrid<T>& OneDGrid<T>::operator=(const OneDGrid<T>& rhs)
{
    // Check for self-assignment.
    if (this == &rhs) {
        return (*this);
    }

    // Free the old memory.
    delete [] mElems;

    // Copy the new memory.
    copyFrom(rhs);
    return (*this);
}

template <typename T>
void OneDGrid<T>::resize(int newSize)
{
    T* newElems = new T[newSize]; // Allocate the new array of the new size

    // Handle the new size being smaller or bigger than the old size.
    for (int i = 0; i < newSize && i < mSize; i++) {
        // Copy the elements from the old array to the new one.
        newElems[i] = mElems[i];
    }
    mSize = newSize; // Store the new size.
    delete [] mElems; // Free the memory for the old array.
    mElems = newElems; // Store the pointer to the new array.
}

template <typename T>
T& OneDGrid<T>::operator[](int x)
{
    return (mElems[x]);
}
```

```
template <typename T>
const T& OneDGrid<T>::operator[](int x) const
{
    return (mElems[x]);
}
```

With this implementation of the OneDGrid, you can create multidimensional grids like this:

```
OneDGrid<int> singleDGrid;
OneDGrid<OneDGrid<int> > twoDGrid;
OneDGrid<OneDGrid<OneDGrid<int> > > threeDGrid;

singleDGrid[3] = 5;
twoDGrid[3][3] = 5;
threeDGrid[3][3][3] = 5;
```

This code works fine, but the declarations are messy. We can do better.

A Real N-Dimensional Grid

You can use template recursion to write a "real" N-dimensional grid because dimensionality of grids is essentially recursive. You can see that in this declaration:

```
OneDGrid<OneDGrid<OneDGrid<int> > > threeDGrid;
```

You can think of each nesting OneDGrid as a recursive step, with the OneDGrid of int as the base case. In other words, a three-dimensional grid is a single-dimensional grid of single-dimensional grids of single-dimensional grids of ints. Instead of requiring the user to do this recursion, you can write a template class that does it for you. Then, you can create N-dimensional grids like this:

```
NDGrid<int, 1> singleDGrid;
NDGrid<int, 2> twoDGrid;
NDGrid<int, 3> threeDGrid;
```

The NDGrid template class takes a type for its element and an integer specifying its "dimensionality." The key insight here is that the element type of the NDGrid is not the element type specified in the template parameter list, but is in fact another NDGrid of dimensionality one less than the current. In other words, a three-dimensional grid is an array of two-dimensional grids; the two-dimensional grids are each arrays of one-dimensional grids.

With recursion, you need a base case. You can write a partial specialization of the NDGrid for dimensionality of 1, in which the element type is not another NDGrid, but is in fact the element type specified by the template parameter.

Here is the general NDGrid template definition, with highlights showing where it differs from the OneDGrid shown above:

```
template <typename T, int N>
class NDGrid
{
    public:
```

```
                NDGrid();
                NDGrid(int inSize);
                NDGrid(const NDGrid<T, N>& src);
                ~NDGrid();

                NDGrid<T, N>& operator=(const NDGrid<T, N>& rhs);
                void resize(int newSize);
                NDGrid<T, N-1>& operator[](int x);
                const NDGrid<T, N-1>& operator[](int x) const;
                int getSize() const { return mSize; }
                static const int kDefaultSize = 10;
        protected:
                void copyFrom(const NDGrid<T, N>& src);
                NDGrid<T, N-1>* mElems;
                int mSize;
    };
```

Note that `mElems` is a pointer to an `NDGrid<T, N-1>`: this is the recursive step. Also, `operator[]` returns a reference to the element type, which is again `NDGrid<T, N-1>`, not `T`.

Here is the template definition for the base case:

```
    template <typename T>
    class NDGrid<T, 1>
    {
        public:
            NDGrid(int inSize = kDefaultSize);
            NDGrid(const NDGrid<T, 1>& src);
            ~NDGrid();
            NDGrid<T, 1>& operator=(const NDGrid<T, 1>& rhs);
            void resize(int newSize);
            T& operator[](int x);
            const T& operator[](int x) const;
            int getSize() const { return mSize; }
            static const int kDefaultSize = 10;
        protected:
            void copyFrom(const NDGrid<T, 1>& src);
            T* mElems;
            int mSize;
    };
```

Here the recursion ends: the element type is `T`, not another template instantiation.

The trickiest aspect of the implementations, other than the template recursion itself, is appropriately sizing each dimension of the array. This implementation creates the N-dimensional array with every dimension of equal size. It's significantly more difficult to specify a separate size for each dimension. However, even with this simplification, there is still a problem: the user should have the ability to create the array with a specified size, such as 20 or 50. Thus, one constructor takes an integer size parameter. However, when you dynamically allocate the nested array of grids, you cannot pass this size value on to the grids because arrays create objects using their default constructor. Thus, you must explicitly call `resize()` on each grid element of the array. That code follows, with the default and one-argument constructors separated for clarity.

The base case doesn't need to resize its elements because the elements are Ts, not grids.

Here are the implementations of the main NDGrid template, with highlights showing the differences from the OneDGrid:

```
template <typename T, int N>
const int NDGrid<T, N>::kDefaultSize;

template <typename T, int N>
NDGrid<T, N>::NDGrid(int inSize) : mSize(inSize)
{
    mElems = new NDGrid<T, N-1>[mSize];
    // Allocating the array above calls the 0-argument
    // constructor for the NDGrid<T, N-1>, which constructs
    // it with the default size. Thus, we must explicitly call
    // resize() on each of the elements.
    for (int i = 0; i < mSize; i++) {
        mElems[i].resize(inSize);
    }
}

template <typename T, int N>
NDGrid<T, N>::NDGrid() : mSize(kDefaultSize)
{
    mElems = new NDGrid<T, N-1>[mSize];
}

template <typename T, int N>
NDGrid<T, N>::NDGrid(const NDGrid<T, N>& src)
{
    copyFrom(src);
}

template <typename T, int N>
NDGrid<T, N>::~NDGrid()
{
    delete [] mElems;
}

template <typename T, int N>
void NDGrid<T, N>::copyFrom(const NDGrid<T, N>& src)
{
    mSize = src.mSize;
    mElems = new NDGrid<T, N-1>[mSize];
    for (int i = 0; i < mSize; i++) {
        mElems[i] = src.mElems[i];
    }
}

template <typename T, int N>
NDGrid<T, N>& NDGrid<T, N>::operator=(const NDGrid<T, N>& rhs)
```

```
    {
        // Check for self-assignment.
        if (this == &rhs) {
            return (*this);
        }
        // Free the old memory.
        delete [] mElems;
        // Copy the new memory.
        copyFrom(rhs);
        return (*this);
    }
```

```
template <typename T, int N>
void NDGrid<T, N>::resize(int newSize)
{
    // Allocate the new array with the new size.
    NDGrid<T, N - 1>* newElems = new NDGrid<T, N - 1>[newSize];
    // Copy all the elements, handling the cases where newSize is
    // larger than mSize and smaller than mSize.
    for (int i = 0; i < newSize && i < mSize; i++) {
        newElems[i] = mElems[i];
        // Resize the nested Grid elements recursively.
        newElems[i].resize(newSize);
    }
    // Store the new size and pointer to the new array.
    // Free the memory for the old array first.
    mSize = newSize;
    delete [] mElems;
    mElems = newElems;
}
```

```
template <typename T, int N>
NDGrid<T, N-1>& NDGrid<T, N>::operator[](int x)
{
    return (mElems[x]);
}
```

```
template <typename T, int N>
const NDGrid<T, N-1>& NDGrid<T, N>::operator[](int x) const
{
    return (mElems[x]);
}
```

Here are the implementations of the partial specialization (base case). Note that you must rewrite a lot of the code because you don't inherit any implementations with specializations. Highlights show the differences from the nonspecialized NDGrid.

```
template <typename T>
const int NDGrid<T, 1>::kDefaultSize;
```

```
template <typename T>
NDGrid<T, 1>::NDGrid(int inSize) : mSize(inSize)
{
    mElems = new T[mSize];
}
```

```
template <typename T>
NDGrid<T, 1>::NDGrid(const NDGrid<T, 1>& src)
{
    copyFrom(src);
}

template <typename T>
NDGrid<T, 1>::~NDGrid()
{
    delete [] mElems;
}

template <typename T>
void NDGrid<T, 1>::copyFrom(const NDGrid<T, 1>& src)
{
    mSize = src.mSize;
    mElems = new T[mSize];
    for (int i = 0; i < mSize; i++) {
        mElems[i] = src.mElems[i];
    }
}

template <typename T>
NDGrid<T, 1>& NDGrid<T, 1>::operator=(const NDGrid<T, 1>& rhs)
{
    // Check for self-assignment.
    if (this == &rhs) {
        return (*this);
    }
    // Free the old memory.
    delete [] mElems;
    // Copy the new memory.
    copyFrom(rhs);
    return (*this);
}

template <typename T>
void NDGrid<T, 1>::resize(int newSize)
{
    T* newElems = new T[newSize];

    for (int i = 0; i < newSize && i < mSize; i++) {
        newElems[i] = mElems[i];
        // Don't need to resize recursively, because this is the base case.
    }
    mSize = newSize;
    delete [] mElems;
    mElems = newElems;
}

template <typename T>
T& NDGrid<T, 1>::operator[](int x)
{
    return (mElems[x]);
}
```

```
template <typename T>
const T& NDGrid<T, 1>::operator[](int x) const
{
    return (mElems[x]);
}
```

Now, you can write code like this:

```
NDGrid<int, 3> my3DGrid;
my3DGrid[2][1][2] = 5;
my3DGrid[1][1][1] = 5;

cout << my3DGrid[2][1][2] << endl;
```

Summary

This chapter taught you how to use templates for generic programming. We hope that you gained an appreciation for the power and capabilities of these features, and an idea of how you could apply these concepts to your own code. Don't worry if you didn't understand all the syntax, or follow all the examples, on your first reading. The concepts can be difficult to grasp when you are first exposed to them, and the syntax is so tricky that the authors of this book consult a reference whenever they want to write templates. When you actually sit down to write a template class or function, you can consult this chapter for a reference on the proper syntax.

This chapter is the main preparation for Chapters 21, 22, and 23 on the standard template library. You can skip straight to Chapters 21 to 23 if you want to read about the STL immediately, but we recommend reading the rest of the chapters in Parts II and III first.

12

Understanding C++ Quirks and Oddities

Many parts of the C++ language have tricky syntax or quirky semantics. As a C++ programmer, you grow accustomed to most of this idiosyncratic behavior; it starts to feel natural. However, some aspects of C++ are a source of perennial confusion. Either books never explain them thoroughly enough, or you forget how they work and continually look them up, or both. This chapter addresses this gap by providing clear explanations for some of C++'s most niggling quirks and oddities.

Many language idiosyncrasies are covered in various chapters throughout this book. This chapter tries not to repeat those topics, by limiting itself to subjects that are not covered in detail elsewhere in the book. There is a bit of redundancy with other chapters, but the material is "sliced" in a different way in order to provide you with a new perspective.

The topics of this chapter include references, `const`, `static`, `extern`, `typedefs`, casts, scope resolution, header files, variable-length argument lists, and preprocessor macros. Although this list might appear to be a hodgepodge of topics, it is a carefully selected collection of some of the most confusing, but commonly used, aspects of the language.

References

Professional C++ code, including much of the code in this book, uses references extensively. It is helpful to step back and think about what exactly references are, and how they behave.

A *reference* in C++ is an *alias* for another variable. All modifications to the reference change the value of the variable to which it refers. You can think of references as implicit pointers that save you the trouble of taking the address of variables and dereferencing the pointer. Alternatively, you can think of references as just another name for the original variable. You can create stand-alone reference variables, use reference data members in classes, accept references as parameters to functions and methods and return references from functions and methods.

Reference Variables

Reference variables must be initialized as soon as they are created, like this:

```
int x = 3;
int& xRef = x;
```

Subsequent to this assignment, xRef is another name for x. Any use of xRef uses the current value of x. Any assignment to xRef changes the value of x. For example, the following code sets x to 10 through xRef:

```
xRef = 10;
```

You cannot declare a reference variable outside of a class without initializing it:

```
int& emptyRef; // DOES NOT COMPILE!
```

> **You must always initialize a reference when it is allocated. Usually, references are allocated when they are declared, but reference data members can be initialized in the initializer list for the containing class.**

You cannot create a reference to an unnamed value such as an integer literal, unless the reference is to a const value:

```
int& unnamedRef = 5; // DOES NOT COMPILE
const int& unnamedRef = 5; // Works as expected
```

Modifying References

A reference always refers to the same variable to which it is initialized; references cannot be changed once they are created. This rule leads to some confusing syntax. If you "assign" a variable to a reference when the reference is declared, the reference refers to that variable. However, if you assign a variable to a reference after that, the variable to which the reference refers is changed to the value of the variable being assigned. The reference is not updated to refer to that variable. Here is a code example:

```
int x = 3, y = 4;
int& xRef = x;
xRef = y; // Changes value of x to 4. Doesn't make xRef refer to y.
```

You might try to circumvent this restriction by taking the address of y when you assign it:

```
int x = 3, y = 4;
int& xRef = x;
xRef = &y; // DOES NOT COMPILE!
```

This code does not compile. The address of y is a pointer, but xRef is declared as a reference to an int, not a reference to a pointer.

Some programmers go even further in attempts to circumvent the intended semantics of references. What if you assign a reference to a reference? Won't that make the first reference refer to the variable to which the second reference refers? You might be tempted to try this code:

```
int x = 3, z = 5;
int& xRef = x;
int& zRef = z;
zRef = xRef; // Assigns values, not references
```

The final line does not change zRef. Instead, it sets the value of z to 3, because xRef refers to x, which is 3.

> **You cannot change the variable to which a reference refers after it is initialized; you can only change the value of that variable.**

References to Pointers and Pointers to References

You can create references to any type, including pointer types. Here is an example of a reference to a pointer to int:

```
int* intP;
int*& ptrRef = intP;
ptrRef = new int;
*ptrRef = 5;
```

The syntax is a little strange: you might not be accustomed to seeing * and & right next to each other. However, the semantics are straightforward: ptrRef is a reference to intP, which is a pointer to int. Modifying ptrRef changes intP. References to pointers are rare, but can occasionally be useful, as discussed in the "Reference Parameters" section later in this chapter.

Note that taking the address of a reference gives the same result as taking the address of the variable to which the reference refers. For example:

```
int x = 3;
int& xRef = x;
int* xPtr = &xRef; // Address of a reference is pointer to value
*xPtr = 100;
```

This code sets xPtr to point to x by taking the address of a reference to x. Assigning 100 to *xPtr changes the value of x to 100.

Finally, note that you cannot declare a reference to a reference or a pointer to a reference:

```
int x = 3;
int& xRef = x;
int&& xDoubleRef = xRef; // DOES NOT COMPILE!
int&* refPtr = &xRef; // DOES NOT COMPILE!
```

Reference Data Members

As you learned in Chapter 9, data members of classes can be references. A reference cannot exist without referring to some other variable. Thus, you must initialize reference data members in the constructor initialization list, not in the body of the constructor. Consult Chapter 9 for details.

Reference Parameters

C++ programmers do not often use stand-alone reference variables or reference data members. The most common use of references is for parameters to functions and methods. Recall that the default parameter-passing semantics are pass-by-value: functions receive copies of their arguments. When those parameters are modified, the original arguments remain unchanged. References allow you to specify alternative pass-by-reference semantics for arguments passed to the function. When you use reference parameters, the function receives references to the function arguments. If those references are modified, the changes are reflected in the original argument variables. For example, here is a simple swap function to swap the values of two ints:

```
void swap(int& first, int& second)
{
    int temp = first;
    first = second;
    second = temp;
}
```

You can call it like this:

```
int x = 5, y = 6;
swap(x, y);
```

When the function swap() is called with the arguments x and y, the first parameter is initialized to refer to x, and the second parameter is initialized to refer to y. When swap() modifies first and second, x and y are actually changed.

Just as you can't initialize normal reference variables with constants, you can't pass constants as arguments to functions that employ pass-by-reference:

```
swap(3, 4); // DOES NOT COMPILE
```

References from Pointers

A common quandary arises when you have a pointer to something that you need to pass to a function or method that takes a reference. You can "convert" a pointer to a reference in this case simply by dereferencing the pointer. This action gives you the value to which the pointer points, which the compiler then uses to initialize the reference parameter. For example, you can call swap() like this:

```
int x = 5, y = 6;
int *xp = &x, *yp = &y;
swap(*xp, *yp);
```

Pass-by-Reference versus Pass-by-Value

Pass-by-reference is required when you want to modify the parameter and see those changes reflected in the variable argument to the function or method However, you should not limit your use of pass-by-reference to only those cases. Pass-by-reference avoids copying the argument to the function, providing two additional benefits in some cases:

1. Efficiency: large objects and `structs` could take a long time to copy. Pass-by-reference passes only a pointer to the object or `struct` into the function.

2. Correctness: not all objects allow pass-by-value. Even those that do allow it might not support deep copying correctly. As you learned in Chapter 9, objects with dynamically allocated memory must provide a custom copy constructor in order to support deep copying.

If you want to leverage these benefits, but do not want to allow the original objects to be modified, you can mark the parameters `const`. This topic is covered in detail later in this chapter.

These benefits to pass-by-reference imply that you should use pass-by-value only for simple built-in types like `int` and `double` for which you don't need to modify the arguments. Use pass-by-reference in all other cases.

Reference Return Values

You can also return a reference from a function or method. The main reason to do so is efficiency. Instead of returning a whole object, return a reference to the object to avoid copying it unnecessarily. Of course, you can only use this technique if the object in question will continue to exist following the function termination.

> **Never return a reference to a variable, such as an automatically allocated variable on the stack, that will be destroyed when the function ends.**

A second reason to return a reference is if you want to be able to assign to the return value directly as an *lvalue* (the left-hand side of an assignment statement).

Several overloaded operators commonly return references. You saw some examples in Chapter 9, and can read about more applications of this technique in Chapter 16.

Deciding between References and Pointers

References in C++ are mostly superfluous: almost everything you can do with references, you can accomplish with pointers. For example, you could write the previously shown `swap()` function like this:

```
void swap(int* first, int* second)
{
    int temp = *first;
    *first = *second;
    *second = temp;
}
```

However, this code is more cluttered than the version with references: references make your programs cleaner and easier to understand. References are also safer than pointers: it's impossible to have an invalid reference, and you don't explicitly dereference references, so you can't encounter any of the dereferencing errors associated with pointers. Most of the time, you can use references instead of pointers. References to objects even support polymorphism in the same way as pointers to objects. The only case in which you need to use a pointer is when you need to change the location to which it points. Recall that you cannot change the variable to which references refer. For example, when you dynamically allocate memory, you need to store a pointer to the result in a pointer rather than a reference.

Another way to distinguish between appropriate use of pointers and references in parameters and return types is to consider who *owns* the memory. If the code receiving the variable is responsible for releasing the memory associated with an object, it must receive a pointer to the object. If the code receiving the variable should not free the memory, it should receive a reference.

> Use references instead of pointers unless you need to dynamically allocate memory or otherwise change, or free, the value to which the pointer points.

This rule applies to stand-alone variables, function or method parameters, and function or method return values.

Strict application of this rule can lead to some unfamiliar syntax. Consider a function that splits an array of `int`s into two arrays: one of even numbers and one of odd numbers. The function doesn't know how many numbers in the source array will be even or odd, so it should dynamically allocate the memory for the destination arrays after examining the source array. It should also return the sizes of the two new arrays. Altogether, there are four items to return: pointers to the two new arrays and the sizes of the two new arrays. Obviously, you must use pass-by-reference. The canonical C way to write the function looks like this:

```
void separateOddsAndEvens(const int arr[], int size, int** odds, int* numOdds,
    int** evens, int* numEvens)
{
    int i;
    // First pass to determine array sizes
    *numOdds = *numEvens = 0;
    for (i = 0; i < size; i++) {
        if (arr[i] % 2 == 1) {
            (*numOdds)++;
        } else {
            (*numEvens)++;
        }
    }

    // Allocate two new arrays of the appropriate size.
    *odds = new int[*numOdds];
    *evens = new int[*numEvens];
```

```
        // Copy the odds and evens to the new arrays
        int oddsPos = 0, evensPos = 0;
        for (i = 0; i < size; i++) {
            if (arr[i] % 2 == 1) {
                (*odds)[oddsPos++] = arr[i];
            } else {
                (*evens)[evensPos++] = arr[i];
            }
        }
    }
```

The final four parameters to the function are the "reference" parameters. In order to change the values to which they refer, `separateOddsAndEvens()` must dereference them, leading to some ugly syntax in the function body.

Additionally, when you want to call `separateOddsAndEvens()`, you must pass the address of two pointers so that the the function can change the actual pointers, and the address of two `int`s so that the function can change the actual `int`s:

```
int unSplit[10] = {1, 2, 3, 4, 5, 6, 6, 8, 9, 10};
int *oddNums, *evenNums;
int numOdds, numEvens;

separateOddsAndEvens(unSplit, 10, &oddNums, &numOdds, &evenNums, &numEvens);
```

If such syntax annoys you (which it should), you can write the same function using references to obtain true pass-by-reference semantics:

```
void separateOddsAndEvens(const int arr[], int size, int*& odds, int& numOdds,
    int*& evens, int& numEvens)
{
    int i;
    numOdds = numEvens = 0;
    for (i = 0; i < size; i++) {
        if (arr[i] % 2 == 1) {
            numOdds++;
        } else {
            numEvens++;
        }
    }

    odds = new int[numOdds];
    evens = new int[numEvens];

    int oddsPos = 0, evensPos = 0;
    for (i = 0; i < size; i++) {
        if (arr[i] % 2 == 1) {
            odds[oddsPos++] = arr[i];
        } else {
            evens[evensPos++] = arr[i];
        }
    }
}
```

In this case, the `odds` and `evens` parameters are references to `int*`s. `separateOddsAndEvents()` can modify the `int*`s that are used as arguments to the function (through the reference), without any explicit dereferencing. The same logic applies to `numOdds` and `numEvens`, which are references to `int`s.

With this version of the function, you no longer need to pass the addresses of the pointers or `int`s. The reference parameters handle it for you automatically:

```
int unSplit[10] = {1, 2, 3, 4, 5, 6, 6, 8, 9, 10};
int *oddNums, *evenNums;
int numOdds, numEvens;

separateOddsAndEvens(unSplit, 10, oddNums, numOdds, evenNums, numEvens);
```

Keyword Confusion

Two keywords in C++ appear to cause more confusion than any others: `const` and `static`. Both of these keywords have several different meanings, and each of their uses presents subtleties that are important to understand.

The const Keyword

The keyword `const` is short for "constant" and specifies, or requires, that something remain unchanged. As you've seen in various places in this book, and probably in real-world code, there are two different, but related, uses of the `const` keyword: for marking variables and for marking methods. This section provides a definitive discussion of these two meanings.

const Variables

You can use `const` to "protect" variables by specifying that they cannot be modified. As you learned in Chapters 1 and 7, one important use of this keyword is as a replacement for `#define` to declare constants. This use of `const` is its most straightforward application. For example, you could declare the constant `PI` like this:

```
const double PI = 3.14159;
```

You can mark any variable `const`, including global variables and class data members.

You can also use `const` to specify that parameters to functions or methods should remain unchanged. You've seen examples of this application in Chapters 1 and 9, and other places throughout the book.

const Pointers

When a variable contains one or more levels of indirection via a pointer, applying `const` becomes trickier. Consider the following lines of code:

```
int* ip;
ip = new int[10];
ip[4] = 5;
```

Suppose that you decide to apply `const` to `ip`. Set aside your doubts about the usefulness of doing so for a moment, and consider what it means. Do you want to prevent the `ip` variable itself from being changed, or do you want to prevent the values to which it points from being changed? That is, do you want to prevent the second line or the third line in the previous example?

In order to prevent the pointed-to value from being modified (as in the third line), you can add the keyword `const` to the declaration of `ip` like this:

```
const int* ip;
ip = new int[10];
ip[4] = 5; // DOES NOT COMPILE!
```

Now you cannot change the values to which `ip` points.

Alternatively, you can write this:

```
int const* ip;
ip = new int[10];
ip[4] = 5; // DOES NOT COMPILE!
```

Putting the `const` before or after the `int` makes no difference in its functionality.

If you want instead to mark `ip` itself `const` (not the values to which it points), you need to write this:

```
int* const ip = NULL;
ip = new int[10]; // DOES NOT COMPILE!
ip[4] = 5;
```

Now that `ip` itself cannot be changed, the compiler requires you to initialize it when you declare it.

You can also mark both the pointer and the values to which it points `const` like this:

```
int const* const ip = NULL;
```

An alternative syntax is the following:

```
const int* const ip = NULL;
```

Although this syntax might seem confusing, there is actually a very simple rule: the `const` keyword applies to whatever is directly to its left. Consider this line again:

```
int const* const ip = NULL;
```

From left to right, the first `const` is directly to the right of the word `int`. Thus, it applies to the `int` to which `ip` points. Therefore, it specifies that you cannot change the values to which `ip` points. The second `const` is directly to the right of the `*`. Thus, it applies to the pointer to the `int`, which is the `ip` variable. Therefore, it specifies that you cannot change `ip` (the pointer) itself.

> **const applies to the level of indirection directly to its left.**

The reason this rule becomes confusing is an exception: the first const can go before the variable like this:

```
const int* const ip = NULL;
```

This "exceptional" syntax is used much more commonly than the other syntax.

You can extend this rule to any number of levels of indirection. For example:

```
const int * const * const * const ip = NULL;
```

const References

const applied to references is usually simpler than const applied to pointers for two reasons. First, references are const by default, in that you can't change to what they refer. So, C++ does not allow you to mark a reference variable explicitly const. Second, there is usually only one level of indirection with references. As explained earlier, you can't create a reference to a reference. The only way to get multiple levels of indirection is to create a reference to a pointer.

Thus, when C++ programmers refer to a "const reference," they mean something like this:

```
int z;
const int& zRef = z;
zRef = 4; // DOES NOT COMPILE
```

By applying const to the int, you prevent assignment to zRef, as shown. Remember that const int& zRef is equivalent to int const& zRef. Note, however, that marking zRef const has no effect on z. You can still modify the value of z by changing it directly instead of through the reference

const references are used most commonly as parameters, where they are quite useful. If you want to pass something by reference for efficiency, but don't want it to be modifiable, make it a const reference. For example:

```
void doSomething(const BigClass& arg)
{
    // Implementation here
}
```

> **Your default choice for passing objects as parameters should be const reference. Only if you explicitly need to change the object should you omit the const.**

const Methods

As you read in Chapter 9, you can mark a class method `const`. That specification prevents the method from modifying any non-`mutable` data members of the class. Consult Chapter 9 for an example.

The static Keyword

Although there are several uses of the keyword `const` in C++, all the uses are related and make sense if you think of `const` as meaning "unchanged." `static` is a different story: there are three uses of the keyword in C++, all seemingly unrelated.

Static Data Members and Methods

As you read in Chapter 9, you can declare static data members and methods of classes. static data members, unlike non-`static` data members, are not part of each object. Instead, there is only one copy of the data member, which exists outside any objects of that class.

`static` methods are similarly at the class level instead of the object level. A static method does not execute in the context of a specific object.

Chapter 9 provides examples of both static members and methods.

Static Linkage

Before covering the use of the `static` keyword for linkage, you need to understand the concept of *linkage* in C++. As you learned in Chapter 1, C++ source files are each compiled independently, and the resulting object files are linked together. Each name in a C++ source file, including functions and global variables, has a linkage that is either *internal* or *external*. External linkage means that the name is available from other source files. Internal linkage (also called *static linkage*) means that it is not. By default, functions and global variables have external linkage. However, you can specify internal (or static) linkage by prefixing the declaration with the keyword static. For example, suppose you have two source files: `FirstFile.cpp` and `AnotherFile.cpp`. Here is `FirstFile.cpp`:

```
// FirstFile.cpp

void f();

int main(int argc, char** argv)
{
    f();
    return (0);
}
```

Note that this file provides a prototype for `f()`, but doesn't show the definition.

Here is `AnotherFile.cpp`:

```
// AnotherFile.cpp

#include <iostream>
using namespace std;

void f();

void f()
{
    cout << "f\n";
}
```

This file provides both a prototype and a definition for `f()`. Note that it is legal to write prototypes for the same function in two different files. That's precisely what the preprocessor does for you if you put the prototype in a header file that you `#include` in each of the source files. The reason to use header files is that it's easier to maintain (and keep synchronized) one copy of the prototype. However, for this example we don't use a header file.

Each of these source files compiles without error, and the program links fine: because `f()` has external linkage, `main()` can call it from a different file.

However, suppose you apply `static` to `f()` in `AnotherFile.cpp`:

```
// AnotherFile.cpp
#include <iostream>
using namespace std;

static void f();

void f()
{
    cout << "f\n";
}
```

Now each of the source files compiles without error, but the linker step fails because `f()` has internal (`static`) linkage, making it unavailable from `FirstFile.cpp`. Some compilers issue a warning when `static` methods are defined but not used in that source file (implying that they shouldn't be `static`, because they're probably used elsewhere).

Note that you don't need to repeat the `static` keyword in front of the definition of `f()`. As long as it precedes the first instance of the function name, there is no need to repeat it.

Now that you've learned all about this use of `static`, you will be happy to know that the C++ committee finally realized that `static` was too overloaded, and deprecated this particular use of the keyword. That means that it continues to be part of the standard for now, but is not guaranteed to be in the future. However, much legacy C++ code still uses `static` in this way.

The supported alternative is to employ *anonymous namespaces* to achieve the same affect. Instead of marking a variable or function `static`, wrap it in an unnamed namespace like this:

```
// AnotherFile.cpp
#include <iostream>
using namespace std;
```

```
namespace {
    void f();

    void f()
    {
        cout << "f\n";
    }
}
```

Entities in an anonymous namespace can be accessed anywhere following their declaration in the same source file, but cannot be accessed from other source files. These semantics are the same as those obtained with the `static` keyword.

The extern Keyword

A related keyword, `extern`, seems like it should be the opposite of `static`, specifying external linkage for the names it precedes. It can be used that way in certain cases. For example, `consts` and `typedefs` have internal linkage by default. You can use `extern` to give them external linkage.

However, `extern` has some complications. When you specify a name as `extern`, the compiler treats it as a declaration, not a definition. For variables, this means the compiler doesn't allocate space for the variable. You must provide a separate definition line for the variable without the `extern` keyword. For example:

```
// AnotherFile.cpp
extern int x;
int x = 3;
```

Alternatively, you can initialize x in the `extern` line, which then serves as the declaration and definition:

```
// AnotherFile.cpp
extern int x = 3;
```

The `extern` in this file is not very useful, because x has external linkage by default anyway. The real use of `extern` is when you want to use x from another source file:

```
// FirstFile.cpp
#include <iostream>
using namespace std;

extern int x;

int main(int argc, char** argv)
{
    cout << x << endl;
}
```

Here `FirstFile.cpp` uses an `extern` declaration so that it can use `x`. The compiler needs a declaration of `x` in order to use it in `main()`. However, if you declared `x` without the `extern` keyword, the compiler would think it's a definition and would allocate space for `x`, causing the linkage step to fail (because there are now two `x` variables in the global scope). With `extern`, you can make variables globally accessible from multiple source files.

However, we do not recommend using global variables at all. They are confusing and error-prone, especially in large programs. For similar functionality, you should use `static` class members and methods.

static Variables in Functions

The final use of the `static` keyword in C++ is to create local variables that retain their values between exits and entrances to their scope. A static variable inside a function is like a global variable that is only accessible from that function. One common use of static variables is to "remember" whether a particular initialization has been performed for a certain function. For example, code that employs this technique might look something like this:

```
void performTask()
{
    static bool inited = false;

    if (!inited) {
        cout << "initing\n";
        // Perform initialization.
        inited = true;
    }

    // Perform the desired task.
}
```

However, `static` variables are confusing, and there are usually better ways to structure your code so that you can avoid them. In this case, you might want to write a class in which the constructor performs the required initialization.

Avoid using stand-alone `static` variables. Maintain state within an object instead.

Order of Initialization of Nonlocal Variables

Before leaving the topic of `static` data members and global variables, consider the order of initialization of these variables. All global variables and `static` class data members in a program are initialized before `main()` begins. The variables in a given source file are initialized in the order they appear in the source file. For example, in the following file `Demo::x` is guaranteed to be initialized before `y`.

```
// source1.cpp

class Demo
{
    public:
        static int x;
};
```

```
int Demo::x = 3;
int y = 4;
```

However, C++ provides no specifications or guarantees about the initialization ordering of nonlocal variables in different source files. If you have a global variable x in one source file and a global variable y in another, you have no way of knowing which will be initialized first. Normally, this lack of specification isn't cause for concern. However, it can be problematic if one global or static variable depends on another. Recall that initialization of objects implies running their constructors. The constructor of one global object might access another global object, assuming that it is already constructed. If these two global objects are declared in two different source files, you cannot count on one being constructed before the other.

> **Initialization order of nonlocal variables in different source files is undefined.**

Types and Casts

Chapter 1 reviewed the basic types in C++. Chapter 8 showed you how to write your own types with classes. This section explores two of the trickier aspects of types: typedefs and casts.

typedefs

A typedef provides a new name for an existing type. You can think of a typedef simply as syntax for introducing a synonym for an existing type name. typedefs do not create new types — they only provide a new way to refer to an old type. You can use the new type name and the old type name interchangeably. Variables created with the new type name are completely compatible with those created with the original type name.

You might be surprised at the simplicity of the previous paragraph's definition for typedefs. You've probably used typedefs in your code, or at least seen code that uses them, and they didn't seem that easy. However, if you examine all the uses, you will see that they are simply providing alternate typenames.

The most common use of typenames is to provide manageable names when the real typenames become too unwieldy. This situation commonly arises with templates. For example, suppose you want to use the Grid template from Chapter 11 to create a spreadsheet, which is a Grid of SpreadsheetCells. Without typedefs, anytime you want to refer to the type of this Grid, for declaring variables, specifying function parameters, and so on, you would have to write Grid<SpreadsheetCell>:

```
int main(int argc, char** argv)
{
    Grid<SpreadsheetCell> mySpreadsheet;
    // Rest of the program . . .
}
```

```
void processSpreadsheet(const Grid<SpreadsheetCell>& spreadsheet)
{
    // Body omitted
}
```

With a `typedef`, you can create a shorter, more meaningful, name:

```
typedef Grid<SpreadsheetCell> Spreadsheet;

int main(int argc, char** argv)
{
    Spreadsheet mySpreadsheet;
    // Rest of the program . . .
}

void processSpreadsheet(const Spreadsheet& spreadsheet)
{
    // Body omitted
}
```

One tricky aspect of `typedef`s is that the typenames can include the scope qualifiers. For example, in Chapter 9, you saw this `typedef`:

```
typedef Spreadsheet::SpreadsheetCell SCell;
```

This `typedef` creates a short name `SCell` to refer to the `SpreadsheetCell` type inside the `Spreadsheet` scope.

The STL uses `typedef`s extensively to provide shorter names for types. For example, `string` is actually a `typdef` that looks like this:

```
typedef basic_string<char> string;
```

Casts

As explained in Chapter 1, the old-style C casts with `()` still work in C++. However, C++ also provides four new casts: `static_cast`, `dynamic_cast`, `const_cast`, and `reinterpret_cast`. You should use the C++ style casts instead of the old C-style casts because they perform more type checking and stand out better syntactically in your code.

This section describes the purposes for each cast and specifies when you would use each of them.

const_cast

The `const_cast` is the most straightforward. You can use it to cast away `const`-ness of a variable. It is the only cast of the four that is allowed to cast away `const`-ness. Theoretically, of course, there should be no need for a `const` cast. If a variable is `const`, it should stay `const`. In practice, however, you sometimes find yourself in a situation where a function is specified to take a `const` variable, which it must then pass to a function that takes a non-`const` variable. The "correct" solution would be to make `const` consistent in the program, but that is not always an option, especially if you are using third-party libraries. Thus, you sometimes need to cast away the `const`-ness of a variable. Here is an example:

```
void g(char* str)
{
    // Function body omitted for brevity
}
```

```
void f(const char* str)
{
    // Function body omitted for brevity
    g(const_cast<char*>(str));
    // Function body omitted for brevity
}
```

static_cast

You can use the static_cast to perform explicitly conversions that are supported directly by the language. For example, if you write an arithmetic expression in which you need to convert an int to a double in order to avoid integer division, use a static_cast:

```
int i = 3;
double result = static_cast<double>(i) / 10;
```

You can also use static_cast to perform explicitly conversions that are allowed because of user-defined constructors or conversion routines. For example, if class A has a constructor that takes an object of class B, you can convert a B object to an A object with a static_cast. In most situations where you want this behavior, however, the compiler will perform the conversion automatically.

Another use for the static_cast is to perform downcasts in an inheritance hierarchy. For example:

```
class Base
{
    public:
        Base() {};
        virtual ~Base() {}
};

class Derived : public Base
{
    public:
        Derived() {}
        virtual ~Derived() {}
};

int main(int argc, char** argv)
{
    Base* b;
    Derived* d = new Derived();

    b = d; // Don't need a cast to go up the inheritance hierarchy
    d = static_cast<Derived*>(b); // Need a cast to go down the hierarchy

    Base base;
    Derived derived;

    Base& br = base;
    Derived& dr = static_cast<Derived&>(br);

    return (0);
}
```

These casts work with both pointers and references. They do not work with objects themselves.

Note that these casts with `static_cast` do not perform runtime type checking. They allow you to convert any `Base` pointer to a `Derived` pointer or `Base` reference to a `Derived` reference, even if the `Base` really isn't a `Derived` at run time. To perform the cast safely, with runtime type checking, use the `dynamic_cast`.

`static_casts` are not all-powerful. You can't `static_cast` pointers of one type to pointers of another unrelated type. You can't `static_cast` pointers to `ints`. You can't `static_cast` directly objects of one type to objects of another type. You can't `static_cast` a `const` type to a non-`const` type. Basically, you can't do anything that doesn't make sense according to the type rules of C++.

reinterpret_cast

The `reinterpret_cast` is a bit more powerful, and concomitantly less safe, than the `static_cast`. You can use it to perform some casts that are not technically allowed by C++ type rules, but which might make sense to the programmer in some circumstances. For example, you can cast a pointer type to any other pointer type, even if they are unrelated by an inheritance hierarchy. Similarly, you can cast a reference to one type to a reference to another type, even if the types are unrelated. You can also cast pointers to `ints` and `ints` to pointers. Here are some examples:

```
class X {};
class Y {};

int main(int argc, char** argv)
{
    int i = 3;

    X x;
    Y y;

    X* xp;
    Y* yp;

    // Need reinterpret cast to perform pointer conversion from unrelated classes
    // static_cast doesn't work.
    xp = reinterpret_cast<X*>(yp);

    // Need reinterpret_cast to go from pointer to int and from int to pointer
    i = reinterpret_cast<int>(xp);
    xp = reinterpret_cast<X*>(i);

    // Need reinterpret cast to perform reference conversion from unrelated classes
    // static_cast doesn't work.
    X& xr = x;
    Y& yr = reinterpret_cast<Y&>(x);

    return (0);
}
```

You should be very careful with the `reinterpret_cast` because it "reinterprets" raw bits as a different type without performing any type checking.

dynamic_cast

As mentioned in the discussion of static_cast, the dynamic_cast provides a run-time check on casts within an inheritance hierarchy. You can use it to cast pointers or references. dynamic_cast checks the runtime type information of the underlying object at run time. If the cast doesn't make sense, dynamic_cast returns NULL (for the pointer version) or throws a bad_cast exception (for the reference version).

Note that the runtime-type information is stored in the vtable of the object. Therefore, in order to use dynamic_cast, your classes must have at least one virtual function.

Here are some examples:

```
#include <typeinfo>
#include <iostream>
using namespace std;

class Base
{
    public:
        Base() {};
        virtual ~Base() {}
};

class Derived : public Base
{
    public:
        Derived() {}
        virtual ~Derived() {}
};

int main(int argc, char** argv)
{
    Base* b;
    Derived* d = new Derived();

    b = d;
    d = dynamic_cast<Derived*>(b);

    Base base;
    Derived derived;

    Base& br = base;

    try {
        Derived& dr = dynamic_cast<Derived&>(br);
    } catch (bad_cast&) {
        cout << "Bad cast!\n";
    }

    return (0);
}
```

In the preceding example, the first cast should succeed, while the second should throw an exception. Chapter 15 covers the details of exception handling.

Note that you can perform the same casts down the inheritance hierarchy with a `static_cast` or `reinterpret_cast`. The difference with `dynamic_cast` is that it performs runtime (dynamic) type checking.

Summary of Casts

The following table summarizes the casts you should use for difference situations.

Situation	Cast
Remove `const`-ness	`const_cast`
Explicit cast supported by language (e.g., `int` to `double`, `int` to `bool`)	`static_cast`
Explicit cast supported by user-defined constructors or conversions	`static_cast`
Object of one class to object of another (unrelated) class	Can't be done
Pointer-to-object of one class to pointer-to-object of another class in the same inheritance hierarchy	`static_cast` or `dynamic_cast`
Reference-to-object of one class to reference-to-object of another class in the same inheritance hierarchy	`static_cast` or `dynamic_cast`
Pointer-to-type to unrelated pointer-to-type	`reinterpret_cast`
Reference-to-type to unrelated reference-to-type	`reinterpret_cast`
Pointer to `int` / `int` to pointer	`reinterpret_cast`
Pointer-to-function to pointer-to-function	`reinterpret_cast`

Scope Resolution

As a C++ programmer, you need to familiarize yourself with the concept of *scope*. Every name in your program, including variable, function, and class names, is in a certain scope. You create scopes with namespaces, function definitions, and class definitions. When you try to access a variable, function, or class, the name is first looked up in the nearest enclosing scope, then the next scope, and so forth, up to the *global scope*. Any name not in a namespace, function, or class is in the global scope.

Sometimes names in scopes hide identical names in other scopes. Other times, the scope you want is not part of the default scope resolution from that particular line in the program. If you don't want the default scope resolution for a name, you can qualify the name with a specific scope using the scope resolution operator : :. For example, to access a static method of a class, you prefix the method name with the name of the class (its scope) and the scope resolution operator:

```cpp
class Demo
{
    public:
        static void method() {}
};

int main(int argc, char** argv)
{
    Demo::method();

    return (0);
}
```

There are other examples of scope resolution throughout this book. One point, however, deserves further attention: accessing the global scope. The global scope is unnamed, so there's no way to access it specifically. Instead, you can use the scope resolution operator by itself (with no name prefix): this always refers to the global scope. Here is an example:

```cpp
int name = 3;

int main(int argc, char** argv)
{
    int name = 4;

    cout << name << endl; // Accesses local name
    cout << ::name << endl; // Accesses global name

    return (0);
}
```

Header Files

Header files are a mechanism for providing an abstract interface to a subsystem or piece of code. One of the trickier parts of using headers is avoiding circular references and multiple includes of the same header file. For example, perhaps you are responsible for writing the Logger class that performs all error message logging tasks. You may end up using another class, `Preferences`, that keeps track of user settings. The `Preferences` class may in turn use the `Logger` class indirectly, through yet another header.

As the following code shows, the `#ifndef` mechanism can be used to avoid circular and multiple includes. At the beginning of each header file, the `#ifndef` directive checks to see if a certain key has *not* been defined. If the key has been defined, the compiler will skip to the matching #endif, which is usually placed at the end of the file If the key has *not* been defined, the file will proceed to define the key so that a subsequent include of the same file will be skipped.

```
// Logger.h

#ifndef __LOGGER__
#define __LOGGER__

#include "Preferences.h"

class Logger
{
    public:
        static void setPreferences(const Preferences& inPrefs);
        static void logError(const char* inError);
};

#endif // __LOGGER__
```

Another tool for avoiding problems with headers is forward references. If you need to refer to a class but you cannot include its header file (for example, because it relies heavily on the class you are writing), you can tell the compiler that such a class exists without providing a formal definition through the `#include` mechanism. Of course, you cannot actually use the class in the code because the compiler knows nothing about it, except that the named class will exist after everything is linked togther However, you can still make use of pointers or references to the class in your class definition. In the following code, the `Logger` class refers to the `Preferences` class without including its header file.

```
// Logger.h

#ifndef __LOGGER__
#define __LOGGER__

class Preferences;

class Logger
{
    public:
        static void setPreferences(const Preferences& inPrefs);
        static void logError(const char* inError);
};

#endif // __LOGGER__
```

C Utilities

Recall that C++ is a superset of C, and thus contains all of its functionality. There are a few obscure C features that have no replacement in C++, and which can occasionally be useful. This section examines two of these features: variable-length argument lists and preprocessor macros.

Variable-Length Argument Lists

Consider the C function `printf()` from `<cstdio>`. You can call it with any number of arguments:

```
#include <cstdio>

int main(int argc, char** argv)
{
    printf("int %d\n", 5);
    printf("String %s and int %d\n", "hello", 5);
    printf("Many ints: %d, %d, %d, %d, %d\n", 1, 2, 3, 4, 5);
}
```

C++ provides the syntax and some utility macros for writing your own functions with a variable number of arguments. These functions usually look a lot like `printf()`. Although you shouldn't need this feature very often, occasionally you run into situations in which it's quite useful. For example, suppose you want to write a quick-and-dirty debug function that prints strings to `stderr` if a debug flag is set, but does nothing if the debug flag is not set. This function should be able to print strings with arbitrary numbers and types of arguments. A simple implementation looks like this:

```
#include <cstdio>
#include <cstdarg>

bool debug = false;

void debugOut(char* str, ...)
{
    va_list ap;
    if (debug) {
        va_start(ap, str);
        vfprintf(stderr, str, ap);
        va_end(ap);
    }
}
```

First, note that the prototype for `debugOut()` contains one typed and named parameter `str`, followed by `...` (ellipses). They stand for any number and types of arguments. In order to access these arguments, you must use macros defined in `<cstdarg>`. You declare a variable of type `va_list`, and initialize it with a call to `va_start`. The second parameter to `va_start()` must be the rightmost named variable in the parameter list. All functions require at least one named parameter. The `debugOut()` function simply passes this list to `vfprintf()` (a standard function in `<cstdio>`). After this function completes, it calls `va_end()` to terminate the access of the variable argument list. You must always call `va_end()` after calling `va_start()` to ensure that the function ends with the stack in a consistent state.

You can use the function in the following way:

```
int main(int argc, char** argv)
{
    debug = true;
    debugOut("int %d\n", 5);
    debugOut("String %s and int %d\n", "hello", 5);
    debugOut("Many ints: %d, %d, %d, %d, %d\n", 1, 2, 3, 4, 5);

    return (0);
}
```

Accessing the Arguments

If you want to access the actual arguments yourself, you can use va_arg() to do so. For example, here's a function that takes any number of ints and prints them out:

```
#include <iostream>
using namespace std;

void printInts(int num, ...)
{
    int temp;
    va_list ap;
    va_start(ap, num);
    for (int i = 0; i < num; i++) {
        temp = va_arg(ap, int);
        cout << temp << " ";
    }
    va_end(ap);
    cout << endl;
}
```

You can call printInts() like this:

```
printInts(5, 5, 4, 3, 2, 1);
```

Why You Shouldn't Use Variable-Length Argument Lists

Accessing variable-length argument lists is not very safe. As you can see from the printInts() function, there are several risks:

❑ You don't know the number of parameters. In the case of printInts(), you must trust the caller to pass the right number of arguments in the first argument. In the case of debugOut(), you must trust the caller to pass the same number of arguments after the character array as there are formatting codes in the character array.

❑ You don't know the types of the arguments. va_arg() takes a type, which it uses to interpret the value it its current spot. However, you can tell va_arg() to interpret the value as any type. There is no way for it to verify the correct type.

> Avoid using variable-length argument lists. It is preferable to pass in an array or vector of variables.

Preprocessor Macros

You can use the C++ preprocessor to write *macros*, which are like little functions. Here is an example:

```
#define SQUARE(x) ((x) * (x)) // No semicolon after the macro definition!

int main(int argc, char** argv)
{
    cout << SQUARE(4) << endl;

    return (0);
}
```

Macros are a remnant from C that are quite similar to `inline` functions, except that they are not type checked, and the preprocessor dumbly replaces any calls to them with their expansions. The preprocessor does not apply true function-call semantics. This behavior can cause unexpected results. For example, consider what would happen if you called the `SQUARE` macro with 2 + 2 instead of 4, like this:

```
cout << SQUARE(2 + 2) << endl;
```

You expect `SQUARE` to calculate 16, which it does. However, what if you left off some parentheses on the macro definition, so that it looks like this?

```
#define SQUARE(x) (x * x)
```

Now, the call to `SQUARE(2 + 2)` generates 8, not 16! Remember that the macro is dumbly expanded without regard to function-call semantics. This means that any x in the macro body is replaced by 2 + 2, leading to this expansion:

```
cout << 2 + 2 * 2 + 2 << endl;
```

Following proper order of operations, this line performs the multiplication first, followed by the additions, generating 8 instead of 16!

Macros also cause problems for debugging because the code you write is not the code that the compiler sees, or that shows up in your debugger (because of the search and replace behavior of the preprocessor). For these reasons, you should avoid macros entirely in favor of inline functions. We show the details here only because quite a bit of C++ code out there employs macros. You need to understand them in order to read and maintain that code.

Summary

This chapter explained some of the aspects of C++ that generate the most confusion. By reading this chapter, you learned a plethora of syntax details about C++. Some of the information, such as the details of references, `const`, scope resolution, the specifics of the C++-style casts, and the techniques for header files, you should use often in your programs. Other information, such as the uses of `static` and `extern`, how to write variable-length argument lists, and how to write preprocessor macros, is important to understand, but not information that you should put into use in your programs on a day-to-day basis. In any case, now that you understand these details, you are poised to tackle the advanced C++ in the rest of the book.

13

Effective Memory Management

In many ways, programming in C++ is like driving without a road. Sure, you can go anywhere you want, but there are no lines or traffic lights to keep you from injuring yourself. C++, like the C language, has a hands-off approach towards its programmers. The language assumes that you know what you're doing. It allows you to do things that are likely to cause problems because C++ is incredibly flexible and sacrifices safety in favor of performance.

Memory allocation and management is a particularly error-prone area of C++ programming. To write high-quality C++ programs, professional C++ programmers need to understand how memory works behind the scenes. This chapter explores the ins and outs of memory management. You will learn about the pitfalls of dynamic memory and some techniques for avoiding and eliminating them.

The chapter begins with an overview on the different ways to use and manage memory. Next, you will read about the often perplexing relationship between arrays and pointers. You will then learn about the creation and management of C-style strings. A low-level look at working with memory comes next. Finally, the last section of this chapter covers some specific problems that you may encounter with memory management and proposes a number of solutions.

Working with Dynamic Memory

When learning to program, dynamic memory is often the first major stumbling block that novice programmers face. Memory is a low-level component of the computer that unfortunately rears its head even in a high-level programming language like C++. Many programmers only understand enough about dynamic memory to get by. They shy away from data structures that use dynamic memory, or get their programs to work by trial and error.

There are two main advantages to using dynamic memory in your programs:

- ❑ Dynamic memory can be shared between different objects and functions.
- ❑ The size of dynamically-allocated memory can be determined at run time.

A solid understanding of how dynamic memory really works in C++ is essential to becoming a professional C++ programmer.

How to Picture Memory

Understanding dynamic memory is much easier if you have a mental model for what objects look like in memory. In this book, a unit of memory is shown as a box with a label. The label indicates the variable name that corresponds to the memory. The data inside the box displays the current value of the memory.

For example, Figure 13-1 shows the state of memory after the following line is executed:

```
int i = 7;
```

As you may recall from Chapter 1, the variable i is allocated on the stack because it is declared as a simple type, not dynamically using the new keyword.

Figure 13-1

When you use the new keyword, memory is allocated in the heap. The following code creates a variable ptr on the stack, and then allocates memory on the heap to which ptr points.

```
int* ptr;
ptr = new int;
```

Figure 13-2 shows the state of memory after this code is executed. Notice that the variable ptr is still on the stack even though it points to memory on the heap. A pointer is just a variable and can live either on the stack or the heap, although this fact is easy to forget. Dynamic memory, however, is always allocated on the heap.

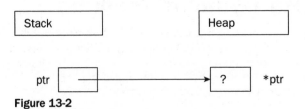

Figure 13-2

The next example shows that pointers can exist both on the stack and on the heap.

```
int** handle;

handle = new int*;
*handle = new int;
```

The preceding code first declares a pointer to a pointer to an integer as the variable `handle`. It then dynamically allocates enough memory to hold a pointer to an integer, storing the pointer to that new memory in `handle`. Next, that memory (`*handle`) is assigned a pointer to another section of dynamic memory that is big enough to hold the integer. Figure 13-3 shows the two levels of pointers with one pointer residing on the stack (`handle`) and the other residing on the heap (`*handle`).

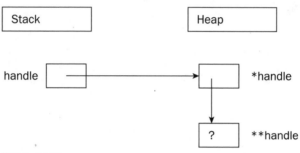

Figure 13-3

The term "handle" is sometimes used to describe a pointer to a pointer to some memory. In some applications, handles are used because they allow the underlying software to move memory around as necessary. This use of the term is more specific than the use in Chapter 5, but follows the same principle of accessing something via a level of indirection.

Allocation and Deallocation

You should already be familiar with the basics of dynamic memory from earlier chapters in this book. To create space for a variable, you use the `new` keyword. To release that space for use by other parts of the program, you use the `delete` keyword. Of course, it wouldn't be C++ if simple concepts such as `new` and `delete` didn't have several variations and intricacies.

Using new and delete

You have already seen the most common way of using `new` above and elsewhere in this book. When you want to allocate a block of memory, you call `new` with the type of the variable for which you need space. `new` returns a pointer to that memory, although it is up to you to store that pointer in a variable. If you ignore the return value of `new`, or if the pointer variable goes out of scope, the memory becomes *orphaned* because you no longer have a way to access it.

For example, the following code orphans enough memory to hold an `int`. Figure 13-4 shows the state of memory after the code is executed. When there are blocks of data in the heap with no access, direct or indirect, from the stack, the memory is orphaned.

```
void leaky()
{
    new int;    // BUG! Orphans memory!

    cout << "I just leaked an int!" << endl;
}
```

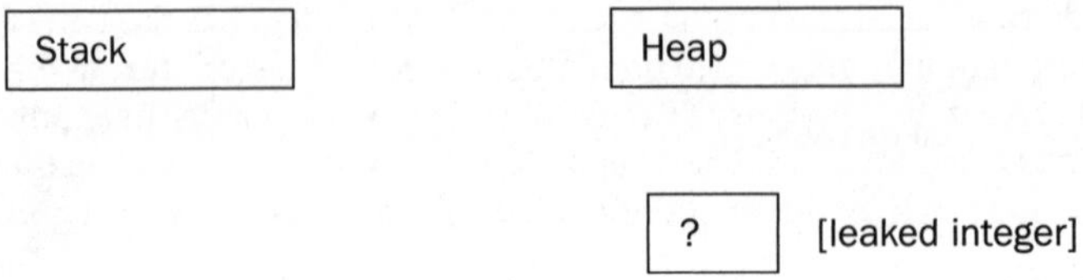

```
  Stack                      Heap


                             ?        [leaked integer]
```

Figure 13-4

Until they find a way to make computers with an infinite supply of fast memory, you will need to tell the compiler when the memory associated with an object can be released and used for another purpose. To free memory on the heap, simply use the `delete` keyword with a pointer to the memory, as shown here:

```
int* ptr;
ptr = new int;
```

```
delete ptr;
```

> As a rule of thumb, every line of code that allocates memory with **new** should correspond to another line of code that releases the same memory with **delete**.

What about My Good Friend malloc?

If you are a C programmer, you may be wondering what was wrong with the `malloc()` function. In C, `malloc()` is used to allocate a given number of bytes of memory. For the most part, using `malloc()` is simple and straightforward. The `malloc()` function still exists in C++, but we recommend avoiding it. The main advantage of `new` over `malloc()` is that `new` doesn't just allocate memory, it constructs objects.

For example, consider the following two lines of code, which use a hypothetical class called `Foo`:

```
Foo* myFoo = (Foo*)malloc(sizeof(Foo));

Foo* myOtherFoo = new Foo();
```

After executing these lines, both `myFoo` and `myOtherFoo` will point to areas of memory in the heap that are big enough for a `Foo` object. Data members and methods of `Foo` can be accessed using both pointers. The difference is that the `Foo` object pointed to by `myFoo` isn't a proper object because it was never constructed. The `malloc()` function only sets aside a piece of memory of a certain size. It doesn't know about or care about objects. In contrast, the call to new will allocate the appropriate size of memory and will also properly construct the object. Chapter 16 describes these two duties of new in more detail.

A similar difference exists between the free() function and the delete function. With free(), the object"s destructor will not be called. With delete, the destructor will be called and the object will be properly cleaned up.

> **Do not mix and match malloc() and free() with new and delete. We recommend using only new and delete.**

When Memory Allocation Fails

Many, if not most, programmers write code with the assumption that new will always be successful. The rationale is that if new fails, it means that memory is very low and life is very, very bad. It is often an unfathomable state to be in because it's unclear what your program could possibly do in this situation.

By default, your program will terminate if new fails. In many programs, this behavior is acceptable. The program exits when new fails because new throws an exception if there is not enough memory available for the request. Chapter 15 explains approaches to recover gracefully from an out-of-memory situation.

There is also an alternative version of new which will not throw an exception. Instead, it will return NULL, similar to the behavior of malloc() in C. The syntax for using this version is shown here:

```
int* ptr = new(nothrow) int;
```

Of course, you still have the same problem as the version that throws an exception — what do you do when the result is NULL? The compiler doesn't require you to check the result, so the nothrow version of new is more likely to lead to other bugs than is the version that throws an exception. For this reason, we suggest that you use the standard version of new. If out-of-memory recovery is important to your program, the techniques covered in Chapter 15 will give you all of the tools that you need.

Arrays

Arrays package multiple variables of the same type into a single variable with indices. Working with arrays quickly becomes natural to a novice programmer because it is easy to think about values in numbered slots. The in-memory representation of an array is not far off from this mental model.

Arrays of Basic Types

When your program allocates memory for an array, it is allocating *contiguous* pieces of memory, where each piece is large enough to hold a single element of the array. For example, an array of five ints would be declared on the stack as follows:

```
int myArray[5];
```

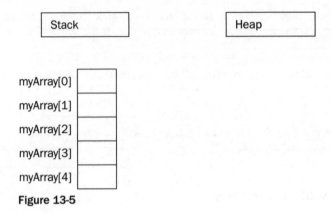

Figure 13-5

Figure 13-5 shows the state of memory after the array is declared. Declaring arrays on the heap is no different, except that you use a pointer to refer to the location of the array. The following code allocates memory for an array of five `ints` and stores a pointer to the memory in a variable called `myArrayPtr`.

```
int* myArrayPtr = new int[5];
```

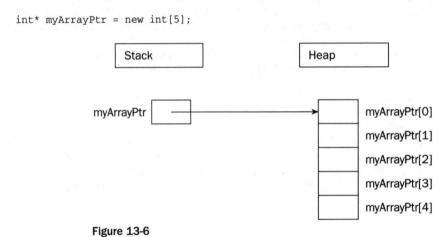

Figure 13-6

As Figure 13-6 illustrates, the heap-based array is similar to the stack-based array, but in a different location. The `myArrayPtr` variable points to the 0th element of the array. The advantage of putting an array on the heap is that you can use dynamic memory to define its size at run time. For example, the following function receives a desired number of documents from a hypothetical function named `askUserForNumberOfDocuments()` and uses that result to create an array of `Document` objects.

```
Document* createDocArray()
{
    int numDocs = askUserForNumberOfDocuments();

    Document* docArray = new Document[numDocs];

    return docArray;
}
```

Some compilers, through mysterious voodoo, allow variable-sized arrays on the stack. This is not a standard feature of C++, so we recommend cautiously backing away when you see it.

In the preceding function, docArray is a dynamically allocated array. Do not get this confused with a *dynamic array*. The array itself is not dynamic because its size does not change once it is allocated. Dynamic memory lets you specify the size of an allocated block at run time, but it does not automatically adjust its size to accommodate the data. There are data structures that do dynamically adjust in size to their data, such as the STL built-in vector class.

There is a function in C++ called realloc(), which is a holdover from the C language. Don't use it! In C, realloc() is used to effectively change the size of an array by allocating a new block of memory of the new size and moving all of the old data to the new location. This approach is extremely dangerous in C++ because user-defined objects will not respond well to bitwise copying.

Do not use **realloc()** in C++. It is not your friend.

Arrays of Objects

Arrays of objects are no different from arrays of simple types. When you use new to allocate an array of *N* objects, enough space is allocated for *N* contiguous blocks where each block is large enough for a single object. Using new, the zero-argument constructor for each of the objects will automatically be called. In this way, allocating an array of objects using new will return a pointer to an array of fully formed and initialized objects.

For example, consider the following class:

```
class Simple
{
    public:
        Simple() { cout << "Simple constructor called!" << endl; }
};
```

If you were to allocate an array of four Simple objects, the Simple constructor would be called four times.

```
int main(int argc, char** argv)
{
    Simple* mySimpleArray = new Simple[4];
}
```

The output of this code is:

```
Simple constructor called!
Simple constructor called!
Simple constructor called!
Simple constructor called!
```

The memory diagram for this array is shown in Figure 13-7. As you can see, it is no different from an array of basic types.

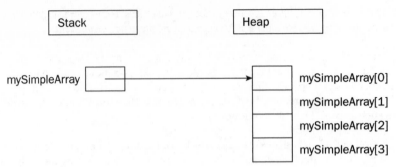

Figure 13-7

Deleting Arrays

When you allocate memory with the array version of new (new[]), you must release it with the array version of delete (delete[]). This version will automatically destruct the objects in the array in addition to releasing the memory associated with them. If you do not use the array version of delete, your program may behave in odd ways. In some compilers, only the destructor for the 0th element of the array will be called because the compiler only knows that you are deleting a pointer to an object. In others, memory corruption may occur because new and new[] can use completely different memory allocation schemes.

```cpp
int main(int argc, char** argv)
{
    Simple* mySimpleArray = new Simple[4];

    // Use mySimpleArray.

    delete[] mySimpleArray;
}
```

Of course, the destructors are only called if the elements of the array are plain objects. If you have an array of pointers, you will still need to delete each element individually just as you allocated each element individually, as shown in the following code:

```cpp
int main(int argc, char** argv)
{
    Simple** mySimplePtrArray = new Simple*[4];

    // Allocate an object for each pointer.
    for (int i = 0; i < 4; i++) {
        mySimplePtrArray[i] = new Simple();
    }

    // Use mySimplePtrArray.

    // Delete each allocated object.
    for (int i = 0; i < 4; i++) {
        delete mySimplePtrArray[i];
    }
    // Delete the array itself.
    delete[] mySimplePtrArray;
}
```

> Do not mix and match **new** and **delete** with **new[]** and **delete[]**

Multidimensional Arrays

Multidimensional arrays extend the notion of indexed values to use multiple indices. For example, a Tic-Tac-Toe game might use a two-dimensional array to represent a three-by-three grid. The following example shows such an array declared on the stack and accessed with some test code.

```
int main(int argc, char** argv)
{
    char board[3][3];

    // Test code
    board[0][0] = 'X';   // X puts marker in position (0,0).
    board[2][1] = 'O';   // O puts marker in position (2,1).
}
```

You may be wondering whether the first subscript in a two-dimensional array is the x-coordinate or the y-coordinate. The truth is that it doesn't really matter, as long as you are consistent. A four-by-seven grid could be declared as `char board[4][7]` or `char board[7][4]`. For most applications, it is easiest to think of the first subscript as the x-axis and the second as the y-axis.

Multidimensional Stack Arrays

In memory, a stack-based two-dimensional array looks like Figure 13-8. Since memory doesn't have two axes (addresses are merely sequential), the computer represents a two dimensional array just like a one-dimensional array. The difference is the size of the array and the method used to access it.

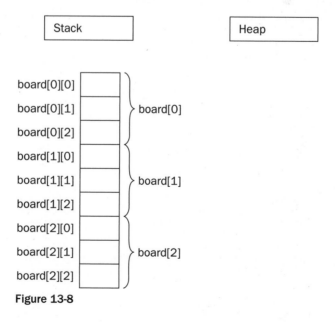

Figure 13-8

The size of a multidimensional array is all of its dimensions multiplied together, then multiplied by the size of a single element in the array. In Figure 13-8, the three-by-three board is 3*3*1 = 9 bytes, assuming that a character is 1 byte. For a four-by-seven board of characters, the array would be 4*7*1 = 28 bytes.

To access a value in a multidimensional array, the computer treats each subscript as accessing another subarray within the multidimensional array. For example, in the three-by-three grid, the expression board[0] actually refers to the subarray highlighted in Figure 13-9. When you add a second subscript, such as board[0][2], the computer is able to access the correct element by looking up the second subscript within the subarray, as shown in Figure 13-10.

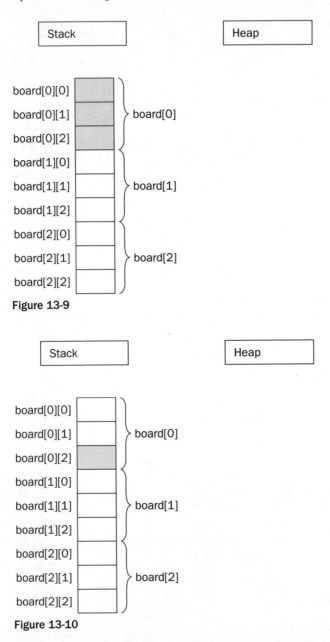

Figure 13-9

Figure 13-10

These techniques are extended to N-dimensional arrays, though dimensions higher than three tend to be difficult to conceptualize and are rarely useful in everyday applications.

Multidimensional Heap Arrays

If you need to determine the dimensions of a multidimensional array at run time, you can use a heap-based array. Just as a single-dimensional dynamically allocated array is accessed through a pointer, a multidimensional dynamically allocated array is also accessed through a pointer. The only difference is that in a two-dimensional array, you need to start with a pointer-to-a-pointer and in an N-dimensional array, you need N levels of pointers. At first, it might seem like the correct way to declare and allocate a dynamically allocated multidimensional array is as follows:

```
char** board = new char[i][j]; // BUG! Doesn't compile
```

This code doesn't compile because heap-based arrays don't work like stack-based arrays. Their memory layout isn't contiguous, so allocating enough memory for a stack-based multidimensional array is incorrect. Instead, you must start by allocating a single contiguous array for the first subscript dimension of a heap-based array. Each element of that array is actually a pointer to another array that stores the elements for the second subscript dimension. This layout for a two-by-two dynamically allocated board is shown in Figure 13-11.

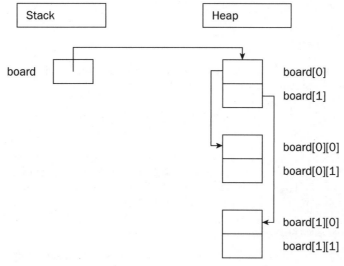

Figure 13-11

Unfortunately, the compiler doesn't allocate memory for the subarrays on your behalf. You can allocate the first dimension array just like a single-dimensional heap-based array, but the individual subarrays must be explicitly allocated. The following function properly allocates memory for a two-dimensional array.

```
char** allocateCharacterBoard(int xDimension, int yDimension)
{
    char** myArray = new char*[xDimension]; // Allocate first dimension

    for (int i = 0; i < xDimension; i++) {
        myArray[i] = new char[yDimension];  // Allocate ith subarray
    }

    return myArray;
}
```

When you wish to release the memory associated with a multidimensional heap-based array, the array delete[] syntax will not clean up the subarrays on your behalf. Your code to release an array should mirror the code to allocate it, as in the following function.

```
void releaseCharacterBoard(char** myArray, int xDimension)
{
    for (int i = 0; i < xDimension; i++) {
        delete[] myArray[i];     // Delete ith subarray
    }

    delete[] myArray;             // Delete first dimension
}
```

Working with Pointers

Pointers get their bad reputation from the relative ease with which you can abuse them. Because a pointer is just a memory address, you could theoretically change that address manually, even doing something as scary as the following line of code:

```
char* scaryPointer = 7;
```

The previous line builds a pointer to the memory address 7, which is likely to be random garbage or memory that is used elsewhere in the application. If you start to use areas of memory that weren't set aside on your behalf with new, eventually you will corrupt the memory associated with an object and your program will crash.

A Mental Model for Pointers

As you read in Chapter 1, there are two ways to think about pointers. More mathematically minded readers might view pointers simply as addresses. This view makes pointer arithmetic, covered later in this chapter, a bit easier to understand. Pointers aren't mysterious pathways through memory; they are simply numbers that happen to correspond to a location in memory. Figure 13-12 illustrates a two-by-two grid in the address-based view of the world.

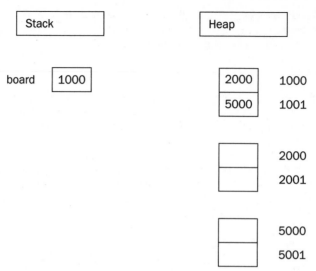

Figure 13-12

Readers who are more comfortable with spatial representations might derive more benefit from the "arrow" view of pointers. A pointer is simply a level of indirection that says to the program "Hey! Look over there." With this view, multiple levels of pointers simply become individual steps on the path to data. Figure 13-11 showed a graphical view of pointers in memory.

When you *dereference* a pointer, by using the * operator, you are telling the program to look one level deeper in memory. In the address-based view, think of a dereference as a jump in memory to the address indicated by the pointer. With the graphical view, every dereference corresponds to following an arrow from its base to its point.

When you take the address of a variable, using the & operator, you are adding a level of indirection in memory. In the address-based view, the program is simply noting the numerical address of the variable, which can be stored in a pointer variable. In the graphical view, the & operator creates a new arrow whose point ends at the variable. The base of the arrow can be attached to a pointer variable.

Casting with Pointers

Since pointers are just memory addresses (or arrows to somewhere), they are somewhat weakly typed. A pointer to an XML Document is the same size as a pointer to an integer. The compiler will let you easily cast any pointer type to any other pointer type using a C-style cast.

```
Document* documentPtr = getDocument();
char* myCharPtr = (char*)documentPtr;
```

A static cast offers a bit more safety. The compiler will refuse to perform a static cast on pointers to different data types.

```
Document* documentPtr = getDocument();
static_cast<char*> (documentPtr);     // BUG! Won't compile
```

361

If the two pointers you are casting are actually pointing to objects that are related through inheritance, the compiler will permit a `static` cast. However, as you read in Chapter 10, a dynamic cast is a safer way to accomplish a cast within an inheritance hierarchy.

const with Pointers

The interaction between the `const` keyword and pointers is a bit confusing, because it is unclear to what you are applying `const`. If you dynamically allocate an array of integers and apply `const` to it, is the array address protected with `const`, or are the individual values protected? The answer depends on the syntax.

If `const` occurs before the type, it means that the pointed-to value is protected. In the case of an array, the individual elements of the array are `const`. The following function receives a pointer to a `const` integer. The first line will not compile because the actual value is protected by `const`. The second line would compile, because the array itself is unprotected.

```
void test(const int* inProtectedInt, int* anotherPtr)
{
    *inProtectedInt = 7;   // BUG! Attempts to write to read-only value
    inProtectedInt = anotherPtr;   // Works fine
}
```

To protect the pointer itself, the `const` keyword immediately precedes the variable name, as shown in the following code. This time, both the pointer and the pointed-to value are protected, so neither line would compile.

```
void test(const int* const inProtectedInt, int* anotherPtr)
{
    *inProtectedInt = 7;   // BUG! Attempts to write to read-only value
    inProtectedInt =  anotherPtr;   // BUG! Attempts to write to read-only value
}
```

In practice, protecting the pointer is rarely necessary. If a function is able to change the value of a pointer that you pass it, it makes little difference. The effect will only be local to the function, and the pointer will still point to its original address as far as the caller is concerned. Marking a pointer as `const` is more useful in documenting its purpose than for any actual protection. Protecting the pointed-to value(s), however, is quite common to protect against overwriting shared data.

Array-Pointer Duality

You have already seen some of the overlap between pointers and arrays. Heap-allocated arrays are referred to by a pointer to their first element. Stack-based arrays are referred to by using the array syntax (`[]`) with an otherwise normal variable declaration. As you are about to learn, however, the overlap doesn't end there. Pointers and arrays have a complicated relationship.

Arrays Are Pointers!

A heap-based array is not the only place where you can use a pointer to refer to an array. You can also use the pointer syntax to access elements of a stack-based array. The address of an array is really the address of the 0th element. The compiler knows that when you refer to an array in its entirety by its variable name, you are really referring to the address of the 0th element. In this way, the pointer works just like a heap-based array. The following code creates an array on the stack, but uses a pointer to access the array.

```
int main(int argc, char** argv)
{
    int myIntArray[10];

    int* myIntPtr = myIntArray;

    // Access the array through the pointer.
    myIntPtr[4] = 5;
}
```

The ability to refer to a stack-based array through a pointer is useful when passing arrays into functions. The following function accepts an array of integers as a pointer. Note that the caller will need to explicitly pass in the size of the array because the pointer implies nothing about size. In fact, C++ arrays of any form, pointer or not, have no built-in notion of size.

```
void doubleInts(int* theArray, int inSize)
{
    for (int i = 0; i < inSize; i++) {
        theArray[i] *= 2;
    }
}
```

The caller of this function can pass a stack-based or heap-based array. In the case of a heap-based array, the pointer already exists and is simply passed by value into the function. In the case of a stack-based array, the caller can pass the array variable and the compiler will automatically treat the array variable as a pointer to the array. Both uses are shown here:

```
int main(int argc, char** argv)
{
    int* heapArray = new int[4];
    heapArray[0] = 1;
    heapArray[1] = 5;
    heapArray[2] = 3;
    heapArray[3] = 4;

    doubleInts(heapArray, 4);

    int stackArray[4] = {5, 7, 9, 11};

    doubleInts(stackArray, 4);
}
```

Even if the function doesn't explicitly have a parameter that is a pointer, the parameter-passing semantics of arrays are uncannily similar to pointers', because the compiler treats an array as a pointer when it
is passed to a function. A function that takes an array as an argument and changes values inside the
array is actually changing the original array, not a copy. Just like a pointer, passing an array effectively
mimics pass-by-reference functionality because what you really pass to the function is the address of the
original array, not a copy. The following implementation of `doubleInts()` changes the original array
even though the parameter is an array, not a pointer.

```
void doubleInts(int theArray[], int inSize)
{
    for (int i = 0; i < inSize; i++) {
        theArray[i] *= 2;
    }
}
```

You may be wondering why things work this way. Why doesn't the compiler just copy the array when
array syntax is used in the function definition? One possible explanation is efficiency — it takes time to
copy the elements of an array, and they potentially take up a lot of memory. By always passing a pointer,
the compiler doesn't need to include the code to copy the array.

To summarize, arrays declared using array syntax can be accessed through a pointer. When an array is
passed to a function, it is always passed as a pointer.

Not All Pointers Are Arrays!

Since the compiler lets you pass in an array where a pointer is expected, as in the `doubleInts()` function shown earlier, you may be lead to believe that pointers and arrays are the same. In fact there are
subtle, but important, differences. Pointers and arrays share many properties and can sometimes be used
interchangeably (as shown earlier), but they are not the same.

A pointer by itself is meaningless. It may point to random memory, a single object, or an array. You can
always use array syntax with a pointer, but doing so is not always appropriate because pointers aren't
always arrays. For example, consider the following code:

```
int* ptr = new int;
```

The pointer `ptr` is a valid pointer, but it is not an array. You can access the pointed-to value using array
syntax (`ptr[0]`), but doing so is stylistically questionable and provides no real benefit. In fact, using
array syntax with nonarray pointers is an invitation for bugs. The memory at `ptr[1]` could be anything!

> Arrays are automatically referenced as pointers, but not all pointers are arrays.

Dynamic Strings

Strings present something of a quandary for programming language designers because they seem like a standard data type, but are not expressed in fixed sizes. Strings are so commonly used, however, that most programming languages need to have a built-in model of a string. In the C language, strings are somewhat of a hack, never given the first-class language feature attention that they deserve. C++ provides a far more flexible and useful representation of a string.

C-Style Strings

In the C language, strings are represented as an array of characters. The last character of a string is a null character (`'\0'`) so that code operating on the string can determine where it ends. Even though C++ provides a better string abstraction, it is important to understand the C technique for strings because they still arise in C++ programming.

By far, the most common mistake that programmers make with C strings is that they forget to allocate space for the `'\0'` character. For example, the string `"hello"` appears to be five characters long, but six characters worth of space are needed in memory to store the value, as shown in Figure 13-13.

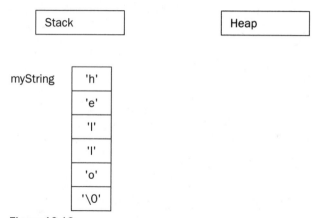

Figure 13-13

C++ contains several functions from the C language that operate on strings. As a general rule of thumb, these functions do not handle memory allocation. For example, the `strcpy()` function takes two strings as parameters. It copies the second string onto the first, whether it fits or not. The following code attempts to build a wrapper around `strcpy()` that allocates the correct amount of memory and returns the result, instead of taking in an already allocated string. It uses the `strlen()` function to obtain the length of the string.

```
char* copyString(const char* inString)
{
    char* result = new char[strlen(inString)];   // BUG! Off by one!

    strcpy(result, inString);

    return result;
}
```

The `copyString()` function as written is incorrect. The `strlen()` function returns the length of the string, not the amount of memory needed to hold it. For the string `"hello"`, `strlen()` will return 5, not 6! The proper way to allocate memory for a string is to add one to the amount of space needed for the actual characters. It seems a little weird at first to have +1 all over, but it quickly becomes natural, and you (hopefully) miss it when it's not there.

```
char* copyString(const char* inString)
{
    char* result = new char[strlen(inString) + 1];

    strcpy(result, inString);

    return result;
}
```

One way to remember that `strlen()` only returns the number of actual characters in the string is to consider what would happen if you were allocating space for a string made up of several others. For example, if your function took in three strings and returned a string that was the concatenation of all three, how big would it be? To hold exactly enough space, it would be the length of all three strings, added together, plus one for the trailing `'\0'` character. If `strlen()` included the `'\0'` in the length of the string, the allocated memory would be too big. The following code uses the `strcpy()` and `strcat()` functions to perform this operation.

```
char* appendStrings(const char* inStr1, const char* inStr2, const char* inStr3)
{
    char* result = new char[strlen(inStr1) + strlen(inStr2) + strlen(inStr3) + 1];

    strcpy(result, inStr1);
    strcat(result, inStr2);
    strcat(result, inStr3);

    return result;
}
```

A complete list of C functions to operate on strings is found in the `<cstring>` header file.

String Literals

You've probably seen strings written in a C++ program with quotes around them. For example, the following code outputs the string `hello` by including the string itself, not a variable that contains it.

```
cout << "hello" << endl;
```

In the preceding line, `"hello"` is a *string literal* because it is written as a value, not a variable. Even though string literals don't have associated variables, they are treated as `const char*`'s (arrays of constant characters).

String literals can be *assigned* to variables, but doing so can be risky. The actual memory associated with a string literal is in a read-only part of memory, which is why it is an array of *constant* characters. This allows the compiler to optimize memory usage by reusing references to equivalent string literals (that is, even if your program uses the string literal `"hello"` 500 times, the compiler can create just one instance of `hello` in memory). The compiler does not, however, force your program to assign a string literal only to a variable of type `const char*` or `const char[]`. You can assign a string to a `char*` without `const`, and the program will work fine unless you attempt to change the string. Generally, attempting to change the string will immediately crash your program, as demonstrated in the following code:

```
char* ptr = "hello";         // Assign the string literal to a variable.

ptr[1] = 'a';                // CRASH! Attempts to write to read-only memory
```

A much safer way to code is to use a pointer to `const` characters when referring to string literals. The code below contains the same bug, but because it assigned the literal to a `const` character array, the compiler will catch the attempt to write to read-only memory.

```
const char* ptr = "hello";   // Assign the string literal to a variable.

ptr[1] = 'a';                // BUG! Attempts to write to read-only memory
```

You can also use a string literal as an initial value for a stack-based character array. Because the stack-based variable cannot in any way refer to memory somewhere else, the compiler will take care of copying the string literal into the stack-based array memory.

```
char stackArray[] = "hello"; // Compiler takes care of copying the array and
                             // creating appropriate size for stack array

stackArray[1] = 'a';         // The copy can be modified.
```

The C++ string Class

As we promised earlier, C++ provides a much-improved implementation of a string as part of the Standard Library. In C++, `string` is a class (actually an instantiation of the `basic_string` template class) that supports many of the same operations as the `<cstring>` functions but, best of all, takes care of memory allocation for you if you use it properly.

What Was Wrong with C-Style Strings?

Before jumping into the new world of the C++ string class, consider the advantages and disadvantages of C-style strings.

Advantages:

❑   They are simple, making use of the underlying basic character type and array structure.

❑   They are lightweight, taking up only the memory that they need if used properly.

❑   They are low level, so you can easily manipulate and copy them as raw memory.

❑   They are well understood by C programmers — why learn something new?

Disadvantages:

- ❏ They are unforgiving and susceptible to difficult memory bugs.
- ❏ They don't leverage the object-oriented nature of C++.
- ❏ They come with a set of poorly named and sometimes confusing helper functions.
- ❏ They require knowledge of their underlying representation on the part of the programmer.

The preceding lists were carefully constructed to make you think that perhaps there is a better way. As you'll learn below, C++ strings solve all of these disadvantages of C strings and make the advantages moot.

Using the string Class

Even though string is a class, you can almost always treat it as though it were a built-in type, like int. In fact, the more you think of it as a simple type, the better off you are. Programmers generally encounter the least trouble with string when they forget that strings are objects.

Through the magic of operator overloading, C++ strings support concatenation with the + operator, assignment with the = operator, comparison with the == operator, and individual character access with the [] operator. These operators are what allow the programmer to treat string like a basic type. As the following code shows, you can perform these operations on a string without worrying about memory allocation.

```cpp
int main(int argc, char** argv)
{
    string myString = "hello";

    myString += ", there";

    string myOtherString = myString;

    if (myString == myOtherString) {
        myOtherString[0] = 'H';
    }

    cout << myString << endl;
    cout << myOtherString << endl;
}
```

The output of this code is:

```
hello, there
Hello, there
```

There are several things to note in this example. First, there are no memory leaks even though strings are allocated and resized left and right. All of these string objects were created as stack variables. While the string class certainly had a bunch of allocating and resizing to do, the objects themselves cleaned up this memory when they went out of scope.

Another point to note is that the operators work the way you would want them to You might be concerned that using = will somehow result in two variables that point to the same memory, but that is not the case. The = operator copies the strings, which is most likely what you wanted. Similarly, the == operator really compares the actual contents of two strings, not the memory locations of the strings. If you are used to working with array-based strings, this will either be refreshingly liberating for you or somewhat confusing. Don't worry – once you learn to trust the `string` class to do the right thing, life gets so much easier.

> For compatibility, you can convert a C++ **string** into a C-style string by using the **c_str()** method. You should call the method just before using the result so that it accurately reflects the current contents of the **string**.

The on-line reference lists all the operations you can perform on `string` objects.

Low-Level Memory Operations

One of the great advantages of C++ over C is that you don't need to worry quite as much about memory. If you code using objects, you just need to make sure that each individual class properly manages its own memory. Through construction and destruction, the compiler helps you manage memory by telling you when to do it. As you saw in the `string` class, hiding the management of memory within classes makes a huge difference in usability.

With some applications, however, you may encounter the need to work with memory at a lower level. Whether for efficiency, debugging, or a sick curiosity, knowing some techniques for working with raw bytes can be helpful.

Pointer Arithmetic

The C++ compiler uses the declared types of pointers to allow you to perform *pointer arithmetic*. If you declare a pointer to an `int` and increase it by 1, the pointer moves ahead in memory by the size of an `int`, not by a single byte. This type of operation is most useful with arrays, since they contain homogeneous data that is sequential in memory. For example, assume you declare an array of `int`s on the heap:

```
int* myArray = new int[8];
```

You are already familiar with the following syntax for setting the value in position 2:

```
myArray[2] = 33;
```

With pointer arithmetic, you can equivalently use the following syntax, which obtains a pointer to the memory that is "2 ints ahead" of `myArray`, then dereferences it to set the value.

```
*(myArray + 2) = 33;
```

As an alternative syntax for accessing individual elements, pointer arithmetic doesn't seem too appealing. Its real power lies in the fact that an expression like myArray + 2 is still a pointer to an int, and thus can represent a smaller int array. Suppose you had a C-style string, as shown below:

```
const char* myString = "Hello, World!";
```

Suppose you also had a function that took in a string and returned a new string that contains a capitalized version of the input:

```
char* toCaps(const char* inString);
```

You could capitalize myString by passing it into this function. However, if you only wanted to capitalize *part* of myString, you could use pointer arithmetic to refer to only a latter part of the string. The following code calls toCaps() on the World part of the string:

```
toCaps(myString + 7);
```

Another useful application of pointer arithmetic involves subtraction. Subtracting one pointer from another of the same type gives you the number of elements of the pointed-to type between the two pointers, not the absolute number of bytes between them.

Custom Memory Management

For 99 percent of the cases you will encounter (some might say 100 percent of the cases), the built-in memory allocation facilities in C++ are adequate. Behind the scenes, new and delete do all the work of handing out memory in properly sized chunks, maintaining a list of available areas of memory, and releasing chunks of memory back to that list upon deletion.

When resource constraints are extremely tight, managing memory on your own may be a viable option. Don't worry — it's not as scary as it sounds. Basically, managing memory yourself generally means that classes allocate a large chunk of memory and dole out that memory in pieces as it is needed.

How is this approach any better? Managing your own memory can potentially reduce overhead. When you use new to allocate memory, the program also needs to set aside a small amount of space to record how much memory was allocated. That way, when you call delete, the proper amount of memory can be released. For most objects, the overhead is so much smaller than the memory allocated that it makes little difference. However, for small objects or programs with enormous numbers of objects, the overhead can have an impact.

When you manage memory yourself, you know the size of each object a priori, so you can avoid the overhead for each object. The difference can be enormous for large numbers of small objects. The syntax for performing custom memory management is described in Chapter 16.

Garbage Collection

At the other end of the memory hygiene spectrum lies garbage collection. With environments that support garbage collection, the programmer rarely, if ever, explicitly frees memory associated with an object. Instead, a low-priority background task keeps an eye on the state of memory and cleans up portions that it decides are no longer needed.

Garbage collection is not built into the C++ language as it is in Java. Most C++ programs manage memory at the object level through `new` and `delete`. It is possible to implement garbage collection in C++, but freeing yourself from the task of releasing memory would probably introduce new headaches.

One approach to garbage collection is called *mark and sweep*. With this approach, the garbage collector periodically examines every single pointer in your program and annotates the fact that the referenced memory is still in use. At the end of the cycle, any memory that hasn't been marked is deemed to be not in use and is freed.

A mark and sweep algorithm could be implemented in C++ if you were willing to do the following:

1. Register all pointers with the garbage collector so that it can easily walk through the list of all pointers

2. Subclass all objects from a mix-in class, perhaps `GarbageCollectible`, that allows the garbage collector to mark an object as in-use

3. Protect concurrent access to objects by making sure that no changes to pointers can occur while the garbage collector is running

As you can see, this simple approach to garbage collection requires quite a bit of diligence on the part of the programmer. It may even be more error-prone than using `delete`! Attempts at a safe and easy mechanism for garbage collection have been made in C++, but even if a perfect implementation of garbage collection in C++ came along, it wouldn't necessarily be appropriate to use for all applications. Among the downsides of garbage collection:

❑ When the garbage collector is actively running, it will likely slow the program down.

❑ If the program is aggressively allocating memory, the garbage collector may be unable to keep up.

❑ If the garbage collector is buggy or thinks an abandoned object is still in use, it can create unrecoverable memory leaks.

Object Pools

Custom memory management, as described above, is the coding equivalent to shopping for a picnic at a warehouse superstore. You fill your SUV with more paper plates than you need right now so that you can avoid the overhead of going back to the store for subsequent picnics. Garbage collection is like leaving any used plates out in the yard where the wind will conveniently blow them into the neighbor's yard. Surely, there must be a more ecological approach to memory management.

Object pools are the analog of recycling. You buy a reasonable number of plates, but you hang onto them after use so that later on you can clean and reuse them. Object pools are ideal for situations where you need to use many objects of the same type over time, and creating each one incurs overhead.

Chapter 17 contains further details about using object pools for performance efficiency.

Function Pointers

You don't normally think about the location of functions in memory, but each function actually lives at a particular address. In C++, you can use *functions as data*. In other words, you can take the address of a function and use it like you use a variable.

Function pointers are typed according to the parameter types and return type of compatible functions. The easiest way to work with function pointers is to use the `typedef` mechanism to assign a type name to the family of functions that have the given characteristics. For example, the following line declares a type called `YesNoFcn` that represents a pointer to any function that has two `int` parameters and returns a `bool`.

```
typedef bool(*YesNoFcn)(int, int);
```

Now that this new type exists, you could write a function that takes a `YesNoFcn` as a parameter. For example, the following function accepts two `int` arrays and their size, as well as a `YesNoFcn`. It iterates through the arrays in parallel and calls the `YesNoFcn` on corresponding elements of both arrays, printing a message if the `YesNoFcn` function returns `true`. Notice that even though the `YesNoFcn` is passed in as a variable, it can be called just like a regular function.

```
void findMatches(int values1[], int values2[], int numValues, YesNoFcn inFunction)
{
    for (int i = 0; i < numValues; i++) {
        if (inFunction(values1[i], values2[i])) {
            cout << "Match found at position " << i <<
                " (" << values1[i] << ", " << values2[i] << ")" << endl;
        }
    }
}
```

To call the `findMatches()` function, all you need is any function that adheres to the defined `YesNoFcn` type — that is, any type that takes in two `int`s and returns a `bool`. For example, consider the following function, which returns `true` if the two parameters are equal:

```
bool intEqual(int inItem1, int inItem2)
{
    return (inItem1 == inItem2);
}
```

Because the `intEqual()` function matches the `YesNoFcn` type, it can be passed as the final argument to `findMatches()`, as in the following program:

```
int main(int argc, char** argv)
{
    int arr1[7] = {2, 5, 6, 9, 10, 1, 1};
    int arr2[7] = {4, 4, 2, 9, 0, 3, 4};

    cout << "Calling findMatches() using intEqual():" << endl;
    findMatches(arr1, arr2, 7, &intEqual);

    return 0;
}
```

Notice that the intEqual() function is passed into the findMatches() function by taking its address. Technically, the & character is optional — if you simply put the function name, the compiler will know that you mean to take its address. The output of this program will be:

```
Calling findMatches() using intEqual():
Match found at position 3 (9, 9)
```

The magic of function pointers lies in the fact that findMatches() is a generic function that compares parallel values in two arrays. As it is used above, it compares based on equality. However, since it takes a function pointer, it could compare based on other criteria. For example, the following function also adheres to the definition of a YesNoFcn:

```
bool bothOdd(int inItem1, int inItem2)
{
    return (inItem1 % 2 == 1 && inItem2 % 2 == 1);
}
```

The following program calls findMatches() using both YesNoFcns:

```
int main(int argc, char** argv)
{
    int arr1[7] = {2, 5, 6, 9, 10, 1, 1};
    int arr2[7] = {4, 4, 2, 9, 0, 3, 4};

    cout << "Calling findMatches() using intEqual():" << endl;
    findMatches(arr1, arr2, 7, &intEqual);

    cout << endl;

    cout << "Calling findMatches() using bothOdd():" << endl;
    findMatches(arr1, arr2, 7, &bothOdd);

    return 0;
}
```

The output of this program will be:

```
Calling findMatches() using intEqual():
Match found at position 3 (9, 9)

Calling findMatches() using bothOdd():
Match found at position 3 (9, 9)
Match found at position 5 (1, 3)
```

By using function pointers, a single function, findMatches(), was customized to different uses based on a parameter, inFunction.

Common Memory Pitfalls

It is difficult to pinpoint the exact situations that can lead to a memory-related bug. Every memory leak or bad pointer has its own nuances. There is no magic bullet for resolving memory issues, but there are several common categories of problems and some tools you can use to detect and resolve them.

Underallocating Strings

As you read above, the most common problem with C-style strings is underallocation. In most cases, this arises when the programmer fails to allocate an extra character for the trailing '\0' sentinel. Underallocation of strings also occurs when programmers assume a certain fixed maximum size. The basic built-in string functions will not adhere to a fixed size — they will happily write off the end of the string into uncharted memory.

The following code reads data off a network connection and puts it in a C-style string. This is done in a loop because the network connection only receives a small amount of data at a time. When NULL is returned from the getMoreData() function, all of the data has been received.

```
char buffer[1024];   // Allocate a whole bunch of memory.
bool done = false;

while (!done) {
    char* nextChunk = getMoreData();
    if (nextChunk == NULL) {
        done = true;
    } else {
        strcat(buffer, nextChunk); // BUG! No guarantees against buffer overrun!
        delete[] nextChunk;
    }
}
```

There are three ways to resolve this problem. In increasing order of preference, they are:

1. Find a version of getMoreData() that takes a maximum size as a parameter. Each time you call getMoreData(), only give it the amount of space that you have left as the maximum size.

2. Keep track of how much space is left in the buffer. When it is no longer big enough for the current chunk, allocate a new buffer with twice as much space and copy the original buffer into the new buffer.

3. Use C++-style strings, which will handle the memory associated with concatenation on your behalf. That's right, let it go!

Memory Leaks

Finding and fixing memory leaks is one of the more frustrating parts of programming in C++. Your program finally works and appears to give the correct results. Then, you start to notice that your program gobbles up more and more memory as it runs. Your program has a memory leak.

Memory leaks occur when you allocate memory and neglect to release it. At first, this sounds like the result of careless programming that could easily be avoided. After all, if every new has a corresponding delete in every class you write, there should be no memory leaks, right? Actually, that's not always true. In the following code, the `Simple` class is properly written to release any memory that it allocates. However, when the `doSomething()` function is called, the pointer is changed to another `Simple` object without deleting the old one. Once you lose a pointer to an object, it's nearly impossible to delete it.

```
#include <iostream>

using namespace std;

class Simple
{
    public:
        Simple() { mIntPtr = new int(); }
        ~Simple() { delete mIntPtr; }

        void setIntPtr(int inInt) { *mIntPtr = inInt; }
        void go() { cout << "Hello there" << endl; }

    protected:
        int* mIntPtr;
};

void doSomething(Simple*& outSimplePtr)
{
    outSimplePtr = new Simple(); // BUG! Doesn't delete the original.
}

int main(int argc, char** argv)
{
    Simple* simplePtr = new Simple(); // Allocate a Simple object.

    doSomething(simplePtr);

    delete simplePtr; // Only cleans up the second object
}
```

In cases like the preceding example, the memory leak probably arose from poor communication between programmers or poor documentation of code. The caller of `doSomething()` may not have realized that the variable was passed by reference and thus had no reason to expect that the pointer would be reassigned. If they did notice that the parameter is a non-`const` reference to a pointer, they may have suspected that something strange was happening, but there is no comment around `doSomething()` that explains this behavior.

Finding and Fixing Memory Leaks

Memory leaks are hard to track down because you can't easily look at memory and see what objects are not in use and where they were originally allocated. Luckily, there are programs that can do this for you. Memory leak detection tools range from expensive professional software packages to free downloadable tools. One such free tool is valgrind, an open-source tool for Linux that, amongst other things, pinpoints the exact line in your code where a leaked object was allocated.

The following output, generated by running valgrind on the previous program, pinpoints the exact location where memory was allocated but never released. In this case, there were two leaks — the first `Simple` object that was never deleted and the heap-based integer that it created.

```
==15606== Memcheck, a.k.a. Valgrind, a memory error detector for x86-linux.
==15606== Copyright (C) 2002-2003, and GNU GPL'd, by Julian Seward.
==15606== Using valgrind-2.0.0, a program supervision framework for x86-linux.
==15606== Copyright (C) 2000-2003, and GNU GPL'd, by Julian Seward.
==15606== Estimated CPU clock rate is 1136 MHz
==15606== For more details, rerun with: -v
==15606==
==15606==
==15606== ERROR SUMMARY: 0 errors from 0 contexts (suppressed: 0 from 0)
==15606== malloc/free: in use at exit: 8 bytes in 2 blocks.
==15606== malloc/free: 4 allocs, 2 frees, 16 bytes allocated.
==15606== For counts of detected errors, rerun with: -v
==15606== searching for pointers to 2 not-freed blocks.
==15606== checked 4455600 bytes.
==15606==
==15606== 4 bytes in 1 blocks are still reachable in loss record 1 of 2
==15606==    at 0x4002978F: __builtin_new (vg_replace_malloc.c:172)
==15606==    by 0x400297E6: operator new(unsigned) (vg_replace_malloc.c:185)
==15606==    by 0x804875B: Simple::Simple() (leaky.cpp:8)
==15606==    by 0x8048648: main (leaky.cpp:24)
==15606==
==15606==
==15606== 4 bytes in 1 blocks are definitely lost in loss record 2 of 2
==15606==    at 0x4002978F: __builtin_new (vg_replace_malloc.c:172)
==15606==    by 0x400297E6: operator new(unsigned) (vg_replace_malloc.c:185)
==15606==    by 0x8048633: main (leaky.cpp:24)
==15606==    by 0x4031FA46: __libc_start_main (in /lib/libc-2.3.2.so)
==15606==
==15606== LEAK SUMMARY:
==15606==    definitely lost: 4 bytes in 1 blocks.
==15606==    possibly lost:   0 bytes in 0 blocks.
==15606==    still reachable: 4 bytes in 1 blocks.
==15606==         suppressed: 0 bytes in 0 blocks.
```

Of course, programs like valgrind can't actually fix the leak for you — what fun would that be? These tools provide information that you can use to find the actual problem. Normally, that involves stepping through the code to find out where the pointer to an object was overwritten without the original object being released. Some debuggers provide "watch point" functionality that can stop execution of the program when this occurs.

Smart Pointers

An increasingly popular technique for avoiding memory leaks is the use of *smart pointers*. Smart pointers are a notion that arose from the fact that most memory-related issues are avoidable by putting everything on the stack. The stack is much safer than the heap because stack variables are automatically destructed and cleaned up when they go out of scope. Smart pointers combine the safety of stack variables with the flexibility of heap variables.

The theory behind a smart pointer is quite simple: it is an object with an associated pointer. When the smart pointer goes out of scope, the associated pointer is deleted. It essentially wraps a heap object inside of a stack-based object.

The C++ standard template library includes a basic implementation of a smart pointer, called `auto_ptr`. Instead of storing dynamically allocated objects in pointers, you can store them in stack-based instances of `auto_ptr`. You won't need to explicitly release memory associated with an `auto_ptr` — it will get cleaned up when the `auto_ptr` goes out of scope.

As an example, consider the following function that blatantly leaks memory by allocating a `Simple` object on the heap and neglecting to release it.

```
void leaky()
{
    Simple* mySimplePtr = new Simple();  // BUG! Memory is never released!

    mySimplePtr->go();
}
```

Using the `auto_ptr` class, the object still is not explicitly deleted. However, when the `auto_ptr` object goes out of scope (at the end of the method) it releases the `Simple` object in its destructor.

```
void notLeaky()
{
    auto_ptr<Simple> mySimpleSmartPtr(new Simple());

    mySimpleSmartPtr->go();
}
```

One of the greatest characteristics of smart pointers is that they provide enormous benefit without requiring the user to learn a lot of new syntax. As you can see in the preceding code, the smart pointer can still be dereferenced (using * or ->) just like a standard pointer.

Chapter 16 provides an actual implementation of a smart pointer template class through operator overloading. Chapter 25 describes an enhanced implementation of smart pointers that includes reference counting.

Double-Deleting and Invalid Pointers

Once you release memory associated with a pointer using `delete`, the memory is available for use by other parts of your program. Nothing stops you, however, from attempting to continue to use the pointer. Double deletion is also a problem. If you use `delete` a second time on a pointer, the program could be releasing memory that has since been assigned to another object.

Double deletion and use of already released memory are both hard problems to track down because the symptoms may not show up immediately. If two deletions occur within a relatively short amount of time, the program might work indefinitely because the associated memory is not reused that quickly. Similarly, if a deleted object is used immediately after being deleted, most likely it will still be intact.

Of course, there is no guarantee that such behavior will work or continue to work. The memory allocator is under no obligation to preserve any object once it has been deleted. Even if it does work, it is extremely poor programming style to use objects that have been deleted.

Many memory leak checking programs, such as valgrind, will also detect double deletion and use of released objects.

Accessing Out-of-Bounds Memory

Earlier in this chapter, you read that since a pointer is just a memory address, it is possible to have a pointer that points to a random location in memory. Such a condition is quite easy to fall into. For example, consider a C-style string that has somehow lost its `'\0'` termination character. The following function, which attempts to fill the string with all `'m'` characters, would instead continue to fill the contents of memory following the string with `'m'`s.

```
void fillWithM(char* inStr)
{
    int i = 0;

    while (inStr[i] != '\0') {
        inStr[i] = 'm';
        i++;
    }
}
```

If an improperly terminated string were handed to this function, it would only be a matter of time before an essential part of memory was overwritten and the program crashed. Consider what might happen if the memory associated with the objects in your program is suddenly overwritten with `'m'`s. It's not pretty!

Bugs that result in writing to memory past the end of an array are often called *buffer overflow errors*. Such bugs have been exploited by several high-profile viruses and worms. A devious hacker can take advantage of the ability to overwrite portions of memory to inject code into a running program.

Luckily, many memory checking tools detect buffer overflows as well. Also, using higher-level constructs like C++ strings and vectors will help prevent numerous bugs associated with writing to C-style strings and arrays.

Summary

In this chapter, you learned the ins and outs of dynamic memory, from the basic syntax to the low-level underpinnings. Aside from memory checking tools and careful coding, there are two keys to avoiding dynamic memory-related problems. First, you need to understand how pointers work under the hood. In reading about two different mental models for pointers, we hope you are confident that you know how the compiler doles out memory. Second, you can avoid all sorts of dynamic memory issues by obscuring pointers with stack-based objects, like the C++ string class and smart pointers.

14

Demystifying C++ I/O

A program's fundamental job is to accept input and produce output. A program that produces no output of any sort would not be very useful. All languages provide some mechanism for I/O, either as a built-in part of the language or through OS-specific hooks. A good I/O system is both flexible and easy to use. Part of being flexible is polymorphism: flexible I/O systems support input and output through a variety of devices, such as files and the user console. They also support the reading and writing of different types of data. I/O is error-prone because data coming from a user can be incorrect or the underlying file system or other data source can be inaccessible. Thus, a good I/O system is also capable of handling error conditions.

If you are familiar with the C language, you have undoubtedly used `printf()` and `scanf()`. As I/O mechanisms, `printf()` and `scanf()` are certainly flexible. Through escape codes and variable placeholders, they can be customized to read in specially formatted data or output anything from an integer to a string. `printf()` and `scanf()`, however, falter on other measures of good I/O systems. They do not handle errors particularly well, they are not flexible enough to handle custom data types, and, worst of all in an object-oriented language like C++, they are not at all object oriented!

C++ provides a more refined method of input and output through a mechanism known as *streams*. Streams are a flexible and object-oriented approach to I/O. In this chapter, you will learn how to use streams for data output and input. You will also learn how to use the stream mechanism to read from various sources and write to various destinations, such as the user console, files, and even strings. This chapter covers the most commonly used I/O features. This chapter also covers the increasingly important topic of writing programs that can be localized to different regions around the world.

Using Streams

The stream metaphor takes a bit of getting used to. At first, streams may seem more complex than traditional C-style I/O, such as `printf()`. In reality, they seem complicated initially only because there is a deeper metaphor behind streams than there is behind `printf()`. Don't worry though; after a few examples, you'll never look back.

What Is a Stream, Anyway?

As you read in Chapter 1, the cout stream is like a laundry chute for data. You throw some variables down the stream, and they are written to the user's screen, or *console*. More generally, all streams can be viewed as data chutes. Streams vary in their direction and their associated source or destination. For example, the cout stream that you are already familiar with is an output stream so its direction is "out." It writes data to the console so its associated destination is "console." There is another standard stream called cin that accepts input from the user. Its direction is in, and its associated source is console. cout and cin are predefined instances of streams that are defined within the std namespace in C++.

> **Every input stream has an associated source. Every output stream has an associated destination.**

Stream Sources and Destinations

Streams as a concept can be applied to any object that accepts data or emits data. You could write a stream-based network class or stream-based access to a MIDI-based instrument. In C++, there are three common sources and destinations for streams.

You have already read many examples of user, or console, streams. Console input streams make programs interactive by allowing input from the user during run time. Console output streams provide feedback to the user and output results.

File streams, as the name implies, read data from a file system and write data to a file system. File input streams are useful for reading in configuration data and saved files or for batch processing file-based data. File output streams are useful for saving state and providing output.

String streams are an application of the stream metaphor to the string type. With a string stream, you can treat character data just as you would treat any other stream. For the most part, this is merely a handy syntax for functionality that could be handled through methods on the string class. However, using stream syntax provides opportunities for optimization and can be far more convenient than direct use of the string class.

The rest of this section deals with console streams (cin and cout). Examples of file and string streams are provided later in this chapter. Other types of streams, such as printer output or network I/O are provided by the operating system and are not built into the language.

Output with Streams

Output using streams was introduced in Chapter 1 and has been used in almost every chapter in this book. This section will briefly revisit some of those basics then will introduce material that is more advanced.

Output Basics

Output streams are defined in the <ostream> header file. Most programmers include <iostream> in their programs, which in turn includes the headers for both input streams and output streams. The <iostream> header also declares the standard console output stream, cout.

The << operator is the simplest way to use output streams. C++ basic types, such as ints, pointers, doubles, and characters, can be output using <<. In addition, the C++ string class is compatible with <<, and C-style strings are properly output as well. Following are some examples of using << and their corresponding output.

```
int i = 7;
cout << i;
```

7

```
char ch = 'a';
cout << ch;
```

a

```
string myString = "Marni is adorable.";
cout << myString;
```

Marni is adorable.

The cout stream is the built-in stream for writing to the console, or *standard output*. Recall that you can "chain" uses of << together to output multiple pieces of data. This is because the << operator returns the stream as its result so you can immediately use << again on the same stream. For example:

```
int i = 11;
cout << "On a scale of 1 to cute, Marni ranks " << i << "!";
```

On a scale of 1 to cute, Marni ranks 11!

C++ streams will correctly parse C-style escape codes, such as strings that contain \n, but it is much more hip to use the built-in endl mechanism for this purpose. The following example uses endl, which is defined in the std namespace to represent an end-of-line character and to flush the output buffer. Several lines of text are output using one line of code.

```
cout << "Line 1" << endl << "Line 2" << endl << "Line 3" << endl;
```

```
Line 1
Line 2
Line 3
```

Methods of Output Streams

The << operator is, without a doubt, the most useful part of output streams. However, there is additional functionality to be explored. If you take a peek at the <ostream> header file, you'll see many lines of overloaded definitions of the << operator. You'll also find some useful public methods.

put() and write()

put() and write() are *raw output methods*. Instead of taking an object or variable that has some defined behavior for output, these methods accept a character or character array, respectively. The data passed to these methods are output as is, without any special formatting or processing. Escape characters, such as \n are still output in their correct form (i.e., a carriage return), but no polymorphic output will occur. The following function takes a C-style string and outputs it to the console without using the << operator:

```
void rawWrite(const char* data, int dataSize)
{
    cout.write(data, dataSize);
}
```

The next function writes the prescribed index of a C-style string to the console using the put method.

```
void rawPutChar(const char* data, int charIndex)
{
    cout.put(data[charIndex]);
}
```

flush()

When you write to an output stream, the stream does not necessarily write the data to its destination right away. Most output streams *buffer*, or accumulate data instead of writing it out as it comes in. The stream will *flush*, or write out the accumulated data, when one of the following conditions occurs:

❑   A sentinel, such as the endl marker, is reached.

❑   The stream goes out of scope and is destructed.

❑   Input is requested from a corresponding input stream (i.e., when you make use of cin for input, cout will flush). In the section on file streams, you will learn how to establish this type of link.

❑   The stream buffer is full.

❑   You explicitly tell the stream to flush its buffer.

One way to explicitly tell a stream to flush is to call its flush() method, as in the code that follows.

```
cout << "abc";
cout.flush();    // abc is written to the console.
cout << "def";
cout << endl;    // def is written to the console.
```

> Not all output streams are buffered. The **cerr** stream, for example, does not buffer its output.

Handling Output Errors

Output errors can arise in a variety of situations. Perhaps you are attempting to write to a file that does not exist or has been given read-only permissions. Maybe a disk error has prevented a write operation from succeeding or the console has somehow gotten into a locked-up state. None of the streams code you have read up until this point has considered these possibilities, mainly for brevity. However, in professional C++ programs, it is vital that you address any error conditions that occur.

When a stream is in its normal usable state, it is said to be "good." The good() method can be called directly on a stream to determine whether or not the stream is currently good.

```
if (cout.good()) {
    cout << "All good" << endl;
}
```

The `good()` method provides an easy way to obtain basic information about the validity of the steam, but it does not tell you why the steam is unusable. There is a method called `bad()` that provides a bit more information. If `bad()` returns `true`, it means that a fatal error has occurred (as opposed to any nonfatal condition like end-of-file). Another method, `fail()`, returns true if the most recent operation has failed, implying that the next operation will also fail. For example, after calling `flush()` on an output stream, you could call `fail()` to make sure the stream is still usable.

```
cout.flush();
if (cout.fail()) {
    cerr << "Unable to flush to standard out" << endl;
}
```

To reset the error state of a stream, use the `clear()` method:

```
cout.clear();
```

Error checking is performed less frequently for console output streams than for file output streams or input streams. The methods discussed here apply for other types of streams as well and are revisited below as each type is discussed.

Output Manipulators

One of the unusual features of streams is that you can throw more than just data down the chute. C++ streams also recognize *manipulators*, objects that make a change to the behavior of the stream instead of, or in addition to, providing data for the stream to work with.

You have already seen one manipulator: `endl`. The `endl` manipulator encapsulates data and behavior. It tells the stream to output a carriage return and to flush its buffer. Following are some other useful manipulators, many of which are defined in the `<ios>` and `<iomanip>` standard header files.

- ❑ **boolalpha and noboolalpha.** Tells the stream to output `bool` values as *true* and *false* (`boolalpha`) or *1* and *0* (`noboolalpha`). The default is `noboolalpha`.

- ❑ **hex, oct, and dec.** Outputs numbers in hexadecimal, octal, and base 10, respectively.

- ❑ **setprecision.** Sets the number of decimal places that are output for fractional numbers. This is a parameterized manipulator (meaning that it takes an argument).

- ❑ **setw.** Sets the field width for outputting numerical data. This is a parameterized manipulator.

- ❑ **setfill.** Specifies the character that is used to pad numbers that are smaller than the specified width. This is a parameterized manipulator.

- ❑ **showpoint and noshowpoint.** Forces the stream to always or never show the decimal point for floats and doubles with no fractional part.

The following program uses several of these manipulators to customize its output.

```
#include <iostream>
#include <iomanip>

using namespace std;
int main(int argc, char** argv)
{
    bool myBool = true;
    cout << "This should be true: " << boolalpha << myBool << endl;
    cout << "This should be 1: " << noboolalpha << myBool << endl;
    double dbl = 1.452;
    cout << "This should be @@1.452: " << setw(7) << setfill('@') << dbl << endl;
}
```

If you don't care for the concept of manipulators, you can usually get by without them. Streams provide much of the same functionality through equivalent methods like setPrecision(). See Appendix B for details.

Input with Streams

Input streams provide a simple way to read in structured or unstructured data. In this section, the techniques for input are discussed within the context of cin, the console input stream.

Input Basics

There are two easy ways to read data using an input stream. The first is an analog of the << operator that outputs data to an output stream. The corresponding operator for reading data is >>. When you use >> to read data from an input stream, the variable you provide is the storage for the received value. For example, the following program reads a line of input from the user and puts it into a string. Then the string is output back to the console.

```
#include <iostream>
#include <string>

using namespace std;

int main(int argc, char** argv)
{
    string userInput;
    cin >> userInput;
    cout << "User input was " << userInput << endl;
}
```

By default, the input stream will *tokenize* values according to white space. For example, if a user runs the previous program and enters hello there as input, only the characters up to the first white space character (the space character in this instance) will be captured into the userInput variable. The output would be:

```
User input was hello
```

The >> operator works with different variable types, just like the << operator. For example, to read an integer, the code differs only in the type of the variable:

```
#include <iostream>
using namespace std;

int main(int argc, char** argv)
{
    int userInput;
    cin >> userInput;
    cout << "User input was " << userInput << endl;
}
```

You can use input streams to read in multiple values, mixing and matching types as necessary. For example, the following function, an excerpt from a restaurant reservation system, asks the user for a last name and number of people in their party.

```
void getReservationData()
{
    string guestName;
    int partySize;

    cout << "Name and number of guests: ";
    cin >> guestName >> partySize;
    cout << "Thank you, " << guestName << "." << endl;
    if (partySize > 10) {
        cout << "An extra gratuity will apply." << endl;
    }
}
```

Note that even though the use of cout does not explicitly flush the buffer using endl or flush(), the text will still be written to the console because the use of cin immediately flushes the cout buffer. cin and cout are linked together in this way.

If you get confused between << and >>, just think of the angles as pointing towards their destination. In an input stream, << points toward the stream itself because data are being sent to the stream. In an output stream, >> points toward the variables because data are being stored.

Input Methods

Just like output streams, input streams have several methods that allow a lower level of access than the functionality provided by the more common >> operator.

get()

The get() method allows raw input of data from a stream. The simplest version of get() simply returns the next character in the stream, though other versions exist that read multiple characters at once. () is most commonly used to avoid the automatic tokenization that occurs with the >> operator. For example, the following function reads a name, which can be made up of several words, from an input stream until the end of the stream is reached.

```
string readName(istream& inStream)
{
    string name;
    while (inStream.good()) {
        int next = inStream.get();
        if (next == EOF) break;
```

```
            name += next;// Implicitly convert to a char and append.
    }

    return name;
}
```

There are several interesting observations to make about the previous function. First, its parameter is a reference to an `istream`, not a `const` reference. The methods that read in data from a stream will change the actual stream (most notably, its position), so they are not `const` methods. Thus, you can't call them on a `const` reference. Second, the return value of `get()` is stored in an `int`, not in a `char`. Because `get()` can return special noncharacter values such as `EOF` (end of file), `int`s are used. When `next` is appended to the `string`, it is implicitly converted to a `char`.

The previous function is a bit strange because there are two ways to get out of the loop. Either the stream can get into a "not good" state, or the end of the stream is reached. A more common pattern for reading from a stream uses a different version of `get()` that takes a reference to a character and returns a reference to the stream. This pattern takes advantage of the fact that evaluating an input stream within a conditional context will result in true only if the stream is available for additional reading. Encountering an error or reaching the end-of-file both cause the stream to evaluate to false. The underlying details of the conversion operations required to implement this feature are explained in Chapter 16. The following version of the same function is a bit more concise.

```
string readName(istream& inStream)
{
    string name;
    char next;    while (inStream.get(next)) {
        name += next;
    }

    return name;
}
```

unget()

For most purposes, the correct way to think of an input stream is as a one-way chute. Data falls down the chute and into variables. The `unget()` method breaks this model in a way by allowing you to push data back up the chute.

A single call to `unget()` causes the stream to back up by one position, essentially putting the last character read back on the stream.

```
char ch1, ch2, ch3;

in >> ch1 >> ch2 >> ch3;
in.unget();
char testChar;
in >> testChar;

// testChar == ch3 at this point
```

putback()

putback(), like unget(), lets you move backward by one character in an input stream. The difference is that the putback() method takes the character being placed back on the stream as a parameter:

```
char ch1;

in >> ch1;
in.putback(ch1);

// ch1 will be the next character read off the stream.
```

peek ()

The peek() method allows you to preview the next value that *would* be returned if you were to call get(). To take the chute metaphor perhaps a bit too far, you could think of it as looking up the chute without a value actually falling down it.

peek() is ideal for any situation where you need to look ahead before reading a value. For example, your program may do something different, depending on whether the next value starts with a number, as in the following code snippet.

```
int next = cin.peek();
if (isdigit(next)) {
    processNumber();
} else {
    processText();
}
```

getline()

Obtaining a single line of data from an input stream is so common that a method exists to do it for you. The getline() method fills a character buffer with a line of data up to the specified size, as in the following code.

```
char buffer[kBufferSize + 1];
cin.getline(buffer, kBufferSize);
```

Note that getline() removes the newline character from the stream. However, the resulting string will not include the newline character. There is a form of get() that performs the same operation as getline(), except that it leaves the newline character in the input stream.

There is also a function called getline() that can be used with C++ strings. It is defined in the std namespace and takes a stream reference, a string reference, and an optional delimiter as parameters:

```
string myString;

std::getline(cin, myString);
```

Handling Input Errors

Input streams have a number of methods to detect unusual circumstances. Most of the error conditions related to input streams occur when there is no data available to read. For example, the end of stream (referred to as *end of file*, even for nonfile streams) may have been reached. The most common way of querying the state of an input stream is to access it within a conditional, as above. You can also call the `good()` method, just like an output stream. There is also an `eof()` method that returns `true` if the stream has reached its end.

You should also get in the habit of checking the stream state after reading data so that you can recover from bad input.

The following program shows the common pattern for reading data from a stream and handling errors. The program reads numbers from standard input and displays their sum once end of file is reached. Note that in most command-line environments, end of file is indicated on the console with `control-D`.

```cpp
#include <iostream>
#include <fstream>
#include <string>

using namespace std;

int main()
{
    int sum = 0;

    if (!cin.good()) {
        cout << "Standard input is in a bad state!" << endl;
        exit(1);
    }

    int number;
    while (true) {
        cin >> number;
        if (cin.good()) {
            sum += number;
        } else if (cin.eof()) {
            break; // Reached end of file
        } else {
            // Error!
            cin.clear(); // Clear the error state.
            string badToken;
            cin >> badToken; // Consume the bad input.
            cerr << "WARNING: Bad input encountered: " << badToken << endl;
        }
    }

    cout << "The sum is " << sum << endl;


    return 0;
}
```

Input Manipulators

The built-in input manipulators, described in the list that follows, can be sent to an input stream to customize the way that data is read.

- ❑ **boolalpha and noboolalpha.** If boolalpha is used, the string *true* will be interpreted as a Boolean value true and *false* will be treated as the Boolean value false. If noboolalpha is set, they will not. The default is noboolalpha.

- ❑ **hex, oct, and dec.** Reads numbers in hexadecimal, octal, and base 10, respectively.

- ❑ **skipws and noskipws.** Tells the stream to either skip white space when tokenizing or to read in white space as its own token.

- ❑ **ws.** A handy manipulator that simply skips over the current series of white space at the present position in the stream.

Input and Output with Objects

As you saw earlier, you can use the << operator to output a C++ string even though it is not a basic type. In C++, objects are able to prescribe how they are output and input. This is accomplished by *overloading* the << operator to understand a new type or class.

Why would you want to overload <<? If you are familiar with the printf() function in C, you know that it is not flexible in this area. printf() knows about several types of data, but there really isn't a way to give it additional knowledge. For example, consider the following simple class:

```
class Muffin
{
    public:
        string      getDescription() const;
        void        setDescription(const string& inDescription);
        int         getSize() const;
        void        setSize(int inSize);
        bool        getHasChocolateChips() const;
        void        setHasChocolateChips(bool inChips);

    protected:
        string      mDescription;
        int         mSize;
        bool        mHasChocolateChips;
};

string Muffin::getDescription() const { return mDescription; }
void Muffin::setDescription(const string& inDescription)
{
    mDescription = inDescription;
}

int Muffin::getSize() const { return mSize; }
void Muffin::setSize(int inSize) { mSize = inSize; }
bool Muffin::getHasChocolateChips() const { return mHasChocolateChips; }
void Muffin::setHasChocolateChips(bool inChips) { mHasChocolateChips = inChips; }
```

To output an object of class Muffin using printf(), it would be nice if you could simply specify it as an argument, perhaps using %m as a placeholder:

```
printf("Muffin output: %m\n", myMuffin); // BUG! printf doesn't understand Muffin.
```

Unfortunately, the `printf()` function knows nothing about the Muffin type and is unable to output an object of type Muffin. Worse still, because of the way the `printf()` function is declared, this will result in a run-time error, not a compile-time error (though a good compiler will give you a warning).

The best you can do with `printf()` is to add a new `output()` method to the Muffin class.

```
class Muffin
{
    public:
        string    getDescription() const;
        void      setDescription(const string& inDescription);
        int       getSize() const;
        void      setSize(int inSize);
        bool      getHasChocolateChips() const;
        void      setHasChocolateChips(bool inChips);

        void output();
    protected:
        string    mDescription;
        int       mSize;
        bool      mHasChocolateChips;
};

string Muffin::getDescription() const { return mDescription; }
void Muffin::setDescription(const string& inDescription) { mDescription =
inDescription; }
int Muffin::getSize() const { return mSize; }
void Muffin::setSize(int inSize) { mSize = inSize; }
bool Muffin::getHasChocolateChips() const { return mHasChocolateChips; }
void Muffin::setHasChocolateChips(bool inChips) { mHasChocolateChips = inChips; }

void Muffin::output()
{
    printf("%s, Size is %d, %s\n", getDescription().c_str(), getSize(),
            (getHasChocolateChips() ? "has chips" : "no chips"));
}
```

Using such a mechanism is cumbersome, however. To output a Muffin in the middle of another line of text, you'd need to split the line into two calls with a call to `Muffin::output()` in between, as shown here:

```
printf("The muffin is ");
myMuffin.output();
printf(" -- yummy!\n");
```

Overloading the << operator lets you output a Muffin just like you output a string — simply by providing it as an argument to <<. Chapter 16 covers the details of overloading the << and >> operators.

String Streams

String streams provide a way to use stream semantics with `strings`. In this way, you can have an *in-memory stream* that represents textual data. Such an approach can be useful in applications where multiple threads are contributing data to the same string, or where you want to pass a `string` around to different functions, while retaining the current read position. String streams are also useful for parsing text, because streams have built-in tokenizing functionality.

The `ostringstream` and `istringstream` classes are used for writing and reading data to/from a string, respectively. They are both defined in the `<sstream>` header file. Because `ostringstream` and `istringstream` inherit the same behavior as `ostream` and `istream`, working with them is pleasantly similar.

The following simple program requests words from the user and outputs them to a single `ostringstream`, separated by the tab character. At the end of the program, the whole stream is turned into a `string` object using the `str()` method and is written to the console.

```cpp
#include <iostream>
#include <sstream>

using namespace std;
int main(int argc, char** argv)
{
    ostringstream outStream;
    while (cin.good()) {
        string nextToken;
        cout << "Next token: ";
        cin >> nextToken;

        if (nextToken == "done") break;
        outStream << nextToken << "\t";
    }

    cout << "The end result is: " << outStream.str() << endl;
}
```

Reading data from a string stream is similarly familiar. The following function creates and populates a `Muffin` object (see earlier example) from a string input stream. The stream data is in a fixed format so that the function can easily turn its values into calls to the `Muffin` setters.

```cpp
Muffin createMuffin(istringstream& inStream)
{
    Muffin muffin;
    // Assume data is properly formatted:
    // Description size chips

    string description;
    int size;
    bool hasChips;
    // Read all three values. Note that chips is represented
    // by the strings "true" and "false"
    inStream >> description >> size >> boolalpha >> hasChips;
    muffin.setSize(size);
    muffin.setDescription(description);
    muffin.setHasChocolateChips(hasChips);

    return muffin;
}
```

*Turning an object into a "flattened" type, like a **string**, is often called marshalling. Marshalling is useful for saving objects to disk or sending them across a network, and is further described in Chapter 24.*

The main advantage of a string stream over a standard C++ `string` is that, in addition to data, the object knows about its current position. There may also be performance benefits depending on the particular implementation of string streams.

File Streams

Files lend themselves very well to the stream abstraction because reading and writing files always involves a position in addition to the data. In C++, the `ofstream` and `ifstream` classes provide output and input functionality for files. They are defined in the header file `<fstream>`.

When dealing with the file system, it is especially important to detect and handle error cases. The file you are working with could be on a network file store that just went offline. You may be trying to write to a file that the current user does not have permissions to edit. These conditions can be detected using the standard error handling mechanisms described earlier.

The only major difference between output file streams and other output streams is that the file stream constructor takes the name of the file and the mode in which you would like to open it. The default mode is write, which starts writing to a file at the beginning, overwriting any existing data. You can also open an output file stream in append mode using the constant `ios_base::app`.

The following simple program opens the file *test* and outputs the arguments to the program.

```
#include <iostream>
#include <fstream>

using namespace std;
int main(int argc, char** argv)
{
    ofstream outFile("test");
    if (!outFile.good()) {
        cerr << "Error while opening output file!" << endl;
        return -1;
    }
    outFile << "There were " << argc << " arguments to this program." << endl;
    outFile << "They are: " << endl;
    for (int i = 0; i < argc; i++) {
        outFile << argv[i] << endl;
    }
}
```

Jumping around with seek() and tell()

The `seek()` and `tell()` methods are present on all input and output streams, but they rarely make sense outside of the context of file streams.

The seek() methods let you move to an arbitrary position within an input or output stream. Such movement breaks the streams metaphor, so it is best to use these methods sparingly. There are several forms of seek(). The methods of seek() within an input stream are actually called seekg() (the g is for *get*), and the versions of seek() in an output stream are called seekp() (the p is for *put*). Each type of stream has two methods of seeking. You can seek to an absolute position in the stream, such as the beginning or the 17th position, or you can seek to an offset, such as the 3rd position from the current marker. Positions are measured in characters.

To seek to an absolute position in an output stream, you can use the one-parameter version of seekp(), as in the following case, which uses the constant ios_base::beg to move to the beginning of the stream. There are also constants provided for the end of the stream (ios_base::end) and the current position of the stream (ios_base::cur).

```
outStream.seekp(ios_base::beg);
```

Seeking within an input stream is exactly the same, except that the seekg() method is used:

```
inStream.seekg(ios_base::beg);
```

The two-argument versions of seek() move to a relative position in the stream. The first argument prescribes how many positions to move and the second argument provides the starting point. To move relative to the beginning of the file, the constant ios_base::beg is used. To move relative to the end of the file, ios_base::end is used. To move relative to the current position, ios_base::cur is used. For example, the following line moves to the second character from the beginning of the stream:

```
outStream.seekp(2, ios_base::beg);
```

The next example moves to the third-to-last position of an input stream.

```
inStream.seekg(-3, ios_base::end);
```

You can also query a stream's current location using the tell() method. tell() returns a ios_base::pos_type that indicates the current position. You can use this result to remember the current marker position before doing a seek() or to query whether you are in a particular location. As with seek(), there are separate versions of tell() for input streams and output streams. Input streams use tellg(), and output streams use tellp().

The following line checks the position of an input stream to determine if it is at the beginning.

```
ios_base::pos_type curPos = inStream.tellg();
if (curPos == ios_base::beg) {
    cout << "We're at the beginning." << endl;
}
```

Below is a sample program that brings it all together. This program writes into a file called test.out and performs the following tests:

1. Outputs the string 12345 to the file
2. Verifies that the marker is at position 5 in the stream
3. Moves to position 2 in the output stream

4. Outputs a 0 in position 2 and flushes the output stream

5. Opens an input stream on the test.out file

6. Reads the first token as an integer

7. Confirms that the value is 12045

```cpp
#include <iostream>
#include <fstream>

using namespace std;

int main(int argc, char** argv)
{
    ofstream fout("test.out");
    if (!fout) {
        cerr << "Error opening test.out for writing\n";
        exit(1);
    }

    // 1. Output the string "12345".
    fout << "12345";

    // 2. Verify that the marker is at the end.
    ios_base::pos_type curPos = fout.tellp();      if (curPos == 5) {
        cout << "Test passed: Currently at position 5" << endl;
    } else {
        cout << "Test failed: Not at position 5" << endl;
    }

    // 3. Move to position 2 in the stream.
    fout.seekp(2, ios_base::beg);

    // 4. Output a 0 in position 2 and flush the stream.
    fout << 0;
    fout.flush();

    // 5. Open an input stream on test.out.
    ifstream fin("test.out");
    if (!fin) {
        cerr << "Error opening test.out for reading\n";
        exit(1);
    }

    // 6. Read the first token as an integer.
    int testVal;
    fin >> testVal;

    // 7. Confirm that the value is 12045.
    if (testVal == 12045) {
        cout << "Test passed: Value is 12045" << endl;
    } else {
        cout << "Test failed: Value is not 12045";
    }
}
```

Linking Streams Together

A link can be established between any input and output streams to give them flush-on-access behavior. In other words, when data is requested from an input stream, its linked output stream will automatically flush. This behavior is available to all streams, but is particularly useful for file streams that may be dependent upon each other.

Stream linking is accomplished with the `tie()` method. To tie an output stream to an input stream, call `tie()` on the input stream, and pass the address of the output stream. To break the link, pass NULL.

The following program ties the input stream of one file to the output stream of an entirely different file. You could also tie it to an output stream on the same file, but bidirectional I/O (covered below) is perhaps a more elegant way to read and write the same file simultaneously.

```cpp
#include <iostream>
#include <fstream>
#include <string>

using namespace std;

int main(int argc, char** argv)
{
    ifstream inFile("input.txt");
    ofstream outFile("output.txt");

    // Set up a link between inFile and outFile.
    inFile.tie(&outFile);

    // Output some text to outFile. Normally, this would
    // not flush because std::endl was not sent.
    outFile << "Hello there!";

    // outFile has NOT been flushed.

    // Read some text from inFile. This will trigger flush()
    // on outFile.
    string nextToken;
    inFile >> nextToken;

    // outFile HAS been flushed.
}
```

The `flush()` method is defined on the `ostream` base class, so you can also link an output stream to another output stream:

```cpp
outFile.tie(&anotherOutputFile);
```

Such a relationship would mean that every time you wrote to one file, the buffered data that had been sent to the other file would be written. You could use this mechanism to keep two related files synchronized.

Bidirectional I/O

So far, this chapter has discussed input and output streams as two separate but related classes. In fact, there is such a thing as a stream that performs both input and output. A *bidirectional stream* operates as both an input stream and an output stream.

Bidirectional streams are subclasses of `iostream`, which in turn subclasses both `istream` and `ostream`, thus serving as an example of useful multiple inheritance. As you would expect, bidirectional streams support both the >> operator and the << operator, as well as the methods of both input streams and output streams.

The `fstream` class provides a bidirectional file stream. `fstream` is ideal for applications that need to replace data within a file because you can read until you find the correct position, then immediately switch to writing. For example, imagine a program that stores a list of mappings between ID numbers and phone numbers. It might use a data file with the following format:

```
123  408-555-0394
124  415-555-3422
164  585-555-3490
100  650-555-3434
```

A reasonable approach to such a program would be to read in the entire data file when the program opens and rewrite the file, with any modifications, when the program closes. If the data set were very large, however, you might not be able to keep everything in memory. With `iostreams`, you don't have to. You can easily scan through the file to find a record, and you can add new records by opening the file for output in append mode. To modify an existing record, you could use a bidirectional stream, as in the following function that changes the phone number for a given ID.

```cpp
void changeNumberForID(const string& inFileName, int inID,
    const string& inNewNumber)
{
    fstream ioData(inFileName.c_str());
    if (!ioData) {
        cerr << "Error while opening file " << inFileName << endl;
        exit(1);
    }

    // Loop until the end of file
    while (ioData.good()) {
        int id;
        string number;

        // Read the next ID.
        ioData >> id;

        // Check to see if the current record is the one being changed.
        if (id == inID) {
            // Seek to the current read position
            ioData.seekp(ioData.tellg());

            // Output a space, then the new number.
            ioData << " " << inNewNumber;
            break;
        }
```

```
        // Read the current number to advance the stream.
        ioData >> number;
    }
}
```

Of course, an approach like this will only work properly if the data is of a fixed size. When the preceding program switched from reading to writing, the output data overwrote other data in the file. To preserve the format of the file, and to avoid writing over the next record, the data had to be the same size.

String streams can also be accessed in a bidirectional manner through the `stringstream` class.

> **Bidirectional streams have separate pointers for the read position and the write position. When switching between reading and writing, you will need to seek to the appropriate position.**

Internationalization

When you're learning how to program in C or C++, it's useful to think of a character as equivalent to a byte and to treat all characters as members of the ASCII (U.S.) character set. In reality, Professional C++ programmers recognize that successful software programs are used throughout the world. Even if you don't initially write your program with international audiences in mind, you shouldn't prevent yourself from *localizing*, or making the software internationally aware, at a later date.

Wide Characters

The problem with viewing a character as a byte is that not all languages, or *character sets*, can be fully represented in 8 bits, or 1 byte. Luckily, C++ has a built-in type called `wchar_t` that holds a *wide character*. Languages with non-ASCII (U.S.) characters such as Japanese and Arabic can be represented in C++ with `wchar_t`.

If there is *any* chance that your program will be used in a non-Western character set context (hint: there is!), you should use wide characters from the beginning. Using `wchar_t` is simple because it works just like a `char`. The only difference is that string and character literals are prefixed with the letter L to indicate that a wide-character encoding should be used. For example, to initialize a `wchar_t` character to be the letter m, you would write it like this:

```
wchar_t myWideCharacter = L'm';
```

There are wide-character versions of all your favorite types and classes. The wide `string` class is `wstring`. The "prefix the letter w" pattern applies to streams as well. Wide-character file output streams are handled with the `wofstream`, and input is handled with the `wifstream`. The joy of pronouncing these class names (*woof-stream? whiff-stream?*) is reason enough to make your programs internationally aware!

In addition to `cout`, `cin`, and `cerr`, there are wide versions of the built-in console and error streams called `wcout`, `wcin`, and `wcerr`. As with the other wide-stream classes and types, using them is no different from using the nonwide versions, as shown by the following simple program:

```
#include <iostream>

using namespace std;

int main(int argc, char** argv)
{
    wcout << L"I am internationally aware." << endl;
}
```

Non-Western Character Sets

Wide characters are a great step forward because they increase the amount of space available to define a single character. The next step is to figure out how that space is used. In traditional (i.e., obsolete) ASCII characters, each letter corresponded to a particular number. Each number could fit in a single byte, so a letter was the same as a number, which was the same as a byte.

Modern character representation isn't very different. The map of characters to numbers (now called code points) is quite a bit larger because it handles many different character sets in addition to the characters that English-speaking programmers are familiar with. The map of characters to code points in all the known character sets is defined by the Unicode standard. For example, the Hebrew character א (pronounced aleph) maps to the Unicode code point 05D0. No other character in any other character set maps to that code point.

To work properly with Unicode text, you also need to know its *encoding*. Different applications can store Unicode characters in different ways. In C++, the standard encoding of wide characters is known as UTF-16 because each character is held in 16 bits.

Locales and Facets

Character sets are only one of the differences in data representation between countries. Even countries that use similar character sets, such as Great Britain and the United States, still differ in how they represent data such as dates and money.

The standard C++ library contains a built-in mechanism that groups specific data about a particular place together into a *locale*. A locale is a collection of settings about a particular location. An individual setting is called a *facet*. An example of a locale is U.S. English. An example of a facet is the format used to display a date. There are several built-in facets that are common to all locales. The language also provides a way to customize or add facets.

Using Locales

From a programmer's perspective, locales are an automatic feature of the language. When using I/O streams, data is formatted according to a particular locale. Locales are simply objects that can be attached to a stream. For example, the following line uses the output stream's imbue() method to attach the U.S. English locale (usually named "en_U") to the wide-character console output stream:

```
wcout.imbue(locale("en_US"));   // locale is defined in the std namespace
```

U.S. English is usually *not* the default locale. The default locale is generally the *classic* locale, which uses ANSI C conventions. The classic C locale is similar to U.S. English settings, but there are slight differences.

For example, if you do not set a locale at all, or set the default locale, and you output a number, it will be presented without any punctuation:

```
wcout.imbue(locale("C"))
wcout << 32767 << endl;
```

The output of this code will be:

```
32767
```

If you set the U.S. English locale, however, the number will be formatted with U.S. English punctuation. The following code to set the locale to U.S. English before outputting the number:

```
wcout.imbue(locale("en_US"));
wcout << 32767 << endl;
```

The output of this code will be:

```
32,767
```

As you may be aware, different regions have different approaches to formatting numerical data, including the punctuation used to separate thousands and denote a decimal place.

The names of locales can be implementation-specific, although most implementations have standardized on the practice of separating the language and the area in two-letter sections with an optional encoding. For example, the locale for the French language, as spoken in France is fr_FR. The locale for Japanese spoken in Japan with Japanese Industrial Standard encoding is ja_JP.jis.

Most operating systems have a mechanism to determine the locale as defined by the user. In C++, you can pass an empty string to the locale object constructor to create a locale from the user's environment. Once this object is created, you can use it to query the locale, possibly making programmatic decisions based on it.

For example, the following program creates a default locale. The name() method is used to get a C++ string that describes the locale. One of two messages is output, depending on whether the locale appears to be U.S. English or not.

```
#include <iostream>
#include <string>

using namespace std;

int main(int argc, char** argv)
{
    locale loc("");

    if (loc.name().find("en_US") == string::npos &&
        loc.name().find("United States") == string::npos) {
        wcout << L"Welcome non-U.S. user!" << endl;
    } else {
        wcout << L"Welcome U.S. user!" << endl;
    }
}
```

Determining a location based on the name of the locale is not necessarily an accurate way to decide where the user is physically located, but it can provide a clue.

Using Facets

You can use the std::use_facet() function to obtain a particular facet in a particular locale. For example, the following expression retrieves the standard monetary punctuation facet of the British English facet.

```
use_facet<moneypunct<wchar_t> >(locale("en_GB"));
```

Note that the innermost template type determines the character type to use. This is usually wchar_t or char. The use of nested template classes is unfortunate, but once you get past the syntax, the result is an object that contains all the information you want to know about British money punctuation. The data available in the standard facets are defined in the <locale> header and its associated files.

The following program brings together locales and facets by printing out the currency symbol in both U.S. English and British English. Note that, depending on your environment, the British currency symbol may appear as a question mark, a box, or not at all. Also note that locale names can vary by platform. If your environment is equipped to handle it, you may actually get the British pound symbol.

```
#include <iostream>
#include <locale>

using namespace std;

int main(int argc, char** argv)
{
    locale locUSEng ("en_US");
    locale locBritishEng ("en_GB");

    wstring dollars = use_facet<moneypunct<wchar_t> >(locUSEng).curr_symbol();
    wstring pounds = use_facet<moneypunct<wchar_t> >(locBritishEng).curr_symbol();

    wcout << L"In the US, the currency symbol is " << dollars << endl;
    wcout << L"In Great Britain, the current symbol is " << pounds << endl;
}
```

Summary

As we hope you have discovered, streams provide a flexible and object-oriented way to perform input and output. The most important message in this chapter, even more important that the use of streams, is the concept of a stream. Some operating systems may have their own file access and I/O facilities, but knowledge of how streams and streamlike libraries work is essential to working with any type of modern I/O system.

We also hope you have gained an appreciation for coding with internationalization in mind. As anyone who has been through a localization effort will tell you, adding support for a new language or locale is infinitely easier if you have planned ahead by using Unicode characters and being mindful of locales.

15

Handling Errors

Inevitably, your C++ programs will encounter errors. The program might be unable to open a file, the network connection might go down, or the user might enter an incorrect value, to name a few possibilities. Professional C++ programs recognize these situations as *exceptional,* but not *unexpected,* and handle them appropriately. The C++ language provides a feature called *exceptions* to support error handling in your programs.

The code examples in this book so far have virtually ignored error conditions for brevity. This chapter rectifies that simplification by teaching you how to incorporate error handling into your programs from their beginnings. It focuses on C++ exceptions, including the details of their syntax, and describes how to employ them effectively to create well-designed error-handling programs. This chapter presents:

❑   An overview of C++ error handling, including pros and cons of exceptions in C++

❑   Syntax of exceptions

   ❑   Throwing and catching exceptions

   ❑   Uncaught exceptions

   ❑   Throw lists

❑   Exception class hierarchies and polymorphism

   ❑   The C++ exception hierarchy

   ❑   Writing your own exception classes

❑   Stack unwinding and cleanup

❑   Common error handling issues

   ❑   Memory allocation errors

   ❑   Errors in constructors and destructors

Errors and Exceptions

Even perfectly written programs encounter errors and exceptional situations. No program exists in isolation; they all depend on external facilities such as networks and file systems, on external code such as third-party libraries, and on user input. Each of these areas can introduce exceptional situations. Thus, anyone who writes a computer program must include error-handling capabilities. Some languages, such as C, do not include many specific language facilities for error handling. Programmers using these languages generally rely on return values from functions and other ad hoc approaches. Other languages, such as Java, enforce the use of a language feature called *exceptions* as an error-handling mechanism. C++ lies between these extremes. It provides language support for exceptions, but does not require their use. However, you can't ignore exceptions entirely in C++ because a few basic facilities, such as memory allocation routines, use them.

What Are Exceptions, Anyway?

Exceptions are a mechanism for a piece of code to notify another piece of code of an "exceptional" situation or error condition without progressing through the normal code paths. The code that encounters the error *throws* the exception, and the code that handles the exception *catches* it. Exceptions do not follow the fundamental rule of step-by-step execution to which you are accustomed. When a piece of code throws an exception, the program control immediately stops executing code step by step and transitions to the exception handler, which could be anywhere from the next line in the same function to several function calls up the stack. If you like sports analogies, you can think of the code that throws an exception as an outfielder throwing a baseball back to the infield, where the nearest infielder (closest exception handler) catches it. Figure 15-1 shows a hypothetical stack of three function calls. Function A() has the exception handler. It calls function B(), which calls function C(), which throws the exception.

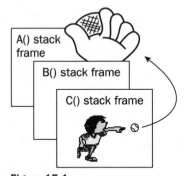

Figure 15-1

Figure 15-2 shows the handler catching the exception. The stack frames for C() and B() have been removed, leaving only A().

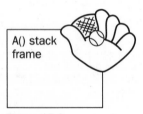

Figure 15-2

Some people who have used C++ for years are surprised to learn that C++ supports exceptions. Programmers tend to associate exceptions with languages like Java, in which they are much more visible. However, C++ has full-fledged support for exceptions.

Why Exceptions in C++ Are a Good Thing

As mentioned above, run-time errors in C++ programs are inevitable. Despite that fact, error handling in most C and C++ programs is messy and ad hoc. The de facto C error-handling standard, which was carried over into many C++ programs, uses integer function return codes and the `errno` macro to signify errors. `errno` acts as a global integer variable that functions can use to communicate errors back to calling functions.

Unfortunately, the integer return codes and `errno` are used inconsistently. Some functions return 0 for success and –1 for an error. If they return –1, they also set `errno` to an error code. Other functions return 0 for success and nonzero for an error, with the actual return value specifying the error code. These functions do not use `errno`. Still others return 0 for failure instead of for success, presumably because 0 always evaluates to false in C and C++.

These inconsistencies can cause problems because programmers encountering a new function often assume that its return codes are the same as other similar functions. That is not always true. On Solaris 9, there are two different libraries of synchronization objects: the POSIX version and the Solaris version. The function to initialize a semaphore in the POSIX version is called `sem_init()`, and the function to initialize a semaphore in the Solaris version is called `sema_init()`. As if that weren't confusing enough, the two functions handle error codes differently! `sem_init()` returns –1 and sets `errno` on error, while `sema_init()` returns the error code directly as a positive integer, and does not set `errno`.

Another problem is that functions in C++ allow only one return value, so if you need to return both an error and a value, you must find an alternative mechanism. One choice is to return the value or error through a reference parameter. Another choice is to make the error code one possible value of the return type, such as a `NULL` pointer.

Exceptions provide an easier, more consistent, and safer mechanism for error handling. There are several specific advantages of exceptions over the ad hoc approaches in C and C++.

❑ Return codes from functions can be ignored. Exceptions cannot be ignored: if your program fails to catch an exception, it will terminate.

❑ Integer return codes do not contain any semantic information. Different numbers can mean different things to different programmers. Exceptions can contain semantic information in both their type names and, if they are objects, in their data.

❑ Integer return codes are devoid of surrounding information. You can use exceptions to pass as much information as you want from the code that finds the error to the code that handles it. Exceptions can also be used to communicate information other than errors, though many programmers consider that an abuse of the exception mechanism.

❑ Exception handling can skip levels of the call stack. That is, a function can handle an error that occurred several function calls down the stack, without error-handling code in the intermediate functions. Return codes require each level of the call stack to clean up explicitly after the previous level.

Why Exceptions in C++ Are a Bad Thing

Despite the advantages of exceptions in general, their specific implementation in C++ makes them undesirable to some programmers. The first problem is performance: the language features added to support exceptions slow down all programs, even those that don't use exceptions. However, unless you're writing high-performance or systems-level software, you should be okay. Chapter 17 discusses this issue in more detail.

A second problem is that exception support in C++ is not an integral part of the language the same way it is in other languages, such as Java. For example, in Java a function that does not specify a list of possible exceptions that it can throw is not allowed to throw any exceptions. That makes sense. In C++, it is just the opposite: a function that does not specify a list of exceptions can throw any exception it wants! Additionally, the exception list is not enforced at compile time in C++, meaning that the exception list of a function can be violated at run time. These, and other, inconsistencies make exceptions in C++ harder to use correctly than they should be, intimidating some programmers.

Finally, the exception mechanism presents problems for dynamically allocated memory and resource cleanup. When you program with exceptions, it is difficult to ensure that you perform proper cleanup. This issue is explored below.

Our Recommendation

Despite the downsides, we recommend exceptions as a useful mechanism for error handling. We feel that the structure and error-handling formalization that exceptions provide outweigh the less desirable aspects. Thus, the remainder of this chapter focuses on exceptions. Even if you do not plan to use exceptions in your programs, you should skim this chapter to gain a familiarity with some of the common error-handling issues in C++ programming.

Exception Mechanics

Exceptional situations arise frequently in the area of file input and output. Below is a simple function to open a file, read a list of integers from the file, and store the integers in the supplied `vector` data structure. Recall from Chapter 4 that the `vector` is a dynamic array. You can add elements to it using the `push_back()` method, and access them with array notation.

```
#include <fstream>
#include <iostream>
#include <vector>
#include <string>
using namespace std;

void readIntegerFile(const string& fileName, vector<int>& dest)
{
    ifstream istr;
    int temp;

    istr.open(fileName.c_str());

    // Read the integers one by one and add them to the vector.
    while (istr >> temp) {
```

```
                dest.push_back(temp);
        }
    }
```

You might use readIntegerFile() like this:

```
int main(int argc, char** argv)
{
    vector<int> myInts;
    const string fileName = "IntegerFile.txt";

    readIntegerFile(fileName, myInts);

    for (size_t i = 0; i < myInts.size(); i++) {
        cout << myInts[i] << " ";
    }
    cout << endl;

    return (0);
}
```

The lack of error handling in these functions should jump out at you. The rest of this section shows you how to add error handling with exceptions.

Throwing and Catching Exceptions

The most likely problem to occur in the readIntegerFile() function is for the file open to fail. That's a perfect situation for throwing an exception. The syntax looks like this:

```
#include <fstream>
#include <iostream>
#include <vector>
#include <string>
#include <exception>
using namespace std;

void readIntegerFile(const string& fileName, vector<int>& dest)
{
    ifstream istr;
    int temp;

    istr.open(fileName.c_str());
    if (istr.fail()) {
        // We failed to open the file: throw an exception.
        throw exception();
    }

    // Read the integers one by one and add them to the vector.
    while (istr >> temp) {
        dest.push_back(temp);
    }
}
```

`throw` is a keyword in C++, and is the only way to throw an exception. C++ provides a class named `exception`, declared in the `<exception>` header file. The `exception()` part of the `throw` line means that you are constructing a new object of type `exception` to throw.

If the function fails to open the file and executes the `throw exception();` line, the rest of the function is skipped, and control transitions to the nearest exception handler.

Throwing exceptions in your code is most useful when you also write code that handles them. Here is a `main()` function that handles the exception thrown in `readIntegerFile()`:

```cpp
int main(int argc, char** argv)
{
    vector<int> myInts;
    const string fileName = "IntegerFile.txt";

    try {
        readIntegerFile(fileName, myInts);
    } catch (const exception& e) {
        cerr << "Unable to open file " << fileName << endl;
        exit (1);
    }

    for (size_t i = 0; i < myInts.size(); i++) {
        cout << myInts[i] << " ";
    }
    cout << endl;

    return (0);
}
```

Exception handling is a way to "try" a block of code, with another block of code designated to react to any problems that might occur. In this particular case, the `catch` statement reacts to any exception of type `exception` that was thrown within the `try` block by printing an error message and exiting. If the `try` block finishes without throwing an exception, the `catch` block is skipped. You can think of `try`/`catch` blocks as glorified `if` statements. If an exception is thrown in the `try` block, execute the `catch` block. Otherwise, skip it.

> *Although by default streams do not throw exceptions, you can tell the streams to throw exceptions for error conditions by calling their **exceptions()** method. However, no less a luminary than Bjarne Stroustrup (who created C++) recommends against this approach. In* The C++ Programming Language, *third edition, he says " . . . I prefer to deal with the stream state directly. What can be handled with local control structures within a function is rarely improved by the use of exceptions." This book follows his guidelines in that regard.*

Exception Types

You can throw an exception of any type. The preceding example throws an object of type `exception`, but exceptions do not need to be objects. You could throw a simple `int` like this:

```cpp
void readIntegerFile(const string& fileName, vector<int>& dest)
{
    // Code omitted
    istr.open(fileName.c_str());
```

```
        if (istr.fail()) {
            // We failed to open the file: throw an exception.
            throw 5;
        }
        // Code omitted
    }
```

You would then need to change the `catch` statement as well:

```
int main(int argc, char** argv)
{
    // code omitted
    try {
        readIntegerFile(fileName, myInts);
    } catch (int e) {
        cerr << "Unable to open file " << fileName << endl;
        exit (1);
    }

    // Code omitted
}
```

Alternatively, you could throw a `char*` C-style string. This technique is sometimes useful because the string can contain information about the exception.

```
void readIntegerFile(const string& fileName, vector<int>& dest)
{
    // Code omitted
    istr.open(fileName.c_str());
    if (istr.fail()) {
        // We failed to open the file: throw an exception.
        throw "Unable to open file";
    }
    // Code omitted
}
```

When you catch the `char*` exception, you can print the result:

```
int main(int argc, char** argv)
{
    // Code omitted
    try {
        readIntegerFile(fileName, myInts);
    } catch (const char* e) {
        cerr << e << endl;
        exit (1);
    }
    // Code omitted
}
```

However, you should generally throw objects as exceptions for two reasons:

❑   Objects convey information simply by their class name.

❑   Objects can store information, such as strings, that describe the exceptions.

The C++ standard library defines eight exception classes, which are described in more detail below. You can also write your own exception classes. How to do so is also detailed below.

Catching Exception Objects by Const and Reference

In the example above in which `readIntegerFile()` throws an object of type `exception`, the `catch` line looks like this:

```
} catch (const exception& e) {
```

However, there is no requirement to catch objects by `const` reference. You could catch the object by value like this:

```
} catch (exception e) {
```

Alternatively, you could catch the object by reference (without the `const`):

```
} catch (exception& e) {
```

Also, as you saw in the `char*` example, you can catch pointers to exceptions, as long as pointers to exceptions are thrown.

> **Your programs can catch exceptions by value, reference, `const` reference, or pointer.**

Throwing and Catching Multiple Exceptions

Failure to open the file is not the only problem `readIntegerFile()` could encounter. Reading the data from the file can cause an error if it is formatted incorrectly. Here is an implementation of `readIntegerFile()` that throws an exception if it cannot either open the file or read the data correctly.

```
void readIntegerFile(const string& fileName, vector<int>& dest)
{
    ifstream istr;
    int temp;

    istr.open(fileName.c_str());
    if (istr.fail()) {
        // We failed to open the file: throw an exception.
        throw exception();
    }

    // Read the integers one by one and add them to the vector.
    while (istr >> temp) {
        dest.push_back(temp);
    }

    if (istr.eof()) {
        // We reached the end-of-file.
        istr.close();
    } else {
        // Some other error. Throw an exception.
```

```
        istr.close();
        throw exception();
    }
}
```

Your code in main() does not need to change because it already catches an exception of type exception. However, that exception could now be thrown in two different situations, so you should modify the error message accordingly:

```
int main(int argc, char** argv)
{
    // Code omitted
    try {
        readIntegerFile(fileName, myInts);
    } catch (const exception& e) {
        cerr << "Unable either to open or to read " << fileName << endl;
        exit (1);
    }
    // Code omitted
}
```

Alternatively, you could throw two different types of exceptions from readIntegerFile(), so that the caller can tell which error occurred. Here is an implementation of readIntegerFile() that throws an exception object of class invalid_argument if the file cannot be opened and an object of class runtime_exception if the integers cannot be read. Both invalid_argument and runtime_exception are classes defined in the header file <stdexcept> as part of the C++ Standard Library.

```
#include <fstream>
#include <iostream>
#include <vector>
#include <string>
#include <stdexcept>

using namespace std;

void readIntegerFile(const string& fileName, vector<int>& dest)
{
    ifstream istr;
    int temp;

    istr.open(fileName.c_str());
    if (istr.fail()) {
        // We failed to open the file: throw an exception.
        throw invalid_argument("");
    }

    // Read the integers one by one and add them to the vector.
    while (istr >> temp) {
        dest.push_back(temp);
    }

    if (istr.eof()) {
        // We reached the end-of-file.
        istr.close();
    } else {
        // Some other error. Throw an exception.
```

```
                    istr.close();
                    throw runtime_error("");
            }
    }
```

There are no public default constructors for `invalid_argument` and `runtime_error`, only `string` constructors.

Now `main()` can catch both `invalid_argument` and `runtime_error` with two `catch` statements:

```
int main(int argc, char** argv)
{
    // Code omitted
    try {
        readIntegerFile(fileName, myInts);
    } catch (const invalid_argument& e) {
        cerr << "Unable to open file " << fileName << endl;
        exit (1);
    } catch (const runtime_error& e) {
        cerr << "Error reading file " << fileName << endl;
        exit (1);
    }

    // Code omitted
}
```

If an exception is thrown inside the `try` block, the compiler will match the type of the exception to the proper catch handler. So, if `readIntegerFile()` is unable to open the file and throws in `invalid_argument` object, it will be caught by the first `catch` statement. If `readIntegerFile()` is unable to read the file properly and throws a `runtime_error`, then the second `catch` statement will catch the exception.

Matching and Const

The `const`-ness specified in the type of the exception you want to catch makes no difference for matching purposes. That is, this line matches any exception of type `runtime_error`.

```
    } catch (const runtime_error& e) {
```

This line also matches any exception of type `runtime_error`:

```
    } catch (runtime_error& e) {
```

> You should generally catch exceptions with `const` to document that you are not modifying them.

Matching Any Exception

You can write a `catch` line that matches any possible exception with the special syntax shown here:

```
int main(int argc, char** argv)
{
    // Code omitted
    try {
```

```
            readIntegerFile(fileName, myInts);
        } catch (...) {
            cerr << "Error reading or opening file " << fileName << endl;
            exit (1);
        }
        // Code omitted
    }
```

The three dots are not a typo. They are a wildcard that match any exception type. When you are calling poorly documented code, this technique can be useful to ensure that you catch all possible exceptions. However, in situations where you have complete information about the set of thrown exceptions, this technique is considered suboptimal because it handles every exception type identically. It's better to match exception types explicitly and take appropriate, targeted action.

Uncaught Exceptions

If your program throws an exception that is not caught anywhere, the program will terminate. This behavior is not usually what you want. The point of exceptions is to give your program a chance to handle and correct undesirable or unexpected situations. If your program didn't catch an exception, there was little point in throwing it to begin with.

> **Catch and handle all possible exceptions thrown in your programs.**

Even if you can't handle a particular exception, you should still write code to catch it and print an appropriate error message before exiting.

It is also possible to change the behavior of your program if there is an uncaught exception. When the program encounters an uncaught exception, it calls the built-in terminate() function, which simply calls abort() from <cstdlib> to kill the program. You can set your own terminate_handler by calling set_terminate() with a pointer to a callback function that takes no arguments and returns no value. terminate(), set_terminate(), and terminate_handler are all declared in the <exception> header. Before you get too excited about this feature, you should know that your callback function must still terminate the program, or else abort() will be called anyway. It can't just ignore the error. However, you can use it to print a helpful error message before exiting. Here is an example of a main() function that doesn't catch the exceptions thrown by readIntegerFile(). Instead, it sets the terminate_handler to a callback that prints an error message before exiting:

```
void myTerminate()
{
    cout << "Uncaught exception!\n";
    exit(1);
}

int main(int argc, char** argv)
{
    vector<int> myInts;
    const string fileName = "IntegerFile.txt";

    set_terminate(myTerminate);

    readIntegerFile(fileName, myInts);
```

```
    for (size_t i = 0; i < myInts.size(); i++) {
        cerr << myInts[i] << " ";
    }
    cout << endl;

    return (0);
}
```

Although not shown in this example, `set_terminate()` returns the old `terminate_handler` when it sets the new one. The `terminate_handler` applies program-wide, so it's considered good style to reset the old `terminate_handler` when you have completed the code that needed the new `terminate_handler`. In this case, the entire program needs the new `terminate_handler`, so there's no point in resetting it.

Although it's important to know about `set_terminate()`, it's not a very effective exception-handling approach. We recommend trying to catch and handle each exception individually in order to provide more precise error handling.

Throw Lists

C++ allows you to specify the exceptions a function or method intends to throw. This specification is called the *throw list* or the *exception specification*. Here is the `readIntegerFile()` function from the earlier example with the proper throw list:

```
void readIntegerFile(const string& fileName, vector<int>& dest)
    throw (invalid_argument, runtime_error)
{
    // Remainder of the function is the same as before
}
```

The throw list simply lists the types of exceptions that can be thrown from the function. Note that the throw list must also be provided for the function prototype:

```
void readIntegerFile(const string& fileName, vector<int>& dest)
    throw (invalid_argument, runtime_error);
```

Unlike `const`, the exception specification is not part of the function or method signature. You cannot overload a function based solely on different exceptions in the throw list.

If a function or method specifies no throw list, it can throw any exception. You've already seen this behavior in the previous implementation of the `readIntegerFile()` function. If you want to specify that a function or method throws no exceptions, you need to write an empty throw list explicitly like this:

```
void readIntegerFile(const string& fileName, vector<int>& dest)
    throw ();
```

If this behavior seems backward to you, you're not alone. However, it's best just to accept it and move on.

> **A function without a throw list can throw exceptions of any type. A function with an empty throw list shouldn't throw any exception.**

Unexpected Exceptions

Unfortunately, the throw list is not enforced at compile time in C++. Code that calls `readIntegerFile()` does not need to catch the exceptions listed in the throw list. This behavior is different from that in other languages, such as Java, which requires a function or method to catch exceptions or declare them in their own function or method throw lists.

Additionally, you could implement `readIntegerFile()` like this:

```
void readIntegerFile(const string& fileName, vector<int>& dest)
    throw (invalid_argument, runtime_error)
{
    throw (5);
}
```

Even though the throw list states that `readIntegerFile()` doesn't throw an int, this code, which obviously throws an int, compiles and runs. However, it won't do what you want. Suppose that you write this `main()` function, assuming that you can catch the int:

```
int main(int argc, char** argv)
{
    vector<int> myInts;
    const string fileName = "IntegerFile.txt";

    try {
        readIntegerFile(fileName, myInts);
    } catch (int x) {
        cerr << "Caught int\n";
    }
}
```

When this program runs and `readIntegerFile()` throws the int exception, the program terminates. It does not allow `main()` to catch the int. However, you can change this behavior.

> **Throw lists don't prevent functions from throwing unlisted exception types, but they prevent the exception from leaving the function.**

When a function throws an exception that is not listed in its throw list, C++ calls a special function `unexpected()`. The built-in implementation of `unexpected()` simply calls `terminate()`. However, just as you can set your own `terminate_handler`, you can set your own `unexpected_handler`. Unlike in the `terminate_handler`, you can actually do something other than just terminate the program in the `unexpected_handler`. Your version of the function must either throw a new exception or terminate the program — it can't just exit the function normally. If it throws a new exception, that exception will be substituted for the unexpected exception as if the new one had been throw originally. If this substituted exception is also not listed in the throw list, the program will do one of two things. If the throw list for the function specifies `bad_exception`, then `bad_exception` will be thrown. Otherwise, the program will terminate. Custom implementations of `unexpected()` are normally used to convert unexpected exceptions into expected exceptions. For example, you could write a version of `unexpected()` like this:

```
void myUnexpected()
{
    cout << "Unexpected exception!\n";
    throw runtime_error("");
}
```

This code converts an unexpected exception to a `runtime_error` exception, which the function `readIntegerFile()` has in its throw list.

You could set this unexpected exception handler in `main()` with the `set_unexpected` function. Like `set_terminate()`, `set_unexpected()` returns the current handler. The `unexpected()` function applies program-wide, not just to this function, so you should reset the handler when you are done with the code that needed your special handler:

```
int main(int argc, char** argv)
{
    vector<int> myInts;
    const string fileName = "IntegerFile.txt";

    unexpected_handler old_handler = set_unexpected(myUnexpected);
    try {
        readIntegerFile(fileName, myInts);
    } catch (const invalid_argument& e) {
        cerr << "Unable to open file " << fileName << endl;
        exit (1);
    } catch (const runtime_error& e) {
        cerr << "Error reading file " << fileName << endl;
        exit (1);
    } catch (int x) {
        cout << "Caught int\n";
    }
    set_unexpected(old_handler);
    // Remainder of function omitted
}
```

Now `main()` handles any exception thrown from `readIntegerFile()` by converting it to a `runtime_error`. However, as with `set_terminate()`, we recommend using this capability judiciously.

`unexpected()`, `set_unexpected()`, and `bad_exception` are all declared in the `<exception>` header file.

Changing the Throw List in Overridden Methods

When you override a `virtual` method in a subclass, you can change the throw list as long as you make it *more restrictive* than the throw list in the superclass. The following changes qualify as more restrictive:

❑ Removing exceptions from the list

❑ Adding subclasses of exceptions that appear in the superclass throw list

The following changes do not qualify as more restrictive:

❑ Adding exceptions to the list that are not subclasses of exceptions in the superclass throw list

❑ Removing the throw list entirely

> If you change throw lists when you override methods, remember that any code that called the superclass version of the method must be able to call the subclass version. Thus, you can't add exceptions.

For example, suppose that you have the following superclass:

```
class Base
{
    public:
        virtual void func() throw(exception) { cout << "Base!\n"; }
};
```

You could write a subclass that overrides func() and specifies that it doesn't throw any exceptions:

```
class Derived : public Base
{
    public:
        virtual void func() throw() { cout << "Derived!\n"; }
};
```

You could also override func() such that it throws a runtime_error as well as an exception, because runtime_error is a subclass of exception.

```
class Derived : public Base
{
    public:
        virtual void func() throw(exception, runtime_error)
            { cout << "Derived!\n"; }
};
```

However, you cannot remove the throw list entirely, because that means func() could throw any exception.

Suppose Base looked like this:

```
class Base
{
    public:
        virtual void func() throw(runtime_error) { cout << "Base!\n"; }
};
```

You cannot then override func() in Derived with a throw list like this:

```
class Derived : public Base
{
    public:
        virtual void func() throw(exception) { cout << "Derived!\n"; } // ERROR!
};
```

exception is a superclass of runtime_error, so you cannot substitute an exception for a runtime_error.

Are Throw Lists Useful?

Given the opportunity to specify the behavior of a function in its signature, it seems wasteful not to take advantage of it. The exceptions thrown from a particular function are an important part of its interface, and should be documented as well as possible.

Unfortunately, most of the C++ code in use today, including the Standard Library, does not follow this advice. That makes it difficult for you to determine which exceptions can be thrown when you use this code. Additionally, it is impossible to specify the exception characteristics of templatized functions and methods. When you don't even know what types will be used to instantiate the template, you have no way to determine the exceptions that methods of those types can throw. As a final problem, the throw list syntax and enforcement is somewhat obscure.

Thus, we leave the decision up to you.

Exceptions and Polymorphism

As described above, you can actually throw any type of exception. However, classes are the most useful types of exceptions. In fact, exception classes are usually written in a hierarchy, so that you can employ polymorphism when you catch the exceptions.

The Standard Exception Hierarchy

You've already seen several exceptions from the C++ standard exception hierarchy: `exception`, `runtime_error`, and `invalid_argument`. Figure 15-3 shows the complete hierarchy:

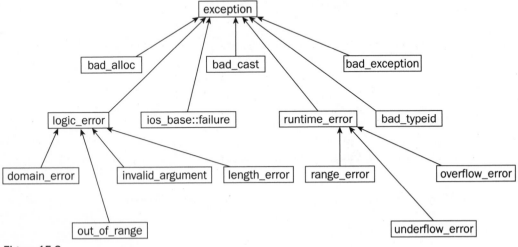

Figure 15-3

All of the exceptions thrown by the C++ Standard Library are objects of classes in this hierarchy. Each class in the hierarchy supports a `what()` method that returns a `char*` string describing the exception. You can use this string in an error message.

All the exception classes except for the base `exception` require you to set in the constructor the string that will be returned by `what()`. That's why you have to specify a string in the constructors for `runtime_error` and `invalid_argument`. Now that you know what the strings are used for, you can make them more useful. Here is an example where the string is used to pass the full error message back to the caller:

```cpp
void readIntegerFile(const string& fileName, vector<int>& dest)
    throw (invalid_argument, runtime_error)
{
    ifstream istr;
    int temp;

    istr.open(fileName.c_str());
    if (istr.fail()) {
        // We failed to open the file: throw an exception.
        string error = "Unable to open file " + fileName;
        throw invalid_argument(error);
    }

    // Read the integers one by one and add them to the vector.
    while (istr >> temp) {
        dest.push_back(temp);
    }

    if (istr.eof()) {
        // We reached the end-of-file.
        istr.close();
    } else {
        // Some other error. Throw an exception.
        istr.close();
        string error = "Unable to read file " + fileName;
        throw runtime_error(error);
    }
}

int main(int argc, char** argv)
{
    // Code omitted
    try {
        readIntegerFile(fileName, myInts);
    } catch (const invalid_argument& e) {
        cerr << e.what() << endl;
        exit (1);
    } catch (const runtime_error& e) {
        cerr << e.what() << endl;
        exit (1);
    }
    // Code omitted
}
```

Catching Exceptions in a Class Hierarchy

The most exciting feature of exception hierarchies is that you can catch exceptions polymorphically. For example, if you look at the two `catch` statements in `main()` following the call to `readIntegerFile()`, you can see that they are identical except for the exception class that they handle. Conveniently, `invalid_argument` and `runtime_error` are both subclasses of exception, so you can replace the two `catch` statements with a single `catch` statement for class exception:

```
int main(int argc, char** argv)
{
    // Code omitted
    try {
        readIntegerFile(fileName, myInts);
    } catch (const exception& e) {
        cerr << e.what() << endl;
        exit (1);
    }
    // Code omitted
}
```

The `catch` statement for an `exception` reference matches any subclasses of `exception`, including both `invalid_argument` and `runtime_error`. Note that the higher in the exception hierarchy that you catch exceptions, the less specific is your error handling. You should generally catch exceptions at as specific a level as possible.

> **When you catch exceptions polymorphically, make sure to catch them by reference. If you catch exceptions by value, you can encounter slicing, in which case you lose information from the object. See Chapter 10 for details on slicing.**

The polymorphic matching rules work on a "first come, first served" basic. C++ attempts to match the exception against each `catch` statement in order. The exception matches a `catch` statement if it is an object of that class or an object of a subclass of the class, even if a more exact match comes in a later `catch` statement. For example, suppose that you want to catch `invalid_argument` from `readIntegerFile()` explicitly, but leave the generic `exception` match for any other exceptions. The correct way to do so is like this:

```
try {
    readIntegerFile(fileName, myInts);
} catch (const invalid_argument& e) { // List the exception subclass first.
    // Take some special action for invalid filenames.
} catch (const exception& e) { // Now list exception
    cerr << e.what() << endl;
    exit (1);
}
```

The first `catch` statement catches `invalid_argument` exceptions, and the second catches any other exceptions. However, if you reverse the order of the `catch` statements, you don't get the same result:

```
try {
    readIntegerFile(fileName, myInts);
} catch (const exception& e) { // BUG: catching superclass first!
    cerr << e.what() << endl;
    exit (1);
} catch (const invalid_argument& e) {
    // Take some special action for invalid filenames.
}
```

With this order, any exception of a class that subclasses `exception` is caught by the first `catch` statement; the second will never be reached. Some compilers issue a warning in this case, but you shouldn't count on it.

Writing Your Own Exception Classes

There are two advantages to writing your own exception classes.

1. The number of exceptions in the C++ Standard Library is limited. Instead of using an exception class with a generic name, such as `runtime_exception`, you can create classes with names that are more meaningful for the particular errors in your program.

2. You can add your own information to these exceptions. The exceptions in the standard hierarchy allow you to set only an error string. You might want to pass different information in the exception.

We recommend that all the exception classes that you write inherit directly or indirectly from the standard `exception` class. If everyone on your project follows that rule, you know that every exception in the program will be a subclass of `exception` (assuming that you aren't using third-party libraries that break this rule). This guideline makes exception handling via polymorphism significantly easier.

For example, `invalid_argument` and `runtime_error` don't capture very well the file opening and reading errors in `readIntegerFile()`. You can define your own error hierarchy for file errors, starting with a generic `FileError` class:

```cpp
class FileError : public runtime_error
{
    public:
        FileError(const string& fileIn) : runtime_error(""), mFile(fileIn) {}
        virtual ~FileError() throw() {}

        virtual const char* what() const throw() { return mMsg.c_str(); }
        string getFileName() { return mFile; }

    protected:
        string mFile, mMsg;
};
```

As a good programming citizen, you should make `FileError` a part of the standard exception hierarchy. It seems appropriate to integrate it as a child of `runtime_error`. When you write a subclass of `runtime_error` (or any other exception in the standard hierarchy), you need to override two methods: `what()` and the destructor.

`what()` has the signature shown and is supposed to return a `char*` string that is valid until the object is destroyed. In the case of `FileError`, this string comes from the `mMsg` data member, which is set to `""` in the constructor. Subclasses of `FileError` must set this `mMsg` string to something different if they want a different message.

You must override the destructor in order to specify the empty throw list. The compiler-generated destructor has no throw list, which won't compile, because `runtime_error` specifies an empty throw list.

The generic `FileError` class also contains a filename and an accessor for that filename.

The first exceptional situation in `readIntegerFile()` occurs if the file cannot be opened. Thus, you might want to write a `FileOpenError` subclass of `FileError`:

```
class FileOpenError : public FileError
{
    public:
        FileOpenError(const string& fileNameIn);
        virtual ~FileOpenError() throw() {}
};

FileOpenError::FileOpenError(const string& fileNameIn) : FileError(fileNameIn)
{
    mMsg = "Unable to open " + fileNameIn;
}
```

The `FileOpenError` changes the `mMsg` string to represent the file-opening error.

The second exceptional situation in `readIntegerFile()` occurs if the file cannot be read properly. It might be useful for this exception to contain the line number of the error in the file, as well as the filename and the error message string returned from `what()`. Here is a `FileReadError` subclass of `FileError`:

```
class FileReadError : public FileError
{
    public:
        FileReadError(const string& fileNameIn, int lineNumIn);
        virtual ~FileReadError() throw() {}
        int getLineNum() { return mLineNum; }

    protected:
        int mLineNum;
};

FileReadError::FileReadError(const string& fileNameIn, int lineNumIn) :
    FileError(fileNameIn), mLineNum(lineNumIn)
{
    ostringstream ostr;

    ostr << "Error reading " << fileNameIn << " at line " << lineNumIn;
    mMsg = ostr.str();
}
```

Of course, in order to set the line number properly, you need to modify your `readIntegerFile()` function to track the number of lines read instead of just reading integers directly. Here is a new `readIntegerFile()` function that uses the new exceptions:

```
void readIntegerFile(const string& fileName, vector<int>& dest)
    throw (FileOpenError, FileReadError)
{
    ifstream istr;
    int temp;
    char line[1024]; // Assume that no line is longer than 1024 characters.
    int lineNumber = 0;

    istr.open(fileName.c_str());
    if (istr.fail()) {
```

```
            // We failed to open the file: throw an exception.
            throw FileOpenError(fileName);
    }

    while (!istr.eof()) {
        // Read one line from the file.
        istr.getline(line, 1024);
        lineNumber++;

        // Create a string stream out of the line.
        istringstream lineStream(line);

        // Read the integers one by one and add them to the vector.
        while (lineStream >> temp) {
            dest.push_back(temp);
        }

        if (!lineStream.eof()) {
            // Some other error. Close the file and throw an exception.
            istr.close();
            throw FileReadError(fileName, lineNumber);
        }
    }
    istr.close();
}
```

Now code that calls `readIntegerFile()` can use polymorphism to catch exceptions of type `FileError` like this:

```
try {
    readIntegerFile(fileName, myInts);
} catch (const FileError& e) {
    cerr << e.what() << endl;
    exit (1);
}
```

There is one trick to writing classes whose objects will be used as exceptions. When a piece of code throws an exception, the object or value thrown is copied. That is, a new object is constructed from the old object using the copy constructor. It must be copied because the original could go out of scope (and be destroyed and have its memory reclaimed) before the exception is caught, higher up in the stack. Thus, if you write a class whose objects will be thrown as exceptions, you must make those objects copyable. This means that if you have dynamically allocated memory, you must write a destructor, copy constructor, and assignment operator, as described in Chapter 9.

Objects thrown as exceptions are always copied by value at least once.

It is possible for exceptions to be copied more than once, but only if you catch the exception by value instead of by reference.

Catch exception objects by reference to avoid unnecessary copying.

421

Stack Unwinding and Cleanup

When a piece of code throws an exception, control jumps immediately to the exception handler that catches the exception. This exception handler could lie one or more function calls up the stack of execution. As the control jumps up in the stack in a process called *stack unwinding*, all code remaining in each function past the current point of execution is skipped. However, local objects and variables in each function that is unwound are destroyed as if the code finished the function normally.

However, in stack unwinding, pointer variables are not freed, and other cleanup is not performed. This behavior can present problems, as the following code demonstrates:

```
#include <fstream>
#include <iostream>
#include <stdexcept>
using namespace std;

void funcOne() throw(exception);
void funcTwo() throw(exception);

int main(int argc, char** argv)
{
    try {
        funcOne();
    } catch (exception& e) {
        cerr << "Exception caught!\n";
        exit(1);
    }

    return (0);
}

void funcOne() throw(exception)
{
    string str1;
    string* str2 = new string();
    funcTwo();
    delete str2;
}

void funcTwo() throw(exception)
{
    ifstream istr;
    istr.open("filename");
    throw exception();
    istr.close();
}
```

When funcTwo() throws an exception, the closest exception handler is in main(). Control then jumps immediately from this line in funcTwo()

```
    throw exception();
```

to this line in main():

```
    cerr << "Exception caught!\n";
```

In `funcTwo()`, control remains at the line that threw the exception, so this subsequent line never gets a chance to run:

```
    istr.close();
```

However, luckily for you, the `ifstream` destructor is called because `istr` is a local variable on the stack. The `ifstream` destructor closes the file for you, so there is no resource leak here. If you had dynamically allocated `istr`, it would not be destroyed, and the file would not be closed.

In `funcOne()`, control is at the call to `funcTwo()`, so this subsequent line never gets a chance to run:

```
    delete str2;
```

In this case, there really is a memory leak. Stack unwinding does not automatically call `delete` on `str2` for you. However, `str1` is destroyed properly because it is a local variable on the stack. Stack unwinding destroys all local variables correctly.

> **Careless exception handling can lead to memory and resource leaks.**

Two techniques for handling this problem follow.

Catch, Cleanup, and Rethrow

The first, and most common, technique for avoiding memory and resource leaks is for each function to catch any possible exceptions, perform necessary cleanup work, and rethrow the exception for the function higher up the stack to handle. Here is a revised `funcOne()` with this technique:

```
void funcOne() throw(exception)
{
    string str1;
    string* str2 = new string();
    try {
        funcTwo();
    } catch (...) {
        delete str2;
        throw; // Rethrow the exception.
    }
    delete str2;
}
```

This function wraps the call to `funcTwo()` with an exception handler that performs the cleanup (calls `delete` on `str2`) and then rethrows the exception. The keyword `throw` by itself simply rethrows whatever exception was caught most recently. Note that the catch statement uses the `...` syntax to catch any exception.

This method works fine, but can be messy. In particular, note that there are now two identical lines that call `delete` on `str2`: one to handle the exception and one if the function exits normally.

Use Smart Pointers

Smart pointers allow you to write code that automatically prevents memory leaks with exception handling. As you read in Chapter 13, smart pointer objects are allocated on the stack, so whenever the smart pointer object is destroyed, it calls `delete` on the underlying dumb pointer. Here is an example of `funcTwo()` using the `auto_ptr` smart pointer template class in the Standard Library:

```
#include <memory>
using namespace std;

void funcOne() throw(exception)
{
    string str1;
    auto_ptr<string> str2(new string("hello"));
    funcTwo();
}
```

With smart pointers, you never have to remember to `delete` the underlying dumb pointer: the smart pointer destructor does it for you, whether you leave the function via an exception or leave the function normally.

Common Error-Handling Issues

Whether or not you use exceptions in your programs is up to you and your colleagues. However, we strongly encourage you to formalize an error-handling plan for your programs, regardless of your use of exceptions. If you use exceptions, it is generally easier to come up with a unified error-handling scheme, but it is not impossible without exceptions. The most important aspect of a good plan is uniformity of error handling throughout all the modules of the program. Make sure that every programmer on the project understands and follows the error-handling rules.

This section discusses the most common error-handling issues in the context of exceptions, but the issues are also relevant to programs that do not use exceptions.

Memory Allocation Errors

Despite the fact that all of our examples so far in this book have ignored the possibility, memory allocation can, and will, fail. However, production code must account for memory allocation failures. C++ provides several different ways to handle memory errors.

The default behaviors of `new` and `new[]` are to throw an exception of type `bad_alloc`, defined in the `<new>` header file, if they cannot allocate memory. Your code should catch these exceptions and handle them appropriately. The definition of "appropriate" depends on your particular application. In some cases, the memory might be crucial for your program to run correctly, in which case printing an error message and exiting is the best course of action. Other times, the memory might be necessary only for a particular operation or task, in which case you can print an error message and fail the particular operation, but keep the program running.

Thus, all your `new` statements should look something like this:

```
try {
    ptr = new int[numInts];
} catch (bad_alloc& e) {
    cerr << "Unable to allocate memory!\n";
    // Handle memory allocation failure.
    return;
}
// Proceed with function that assumes memory has been allocated.
```

You could, of course, bulk handle many possible new failures with a single `try`/`catch` block at a higher point on the program, if it will work for your program.

Another consideration is that logging an error might try to allocate memory. If new fails, there might not be enough memory left even to log the error message.

Nothrow new

As mentioned in Chapter 13, if you don't like exceptions, you can revert to the old C model in which memory allocation routines return the NULL pointer if they cannot allocate memory. C++ provides *nothrow* versions of new and new[ ], which return NULL instead of throwing an exception if they fail to allocate memory.

```
ptr = new(nothrow) int[numInts];
if (ptr == NULL) {
    cerr << "Unable to allocate memory!\n";
    // Handle memory allocation failure.
    return;
}
// Proceed with function that assumes memory has been allocated.
```

The syntax is a little strange: you really do write "nothrow" as if it's an argument to new (which it is).

Customizing Memory Allocation Failure Behavior

C++ allows you to specify a *new handler* callback function. By default, there is no new handler, so new and new[ ] just throw bad_alloc exceptions. However, if there is a new handler, the memory allocation routine calls the new handler upon memory allocation failure instead of throwing an exception. If the new handler returns, the memory allocation routines attempt to allocate memory again, calling the new handler again if they fail. This cycle could become an infinite loop unless your new handler changes the situation with one of four alternatives. Practically speaking, some of the four options are better than others. Here is the list with commentary:

❑ **Make more memory available.** One trick to expose space is to allocate a large chunk of memory at program start-up, and then to free it with delete in the new handler. If the current request for memory is for a size smaller than the one you free in the new handler, the memory allocation routine will now be able to allocate it. However, this technique doesn't buy you much. If you hadn't preallocated that chunk of memory, the request for memory would have succeeded in the first place and wouldn't have needed to call the new handler. One of the only benefits is that you can log a warning message about low memory in the new handler.

❑ **Throw an exception.** new and new[ ] have throw lists that say they will throw exceptions only of type bad_alloc. So, unless you want to create a call to unexpected(), if you throw an exception from the new handler, throw bad_alloc or a subclass. However, you don't need a new handler to throw an exception: the default behavior does so for you. Thus, if that's all your new handler does, there's no reason to write a new handler in the first place.

❑ **Set a different new handler.** Theoretically, you could have a series of new handlers, each of which tries to create memory and sets a different new handler if it fails. However, such a scenario is usually more complicated than useful.

❑ **Terminate the program.** This option is the most practical and useful of the four. Your new handler can simply log an error message and terminate the program. The advantage of using a new handler over catching the `bad_alloc` exception and terminating in the exception handler is that you centralize the failure handling to one function, and you don't need to litter your code with `try`/`catch` blocks. If there are some memory allocations that can fail but still allow your program to succeed, you can simply set the new handler back to its default of NULL temporarily before calling new in those cases.

If you don't do one of these four things in your new handler, any memory allocation failure will cause an infinite loop.

You set the new handler with a call to `set_new_handler()`, declared in the `<new>` header file. `set_new_handler()` completes the trio of C++ functions to set callback functions. The other two are `setterminate()` and `set_unexpected()`, which are discussed earlier in the chapter. Here is an example of a new handler that logs an error message and aborts the program:

```
void myNewHandler()
{
    cerr << "Unable to allocate memory. Terminating program!\n";
    abort();
}
```

The new handler must take no arguments and return no value. This new handler calls the `abort()` function declared in `<cstdlib>` to terminate the program.

You can set the new handler like this:

```
#include <new>
#include <cstdlib>
#include <iostream>

using namespace std;

int main(int argc, char** argv)
{
    // Code omitted

    // Set the new new_handler and save the old.
    new_handler oldHandler = set_new_handler(myNewHandler);
    // Code that calls new

    // Reset the old new_handler.
    set_new_handler(oldHandler);
    // Code omitted
    return (0);
}
```

Note that `new_handler` is a `typedef` for the type of function pointer that `set_new_handler()` takes.

Errors in Constructors

Before C++ programmers discover exceptions, they are often stymied by error handling and constructors. What if a constructor fails to construct the object properly? Constructors don't have a return value, so the standard preexception error-handling mechanism doesn't work. Without exceptions, the best you can do is to set a flag in the object specifying that it is not constructed properly. You can provide a method, with a name like checkConstructionStatus(), which returns the value of that flag, and hope that clients remember to call the function on the object after constructing it.

Exceptions provide a much better solution. You can throw an exception from a constructor, even though you can't return a value. With exceptions you can easily tell clients whether or not construction of the object succeeded. However, there is one major problem: if an exception leaves a constructor, the destructor for that object will never be called. Thus, you must be careful to clean up any resources and free any allocated memory in constructors before allowing exceptions to leave the constructor. This problem is the same as in any other function, but it is subtler in constructors because you're accustomed to letting the destructors take care of the memory deallocation and resource freeing.

Here is an example of the constructor from the GameBoard class from Chapter 11 retrofitted with exception handling:

```
GameBoard::GameBoard(int inWidth, int inHeight) throw(bad_alloc) :
    mWidth(inWidth), mHeight(inHeight)
{
    int i, j;
    mCells = new GamePiece* [mWidth];

    try {
        for (i = 0; i < mWidth; i++) {
            mCells[i] = new GamePiece[mHeight];
        }
    } catch (...) {
        //
        // Clean up any memory we already allocated, because the destructor
        // will never be called. The upper bound of the for loop is the index
        // of the last element in the mCells array that we tried to allocate
        // (the one that failed). All indices before that one store pointers to
        // allocated memory that must be freed.
        //
        for (j = 0; j < i; j++) {
            delete [] mCells[j];
        }
        delete [] mCells;

        // Translate any exception to bad_alloc.
        throw bad_alloc();
    }
}
```

It doesn't matter if the first new throws an exception because the constructor hasn't allocated anything else yet that needs freeing. If any of the subsequent new calls throw exceptions, though, the constructor must clean up all of the memory already allocated. It catches any exception via . . . because it doesn't know what exceptions the GamePiece constructors themselves might throw.

You might be wondering what happens when you add inheritance into the mix. Superclass constructors run before subclass constructors. If a subclass constructor throws an exception, how are the resources that the superclass constructor allocated freed? The answer is that C++ guarantees that it will run the destructor for any fully constructed "subobjects." Therefore, any constructor that completes without an exception will cause the corresponding destructor to be run.

Errors in Destructors

You should handle all error conditions that arise in destructors in the destructors themselves. You should not let any exceptions be thrown from destructors, for three reasons:

1. Destructors can run while there is another pending exception, in the process of stack unwinding. If you throw an exception from the destructor while another exception is active, the program will terminate. For the brave and curious, C++ does provide the ability to determine, in a destructor, whether you are executing as a result of a normal function exit or delete call, or because of stack unwinding. The function uncaught_exception(), declared in the <exception> header file, returns true if there is an uncaught exception and you are in the middle of stack unwinding. Otherwise, it returns false. However, this approach is messy and should be avoided.

2. What action would clients take? Clients don't call destructors explicitly: they call delete, which calls the destructor. If you throw an exception from the destructor, what is a client supposed to do? It can't call delete on the object again, and it shouldn't call the destructor explicitly. There is no reasonable action the client can take, so there is no reason to burden that code with exception handling.

3. The destructor is your one chance to free memory and resources used in the object. If you waste your chance by exiting the function early due to an exception, you will never be able to go back and free the memory or resources.

Therefore, be careful to catch in a destructor any exceptions that can be thrown by calls you make from the destructor. Normally, destructors call only delete and delete[], which cannot throw exceptions, so there should be no problem.

Putting It All Together

Now that you've learned about error handling and exceptions, here is the entire GameBoard class from Chapter 11 retrofitted with exceptions.

First, here is the class definition:

```
#include <stdexcept>
#include <new>
using std::bad_alloc;
using std::out_of_range;

class GameBoard
{
    public:
        GameBoard(int inWidth = kDefaultWidth, int inHeight = kDefaultHeight)
            throw(bad_alloc);
        GameBoard(const GameBoard& src) throw(bad_alloc);
        ~GameBoard() throw();
```

```
        GameBoard& operator=(const GameBoard& rhs) throw(bad_alloc);

        void setPieceAt(int x, int y, const GamePiece& inPiece)
            throw(out_of_range);
        GamePiece& getPieceAt(int x, int y) throw(out_of_range);
        const GamePiece& getPieceAt(int x, int y) const throw(out_of_range);

        int getHeight() const throw() { return mHeight; }
        int getWidth() const throw() { return mWidth; }

        static const int kDefaultWidth = 100;
        static const int kDefaultHeight = 100;

    protected:
        void copyFrom(const GameBoard& src) throw(bad_alloc);

        GamePiece** mCells;
        int mWidth, mHeight;
};
```

The constructors and `operator=` all throw `bad_alloc` because they perform memory allocation. The destructor, `getHeight()`, and `getWidth()` throw no exceptions. `setPeiceAt()` and `getPieceAt()` throw `out_of_range` if the caller supplies an invalid width or height.

You've already seen the implementation of the constructor in the previous section. Here are the implementations of the `copyFrom()`, `setPieceAt()`, and `getPieceAt()` methods with exception handling. The implementations of the copy constructor and `operator=` did not change except for their throw lists because all the work is in `copyFrom()`, so their implementations are not shown. The destructor also did not change, so its implementation is not shown. Refer to Chapter 11 for details.

```
void GameBoard::copyFrom(const GameBoard& src) throw(bad_alloc)
{
    int i, j;
    mWidth = src.mWidth;
    mHeight = src.mHeight;

    mCells = new GamePiece *[mWidth];

    try {
        for (i = 0; i < mWidth; i++) {
            mCells[i] = new GamePiece[mHeight];
        }
    } catch (...) {
        // Clean up any memory we already allocated.
        // If this function is called from the copy constructor,
        // the destructor will never be called.
        // Use the same upper bound on the loop as described in the constructor.
        for (j = 0; j < i; j++) {
            delete [] mCells[j];
        }
        delete [] mCells;

        // Set mCells and mWidth to values that will allow the
        // destructor to run without harming anything.
        // This function is called from operator=, in which case the
```

```
            // object was already constructed, so the destructor will be
            // called.
            mCells = NULL;
            mWidth = 0;
            throw bad_alloc();
        }

    for (i = 0; i < mWidth; i++) {
        for (j = 0; j < mHeight; j++) {
            mCells[i][j] = src.mCells[i][j];
        }
    }
}

void GameBoard::setPieceAt(int x, int y, const GamePiece& inElem)
    throw(out_of_range)
{
    // Check for out of range arguments.
    if (x < 0 || x >= mWidth || y < 0 || y >= mHeight) {
        throw out_of_range("Invalid width or height");
    }
    mCells[x][y] = inElem;
}

GamePiece& GameBoard::getPieceAt(int x, int y) throw(out_of_range)
{
    // Check for out of range arguments.
    if (x < 0 || x >= mWidth || y < 0 || y >= mHeight) {
        throw out_of_range("Invlalid width or height");
    }
    return (mCells[x][y]);
}

const GamePiece& GameBoard::getPieceAt(int x, int y) const throw(out_of_range)
{
    // Check for out of range arguments.
    if (x < 0 || x >= mWidth || y < 0 || y >= mHeight) {
        throw out_of_range("Invlalid width or height");
    }
    return (mCells[x][y]);
}
```

Summary

This chapter described the issues related to error handling in C++ programs, and emphasized that you must design and code your programs with an error-handling plan. By reading this chapter, you learned the details of C++ exceptions syntax and behavior. The chapter also covered some of the areas in which error handling plays a large role, including I/O streams, memory allocation, constructors, and destructors. Finally, you saw an example of error handling in the GameBoard class.

The next few chapters continue to cover advanced C++ language topics. Chapter 16 describes operator overloading, Chapter 17 covers performance issues in C++, and Chapter 18 teaches you how to combine C++ with other languages and run your programs on multiple platforms.

16

Overloading C++ Operators

C++ allows you to redefine the meanings of operators, such as +, -, and =, for your classes. Many object-oriented languages do not provide this capability, so you might be tempted to disregard its usefulness in C++. However, it can be beneficial for making your classes behave similarly to built-in types such as `ints` and `doubles`. It is even possible to write classes that look like arrays, functions, or pointers!

Chapters 3 and 5 introduced object-oriented design and operator overloading, respectively. Chapters 8 and 9 presented the syntax details for objects and for basic operator overloading. This chapter picks up operator overloading where Chapter 9 left off. The STL, introduced in Chapter 4, and described in detail in Chapters 21 to 23, uses operator overloading extensively. You should read and understand this chapter before tackling Chapters 21 to 23.

This chapter focuses on the syntax and basic semantics of operator overloading. Practical examples are provided for most of the operators, but for a few of them, practical examples are postponed until later chapters.

This chapter does not repeat information contained in Chapter 9.

The contents of this chapter include:

- ❑ An overview of operator overloading
    - ❑ Rationale for overloading operators
    - ❑ Limitations, caveats, and choices in operator overloading
    - ❑ Summary of operators you can, cannot, and should not overload
- ❑ How to overload unary plus, unary minus, increment, and decrement
- ❑ How to overload the I/O streams operators (`operator<<` and `operator>>`)
- ❑ How to overloading the subscripting (array index) operator

Chapter 16

❏   How to overload the function call operator

❏   How to overload the dereferencing operators (* and ->)

❏   How to write conversion operators

❏   How to overload the memory allocation and deallocation operators

Overview of Operator Overloading

As Chapter 1 reviewed, operators in C++ are symbols such as +, <, *, and <<. They work on built-in types such as int and double to allow you to perform arithmetic, logical, and other operations. There are also operators such as -> and & that allow you to dereference pointers. The concept of operators in C++ is broad, and even includes [] (array index), () (function call), and the memory allocation and deallocation routines.

Operator overloading allows you to change the behavior of language operators for your classes. However, this capability comes with rules, limitations, and choices.

Why Overload Operators?

Before learning how to overload operators, you probably want to know why you would ever want to do so. The reasons vary for the different operators, but the general guiding principle is to make your classes behave like built-in types. The closer your classes are to built-in types, the easier they will be for clients to use. For example, if you want to write a class to represent fractions, it's quite helpful to have the ability to define what +, -, *, and / mean when applied to objects of that class.

The second reason to overload operators is to gain greater control over behavior in your program. For example, you can overload memory allocation and deallocation routines for your classes to specify exactly how memory should be distributed and reclaimed for each new object.

It's important to emphasize that operator overloading doesn't necessarily make things easier for you as the class developer; its main purpose is to make things easier for clients of the class.

Limitations to Operator Overloading

Here is a list of things you cannot do when you overload operators:

❏   You cannot add new operator symbols. You can only redefine the meanings of operators already in the language. The table in the "Summary of Overloadable Operators" section lists all of the operators that you can overload.

❏   There are a few operators that you cannot overload, such as . (member access in an object), :: (scope resolution operator), sizeof, ?: (the ternary operator), and a few others. The table lists all the operators that you *can* overload. The operators that you can't overload are usually not those you would care to overload anyway, so we don't think you'll find this restriction limiting.

❏   You cannot change the *arity* of the operator. The arity describes the number of arguments, or *operands*, associated with the operator. Unary operators, such as ++, work on only one operand. Binary operators, such as +, work on two operands. There is only one ternary operator: ?:. The main place where this limitation might bother you is when overloading [] (array brackets), as discussed below.

❑ You cannot change the *precedence* or *associativity* of the operator. These rules determine in which order operators are evaluated in a statement. Again, this constraint shouldn't be cause for concern in most programs because there are rarely benefits to changing the order of evaluation.

❑ You cannot redefine operators for built-in types. The operator must be a method in a class, or at least one of the arguments to a global overloaded operator function must be a user-defined type (e.g., a class). This means that you can't do something ridiculous such as redefine + for ints to mean subtraction (though you could do so for your classes). The one exception to this rule is the memory allocation and deallocation routines; you can replace the global routines for all memory allocation in your program.

Some of the operators already mean two different things. For example, the – operator can be used as a binary operator, as in x = y - z or as a unary operator, as in x = -y;. The * operator can be used for multiplication or for dereferencing a pointer. The << operator is the insertion operator or the left-shift operator, depending on context. You can overload both meanings of operators with dual meanings.

Choices in Operator Overloading

When you overload an operator, you write a function or method with the name operator*X*, where *X* is the symbol for some operator. For example, in Chapter 9, you saw operator+ declared for SpreadsheetCell objects like this:

```
friend const SpreadsheetCell operator+(const SpreadsheetCell& lhs,
    const SpreadsheetCell& rhs);
```

There are several choices involved in each overloaded operator function or method you write.

Method or Global Function

First, you must decide whether your operator should be a method of your class or a global function (usually a friend of the class). How do you choose? First, you need to understand the difference between these two choices. When the operator is a method of a class, the left-hand-side of the operator expression must always be an object of that class. If you write a global function, the left-hand-side can be an object of a different type.

There are three different types of operators:

❑ **Operators that must be methods.** The C++ language requires some operators to be methods of a class because they don't make sense outside of a class. For example, operator= is tied so closely to the class that it can't exist anywhere else. The table in the "Summary of Overloadable Operators" section lists those operators that must be methods. For these, the choice of method or global function is simple! However, most operators do not impose this requirement.

❑ **Operators that must be global functions.** Whenever you need to allow the left-hand side of the operator to be a variable of a different type from your class, you must make the operator a global function. This rule applies specifically to operator<< and operator>>, where the left-hand side is the iostream object, not an object of your class. Additionally, commutative operators like binary + and – should allow variables that are not objects of your class on the left-hand side. This problem was explained previously in Chapter 9.

❑ **Operators that can be either methods or global functions.** There is some disagreement in the C++ community on whether it's better to write methods or global functions to overload operators. However, we recommend the following rule: make every operator a method unless you must make it a global function as described previously. One major advantage to this rule is that methods can be `virtual`, but friend functions cannot. Therefore, when you plan to write overloaded operators in an inheritance tree, you should make them methods if possible.

When you write an overloaded operator as a method, you should mark the entire method `const` if it doesn't change the object. That way, it can be called on `const` objects.

Choosing Argument Types

You are somewhat limited in your choice of argument types because you can't usually change the number of arguments (although there are exceptions, which are explained later in this chapter). For example, `operator+` must always have two arguments if it is a global function; one argument if it's a method. The compiler issues an error if it differs from this standard. In this sense, the operator functions are different from normal functions, which you can overload with any number of parameters. Additionally, although you can write the operator for whichever types you want, the choice is usually constrained by the class for which you are writing the operator. For example, if you want to implement addition for class `T`, you wouldn't write an `operator+` that takes two `strings`! The real choice arises when you try to determine whether to take parameters by value or by reference, and whether or not to make them `const`.

The choice of value vs. reference is easy: you should take every parameter by reference. As explained in Chapters 9 and 12, never pass objects by value if you can pass-by-reference instead!

The `const` decision is also trivial: mark every parameter `const` unless you actually modify it. The table in the "Summary of Overloadable Operators" section shows sample prototypes for each operator, with the arguments marked `const` and reference as appropriate.

Choosing Return Types

Recall that C++ doesn't determine overload resolution based on return type. Thus, you can specify any return type you want when you write overloaded operators. However, just because you *can* do something doesn't mean you *should* do it. This flexibility implies that you could write confusing code in which comparison operators return pointers, and arithmetic operators return `bools`! However, you shouldn't do that. Instead, you should write your overloaded operators such that they return the same types as the operators do for the built-in types. If you write a comparison operator, return a `bool`. If you write an arithmetic operator, return an object representing the result of the arithmetic. Sometimes the return type is not obvious at first. For example, as you learned in Chapter 8, `operator=` should return a reference to the object on which it's called in order to support nested assignment. Other operators have similarly tricky return types, all of which are summarized in the table in the "Summary of Overloadable Operators" section.

The same choices of reference and `const` apply to return types as well. However, for return values, the choices are more difficult. The general rule for value or reference is to return a reference if you can; otherwise, return a value. How do you know when you can return a reference? This choice applies only to operators that return objects: the choice is moot for the comparison operators that return `bool`, the conversion operators that have no return type, and the function call operator, which may return any type you want. If your operator constructs a new object, then you must return that new object by value. If it does not construct a new object, you can return a reference to the object on which the operator is called, or one of its arguments. The table in the "Summary of Overloadable Operators" section shows examples.

A return value that can be modified as an *lvalue* (the left-hand-side of an assignment expression) must be non-`const`. Otherwise, it should be `const`. More operators than you might think at first return lvalues, including all of the assignment operators (`operator=`, `operator+=`, `operator-=`, etc.).

If you are in doubt about the appropriate return type, simply consult the table in the "Summary of Overloadable Operators" section.

Choosing Behavior

You can provide whichever implementation you want in an overloaded operator. For example, you could write an `operator+` that launches a game of Scrabble. However, as described in Chapter 5, you should generally constrain your implementations to provide behaviors that clients expect. Write `operator+` so that it performs addition, or something like addition, such as string concatenation.

This chapter explains how you *should* implement your overloaded operators. In exceptional circumstances, you might want to differ from these recommendations, but, in general, you should follow the standard patterns.

Operators You Shouldn't Overload

There are a few operators that it is rarely a good idea to overload, even though it is permitted. Specifically, the address-of operator (`operator&`) is not particularly useful to overload, and leads to confusion if you do because you are changing fundamental language behavior (taking addresses of variables) in potentially unexpected ways.

Additionally, you should avoid overloading the binary Boolean operators `operator&&` and `operator||` because you lose C++'s short-circuit evaluation rules.

Finally, you should not overload the comma operator (`operator,`). Yes, you read that correctly: there really is a comma operator in C++. It's also called the *sequencing operator*, and is used to separate two expressions in a single statement, while guaranteeing that they are evaluated left to right. There is rarely (if ever) a good reason to overload this operator.

Summary of Overloadable Operators

The following table lists all of the operators that you can overload, specifies whether they should be methods of the class or global friend functions, summarizes when you should (or should not) overload them, and provides sample prototypes, showing the proper return values.

This table should be a useful reference in the future when you want to sit down and write an overloaded operator. You're bound to forget which return type you should use, and whether or not the function should be a method. We're looking forward to referring to this table ourselves!

In this table, `T` is the name of the class for which the overloaded operator is written, and `E` is a different type (not the name of the class).

Operator	Name or Category	Method or Global Friend Function	When to Overload	Sample Prototype
operator+ operator- operator* operator/ operator%	Binary arithmetic	Global friend function recommended	Whenever you want to provide these operations for your class	`friend const T operator+(const T&, const T&);`
operator- operator+ operator~	Unary arithmetic and bitwise operators	Method recommended	Whenever you want to provide these operations for your class	`const T operator-() const;`

operator++
operator--
	Increment and decrement	Method recommended	Whenever you overload binary + and -	`T& operator++();`
				
				`const T operator++(int);`

operator=	Assignment operator	Method required	Whenever you have dynamically allocated memory in the object or want to prevent assignment, as described in Chapter 9	`T& operator=(const T&);`
operator+= operator-= operator*/ operator/= operator%=	Shorthand arithmetic operator assignments	Method recommended	Whenever you overload the binary arithmetic operators	`T& operator+=(const T&);`
operator<< operator>> operator& operator| operator^	Binary bitwise operators	Global friend function recommended	Whenever you want to provide these operations	`friend const T operator<<(const T&, const T&);`
operator<<= operator>>= operator&= operator|= operator^=	Shorthand bitwise operator assignments	Method recommended	Whenever you overload the binary bitwise operators	`T& operator<<= (const T&);`

Operator	Name or Category	Method or Global Friend Function	When to Overload	Sample Prototype
operator< operator> operator<= operator>= operator==	Binary comparison operators	Global friend function recommended	Whenever you want to provide these operations	`friend bool operator<(const T&, const T&);`

operator<<
operator>>
	I/O stream operators (insertion and extraction)	Global friend function recommended	Whenever you want to provide these operations	`friend ostream &operator<< (ostream&, const T&);`
				
				`friend istream &operator>> (istream&, T&);`

operator!	Boolean negation operator	Member function recommended	Rarely; use bool or void* conversion instead	`bool operator!() const;`

operator&&
operator||
	Binary Boolean operators	Global friend function recommended	Rarely	`friend bool operator&&(const T& lhs, const T& rhs);`
				
				`friend bool operator||(const T& lhs, const T& rhs);`

operator[]	Subscripting (array index) operator	Method required	When you want to support subscripting: in array-like classes	`E& operator[](int);`
				
				`const E& operator[](int) const;`

operator()	Function call operator	Method required	When you want objects to behave like function pointers	Return type and arguments can vary; see examples in this chapter

operator new
operator new[]
	Memory allocation routines	Method recommended	When you want to control memory allocation for your classes (rarely)	`void* operator new(size_t size) throw(bad_alloc);`
				
				`void* operator new[](size_t size) throw(bad_alloc);`

Table continued on following page

Operator	Name or Category	Method or Global Friend Function	When to Overload	Sample Prototype

operator delete operator delete[]	Memory deallocation routines	Method recommended	Whenever you overload the memory allocation routines	void operator delete(void* ptr) throw();
				
				 void operator delete[](void* ptr) throw();

operator* operator->	Dereferencing operators	Method required for operator-> Method recommended for operator*	Useful for smart pointers	E& operator*() const; E* operator->() const;
operator&	Address-of operator	N/A	Never	N/A
operator->*	Dereference pointer-to-member	N/A	Never	N/A
operator,	Comma operator	N/A	Never	N/A
operator type()	Conversion, or cast, operators (separate operator for each type)	Method required	When you want to provide conversions from your class to other types	operator type() const;

Overloading the Arithmetic Operators

In Chapter 9, you learned how to write the binary arithmetic operators and the shorthand arithmetic assignment operators. However, you did not yet learn how to overload all of the arithmetic operators.

Overloading Unary Minus and Unary Plus

C++ has several unary arithmetic operators. Two of these are unary minus and unary plus. You've probably used unary minus, but you might be surprised to learn about unary plus. Here is an example of these operators using ints:

```
int i, j = 4;
i = -j; // Unary minus
i = +i; // Unary plus
j = +(-i); // Apply unary plus to the result of applying unary minus to i.
j = -(-i); // Apply unary minus to the result of applying unary minus to i.
```

Unary minus negates the operand, while unary plus returns the operand directly. The result of unary plus or minus is not an lvalue: you can't assign to it. This means you should return a const object when you overload them. However, note that you can apply unary plus or unary minus to the result of unary plus or unary minus. Because you're applying these operations to a const temporary object, you must make operator- and operator+ themselves const; otherwise, the compiler won't let you call them on the const temporary.

Here is an example of a SpreadsheetCell class definition with an overloaded operator-. Unary plus is usually a no-op, so this class doesn't bother to overload it.

```
class SpreadsheetCell
{
    public:
        // Omitted for brevity. Consult Chapter 9 for details.

        friend const SpreadsheetCell operator+(const SpreadsheetCell& lhs,
            const SpreadsheetCell& rhs);
        friend const SpreadsheetCell operator-(const SpreadsheetCell& lhs,
            const SpreadsheetCell& rhs);
        friend const SpreadsheetCell operator*(const SpreadsheetCell& lhs,
            const SpreadsheetCell& rhs);
        friend const SpreadsheetCell operator/(const SpreadsheetCell& lhs,
            const SpreadsheetCell& rhs);
        SpreadsheetCell& operator+=(const SpreadsheetCell& rhs);
        SpreadsheetCell& operator-=(const SpreadsheetCell& rhs);
        SpreadsheetCell& operator*=(const SpreadsheetCell& rhs);
        SpreadsheetCell& operator/=(const SpreadsheetCell& rhs);
        const SpreadsheetCell operator-() const;
    protected:
        // Omitted for brevity. Consult Chapter 9 for details.
};
```

Here is the definition of the unary operator-.

```
const SpreadsheetCell SpreadsheetCell::operator-() const
{
    SpreadsheetCell newCell(*this);
    newCell.set(-mValue); // call set to update mValue and mStr

    return (newCell);
}
```

operator- doesn't change the operand, so this method must construct a new SpreadsheetCell with the negated value, and return a copy of it. Thus, it can't return a reference.

Overloading Increment and Decrement

Recall that there are four ways to add one to a variable:

```
i = i + 1;
i += 1;
++i;
i++;
```

The last two are called the *increment* operators. The first form is *prefix increment*, which adds one to the variable, then returns the newly incremented value for use in the rest of the expression. The second form is *postfix increment*, which returns the old (nonincremented) value for use in the rest of the expression. The decrement operators function similarly.

The two possible meanings for `operator++` and `operator--` (prefix and postfix) present a problem when you want to overload them. When you write an overloaded `operator++`, for example, how do you specify whether you are overloading the prefix or the postfix version? C++ introduced a hack to allow you to make this distinction: the prefix versions of `operator++` and `operator--` take no arguments, while the postfix versions take one unused argument of type `int`.

If you want to overload these operators for your `SpreadsheetCell` class, the prototypes would look like this:

```
class SpreadsheetCell
{
    public:
        // Omitted for brevity. Consult Chapter 9 for details.
        SpreadsheetCell& operator++(); // Prefix
        const SpreadsheetCell operator++(int); // Postfix
        SpreadsheetCell& operator--(); // Prefix
        const SpreadsheetCell operator--(int); // Postfix
    protected:
        // Omitted for brevity. Consult Chapter 9 for details.
};
```

The C++ standard specifies that the prefix versions of increment and decrement return an lvalue, so they can't return a `const` value. The return value in the prefix forms is the same as the end value of the operand, so prefix increment and decrement can return a reference to the object on which they are called. The postfix versions of increment and decrement, however, return values that are different from the end values of the operands, so they cannot return references.

Here are the implementations of these operators:

```
SpreadsheetCell& SpreadsheetCell::operator++()
{
    set(mValue + 1);
    return (*this);
}

const SpreadsheetCell SpreadsheetCell::operator++(int)
{
    SpreadsheetCell oldCell(*this); // Save the current value before incrementing
    set(mValue + 1); // Increment
    return (oldCell); // Return the old value.
}

SpreadsheetCell& SpreadsheetCell::operator--()
```

```
    {
        set(mValue - 1);
        return (*this);
    }

    const SpreadsheetCell SpreadsheetCell::operator--(int)
    {
        SpreadsheetCell oldCell(*this); // Save the current value before incrementing
        set(mValue - 1); // Increment
        return (oldCell); // Return the old value.
    }
```

Now you can increment and decrement your SpreadsheetCell objects to your heart's content!

```
    SpreadsheetCell c1, c2;
    c1.set(4);
    c2.set(4);

    c1++;
    ++c1;
```

Recall that increment and decrement also work on pointers. When you write classes that are smart pointers or iterators, you can overload operator++ and operator-- to provide pointer incrementing and decrementing. You can see this topic in action in Chapter 23, in which you learn how to write your own STL iterators.

Overloading the Bitwise and Binary Logical Operators

The bitwise operators are similar to the arithmetic operators, and the bitwise shorthand assignment operators are similar to the arithmetic shorthand assignment operators. However, they are significantly less common, so we do not show examples here. The table in the "Summary of Overloadable Operators" section shows sample prototypes, so you should be able to implement them easily if the need ever arises.

The logical operators are trickier. We don't recommend overloading && and ||. These operators don't really apply to individual types: they aggregate results of Boolean expressions. Additionally, you lose the short-circuit evaluation. Thus, it rarely makes sense to overload them for specific types.

Overloading the Insertion and Extraction Operators

In C++, you use operators not only for arithmetic operations, but also for reading from and writing to streams. For example, when you write ints and strings to cout you use the insertion operator, <<:

```
    int number = 10;
    cout << "The number is " << number << endl;
```

When you read from streams you use the extraction operator, >>:

```
    int number;
    string str;
    cin >> number >> str;
```

You can write insertion and extraction operators that work on your classes as well, so that you can read and write them like this:

```
    SpreadsheetCell myCell, anotherCell, aThirdCell;

    cin >> myCell >> anotherCell >> aThirdCell;
    cout << myCell << " " << anotherCell << " " << aThirdCell << endl;
```

Before you write the insertion and extraction operators, you need to decide how you want to stream your class out and how you want to read it in. For `SpreadsheetCell`s it makes sense to read and write `string`s because all `double`s can be read as `string`s (and converted back to `double`s), but not vice versa.

The object on the left of an insertion or extraction operator is the `istream` or `ostream` (such as `cin` or `cout`), not a `SpreadsheetCell` object. Because you can't add a method to the `istream` or `ostream` class, you should write the insertion and extraction operators as global `friend` functions of the `SpreadsheetCell` class. The declaration of these functions in your `SpreadsheetCell` class looks like this:

```
    class SpreadsheetCell
    {
        public:
            // Omitted for brevity
            friend ostream& operator<<(ostream& ostr, const SpreadsheetCell& cell);
            friend istream& operator>>(istream& istr, SpreadsheetCell& cell);
            // Omitted for brevity
    };
```

By making the insertion operator take a reference to an `ostream` as its first parameter, you allow it to be used for file output streams, string output streams, `cout`, and `cerr`. See Chapter 14 for details. Similarly, by making the extraction operator take a reference to an `istream`, you can make it work on file input streams, string input streams, and `cin`.

The second parameter to `operator<<` and `operator>>` is a reference to the `SpreadsheetCell` object that you want to read or write. The insertion operator doesn't change the `SpreadsheetCell` it writes, so that reference can be `const`. The extraction operator, however, modifies the `SpreadsheetCell` object, requiring the argument to be a non-`const` reference.

Both operators return a reference to the stream they were given as their first argument so that calls to the operator can be nested. Remember that the operator syntax is shorthand for calling the global `operator>>` or `operator<<` functions explicitly. Consider this line:

```
    cin >> myCell >> anotherCell >> aThirdCell;
```

It's actually shorthand for this line:

```
    operator>>(operator>>(operator>>(cin, myCell), anotherCell), aThirdCell);
```

As you can see, the return value of the first call to `operator>>` is used as input to the next. Thus, you must return the stream reference so that it can be used in the next nested call. Otherwise, the nesting won't compile.

Here are the implementations for `operator<<` and `operator>>` for the `SpreadsheetCell` class:

```
ostream& operator<<(ostream& ostr, const SpreadsheetCell& cell)
{
    ostr << cell.mString;
    return (ostr);
}

istream& operator>>(istream& istr, SpreadsheetCell& cell)
{
    string temp;
    istr >> temp;
    cell.set(temp);
    return (istr);
}
```

The trickiest part of these functions is that, in order for `mValue` to be set correctly, `operator>>` must remember to call the `set()` method on the `SpreadsheetCell` instead of setting `mString` directly.

Overloading the Subscripting Operator

Pretend, for a few minutes, that you have never heard of the vector template class in the STL, and so you have decided to write your own dynamically allocated array class. This class would allow you to set and retrieve elements at specified indices, and would take care of all memory allocation "behind the scenes." A first stab at the class definition for a dynamically allocated integer array might look like this:

```
class Array
{
    public:
        // Creates an array with a default size that will grow as needed.
        Array();
        ~Array();

        // Returns the value at index x. If index x does not exist in the array,
        // throws an exception of type out_of_range.
        int getElementAt(int x) const;

        // Sets the value at index x to val. If index x is out of range,
        // allocates more space to make it in range.
        void setElementAt(int x, int val);

    protected:
        static const int kAllocSize = 4;
        void resize(int newSize);
        int* mElems;
        int mSize;
    private:
        // Disallow assignment and pass by value.
        Array(const Array& src);
        Array& operator=(const Array& rhs);
};
```

In order to present only the salient points, we have omitted exception throw lists and have not made this class a template. The interface supports setting and accessing elements. It provides random-access guarantees: a client could create an array and set elements 1, 100, and 1000 without worrying about memory management.

Here are the implementations of the methods:

```
#include "Array.h"

const int Array::kAllocSize;

Array::Array()
{
    mSize = kAllocSize;
    mElems = new int[mSize];
}

Array::~Array()
{
    delete [] mElems;
}

int Array::getElementAt(int x) const
{
    if (x < 0 || x >=mSize) {
        throw out_of_range(".");
    }
    return (mElems[x]);
}

void Array::setElementAt(int x, int val)
{
    if (x < 0) {
        throw out_of_range("");
    }
    if (x >= mSize) {
        // Allocate kAllocSize past the element the client wants
        resize (x + kAllocSize);
    }
    mElems[x] = val;
}

void Array::resize(int newSize)
{
    int* newElems = new int[newSize]; // Allocate the new array of the new size.

    // The new size is always bigger than the old size.
    for (int i = 0; i < newSize; i++) {
        // Copy the elements from the old array to the new one.
        newElems[i] = mElems[i];
    }
    mSize = newSize; // Store the new size.
    delete [] mElems; // Free the memory for the old array.
    mElems = newElems; // Store the pointer to the new array.
}
```

Here is a small example of how you could use this class:

```
Array arr;
int i;

for (i = 0; i < 10; i++) {
    arr.setElementAt(i, 100);
}

for (i = 0; i < 10; i++) {
    cout << arr.getElementAt(i) << " ";
}
cout << endl;
```

As you can see, you never have to tell the array how much space you need. It allocates as much space as it requires to store the elements you give it. However, it's inconvenient to use the setElementAt() and getElementAt() functions. It would be nice to be able use real array index notation like this:

```
Array arr;
int i;

for (i = 0; i < 10; i++) {
    arr[i] = 100;
}

for (i = 0; i < 10; i++) {
    cout << arr[i] << " ";
}
cout << endl;
```

This is where the overloaded subscripting operator comes in. You can replace getElementAt() and setElementAt() in your class with an operator[] like this:

```
class Array
{
    public:
        Array();
        ~Array();
        int& operator[](int x)
    protected:
        static const int kAllocSize = 4;
        void resize(int newSize);
        int* mElems;
        int mSize;
    private:
        // Disallow assignment and pass by value.
        Array(const Array& src);
        Array& operator=(const Array& rhs);
};
```

The preceding code using array index notation on the array now compiles. The operator[] can replace both setElementAt() and getElementAt() because it returns a reference to the element at location x. This reference can be an lvalue, so it can be used to assign to that element. Here is the implementation of the operator:

```
int& Array::operator[](int x)
{
    if (x < 0) {
        throw out_of_range("");
    }
    if (x >= mSize) {
        // Allocate kAllocSize past the element the client wants.
        resize (x + kAllocSize);
    }
    return (mElems[x]);
}
```

When `operator[]` is used on the left-hand-side of an assignment statement, the assignment actually changes the value at location x in the `mElems` array.

Providing Read-Only Access with operator[]

Although it's sometimes convenient for `operator[]` to return an element that can serve as an lvalue, you don't always want that behavior. It would be nice to be able to provide read-only access to the elements of the array as well, by returning a const value or const reference. Ideally, you would provide two `operator[]`s: one returns a reference and one returns a const reference.

```
class Array
{
    public:
        Array();
        ~Array();
        int& operator[](int x);
        const int& operator[](int x);  // BUG! Can't overload based on return type
    protected:
        static const int kAllocSize = 4;
        void resize(int newSize);
        int* mElems;
        int mSize;
    private:
        // Disallow assignment and pass by value.
        Array(const Array& src);
        Array& operator=(const Array& rhs);
};
```

However, there is one small problem: you can't overload a method or operator based only on return type. The above code doesn't compile. Luckily, C++ provides a way around this restriction: if you mark the second `operator[]` const, then the compiler can distinguish between the two. If you call `operator[]` on a const object, it will use the const `operator[]`, and, if you call it on a non-const object, it will use the non-const `operator[]`. Here are the two operators with the correct signatures:

```
int& operator[](int x);
const int& operator[](int x) const;
```

Here is the implementation of the const `operator[]`. It throws an exception if the index is out of range instead of trying to allocate new space. It doesn't make sense to allocate new space when you're only trying to read the element value.

```
const int& Array::operator[](int x) const
{
    if (x < 0 || x >=mSize) {
        throw out_of_range("");
    }
    return (mElems[x]);
}
```

The following code demonstrates these two forms of `operator[]`:

```
#include "Array.h"

void printArray(const Array& arr, int size);

int main(int argc, char** argv)
{
    Array arr;
    int i;

    for (i = 0; i < 10; i++) {
        arr[i] = 100; // Calls the non-const operator[] because
                      // arr is a non-const object.
    }
    printArray(arr, 10);
    return (0);
}

void printArray(const Array& arr, int size)
{
    for (int i = 0; i < size; i++) {
        cout << arr[i] << " "; // Calls the const operator[] because arr is a const
                               // object.
    }
    cout << endl;
}
```

Note that the const `operator[]` is called in `printArray()` only because `arr` is `const`. If `arr` were not const, the non-`const` `operator[]` would be called, despite the fact that the result is not modified.

Non-Integral Array Indices

You can also write an `operator[]` that uses a different, non-integral, type as its index. For example, you could create an *associative array*, in which you use `string` keys instead of integers. Here is the definition for an associative array class that stores `ints`:

```
class AssociativeArray
{
    public:
        AssociativeArray();
        ~AssociativeArray();

        int& operator[](const string& key);
        const int& operator[](const string& key) const;
```

```
    private:
        // Implementation details omitted
};
```

We leave the implementation of this class as an exercise for the reader. You might also be interested to know that the STL `map` provides associative array-like functionality, including the use of `operator[]` with any possible type as the key.

> You cannot overload the subscripting operator to take more than one parameter. If you want to provide subscripting on more than one index, you can use the function call operator.

Overloading the Function Call Operator

C++ allows you to overload the function call operator, written as `operator()`. If you write an `operator()` for your class, you can use objects of that class as if they were function pointers. You can only overload this operator as a non-`static` method in a class. Here is an example of a simple class with an overloaded `operator()` and a class method with the same behavior:

```
class FunctionObject
{
    public:
        int operator() (int inParam); // Function-call operator
        int aMethod(int inParam); // Normal method
};

//Implementation of overloaded function-call operator
int FunctionObject::operator() (int inParam)
{
    return (inParam * inParam);
}

// Implementation of normal method
int FunctionObject::aMethod(int inParam)
{
    return (inParam * inParam);
}
```

Here is an example of code that uses the function-call operator, contrasted with the call to a normal method of the class:

```
int main(int argc, char** argv)
{
    int x = 3, xSquared, xSquaredAgain;
    FunctionObject square;

    xSquared = square(x); // Call the function-call operator
    xSquaredAgain = square.aMethod(x); // Call the normal method
}
```

An object of a class with a function call operator is called a *function object*, or *functor* for short.

At first, the function call operator probably seems a little strange. Why would you want to write a special method for a class to make objects of the class look like function pointers? Why wouldn't you just write a function or a standard method of a class? The advantage of function objects over standard methods of objects is simple: these objects can sometimes masquerade as function pointers. You can pass function objects as callback functions to routines that expect function pointers, as long as the function pointer types are templatized. See Chapter 22 for details.

The advantages of function objects over global functions are more intricate. There are two main benefits:

❑ Objects can retain information in their data members between repeated calls to their function-call operators. For example, a function object might be used to keep a running sum of numbers collected from each call to the function-call operator.

❑ You can customize the behavior of a function object by setting data members. For example, you could write a function object to compare an argument to the function against a data member. This data member could be configurable so that the object could be customized for whatever comparison you want.

Of course, you could implement either of the preceding benefits with global or `static` variables. However, function objects provide a cleaner way to do it. The true benefits of function objects will become apparent when you learn more about the STL in Chapters 21 and 23.

By following the normal method overloading rules, you can write as many `operator()`s for your classes as you want. Specifically, the various `operator()`s must have different numbers of types of parameters. For example, you could add an `operator()` to the `FunctionObject` class that takes a `string` reference:

```
class FunctionObject
{
    public:
        int operator() (int inParam);
        void operator() (string& str);
        int aMethod(int inParam);
};
```

The function call operator can also be used to provide subscripting for multiple indices of an array. Simply write an `operator()` that behaves like `operator[]` but allows more than one parameter. The only problem with this technique is that now you have to use `()` to index instead of `[]`, as in `myArray(3, 4) = 6;`

Overloading the Dereferencing Operators

There are three de-referencing operators you can overload: `*`, `->`, and `->*`. Ignoring `->*` for the moment (we'll get back to it later), consider the built-in meanings of `*` and `->`. `*` dereferences a pointer to give you direct access to its value, while `->` is shorthand for a `*` dereference followed by a `.` member selection. The following code shows the equivalences:

```
SpreadsheetCell* cell1 = new SpreadsheetCell;
(*cell1).set(5); // Dereference plus member selection
cell1->set(5); // Shorthand arrow dereference and member selection together
```

You can overload the dereferencing operators for your classes in order to make objects of the classes behave like pointers. The main use of this capability is for implementing smart pointers, which you learned about in Chapters 4, 13, and 15. It is also useful for iterators, which the STL uses and which you can think of as fancy smart pointers. Chapters 21 to 23 cover iterators in more detail, and Chapter 25 provides a sample implementation of a smart pointer class. This chapter teaches you the basic mechanics for over-loading the relevant operators in the context of a simple smart pointer template class.

Here is the smart pointer template class definition, without the dereference operators filled in yet:

```
template <typename T>
class Pointer
{
    public:
        Pointer(T* inPtr);
        ~Pointer();

        // Dereference operators will go here.
    protected:
        T* mPtr;
    private:
        // Prevent assignment and pass by reference.
        Pointer(const Pointer<T>& src);
        Pointer<T>& operator=(const Pointer<T>& rhs);
};
```

This smart pointer is about as simple as you can get. All it does is store a dumb pointer and delete it when the object is destroyed. The implementations are equally simple: the constructor takes a real ("dumb") pointer, which is stored as the only data member in the class. The destructor frees the pointer.

```
template <typename T>
Pointer<T>::Pointer(T* inPtr)
{
    mPtr = inPtr;
}

template <typename T>
Pointer<T>::~Pointer()
{
    delete mPtr;
}
```

You would like to be able to use the smart pointer template like this:

```
#include "Pointer.h"
#include "SpreadsheetCell.h"
#include <iostream>
using namespace std;

int main(int argc, char** argv)
{
    Pointer<int> smartInt(new int);

    *smartInt = 5; // Dereference the smart pointer.
    cout << *smartInt << endl;
```

```
        Pointer<SpreadsheetCell> smartCell(new SpreadsheetCell);

        smartCell->set(5); // Dereference and member select the set method.
        cout << smartCell->getValue() << endl;

        return (0);
}
```

As you can see, you need to provide implementations of * and -> for this class.

> **You should rarely write** `operator*` **or** `operator->` **alone. Always implement both together if they have appropriate semantics for your class. It would be confusing for a smart pointer–like object to support** -> **but not** *, **or vice-versa.**

Implementing operator*

When you dereference a pointer, you expect to be able to access the memory to which the pointer points. If that memory contains a simple type such as an `int`, you should be able to change its value directly. If the memory contains a more complicated type, such as an object, you should be able to access its data members or methods with the . operator.

To provide these semantics, you should return a reference to a variable or object from `operator*`. In the `Pointer` class, the declaration and definition look like this:

```
template <typename T>
class Pointer
{
    public:
        Pointer(T* inPtr);
        ~Pointer();
        T& operator*();
        const T& operator*() const;
    protected:
        T* mPtr;
    private:
        Pointer(const Pointer<T>& src);
        Pointer<T>& operator=(const Pointer<T>& rhs);
};

template <typename T>
T& Pointer<T>::operator*()
{
    return (*mPtr);
}
```

As you can see, `operator*` returns a reference to the object or variable to which the underlying dumb pointer points. As in overloading the subscripting operators, it's useful to provide both `const` and non-`const` versions of the method, which return a `const` reference and reference, respectively. The `const` version is implemented identically to the non-`const` version, so its implementation is not shown here.

Implementing operator->

The arrow operator is a bit trickier. The result of applying the arrow operator should be a member or method of an object. However, in order to implement it like that, you would have to be able to implement the equivalent of `operator*` followed by `operator.`. C++ doesn't allow you to overload `operator.` for good reason: it's impossible to write a single prototype that allows you to capture any possible member or method selection. Similarly, you couldn't write an `operator->` with such semantics.

Therefore, C++ treats `operator->` as a special case. Consider this line:

```
smartCell->set(5);
```

C++ translates the preceding to:

```
(smartCell.operator->())->set(5);
```

As you can see, C++ applies another `operator->` to whatever you return from your overloaded `operator->`. Therefore, you must return a pointer to an object like this:

```
template <typename T>
class Pointer
{
    public:
        Pointer(T* inPtr);
        ~Pointer();
        T& operator*();
        const T& operator*() const;
        T* operator->();
        const T* operator->() const;
    protected:
        T* mPtr;
    private:
        Pointer(const Pointer<T>& src);
        Pointer<T>& operator=(const Pointer<T>& rhs);
};

template <typename T>
T* Pointer<T>::operator->()
{
    return (mPtr);
}
```

Again, you should write both `const` and non-`const` forms of the operator. The implementation of the `const` version is identical to the non-`const`, so it is not shown here.

It's unfortunate that `operator*` and `operator->` are asymmetric, but, once you see them a few times, you'll get used to it.

What in the World Is operator->* ?

Recall from Chapter 9 that you can manipulate pointers to members and methods of a class. When you try to dereference the pointer, it must be in the context of an object of that class. Here is the example from Chapter 9:

```
SpreadsheetCell myCell;
double (SpreadsheetCell::*methodPtr) () const = &SpreadsheetCell::getValue;
cout << (myCell.*methodPtr)() << endl;
```

Note the use of the `.*` operator to derefence the method pointer and call the method. There is also an equivalent `operator->*` for calling methods via pointers when you have a pointer to an object instead of the object itself. The operator looks like this:

```
SpreadsheetCell* myCell = new SpreadsheetCell();
double (SpreadsheetCell::*methodPtr) () const = &SpreadsheetCell::getValue;
cout << (myCell->*methodPtr)() << endl;
```

C++ does not allow you to overload `operator.*` (just as you can't overload `operator.`), but you could overload `operator->*`. However, it is very tricky, and, given that most C++ programmers don't even know that you can access methods and members through pointers, it's probably not worth the trouble. The `auto_ptr` template in the standard library does not overload `operator->*`.

Writing Conversion Operators

Going back to the `SpreadsheetCell` example, consider these two lines of code:

```
SpreadsheetCell cell1;
string s1 = cell1; // DOES NOT COMPILE!
```

A `SpreadsheetCell` contains a string representation, so it seems logical that you could assign it to a `string` variable. Well, you can't. The compiler tells you that it doesn't know how to convert a `SpreadsheetCell` to a `string`. You might be tempted to try forcing the compiler to do what you want like this:

```
string s1 = (string) cell1; // STILL DOES NOT COMPILE!
```

First, the preceding code still doesn't compile because the compiler still doesn't know *how* to convert the `SpreadsheetCell` to a string. It already knew from the first line what you wanted it to do, and it would do it if it could. Second, it's a bad idea in general to add gratuitous casts to your program. Even if the compiler allowed this cast to compile, it probably wouldn't do the right thing at run time. For example, it might try to interpret the bits representing your object as a `string`.

If you want to allow this kind of assignment, you must tell the compiler how to perform it. Specifically, you can write a conversion operator to convert `SpreadsheetCells` to `strings`. The prototype looks like this:

```
class SpreadsheetCell
{
    public:
        // Omitted for brevity
        operator string() const;
        // Omitted for brevity
};
```

The name of the function is `operator string`. It has no return type because the return type is specified by the name of the operator: `string`. It is `const` because it doesn't change the object on which it is called. Yes, it looks odd at first, but you'll get used to it. The implementation looks like this:

```
SpreadsheetCell::operator string() const
{
    return (mString);
}
```

That's all you need to do to write a conversion operator from `SpreadsheetCell` to `string`. Now the compiler accepts this line and does the right thing at run time:

```
SpreadsheetCell cell1;
string s1 = cell1; // Works as expected
```

You can write conversion operators for any type with this same syntax. For example, here is the prototype for a `double` conversion operator from `SpreadsheetCell`:

```
class SpreadsheetCell
{
    public:
        // Omitted for brevity
        operator string() const;
        operator double() const;
        // Omitted for brevity
};
```

The implementation looks like this:

```
SpreadsheetCell::operator double() const
{
    return (mValue);
}
```

Now you can write code like the following:

```
SpreadsheetCell cell1;
double d2 = cell1;
```

Ambiguity Problems with Conversion Operators

Unfortunately, writing the `double` conversion operator for the `SpreadsheetCell` object introduces an *ambiguity* problem. Consider this line:

```
SpreadsheetCell cell1;
double d1 = cell1 + 3.3; // DOES NOT COMPILE IF YOU DEFINE operator double()
```

This line now fails to compile. It worked before you wrote `operator double()`, so what's the problem now? The issue is that the compiler doesn't know if it should convert `cell1` to a `double` with `operator double()` and perform `double` addition, or convert `3.3` to a `SpreadsheetCell` with the `double` constructor and perform `SpreadsheetCell` addition. Before you wrote `operator double()`, the compiler had only one choice: convert `3.3` to a `SpreadsheetCell` with the `double` constructor and perform

`SpreadsheetCell` addition. However, now the compiler could do either. It doesn't want to make a choice for you, which you might not like, so it refuses to make any choice at all.

The usual solution to this conundrum is to make the constructor in question `explicit`, so that the automatic conversion using that constructor is prevented. Unfortunately, we don't want that constructor to be `explicit` because we generally like the automatic conversion of `double`s to `SpreadsheetCell`s, as explained in Chapter 9. In this case, it's probably better not to write the `double` conversion operator for the `SpreadsheetCell` class.

Conversions for Boolean Expressions

Sometimes it is useful to be able to use objects in Boolean expressions. For example, programmers often use pointers in conditional statements like this:

```
if (ptr != NULL) {
    // Perform some dereferencing action.
}
```

Sometimes they write shorthand conditions such as:

```
if (ptr) {
    // Perform some dereferencing action.
}
```

Other times, you see code like the following:

```
if (!ptr) {
    // Do something.
}
```

Currently, none of the preceding expressions compiles with the `Pointer` smart pointer class defined earlier. However, you can add a conversion operator to the class to convert it to a pointer type. Then, the comparisons to `NULL`, as well as the object alone in an `if` statement, trigger the conversion to the pointer type. The usual pointer type for the conversion operator is `void*`. Here is the modified `Pointer` class:

```
template <typename T>
class Pointer
{
    public:
        Pointer(T* inPtr);
        ~Pointer();
        T& operator*();
        const T& operator*() const;
        T* operator->();
        const T* operator->() const;
        operator void*() const { return mPtr; }
    protected:
        T* mPtr;
    private:
        Pointer(const Pointer<T>& src);
        Pointer<T>& operator=(const Pointer<T>& rhs);
};
```

Now the following statements all compile and do what you expect:

```
Pointer<SpreadsheetCell> smartCell(new SpreadsheetCell);
smartCell->set(5);
if (smartCell != NULL) {
    cout << "not NULL!\n";
}
if (smartCell) {
    cout << "not NULL!\n";
}
if (!smartCell) {
    cout << "NULL\n";
}
```

Another alternative is to overload `operator bool` instead of `operator void*`. After all, you're using the object in a Boolean expression; why not convert it directly to a `bool`? You could write your `Pointer` class like this:

```
template <typename T>
class Pointer
{
    public:
        Pointer(T* inPtr);
        ~Pointer();
        T& operator*();
        const T& operator*() const;
        T* operator->();
        const T* operator->() const;
        operator bool() const { return (mPtr != NULL); }
    protected:
        T* mPtr;
    private:
        Pointer(const Pointer<T>& src);
        Pointer<T>& operator=(const Pointer<T>& rhs);
};
```

All three of the preceding tests continue to work, though the comparison to NULL explicitly might cause your compiler to generate warnings. This technique seems especially appropriate for objects that don't represent pointers and for which conversion to a pointer type really doesn't make sense. Unfortunately, adding a conversion operator to `bool` presents some unanticipated consequences. C++ applies "promotion" rules to silently convert `bool` to `int` whenever the opportunity arises. Therefore, with the preceding conversion operator, such code compiles and runs:

```
Pointer<SpreadsheetCell> smartCell(new SpreadsheetCell);
int i = smartCell; // Converts smartCell Pointer to bool to int.
```

That's usually not behavior that you expect or desire. Thus, many programmers prefer `operator void*` to `operator bool`. In fact, recall the following use of streams from Chapter 14:

```
ifstream istr;
int temp;
// Open istr
while (istr >> temp) {
    // Process temp
}
```

In order to allow stream objects to be used in Boolean expressions, but prohibit their undesired promotion to int, the `basic_ios` class defines `operator void*` instead of `operator bool`.

A third alternative is to implement `operator!` and require clients of the class to use only negative comparisons, such as:

```
if (!smartCell) {
    cout << "NULL\n";
}
```

As you can see, there is a design element to overloading operators. Your decisions about which operators to overload directly influence the ways in which clients can use your classes.

Overloading the Memory Allocation and Deallocation Operators

C++ gives you the ability to redefine the way memory allocation and deallocation work in your programs. You can provide this customization both on the global level and the class level. This capability is most useful when you are worried about performance and would like to provide more efficient memory management than is provided by default. For example, instead of going to the default C++ memory allocation each time you need memory, you could write a memory pool allocator that reuses fixed-size chunks of memory. This section explains the subtleties of the memory allocation and deallocation routines and shows you how to customize them. With these tools, you should be able to write a memory pool if the need ever arises.

> **Unless you know a lot about memory allocation strategies, attempts to overload the memory allocation routines are rarely worth the trouble. Don't overload them just because it sounds like a neat idea. Only do so if you have a genuine performance or space requirement and the necessary knowledge.**

How new and delete Really Work

One of the trickiest aspects of C++ is the details of `new` and `delete`. Consider this line of code:

```
SpreadsheetCell* cell = new SpreadsheetCell();
```

The `new SpreadsheetCell()` is called the *new expression*. It does two things. First, it allocates space for the `SpreadsheetCell` object by making a call to `operator new`. Second, it calls the constructor for the object. Only after the constructor has completed does it return the pointer to you.

`delete` functions similarly. Consider this line of code:

```
delete cell;
```

This line is called the *delete expression*. It first calls the destructor for `cell`, then calls `operator delete` to free the memory.

> When you use the keyword **new** to allocate memory, you are not directly calling
> `operator new`. When you use the keyword **delete** to free memory, you are not
> directly calling `operator delete`.

You can overload `operator new` and `operator delete` to control memory allocation and deallocation,
but you cannot overload the new expression or the delete expression. Thus, you can customize the
actual memory allocation and deallocation, but not the calls to the constructor and destructor.

The New Expression and operator new

There are six different forms of the new expression, each of which has a corresponding `operator new`.
You've already seen the first four new expressions in Chapters 13 and 15: new, new[], nothrow new, and
nothrow new[]. The `operator new`s for each them are defined in the header file <new> and are reproduced here respectively:

```
void* operator new(size_t size) throw(bad_alloc); // For new
void* operator new[](size_t size) throw(bad_alloc); // For new[]
void* operator new(size_t size, const nothrow_t&) throw(); // For nothrow new
void* operator new[](size_t size, const nothrow_t&) throw(); // For nothrow new[]
```

The fifth and sixth forms of new are called *placement new* (including both single and array forms). They
allow you to construct an object in preexisting memory like this:

```
void* ptr = allocateMemorySomehow();
SpreadsheetCell* cell = new (ptr) SpreadsheetCell();
```

This feature is a bit obscure, but it's important to realize that it exists. It can come in handy if you want
to implement memory pools such that you reuse memory without freeing it in between. The corresponding `operator new`s look like this:

```
void* operator new(size_t size, void* p) throw();
void* operator new[](size_t size, void* p) throw();
```

The Delete Expression and operator delete

There are only two different forms of the delete expression that you can call: delete, and delete[];
there are no `nothrow` or placement forms. However, there are all six forms of `operator delete`. Why
the asymmetry? The four `nothrow` and placement forms are used only if an exception is thrown from a
constructor. In that case, the `operator delete` is called that matches the `operator new` that was used
to allocate the memory prior to the constructor call. However, if you delete a pointer normally, delete
will call either `operator delete` or `operator delete[]` (never the `nothrow` or placement forms).
Practically, this doesn't really matter: delete never throws an exception anyway, so the `nothrow` version
of `operator delete` is superfluous, and placement delete should be a no-op. (The memory wasn't allocated in placement `operator new`, so there's nothing to free). Here are the prototypes for the `operator
delete` forms:

```
void operator delete(void* ptr) throw();
void operator delete[](void* ptr) throw();
void operator delete(void* ptr, const nothrow_t&) throw();
```

```
void operator delete[](void* ptr, const nothrow_t&) throw();
void operator delete(void* p, void*) throw();
void operator delete[](void* p, void*) throw();
```

Overloading operator new and operator delete

You can actually replace the global operator new and operator delete routines if you want. These functions are called for every new expression and delete expression in the program, unless there are more specific routines in individual classes. However, to quote Bjarne Stroustrup, ". . . replacing the global operator new() and operator delete() is not for the fainthearted." (*The C++ Programming Language*, third edition). We don't recommend it either!

> If you fail to heed our advice and decide to replace the global operator new, keep in mind that you cannot put any code in the operator that makes a call to new: an infinite loop would result. For example, you cannot write a message to console with cout.

A more useful technique is to overload operator new and operator delete for specific classes. These overloaded operators will be called only when you allocate and deallocate objects of that particular class. Here is an example of a class that overloads the four nonplacement forms of operator new and operator delete:

```cpp
#include <new>
using namespace std;

class MemoryDemo
{
    public:
        MemoryDemo() {}
        ~MemoryDemo() {}

        void* operator new(size_t size) throw(bad_alloc);
        void operator delete(void* ptr) throw();

        void* operator new[](size_t size) throw(bad_alloc);
        void operator delete[](void* ptr) throw();

        void* operator new(size_t size, const nothrow_t&) throw();
        void operator delete(void* ptr, const nothrow_t&) throw();

        void* operator new[](size_t size, const nothrow_t&) throw();
        void operator delete[](void* ptr, const nothrow_t&) throw();
};
```

Here are simple implementations of these operators that pass the argument through to calls to the global versions of the operators. Note that nothrow is actually a variable of type nothrow_t.

```cpp
#include "MemoryDemo.h"
#include <iostream>
using namespace std;
```

```
void* MemoryDemo::operator new(size_t size) throw(bad_alloc)
{
    cout << "operator new\n";
    return (::operator new(size));
}

void MemoryDemo::operator delete(void* ptr) throw()
{
    cout << "operator delete\n";
    ::operator delete(ptr);
}

void* MemoryDemo::operator new[](size_t size) throw(bad_alloc)
{
    cout << "operator new[]\n";
    return (::operator new[](size));
}

void MemoryDemo::operator delete[](void* ptr) throw()
{
    cout << "operator delete[]\n";
    ::operator delete[](ptr);
}

void* MemoryDemo::operator new(size_t size, const nothrow_t&) throw()
{
    cout << "operator new nothrow\n";
    return (::operator new(size, nothrow));
}

void MemoryDemo::operator delete(void* ptr, const nothrow_t&) throw()
{
    cout << "operator delete nothrow\n";
    ::operator delete[](ptr, nothrow);
}

void* MemoryDemo::operator new[](size_t size, const nothrow_t&) throw()
{
    cout << "operator new[] nothrow\n";
    return (::operator new[](size, nothrow));
}

void MemoryDemo::operator delete[](void* ptr, const nothrow_t&) throw()
{
    cout << "operator delete[] nothrow\n";
    ::operator delete[](ptr, nothrow);
}
```

Here is some code that allocates and frees objects of this class in several ways:

```
#include "MemoryDemo.h"

int main(int argc, char** argv)
{
    MemoryDemo* mem = new MemoryDemo();
```

```
        delete mem;

        mem = new MemoryDemo[10];
        delete [] mem;

        mem = new (nothrow) MemoryDemo();
        delete mem;

        mem = new (nothrow) MemoryDemo[10];
        delete [] mem;

        return (0);
}
```

Here is the output from running the program:

```
operator new
operator delete
operator new[]
operator delete[]
operator new nothrow
operator delete
operator new[] nothrow
operator delete[]
```

These implementations of `operator new` and `operator delete` are obviously trivial and not particularly useful. They are intended only to give you an idea of the syntax in case you ever want to implement nontrivial versions of them.

> **Whenever you overload `operator new`, overload the corresponding form of
> `operator delete`. Otherwise, memory will be allocated as you specify but freed
> according to the built-in semantics, which may not be compatible.**

It might seem overkill to overload all of the various forms of `operator new`. However, it's generally a good idea to do so in order to prevent inconsistencies in the memory allocations. If you don't want to provide implementations, you can declare the function as `protected` or `private` in order to prevent anyone from using it.

> **Overload all forms of `operator new`, or provide `private` declarations without
> implementations to prevent their use.**

Overloading operator new and operator delete with Extra Parameters

In addition to overloading the standard forms of `operator new`, you can write your own versions with extra parameters. For example, here is the `MemoryDemo` class showing an additional `operator new` with an extra integer parameter:

```
#include <new>
using namespace std;

class MemoryDemo
{
    public:
        MemoryDemo();
        ~MemoryDemo();
        void* operator new(size_t size) throw(bad_alloc);
        void operator delete(void* ptr) throw();
        void* operator new[](size_t size) throw(bad_alloc);
        void operator delete[](void* ptr) throw();
        void* operator new(size_t size, const nothrow_t&) throw();
        void operator delete(void* ptr, const nothrow_t&) throw();
        void* operator new[](size_t size, const nothrow_t&) throw();
        void operator delete[](void* ptr, const nothrow_t&) throw();
        void* operator new(size_t size, int extra) throw(bad_alloc);
};

void* MemoryDemo::operator new(size_t size, int extra) throw(bad_alloc)
{
    cout << "operator new with extra int arg\n";
    return (::operator new(size));
}
```

When you write an overloaded `operator new` with extra parameters, the compiler will automatically allow the corresponding new expression. So, you can now write code like this:

```
int x = 5;
MemoryDemo* memp = new(5) MemoryDemo();
delete memp;
```

The extra arguments to `new` are passed with function call syntax (as in `nothrow new`). These extra arguments can be useful for passing various flags or counters to your memory allocation routines.

You cannot add arbitrary extra arguments to `operator delete`. However, an alternate form of `operator delete` gives you the size of the memory that should be freed as well as the pointer. Simply declare the prototype for `operator delete` with an extra size parameter.

> **If your class declares two identical versions of `operator delete` except that one takes the size parameter and the other doesn't, the version without the size parameter will always get called. If you want the version with the size to be used, write only that version.**

You can replace `operator delete` with the version that takes a size for any of the versions of `operator delete` independently. Here is the `MemoryDemo` class definition with the first `operator delete` modified to take the size of the memory to be deleted.

```
#include <new>
using namespace std;
```

```
class MemoryDemo
{
    public:
        MemoryDemo();
        ~MemoryDemo();
        void* operator new(size_t size) throw(bad_alloc);
        void operator delete(void* ptr, size_t size) throw();
        void* operator new[](size_t size) throw(bad_alloc);
        void operator delete[](void* ptr) throw();
        void* operator new(size_t size, const nothrow_t&) throw();
        void operator delete(void*ptr, const nothrow_t&) throw();
        void* operator new[](size_t size, const nothrow_t&) throw();
        void operator delete[](void* ptr, const nothrow_t&) throw();
        void* operator new(size_t size, int extra) throw(bad_alloc);
};
```

The implementation of this operator delete calls the global operator delete without the size parameter because there is no global operator delete that takes the size.

```
void MemoryDemo::operator delete(void* ptr, size_t size) throw()
{
    cout << "operator delete with size\n";
    ::operator delete(ptr);
}
```

This capability is useful only if you are writing a complicated memory allocation and deallocation scheme for your classes.

Summary

This chapter summarized the rationale for operator overloading, and provided examples and explanations for overloading the various categories of operators. We hope that this chapter taught you to look past the ugly syntax of operator overloading, and to appreciate the power that it gives you.

Subsequent chapters in this book employ operator overloading to provide abstractions, including iterators in Chapter 23 and smart pointers in Chapter 25.

17

Writing Efficient C++

The efficiency of your programs is important regardless of your application domain. If your product competes with others in the marketplace, speed can be a major differentiator: given the choice between a slower and a faster program, which one would you choose? No one would buy an operating system that takes two weeks to boot up, unless it was the only option. Even if you don't intend to sell your products, they will have users. Those users will not be happy with you if they end up wasting time waiting for your programs to complete tasks.

Now that you understand the concepts of Professional C++ design and coding, and have tackled some of the more complex facilities that the language provides, you are ready to incorporate performance into your programs. Writing efficient programs involves thought at the design level, as well as details at the implementation level. Although this chapter falls late in this book, remember to consider performance from the beginning of your program life cycle.

This chapter first provides working definitions of "efficiency" and "performance" as they relate to software, describes the two levels at which you can increase efficiency in your programs, and discusses the two major classes of applications. Specific strategies follow for writing efficient programs, including language-level optimizations and design-level guidelines. Finally, the chapter provides an in-depth discussion of profiling tools.

Overview of Performance and Efficiency

Before delving further into the details, it's helpful to define the terms performance and efficiency, as used in this book. The *performance* of a program can refer to several areas, such as speed, memory usage, disk access, and network use. This chapter focuses on speed performance. The term *efficiency*, when applied to programs, means running without wasted effort. An efficient program completes its tasks as quickly as possible within the given circumstances. A program can be efficient without being fast, if the application domain is inherently prohibitive to quick execution.

> An efficient, or *high-performance*, program runs as fast as is possible for the particular tasks.

Note that the title of this chapter, "Writing Efficient C++," means writing programs that run efficiently, not efficiently writing programs. That is, the time you learn to save by reading this chapter will be your users', not your own!

Two Approaches to Efficiency

The traditional approach to writing efficient programs is to aim for *optimizing*, or improving the performance of, preexisting code. This technique usually involves only *language-level efficiency:* specific, independent, code changes such as passing objects by reference instead of by value. That approach will only get you so far. If you want to write truly high-performance applications, you must think about efficiency from the beginning of your design. This *design-level efficiency* includes choosing efficient algorithms, avoiding unnecessary steps and computations, and selecting appropriate design optimizations.

Two Kinds of Programs

As noted, efficiency is important for all application domains. Additionally, there is a small subset of programs, such as systems-level software, embedded systems, intensive computational applications, and real-time games, which require extremely high levels of efficiency. Most programs don't. Unless you write those types of high-performance applications, you probably don't need to worry about squeezing every ounce of speed out of your C++ code. Think of it as the difference between building normal family cars and building sports cars. Every car must be reasonably efficient, but sports cars require extremely high performance. You wouldn't want to waste your time optimizing family cars for speed when they'll never go faster than 70 miles per hour.

Is C++ an Inefficient Language?

C programmers often resist using C++ for high-performance applications. They claim that the language is inherently less efficient than C or a similar procedural language. On the surface, the argument is compelling: C++ includes high-level constructs, such as exceptions and virtual methods, which are fundamentally slow. However, there are problems with the argument.

First, you cannot ignore the effect of compilers. When discussing the efficiency of a language, you must separate the performance capabilities of the language itself from the effectiveness of its compilers at optimizing it. Recall that the C or C++ code you write is not the code that the computer executes. A compiler first translates that code into machine language, applying optimizations in the process. This means that you can't simply run benchmarks of C and C++ programs and compare the result. You're really comparing the compiler optimizations of the languages, not the languages themselves. C++ compilers can "optimize away" many of the high-level constructs in the language to generate machine code similar to that generated from a comparable C program.

Critics, however, still maintain that some features of C++ cannot be optimized away. For example, as explained in Chapter 10, virtual methods require the existence of a vtable and an additional level of indirection at run time, making them unarguably slower than regular nonvirtual function calls. However, when you really think about it, this argument is still unconvincing. Virtual method calls provide more than just a function call: they also give you a run-time choice of which function to call. A comparable nonvirtual function call would need a conditional statement to decide which function to call. If you don't need those extra semantics, you can use a nonvirtual function (although for safety and style reasons, we recommend you don't). A general design rule in the C++ language is, "if you don't use it, you don't need to pay for it." If you don't use virtual methods, you pay no performance penalty for the fact that you could use them. Thus, nonvirtual function calls in C++ are identical to function calls in C in terms of performance.

The critics might be right in one sense, however: some aspects of C++ make it easy to write inefficient code at the language-level. Using exceptions and virtual functions indiscriminately can slow down your program. However, this issue is insubstantial in light of the advantages C++ offers for your algorithms and overall design. The high-level constructs of C++ enable you to write cleaner programs that are more efficient at the design level, are more easily maintained, and avoid accumulating unnecessary and dead code.

Finally, both authors of this book have used C++ for successful systems level software where high-performance was required. We believe that you will be better served in your development, performance, and maintenance by choosing C++ instead of a procedural language.

Language-Level Efficiency

Many books, articles, and programmers spend a lot of time trying to convince you to apply language-level optimizations to your code. These tips-and-tricks are important, and can speed up your programs in some cases. However, they are far less important than the overall design and algorithm choices in your program. You can pass-by-reference all you want, but it won't ever make your program fast if you perform twice as many disk writes as you need. It's easy to get bogged down in references and pointers and forget about the big picture.

Furthermore, some of these language-level tricks can be performed automatically by good optimizing compilers. Check your compiler documentation for details before spending time optimizing a particular area yourself.

In this book, we've tried to present a balance of strategies. Thus, we've included here what we feel are the most useful language-level optimizations. This list is not comprehensive, but should give you a good start if you want to optimize your code. However, make sure to read, and practice, the design-level efficiency advice described later in this chapter as well.

> **Apply language-level optimizations judiciously.**

Handle Objects Efficiently

C++ does a lot of work for you behind the scenes, particularly with regard to objects. You should always be aware of the performance impact of the code you write. If you follow a few simple guidelines, your code will become significantly more efficient.

Pass-by-Reference

This rule is discussed elsewhere in this book, but it's worth repeating here.

Objects should rarely be passed by value to a function or method.

Pass-by-value incurs copying costs that are avoided by pass-by-reference. One reason why this rule can be difficult to remember is that on the surface there doesn't appear to be any problem when you pass-by-value. Consider a class to represent a person that looks like this:

```cpp
class Person
{
    public:
        Person();
        Person(const string& inFirstName, const string& inLastName, int inAge);
        string getFirstName() { return firstName; }
        string getLastName() { return lastName; }
        int getAge() { return age; }

    private:
        string firstName, lastName;
        int age;
};
```

You could write a function that takes a `Person` object in the following way:

```cpp
void processPerson(Person p)
{
    // Process the person.
}
```

You might call it like this:

```cpp
Person me("Nicholas", "Solter", 28);
processPerson(me);
```

This doesn't look like there's any more code than if you instead wrote the function like this:

```cpp
void processPerson(const Person& p)
{
    // Process the person.
}
```

The call to the function remains the same. However, consider what happens when you pass-by-value in the first version of the function. In order to initialize the p parameter of `processPerson()`, me must be copied with a call to its copy constructor. Even though you didn't write a copy constructor for the `Person` class, the compiler generates one that copies each of the data members. That still doesn't look so bad: there are only three data members. However, two of those are `strings`, which are themselves objects with copy constructors. So, each of their copy constructors will be called as well. The version of `processPerson()` that takes p by reference incurs no such copying costs. Thus, pass-by-reference in this example avoids three function calls when the code enters the function.

And you're still not done. Remember that p in the first version of `processPerson()` is a local variable to the `processPerson()` function, and so must be destroyed when the function exits. This destruction requires a call to the `Person` destructor. Because you didn't write a destructor, the default destructor simply calls the destructor of all of the data members. `strings` have destructors, so exiting this function (if you passed by value) incurs calls to three destructors. None of those calls are needed if the `Person` object is passed by reference.

In summary, if a function must modify an object, you can simply pass the object by reference. If the function should not modify the object, you can pass it by `const` reference, as in the preceding example. See Chapter 12 for details on reference and `const`.

Return by Reference

Just as you should pass objects by reference to functions, you should also return them by reference from functions in order to avoid copying the objects unnecessarily. Unfortunately, it is sometimes impossible to return objects by reference, such as when you write overloaded `operator+` and other similar operators. You should never return a reference or a pointer to a local object that will be destroyed when the function exits!

Catch Exceptions by Reference

As noted in Chapter 15, you should catch exceptions by reference in order to avoid an extra copy. As described later in this section, exceptions are heavy in terms of performance, so any little thing you can do to improve their efficiency will help.

Avoid Creating Temporary Objects

The compiler creates temporary, unnamed objects in several circumstances. Recall from Chapter 9 that after writing a global `operator+` for a class, you can add objects of that class to other types, as long as those types can be converted to objects of that class. For example, the `SpreadsheetCell` class definition looks in part like the following:

```
class SpreadsheetCell
{
    public:
        // Other constructors omitted for brevity
        SpreadsheetCell(double initialValue);

        friend const SpreadsheetCell operator+(const SpreadsheetCell& lhs,
            const SpreadsheetCell& rhs);

        // Remainder omitted for brevity
};
```

The constructor that takes a `double` allows you to write code like this:

```
SpreadsheetCell myCell(4), aThirdCell;

aThirdCell = myCell + 5.6;
aThirdCell = myCell + 4;
```

The first addition line constructs a temporary `SpreadsheetCell` object from the `5.6` argument, then calls the `operator+` with `myCell` and the temporary object as arguments. The result is stored in `aThirdCell`. The second addition line does the same thing, except that 4 must be coerced to a `double` in order to call the `double` constructor of the `SpreadsheetCell`.

The important point in the above example is that the compiler generates code to create an extra, unnamed `SpreadsheetCell` object for each addition line. That object must be constructed and destructed with calls to its constructor and destructor. If you're still skeptical, try inserting `cout` statements in your constructor and destructor and watching the printout.

In general, the compiler constructs a temporary object whenever your code converts a variable of one type to another type for use in a larger expression. This rule applies mostly to function calls. For example, suppose that you write a function with this signature:

```
void doSomething(const SpreadsheetCell& s);
```

You can call it like this:

```
doSomething(5.56);
```

The compiler constructs a temporary `SpreadsheetCell` object from `5.56` using the `double` constructor, which it passes to `doSomething()`. Note that if you remove the `const` from the s parameter, you can no longer call `doSomething()` with a constant: you must pass a variable. Temporary objects can only serve as targets of a `const` reference, not a non-`const` reference.

You should generally attempt to avoid cases in which the compiler is forced to construct temporary objects. Although it is impossible to avoid in some situations, you should at least be cognizant of the existence of this "feature" so you aren't surprised by performance and profiling results.

The Return-Value Optimization

A function that returns an object by value can cause the creation of a temporary object. Continuing with the `Person` example, consider this function:

```
Person createPerson()
{
    Person newP;
    return (newP);
}
```

Suppose that you call it like this (assuming that `operator<<` is implemented for the `Person` class):

```
cout << createPerson();
```

Even though this call does not store the result of `createPerson()` anywhere, the result must be stored somewhere in order to pass to the `operator<<` call. In order to generate code for this behavior, the compiler is allowed to create a temporary variable in which to store the `Person` object returned from `createPerson()`.

Even if the result of the function is not used anywhere, the compiler might still generate code to create the temporary object. For example, suppose that you have this code:

```
createPerson();
```

The compiler might generate code to create a temporary object for the return value, even though it is not used.

However, you usually don't need to worry about this issue because the compiler will optimize away the temporary variable in most cases. This optimization is called the *return value optimization*.

Don't Overuse Costly Language Features

Several C++ features are costly in terms of execution speed: exceptions, virtual methods, and RTTI are the biggest offenders. If you are worried about efficiency, you should consider avoiding these features. Unfortunately, support for exceptions and RTTI incurs performance overhead even if you don't explicitly use the features in your program. Support for only the possible use of those features requires extra steps during execution. Thus, many compilers allow you to specify that your program should be compiled without support for these features at all. For example, consider the following simple program that uses both exceptions and RTTI:

```cpp
// test.cpp
#include <iostream>
#include <exception>
using namespace std;

class base
{
    public:
        base() {}
        virtual ~base() {}
};

class derived : public base {};

int main(int argc, char** argv)
{
    base* b = new derived();
    derived* d = dynamic_cast<derived*>(b); // Use RTTI.
    if (d == NULL) {
        throw exception(); // Use exceptions.
    }
    return (0);
}
```

Using g++ 3.2.2 on Linux, you can compile the program in the following way:

```
>g++ test.cpp
```

If you specify the g++ flag to disable exceptions, your attempt to compile looks like this:

```
>g++ -fno-exceptions test.cpp
test.cpp: In function `int main (int, char**)':
test.cpp:20: exception handling disabled, use -fexceptions to enable
```

Strangely, if you specify the g++ flag to disable RTTI, the compiler successfully compiles the program, despite the obvious use of `dynamic_cast`:

```
>g++ -fno-rtti test.cpp
>
```

However, the use of RTTI fails at run time, causing the program to generate a segmentation violation.

Consult your compiler documentation for the proper flags to disable these features.

> **Disabling support for language features is risky. You never know when a third-party library will suddenly throw an exception or rely on RTTI for correct behavior. Thus, you should only disable support for exceptions and RTTI when you are sure that none of your code and none of the library code you use require those features, and when you are writing a performance-critical application.**

Use Inline Methods and Functions

As described in Chapter 9, the code for an `inline` method or function is inserted directly into the code where it is called, avoiding the overhead of a function call. You should mark as `inline` all functions and methods that you think can qualify for this optimization. However, remember that inlining requests by the programmer are only a recommendation to the compiler. It can refuse to inline the function that you want it to inline.

On the other hand, some compilers inline appropriate functions and methods during their optimization steps, even if those functions aren't marked with the `inline` keyword. Thus, you should read your compiler documentation before wasting a lot of effort deciding which functions to inline.

Design-Level Efficiency

The design choices in your program affect its performance far more than do language details such as pass-by-reference. For example, if you choose an algorithm for a fundamental task in your application that runs in $O(n^2)$ time instead of a simpler one that runs in $O(n)$ time, you could potentially perform the square of the number of operations that you really need. To put numbers on that, a task that uses an $O(n^2)$ algorithm and performs one million operations would perform only one thousand with an $O(n)$ algorithm Even if that operation is optimized beyond recognition at the language level, the simple fact that you perform one million operations when a better algorithm would only use one thousand will make your program very inefficient. Remember, though, that big-O notation ignores constant factors, so it's not always the most valid guideline. Nonetheless, you should choose your algorithms carefully. Refer to Part I, specifically Chapter 4, of this book for a detailed discussion of algorithm design choices.

In addition to your choice of algorithms, design-level efficiency includes specific tips and tricks. The remainder of this section presents three design techniques for optimizing your program: caching, object pools, and thread pools.

Cache as Much as Possible

Caching means storing items for future use in order to avoid retrieving or recalculating them. You might be familiar with the principle from its use in computer hardware. Modern computer processors are built with memory caches that store recently and frequently accessed memory values in a location that is quicker to access than main memory. Most memory locations that are accessed at all are accessed more than once in a short time period, so caching at the hardware level can significantly speed up computations.

Caching in software follows the same approach. If a task or computation is particularly slow, you should make sure that you are not performing it more than necessary. Store the results in memory the first time you perform the task so that they are available for future needs. Here is a list of tasks that are usually slow:

❑ **Disk access.** You should avoid opening and reading the same file more than once in your program. If memory is available, save the file contents in RAM if you need to access it frequently.

❑ **Network communication.** Whenever you need to communicate over a network, your program is subject to the vagaries of the network load. Treat network accesses like file accesses, and cache as much static information as possible.

❑ **Mathematical computations.** If you need the result of a computation in more than one place in your program, perform the calculation once and share the result.

❑ **Object allocation.** If you need to create and use a large number of short-lived objects in your program, consider using an object pool, which is described in the next section.

❑ **Thread creation.** This task can also be slow. You can "cache" threads in a thread-pool. See the section on Thread Pools below.

Cache Invalidation

One common problem with caching is that the data you store are often only copies of the underlying information. The original data might change during the lifetime of the cache. For example, you might want to cache the values in a configuration file so that you don't need to read it repeatedly. However, the user might be allowed to change the configuration file while your program is running, which would make your cached version of the information obsolete. In cases like this, you need a mechanism for *cache invalidation:* when the underlying data change, you must either stop using your cached information, or repopulate your cache.

One technique for cache invalidation is to request that the entity managing the underlying data notify your program if the data change. It could do this through a *callback* that your program registers with the manager. Alternatively, your program could poll for certain events that would trigger it to repopulate the cache automatically. Regardless of your specific cache invalidation implementation, make sure that you think about these issues before relying on a cache in your program.

Use Object Pools

As you learned in Chapter 13, object pools are a technique for avoiding the creation and deletion of a large number of objects throughout the lifetime of your program. If you know that your program needs a large number of short-lived objects of the same type, you can create a *pool*, or cache, of those objects. Whenever you need an object in your code, you ask the pool for one. When you are done with the object, you return it to the pool. The object pool creates the objects only once, so their constructor is called only once, not each time they are used. Thus, object pools are appropriate when the constructor performs some setup actions that apply to many uses of the object, and when you can set instance-specific parameters on the object through nonconstructor method calls.

An Object Pool Implementation

This section provides an implementation of a pool class template that you can use in your programs. The pool allocates a *chunk* of objects of the specified class when it is constructed and hands them out via the `acquireObject()` method. When the client is done with the object, she returns it via the `releaseObject()` method. If `aquireObject()` is called but there are no free objects, the pool allocates another chunk of objects.

The most difficult aspect of an object pool implementation is keeping track of which objects are free and which are in use. This implementation takes the approach of storing free objects on a queue. Each time a client requests an object, the pool gives that client the top object from the queue. The pool does not explicitly track objects that are in use. It trusts the clients to return them correctly to the pool when the clients are finished with them. Separately, the pool keeps track of all allocated objects in a vector. This vector is used only when the pool is destroyed in order to free the memory for all the objects, thereby preventing memory leaks.

The code uses the STL implementations of `queue` and `vector`, which were introduced in Chapter 4. The `queue` container allows clients to add elements with `push()`, remove them with `pop()`, and examine the top element with `front()`. The `vector` allows clients to add elements with `push_back()`. Consult Chapters 21 through 23 for more details of these two containers.

Here is the class definition, with comments that explain the details. Note that the template is parameterized on the class type from which the objects in the pool are to be constructed.

```
#include <queue>
#include <vector>
#include <stdexcept>
#include <memory>

using std::queue;
using std::vector;

//
// template class ObjectPool
//
// Provides an object pool that can be used with any class that provides a
// default constructor
//
// The object pool constructor creates a pool of objects, which it hands out
// to clients when requested via the acquireObject() method. When a client is
// finished with the object it calls releaseObject() to put the object back
// into the object pool.
//
// The constructor and destructor on each object in the pool will be called only
// once each for the lifetime of the program, not once per acquisition and release.
//
// The primary use of an object pool is to avoid creating and deleting objects
// repeatedly. The object pool is most suited to applications that use large
// numbers of objects for short periods of time.
//
// For efficiency, the object pool doesn't perform sanity checks.
// It expects the user to release every acquired object exactly once.
// It expects the user to avoid using any objects that he or she has released.
//
// It expects the user not to delete the object pool until every object
// that was acquired has been released. Deleting the object pool invalidates
// any objects that the user has acquired, even if they have not yet been released.
//
template <typename T>
class ObjectPool
{
```

```
public:
    //
    // Creates an object pool with chunkSize objects.
    // Whenever the object pool runs out of objects, chunkSize
    // more objects will be added to the pool. The pool only grows:
    // objects are never removed from the pool (freed), until
    // the pool is destroyed.
    //
    // Throws invalid_argument if chunkSize is <= 0
    //
    ObjectPool(int chunkSize = kDefaultChunkSize)
        throw(std::invalid_argument, std::bad_alloc);

    //
    // Frees all the allocated objects. Invalidates any objects that have
    // been acquired for use
    //
    ~ObjectPool();

    //
    // Reserve an object for use. The reference to the object is invalidated
    // if the object pool itself is freed.
    //
    // Clients must not free the object!
    //
    T& acquireObject();

    //
    // Return the object to the pool. Clients must not use the object after
    // it has been returned to the pool.
    //
    void releaseObject(T& obj);

protected:
    //
    // mFreeList stores the objects that are not currently in use
    // by clients.
    //
    queue<T*> mFreeList;
    //
    // mAllObjects stores pointers to all the objects, in use
    // or not. This vector is needed in order to ensure that all
    // objects are freed properly in the destructor.
    //
    vector<T*> mAllObjects;

    int mChunkSize;
    static const int kDefaultChunkSize = 10;

    //
    // Allocates mChunkSize new objects and adds them
    // to the mFreeList
    //
    void allocateChunk();
    static void arrayDeleteObject(T* obj);
```

Chapter 17

```
    private:
        // Prevent assignment and pass-by-value.
        ObjectPool(const ObjectPool<T>& src);
        ObjectPool<T>& operator=(const ObjectPool<T>& rhs);
};
```

There are a few points to emphasize about this class definition. First, note that objects are acquired and released by reference, instead of by pointer, in order to discourage clients from manipulating them or freeing them through pointers. Next, note that the user of the object pool specifies through the template parameter the name of the class from which objects can be created, and through the constructor the allocation "chunk size." This "chunk size" controls the number of objects created at one time. Here is the code that defines the kDefaultChunkSize:

```
template<typename T>
const int ObjectPool<T>::kDefaultChunkSize;
```

The default of 10, given in the class definition, is probably too small for most uses. If your program requires thousands of objects at once, you should use a larger, more appropriate, value.

The constructor validates the chunkSize parameter, and calls the allocateChunk() helper method to obtain a starting allocation of objects.

```
template <typename T>
ObjectPool<T>::ObjectPool(int chunkSize) throw(std::invalid_argument,
    std::bad_alloc) : mChunkSize(chunkSize)
{
    if (mChunkSize <= 0) {
        throw std::invalid_argument("chunk size must be positive");
    }
    // Create mChunkSize objects to start.
    allocateChunk();
}
```

The allocateChunk() method allocates mChunkSize elements in contiguous storage. It stores a pointer to the array of objects in the mAllObjects vector, and pushes each individual object onto the mFreeLlist queue.

```
//
// Allocates an array of mChunkSize objects because that's
// more efficient than allocating each of them individually.
// Stores a pointer to the first element of the array in the mAllObjects
// vector. Adds a pointer to each new object to the mFreeList.
//
template <typename T>
void ObjectPool<T>::allocateChunk()
{
    T* newObjects = new T[mChunkSize];
    mAllObjects.push_back(newObjects);
    for (int i = 0; i < mChunkSize; i++) {
        mFreeList.push(&newObjects[i]);
    }
}
```

The destructor simply frees all of the arrays of objects that were allocated in `allocateChunk()`. However, it uses the `for_each()` STL algorithm to do so, passing it a pointer to the `arrayDelete()` static method, which in turn makes the actual delete call on each object array. Consult the STL chapters, Chapters 21 through 23, for details if this code confuses you.

```
//
// Freeing function for use in the for_each algorithm in the
// destructor
//
template<typename T>
void ObjectPool<T>::arrayDeleteObject(T* obj)
{
    delete [] obj;
}

template <typename T>
ObjectPool<T>::~ObjectPool()
{
    // Free each of the allocation chunks.
    for_each(mAllObjects.begin(), mAllObjects.end(), arrayDeleteObject);
}
```

`acquireObject()` returns the top object from the free list, first calling `allocateChunk()` if there are no free objects.

```
template <typename T>
T& ObjectPool<T>::acquireObject()
{
    if (mFreeList.empty()) {
        allocateChunk();
    }
    T* obj = mFreeList.front();
    mFreeList.pop();
    return (*obj);
}
```

Finally, `releaseObject()` returns the object to the tail of the free list.

```
template <typename T>
void ObjectPool<T>::releaseObject(T& obj)
{
    mFreeList.push(&obj);
}
```

Using the Object Pool

Consider an application that is structured around obtaining requests for actions from users and processing those requests. This application would most likely be the middleware between a graphical front-end and a back-end database. For example, it could be part of an airline reservation system or an online banking application. You might want to encode each user request in an object, with a class that looks something like this:

```
class UserRequest
{
    public:
        UserRequest() {}
        ~UserRequest() {}

        // Methods to populate the request with specific information
        // Methods to retrieve the request data
        // (not shown)

    protected:
        // Data members (not shown)
};
```

Instead of creating and deleting large numbers of requests throughout the lifetime of your program, you could use an object pool. Your program structure would then be something like the following:

```
UserRequest& obtainUserRequest(ObjectPool<UserRequest>& pool)
{
    // Obtain a UserRequest object from the pool.
    UserRequest& request = pool.acquireObject();

    // Populate the request with user input
    // (not shown).

    return (request);
}

void processUserRequest(ObjectPool<UserRequest>& pool, UserRequest& req)
{
    // Process the request
    // (not shown).

    // Return the request to the pool.
    pool.releaseObject(req);
}

int main(int argc, char** argv)
{
    ObjectPool<UserRequest> requestPool(1000);

    // Set up program
    // (not shown).

    while (/* program is running */) {
        UserRequest& req = obtainUserRequest(requestPool);
        processUserRequest(requestPool, req);
    }

    return (0);
}
```

Use Thread Pools

Thread pools are very similar to object pools. Instead of creating and deleting threads dynamically throughout your program lifetime, you can create a pool of threads that can be used as needed. This technique is often used in programs that process incoming network requests. Your Web server might keep a pool of threads ready to lookup pages in response to each client request that arrives.

As discussed further in Chapter 18, threading support is platform-specific, so we do not show an example of a thread pool here. However, you can write one in a similar way to an object pool.

Profiling

Although we urge you to think about efficiency as you design and code, you should accept that not every finished application will perform as well as it could. It is easy for efficiency to fall by the wayside in an attempt to generate a functional program; in our experience, most efficiency optimization is performed on already working programs. Even if you did consider efficiency in your development, you might not have optimized the right parts of the program! Recall from Chapter 4 that 90 percent of the running time of most programs is spent in only 10 percent of the code. This means that you could optimize 90 percent of your code out of existence, but still only improve the running time of the program by 10 percent. Obviously, you want to optimize the parts of the code that are exercised the most for the specific workload that you expect the program to run.

Consequently, it is often helpful to *profile* your program to determine which parts of the code require optimization. There are many *profiling tools* available that analyze programs as they run in order to generate data about their performance. Most profiling tools provide analysis at the function level by specifying the amount of time (or percent of total execution time) spent in each function in the program. After running a profiler on your program, you can usually tell immediately which parts of the program need optimization. Profiling before and after optimizing is also useful to prove that your optimizations had an effect.

In our experience, the best profiling tool is Rational Quantify from IBM. It requires significant license fees, but you should check if your company or academic institution has a license for its use. If the license restriction is prohibitive, there are several free profiling tools. One of the most well-known is gprof, which can be found on most Unix systems, including Solaris and Linux.

Profiling Example with gprof

The power of profiling can best be seen with a real coding example. As a disclaimer, the performance bugs in the first attempt shown are not subtle. Real efficiency issues would probably be more complex, but a program long enough to demonstrate them would be too lengthy for this book.

Suppose that you work for the United States Social Security Administration. Every year the administration puts up a Web site that allows users to look up the popularity of new baby names from the previous year. Your job is to write the back-end program that looks up names for users. Your input is a file containing the name of every new baby. This file will obviously contain redundant names. For example, in the file for boys for 2003, the name Jacob was the most popular, showing up 29,195 times. Your program must read the file to construct an in-memory database. A user may then request the absolute number of babies with a given name, or the rank of that name among all the babies.

First Design Attempt

A logical design for this program consists of a NameDB class with the following public methods:

```cpp
#include <string>
#include <stdexcept>

using std::string;

class NameDB
{
    public:
        // Reads the list of baby names in nameFile to populate the database.
        // Throws invalid_argument if nameFile cannot be opened or read.
        NameDB(const string& nameFile) throw (std::invalid_argument);

        // Returns the rank of the name (1st, 2nd, etc).
        // Returns -1 if the name is not found.
        int getNameRank(const string& name) const;

        // Returns the number of babies with this name.
        // Returns -1 if the name is not found.
        int getAbsoluteNumber(const string &name) const;

        // Protected and private members and methods not shown
};
```

The hard part is choosing a good data structure for the in-memory database. A first attempt might be an array, or a vector from the STL, of name/count pairs. Each entry in the vector would store one of the names, along with a count of the number of times that name shows up in the raw data file. Here is the complete class definition with such a design:

```cpp
#include <string>
#include <stdexcept>
#include <vector>

using std::string;

class NameDB
{
    public:
        NameDB(const string& nameFile) throw (std::invalid_argument);

        int getNameRank(const string& name) const;
        int getAbsoluteNumber(const string& name) const;

    protected:
        std::vector<std::pair<string, int> > mNames;

        // Helper methods
        bool nameExists(const string& name) const;
        void incrementNameCount(const string& name);
        void addNewName(const string& name);

    private:
```

```
            // Prevent assignment and pass-by-value.
            NameDB(const NameDB& src);
            NameDB& operator=(const NameDB& rhs);
    };
```

Note the use of the STL vector and pair. A pair is simply a utility class that combines two variables of different types. Consult Chapters 21 to 23 for details on the STL.

Here is the implementation of the constructor and the helper functions nameExists(), incrementNameCount(), and addNewName(). If you're unfamiliar with the STL, you might be confused by the loops in nameExists() and incrementNameCount(). They simply iterate over all the elements of the mNames vector.

```
//
// Reads the names from the file and populates the database.
// The database is vector of name/count pairs, storing the
// number of times each name shows up in the raw data.
//
NameDB::NameDB(const string& nameFile) throw (invalid_argument)
{
    // Open the file and check for errors.
    ifstream inFile(nameFile.c_str());
    if (!inFile) {
        throw invalid_argument("Unable to open file\n");
    }

    // Read the names one at a time.
    string name;
    while (inFile >> name) {
        // Look up the name in the database so far.
        if (nameExists(name)) {
            // If the name exists in the database, just
            // increment the count.
            incrementNameCount(name);
        } else {
            // If the name doesn't yet exist, add it with
            // a count of 1.
            addNewName(name);
        }
    }
    inFile.close();
}

//
// nameExists
//
// Returns true if the name exists in the database. Returns false otherwise.
//
bool NameDB::nameExists(const string& name) const
{
    // Iterate through the vector of names looking for the name.
    for (vector<pair<string, int> >::const_iterator it = mNames.begin();
        it != mNames.end(); ++it) {
        if (it->first == name) {
```

```
            return (true);
        }
    }
    return (false);
}


//
// incrementNameCount
//
// Precondition: name exists in the vector of names.
// Postcondition: the count associated with name is incremented.
//
void NameDB::incrementNameCount(const string& name)
{
    for (vector<pair<string, int> >::iterator it = mNames.begin();
        it != mNames.end(); ++it) {
        if (it->first == name) {
            it->second++;
            return;
        }
    }
}


//
// addNewName
//
// Adds a new name to the database
//
void NameDB::addNewName(const string& name)
{
    mNames.push_back(make_pair<string, int>(name, 1));
}
```

Note that in the preceding example, you could use an algorithm like find_if to accomplish the same thing as the loops in nameExists() and incrementNameCount(). We show the loops explicitly in order to emphasize the performance problems.

The savvy reader might notice some performance problems already. What if there are hundreds of thousands of names? The many linear searches involved in populating the database might become slow.

In order to complete the example, here are the implementations of the two public methods:

```
//
// getNameRank
//
// Returns the rank of the name.
// First looks up the name to obtain the number of babies with that name.
// Then iterates through all the names, counting all the names with a higher
// count than the specified name. Returns that count as the rank.
//
int NameDB::getNameRank(const string& name) const
{
    // Make use of the getAbsoluteNumber() method.
    int num = getAbsoluteNumber(name);
```

```
        // Check if we found the name.
        if (num == -1) {
            return (-1);
        }

        //
        // Now count all the names in the vector that have a
        // count higher than this one. If no name has a higher count,
        // this name is rank number 1. Every name with a higher count
        // decreases the rank of this name by 1.
        //
        int rank = 1;
        for (vector<pair<string, int> >::const_iterator it = mNames.begin();
             it != mNames.end(); ++it) {
            if (it->second > num) {
                rank++;
            }
        }

        return (rank);
}

//
// getAbsoluteNumber
//
// Returns the count associated with this name
//
int NameDB::getAbsoluteNumber(const string& name) const
{
    for (vector<pair<string, int> >::const_iterator it = mNames.begin();
         it != mNames.end(); ++it) {
        if (it->first == name) {
            return(it->second);
        }
    }
    return (-1);
}
```

Profile of the First Attempt

In order to test the program, you need a main function:

```
#include "NameDB.h"

int main(int argc, char** argv)
{
    NameDB boys("boys_long.txt");

    cout << boys.getNameRank("Daniel") << endl;
    cout << boys.getNameRank("Jacob") << endl;
    cout << boys.getNameRank("William") << endl;

    return (0);
}
```

483

This main creates one `NameDB` database called `boys`, telling it to populate itself with the file `boys_long` `.txt` This file contains 500,500 names.

There are three steps to using gprof:

1. Compile your program with a special flag that causes it to log raw execution information next time it is run. On Solaris 9, using the SunOne Studio 8 C++ Compiler, the flag is `-xpg`:

```
> CC -o namedb -xpg main.cpp NameDB.cpp
```

2. Next, run your pogram. This run should generate a file gmon.out in the working directory.

3. The final step is to run the gprof command in order to analyze the `gmon.out` profiling information and produce a (somewhat) readable report. The –C option tells gprof to *demangle* C++ function names so they are more readable. gprof outputs to standard out, so you should redirect the output to a file:

```
> gprof -C namedb gmon.out > gprof_analysis.out
```

Now you can analyze the data. Unfortunately, the output file is somewhat cryptic and intimidating. It takes a little while to learn how to interpret it. gprof provides two separate sets of information. The second set summarizes the amount of time spent executing each function in the program. The first, and more useful, set summarizes the amount of time spent executing each function *and its descendents*. Here is some of the output from the gprof_analysis.out file, edited to make it more readable:

```
[2]    85.1    0.00    48.21        1            main [2]
```

The preceding line means that `main()` and its descendents took 85.1 percent of the total execution time of the program, for a total of 48.21 seconds. The remaining 14.9 percent of the time was spent performing other tasks like looking for dynamically linked libraries and initializing global variables. The next entry shows that the `NameDB` constructor and its descendents took 48.18 seconds, which is almost the entire time of `main()`. The nested entries below `NameDB::NameDB` show which of its descendents took the most time. Here you can see that `nameExists()` and `incrementNameCount()` both took approximately 14 seconds. Remember that these times are the sums of all the calls to the functions. The third column in those lines shows the number of calls to the function (500,500 to `nameExists()` and 499,500 to `incrementNameCont()`). No other function took a significant amount of the `NameDB` time.

```
[3]    85.1    0.03    48.18        1            NameDB::NameDB
              9.60   14.04  500500/500500         bool NameDB::nameExists
              8.36   14.00  499500/499500         void NameDB::incrementNameC
ount
```

Without going any further in this analysis, two things should jump out at you:

1. 48 seconds to populate the database of approximately 500,000 names is slow. Perhaps you need a better data structure.

2. `nameExists()` and `incrementNameCount()` take almost identical time, and are called almost the same number of times. If you think about the application domain, that makes sense: most names in the text file input are duplicates, so the vast majority of the calls to `nameExists()` are followed by a call to `incrementNameCount()`. If you look back at the code, you can see that these functions are almost identical; they could probably be combined. In addition, most of what they are doing is searching the `vector`. It would probably be better to use a sorted data structure to reduce the searching time.

Second Attempt

With these two observations from the gprof output, it's time to redesign the program. The new design uses a `map` instead of a `vector`. Recall from Chapter 4 that the STL `map` employs an underlying tree structure that keeps the entries sorted, and provides O(log *n*) lookup instead of the O(*n*) searches in the vector.

The new version of the program also combines `nameExists()` and `incrementNameCount()` into one `nameExistsAndIncrement()` function.

Here is the new class definition:

```
#include <string>
#include <stdexcept>
#include <map>

using std::string;

class NameDB
{
    public:
        NameDB(const string& nameFile) throw (std::invalid_argument);

        int getNameRank(const string& name) const;
        int getAbsoluteNumber(const string& name) const;

    protected:
        std::map<string, int> mNames;

        bool nameExistsAndIncrement(const string& name);
        void addNewName(const string& name);

    private:
        // Prevent assignment and pass-by-value
        NameDB(const NameDB& src);
        NameDB& operator=(const NameDB& rhs);
};
```

Here are the new method implementations:

```
//
// Reads the names from the file and populates the database.
// The database is a map associating names with their frequency.
//
NameDB::NameDB(const string& nameFile) throw (invalid_argument)
{
    //
    // Open the file and check for errors.
    //
    ifstream inFile(nameFile.c_str());
        if (!inFile) {
            throw invalid_argument("Unable to open file\n");
        }
```

```
    //
    // Read the names one at a time.
    //
    string name;
    while (inFile >> name) {
        //
        // Look up the name in the database so far.
        //
        if (!nameExistsAndIncrement(name)) {
            //
            // If the name exists in the database, the
            // function incremented it, so we just continue.
            // We get here if it didn't exist, in case which
            // we add it with a count of 1.
            //
            addNewName(name);
        }
    }
    inFile.close();
}
```

```
//
// nameExistsAndIncrement
//
// Returns true if the name exists in the database. false
// otherwise. If it finds it, it increments it.
//
bool NameDB::nameExistsAndIncrement(const string& name)
{
    //
    //Find the name in the map.
    //
    map<string, int>::iterator res = mNames.find(name);
    if (res != mNames.end()) {
        res->second++;
        return (true);
    }
    return (false);
}
```

```
//
// addNewName
//
// Adds a new name to the database
//
void NameDB::addNewName(const string& name)
{
    mNames.insert(make_pair<string, int>(name, 1));
}
```

```
//
// getNameRank
//
// Returns the
```

```
int NameDB::getNameRank(const string& name) const
{
    int num = getAbsoluteNumber(name);

    //
    // Check if we found the name.
    //
    if (num == -1) {
        return (-1);
    }

    //
    // Now count all the names in the map that have
    // count higher than this one. If no name has a higher count,
    // this name is rank number 1. Every name with a higher count
    // decreases the rank of this name by 1.
    //
    int rank = 1;
    for (map<string, int>::const_iterator it = mNames.begin();
         it != mNames.end(); ++it) {
        if (it->second > num) {
            rank++;
        }
    }

    return (rank);
}

//
// getAbsoluteNumber
//
// Returns the count associated with this name
//
int NameDB::getAbsoluteNumber(const string& name) const
{
    map<string, int>::const_iterator res = mNames.find(name);
    if (res != mNames.end()) {
        return (res->second);
    }

    return (-1);
}
```

Profile of the Second Attempt

By following the same steps shown earlier, you can obtain the gprof performance data on the new version of the program. The data are quite encouraging:

```
[2]     85.3    0.00    3.19    1       main [2]
```

main() now takes only 3.19 seconds: a 15-fold improvement! There are certainly further improvements that you could make on this program, but we leave those as an exercise for the reader. One hint is that caching could come in handy for ranking the names.

Summary

This chapter discussed the key aspects of efficiency and performance in C++ programs, and provided several specific tips and techniques for designing and writing more efficient applications. We hope you gained an appreciation for the importance of performance and for the power of profiling tools. Remember to think about performance and efficiency from the beginning of your program life cycle: design-level efficiency is far more important than is language-level efficiency.

18

Developing Cross-Platform and Cross-Language Applications

C++ programs can be compiled to run on a variety of computing platforms and the language has been rigorously defined to ensure that programming in C++ for one platform is very similar to programming in C++ for another. Yet, despite the standardization of the language, platform differences eventually come into play when writing professional-quality programs in C++. Even when development is limited to a particular platform, small differences in compilers can elicit major programming headaches. This chapter examines the necessary complication of programming in a world with multiple platforms and multiple programming languages.

The first part of this chapter surveys the platform-related issues that C++ programmers encounter. A *platform* is the collection of all of the details that make up your development and/or run-time system. For example, your platform may be a Microsoft C++ compiler running on Windows XP on a Pentium processor. Alternatively, your platform might be the gcc compiler running on Linux on a PowerPC processor. Both of these platforms are able to compile and run C++ programs, but there are significant differences between them.

The second part of this chapter looks at how C++ can interact with other programming languages. While C++ is a general-purpose language, it may not always be the right tool for the job. Through a variety of mechanisms, you can integrate C++ with other languages that may better serve your needs.

Cross-Platform Development

There are several reasons why the C++ language encounters platform issues. Even though C++ is a high-level language, its definition includes low-level implementation details. For example, C++ arrays are defined to live in contiguous blocks of memory. Such a specific implementation detail exposes the language to the possibility that not all systems arrange and manage their memory in the same way. C++ also faces the challenge of providing a standard language and a standard library without a standard implementation. Varying interpretations of the specification among C++ compiler and library vendors can lead to trouble when moving from one system to another. Finally, C++ is selective in what the language provides as standard. Despite the presence of a standard library, sophisticated programs often need functionality that is not provided by the language. This functionality generally comes from third-party libraries or the platform, and can vary greatly.

Architecture Issues

The term *architecture* generally refers to the processor, or family of processors, on which a program runs. A standard PC running Windows or Linux generally runs on the x86 architecture and Mac OS is usually found on the PowerPC architecture. As a high-level language, C++ shields you from the differences between these architectures. For example, a Pentium processor may have a single instruction that performs the same functionality as six PowerPC instructions. As a C++ programmer, you don't need to know what this difference is or even that it exists. One advantage to using a high-level language is that the compiler takes care of converting your code into the processor's native assembly code format.

Processor differences do, however, rise up to the level of C++ code at times. You won't face most of these issues unless you are doing particularly low-level work, but you should be aware that they exist.

Binary Compatibility

As you probably already know, you cannot take a program written and compiled for a Pentium computer and run it on a Mac. These two platforms are not *binary compatible* because their processors do not support the same set of instructions. Recall that when you compile a C++ program, your source code is turned into binary instructions that the computer executes. That binary format is defined by the platform, not by the C++ language.

The solution for binary compatibility issues is usually *cross-compiling*. When you cross-compile a program, you build a separate version for each architecture on which it is destined to run. Some compilers support cross-compiling directly. Others require that you build each version separately on the destination architecture.

Another solution to differences in binary representation is *open source distribution*. By making your source available to the end user, she can compile it natively on her system and build a version of the program that is in the correct binary format for her machine. As discussed in Chapter 4, open-source software has become increasingly popular in the last several years. One of the major reasons is that it allows programmers to collaboratively develop software and increase the number of platforms on which it can run.

Word and Type Sizes

A *word* is the fundamental unit of storage for computer architectures. In most systems, a word is the size of an address and/or a single processor instruction. When someone describes an architecture as *32-bit*, they most likely mean that the word size is 32 bits, or 4 bytes. In general, a system with a larger word size can handle more memory and operate more quickly on complex programs.

Since pointers are memory addresses, they are inherently tied to word sizes. Many programmers are taught that pointers are always 4 bytes, but this is not always the case. For example, consider the following program, which outputs the size of a pointer.

```
#include <iostream>

using namespace std;

int main(int argc, char** argv)
{
    int *ptr;

    cout << "ptr size is " << sizeof(ptr) << " bytes" << endl;
}
```

If this program is run on a 32-bit Pentium architecture, the output is:

```
ptr size is 4 bytes
```

On a 64-bit Itanium system, the output is:

```
ptr size is 8 bytes
```

From a programmer's point of view, the upshot of varying pointer sizes is simply that you cannot equate a pointer with 4 bytes. More generally, you need to be aware that most sizes are not prescribed by the C++ standard. The standard only says that a short integer has as much, or less, space as an integer, which has as much, or less, space as a long integer. An integer itself is supposed to contain enough space to hold a word, but as you saw above, this number can vary.

Word Order

All modern computers store numbers in a binary representation, but the representation of the same number on two platforms may not be identical. This sounds contradictory, but as you'll see, there are two approaches to reading numbers that both make sense.

A single slot in your computer's memory is usually a byte because most computers are *byte addressable*. Number types in C++ are usually multiple bytes. For example, a short may be 2 bytes. Imagine that your program contains the following line:

```
short myShort = 513;
```

In binary, the number 513 is 0000001000000001. This number contains 16 1s and 0s, or 16 bits. Because there are 8 bits in a byte, the computer would need 2 bytes to store the number. Because each individual memory address contains 1 byte, the computer needs to split the number up into multiple bytes. Assuming that a short is 2 bytes, the number will get split into two even parts. The higher part of the number is put into the *high-order byte* and the lower part of the number is put into the *low-order byte*. In this case, the high-order byte is 00000010 and the low-order byte is 00000001.

Now that the number has been split up into memory-sized parts, the only question that remains is how to store them in memory. Two bytes are needed, but the order of the bytes is unclear and in fact depends on the architecture of the system in question.

One way to represent the number is to put the high-order byte first in memory and the low-order byte next. This strategy is called *big-endian ordering* because the bigger part of the number comes first. PowerPC and Sparc processors use a big-endian approach. Some other processors, such as x86, order the bytes in the opposite order, putting the low-order byte first in memory. This approach is called *little-endian ordering* because the smaller part of the number comes first. An architecture may choose one approach or the other, usually based on backward compatibility. For the curious, the terms "big-endian" and "little-endian" predate modern computers by several hundred years. Jonathan Swift coined the terms in his eighteenth-century novel *Gulliver's Travels* to describe the opposing camps of a debate about the proper end on which to break an egg. Many computer scientists feel that the current debate about endianness is at least as silly as the one described by Swift.

Regardless of the *word ordering* a particular architecture uses, your program can continue to use numerical values without paying any attention to whether the machine uses big-endian ordering or little-endian ordering. The word ordering only comes into play when data moves between architectures. For example, if you are sending binary data across a network, you may need to consider the word ordering of the other system. Similarly, if you are writing binary data to a file, you may need to consider what will happen if that file is opened on a system with opposite word ordering.

Implementation Issues

When a C++ compiler is written, it is designed by a human being who attempts to adhere to the C++ standard. Unfortunately, the C++ standard is several hundred pages long and written in a combination of prose, language grammars, and examples. Two human beings implementing a compiler according to such a standard are unlikely to interpret every piece of prescribed information in the exact same way or to catch every single edge case. As difficult as it is to believe, even compilers have bugs.

Compiler Quirks and Extensions

The first compiler bug you encounter is a surreal experience. After all these years of tracking down and correcting your own bugs, you've finally discovered that the very program you have been depending on contains flaws! C++ compilers have improved greatly since the creation of the language, but bugs do exist in C++ compilers. At best, these are simply different interpretations of the specification or omitted language features. From time to time, however, you may find a case where the compiler simply does the wrong thing.

There is no simple rule for finding or avoiding compiler bugs. The best you can do is stay up to date on compiler updates and perhaps subscribe to a mailing list or newsgroup for your compiler. If you suspect that you have encountered a compiler bug, a simple Web search for the error message or condition you have witnessed could uncover a workaround or patch.

One area that compilers are notorious for having trouble with is the set of more recent language additions. For example, some of the template and run-time type features in C++ weren't originally part of the language. As mentioned in Chapter 11, some compilers still don't properly support these features.

Another issue to be aware of is that compilers often include their own language extensions without making it obvious to the programmer. For example, variable-sized stack-based arrays are not part of the C++ language, yet the following line compiles with the g++ compiler:

```
int i = 4;
char myStackArray[i];   // Not a standard language feature!
```

Some compiler extensions may be useful, but if there is a chance that you will switch compilers at some point, you should see if your compiler has a strict mode where it will avoid such extensions. For example, compiling the previous line with the `pedantic` flag passed to g++ will yield the following warning:

```
warning: ISO C++ forbids variable-size array 'myStackArray'
```

The C++ specification allows for a certain type of compiler-defined language extension through the #pragma mechanism. #pragma is a precompiler directive whose behavior is defined by the implementation. If the implementation does not understand the directive, it simply ignores it. For example, some compilers allow the programmer to turn compiler warnings off temporarily with #pragma. However, this behavior is compiler-dependent and you should not rely on it.

Library Implementations

Most likely, your compiler includes an implementation of the C++ standard library, including the standard template library. Since the STL is written in C++, however, you aren't required to use the one that came bundled with your compiler. You could use a third-party STL that has been optimized for speed or you could even write your own.

Of course, STL implementers face the same problem that compiler writers face — the standard is subject to interpretation. In addition, certain implementations may make tradeoffs that are incompatible with your needs. For example, some implementations may increase their single-processor performance profile by giving up multiple-processor support. Others may be tuned especially for multiple processors.

When working with an STL implementation, or indeed any third-party library, it is important to consider the tradeoffs that the designer made during development. If the library is open source, you may be able to find a current list of open issues or a bug database. Chapter 4 contains a more detailed discussion of the issues involved in using libraries.

Platform-Specific Features

C++ is a great general-purpose language. With the addition of the Standard Library, the language is packed full of so many features that a casual programmer could happily code in C++ for years without going beyond what is built in. However, professional programs require facilities that C++ does not provide. This section lists several important features that are provided by the platform, not by the C++ language.

- ❑ **Graphical user interfaces.** Most commercial programs today run on an operating system that has a graphical user interface, containing such elements as clickable buttons, movable windows, and hierarchical menus. C++, like the C language, has no notion of these elements. To write a graphical application in C++, you need to use platform-specific libraries that allow you to draw windows, accept input through the mouse, and perform other graphical tasks. Chapter 25 describes object-oriented graphical frameworks as one way that platforms provide this functionality.

- ❑ **Networking.** The Internet has changed the way we write applications. These days, it's not uncommon for an application to check for updates through the Web or for a game to provide a networked multiplayer mode. C++ does not provide a mechanism for networking, though several standard libraries exist. The most common means of writing networking software is through an abstraction called *sockets*. A socket library implementation can be found on most platforms and it provides a simple procedure-oriented way to transfer data over a network. Some platforms support a streams-based networking system that operates like I/O streams in C++.

- ❑ **OS Events and application interaction.** In pure C++ code, there is little interaction with the surrounding operating system and other applications. The command-line arguments are about all

Chapter 18

you get in a standard C++ program without platform extensions. For example, operations such as copy and paste are not directly supported in C++ and require platform-provided libraries.

❑ **Low-level files.** In Chapter 14, you read about standard I/O in C++, including reading and writing files. Many operating systems provide their own file APIs, which are sometimes incompatible with the standard file classes in C++. These libraries often provide OS-specific file tools, such as a mechanism to get the home directory of the current user or access to OS configuration files. In general, once you start using the APIs for a particular platform, you should switch from C++ I/O classes to the platform's I/O classes if any exist.

❑ **Threads.** Concurrent threads of execution within a single program are not directly supported in C++. Their implementation depends heavily on the inner workings of the operating system, so threads were not included in the language. The most commonly used thread library is called `pthreads`. Many operating systems and object-oriented frameworks also provide their own threading models.

Cross-Language Development

For certain types of programs, C++ may not be the best tool for the job. For example, if your Unix program needs to interact closely with the shell environment, you may be better off writing a shell script than a C++ program. If your program performs heavy text parsing, you may decide that the Perl language is the way to go. Sometimes what you want is a language that blends the general features of C++ with the specialized features of another language. Fortunately, there are some techniques you can use to get the best of both worlds — the flexibility of C++ combined with the unique specialty of another language.

Mixing C and C++

As you already know, the C++ language is a superset of the C language. All C programs will compile and run in C++ with a few minor exceptions. These exceptions usually have to do with reserved words. In C, for example, the term *class* has no particular meaning. Thus, it could be used as a variable name, as in the following C program.

```
#include <stdio.h>

int main(int argc, char** argv)
{
    int class = 1; // Compiles in C, not C++

    printf("class is %d\n", class);
}
```

This program will compile and run in C, but will yield an error when compiled as C++ code. When you translate, or *port*, a program from C to C++, this is the type of error you will face. Fortunately, the fixes are usually quite simple. In this case, simply rename the `class` variable to `classID` and the code will compile.

The ease of incorporating C code in a C++ program comes in handy when you encounter a useful library or legacy code that was written in C. Functions and classes, as you've seen many times in this book, work just fine together. A class method can call a function, and a function can make use of objects.

494

Shifting Paradigms

One of the dangers of mixing C and C++ is that your program may start to lose its object-oriented properties. For example, if your object-oriented Web browser is implemented with a procedural networking library, the program will be mixing these two paradigms. Given the importance and quantity of networking tasks in such an application, you might consider writing an *object-oriented wrapper* around the procedural library.

For example, imagine that you are writing a Web browser in C++, but you are using a C networking library that contains the functions declared in the following code. Note that the `HostRecord` and `Connection` data structures have been omitted for brevity.

```
// netwrklib.h

#include "hostrecord.h"
#include "connection.h"

/**
 * Gets the host record for a particular Internet host given
 * its hostname (i.e. www.host.com)
 */
HostRecord* lookupHostByName(char* inHostName);

/**
 * Connects to the given host
 */
Connection* connectToHost(HostRecord* inHost);

/**
 * Retrieves a Web page from an already-opened connection
 */
char* retrieveWebPage(Connection* inConnection, char* page);
```

The `netwrklib.h` interface is fairly simple and straightforward. However, it is not object-oriented, and a C++ programmer who uses such a library is bound to feel *icky*, to use a technical term. This library isn't organized into a cohesive class and it isn't even `const`-correct! Of course, a talented C programmer could have written a better interface, but as the user of a library, you have to accept what you are given. Writing a wrapper is your opportunity to customize the interface.

Before we build an object-oriented wrapper for this library, take a look at how it might be used as is to gain an understanding of actual usage. In the following program, the `netwrklib` library is used to retrieve the Web page at www.wrox.com/index.html.

```
#include <iostream>
#include "netwrklib.h"

using namespace std;

int main(int argc, char** argv)
{
    HostRecord* myHostRecord = lookupHostByName("www.wrox.com");
    Connection* myConnection = connectToHost(myHostRecord);
```

```
        char* result = retrieveWebPage(myConnection, "/index.html");

        cout << "The result is " << result << endl;
}
```

A possible way to make the library more object-oriented is to provide a single abstraction that recognizes the links between looking up a host, connecting to the host, and retrieving a Web page. A good object-oriented wrapper could hide the unnecessarily complexity of the HostRecord and Connection types.

Recalling the design principles you read about in Chapters 3 and 5, the new class should capture the common use case for the library. The previous example shows the most frequently used pattern — first a host is looked up, then a connection is established, then a page is retrieved. It is also likely that subsequent pages will be retrieved from the same host so a good design will accommodate that mode of use as well.

Following is the public portion of the definition for the WebHost class. This class makes the common case easy for the client programmer.

```
// WebHost.h

class WebHost {

public:
    /**
     * Constructs a WebHost object for the given host
     */
    WebHost(const string& inHost);

    /**
     * Obtains the given page from this host
     */
    string getPage(const string& inPage);

};
```

Consider the way a client programmer would use this class. To repeat the example used for the netwrk-lib library:

```
#include <iostream>
#include "WebHost.h"

int main(int argc, char** argv)
{
    WebHost myHost("www.wrox.com");
    string result = myHost.getPage("/index.html");

    cout << "The result is " << result << endl;
}
```

The WebHost class effectively encapsulates the behavior of a host and provides useful functionality without unnecessary calls and data structures. The class even provides a useful new piece of functionality — once a WebHost is created, it can be used to obtain multiple Web pages, saving code and possibly making the program run faster.

The implementation of the `WebHost` class makes extensive use of the `netwrklib` library without exposing any of its workings to the user. To enable this abstraction, the class needs a data member, as shown in the revised header file below.

```
// WebHost.h

#include "netwrklib.h"

class WebHost {

public:
    /**
     * Constructs a WebHost object for the given host
     */
    WebHost(const string& inHost);

    /**
     * Obtains the given page from this host
     */
    string getPage(const string& inPage);

protected:
    Connection* mConnection;
};
```

The corresponding source file puts a new face on the functionality contained in the `netwrklib` library. First, the constructor builds a `HostRecord` for the specified host. Because the `WebHost` class deals with C++ strings instead of C-style strings, it uses the `c_str()` method on `inHost` to obtain a `const char*`, then performs a `const` cast to make up for `netwrklib`'s const-incorrectness. The resulting `HostRecord` is used to create a `Connection`, which is stored in the `mConnection` data member for later use.

```
WebHost::WebHost(const string& inHost)
{
    const char* host = inHost.c_str();

    HostRecord* theHost = lookupHostByName(const_cast<char*>(host));

    mConnection = connectToHost(theHost);
}
```

Subsequent calls to `getPage()` pass the stored connection to `netwrklib`'s `retrieveWebPage()` function and return the value as a C++ string.

```
string getPage(const string& inPage)
{
    const char* page = inPage.c_str();

    string result = retrieveWebPage(mConnection, const_cast<char*>(page));

    return result;
}
```

Networking-savvy readers may note that keeping a connection open to a host indefinitely is considered bad practice and doesn't adhere to the HTTP specification. We've chosen elegance over etiquette in this example.

As you can see, the `WebHost` class provides an object-oriented wrapper around the C library. By providing an abstraction, you can change the underlying implementation without affecting client code or provide additional features, such as connection reference counting or parsing of pages.

Linking with C Code

In the previous example, we assumed that you had the raw C code to work with. The example took advantage of the fact that most C code will successfully compile with a C++ compiler. If you only have compiled C code, perhaps in the form of a library, you can still use it in your C++ program, but you need to take a few extra steps.

Compiled C code is in a different format from compiled C++ code, so you need to tell the compiler that certain functions are written in C so that the linker can properly make use of them. This is done with the `extern` keyword.

In the following code, the function prototype for `doCFunction()` is specified as an external C function.

```
extern "C" {
    void doCFunction(int i);
}

int main(int argc, char** argv)
{
    // Call the C function.
    doCFunction(8);
}
```

The actual definition for `doCFunction()` is provided in a compiled binary file that is attached in the link phase. The `extern` keyword above simply informs the compiler that the linked-in code was compiled in C.

A more common pattern for using `extern` is at the header level. For example, if you are using a graphics library written in C, it probably came with a `.h` file for you to use. You can write another header file that wraps the original one in an `extern` block to specify that the entire header defines functions written in C. The wrapper `.h` file is often named with `.hpp` to distinguish it from the C version of the header:

```
// graphicslib.hpp

extern "C" {
    #include "graphicslib.h"
}
```

Whether you are including C code in your C++ program or linking against a compiled C library, remember that even though C++ is essentially a superset of C, they are different languages with different design goals. Adapting C code to work in C++ is quite common, but providing an object-oriented C++ wrapper around procedural C code is often much better.

Mixing Java and C++ with JNI

Even though this is a C++ book, we won't pretend that there aren't newer and snazzier languages out there. The Java language took the programming world by storm in the mid-1990s and has grown immensely in popularity ever since. Java and C++ are similar languages to an extent, but they have different strengths. Without getting into a religious war, the most commonly cited advantage of C++ is its speed, and the most commonly cited advantages of Java are its built-in libraries for network programming and graphical interfaces.

The *Java Native Interface*, or JNI, is a part of the Java language that allows the programmer to access functionality that was not written in Java. Because Java is a cross-platform language, the original intent was to make it possible for Java programs to interact with the operating system. JNI also allows programmers to make use of libraries written in other languages, such as C++. Access to C++ libraries may be useful to a Java programmer who has a performance-critical piece of his application or who needs to use legacy code.

JNI can also be used to execute Java code within a C++ program, but such a use is far less common. There is currently much more legacy C++ code than legacy Java code, so most applications that use Java code are Java through-and-through. Because this is a C++ book, we do not include an introduction to the Java language. This section is targeted at readers who already know Java and wish to incorporate C++ code into their Java code.

To begin your cross-language adventure, start with the Java program. For this example, the simplest of Java programs will suffice:

```
public class HelloCpp {

    public static void main(String[] args)
    {
        System.out.println("Hello from Java!\n");
    }
}
```

The next step is a little strange. You need to declare a Java method that will be written in another language. To do this, you use the `native` keyword and leave out the implementation:

```
public class HelloCpp {

    // This will be implemented in C++.
    public native void callCpp();

    public static void main(String[] args)
    {
        System.out.println("Hello from Java!\n");
    }
}
```

C++ code will eventually be compiled into a shared library that gets dynamically loaded into the Java program. You need to load this library inside of a Java static block so that it is loaded when the Java program begins executing. The name of the library can be whatever you want this example uses `hellocpp.so`. A file ending in `.so` is a shared library on Unix systems. Windows users would most likely use a `.dll` file.

```
public class HelloCpp {

    static {
        System.load("hellocpp.so");
    }

    // This will be implemented in C++.
    public native void callCpp();

    public static void main(String[] args)
    {
        System.out.println("Hello from Java!\n");
    }
}
```

Finally, you need to actually call the C++ code from within the Java program. The callCpp() Java method serves as a placeholder for the not-yet-written C++ code. Because callCpp() is a method of the HelloCpp class, simply create a new HelloCpp object and call the callCpp() method.

```
public class HelloCpp {

    static {
        System.load("hellocpp.so");
    }

    // This will be implemented in C++.
    public native void callCpp();

    public static void main(String[] args)
    {
        System.out.println("Hello from Java!\n");

        HelloCpp cppInterface = new HelloCpp();
        cppInterface.callCpp();
    }
}
```

That's all for the Java side! Now, just compile the Java program as you normally would:

```
javac HelloCpp.java
```

Then use the javah program (the authors like to pronounce it *jav-AHH!*) to create a header file for the native method:

```
javah HelloCpp
```

After running javah, you will find a file named HelloCpp.h, which is a fully working (if somewhat ugly) C/C++ header file. Inside of that header file is a C function definition for a function called Java_HelloCpp_callCpp(). Your C++ program will need to implement this function to be called from within the Java program. The full signature is:

```
void Java_HelloCpp_callCpp(JNIEnv* env, jobject javaobj);
```

Your C++ implementation of this function can make full use of the language. This example simply outputs some text from C++. First, you need to include the `jni.h` header file and the `HelloCpp.h` file that was created by `javah`. You will also need to include any C or C++ headers that you intend to use.

```
#include <jni.h>
#include "HelloCpp.h"
#include <iostream>
```

The C++ function is written as normal. Keep in mind that you are implementing a function, not writing a program. You will not need a `main()`. The parameters to the function allow interaction with the Java environment and the object that called the native code. They are beyond the scope of this example.

```
#include <jni.h>
#include "HelloCpp.h"
#include <iostream>

void Java_HelloCpp_callCpp(JNIEnv* env, jobject javaobj)
{
    std::cout << "Hello from C++!" << std::endl;
}
```

Compiling this code depends on your environment, but you will most likely need to tweak your compiler's settings to include the JNI headers and the location of the native Java library files. Using the gcc compiler on Linux, your compile command might look like this:

```
g++ -shared -I/usr/java/jdk/include/ -I/usr/java/jdk/include/linux HelloCpp.cpp \
-o hellocpp.so
```

The output from the compiler is the library that is used by the Java program. As long as the shared library is somewhere in the Java class path, you can execute the Java program normally:

```
java HelloCpp
```

You should see the following result:

```
Hello from Java!

Hello from C++!
```

Of course, this example just scratches the surface of what is possible through JNI. You can use JNI to interface with OS-specific features or hardware drivers. For complete coverage of JNI, you should consult a Java text.

Mixing C++ with Perl and Shell Scripts

C++ contains a built-in general-purpose mechanism to interface with other languages and environments. You've already used it many times, probably without paying it much attention — it's the arguments to and return value from the `main()` function.

C and C++ were designed with command-line interfaces in mind. The `main()` function receives the arguments that a user types at the command line and returns a status code that can be interpreted by the caller. Many large graphical applications ignore the parameters to `main()` because graphical interfaces tend to avoid passing arguments. However, in a scripting environment, arguments to your program can be a powerful mechanism that allows you to interface with the environment.

Scripting versus Programming

Before delving into the details of mixing C++ and scripts, consider whether your project is an *application* or a *script*. The difference is subtle and subject to debate. The following descriptions are just guidelines. Many so-called scripts are just as sophisticated as full-blown applications. The question isn't whether or not something can be done as a script, but whether or not a scripting language is the best tool.

An application is a program that performs a particular task. Modern applications typically involve some sort of user interaction. In other words, applications tend to be driven by the user, who directs the application to take certain actions. Applications often have multiple capabilities. For example, a user can use a photo editing application to scale an image, paint over an image, or print an image. Most of the software you would buy in a box is an application. Applications tend to be relatively large and often complex programs.

A script generally performs a single task, or a set of related tasks. You might have a script that automatically sorts your email, or backs up your important files. Scripts often run without user interaction, perhaps at a particular time each day or triggered by an event, such as the arrival of new mail. Scripts can be found at the OS level (such as a script that compresses files every night) or at the application level (such as a script that automates the process of shrinking and printing images). Automation is an important part of the definition of a script — scripts are usually written to codify a sequence of steps that a user would otherwise perform manually.

Now, consider the difference between a *scripting language* and a *programming language*. Not all scripts are necessarily written in scripting languages. You could write a script that sorts your email using the C programming language, or you could write an equivalent script using the Perl scripting language. Similarly, not all applications are written in programming languages. A suitably motivated coder could write a Web browser in Perl if she really wanted to. The line is blurry. In fact, the Perl language is so flexible that many programmers consider it both a programming language and a scripting language.

In the end, what matters most is which language provides the functionality you need. If you are going to be interacting with the operating system heavily, you might consider a scripting language because scripting languages tend to have better support for OS interaction. If your project is going to be larger in scope and involve heavy user interaction, a programming language will probably be easier in the long run.

A Practical Example — Encrypting Passwords

Assume that you have a system that writes everything a user sees and types to a file for auditing purposes. The file can be read only by the system administrator so that she can figure out who to blame if something goes wrong. An excerpt of such a file might look like this:

```
Login: bucky-bo
Password: feldspar

bucky-bo> mail

bucky-bo has no mail

bucky-bo> exit
```

While the system administrator may want to keep a log of all user activity, she may wish to obscure everybody's passwords in case the file is somehow obtained by a hacker. A script seems like the natural choice for this project because it should happen automatically, perhaps at the end of every day. There is, however, one piece of the project that might not be best suited for a scripting language. Encryption libraries tend to exist mainly for high-level languages such as C and C++. Therefore, one possible implementation is to write a script that calls out to a C++ program to perform the encryption.

The following script uses the Perl language, though almost any scripting language could accomplish this task. We chose Perl because it is cross-platform and has facilities that make text parsing simple. If you don't know Perl, you will still be able to follow along. The most important element of Perl syntax for this example is the ` character. The ` character instructs the Perl script to *shell out* to an external command. In this case, the script will shell out to a C++ program called encryptString.

The strategy for the script is to loop over every line of a file looking for lines that contain a password prompt. The script will write a new file, userlog.out, which contains the same text as the source file, except that all passwords are encrypted. The first step is to open the input file for reading and the output file for writing. Then, the script needs to loop over all the lines in the file. Each line in turn is placed in a variable called $line.

```
open (INPUT, "userlog.txt") or die "Couldn't open input file!";
open (OUTPUT, ">userlog.out") or die "Couldn't open output file!";

while ($line = <INPUT>) {
```

Next, the current line is checked against a *regular expression* to see if this particular line contains the Password: prompt. If it does, Perl will store the password in the variable $1.

```
    if ($line =~ m/^Password: (.*)/) {
```

Since a match has been found, the script calls the encryptString program with the detected password to obtain an encrypted version of it. The output of the program is stored in the $result variable, and the result status code from the program is stored in the variable $?. The script checks $? and quits immediately if there was a problem. If everything is okay, the password line is written to the output file with the encrypted password instead of the original one.

```
        $result = `encryptString $1`;
        if ($? != 0) { exit(-1) }
        print OUTPUT "Password: $result\n";
```

If the current line was not a password prompt, the script simply writes the line as is to the output file. At the end of the loop, it closes both files and exits.

```
    } else {
        print OUTPUT "$line";
    }
}

close (INPUT);
close (OUTPUT);
```

That's it! The only other required piece is the actual C++ program. Implementation of a cryptographic algorithm is beyond the scope of this book. The important piece is the `main()` function because it accepts the string that should be encrypted as an argument.

Arguments are contained in the `argv` array of C-style strings. You should always consult the `argc` parameter before accessing an element of `argv`. Remember that if `argc` is 1, there is one element in the argument list and it is accessible at `argv[0]`. The 0th element of the `argv` array is generally the name of the program, so actual parameters begin at `argv[1]`.

Following is the `main()` function for a C++ program that encrypts the input string. Notice that the program returns 0 for success and non-0 for failure, as is standard in Unix.

```
int main(int argc, char** argv)
{
    if (argc < 2) {
        cerr << "Usage: " << argv[0] << " string-to-be-encrypted" << endl;
        return -1;
    }

    cout << encrypt(argv[1]);

    return 0;
}
```

There is actually a blatant security hole in this code. When the to-be-encrypted string is passed to the C++ program as a command-line argument, it may be visible to other users through the process table. A more secure way to get the information into the C++ program would be to send it through standard input, which is the forte of the **expect** *scripting language.*

Now that you've seen how easily C++ programs can be incorporated into scripting languages, you can combine the strengths of the two languages for your own projects. You can use a scripting language to interact with the OS and control the flow of the script, and a traditional programming language for the heavy lifting.

Mixing C++ with Assembly Code

C++ is generally considered a fast language, especially relative to other object-oriented languages. Yet, there is simply no way to beat raw assembly code when speed is absolutely critical. Recall that when your program is compiled, it is turned from high-level C++ into low-level assembly. The automatically generated assembly code is fast enough for most purposes. Optimizers are often run over the generated assembly code to make it even faster. Yet, for all the advances in compiler writing, a talented human being can often write assembly code that outperforms compiled C++ code.

In C++, the keyword `asm` is used by many compilers to allow the programmer to insert raw assembly code. The keyword is part of the C++ standard, but its implementation is compiler-defined. In most compilers, you can use `asm` to drop from C++ down to the level of assembly right in the middle of your program.

Inline assembly can be very useful in certain applications, such as intensive 3-D graphics, but we don't recommend it for most programs. There are several reasons to avoid inline assembly code:

❑   Your code is no longer portable to another processor once you start including raw assembly code for your platform.

❑   Most programmers don't know assembly languages and won't be able to modify or maintain your code.

❑   Assembly code is not known for its readability. It can hurt your program's use of style.

❑   Most of the time, it is simply not necessary. If your program is slow, look for algorithmic problems or consult some of the other performance suggestions in Chapter 17.

Summary

If you take away one point from this chapter, it should be that C++ is a flexible language. It exists in the sweet spot between languages that are too tied to a particular platform and languages that are too high-level and generic. Rest assured that when you develop code in C++, you aren't locking yourself into the language forever. C++ can be mixed with other technologies and has a solid history and code base that help guarantee its relevance in the future.

Becoming Adept at Testing

A programmer has overcome a major hurdle in her career when she realizes that testing is a part of the software development process. Bugs are not an occasional occurrence. They are found in *every* project of significant size. A good *quality-assurance* (QA) team is invaluable, but the full burden of testing cannot be placed on QA alone. Your responsibility as a programmer is to write code that works and tests to prove its correctness.

A distinction is often made between *white box testing*, in which the tester is aware of the inner workings of the program, and *black box testing*, which tests the program's functionality without concern for its implementation. Both forms of testing are important to professional-quality projects. Black box testing is the most fundamental approach because it typically models the behavior of a user. For example, a black box test can examine interface components like buttons. If the tester clicks the button and nothing happens, there is obviously a bug in the program.

Black box testing cannot cover everything. Modern programs are too large to employ a simulation of clicking every button, providing every kind of input, and performing all combinations of commands. White box testing is necessary because it is easier to ensure test coverage when tests are written at the object or subsystem level. White box tests are often easier to write and automate than black box tests. This chapter focuses on topics that would generally be considered white box testing techniques because the programmer can use these techniques during development.

This chapter begins with a high-level discussion of quality control, including some approaches to viewing and tracking bugs. A section on unit testing, one of the simplest and most useful types of testing, follows this introduction. You will read about the theory and practice of unit testing, as well as several examples of unit tests in action. Next, higher-level tests are covered, including integration tests, system tests, and regression tests. Finally, this chapter ends with a list of tips for successful testing.

Quality Control

Large programming projects are rarely finished when a feature-complete goal is reached. There are always bugs to find and fix, both during and after the main development phase. Understanding the shared responsibility of quality control and the life cycle of a bug is essential to performing well in a group.

Whose Responsibility Is Testing?

Software development organizations have different approaches to testing. In a small startup, there may not be a group of people whose full-time job is testing the product. Testing may be the responsibility of the individual developers, or all the employees of the company may be asked to lend a hand and try to break the product before its release. In larger organizations, a full-time quality assurance staff probably qualifies a release by testing it according to a set of criteria. Nonetheless, some aspects of testing may still be the responsibility of the developers. Even in organizations where the developers have no role in formal testing, you still need to be aware of what your responsibilities are in the larger process of quality assurance.

The Life Cycle of a Bug

All good engineering groups recognize that bugs will occur in software both before and after its release. There are many different ways to deal with these problems. Figure 19-1 shows a formal bug process, expressed as a flow chart. In this particular process, a bug is always filed by a member of the QA team. The bug reporting software sends a notification to the development manager, who sets the priority of the bug and assigns the bug to the appropriate module owner. The module owner can accept the bug or explain why the bug actually belongs in a different module or is invalid, giving the development manager the opportunity to assign it to someone else. Once the bug has found its rightful owner, a fix is made and the developer marks the bug as "fixed." At this point, the QA engineer verifies that the bug no longer exists and marks the bug as "closed" or reopens the bug if it is still present.

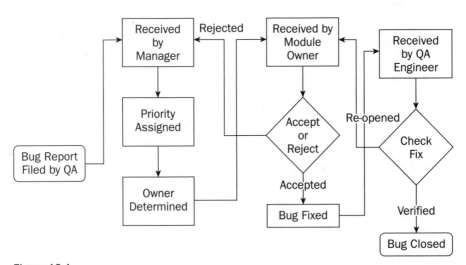

Figure 19-1

A less formal approach is shown in Figure 19-2. In this workflow, anybody can file a bug and assign an initial priority and a module. The module owner receives the bug report and can either accept it or reassign it to another engineer or module. When a correction is made, the bug is marked as "fixed." Toward the end of the testing phase, all the implementation and QA engineers divide up the fixed bugs and verify that each bug is no longer present in the current build. The release is ready when all bugs are marked as "closed."

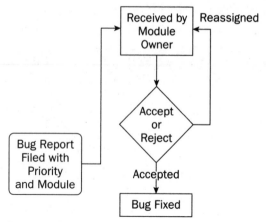

Figure 19-2

Bug-Tracking Tools

There are many ways to keep track of software bugs, from informal email- or spreadsheet-based schemes to expensive third-party bug-tracking software. The appropriate solution for your organization depends on the group's size, the nature of the software, and the level of formality you wish to build around bug fixing.

Bugzilla is a popular free tool for bug tracking, written by the authors of the Mozilla Web browser. As an open-source project, Bugzilla has gradually accumulated a number of useful features to the point where it now rivals expensive bug-tracking software packages. Among its many features are:

- ❏ Customizable settings for a bug, including its priority, associated component, status, and so on

- ❏ Email notification of new bug reports or changes to an existing report

- ❏ Tracking of dependencies between bugs and resolution of duplicate bugs

- ❏ Reporting and searching tools

- ❏ A Web-based interface for filing and updating bugs

Figure 19-3 shows a bug being entered into a Bugzilla project that we set up for this book. For our purposes, each chapter was input as a Bugzilla component. The filer of the bug can specify the severity of the bug (how big of a deal it is) as well as the priority of the bug (how soon it needs to be fixed). A summary and description are included to make it possible to search for the bug or list it in a report format.

Bug-tracking tools like Mozilla are becoming essential components of a professional software development environment. In addition to supplying a central list of currently open bugs, bug-tracking tools provide an important archive of previous bugs and their fixes. A support engineer, for instance, might use Bugzilla to search for a problem similar to one reported by a customer. If a fix was made, the support person will be able to tell the customer to which version they need to update or how to work around the problem.

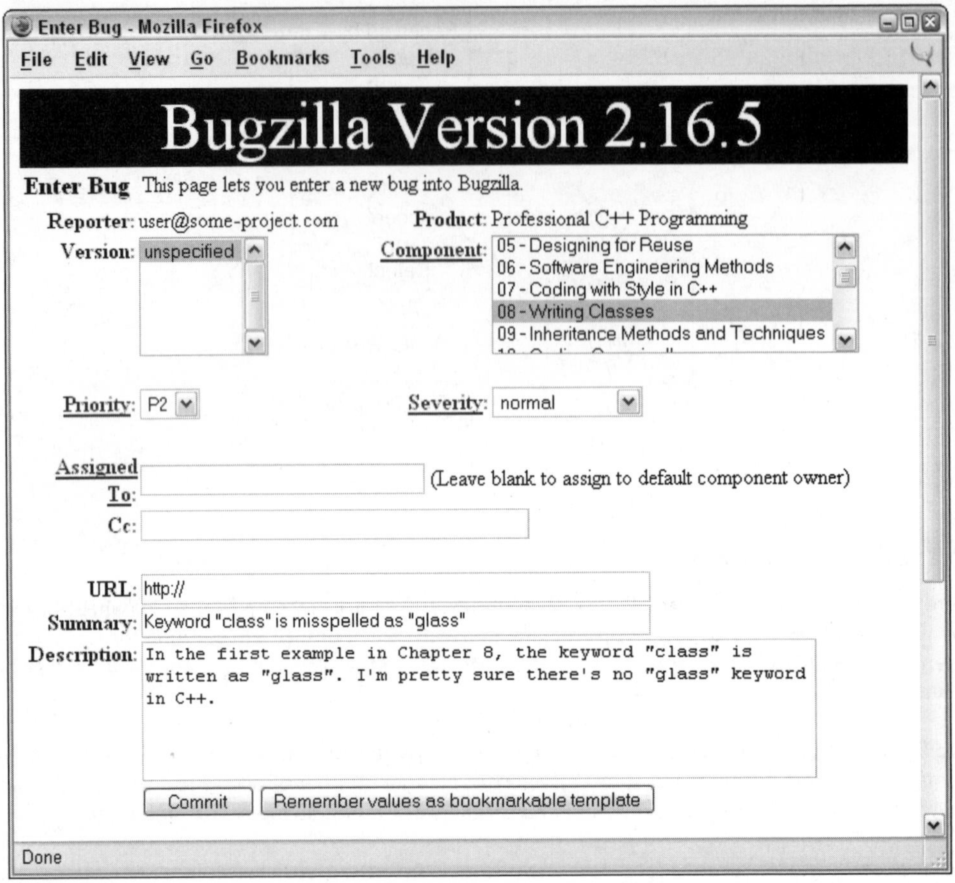

Figure 19-3

Unit Testing

The only way to find bugs is through testing. One of the most important types of tests from a developer's point of view is the unit test. Unit tests are pieces of code that exercise specific functionality of a class or subsystem. These are the most granular tests that you could possibly write. Ideally, one or more unit tests should exist for every low-level task that your code can perform. For example, imagine that you are writing a math library that can perform addition and multiplication. Your suite of unit tests might contain the following tests:

❑   Basic test of addition

❑   Test addition of large numbers

❑   Test addition of negative numbers

❑   Test addition of zero to a number

- ❑ Test the commutative property of addition

- ❑ Basic test of multiplication

- ❑ Test multiplication of large numbers

- ❑ Test multiplication of negative numbers

- ❑ Test multiplication by zero

- ❑ Test the commutative property of multiplication

Well-written unit tests protect you in many ways. First, they prove that a piece of functionality actually works. Until you have some code that actually makes use of your class, its behavior is a major unknown. Second, they provide a first alert when a recently introduced change breaks something. This specific usage, called a *regression test*, is covered later in this chapter. Third, when used as part of the development process, they force the developer to fix problems from the start. If you are prevented from checking in your code with failed unit tests, you're forced to address problems right away. Fourth, unit tests let you try code out before other code is in place. When you first started programming, you could write a whole program and then run it for the first time. Professional programs are too big for that approach, so you need to be able to test components in isolation. Last, but certainly not least, they provide an example of usage. Almost as a side effect, unit tests make great reference code for other programmers. If a coworker wants to know how to perform matrix multiplication using your math library, you can point her to the appropriate test.

Approaches to Unit Testing

It's hard to go wrong with unit tests, unless you don't write them or write them poorly. In general, the more tests you have, the more coverage you have. The more coverage you have, the less likely it is for bugs to fall through the cracks and for you to have to tell your boss, or worse, your customer, "Oh, we never tested that."

There are several methodologies for writing unit tests most effectively. The Extreme Programming methodology, explained in Chapter 6, instructs its followers to write unit tests *before* writing code. In theory, writing tests first helps you solidify the requirements for the component and provide a metric that can be used to determine when it is done. Writing tests first can be tricky and requires diligence on the part of the programmer. For some programmers, it simply doesn't mesh well with their coding style. A less rigid approach is to design the tests before coding, but implement them later in the process. This way, the programmer is still forced to understand the requirements of the module but doesn't have to write code that makes use of nonexistent classes.

In some groups, the author of a particular subsystem doesn't write the unit tests for that subsystem. The theory is that if you write the tests for your own code, you might subconsciously work around problems that you know about, or only cover certain cases that you know your code handles well. In addition, it's sometimes difficult to get excited about finding bugs in code you just wrote, so you might only put in a half-hearted effort. In practice, having one developer write unit tests for another developer's code requires a lot of extra overhead and coordination. When such coordination is accomplished, however, this approach helps guarantee more effective tests.

Another way to ensure that unit tests are actually testing the right parts of the code is to write them so that they maximize *code coverage*. You can use a code coverage tool, such as gcov, or have your resident Perl hacker write a script that will tell you what percentage of public methods are called by unit tests. In theory, a properly tested class has unit tests for all of its public methods.

The Unit Testing Process

The process of providing unit tests for your code begins before the code is written. Even if you do not subscribe to the methodology of writing unit tests before you write code, you should take the time to consider what sorts of tests you will provide. This way, you can break the task up into well-defined chunks, each of which has its own test-validated criteria. For example, if your task is to write a database access class, you might first write the functionality that inserts data into the database. Once that is fully tested with a suite of unit tests, you can continue to write the code to support updates, deletes, and selects, testing each piece as you go.

The following list of steps is a suggested approach for designing and implementing unit tests. As with any programming methodology, the best process is the one that yields the best results. We suggest that you experiment with different ways of using unit tests to discover what works best for you.

Define the Granularity of Your Tests

Before you start designing the individual tests, you need to do a reality check. Given the requirements of your component, its complexity, and the amount of time available, what level of unit testing can you provide? In an ideal world, you would write more tests than code to thoroughly validate the functionality of a program (though if it were truly an ideal world, we probably wouldn't need tests because everything would work!) In reality, you are probably already crunched for time, and your initial task is to maximize the effectiveness of unit tests given the constraints placed upon you.

The *granularity* of tests refers to their scope. As the following table illustrates, you can unit test a database class with just a few test functions or you can go nuts and really ensure that everything works as it should.

Large-Grained Tests	Medium-Grained Tests	Fine-Grained Tests
testConnection()	[all of the large-grained tests]	[all large and medium-grained tests]
testInsert()	testConnectionDroppedError()	testConnectionThroughHTTP()
testUpdate()	testInsertBadData()	testConnectionLocal()
testDelete()	testInsertStrings()	testConnectionErrorBadHost()
testSelect()	testInsertIntegers()	testConnectionErrorServerBusy()
	testUpdateStrings()	testInsertWideCharacters()
	testUpdateIntegers()	testInsertLargeData()
	testDeleteNonexistentRow()	testInsertMalformed()
	testSelectComplicated()	testUpdateWideCharacters()
	testSelectMalformed()	testUpdateLargeData()
		testUpdateMalformed()test DeleteWithoutPermissions()
		testDeleteThenUpdate()
		testSelectNested()
		testSelectWideCharacters()
		testSelectLargeData()

As you can see, each successive column brings in more specific tests. As you move from large-grained tests to more finely grained tests, you start to consider error conditions, different input data sets, and different modes of operation.

Of course, the decision you make initially when choosing the granularity of your tests is not set in stone. Perhaps the database class is just being written as a proof-of-concept and might not even be used. A few simple tests may be adequate now, and you can always add more later. Or perhaps the use case changes at a later date. The database class might not initially have been written with international characters in mind. Once such features are added, they should be tested with specific targeted unit tests.

If you plan to revisit or refine the tests at a later date, you should make every effort to actually do so. Consider the unit tests to be part of the actual implementation. When you make a modification, don't just modify the tests so that they continue to work, write new tests and reevaluate the existing ones.

> **Unit tests are part of the subsystem that they are testing. As you enhance and refine the subsystem, enhance and refine the tests.**

Brainstorm the Individual Tests

Over time, you will gain an intuition for which aspects of a piece of code should turn into a unit test. Certain methods or inputs just feel like they should be tested. This intuition is gained through trial and error and by looking at unit tests that other people in your group have written. It should be pretty easy to pick out which programmers are the best unit testers. Their tests tend to be organized and frequently modified.

Until unit test creation becomes second nature, approach the task of figuring out which tests to write by brainstorming. To get some ideas flowing, consider the following questions.

1. What are the things that this piece of code was written to do?

2. What are the typical ways each method would be called?

3. What preconditions of the methods could be violated by the caller?

4. How could each method be misused?

5. What kinds of data are you expecting as input?

6. What kinds of data are you *not* expecting as input?

7. What are the edge cases or exceptional conditions?

You don't need to write formal answers to those questions (unless your manager is a particularly fervent devotee of this book), but they should help you generate some ideas for unit tests. The table of tests for the database class contained test functions that each arose from one of these questions.

Once you have generated ideas for some of the tests you would like to use, consider how you might organize them into categories and the breakdown of tests will fall into place. In the database class example, the tests could be split into the following categories:

❑ Basic tests

❑ Error tests

❑ Internationalization tests

❑ Bad input tests

❑ Complicated tests

Splitting your tests into categories makes them easier to identify and augment. It might also make it easier to realize which aspects of the code are thoroughly tested and which could use a few more unit tests.

> **It's easy to write a massive number of simple tests, but don't forget about the more complicated cases!**

Create Sample Data and Results

The most common trap to fall into when writing unit tests is to match the test to the behavior of the code instead of using the test to validate the code. If you write a unit test that performs a database select and the test fails, is it a problem with the code or a problem with the test? It's usually easier to assume that the code is right and to modify the test to match. This approach is usually wrong.

To avoid this pitfall, you should understand the inputs to the test and the expected output before you try it out. This is sometimes easier said than done. For example, say you wrote some code to encrypt an arbitrary block of text using a particular key. A reasonable unit test would take a fixed string of text and pass it in to the encryption module. Then, it would examine the result to see if it was correctly encrypted. When you go to write such a test, it is tempting to try out the behavior with the encryption module first and see the result. If it looks reasonable, you might write a test to look for that value. Doing so really doesn't prove anything, however. You haven't actually tested the code — you've just written a test that guarantees it will continue to return that same value. Often times writing the test requires some real work — you would need to encrypt the text independently of your encryption module to get an accurate result.

> **Decide on the correct output for your test *before* you ever run the test.**

Write the Tests

The exact code behind a test will vary depending on what type of test framework you have in place. One framework, `cppunit`, is discussed below. Independent of the actual implementation, however, the following guidelines will help ensure effective tests:

- ❏ Make sure that you're only testing one thing in each test. That way, if a test fails, it will point to a specific piece of functionality.

- ❏ Be specific inside the test. Did the test fail because an exception was thrown or because the wrong value was returned?

- ❏ Use logging extensively inside of test code. If the test fails some day, you will have some insight into what happened.

- ❏ Avoid tests that depend on earlier tests or are otherwise interrelated. Tests should be as atomic and isolated as possible.

- ❏ If the test requires the use of other subsystems, consider writing *stub versions* of those subsystems that simulate the modules' behavior so that changes in loosely related code don't cause the test to fail.

- ❏ Ask your code reviewers to look at your unit tests as well. When you do a code review, tell the other engineer where you think additional tests could be added.

As you will see in the example below, unit tests are usually very small and simple pieces of code. In most cases, writing a single unit test will only take a few minutes, making them one of the most productive uses of your time.

Run the Tests

When you're done writing a test, you should run it right away before the anticipation of the results becomes too much to bear. The joy of a screen full of passing unit tests shouldn't be minimized. For most programmers, this is the easiest way to see quantitative data that declare your code useful and correct.

Even if you adopt the methodology of writing tests prior to writing code, you should still run the tests immediately after they are written. This way, you can prove to yourself that the test fails initially. Once the code is in place, you have tangible data that shows that it accomplished what it was supposed to accomplish.

It's unlikely that every test you write will have the expected result the first time. In theory, if you are writing tests before writing code, all of your tests should fail. If one passes, either the code magically appeared or there is a problem with a test. If the code is done and tests still fail (some would say that if the tests fail, the code is actually *not* done!), there are two possibilities. The code could be wrong or the test could be wrong. As mentioned previously, it's often quite tempting to turn to the test and twiddle some Booleans to make everything work. Resist this urge!

Unit Testing in Action

Now that you've read about unit testing in theory, it's time to actually write some tests. The following example draws on the object pool example from Chapter 17. As a brief recap, the object pool is a class that can be used to avoid excessive object creation. By keeping track of already created objects, the pool acts as a broker between code that needs a certain type of object and such objects that already exist.

The public interface for `ObjectPool` is shown here:

```
//
// template class ObjectPool
//
// Provides an object pool that can be used with any class that provides a
// default constructor.
//
// The object pool constructor creates a pool of objects, which it hands out
// to clients when requested via the acquireObject() method. When a client is
// finished with the object it calls releaseObject() to put the object back
// into the object pool.
//
// The constructor and destructor on each object in the pool will be called only
// once each for the lifetime of the program, not once per acquisition and release.
//
// The primary use of an object pool is to avoid creating and deleting objects
// repeatedly. The object pool is most suited to applications that use large
// numbers of objects for short periods of time.
//
// For efficiency, the object pool doesn't perform sanity checks.
// Expects the user to release every acquired object exactly once.
// Expects the user to avoid using any objects that he or she has released.
//
```

```
// Expects the user not to delete the object pool until every object
// that was acquired has been released. Deleting the object pool invalidates
// any objects that the user had acquired, even if they had not yet been released.
//
template <typename T>
class ObjectPool
{
    public:
        //
        // Creates an object pool with chunkSize objects.
        // Whenever the object pool runs out of objects, chunkSize
        // more objects will be added to the pool. The pool only grows:
        // objects are never removed from the pool (freed), until
        // the pool is destroyed.
        //
        // Throws invalid_argument if chunkSize is <= 0.
        //
        ObjectPool(int chunkSize = kDefaultChunkSize)
            throw(std::invalid_argument, std::bad_alloc);

        //
        // Frees all the allocated objects. Invalidates any objects that have
        // been acquired for use.
        //
        ~ObjectPool();

        //
        // Reserve an object for use. The reference to the object is invalidated
        // if the object pool itself is freed.
        //
        // Clients must not free the object!
        //
        T& acquireObject();

        //
        // Return the object to the pool. Clients must not use the object after
        // it has been returned to the pool.
        //
        void releaseObject(T& obj);


    // [Private/Protected methods and data omitted]
};
```

If the notion of an object pool is new to you, you may wish to peruse Chapter 17 before continuing with this example.

Introducing cppunit

cppunit is an open-source unit testing framework for C++ that is based on a Java package called junit. The framework is fairly lightweight (in a good way), and it is very easy to get started. The advantage of using a framework such as cppunit is that it allows the developer to focus on writing tests instead of dealing with setting up tests, building logic around tests, and gathering results. cppunit includes a number of helpful utilities for test developers and automatic output in various formats. The full breadth of features is not covered here. We suggest you read up on cppunit at http://cppunit.sourceforge.net.

The most common way of using cppunit is to subclass the CppUnit::TestFixture class (note that CppUnit is the namespace and TestFixture is the class). A *fixture* is simply a logical group of tests. A TestFixture subclass can override the setUp() method to perform any tasks that need to happen prior to the tests running as well as the tearDown() method, which can be used to clean up after the tests have run. A fixture can also maintain state with member variables. A skeleton implementation of ObjectPoolTest, a class for testing the ObjectPool class, is shown here:

```
// ObjectPoolTest.h

#include <cppunit/TestFixture.h>

class ObjectPoolTest : public CppUnit::TestFixture
{
    public:
        void setUp();
        void tearDown();
};
```

Because the tests for ObjectPool are relatively simple and isolated, empty definitions will suffice for setUp() and tearDown(). The beginning stage of the source file is shown here:

```
// ObjectPoolTest.cpp

#include "ObjectPoolTest.h"

void ObjectPoolTest::setUp()
{
}

void ObjectPoolTest::tearDown()
{
}
```

That's all the initial code we need to start developing unit tests!

Writing the First Test

Since this may be your first exposure to cppunit, or to unit tests at large, the first test will be a very simple one. It simply tests whether 0 < 1.

An individual unit test in cppunit is just a method of the fixture class. To create a simple test, add its declaration to the ObjectPoolTest.h file:

```
// ObjectPoolTest.h

#include <cppunit/TestFixture.h>

class ObjectPoolTest : public CppUnit::TestFixture
{
    public:
        void setUp();
        void tearDown();
```

```
            // Our first test!
            void testSimple();
};
```

The test definition uses the CPPUNIT_ASSERT macro to perform the actual test. CPPUNIT_ASSERT, like other assert macros you may have used, simply surrounds an expression that *should* be true. See Chapter 20 for details on assert. In this case, the test claims that 0 is less than 1, so it surrounds the statement 0 < 1 in a CPPUNIT_ASSERT macro call. This macro is defined in the cppunit/TestAssert.h file.

```
// ObjectPoolTest.cpp

#include "ObjectPoolTest.h"
#include <cppunit/TestAssert.h>

void ObjectPoolTest::setUp()
{
}

void ObjectPoolTest::tearDown()
{
}

void ObjectPoolTest::testSimple()
{
    CPPUNIT_ASSERT(0 < 1);
}
```

That's it! Of course, most of your unit tests will do something a bit more interesting than a simple assert. As you will see, the common pattern is to perform some sort of calculation and assert that the result is the value you expected. With cppunit, you don't even need to worry about exceptions — the framework will catch and report them as necessary.

Building a Suite of Tests

There are a few more steps before the simple test can be run. cppunit runs a group of tests as a *suite*. A suite tells cppunit which tests to run, as opposed to a fixture, which simply groups tests together logically. The common pattern is to give your fixture class a static method that builds a suite containing all of its tests. In the updated versions of ObjectPoolTest.h and ObjectPoolTest.cpp, the suite() method is used for this purpose.

```
// ObjectPoolTest.h

#include <cppunit/TestFixture.h>
#include <cppunit/TestSuite.h>
#include <cppunit/Test.h>

class ObjectPoolTest : public CppUnit::TestFixture
{
    public:
        void setUp();
        void tearDown();

        // Our first test!
        void testSimple();
```

```
        static CppUnit::Test* suite();
};
```

```
// ObjectPoolTest.cpp

#include "ObjectPoolTest.h"
#include <cppunit/TestAssert.h>

void ObjectPoolTest::setUp()
{
}

void ObjectPoolTest::tearDown()
{
}

void ObjectPoolTest::testSimple()
{
    CPPUNIT_ASSERT(0 < 1);
}
```

```
CppUnit::Test* ObjectPoolTest::suite()

  CppUnit::TestSuite* suiteOfTests = new CppUnit::TestSuite("ObjectPoolTest");
  suiteOfTests->addTest(new CppUnit::TestCaller<ObjectPoolTest>(
                              "testSimple",
                              &ObjectPoolTest::testSimple ) );
  return suiteOfTests; // Note that Test is a superclass of TestSuite
}
```

The template syntax for creating a `TestCaller` is a bit dense, but just about every single test you write will follow this exact pattern, so you can ignore the implementation of `TestSuite` and `TestCaller` for the most part.

To actually run the suite of tests and see the results, you will need a *test runner*. cppunit is a flexible framework. It contains several different runners that operate in different environments, such as the MFC Runner, which is designed to run within a program written with the Microsoft Foundation Classes. For a text-based environment, you should use the Text Runner, which is defined in the `CppUnit::TextUi` namespace.

The code to run the suite of tests defined by the `ObjectPoolTest` fixture follows. It simply creates a runner, adds the tests returned by the `suite()` method, and calls `run()`.

```
// main.cpp

#include "ObjectPoolTest.h"
#include <cppunit/ui/text/TestRunner.h>

int main(int argc, char** argv)
{
  CppUnit::TextUi::TestRunner runner;
  runner.addTest(ObjectPoolTest::suite());
```

```
    runner.run();
}
```

After the code is all compiled, linked, and run, you should see output similar to the following:

```
OK (1 tests)
```

If you modify the code to assert that 1 < 0, the test will fail, cppunit will report the failure as follows:

```
!!!FAILURES!!!
Test Results:
Run:  1    Failures: 1    Errors: 0


1) test: testSimple (F) line: 21 ObjectPoolTest.cpp
assertion failed
- Expression: 1 < 0
```

Note that by using the CPPUNIT_ASSERT macro, the framework was able to pinpoint the exact line on which the test failed — a useful piece of information for debugging!

Adding the Real Tests

Now that the framework is all set up and a simple test is working, it's time to turn your attention to the ObjectPool class and write some code that actually tests it. All of the following tests will be added to ObjectPoolTest.h and ObjectPoolTest.cpp, just like the earlier simple test.

Before you can write the tests, you'll need a helper object to use with the ObjectPool class. As you recall, the ObjectPool creates *chunks* of objects of a certain type and hands them out to the caller as requested. Some of the tests will need to check if a retrieved object is the same as a previously retrieved object. One way to do this is to create a pool of serial objects — objects that have a monotonically increasing serial number. The following code defines such a class:

```
// Serial.h

class Serial
{
    public:
        Serial();

        int getSerialNumber() const;

    protected:
        static int sNextSerial;

        int mSerialNumber;
};
```

```
// Serial.cpp

#include "Serial.h"
```

```
Serial::Serial()
{
    // A new object gets the next serial number.
    mSerialNumber = sNextSerial++;
}

int Serial::getSerialNumber() const
{
    return mSerialNumber;
}

int Serial::sNextSerial = 0;   // The first serial number is 0.
```

On to the tests! As an initial sanity check, you might want a test that simply creates an object pool. If any exceptions are thrown during creation, cppunit will report an error:

```
void ObjectPoolTest::testCreation()
{
  ObjectPool<Serial> myPool;
}
```

The next test is a *negative test* because it is doing something that *should* fail. In this case, the test tries to create an object pool with an invalid chunk size of 0. The object pool constructor should throw an exception. Normally, cppunit would catch the exception and report an error. However, since that is the desired behavior, the test catches the exception explicitly and sets a flag. The final step of the test is to assert that the flag was set. Thus, if the constructor does *not* throw an exception, the test will fail:

```
void ObjectPoolTest::testInvalidChunkSize()
{
    bool caughtException = false;

    try {
        ObjectPool<Serial> myPool(0);
    } catch (const invalid_argument& ex) {
        // OK. We were expecting an exception.
        caughtException = true;
    }

    CPPUNIT_ASSERT(caughtException);
}
```

testAcquire() tests a specific piece of public functionality — the ability of the ObjectPool to give out an object. In this case, there is not much to assert. To prove validity of the resulting Serial reference, the test asserts that its serial number is greater than or equal to zero.

```
void ObjectPoolTest::testAcquire()
{
    ObjectPool<Serial> myPool;

    Serial& serial = myPool.acquireObject();

    CPPUNIT_ASSERT(serial.getSerialNumber() >= 0);
}
```

The next test is a bit more interesting. The `ObjectPool` should not give out the same `Serial` object twice (unless it is explicitly released). This test checks the exclusivity property of the `ObjectPool` by creating a pool with a fixed chunk size and retrieving exactly that many objects. If the pool is properly dishing out unique objects, none of their serial numbers should match. Note that this test only covers objects created as part of a single chunk. A similar test for multiple chunks would be an excellent idea.

```
void ObjectPoolTest::testExclusivity()
{
    const int poolSize = 5;
    ObjectPool<Serial> myPool(poolSize);
    set<int> seenSerials;

    for (int i = 0; i < poolSize; i++) {
        Serial& nextSerial = myPool.acquireObject();

        // Assert that this number hasn't been seen before.
        CPPUNIT_ASSERT(seenSerials.find(nextSerial.getSerialNumber()) ==
                       seenSerials.end());

        // Add this number to the set.
        seenSerials.insert(nextSerial.getSerialNumber());
    }
}
```

This implementation uses the `set` container from the STL. Consult Chapter 21 for details if you are unfamiliar with this container.

The final test (for now) checks the release functionality. Once an object is released, the `ObjectPool` can give it out again. The pool shouldn't create additional chunks until it has *recycled* all released objects. This test first retrieves a `Serial` from the pool and records its serial number. Then, the object is immediately released back into the pool. Next, objects are retrieved from the pool until either the original object is recycled (identified by its serial number) or the chunk has been used up. If the code gets all the way through the chunk without seeing the recycled object, the test fails.

```
void ObjectPoolTest::testRelease()
{
    const int poolSize = 5;
    ObjectPool<Serial> myPool(poolSize);

    Serial& originalSerial = myPool.acquireObject();

    int originalSerialNumber = originalSerial.getSerialNumber();

    // Return the original object to the pool.
    myPool.releaseObject(originalSerial);

    // Now make sure that the original object is recycled before
    // a new chunk is created.
    bool wasRecycled = false;
    for (int i = 0; i < poolSize; i++) {
        Serial& nextSerial = myPool.acquireObject();
        if (nextSerial.getSerialNumber() == originalSerialNumber) {
            wasRecycled = true;
            break;
```

```
        }
    }

    CPPUNIT_ASSERT(wasRecycled);
}
```

Once these tests are added to the suite, you should be able to run them, and they should all pass. Of course, if one or more tests fails, you are presented with the quintessential issue in unit tests — is it the test or the code that is broken?

Basking in the Glorious Light of Unit Test Results

Hopefully, the tests in the previous section gave you a good idea of how to get started writing actual professional-quality tests for real code. It's just the tip of the iceberg though. The previous examples should help you think of additional tests that you could write for the `ObjectPool` class. For example, none of the tests dealt with allocation of multiple chunks — there should definitely be coverage of that functionality. There also weren't complex tests that acquired and released the same object multiple times.

There is no end to the number of unit tests you could write for a given piece of code, and that's the best thing about unit tests! If you find yourself wondering how your code might react to a certain situation, that's a unit test! If a particular aspect of your subsystem seems to be presenting problems, increase unit test coverage of that particular area. Even if you simply want to put yourself in the client's shoes to see what it's like to work with your class, writing unit tests is a great way to get a different perspective.

Higher-Level Testing

While unit tests are the best first line of defense against bugs, they are only part of the larger testing process. Higher-level tests focus on how pieces of the product work together, as opposed to the relatively narrow focus of unit tests. In a way, higher-level tests are more challenging to write because it's less clear what tests need to be written. Yet, you cannot really claim that the program works until you have tested how its pieces work together.

Integration Tests

An *integration test* covers areas where components meet. Unlike a unit test, which generally acts on the level of a single class, an integration test usually involves two or more classes. Integration tests excel at testing interactions between two components, often written by two different programmers. In fact, the process of writing an integration test often reveals important incongruities in designs.

Sample Integration Tests

Since there are no hard-and-fast rules to determine what integration tests you should write, some examples might help you get a sense of when integration tests are useful. The following scenarios depict cases where an integration test is appropriate, but they do not cover every possible case. Just as with unit tests, over time you will refine your intuition for useful integration tests.

An XML-Based File Serializer

Suppose that your project includes a persistence layer that is used to save certain types of objects to disk and to read them back in. The hip way to serialize data is to use the XML format, so a logical breakdown of components might include an XML conversion layer sitting on top of a custom file API. Both of these components can be thoroughly unit tested. The XML layer would have unit tests that ensure that different types of objects are correctly converted to XML and populated from XML. The file API would have tests that read, write, update, and delete files on disk. When these modules start to work together, integration tests are appropriate. At the very least, you should have an integration test that saves an object to disk through the XML layer, then reads it back in and does a comparison to the original. Because the test covers both modules, it is a basic integration test.

Readers and Writers to a Shared Resource

Imagine a program that contains a data space shared by different components. For example, a stock-trading program might have a queue of buy and sell requests. Components related to receiving stock transaction requests would add orders to the queue, and components related to performing stock trades would take data off the queue. You could unit test the heck out of the queue class, but until it is tested with the actual components that will be using it, you really don't know if any of your assumptions are wrong. A good integration test would use the stock request components and the stock trade components as clients of the queue class. You would write some sample orders and make sure that they successfully entered and exited the queue through the client components.

Wrapper around a Third-Party Library

Integration tests do not always need to occur at integration points in your own code. Many times, integration tests are written to test the interaction between your code and a third-party library. For example, you may be using a database connection library to talk to a relational database system. Perhaps you built an object-oriented wrapper around the library that adds support for connection caching or provides a friendlier interface. This is a very important integration point to test because, even though the wrapper probably provides a more useful interface to the database, it introduces possible misuse of the original library. In other words, writing a wrapper is a good thing, but writing a wrapper that introduces bugs is going to be a disaster.

Methods of Integration Testing

When it comes to actually writing integration tests, there is often a fine line between integration and unit tests. If a unit test is modified so that it touches another component, is it suddenly an integration test? In a way, the answer is moot because a good test is a good test regardless of the type of test. We recommend that you use the concepts of integration and unit testing as two *approaches* to testing, but avoid getting caught up in labeling the category of every single test.

In terms of implementation, integration tests are often written using a unit testing framework, further blurring their distinction. As it turns out, unit testing frameworks provide an easy way to write a yes/no test and produce useful results. Whether the test is looking at a single unit of functionality or the intersection of two components hardly makes a difference from the framework's point of view.

For performance and organizational reasons, you may wish to attempt to separate unit tests from integration tests. For example, your group may decide that everybody must run integration tests before checking in new code, but be a bit more lax on running unrelated unit tests. Separating the two types of tests also increases the value of results. If a test failure occurs within the XML class tests, it will be clear that it's a bug in that class, not in the interaction between that class and the file API.

System Tests

System tests operate at an even higher level than integration tests. These tests examine the program as a whole. System tests often make use of a *virtual user* that simulates a human being working with the program. Of course, the virtual user must be programmed with a script of actions to perform. Other system tests rely on scripts or a fixed set of inputs and expected outputs.

Much like unit and integration tests, an individual system test performs a specific test and expects a specific result. It is not uncommon to use system tests to make sure that different features work in combination with one another. In theory, a fully system-tested program would contain a test for every permutation of every feature. This approach quickly grows unwieldy but you should still make an effort to test many features in combination. For example, a graphics program could have a system test that imports an image, rotates it, performs a blur filter, converts it to black and white, and then saves it. The test would compare the saved image to a file that contains the expected result.

Unfortunately, few specific rules can be stated about system tests because they are highly dependent on the actual application. For applications that process files with no user interaction, system tests can be written much like unit and integration tests. For graphical programs, a virtual user approach may be best. For server applications, you might need to build stub clients that simulate network traffic. The important part is that you are actually testing real use of the program, not just a piece of it.

Regression Tests

Regression testing is more of a testing concept than a specific type of test. The idea is that once a feature works, developers tend to put it aside and assume that it will continue to work. Unfortunately, new features and other code changes often conspire to break previously working functionality. Regression tests are often put in place as a sanity check for features that are, more or less, complete and working. If the regression test is well written, it will cease to pass when a change is introduced that breaks the feature.

If your company has an army of quality-assurance testers, regression testing may take the form of manual testing. The tester acts as a user would and goes through a series of steps, gradually testing every feature that worked in the previous release. This approach is thorough and accurate if carefully performed, but not particularly scalable. At the other extreme, you could build a completely automated system that performs each function as a virtual user. This would be a scripting challenge, though several commercial and noncommercial packages exist to ease the scripting of various types of applications. A middle ground is known as *smoke testing*. Some tests will only test the subset of the most important features that should work. The idea is that if something is broken, it should show up right away. If smoke tests pass, they could be followed by more rigorous manual or automated testing.

Some bugs are like the dream where you show up for school in your underwear — they are both terrifying and recurring. Recurring bugs are frustrating and a poor use of engineering resources. Even if, for some reason, you decide not to write a suite of regression tests, you should *still* write regression tests for bugs that you fix. By writing a test for a bug fix, you both prove that the bug is fixed and set up an alert that is triggered if the bug ever comes back (for example, if your change is rolled back or otherwise undone). When a regression test of a previously fixed bug fails, it should be easy to fix because the regression test can refer to the original bug number and describe how it was fixed the first time.

Tips for Successful Testing

As a software engineer, your role in testing may range anywhere from basic unit testing responsibility to complete management of an automated test system. Because testing roles and styles vary so much, we have assembled several tips from our experiences that may help you in various testing situations.

❑   Spend some time designing your automated test system. A system that runs constantly throughout the day will detect failures quickly. A system that sends email to engineers automatically or sits in the middle of the room loudly playing show tunes when a failure occurs will result in increased visibility of problems.

❑   Don't forget about stress testing. Even though a full suite of unit tests passes for your database access class, it could still fall down when used by several dozen threads simultaneously. You should test your product under the most extreme conditions it could face in the real world.

❑   Test on a variety of platforms or a platform that closely mirrors the customer's system. One method of testing on multiple operating systems is to use a third-party virtual machine environment that allows you to run several different operating systems on the same machine.

❑   Some tests can be written to intentionally inject faults in a system. For example, you could write a test that deletes a file while it is being read or simulates a network outage during a network operation.

❑   Bugs and tests are closely related. Bug fixes should be proven by writing a regression test. The comment with the test should refer to the original bug number.

❑   Don't simply comment out the tests that are failing. When a coworker is slaving over a bug and finds your commented out tests, he will come looking for you!

The most important tip we can give you is to remember that testing is a part of software development. If you agree with that and accept it before you start coding, it won't be quite as unexpected when the feature is finished but there is still more work to do to prove that it works.

Summary

This chapter has covered the basic information that all professional programmers should know about testing. Unit testing in particular is the easiest and most effective way to increase the quality of your own code. Higher-level tests provide coverage of use cases, synchronicity between modules, and protection against regressions. No matter what your role is with regard to testing, you should now be able to confidently design, create, and review tests at various levels.

Now that you know how to find bugs, it's time to learn how to fix them. To that end, Chapter 20 covers techniques and strategies for effective debugging.

20

Conquering Debugging

Your code will contain bugs. Every professional programmer would like to write bug-free code, but the reality is that few software engineers succeed in this endeavor. As computer users know, bugs are endemic in computer software. The software that you write is probably no exception. Therefore, unless you plan to bribe your coworkers into fixing all your bugs, you cannot be a Professional C++ programmer without knowing how to debug C++ code. One factor that often distinguishes an experienced programmer from a novice is his or her debugging skills.

Despite the obvious importance of debugging, it is rarely given enough attention in courses and books. Debugging seems to be the type of skill that everyone wants you to know, but no one knows how to teach. This chapter attempts to provide you with concrete guidelines and techniques for debugging even the most galling problems. The contents include an introduction to the Fundamental Law of Debugging and bug taxonomies, followed by tips for avoiding bugs. Techniques for planning for bugs include error logging, debug traces, and asserts. The chapter concludes with specific tips for debugging the problems that arise, including techniques for reproducing bugs, debugging reproducible bugs, debugging nonreproducible bugs, debugging memory errors, and debugging multi-threaded programs. The chapter concludes with a step-by-step debugging example.

The Fundamental Law of Debugging

The first rule of debugging is to be honest with yourself and admit that your program will contain bugs. This realistic assessment enables you to put your best effort into preventing bugs from crawling into your program in the first place while you simultaneously include the necessary features to make debugging as easy as possible.

> The Fundamental Law of Debugging: avoid bugs when you're coding, but plan for bugs in your code.

Bug Taxonomies

A *bug* in a computer program is incorrect run-time behavior. This undesirable behavior includes both *catastrophic bugs* that cause program death, data corruption, operating system panics, or some other similarly horrific outcome and *noncatastrophic bugs* that cause the program to behave incorrectly in more subtle ways. For example, a Web browser might return the wrong Web page, or a spreadsheet application might calculate the standard deviation of a column incorrectly. The underlying cause, or *root cause*, of the bug is the mistake in the program that causes this incorrect behavior. The process of debugging a program includes both determining the root cause of the bug and fixing the code so that the bug will not occur again.

> *Programmers often use the term root-cause as a verb, as in "Have you root-caused that core dump yet?"*

Avoiding Bugs

The powerful features of C++ make it an especially error-prone language, so debugging skills are even more important when coding in C++ than when using most other languages. Here are a few tips for avoiding bugs in your programs:

❑   Read this book from cover to cover. Learn the C++ language intimately, especially pointers and memory management. Then, recommend this book to your friends and coworkers so they avoid bugs too!

❑   Follow the style guidelines in this book, specifically those described in Chapter 7. They will lead to fewer bugs because you, and other people, will be able to understand your programs.

❑   Design before you code. Designing while you code tends to lead to convoluted designs that are harder to understand and are more error-prone. It also makes you more likely to omit possible edge cases and error conditions.

❑   Utilize code reviews: At least two people should look at every line of code that you write. Sometimes it takes a fresh perspective to notice problems.

❑   Test, test, and test again. Follow the guidelines in Chapter 19.

❑   Expect error conditions, and handle them appropriately. In particular, plan for and handle out-of-memory conditions. They will occur. See Chapter 15.

❑   Last, and probably most importantly, use smart pointers to avoid memory leaks. See Chapters 13, 15, and 25 for details.

Planning for Bugs

Your programs should contain features that enable easier debugging when the inevitable bugs arise. This section describes these features and presents sample implementations that you can incorporate into your own programs.

Error Logging

Imagine this scenario: You have just released a new version of your flagship product, and one of the first users reports that the program "stopped working." You attempt to pry more information from the user, and eventually discover that the program died in the middle of an operation. The user can't quite remember what he was doing, or if there were any error messages. How will you debug this problem?

Now imagine the same scenario, but in addition to the limited information from the user, you are also able to examine the error log on the user's computer. In the log you see a message from your program that says "Error: unable to allocate memory." Looking at the code near the spot where that error message was generated, you find a line in which you dereferenced a pointer without checking for NULL. You've found the root cause of your bug!

Error logging is the process of writing error messages to persistent storage so that they will be available following an application, or even machine, death. Despite the example scenario, you might still have doubts about this strategy. Won't it be obvious by your program's behavior if it encounters errors? Won't the user notice if something goes wrong? As the preceding example shows, user reports are not always accurate or complete. In addition, many programs, such as the operating system kernel and long-running daemons like inetd or syslogd on Unix, are not interactive and run unattended on a machine. The only way these programs can communicate with users is through error logging.

Thus, your program should log errors as it encounters them. That way, if a user reports a bug, you will be able to examine the log files on the machine to see if your program reported any errors prior to encountering the bug. Unfortunately, error logging is platform dependent: C++ does not contain a standard logging mechanism. Examples of platform-specific logging mechanisms include the syslog facility in Unix and the event reporting API in Windows. You should consult the documentation for your development platform. There are also some open-source implementations of cross-platform logging classes, including log4cpp (available at http://sourceforge.net).

Now that you're convinced that error logging is a great feature to add to your programs, you might be tempted to log error messages every few lines in your code, so that, in the event of any bug, you'll be able to trace the code path that was executing. These types of error messages are appropriately called "traces." However, you should not write these traces to error logs for two reasons. First, writing to persistent storage is slow. Even on systems that write the logs asynchronously, logging that much information will slow down your program. Second, and most importantly, most of the information that you would put in your traces is not appropriate for the end user to see. It will just confuse the user, leading to unwarranted service calls. That said, tracing is an important debugging technique under the correct circumstances, as described in the next section.

Here are some specific guidelines for the types of errors your programs should log:

❑ Unrecoverable errors, such as an inability to allocate memory or a system call failing unexpectedly. These errors will usually directly precede an application exit or memory core dump.

❑ Errors for which an administrator can take action, such as low memory, an incorrectly formatted data file, an inability to write to disk, or a network connection being down.

❑ Unexpected errors such as a code path that you never expected to take or variables with unexpected values. Note that your code should "expect" users to enter invalid data and should handle it appropriately. An unexpected error would represent a bug in your program.

❑ Security breaches such as a network connection attempted from an unauthorized address or too many network connections attempted (denial of service).

Additionally, most APIs allow you to specify a *log level* or *error level*. You can log nonerror conditions under a log level that is less severe than "error." For example, you might want to log significant state changes in your application, or startup and shutdown of the program. You also might consider giving your users a way to adjust the log level of your program at run time so that they can customize the amount of logging that occurs.

Debug Traces

When debugging complicated problems, public error messages generally do not contain enough information. You often need a complete trace of the code path taken or values of variables before the bug showed up. In addition to basic messages, it's sometimes helpful to include the following information in debug traces:

- ❑ The thread ID, if a multithreaded program.

- ❑ The name of the function that generated the trace.

- ❑ The name of the source file in which the code that generates this trace lives.

You can add this tracing to your program through a special debug mode, or via a *ring buffer*. Both of these methods are explained in detail below.

Debug Mode

The first technique to add debug traces is to provide a debug mode for your program. In debug mode, the program writes trace output to standard error or to a file, and perhaps does extra checking during execution. There are several ways to add a debug mode to your program.

Compile-Time Debug Mode

You can use preprocessor #ifdefs to selectively compile the debug code into your program. The advantage of this method is that your debug code is not compiled into the "release" binary, and so does not increase its size. The disadvantages are that there is no way to enable debugging at a customer site for testing or following the discovery of a bug, and your code starts to look cluttered and indecipherable.

The rest of this section shows an example of a simple program instrumented with a compile-time debug mode. This program doesn't do anything useful: it is only for demonstrating the technique.

In order to generate a debug version of the program, it should be compiled with the symbol DEBUG_MODE defined. Your compiler should allow you to specify symbols to define during compilation; consult your documentation for details. For example, g++ allows you to specify –Dsymbol on the compile command.

Note that this example uses a global variable for the ofstream object. This example is one of the only times that we recommend using global variables! It's acceptable here because debug mode should not interfere with the rest of the program. If the ofstream object were not global, you would have to pass it to each function, requiring changes to all the function prototypes in the whole program.

```
// CTDebug.cpp
#include <exception>
#include <fstream>
#include <iostream>
using namespace std;
```

```cpp
#ifdef DEBUG_MODE
ofstream debugOstr;

const char* debugFileName = "debugfile.out";
#endif

class ComplicatedClass
{
    public:
        ComplicatedClass() {}

    // Class details omitted for brevity
};

class UserCommand
{
    public:
        UserCommand() {}

    // Class details not shown for brevity
};

ostream& operator<<(ostream& ostr, const ComplicatedClass& src);
ostream& operator<<(ostream& ostr, const UserCommand& src);
UserCommand getNextCommand(ComplicatedClass* obj);
void processUserCommand(UserCommand& cmd);
void trickyFunction(ComplicatedClass* obj) throw(exception);

int main(int argc, char** argv)
{
#ifdef DEBUG_MODE
    // Open the output stream.
    debugOstr.open(debugFileName);
    if (debugOstr.fail()) {
        cout << "Unable to open debug file!\n";
        return (1);
    }

    // Print the command-line arguments to the trace.
    for (int i = 0; i < argc; i++) {
        debugOstr << argv[i] << " ";
        debugOstr << endl;
    }
#endif

    // Rest of the function not shown
    return (0);
}

ostream& operator<<(ostream& ostr, const ComplicatedClass& src)
{
    ostr << "ComplicatedClass";
    return (ostr);
}
```

```
ostream& operator<<(ostream& ostr, const UserCommand& src)
{
    ostr << "UserCommand";
    return (ostr);
}

UserCommand getNextCommand(ComplicatedClass* obj)
{
    UserCommand cmd;
    return (cmd);
}

void processUserCommand(UserCommand& cmd)
{
    // Details omitted for brevity
}


void trickyFunction(ComplicatedClass* obj) throw(exception)
{
#ifdef DEBUG_MODE
    // If in debug mode, print the values with which this function starts
    debugOstr << "trickyFunction(): given argument: " << *obj << endl;
#endif

    while (true) {
        UserCommand cmd = getNextCommand(obj);

#ifdef DEBUG_MODE
        debugOstr << "trickyFunction(): retrieved cmd " << cmd << endl;
#endif
        try {
            processUserCommand(cmd);
        } catch (exception& e) {
#ifdef DEBUG_MODE
            debugOstr << "trickyFunction(): "
                << " received exception from procesUserCommand(): "
                << e.what() << endl;
#endif
            throw;
        }
    }
}
```

Start-Time Debug Mode

Start-time debug mode is an alternative to #ifdefs that is just as simple to implement. A command-line argument to the program can specify whether it should run in debug mode. Unlike compile-time debug mode, this strategy includes the debug code in the "release" binary, and allows debug mode to be enabled at a customer site. However, it still requires users to restart the program in order to run it in debug mode, which is not always an attractive alternative for customers, and which may prevent you from obtaining useful information about bugs.

The following example of start-time debug mode uses the same program as that shown for compile-time debug mode so that you can directly compare the differences. This version of the program again uses global variables: this time for the `ofstream` and the Boolean specifying whether the program is in debug mode. This choice is acceptable here to avoid imposing extra debug arguments on all the function prototypes.

One aspect of this program needs further comment: there is no standard library functionality in C++ for parsing command-line arguments. This program uses a simple function `isDebugSet()` to check for the debug flag among all the command-line arguments, but a function to parse all command-line arguments would need to be more sophisticated.

```cpp
// STDebug.cpp
#include <exception>
#include <fstream>
#include <iostream>
using namespace std;

ofstream debugOstr;
bool debug = false;

const char* debugFileName = "debugfile.out";

class ComplicatedClass
{
    public:
        ComplicatedClass() {}
        ~ComplicatedClass() {}
};

class UserCommand
{
    public:
        UserCommand() {}
};

bool isDebugSet(int argc, char** argv);
ostream& operator<<(ostream& ostr, const ComplicatedClass& src);
ostream& operator<<(ostream& ostr, const UserCommand& src);
UserCommand getNextCommand(ComplicatedClass* obj);
void processUserCommand(UserCommand& cmd);
void trickyFunction(ComplicatedClass* obj) throw(exception);

int main(int argc, char** argv)
{

    debug = isDebugSet(argc, argv);
    if (debug) {
        // Open the output stream.
        debugOstr.open(debugFileName);
        if (debugOstr.fail()) {
            cout << "Unable to open debug file!\n";
            return (1);
        }

        // Print the command-line arguments.
```

```
            for (int i = 0; i < argc; i++) {
                debugOstr << argv[i] << " ";
                debugOstr << endl;
            }
        }

        // Rest of the function not shown
        return (0);
}

bool isDebugSet(int argc, char** argv)
{
    for (int i = 0; i < argc; i++) {
        if (strcmp(argv[i], "-d") == 0) {
            return (true);
        }
    }
    return (false);
}

ostream& operator<<(ostream& ostr, const ComplicatedClass& src)
{
    ostr << "ComplicatedClass";
    return (ostr);
}

ostream& operator<<(ostream& ostr, const UserCommand& src)
{
    ostr << "UserCommand";
    return (ostr);
}

UserCommand getNextCommand(ComplicatedClass* obj)
{
    UserCommand cmd;
    return (cmd);
}

void processUserCommand(UserCommand& cmd)
{
    // Details omitted for brevity
}

void trickyFunction(ComplicatedClass* obj) throw(exception)
{
    if (debug) {
        // If in debug mode, print the values with which this function starts
        debugOstr << "trickyFunction(): given argument: " << *obj << endl;
    }

    while (true) {
        UserCommand cmd = getNextCommand(obj);
        if (debug) {
            debugOstr << "trickyFunction(): retrieved cmd " << cmd << endl;
        }
```

```
            try {
                processUserCommand(cmd);
            } catch (exception& e) {
                if (debug) {
                    debugOstr << "trickyFunction(): "
                        << " received exception from procesUserCommand(): "
                        << e.what() << endl;
                }
                throw;
            }
        }
    }
```

Run-Time Debug Mode

The most flexible way to provide a debug mode is to allow it to be enabled or disabled at run time. One way to provide this feature is to supply an asynchronous interface that controls debug mode on the fly. In a GUI program, this interface could take the form of a menu command. In a CLI program, this interface could be an asynchronous command that makes an interprocess call into the program (using sockets, signals, or remote procedure calls for example). C++ provides no standard way to perform interprocess communication or GUIs, so we do not show an example of this technique.

Ring Buffers

Debug mode is useful for debugging reproducible problems and for running tests. However, bugs often appear when the program is running in nondebug mode, and by the time you or the customer enables debug mode, it is too late to gain any information about the bug. One solution to this problem is to enable tracing in your program at all times. You usually need only the most recent traces to debug a program, so you should store only the most recent traces at any point in a program's execution. One way to provide this limitation is through careful use of log file rotations.

However, in order to avoid the problems with logging traces described earlier in the "Error Logging" section, it is better if your program doesn't log these traces at all; it should store them in memory. Then, it should provide a mechanism to dump all the trace messages to standard error or to a log file if the need arises. A common technique is to use a *ring buffer* to store a fixed number of messages, or messages in a fixed amount of memory. When the buffer fills up, it starts writing messages at the beginning of the buffer again, overwriting the older messages. This cycle can repeat indefinitely. The following sections provide an implementation of a ring buffer and show you how you can use it in your programs.

Ring Buffer Interface

```cpp
#include <vector>
#include <string>
#include <fstream>

using std::string;
using std::vector;
using std::ostream;

//
// class RingBuffer
//
// Provides a simple debug buffer. The client specifies the number
// of entries in the constructor and adds messages with the addEntry()
```

```
// method. Once the number of entries exceeds the number allowed, new
// entries overwrite the oldest entries in the buffer.
//
// The buffer also provides the option to print entries as they
// are added to the buffer. The client can specify an output stream
// in the constructor, and can reset it with the setOutput() method.
//
// Finally, the buffer supports streaming to an output stream.
//
class RingBuffer
{
    public:
        //
        // Constructs a ring buffer with space for numEntries.
        // Entries are written to *ostr as they are queued.
        //
        RingBuffer(int numEntries = kDefaultNumEntries, ostream* ostr = NULL);
        ~RingBuffer();

        //
        // Adds the string to the ring buffer, possibly overwriting the
        // oldest string in the buffer (if the buffer is full).
        //
        void addEntry(const string& entry);

        //
        // Streams the buffer entries, separated by newlines, to ostr.
        //
        friend ostream& operator<<(ostream& ostr, const RingBuffer& rb);

        //
        // Sets the output stream to which entries are streamed as they are added.
        // Returns the old output stream.
        //
        ostream* setOutput(ostream* newOstr);

    protected:
        vector<string> mEntries;
        ostream* mOstr;

        int mNumEntries, mNext;
        bool mWrapped;

        static const int kDefaultNumEntries = 500;

    private:
        // Prevent assignment and pass-by-value.
        RingBuffer(const RingBuffer& src);
        RingBuffer& operator=(const RingBuffer& rhs);
};
```

Ring Buffer Implementation

This implementation of the ring buffer stores a fixed number of strings. Each of these strings must be copied into the ring buffer, requiring dynamic allocation of memory. This approach certainly is not the most efficient solution. Other possibilities would be to provide a fixed number of bytes of memory for the buffer. However, that requires mucking with low-level C-strings and memory management, which you should avoid whenever possible. This implementation should be sufficient unless you're writing a high-performance application.

This ring buffer uses the STL vector to store the string entries. You could also use a standard C-style array. The use of the STL is straightforward except for the implementation of `operator<<` for the `RingBuffer`, which employs some fancy iterators. Consult Chapters 21, 22, and 23 for the details of iterators and the copy algorithm.

```cpp
#include <algorithm>
#include <iterator>
#include <iostream>
#include "RingBuffer.h"

using namespace std;

const int RingBuffer::kDefaultNumEntries;

//
// Initialize the vector to hold exactly numEntries. The vector size
// does not need to change during the lifetime of the object.
//
// Initialize the other members.
//
RingBuffer::RingBuffer(int numEntries, ostream* ostr) : mEntries(numEntries),
    mOstr(ostr), mNumEntries(numEntries), mNext(0), mWrapped(false)
{
}

RingBuffer::~RingBuffer()
{
}

//
// The algorithm is pretty simple: add the entry to the next
// free spot, then reset mNext to indicate the free spot after
// that. If mNext reaches the end of the vector, it starts over at 0.
//
// The buffer needs to know if the buffer has wrapped or not so
// that it knows whether to print the entries past mNext in operator<<
//
void RingBuffer::addEntry(const string& entry)
{
    // Add the entry to the next free spot and increment
    // mNext to point to the free spot after that.
    mEntries[mNext++] = entry;

    // Check if we've reached the end of the buffer. If so, we need to wrap.
    if (mNext >= mNumEntries) {
        mNext = 0;
        mWrapped = true;
    }

    // If there is a valid ostream, write this entry to it.
```

```cpp
    if (mOstr != NULL) {
        *mOstr << entry << endl;
    }
}

ostream* RingBuffer::setOutput(ostream* newOstr)
{
    ostream* ret = mOstr;
    mOstr = newOstr;
    return (ret);
}


//
// This function uses an ostream_iterator to "copy" entries directly
// from the vector to the output stream.
//
// This function must print the entries in order. If the buffer has wrapped,
// the earliest entry is one past the most recent entry, which is the entry
// indicated by mNext. So first print from entry mNext to the end.
//
// Then (even if the buffer hasn't wrapped) print from the beginning to mNext - 1.
//
ostream& operator<<(ostream& ostr, const RingBuffer& rb)
{
    if (rb.mWrapped) {
        //
        // If the buffer has wrapped, print the elements from
        // the earliest entry to the end.
        //
        copy (rb.mEntries.begin() + rb.mNext, rb.mEntries.end(),
            ostream_iterator<string>(ostr, "\n"));
    }

    //
    // Now print up to the most recent entry.
    // Go up to begin() + mNext because the range is not inclusive on the
    // right side.
    //
    copy (rb.mEntries.begin(), rb.mEntries.begin() + rb.mNext,
        ostream_iterator<string>(ostr, "\n"));

    return (ostr);
}
```

Using the Ring Buffer

In order to use the ring buffer, you can simply declare an object and start adding messages to it. When you want to print the buffer, just use `operator<<` to print it to the appropriate `ostream`. Here is the earlier start-time debug mode program modified to show use of a ring buffer instead:

```cpp
#include "RingBuffer.h"
#include <exception>
#include <fstream>
#include <iostream>
#include <cassert>
```

```cpp
#include <sstream>
using namespace std;

RingBuffer debugBuf;

class ComplicatedClass
{
    public:
        ComplicatedClass() {}
        ~ComplicatedClass() {}
};

class UserCommand
{
    public:
        UserCommand() {}
};

ostream& operator<<(ostream& ostr, const ComplicatedClass& src);
ostream& operator<<(ostream& ostr, const UserCommand& src);
UserCommand getNextCommand(ComplicatedClass* obj);
void processUserCommand(UserCommand& cmd);
void trickyFunction(ComplicatedClass* obj) throw(exception);

int main(int argc, char** argv)
{
    // Print the command-line arguments.
    for (int i = 0; i < argc; i++) {
        debugBuf.addEntry(argv[i]);
    }

    trickyFunction(new ComplicatedClass());

    // Print the current contents of the debug buffer to cout.
    cout << debugBuf;

    return (0);
}

ostream& operator<<(ostream& ostr, const ComplicatedClass& src)
{
    ostr << "ComplicatedClass";
    return (ostr);
}

ostream& operator<<(ostream& ostr, const UserCommand& src)
{
    ostr << "UserCommand";
    return (ostr);
}

UserCommand getNextCommand(ComplicatedClass* obj)
{
    UserCommand cmd;
    return (cmd);
}
```

```
void processUserCommand(UserCommand& cmd)
{
    // Details omitted for brevity
}

void trickyFunction(ComplicatedClass* obj) throw(exception)
{
    assert(obj != NULL);

    // Trace log the values with which this function starts.
    ostringstream ostr;
    ostr << "trickyFunction(): given argument: " << *obj;
    debugBuf.addEntry(ostr.str());

    while (true) {
        UserCommand cmd = getNextCommand(obj);

        ostringstream ostr;
        ostr << "trickyFunction(): retrieved cmd " << cmd;
        debugBuf.addEntry(ostr.str());

        try {
            processUserCommand(cmd);
        } catch (exception& e) {
            string msg = "trickyFunction(): received exception from procesUserCommand():";
            msg += e.what();
            debugBuf.addEntry(msg);
            throw;
        }
        break;
    }
}
```

Note that this interface to the ring buffer sometimes requires you to construct strings using `ostringstream`s or `string` concatenation before adding entries to the buffer.

Displaying the Ring Buffer Contents

Storing trace debug messages in memory is a great start, but in order for them to be useful, you need a way to access these traces for debugging. Your program should provide a "hook" to tell it to print the messages. This hook could be similar to the interface you would use to enable debugging at run time. Additionally, if your program encounters a fatal error that causes it to exit, it should print the ring buffer to standard error or to a log file before exiting.

Another way to retrieve these messages is to obtain a memory dump of the program. Each platform handles memory dumps differently, so you should consult a book or expert on your platform.

Asserts

The `assert` macro in the `<cassert>` library is a powerful tool. It takes a Boolean expression and, if the expression evaluates to `false`, prints an error message and terminates the program. If the expression evaluates to `true`, it does nothing. Although this behavior may not sound particularly helpful, it turns out to be quite useful in some cases. It allows you to "force" your program to exhibit a bug at the exact point where that bug originates. If you didn't assert at that point, your program might proceed with those incorrect values, and the bug might not show up until much later. Thus, asserts allow you to detect bugs earlier than you otherwise would.

> *The behavior of **assert** depends on the **NDEBUG** preprocessor symbol: if the symbol is not defined, the assertion takes place, otherwise it is ignored. Compilers often define this symbol when compiling "debug" builds. If you want to leave asserts in run time code, you must specify your compiler settings, or write your own version of **assert** that isn't affected by the value of **NDEBUG**.*

You should use asserts in your code whenever you are "assuming" something about the state of your variables. For example, if you call a library function that is supposed to return a pointer and claims never to return NULL, throw in an assert after the function call to make sure that pointer isn't NULL.

Note that you should assume as little as possible. For example, if you are writing a library function, don't assert that the parameters are valid. Instead, check the parameters and return an error code or throw an exception if they are invalid. Asserts should be reserved for cases in which you have no other option. For example, in the start-time debugging example, the function trickyFunction() takes a parameter of type ComplicatedClass*. Instead of assuming that the argument is valid, it might be a good idea to assert it like this:

```
#include <cassert>

void trickyFunction(ComplicatedClass* obj) throw(exception)
{
    assert(obj != NULL);
    // Remainder of the function omitted for brevity
}
```

> **Be careful not to put any code that must be executed for correct program functioning inside** asserts. **For example, a line like this is asking for trouble:** assert(myFunctionCall() != NULL). **If a release build in your code strips** asserts, **then the call to** myFunctionCall() **will be missing as well!**

Debugging Techniques

Debugging a program can be incredibly frustrating. However, with a systematic approach it becomes significantly easier. Your first step in trying to debug a program should always be to reproduce the bug. Depending on whether or not you can reproduce the bug, your subsequent approach will differ. The next three sections explain how to reproduce bugs, how to debug reproducible bugs, and how to debug nonreproducible bugs. Additional sections explain details about debugging memory errors and debugging multithreaded programs.

Reproducing Bugs

If you can reproduce the bug consistently, it will be much easier to determine the root cause. Any reproducible bug can be root-caused and fixed. Bugs that are not reproducible are difficult, if not impossible, to root-cause. As a first step to reproduce the bug, run the program with exactly the same inputs as the run when the bug first appeared. Be sure to include all inputs, from the program's startup to the time of the bug's appearance. A common mistake is to attempt to reproduce the bug by performing only the triggering action. This technique may not reproduce the bug because the bug might be caused by an entire sequence of actions. For example, if your Web browser program dies with a segmentation violation when you request a certain Web page, it may be due to memory corruption triggered by that particular request's network address. On the other hand, it may be because your program records all requests in a queue, with space for one million entries, and this entry was number one million and one. Starting the program over and sending one request certainly wouldn't trigger the bug in that case.

Sometimes it is impossible to emulate the entire sequence of events that leads to the bug. Perhaps the bug was reported by someone who can't remember everything that he or she did. Alternatively, maybe the program was running for too long to emulate every input. In that case, simply do your best to reproduce the bug. It takes some guesswork, and can be time-consuming, but effort at this point will save time later in the debugging process. Here are some techniques you can try:

- Repeat the triggering action in the correct environment and with as many inputs as possible similar to the initial report.

- Run automated tests that exercise similar functionality. Reproducing bugs is one benefit of automated tests. If it takes 24 hours of testing before the bug shows up, it's preferable to let those tests run on their own rather than spend 24 hours of your time trying to reproduce it.

- If you have the necessary hardware available, running slight variations of tests concurrently on different machines can sometimes save time.

- Run stress tests that exercise similar functionality. If your program is a Web server that died on a particular request, try running millions of browsers simultaneously that make that request.

After you are able to reproduce the bug consistently, you should attempt to determine the simplest and most efficient test case to reproduce it. That makes it simpler to root-cause the problem and easier to verify the fix.

Debugging Reproducible Bugs

When you can reproduce a bug consistently and efficiently, it's time to figure out the problem in the code that causes the bug. Your goal at this point is to find the exact lines of code that trigger the problem. You can use two different strategies:

1. `cout` **debugging.** By adding enough debug messages to your program and watching its output when you reproduce the bug, you should be able to pinpoint the exact lines of code where the bug occurs. If you have a debugger at your disposal, this method is usually not recommended because it requires modifications to the program and can be time-consuming. However, if you have already instrumented your program with debug messages as described earlier, you might be able to root-cause your bug simply by running your program in debug mode while reproducing the bug. This technique may actually be faster than firing up a debugger.

2. **Using a debugger.** We hope that you are familiar with debuggers, which allow you to step through the execution of your program and to view the state of memory and the values of variables at various points. If you have not yet used debuggers, you should learn to use them as soon as possible. They are often indispensable tools for root-causing bugs. When you have access to the source code, you will use a *symbolic debugger*: a debugger that utilizes the variable

names, class names, and other symbols in your code. In order to use a symbolic debugger you must compile your program with debugging information included. Otherwise, the symbol information is stripped from the program executable and is not available in the debugger.

The debugging example at the end of this chapter demonstrates both these approaches.

Debugging Nonreproducible Bugs

Fixing bugs that are not reproducible is significantly more difficult than root-causing reproducible bugs. You often have very little information and must employ a lot of guesswork. Nevertheless, a few strategies can aid you:

1. Try to turn a nonreproducible bug into a reproducible bug. By using educated guesses, you can often determine approximately where the bug lies. It's worthwhile to spend some time trying to reproduce the bug. Once you have a reproducible bug you can figure out its root cause using the techniques described earlier.

2. Analyze error logs. Hopefully, you instrumented your program with error log generation as described previously. You should sift through this information because any errors that were logged directly before the bug occurred are likely to have contributed to the bug itself. If you're lucky (or if you coded your program well), your program will have logged the exact reason for the bug at hand!

3. Obtain and analyze traces. Hopefully you instrumented your program with tracing output via a ring buffer as described previously. At the time of the bug's occurrence, you hopefully obtained a copy of the traces. These traces should lead you right to the location of the bug in your code.

4. Examine a *memory dump* file, if it exists. Some platforms generate memory dump files of applications that terminate abnormally. On Unix these memory dumps are called *core files*. Each platform provides tools for analyzing these memory dumps. Even without symbolic debugging information, you can often obtain a surprising amount of information from these files. For example, you can usually generate a stack trace of the application before its death because global symbols such as function and method names are usually available in stripped binaries. If you are familiar with the assembly of your platform, you can disassemble the machine code to get assembly code. In addition, you can view the contents of memory, although without symbols it is untyped and unnamed.

5. Inspect the code. Unfortunately, this is often the only strategy to determine the cause of a nonreproducible bug. Surprisingly, it often works. When you examine code, even code that you wrote yourself, with the perspective of the bug that just occurred, you can often find mistakes that you overlooked previously. We don't recommend spending hours staring at your code, but tracing through the code path by hand will often lead you directly to the problem.

6. Use a memory-watching tool, such as one of those described in the "Debugging Memory Problems" section, which follows. Such tools will often alert you to memory errors that don't always cause your program to misbehave, but could potentially be the cause of the bug at hand.

7. File or update a bug report. Even if you can't find the root cause of the bug right away, the report will be a useful record of your attempts if the problem is encountered again. Consult Chapter 19 for details on bug-tracking systems.

Once you have root-caused a nonreproducible bug, you should create a reproducible test case and move it to the "reproducible bugs" category. It is important to be able to reproduce a bug before you actually fix it. Otherwise, how will you test the fix? A common mistake when debugging nonreproducible bugs is to fix the wrong problem in the code. Because you can't reproduce the bug, you don't know if you've really fixed it, so don't be surprised when it shows up again a month later.

Debugging Memory Problems

Most catastrophic bugs, such as application death, are caused by memory errors. Many noncatastrophic bugs are triggered by memory errors as well. Some memory bugs are obvious: if your program attempts to dereference a NULL pointer, it will terminate immediately. However, others are more insidious. If you write past the end of an array in C++, your program will probably not crash directly at that point. However, if that array was on the stack, you may have written into a different variable or array, changing values that won't show up until later in the program. Alternatively, if the array was on the heap, you could cause memory corruption in the heap, which will cause errors later when you attempt to allocate or free more memory dynamically. Chapter 13 introduced some of the common memory errors from the perspective of what to avoid when you're coding. This section discusses memory errors from the perspective of identifying problems in code that exhibits bugs. You should be familiar with the discussion in Chapter 13 before reading this section.

Categories of Memory Errors

In order to debug memory problems you should be familiar with the types of errors that can occur. This section describes the major categories of memory errors. Each memory error includes a small code example demonstrating the error and a list of possible *symptoms* that you might observe. Note that a symptom is not the same thing as a bug itself: a symptom is an observable behavior caused by a bug.

Memory Freeing Errors

This following table summarizes the five major errors involving freeing memory.

Error Type	Symptoms	Example

Memory leak	Process grows over time. Process runs slower over time. Eventually, commands and system calls fail because of lack of memory.	```void memoryLeak()
		{
		    int* ip = new int[1000];
		    return; // Bug! Not freeing ip.
		}```

Using mismatched allocation and free commands	Does not usually cause a program crash immediately. Can cause memory corruption on some platforms, which might show up as a program crash (segmentation violation) later in the program.	```void mismatchedFree()
		{
		    int* ip1 = (int *)malloc(sizeof(int));
		    int* ip2 = new int;
		    int* ip3 = new int[1000];
		
		    delete ip1; // BUG! Should use free
		    delete[] ip2; // BUG! Should use delete
		    free (ip3); // BUG! Should use delete[]
		}```

Error Type	Symptoms	Example
Freeing memory more than once	Can cause a program crash (segmentation violation) If the memory at that location has been handed out in another allocation between the two calls to delete.	```void doubleFree()\n{\n int* ip1 = new int[1000];\n delete[] ip1;\n int* ip2 = new int[1000];\n delete[] ip1; // BUG! freeing ip1 twice\n}```
Freeing unallocated memory	Will usually cause a program crash (segmentation violation or bus error).	```void freeUnallocated()\n{\n int* ip1 =\n reinterpret_cast<int*>(10000);\n // BUG! ip1 is not a valid pointer.\n delete ip1;\n}```
Freeing stack memory	Technically a special case of freeing unallocated memory. Will usually cause a program crash.	```void freeStack()\n{\n int x;\n int* ip = &x;\n delete ip; // BUG! Freeing stack memory\n}```

As you can see, some of the memory free errors do not cause immediate program termination. These bugs are more subtle, leading to problems later in the run of the program.

Memory Access Errors

The second category of memory errors involves the actual reading and writing of memory.

Error Type	Symptoms	Example
Accessing Invalid Memory	Almost always causes program to crash immediately.	```void accessInvalid()\n{\n int* ip1 =\n reinterpret_cast<int*>(10000);\n // BUG! ip1 is not a valid pointer.\n *ip1 = 5;\n}```

Table continued on following page

Error Type	Symptoms	Example
| Accessing Freed Memory | Does not usually cause a program crash. If the memory has been handed out in another allocation, can cause "strange" values to appear unexpectedly. | ```cpp
void accessFreed()
{
    int* ip1 = new int;
    delete ip1;
    int* ip2 = new int;

    // BUG! The memory pointed to by ip1
    // has been freed.
    *ip1 = 5;
}
``` |
| Accessing Memory in a Different Allocation | Does not cause a program crash. Can cause "strange" values to appear unexpectedly. | ```cpp
void accessElsewhere()
{
    int x, y[10], z;
    x = 0;
    z = 0;

    // BUG! element 10 is past the
    // end of the array.
    for (int i = 0; i <= 10; i++) {
        y[i] = 10;
    }
}
``` |
| Reading Uninitialized Memory | Does not cause a program crash unless you use the uninitialized value as a pointer and dereference it (as in the example). Even then, it will not always cause a program crash. | ```cpp
void readUninitialized()
{
    int* ip;

    // BUG! ip is uninitialized.
    cout << *ip << endl;
}
``` |

Memory access errors are more likely than memory free errors to cause program crashes. However, they don't always do so. They can instead lead to subtle noncatastrophic bugs in your program.

Tips for Debugging Memory Errors

Memory-related bugs often show up in slightly different places in the code each time you run the program. This is usually the case with heap memory corruption. Heap memory corruption is like a time bomb, ready to explode at some attempt to allocate, free, or use memory on the heap. So, when you see a bug that is reproducible, but shows up in slightly different places, suspect memory corruption. For example, the program might get a segmentation violation one time followed by a bus error the next time.

If you suspect a memory bug, your best option is to use a memory-checking tool for C++. Debuggers often provide options to run the program while checking for memory errors. Additionally, there are some excellent third-party tools such as purify from Rational Software (now owned by IBM) or valgrind for Linux (discussed in Chapter 13). These debuggers and tools work by interposing their own memory allocation and freeing routines in order to check for any misuse of dynamic memory, such as freeing unallocated memory, dereferencing unallocated memory, or writing off the end of an array.
```

If you don't have a memory-checking tool at your disposal, and the normal strategies for debugging are not helping, you may need to resort to code inspection. Once you've narrowed down the part of the code containing the bug, here are some specific items to look for.

Object and Class-related Errors

❑ Verify that your classes with dynamically allocated memory have destructors that free exactly the memory that's allocated in the object: no more, and no less.

❑ Ensure that your classes handle copying and assignment correctly with copy constructors and assignment operators, as described in Chapter 9.

❑ Check for suspicious casts. If you are casting a pointer to an object from one type to another, make sure that it's valid.

General Memory Errors

❑ Make sure that every call to new is matched with exactly one call to delete. Similarly, every call to malloc, alloc, or calloc should be matched with one call to free. And every call to new[] should be matched with one call to delete[]. Although duplicate free calls are generally harmless, they can cause problems if that same memory was handed out in a different memory allocation call after the first free.

❑ Check for buffer overruns. Anytime you iterate over an array or write into or read from a C-style string, verify that you are not accessing memory past the end of the array.

❑ Check for dereferencing invalid pointers.

Debugging Multithreaded Programs

Unlike in Java, the C++ language does not provide any mechanisms for threading and synchronization between threads. However, multithreaded C++ programs are common, so it is important to think about the special issues involved in debugging a multithreaded program. Bugs in multithreaded programs are often caused by variations in timing in the operating system scheduling, and can be difficult to reproduce. Thus, debugging multithreaded programs takes a special set of techniques:

1. Use cout debugging. When debugging multithreaded programs, cout debugging is often more effective than using a debugger. Most debuggers do not handle multiple threads of execution very well, or at least don't make it easy to debug a multithreaded program. It is difficult to step through your program when you don't know which thread will run at any given time. Add debug statements to your program before and after critical sections, and before acquiring and after releasing locks. Often by watching this output, you will be able to detect deadlocks and race conditions because you will be able to see that two threads are in a critical section at the same time or that one thread is stuck waiting for a lock.

2. Insert forced sleeps and context switches. If you are having trouble reproducing the problem consistently, or have a hunch about the root cause but want to verify it, you can force certain thread-scheduling behavior by making your threads sleep for specified amounts of time. Although there is no standard way in C++ to make a thread sleep, most platforms provide a call, often called sleep(). Sleeping for several seconds right before releasing a lock, immediately before signaling a condition variable, or directly before accessing shared data can reveal race conditions that would otherwise go undetected.

Debugging Example: Article Citations

This section presents a buggy program and shows you the steps to take in order to debug it and fix the problem.

Suppose that you're part of a team writing a Web page that allows users to search for the research articles that cite a particular paper. This type of service is useful for authors who are trying to find work similar to their own. Once they find one paper representing a related work, they can look for every paper that cites that one to find other related work.

In this project, you are responsible for the code that reads the raw citations data from text files. For simplicity, assume that the citation info for each paper is found in its own file. Furthermore, assume that the first line of each file contains the author, title, and publication info for the paper; the second line is always empty; and all subsequent lines contain the citations from the article (one on each line). Here is an example file for one of the most important papers in Computer Science:

```
Alan Turing,"On Computable Numbers with an Application to the Entscheidungsproblem",\
Proceedings of the London Mathematical Society, Series 2, Vol.42 (1936 - 37) pages\
230 to 265.
Godel, "Uber formal unentscheidbare Satze der Principia Mathernatica und verwant der\
Systeme, I", Monatshefte Math. Phys., 38 (1931). 173-198.
Alonzo Church. "An unsolvable problem of elementary number theory", American J of\
Math., 58(1936), 345 363.
Alonzo Church. "A note on the Entscheidungsproblem", J. of Symbolic logic, 1 (1930),\
40 41.
Cf. Hobson, "Theory of functions of a real variable (2nd ed., 1921)", 87, 88.\
Proc. London Math. Soc (2) 42 (1936 7), 230 265.
```

Note that the \ character is the continuation character to ensure that the computer treats the multiple lines as a single line during processing.

Buggy Implementation of an ArticleCitations Class

You decide to structure your program by writing an ArticleCitations class that reads the file and stores the information. This class stores the article info from the first line in one string, and the citations info in an array of strings. Please note that this design decision is not necessarily the best possible. However, for the purposes of illustrating buggy applications, it's perfect! The class definition looks like this:

```cpp
#include <string>
using std::string;

class ArticleCitations
{
    public:
        ArticleCitations(const string& fileName);
        ~ArticleCitations();
        ArticleCitations(const ArticleCitations& src);
        ArticleCitations& operator=(const ArticleCitations& rhs);
```

```
        string getArticle() const { return mArticle; }
        int getNumCitations() const { return mNumCitations; }
        string getCitation(int i) const { return mCitations[i]; }

    protected:
        void readFile(const string& fileName);

        string mArticle;
        string* mCitations;
        int mNumCitations;
};
```

The implementations of the methods follow. This program is buggy! Don't use it verbatim or as a model.

```
#include "ArticleCitations.h"
#include <iostream>
#include <fstream>
#include <string>
#include <stdexcept>
using namespace std;

ArticleCitations::ArticleCitations(const string& fileName)
{
    // All we have to do is read the file.
    readFile(fileName);
}

ArticleCitations::ArticleCitations(const ArticleCitations& src)
{
    // Copy the article name, author, etc.
    mArticle = src.mArticle;
    // Copy the number of citations.
    mNumCitations = src.mNumCitations;
    // Allocate an array of the correct size.
    mCitations = new string[mNumCitations];
    // Copy each element of the array.
    for (int i = 0; i < mNumCitations; i++) {
        mCitations[i] = src.mCitations[i];
    }
}

ArticleCitations& ArticleCitations::operator=(const ArticleCitations& rhs)
{
    // Check for self-assignment.
    if (this == &rhs) {
        return (*this);
    }
    // Free the old memory.
    delete [] mCitations;
    // Copy the article name, author, etc.
    mArticle = rhs.mArticle;
    // Copy the number of citations.
    mNumCitations = rhs.mNumCitations;
    // Allocate a new array of the correct size.
    mCitations = new string[mNumCitations];
```

```
        // Copy each citation.
        for (int i = 0; i < mNumCitations; i++) {
            mCitations[i] = rhs.mCitations[i];
        }
        return (*this);
}

ArticleCitations::~ArticleCitations()
{
    delete[] mCitations;
}

void ArticleCitations::readFile(const string& fileName)
{
    // Open the file and check for failure.
    ifstream istr(fileName.c_str());
    if (istr.fail()) {
        throw invalid_argument("Unable to open file\n");
    }
    // Read the article author, title, etc. line.
    getline(istr, mArticle);

    // Skip the white space before the citations start.
    istr >> ws;

    int count = 0;
    // Save the current position so we can return to it.
    int citationsStart = istr.tellg();
    // First count the number of citations.
    while (!istr.eof()) {
        string temp;
        getline(istr, temp);
        // Skip white space before the next entry.
        istr >> ws;
        count++;
    }

    if (count != 0) {
        // Allocate an array of strings to store the citations.
        mCitations = new string[count];
        mNumCitations = count;
        // Seek back to the start of the citations.
        istr.seekg(citationsStart);
        // Read each citation and store it in the new array.
        for (count = 0; count < mNumCitations; count++) {
            string temp;
            getline(istr, temp);
            mCitations[count] = temp;
        }
    }
}
```

Testing the ArticleCitations class

Following the advice of Chapter 19, you decide you unit test your ArticleCitations class before proceeding, though for simplicity in this example, the unit test does not use a test framework. The following program asks the user for a filename, constructs an `ArticleCitations` class with that filename, and passes the object by value to the `processCitations()` function, which prints out the info using the public accessor methods on the object.

```
#include "ArticleCitations.h"
#include <iostream>
using namespace std;

void processCitations(ArticleCitations cit);

int main(int argc, char** argv)
{
    string fileName;

    while (true) {
        cout << "Enter a file name (\"STOP\" to stop): ";
        cin >> fileName;

        if (fileName == "STOP") {
            break;
        }
        // Test constructor
        ArticleCitations cit(fileName);
        processCitations(cit);
    }
    return (0);
}

void processCitations(ArticleCitations cit)
{
    cout << cit.getArticle() << endl;
    int num = cit.getNumCitations();
    for (int i = 0; i < num; i++) {
        cout << cit.getCitation(i) << endl;
    }
}
```

cout Debugging

You decide to test the program on the Alan Turing example (stored in a file called `paper1.txt`). Here is the output:

```
Enter a file name ("STOP" to stop): paper1.txt
Alan Turing."On Computable Numbers with an Application to the
Entscheidungsproblem", Proceedings of the London Mathematical Society, Series 2,
Vol.42 (1936 - 37) pages 230 to 265.




Enter a file name ("STOP" to stop): STOP
```

That doesn't look right! There are supposed to be five citations printed instead of five blank lines.

For this bug, you decide to try good ole cout debugging. In this case, it makes sense to start by looking at the function that reads the citations from the file. If that doesn't work right, then obviously the object won't have the citations. You can modify readFile() as follows:

```
void ArticleCitations::readFile(const string& fileName)
{
    // Open the file and check for failure.
    ifstream istr(fileName.c_str());
    if (istr.fail()) {
        throw invalid_argument("Unable to open file\n");
    }
    // Read the article author, title, etc. line.
    getline(istr, mArticle);

    // Skip the white space before the citations start.
    istr >> ws;

    int count = 0;
    // Save the current position so we can return to it.
    int citationsStart = istr.tellg();
    // First count the number of citations.
    cout << "readFile(): counting number of citations\n";
    while (!istr.eof()) {
        string temp;
        getline(istr, temp);
        // Skip white space before the next entry.
        istr >> ws;
        cout << "Citation " << count << ": " << temp << endl;
        count++;
    }

    cout << "Found " << count << " citations\n" << endl;
    cout << "readFile(): reading citations\n";
    if (count != 0) {
        // Allocate an array of strings to store the citations.
        mCitations = new string[count];
        mNumCitations = count;
        // Seek back to the start of the citations.
        istr.seekg(citationsStart);
        // Read each citation and store it in the new array.
        for (count = 0; count < mNumCitations; count++) {
            string temp;
            getline(istr, temp);
            cout << temp << endl;
            mCitations[count] = temp;
        }
    }
}
```

Running the same test on this program gives this output:

```
Enter a file name ("STOP" to stop): paper1.txt
readFile(): counting number of citations
Citation 0: Godel, "Uber formal unentscheidbare Satze der Principia Mathematica
und verwant der Systeme, I", Monatshefte Math. Phys., 38 (1931). 173-198.
```

Citation 1: Alonzo Church. "An unsolvable problem of elementary number theory", American J of Math., 58(1936), 345 363.
Citation 2: Alonzo Church. "A note on the Entscheidungsproblem", J. of Symbolic logic, 1 (1930), 40 41.
Citation 3: Cf. Hobson, "Theory of functions of a real variable (2nd ed., 1921)", 87, 88.
Citation 4: Proc. London Math. Soc (2) 42 (1936 7), 230 265.
Found 5 citations

readFile(): reading citations

Alan Turing,"On Computable Numbers with an Application to the
Entscheidungsproblem", Proceedings of the London Mathematical Society, Series 2,
Vol.42 (1936 - 37) pages 230 to 265.

Enter a file name ("STOP" to stop):

As you can see from the output, the first time the program reads the citations from the file, in order to count them, they are read correctly. However, the second time, they are not read correctly. Why not? One way to delve deeper into this issue is to add some debugging code to check the state of the file stream after each attempt to read a citation:

```cpp
void printStreamState(const istream& istr)
{
    if (istr.good()) {
        cout << "stream state is good\n";
    }
    if (istr.bad()) {
        cout << "stream state is bad\n";
    }
    if (istr.fail()) {
        cout << "stream state is fail\n";
    }
    if (istr.eof()) {
        cout << "stream state is eof\n";
    }
}
```

```cpp
void ArticleCitations::readFile(const string& fileName)
{
    // Open the file and check for failure.
    ifstream istr(fileName.c_str());
    if (istr.fail()) {
        throw invalid_argument("Unable to open file\n");
    }
    // Read the article author, title, etc. line.
    getline(istr, mArticle);
```

```
        // Skip the white space before the citations start.
        istr >> ws;

        int count = 0;
        // Save the current position so we can return to it.
        int citationsStart = istr.tellg();
        // First count the number of citations.
        cout << "readFile(): counting number of citations\n";
        while (!istr.eof()) {
            string temp;
            getline(istr, temp);
            // Skip white space before the next entry.
            istr >> ws;
            printStreamState(istr);
            cout << "Citation " << count << ": " << temp << endl;
            count++;
        }

        cout << "Found " << count << " citations\n" << endl;
        cout << "readFile(): reading citations\n";
        if (count != 0) {
            // Allocate an array of strings to store the citations.
            mCitations = new string[count];
            mNumCitations = count;
            // Seek back to the start of the citations.
            istr.seekg(citationsStart);
            // Read each citation and store it in the new array.
            for (count = 0; count < mNumCitations; count++) {
                string temp;
                getline(istr, temp);
                printStreamState(istr);
                cout << temp << endl;
                mCitations[count] = temp;
            }
        }
    }
```

When you run your program this time, you find some interesting information:

```
Enter a file name ("STOP" to stop): paper1.txt
readFile(): counting number of citations
stream state is good
Citation 0: Godel, "Uber formal unentscheidbare Satze der Principia Mathernatica
und verwant der Systeme, I", Monatshefte Math. Phys., 38 (1931). 173-198.
stream state is good
Citation 1: Alonzo Church. "An unsolvable problem of elementary number theory",
American J of Math., 58(1936), 345 363.
stream state is good
Citation 2: Alonzo Church. "A note on the Entscheidungsproblem", J. of Symbolic
logic, 1 (1930), 40 41.
stream state is good
Citation 3: Cf. Hobson, "Theory of functions of a real variable (2nd ed., 1921)",
87, 88.
stream state is eof
Citation 4: Proc. London Math. Soc (2) 42 (1936 7), 230 265.
Found 5 citations
```

```
readFile(): reading citations
stream state is fail
stream state is eof

stream state is fail
stream state is eof

stream state is fail
stream state is eof

stream state is fail
stream state is eof

stream state is fail
stream state is eof
```

Alan Turing,"On Computable Numbers with an Application to the Entscheidungsproblem", Proceedings of the London Mathematical Society, Series 2, Vol.42 (1936 - 37) pages 230 to 265.

Enter a file name ("STOP" to stop):

It looks like the stream state is good until after the final citation is read for the first time. Then, the stream state is `eof`, because the end-of-file has been reached. That is expected. What is not expected is that the stream state is both `fail` and `eof` after all attempts to read the citations a second time. That doesn't appear to make sense at first: the code uses `seekg()` to seek back to the beginning of the citations before reading them a second time, so the file shouldn't still be at the end. However, recall from Chapter 13 that streams maintain their error and `eof` states until you clear them explicitly. `seekg()` doesn't clear the `eof` state automatically. When in an error or `eof` state, streams fail to read data correctly, which explains why the stream state is `fail` also after trying to read the citations a second time. A closer look at your method reveals that it fails to call `clear()` on the `istream` after reaching the end of file. If you modify the method by adding a call to `clear()`, it will read the citations properly.

Here is the corrected `readFile()` method without the debugging `cout` statements:

```cpp
void ArticleCitations::readFile(const string& fileName)
{
    // CODE OMMITTED FOR BREVITY

    if (count != 0) {
        // Allocate an array of strings to store the citations.
        mCitations = new string[count];
        mNumCitations = count;
        // Clear the previous eof.
        istr.clear();
        // Seek back to the start of the citations.
        istr.seekg(citationsStart);
        // Read each citation and store it in the new array.
        for (count = 0; count < mNumCitations; count++) {
            string temp;
```

```
                getline(istr, temp);
                mCitations[count] = temp;
            }
        }
    }
```

Using a Debugger

The following example uses the gdb debugger on the Linux operating system.

Now that your `ArticleCitations` class seems to work well on one citations file, you decide to blaze ahead and test some special cases, starting with a file with no citations. The file looks like this, and is stored in a file named `paper2.txt`:

```
Author with no citations
```

When you try to run your program on this file, you get the following result:

```
Enter a file name ("STOP" to stop): paper1.txt
Alan Turing."On Computable Numbers with an Application to the
Entscheidungsproblem", Proceedings of the London Mathematical Society, Series 2,
Vol.42 (1936 - 37) pages 230 to 265.
Godel, "Uber formal unentscheidbare Satze der Principia Mathernatica und verwant
der Systeme, I", Monatshefte Math. Phys., 38 (1931). 173-198.
Alonzo Church. "An unsolvable problem of elementary number theory", American J of
Math., 58(1936), 345 363.
Alonzo Church. "A note on the Entscheidungsproblem", J. of Symbolic logic, 1
(1930), 40 41.
Cf. Hobson, "Theory of functions of a real variable (2nd ed., 1921)", 87, 88.
Proc. London Math. Soc (2) 42 (1936 7), 230 265.
Enter a file name ("STOP" to stop): paper2.txt
Author with no citations
Segmentation fault
```

Oops. There must be some sort of memory error. This time you decide to give the debugger a shot. The Gnu DeBugger (gdb) is widely available on Unix platforms, and works quite well. First, you must compile your program with debugging info (-g with g++). After that, you can launch the program under gdb. Here's an example session using the debugger to root-cause this problem:

```
>gdb buggyprogram
GNU gdb Red Hat Linux (5.2-2)
Copyright 2002 Free Software Foundation, Inc.
GDB is free software, covered by the GNU General Public License, and you are
welcome to change it and/or distribute copies of it under certain conditions.
Type "show copying" to see the conditions.
There is absolutely no warranty for GDB.  Type "show warranty" for details.
This GDB was configured as "ia64-redhat-linux"...
(gdb) run
Starting program: buggyprogram
Enter a file name ("STOP" to stop): paper1.txt
Alan Turing."On Computable Numbers with an Application to the
Entscheidungsproblem", Proceedings of the London Mathematical Society, Series 2,
Vol.42 (1936 - 37) pages 230 to 265.
```

```
Godel, "Uber formal unentscheidbare Satze der Principia Mathernatica und verwant
der Systeme, I", Monatshefte Math. Phys., 38 (1931). 173-198.
Alonzo Church. "An unsolvable problem of elementary number theory", American J of
Math., 58(1936), 345 363.
Alonzo Church. "A note on the Entscheidungsproblem", J. of Symbolic logic, 1
(1930), 40 41.
Cf. Hobson, "Theory of functions of a real variable (2nd ed., 1921)", 87, 88.
Proc. London Math. Soc (2) 42 (1936 7), 230 265.
Enter a file name ("STOP" to stop): paper2.txt
Author with no citations

Program received signal SIGSEGV, Segmentation fault.
__libc_free (mem=0x6000000000010320) at malloc.c:3143
3143     malloc.c: No such file or directory.
         in malloc.c
Current language:  auto; currently c
```

When the SEGV occurs, the debugger allows you to poke around in the state of program at the time. The bt command shows the current stack trace. You can move up and down the function calls in the stack with up and down.

```
(gdb) bt
#0  __libc_free (mem=0x6000000000010320) at malloc.c:3143
#1  0x2000000000089010 in __builtin_delete ()
    from /usr/lib/libstdc++-libc6.2-2.so.3
#2  0x2000000000089050 in __builtin_vec_delete ()
    from /usr/lib/libstdc++-libc6.2-2.so.3
#3  0x400000000000a820 in ArticleCitations::~ArticleCitations (
    this=0x80000fffffffb920, __in_chrg=2) at ArticleCitations.cpp:51
#4  0x4000000000004f40 in main (argc=1, argv=0x80000fffffffb968)
    at BuggyProgram.cpp:20
```

One item of interest in this stack trace is that delete calls free(). It's actually fairly common for new and delete to be implemented in terms of malloc() and free(). More importantly, from this stack trace you can see that there seems to be some sort of problem in the ArticleCitations destructor. The list command shows the code in the current stack frame.

```
(gdb) up 3
#3  0x400000000000a820 in ArticleCitations::~ArticleCitations (
    this=0x80000fffffffb920, __in_chrg=2) at ArticleCitations.cpp:51
51         delete [] mCitations;
Current language:  auto; currently c++
(gdb) list
46         return (*this);
47      }
48
49      ArticleCitations::~ArticleCitations()
50      {
51         delete [] mCitations;
52      }
53
54      void ArticleCitations::readFile(const string& fileName)
{
```

The only thing in the destructor is a single `delete[]` call. In gdb, you can print values available in the current scope with `print`. In order to root-cause the problem, you can try printing some of the object member variables. Recall that the `string` type in C++ is really a `typedef` of the `basic_string` template instantiated for `chars`.

```
(gdb) print mCitations
$3 = (
    basic_string<char,string_char_traits<char>,__default_alloc_template<true, 0> >
*) 0x6000000000010338
```

Hmm, `mCitations` looks like a valid pointer (though it's hard to tell, of course).

```
(gdb) print mNumCitations
$2 = 5
```

Ah ha! Here's the problem. This article isn't supposed to have any citations. Why is `mNumCitations` set to 5? Take another look at the code in `readFile()` for the case that there are no citations. In that case, it looks like it never initializes `mNumCitations` and `mCitations`! The code is left with whatever junk is in memory already in those locations. In this case, the previous `ArticleCitations` object had the value 5 in `mNumCitations`. The second `ArticleCitations` object must have been placed in the same location in memory and so received that same value. However, the pointer value that it was assigned randomly is certainly not a valid pointer to delete! You need to initialize `mCitations` and `mNumCitations` whether or not you actually find any citations in the file. Here is the fixed code:

```
void ArticleCitations::readFile(const string& fileName)
{
    // CODE OMMITTED FOR BREVITY

    mCitations = NULL;
    mNumCitations = 0;
    if (count != 0) {
        // Allocate an array of strings to store the citations.
        mCitations = new string[count];
        mNumCitations = count;
        // Clear the previous eof.
        istr.clear();
        // Seek back to the start of the citations.
        istr.seekg(citationsStart);
        // Read each citation and store it in the new array.
        for (count = 0; count < mNumCitations; count++) {
            string temp;
            getline(istr, temp);
            mCitations[count] = temp;
        }
    }
}
```

As this example shows, memory errors don't always show up right away. It often takes a debugger and some persistence to figure them out.

If you attempt to replicate this debugging session on a different platform, you may find that, due to the vagaries of memory errors, the program crashes in a different place than this example shows.

Lessons from the ArticleCitations Example

You might be inclined to disregard this example as too small to be representative of real debugging. Although the buggy code is not lengthy, many classes that you write will not be much bigger, even in large projects. Thus, this example corroborates the message from Chapter 19 about the importance of unit testing. Imagine if you had failed to test this example thoroughly before integrating it with the rest of the project. If these bugs showed up later, you and other engineers would have to spend more time narrowing down the problem before you could debug it as shown here. Additionally, the techniques shown in this example apply to all debugging, large scale or small.

Summary

The most important concept in this chapter was the Fundamental Law of Debugging: avoid bugs when you're coding, but plan for bugs in your code. The reality of programming is that bugs will appear. If you've prepared your program properly, with error logging, debug traces in a ring buffer, and asserts, then the actual debugging will be significantly easier.

In addition to these techniques, this chapter also presented specific approaches for debugging bugs. The most important rule when actually debugging is to reproduce the problem. Then, you can use `cout` debugging or a symbolic debugger to track down the root cause. Memory errors present particular difficulties, and account for the majority of bugs in C++ code. This chapter described the various categories of memory bugs and their symptoms, and showed several examples of debugging errors in a program.

21

Delving into the STL: Containers and Iterators

Many programmers who claim to know C++ have never heard of the standard template library. As a Professional C++ programmer, it behooves you to familiarize yourself with its powerful capabilities. You can save yourself immeasurable time and energy by incorporating the STL containers and algorithms into your programs instead of writing and debugging your own versions. Now that you have read Chapters 1 through 20, and are an expert C++ designer, coder, tester, and debugger, it's time to master the STL.

Chapter 4 introduced the STL, described its basic philosophy and provided an overview of the various containers and algorithms. You should be familiar with that section of Chapter 4, as well as the content of most of the Chapters in Parts II and III, specifically Chapter 11 and Chapter 16.

This chapter begins a three-part tour of the STL by covering the STL containers, including:

- ❑ Containers Overview: requirements on elements, general error handling, and iterators.
- ❑ Sequential Containers: `vector`, `deque`, and `list`.
- ❑ Container Adapters: `queue`, `priority_queue`, and `stack`.
- ❑ Associative Containers: the `pair` utility, `map`, `multimap`, `set`, and `multiset`.
- ❑ Other Containers: arrays, `strings`, streams, and `bitset`.

Chapter 22 continues the STL by describing and showing examples of the generic algorithms that you can use on container elements. The chapter also describes the predefined function object classes in the STL and shows you how to use them effectively as callbacks with the algorithms.

Chapter 23 examines some advanced aspects of STL programming with a focus on customizing and extending the library. It covers using and writing allocators, using iterator adapters, writing algorithms, writing containers, and writing iterators.

Despite the depth of material found in this chapter and the next two, the standard template library is too large for this book to cover exhaustively. The resource material on the Web site contain a reference for the most useful parts of the standard library. Standard Library Header Files provides a summary of all the header files in the standard library, while the Standard Library Reference presents a reference for the various classes and algorithms in the STL. You should read Chapters 21 to 23 to learn about the STL, but keep in mind that they don't mention every method and member that the various classes provide, or show you the prototypes of every algorithm. Consult the appendices for those details.

Containers Overview

Recall from Chapter 4 that the containers in the STL are generic data structures useful for storing collections of data. You should rarely need to use a C-style array, write a linked list, or design a stack when you use the STL. The containers are implemented as templates, which allows you to instantiate them for any type that meets certain basic conditions outlined below.

The STL provides 11 containers, divided into four categories. The *sequential containers* include the vector (dynamic array), list, and deque. The *associative containers* include the map, multimap, set, and multiset. The *container adapters* include the queue, priority_queue, and stack. The final container, the bitset, is in a class of its own. Additionally, C-style arrays, C++ strings, and streams all can be used as STL containers to a certain degree.

> There is some debate about exactly which containers in C++ qualify as being part of the STL. This book is somewhat more inclusive in its definition than are others. Some people feel that only the sequential and associative containers qualify. Others allow strings, but not **bitset** and container adapters.

In our experience, the containers are the most valuable part of the STL (although some C++ aficionados find that statement heretical.) If you don't have much time or interest to pursue the STL in detail, at least consider learning about the containers. Once you get past a few syntax details, they are not difficult to use, and will save you debugging time down the road.

Everything in the STL is in the std namespace. The examples in this book usually use the blanket using namespace std; statement in source files, but you can be more selective in your own programs about which symbols from std to use.

Requirements on Elements

STL containers use *value semantics* on elements. That is, they store a copy of the element that they are given, and return copies of elements when requested. They also assign to elements with the assignment operator and destroy elements with the destructor. Thus, when you write classes that you intend to use with the STL, make sure that it's okay to have multiple copies of an object in the program at the same time.

If you prefer reference semantics, you must implement them yourself by storing pointers to elements instead of the elements themselves. When the containers copy a pointer, the result still refers to the same element.

> If you store pointers in containers, we recommend using reference-counted smart pointers in order to handle the memory management properly. However, you cannot use the C++ `auto_ptr` class in containers because it does not implement copying correctly (as far as the STL is concerned). See Chapter 25 for a `SuperSmartPointer` class that you can use in the STL containers.

The specific requirements on elements in containers are shown in the following table:

Method	Desription	Notes
Copy Constructor	Creates a new element that is "equal" to the old one, but that can safely be destructed without affecting the old one.	Used every time you insert an element.
Assignment Operator	Replaces the contents of an element with a copy of the source element.	Used every time you modify an element.
Destructor	Cleans up an element.	Used every time you remove an element.
Default Constructor	Constructs an element without any arguments.	Required only for certain operations such as vector `resize()` method and the map `operator[]` access.
`operator==`	Compares two elements for equality.	Required only for certain operations such as `operator==` on two containers.
`operator<`	Determines if one element is less than another.	Required only for certain operations such as `operator<` on two containers. `operator<` is also the default comparison for keys in associative containers.

Consult Chapters 9 and 16 for details about writing these methods.

> The STL containers call the copy constructor and assignment operator for elements often, so make those operations efficient.

Exceptions and Error Checking

The STL containers provide limited error checking. Clients are expected to ensure that their uses are valid. However, some container methods and functions throw exceptions in certain conditions such as out-of-bounds indexing. This chapter mentions exceptions where appropriate. The Standard Library Reference resource on the Web site attempts to catalog the possible exceptions thrown from each method. However, it is impossible to list exhaustively the exceptions that can be thrown from these methods because they perform operations on user-specified types with unknown exception characteristics.

Iterators

As described in Chapter 4, the STL uses the iterator pattern to provide a generic abstraction for accessing the elements of the containers. Each container provides a container-specific iterator, which is a glorified smart pointer that knows how to iterate over the elements of that specific container. The iterators for all the different containers adhere to a specific interface defined in the C++ standard. Thus, even though the containers provide different functionality, the iterators present a common interface to code that wishes to work with elements of the containers.

You can think of an iterator as a pointer to a specific element of the container. Like pointers to elements in an array, iterators can move to the next element with `operator++`. Similarly, you can usually use `operator*` and `operator->` on the iterator to access the actual element or field of the element. Some iterators allow comparison with `operator==` and `operator!=`, and support `operator--` for moving to previous elements. Different containers provide iterators with slightly different capabilities. The standard defines five categories of iterators, summarized in the following table.

Iterator Category	Operations Supported	Comments
Input	operator++ operator* operator-> copy constructor operator= operator== operator!=	Provides read-only access, forward-only (no `operator--` to move backward). Iterators can be assigned and copied with assignment operator and copy constructor. Iterators can be compared for equality.
Output	operator++ operator* copy constructor	Provides write-only access, forward only. Iterators cannot be assigned or copied. Iterators cannot be compared for equality. Note the absence of `operator->`.
Forward	operator++ operator* operator-> copy constructor default constructor operator= operator== operator!=	Provides read/write access, forward only. Iterators can be assigned and copied with assignment operator and copy constructor. Iterators can be compared for equality.
Bidirectional	Capbilities of Forward iterators, plus: operator--	Provides everything forward iterator provides Iterators can also move backward to previous element.
Random Access	Bidirectional capability, plus: operator+, operator-, operator+=, operator-= operator<, operator>, operator<=, operator>= operator[]	Equivalent to dumb pointers: iterators support pointer arithmetic, array index syntax, and all forms of comparison.

The standard containers that provide iterators all furnish either random access or bidirectional iterators.

Iterators are implemented similarly to smart pointer classes in that they overload the specific desired operators. Consult Chapter 16 for details on operator overloading. See Chapter 23 for a sample iterator implementation.

The basic iterator operations are similar to those supported by dumb pointers, so a dumb pointer is a legitimate iterator for certain containers. In fact, the `vector` iterator is often implemented as simply a dumb pointer. However, as a client of the containers, you need not worry about the implementation details; you can simply use the iterator abstraction.

Iterators might not be implemented internally as pointers, so this text uses the term "refers to" instead of "points to" when discussing the elements accessible via an iterator.

Chapters 22 and 23 delve into more detail about iterators and the STL algorithms that use them. This chapter simply shows you the basics of using the iterators for each container.

> **Only the sequential and associative containers provide iterators. The container adapters and bitmap do not support iteration over their elements.**

Common Iterator Typedefs and Methods

Every container class in the STL that supports iterators provides public `typedefs` for its iterator types called `iterator` and `const_iterator`. That way, clients can use the container iterators without worrying about the actual types.

> `const_iterators` **provide read-only access to elements of the container.**

The containers also provide a method `begin()` that returns an iterator referring to the first element in the container. The `end()` method returns a reference to the "past-the-end" value of the sequence of elements. That is, `end()` returns an iterator that is equal to the result of applying `operator++` to an iterator referring to the last element in the sequence. Together `begin()` and `end()` provide a *half-open range* that includes the first element but not the last. The reason for this apparent complication is to support empty ranges (containers without any elements), in which case `begin()` is equal to `end()`. The half-open range bounded by iterators `start` and `end` is often written mathematically like this: [start,end).

> **The half-open range concept also applies to iterator ranges that are passed to container methods such as `insert()` and `erase()`. See the specific container descriptions in this chapter for details.**

Sequential Containers

The `vector`, `deque`, and `list` are called the sequential containers because they store elements in a client-visible order. The best way to learn about the sequential containers is to jump in with an example of the `vector`, which is the container most commonly used. This section describes the `vector` in detail as an example of a sequential container, followed by briefer descriptions of the deque and the list. Once you become familiar with the sequential containers, it's trivial to switch between them.

Vector

As described in Chapter 4, the STL vector is similar to an array: the elements are stored in contiguous memory, each in its own "slot." You can index into the vector, as well as add new elements to the back or insert them anywhere else. Inserting and deleting elements into and from the vector generally takes linear time, though these operations actually run in *amortized constant* time (explained in the "Vector Memory Allocation Scheme" section) at the end of the vector. Random access of individual elements is constant complexity.

Vector Overview

The vector is defined in the `<vector>` header file as a class template with two type parameters: the element type to store in the vector, and an *allocator* type.

```
template <typename T, typename Allocator = allocator<T> > class vector;
```

The Allocator parameter specifies the type for a memory allocator object that the client can set in order to use custom memory allocation. The template parameter has a default value, which uses the element type parameter T. See Chapter 11 for details on template parameters.

> The default value for the Allocator type parameter is sufficient for most applications. Programmers do not usually find it useful to customize allocators, but Chapter 23 provides more detail in case you are interested. This chapter assumes that you always use the default allocator.

Fixed-Length Vectors

The simplest way to use a vector is as a fixed-length array. The vector provides a constructor that allows you to specify the number of elements, and provides overloaded operator[] in order to access and modify those elements.

> Like "real" array indexing, the vector **operator[]** does not provide bounds checking.

For example, here is a small program to "normalize" test scores so that the highest score is set to 100, and all other scores are adjusted accordingly. The program creates a vector of 10 doubles, reads in 10 values from the user, divides each value by the max score (times 100), and prints out the new values. For the sake of brevity, the program forsakes error checking.

```
#include <vector>
#include <iostream>
using namespace std;

int main(int argc, char** argv)
{
```

```
    vector<double> doubleVector(10); // Create a vector of 10 doubles.
    double max;
    int i;

    for (i = 0; i < 10; i++) {
        doubleVector[i] = 0;
    }

    // Read the first score before the loop in order to initialize max.
    cout << "Enter score 1: ";
    cin >> doubleVector[0];
    max = doubleVector[0];

    for (i = 1; i < 10; i++) {
        cout << "Enter score " << i + 1 << ": ";
        cin >> doubleVector[i];
        if (doubleVector[i] > max) {
            max = doubleVector[i];
        }
    }

    max /= 100;
    for (i = 0; i < 10; i++) {
        doubleVector[i] /= max;
        cout << doubleVector[i] << " ";
    }
    cout << endl;
    return (0);
}
```

As you can see from this example, you can use a vector just as you would use an array.

The vector `operator[]` normally returns a reference to the element, which can be used on the left-hand side of assignment statements. If `operator[]` is called on a `const` vector object, it returns a reference to a `const` element, which cannot be used as the target of an assignment. See Chapter 16 for details on how this trick is implemented.

Specifying an Initial Element Value

You can specify an initial value for the elements when you create the `vector` like this:

```
#include <vector>
#include <iostream>
using namespace std;

int main(int argc, char** argv)
{
    vector<double> doubleVector(10, 0); // Creates vector of 10 doubles of value 0
    double max;
    int i;

    // No longer need to initialize each element: the ctor did it for you.
```

```
    // Read the first score before the loop in order to initialize max.
    cout << "Enter score 1: ";
    cin >> doubleVector[0];
    max = doubleVector[0];

    for (i = 1; i < 10; i++) {
        cout << "Enter score " << i + 1 << ": ";
        cin >> doubleVector[i];
        if (doubleVector[i] > max) {
            max = doubleVector[i];
        }
    }

    max /= 100;
    for (i = 0; i < 10; i++) {
        doubleVector[i] /= max;
        cout << doubleVector[i] << " ";
    }
    cout << endl;
    return (0);
}
```

Other Vector Element Access Methods

In addition to using `operator[]`, you can access `vector` elements via `at()`, `front()`, and `back()`. `at()` is identical to `operator[]`, except that it performs bounds checking, and throws an `out_of_range` exception if the index is out of bounds. `front()` and `back()` return the references to the first and last elements of the `vector`, respectively.

> **All `vector` element accesses run in constant complexity.**

Dynamic-Length Vectors

The real power of the `vector` lies in its ability to grow dynamically. For example, consider the test score normalization program from the previous section with the additional requirement that it handle any number of test scores. Here is the new version:

```
int main(int argc, char** argv)
{
    vector<double> doubleVector; // Create a vector with zero elements.
    double max, temp;
    size_t i;

    // Read the first score before the loop in order to initialize max.
    cout << "Enter score 1: ";
    cin >> max;
    doubleVector.push_back(max);

    for (i = 1; true; i++) {
        cout << "Enter score " << i + 1 << " (-1 to stop): ";
        cin >> temp;
        if (temp == -1) {
```

```
            break;
        }
        doubleVector.push_back(temp);
        if (temp > max) {
            max = temp;
        }
    }

    max /= 100;
    for (i = 0; i < doubleVector.size(); i++) {
        doubleVector[i] /= max;
        cout << doubleVector[i] << " ";
    }
    cout << endl;
    return (0);
}
```

This version of the program uses the default constructor to create a vector with zero elements. As each score is read, it's added to the vector with the push_back() method. push_back() takes care of allocating space for the new element. Note that the last for loop uses the size() method on the vector to determine the number of elements in the container. size() returns an unsigned integer, so the type of i was changed to size_t for compatibility.

Vector Details

Now that you've had a taste of the power of vectors, it's time to delve into their details.

Constructors and Destructors

The default constructor creates a vector with 0 elements.

```
#include <vector>
using namespace std;

int main(int argc, char** argv)
{
    vector<int> intVector; // Creates a vector of ints with zero elements
    return (0);
}
```

As you've already seen, you can specify a number of elements and, optionally, a value for those elements, like this:

```
#include <vector>
using namespace std;

int main(int argc, char** argv)
{
    vector<int> intVector(10, 100); // Creates a vector of 10 ints with value 100
    return (0);
}
```

If you omit the default value, the new objects are zero-initialized. As described in Chapter 11, zero-initialization constructs objects with the default constructor and initializes primitives such as int and double with 0.

You can also create vectors of built-in classes like this:

```
#include <vector>
#include <string>
using namespace std;

int main(int argc, char** argv)
{
    vector<string> stringVector(10, "hello");
    return (0);
}
```

Finally, you can create vectors of user-defined classes:

```
#include <vector>
using namespace std;

class Element
{
    public:
        Element() {}
        ~Element() {}
};

int main(int argc, char** argv)
{
    vector<Element> elementVector;
    return (0);
}
```

The `vector` stores copies of the objects, and its destructor calls the destructor for each of the objects.

You can allocate vectors in the heap as well:

```
#include <vector>
using namespace std;

class Element
{
    public:
        Element() {}
        ~Element() {}
};

int main(int argc, char** argv)
{
    vector<Element>*  elementVector = new vector<Element>(10);
    delete elementVector;
    return (0);
}
```

Remember to call `delete` when you are finished with a `vector` that you allocated with new!

> **Use** `delete`, **not** `delete[]`, **to free vectors. Even though the** `vector` **is implemented as an array, you are deleting only the vector object. The vector handles the underlying array itself.**

Copying and Assigning Vectors

The copy constructor and assignment operator for the `vector` class perform deep copies of all the elements in the vector. Thus, for efficiency, you should pass `vectors` by reference or `const` reference to functions and methods. Consult Chapter 11 for the details on writing functions that take template instantiations as parameters.

In addition to normal copying and assignment, `vectors` provide an `assign()` method that allows you to remove all the current elements and add any number of new elements. This method is useful if you want to reuse a `vector`. Here is a trivial example:

```
vector<int> intVector(10, 0);
// Other code . . .
intVector.assign(5, 100);
```

Vectors also provide a `swap()` method that allows you to swap the contents of two `vectors`. Here is a simple example:

```
vector<int> vectorOne(10, 0);
vector<int> vectorTwo(5, 100);

vectorOne.swap(vectorTwo);
// vectorOne now has 5 elements with the value 100.
// vectorTwo now has 10 elements with the value 0.
```

Comparing Vectors

The STL provides the usual six overloaded comparison operators for `vectors`: `==`, `!=`, `<`, `>`, `<=`, `>=`. Two `vectors` are equal if they have the same number of elements and all the corresponding elements in the two `vectors` are equal to each other. One `vector` is "less than" another if all elements 0 through `i` -1 in the first vector are equal to 0 through `i` $-$ 1 in the second `vector`, but element `i` in the first is less than element `i` in the second.

> **Comparing two vectors with `operator==` or `operator!=` requires the individual elements to be comparable with `operator==`. Comparing two vectors with `operator<`, `operator>`, `operator<=`, or `operator>=` requires the individual elements to be comparable with `operator<`. If you intend to store objects of a custom class in a vector, make sure to write those operators.**

Here is an example of a simple program that compares `vectors` of `ints`:

```
#include <vector>
#include <iostream>
using namespace std;
```

```
int main(int argc, char** argv)
{
    vector<int> vectorOne(10, 0);
    vector<int> vectorTwo(10, 0);

    if (vectorOne == vectorTwo) {
        cout << "equal!\n";
    } else {
        cout << "not equal!\n";
    }

    vectorOne[3] = 50;

    if (vectorOne < vectorTwo) {
        cout << "vectorOne is less than vectorTwo\n";
    } else {
        cout << "vectorOne is not less than vectorTwo\n";
    }
    return (0);
}
```

The output of the program is:

```
equal!
vectorOne is not less than vectorTwo
```

Vector Iterators

The section on "Iterators" at the beginning of this chapter explained the basics of container iterators. The discussion can get a bit abstract, so it's helpful to jump in and look at a code example. Here is the test score normalization program from earlier with the `for` loop previously using `size()` replaced by a `for` loop using an iterator.

```
#include <vector>
#include <iostream>
using namespace std;

int main(int argc, char** argv)
{
    vector<double> doubleVector;
    double max, temp;
    int i;

    // Read the first score before the loop in order to initialize max.
    cout << "Enter score 1: ";
    cin >> max;
    doubleVector.push_back(max);

    for (i = 1; true; i++) {
        cout << "Enter score " << i + 1 << " (-1 to stop): ";
        cin >> temp;
        if (temp == -1) {
            break;
        }
        doubleVector.push_back(temp);
```

```
            if (temp > max) {
                max = temp;
            }
        }

    max /= 100;
    for (vector<double>::iterator it = doubleVector.begin();
        it != doubleVector.end(); ++it) {
        *it /= max;
        cout << *it << " ";
    }
    cout << endl;
    return (0);
}
```

You see `for` loops like the new one in this example quite a bit in STL code. First, take a look at the `for` loop initialization statement:

```
vector<double>::iterator it = doubleVector.begin();
```

Recall that every container defines a type named `iterator` to represent iterators for that type of container. `begin()` returns an iterator of that type referring to the first element in the container. Thus, the initialization statement obtains in the variable `it` an iterator referring to the first element of `doubleVector`. Next, look at the `for` loop comparison:

```
it != doubleVector.end();
```

This statement simply checks if the iterator is past the end of the sequence of elements in the `vector`. When it reaches that point, the loop terminates. The increment statement, `++it`, increments the iterator to refer to the next element in the `vector`.

> Use preincrement instead of postincrement when possible because preincrement is at least as efficient, and usually more efficient. `it++` must return a new iterator object, while `++it` can simply return a reference to `it`. See Chapter 16 for details on implementing **operator++**, and Chapter 23 for details on writing iterators.

The for loop body contains these two lines:

```
        *it /= max;
        cout << *it << " ";
```

As you can see, your code can both access and modify the elements over which it iterates. The first line uses `*` to dereference `it` to obtain the element to which it refers, and assigns to that element. The second line dereferences `it` again, but this time only to stream the element to `cout`.

Accessing Fields of Object Elements

If the elements of your container are objects, you can use the `->` operator on iterators to call methods or access members of those objects. For example, the following small program creates a `vector` of 10 strings, then iterates over all of them appending a new `string` to the old one:

```
#include <vector>
#include <string>
using namespace std;

int main(int argc, char** argv)
{
    vector<string> stringVector(10, "hello");

    for (vector<string>::iterator it = stringVector.begin();
        it != stringVector.end(); ++it) {
        it->append(" there");
    }
}
```

const_iterator

The normal `iterator` is read/write. However, if you call `begin()` and `end()` on a `const` object, you receive a `const_iterator`. The `const_iterator` is read-only; you cannot modify the elements. An `iterator` can always be converted to a `const_iterator`, so it's always safe to write something like this:

```
vector<type>::const_iterator it = myVector.begin();
```

However, a `const_iterator` cannot be converted to an `iterator`. If `myVector` is `const`, the following line doesn't compile:

```
vector<type>::iterator it = myVector.begin();
```

Thus, if you do not need to modify the elements of a `vector`, you should use a `const_iterator`. This rule will make your code more generic.

Iterator Safety

Generally, iterators are about as safe as pointers: extremely insecure. For example, you can write code like this:

```
vector<int> intVector;

vector<int>::iterator it = intVector.end();
*it = 10; // BUG! it doesn't refer to a valid element.
```

Recall that the iterator returned by `end()` is past the end of the `vector`. Trying to dereference it is undefined, which usually means that your program will crash. However, the iterators themselves are not required to perform any verification.

> Remember that `end()` returns an iterator past the end of the container, not the iterator referring to the last element of the container.

Another problem can occur if you use mismatched iterators. For example, the following code initializes an iterator from `vectorTwo` and tries to compare it to the end iterator for `vectorOne`. Needless to say, this loop will not do what you intended, and may never terminate.

```
vector<int> vectorOne(10);
vector<int> vectorTwo(10);

// Fill in the vectors.

// BUG! Infinite loop
for (vector<int>::iterator it = vectorTwo.begin(); it != vectorOne.end();
    ++it) {
    // Loop body
}
```

Other Iterator Operations

The vector iterator is random access, which means that you can move it backward or forward, or jump around. For example, the following code eventually changes the fifth element (index 4) in the `vector` to the value 4:

```
vector<int> intVector(10, 0);

vector<int>::iterator it = intVector.begin();
it += 5;
--it;
*it = 4;
```

Chapter 23 provides more information on the different categories of iterators.

Iterators versus Indexing

Given that you can write a `for` loop that uses a simple index variable and the `size()` method to iterate over the elements of the `vector`, why should you bother using iterators? That's a valid question, for which there are three main answers:

❑   Iterators allow you to insert and delete elements and sequences of elements at any point in the container. See the following "Adding and Removing Elements" section.

❑   Iterators allow you to use the STL algorithms, which are discussed in Chapter 22.

❑   Using an iterator to access each element sequentially is often more efficient than indexing the container to retrieve each element individually. This generalization is not true for `vectors`, but applies to `lists`, `maps`, and `sets`.

Adding and Removing Elements

As you have already read, you can append an element to a `vector` with the `push_back()` method. The `vector` provides a parallel remove method called `pop_back()`.

> **pop_back()** does not return the element that it removed. If you want the element you must first retrieve it with **back()**.

You can also insert elements at any point in the vector with the `insert()` method. `insert()` adds one or more elements to a position specified by an iterator, shifting all subsequent elements down to make room for the new ones. There are three different overloaded forms of insert(): one that inserts a single element, one that inserts n copies of a single element, and one that inserts elements from an iterator range. Recall that the iterator range is half-open, such that it includes the element referred to by the starting iterator but not the one referred to by the ending iterator.

> push_back() and insert() take const references to elements, allocate memory as needed to store the new elements, and store copies of the element arguments.

You can similarly remove elements from any point in the vector with erase(). There are two forms of erase(): single element and range specified by an iterator. You can remove all elements with clear().

Here is a small program that demonstrates the methods for adding and removing elements. It uses a helper function printVector() that prints the contents of the vector to cout, but whose implementation is not shown here because it uses algorithms covered in the next two chapters.

```
int main(int argc, char** argv)
{
    vector<int> vectorOne, vectorTwo;
    int i;

    vectorOne.push_back(1);
    vectorOne.push_back(2);
    vectorOne.push_back(3);
    vectorOne.push_back(5);

    // Oops, we forgot to add 4. Insert it in the correct place.
    vectorOne.insert(vectorOne.begin() + 3, 4);

    // Add elements 6 through 10 to vectorTwo.
    for (i = 6; i <= 10; i++) {
        vectorTwo.push_back(i);
    }

    printVector(vectorOne);
    printVector(vectorTwo);

    // Add all the elements from vectorTwo to the end of vectorOne.
    vectorOne.insert(vectorOne.end(), vectorTwo.begin(), vectorTwo.end());

    printVector(vectorOne);

    // Clear vectorTwo entirely.
    vectorTwo.clear();

    // And add 10 copies of the value 100.
    vectorTwo.insert(vectorTwo.begin(), 10, 100);

    // Decide we only want 9 elements.
    vectorTwo.pop_back();

    // Now erase the numbers 2 through 5 in vectorOne.
    vectorOne.erase(vectorOne.begin() + 1, vectorOne.begin() + 5);
```

```
        printVector(vectorOne);
        printVector(vectorTwo);

        return (0);
}
```

The output of the program is:

```
1 2 3 4 5
6 7 8 9 10
1 2 3 4 5 6 7 8 9 10
1 6 7 8 9 10
100 100 100 100 100 100 100 100 100
```

Recall that iterator pairs represent a half-open range, and `insert()` adds elements before the element referred to by the iterator position. Thus, you can insert the entire contents of `vectorTwo` into the end of `vectorOne`, like this:

```
vectorOne.insert(vectorOne.end(), vectorTwo.begin(), vectorTwo.end());
```

> Methods such as `insert()` and `erase()` that take a `vector` range as arguments assume that the beginning and ending iterators refer to elements in the same container, and that the end iterator refers to an element at or past the begin iterator. The methods will not work correctly if these preconditions are not met!

Algorithmic Complexity and Iterator Invalidation

Inserting or erasing elements in a `vector` causes all subsequent elements to shift up or down to make room for, or fill in the holes left by, the affected elements. Thus, these operations take linear complexity. Furthermore, all iterators referring to the insertion or removal point or subsequent positions are invalid following the action. The iterators are not "magically" moved to keep up with the elements that are shifted up or down in the `vector`.

Also keep in mind that an internal `vector` reallocation can cause invalidation of all iterators referring to elements in the vector, not just those referring to elements past the point of insertion or deletion. See the next section for details.

The Vector Memory Allocation Scheme

The `vector` allocates memory automatically to store the elements that you insert. Recall that the `vector` requirements dictate that the elements must be in contiguous memory, like in C-style arrays. Because it's impossible to request to add memory to the end of a current chunk of memory, every time the `vector` allocates more memory it must allocate a new, larger, chunk in a separate memory location and copy all the elements to the new chunk. This process is time-consuming, so the vector implementations attempt to avoid it by allocating more space than needed when they have to perform a reallocation. That way, they can avoid reallocating memory every time you insert an element.

One obvious question at this point is why you, as a client of the vector, care how it manages its memory internally. You might think that the principle of abstraction should allow you to disregard the internals of the `vector` memory allocation scheme. Unfortunately, there are two reasons why you need to understand how it works:

1. **Efficiency.** The vector allocation scheme can guarantee that element insert runs in *amortized constant time*: most of the time the operation is constant, but once in a while (if it requires a reallocation), it's linear. If you are worried about efficiency you can control when the vector performs reallocations.

2. **Iterator invalidations.** A reallocation invalidates all iterators referring to elements in the vector.

Thus, the vector interface allows you to query and control the vector reallocations. If you don't control the reallocations explicitly, you should assume that all insertions cause a reallocation and thus invalidate all iterators.

Size and Capacity

The vector provides two methods for obtaining information about its size: size() and capacity(). size() returns the number of elements in the vector, while capacity() returns the number of elements that it can hold without a reallocation. Thus, the number of elements that you can insert without causing a reallocation is capacity() - size().

> You can query whether a vector is empty with the empty() method. A vector can be empty but have nonzero capacity.

Reserving Capacity

If you don't care about efficiency or iterator invalidations, there is never a need to control the vector memory allocation explicitly. However, if you want to make your program as efficient as possible, or want to guarantee that iterators will not be invalidated, you can force the vector to preallocate enough space to hold all of its elements. Of course, you need to know how many elements it will hold, which is sometimes impossible to predict.

One way to preallocate space is to call reserve(). That method allocates enough memory to hold the specified number of elements. The next section shows an example of the reserve() method in action.

> Reserving space for elements changes the capacity, but not the size. That is, it doesn't actually create elements. Don't access elements past the vector size.

Another way to preallocate space is to specify, in the constructor, how many elements you want the vector to store. This method actually creates a vector of that size (and probably of that capacity).

Vector Example: A Round-Robin Class

A common problem in computer science is distributing requests among a finite list of resources. For example, a network load balancer distributes incoming network connections among the various hosts that can service the request. Ideally, each of the hosts would be kept equally busy. One of the simplest algorithmic solutions to this problem is *round-robin scheduling*, in which the resources are used or processed in order. When the last resource has been used, the scheduler starts over again at the beginning. For example, in the case of a network load balancer with three hosts, the first request would go the first host, the second to the second host, the third to the third host, and the fourth back to the first host. The cycle would continue in this way indefinitely.

Suppose that you decide to write a generic round-robin scheduling class that can be used with any type of resource. The class should support adding and removing resources, which occurs infrequently, and should support cycling through the resources in order to obtain the next one. You could use the STL `vector` directly, but it's often helpful to write a wrapper class that provides more directly the functionality you need for your specific application. The following example shows a `RoundRobin` class template with comments explaining the code. First, here is the class definition:

```cpp
#include <stdexcept>
#include <vector>
using std::vector;

//
// Class template RoundRobin
//
// Provides simple round-robin semantics for a list of elements.
// Clients add elements to the end of the list with add().
//
// getNext() returns the next element in the list, starting with the first,
// and cycling back to the first when the end of the list is reached.
//
// remove() removes the element matching the argument.
//
template <typename T>
class RoundRobin
{
    public:
        //
        // Client can give a hint as to the number of expected elements for
        // increased efficiency.
        //
        RoundRobin(int numExpected = 0);
        ~RoundRobin();

        //
        // Appends elem to the end of the list. May be called
        // between calls to getNext().
        //
        void add(const T& elem);

        //
        // Removes the first (and only the first) element
        // in the list that is equal (with operator==) to elem.
        // May be called between calls to getNext().
        //
        void remove(const T& elem);

        //
        // Returns the next element in the list, starting from 0 and continuously
        // cycling, taking into account elements that are added or removed.
        //
        T& getNext() throw(std::out_of_range);
    protected:
        vector<T> mElems;
        typename std::vector<T>::iterator mCurElem;
```

```
        private:
            // Prevent assignment and pass-by-reference.
            RoundRobin(const RoundRobin& src);
            RoundRobin& operator=(const RoundRobin& rhs);
};
```

As you can see, the public interface is straightforward: only three methods plus the constructor and destructor. The resources are stored in the vector mElems. mCurElem is an iterator that always refers to the next element in mElems that should be used in the round-robin scheme. Note the use of the typename keyword in front of the line declaring mCurElem. So far, you've only seen that keyword used to specify template parameters, but there is another use for it. You must specify typename explicitly whenever you access a type based on one or more template parameters. In this case, the template parameter T is used to access the iterator type. Thus, you must specify typename. This is another example of arcane C++ syntax.

The implementation of the RoundRobin class follows. Note the use of reserve() in the constructor, and the extensive use of the iterator in add(), remove(), and getNext(). The trickiest aspect is keeping mCurElem valid and referring to the correct element following add() or remove().

```
template <typename T>
RoundRobin<T>::RoundRobin(int numExpected)
{
    // If the client gave a guideline, reserve that much space.
    mElems.reserve(numExpected);

    // Initialize mCurElem even though it isn't used until
    // there's at least one element.
    mCurElem = mElems.begin();
}

template <typename T>
RoundRobin<T>::~RoundRobin()
{
    // Nothing to do here--the vector will delete all the elements
}

//
// Always add the new element at the end.
//
template <typename T>
void RoundRobin<T>::add(const T& elem)
{
    //
    // Even though we add the element at the end,
    // the vector could reallocate and invalidate the iterator.
    // Take advantage of the random access iterator features to save our
    // spot.
    //
    int pos = mCurElem - mElems.begin();

    // Add the element.
    mElems.push_back(elem);

    // If it's the first element, initialize the iterator to the beginning.
```

```
        if (mElems.size() == 1) {
            mCurElem = mElems.begin();
        } else {
            // Set it back to our spot.
            mCurElem = mElems.begin() + pos;
        }
    }
}

template <typename T>
void RoundRobin<T>::remove(const T& elem)
{
    for (typename std::vector<T>::iterator it = mElems.begin(); it != mElems.end();
        ++it) {
        if (*it == elem) {
            //
            // Removing an element will invalidate our mCurElem iterator if
            // it refers to an element past the point of the removal.
            // Take advantage of the random access features of the iterator
            // to track the position of the current element after the removal.
            //
            int newPos;

            // If the current iterator is before or at the one we're removing,
            // the new position is the same as before.
            if (mCurElem <= it) {
                newPos = mCurElem - mElems.begin();
            } else {
                // Otherwise, it's one less than before.
                newPos = mCurElem - mElems.begin() - 1;
            }
            // Erase the element (and ignore the return value).
            mElems.erase(it);

            // Now reset our iterator.
            mCurElem = mElems.begin() + newPos;

            // If we were pointing to the last element and it was removed,
            // we need to loop back to the first.
            if (mCurElem == mElems.end()) {
                mCurElem = mElems.begin();
            }
            return;
        }
    }
}

template <typename T>
T& RoundRobin<T>::getNext()throw(std::out_of_range)
{
    // First, make sure there are any elements.
    if (mElems.empty()) {
        throw std::out_of_range("No elements in the list");
    }

    // Retrieve a reference to return.
    T& retVal = *mCurElem;
```

```
        // Increment the iterator modulo the number of elements.
        ++mCurElem;
        if (mCurElem == mElems.end()) {
            mCurElem = mElems.begin();
        }

        // Return the reference.
        return (retVal);
    }
```

Here's a simple implementation of a load balancer that uses the `RoundRobin` class template. The actual networking code is omitted because networking is operating system specific.

```cpp
#include "RoundRobin.h"

//
// Forward declaration for NetworkRequest
// Implementation details omitted
//
class NetworkRequest;

//
// Simple Host class that serves as a proxy for a physical machine.
// Implementation details omitted.
//
class Host
{
    public:
        //
        // Implementation of processRequest would forward
        // the request to the network host represented by the
        // object. Omitted here.
        //
        void processRequest(NetworkRequest& request) {}
};

//
// Simple load balancer that distributes incoming requests
// to its hosts using a round-robin scheme
//
class LoadBalancer
{
    public:
        //
        // Constructor takes a vector of hosts.
        //
        LoadBalancer(const vector<Host>& hosts);
        ~LoadBalancer() {}

        //
        // Ship the incoming request to the next host using
        // a round-robin scheduling algorithm.
        //
        void distributeRequest(NetworkRequest& request);
```

```
    protected:
        RoundRobin<Host> rr;
};

LoadBalancer::LoadBalancer(const vector<Host>& hosts)
{
    // Add the hosts.
    for (size_t i = 0; i < hosts.size(); ++i) {
        rr.add(hosts[i]);
    }
}

void LoadBalancer::distributeRequest(NetworkRequest& request)
{
    try {
        rr.getNext().processRequest(request);
    } catch (out_of_range& e) {
        cerr << "No more hosts.\n";
    }
}
```

The vector<bool> Specialization

The standard requires a partial specialization of vector for bools, with the intention that it optimize space allocation by "packing" the Boolean values. Recall that a bool is either true or false, and thus could be represented by a single bit, which can take on exactly two values. However, most C++ compilers make bools the same size as ints. The vector<bool> is supposed to store the "array of bools" in single bits, thus saving space.

> You can think of the **vector<bool>** as a bit-field instead of a **vector**. The **bitset** container described below provides a more full-featured bit-field implementation than does **vector<bool>**. However, the benefit of **vector<bool>** is that it can change size dynamically.

In a half-hearted attempt to provide some bit-field routines for the vector<bool>, there is one additional method: flip(). This method can be called on either the container, in which case it negates all the elements in the container, or a single reference returned from operator[] or a similar method, in which case it negates that element.

At this point, you should be wondering how you can call a method on a reference to bool. The answer is that you can't. The vector<bool> specialization actually defines a class called reference that serves as a proxy for the underlying bool (or bit). When you call operator[], at(), or a similar method, the vector<bool> returns a reference object, which is a proxy for the real bool.

> The fact that references returned from **vector<bool>** are really proxies means that you can't take their addressees to obtain pointers to the actual elements in the container. The *proxy* design pattern is covered in detail in Chapter 26.

In practice, the little amount of space saved by packing `bool`s hardly seems worth the extra effort. However, you should be familiar with this partial instantiation because of the additional `flip()` method, and because of the fact that references are actually proxy objects. Many C++ experts recommend avoiding `vector<bool>` in favor of the `bitset`, unless you really need a dynamically sized bit-field.

deque

The `deque` is almost identical to the `vector`, but is used far less frequently. The principle differences are:

❑ The implementation is not required to store elements contiguously in memory.

❑ The `deque` supports constant-time insertion and removal of elements at both the front and the back (the `vector` supports amortized constant time at just the back).

❑ The `deque` provides `push_front()` and `pop_front()`, which the `vector` omits.

❑ The `deque` does not expose its memory management scheme via `reserve()` or `capacity()`.

Rarely will your applications require a `deque`, as opposed to a `vector` or `list`. Thus, we leave the details of the `deque` methods to the Standard Library Reference resource on the Web site.

list

The STL `list` is a standard doubly linked list. It supports constant-time insertion and deletion of elements at any point in the list, but provides slow (linear) time access to individual elements. In fact, the list does not even provide random access operations like `operator[]`. Only through iterators can you access individual elements.

Most of the `list` operations are identical to those of the `vector`, including the constructors, destructor, copying operations, assignment operations, and comparison operations. This section focuses on those methods that differ from those of `vector`. Consult the Standard Library Reference resource on the Web site for details on the `list` methods not discussed here.

Accessing Elements

The only methods provided by the `list` to access elements are `front()` and `back()`, both of which run in constant time. All other element access must be performed through iterators.

> Lists do not provide random access to elements.

Iterators

The `list` iterator is bidirectional, not random access like the `vector` iterator. That means that you cannot add and subtract `list` iterators from each other, or perform other pointer arithmetic on them.

Adding and Removing Elements

The `list` supports the same element add and remove methods that does the `vector`, including `push_back()`, `pop_back()`, the three forms of `insert()`, the two forms of `erase()`, and `clear()`.

Like the `deque`, it also provides `push_front()` and `pop_front()`. The amazing thing about the list is that all these methods (except for `clear()`) run in constant time, once you've found the correct position. Thus, the list is appropriate for applications that perform many insertions and deletions from the data structure, but do not need quick index-based element access.

List Size

Like `deques`, and unlike `vectors`, `lists` do not expose their underlying memory model. Consequently, they support `size()` and `empty()`, but not `resize()` or `capacity()`.

Special List Operations

The `list` provides several special operations that exploit its quick element insertion and deletion. This section provides an overview and examples. The Standard Library Reference resource on the Web site gives a thorough reference for all the methods.

Splicing

The linked-list characteristics of the `list` class allow it to *splice*, or insert, an entire `list` at any position in another `list` in constant time. The simplest version of this method works like this:

```
#include <list>
#include <string>
#include <iostream>
using namespace std;

int main(int argc, char** argv)
{
    list<string> dictionary, bWords;

    // Add the a words.
    dictionary.push_back("aardvark");
    dictionary.push_back("ambulance");
    dictionary.push_back("archive");

    // Add the c words.
    dictionary.push_back("canticle");
    dictionary.push_back("consumerism");
    dictionary.push_back("czar");

    // Create another list, of the b words.
    bWords.push_back("bathos");
    bWords.push_back("balderdash");
    bWords.push_back("brazen");

    // Splice the b words into the main dictionary.
    list<string>::iterator it;
    int i;

    // Iterate up to the spot where we want to insert bs
    // for loop body intentionally empty--we're just moving up three elements.
    for (it = dictionary.begin(), i = 0; i < 3; ++it, ++i);

    // Add in the bwords. This action removes the elements from bWords.
    dictionary.splice(it, bWords);
```

```
    // Print out the dictionary.
    for (it = dictionary.begin(); it != dictionary.end(); ++it) {
        cout << *it << endl;
    }

    return (0);
}
```

The result from running this program looks like this:

```
aardvark
ambulance
archive
bathos
balderdash
brazen
canticle
consumerism
czar
```

There are also two other forms of splice(): one that inserts a single element from another list and one that inserts a range from another list. See the Standard Library Reference resource on the Web site for details.

> **Splicing is destructive to the list passed as a parameter: it removes the spliced elements from one list in order to insert them into the other.**

More Efficient Versions of Algorithms

In addition to splice(), the list class provides special implementations of several of the generic STL algorithms. The generic forms are covered in Chapter 22. Here we discuss only the specific versions provided by list.

> **When you have a choice, use the list methods rather than the generic algorithms because the former are more efficient.**

The following table summarizes the algorithms for which list provides special implementations as methods. See the Standard Library Reference resource on the Web site and Chapter 22 for prototypes, details on the algorithms, and their specific running time when called on list.

Method	Description
remove() remove_if()	Removes certain elements from the list.
unique()	Removes duplicate consecutive elements from the list.
merge()	Merges two lists. Both lists must be sorted to start. Like splice(), merge() is destructive to the list passed as an argument.

Method	Description
sort()	Performs a stable sort on elements in the list.
reverse()	Reverses the order of the elements in the list.

The following program demonstrates most of these methods.

List Example: Determining Enrollment

Suppose that you are writing a computer registration system for a university. One feature you might provide is the ability to generate a complete list of enrolled students in the university from lists of the students in each class. For the sake of this example, assume that you must write only a single function that takes a vector of lists of student names (as strings), plus a list of students that have been dropped from their courses because they failed to pay tuition. This method should generate a complete list of all the students in all the courses, without any duplicates, and without those students who have been dropped. Note that students might be in more than one course.

Here is the code for this method. With the power of the STL lists, the method is practically shorter than its written description! Note that the STL allows you to "nest" containers: in this case, you can use a vector of lists.

```cpp
#include <list>
#include <vector>
#include <string>
using namespace std;

//
// classLists is a vector of lists, one for each course. The lists
// contain the students enrolled in those courses. They are not sorted.
//
// droppedStudents is a list of students who failed to pay their
// tuition and so were dropped from their courses.
//
// The function returns a list of every enrolled (nondropped) student in
// all the courses.
//
list<string>
getTotalEnrollment(const vector<list<string> >& classLists,
    const list<string>& droppedStudents)
{
    list<string> allStudents;

    // Concatenate all the course lists onto the master list.
    for (size_t i = 0; i < classLists.size(); ++i) {
        allStudents.insert(allStudents.end(), classLists[i].begin(),
            classLists[i].end());
    }

    // Sort the master list.
    allStudents.sort();

    // Remove duplicate student names (those who are in multiple courses).
    allStudents.unique();
```

```
//
// Remove students who are on the dropped list.
// Iterate through the dropped list, calling remove on the
// master list for each student in the dropped list.
//
for (list<string>::const_iterator it = droppedStudents.begin();
     it != droppedStudents.end(); ++it) {
     allStudents.remove(*it);
}


// Done!
return (allStudents);
}
```

Container Adapters

In addition to the three standard sequential containers, the STL provides three container adapters: the
queue, priority_queue, and stack. Each of these adapters is a wrapper around one of the sequential
containers. The intent is to simplify the interface and to provide only those features that are appropriate
for the stack or queue abstraction. For example, the adapters don't provide iterators or the capability to
insert or erase multiple elements simultaneously.

> The container adapters' interfaces may be too limiting for your needs. If so, you can
> use the sequential containers directly or write your own, more full-featured,
> adapters. See Chapter 26 for details on the *adapter* design pattern.

queue

The queue container adapter, defined in the header file <queue>, provides standard "first-in, first-out"
(FIFO) semantics. As usual, it's written as a class template, which looks like this:

```
template <typename T, typename Container = deque<T> > class queue;
```

The T template parameter specifies the type that you intend to store in the queue. The second template
parameter allows you to stipulate the underlying container that the queue adapts. However, the queue
requires the sequential container to support both push_back() and pop_front(), so you only have
two built-in choices: deque and list. For most purposes, you can just stick with the default deque.

Queue Operations

The queue interface is extremely simple: there are only six methods plus the constructor and the normal
comparison operators. The push() method adds a new element to the tail of the queue, and pop()
removes the element at the head of the queue. You can retrieve references to, without removing, the first
and last elements with front() and back(), respectively. As usual, when called on const objects,
front() and back() return const references, and when called on non-const objects they return
non-const (read/write) references.

> pop() does not return the element popped. If you want to retain a copy, you must first retrieve it with front().

The queue also supports size() and empty(). See the Standard Library Reference resource on the Web site for details.

Queue Example: A Network Packet Buffer

When two computers communicate over a network, they send information to each other divided up into discrete chunks called *packets*. The networking layer of the computer's operating system must pick up the packets and store them as they arrive. However, the computer might not have enough bandwidth to process all of them at once. Thus, the networking layer usually *buffers*, or stores, the packets until the higher layers have a chance to attend to them. The packets should be processed in the order they arrive, so this problem is perfect for a queue structure. Following is a small PacketBuffer class that stores incoming packets in a queue until they are processed. It's a template so that different layers of the networking layer can use it for different kinds of packets, such as IP packets or TCP packets. It allows the client to specify a max size because operating systems usually limit the number of packets that can be stored, so as not to use too much memory. When the buffer is full, subsequently arriving packets are ignored

```
#include <queue>
#include <stdexcept>
using std::queue;

template <typename T>
class PacketBuffer
{
    public:
        //
        // If maxSize is nonpositive, the size is unlimited.
        // Otherwise only maxSize packets are allowed in
        // the buffer at any one time.
        //
        PacketBuffer(int maxSize = -1);

        //
        // Stores the packet in the buffer.
        // Throws overflow_error is the buffer is full.
        //
        void bufferPacket(const T& packet);

        //
        // Returns the next packet. Throws out_of_range
        // if the buffer is empty.
        //
        T getNextPacket() throw (std::out_of_range);

    protected:
        queue<T> mPackets;
        int mMaxSize;

    private:
        // Prevent assignment and pass-by-value.
```

```
        PacketBuffer(const PacketBuffer& src);
        PacketBuffer& operator=(const PacketBuffer& rhs);
};

template <typename T>
PacketBuffer<T>::PacketBuffer(int maxSize)
{
    mMaxSize = maxSize;
}

template <typename T>
void PacketBuffer<T>::bufferPacket(const T& packet)
{
    if (mMaxSize > 0 && mPackets.size() ==
        static_cast<size_t>(mMaxSize)) {
        // No more space. Just drop the packet.
        return;
    }

    mPackets.push(packet);
}

template <typename T>
T PacketBuffer<T>::getNextPacket() throw (std::out_of_range)
{
    if (mPackets.empty()) {
        throw (std::out_of_range("Buffer is empty"));
    }
    // Retrieve the head element.
    T temp = mPackets.front();
    // Pop the head element.
    mPackets.pop();
    // Return the head element.
    return (temp);
}
```

A practical application of this class would require multiple threads. However, here is a quick unit testlike example of its use:

```
#include "PacketBuffer.h"
#include <iostream>
using namespace std;

class IPPacket {};

int main(int argc, char** argv)
{
    PacketBuffer<IPPacket> ipPackets(3);

    ipPackets.bufferPacket(IPPacket());
    ipPackets.bufferPacket(IPPacket());
    ipPackets.bufferPacket(IPPacket());
    ipPackets.bufferPacket(IPPacket());
```

```
    while (true) {
        try {
            IPPacket packet = ipPackets.getNextPacket();
        } catch (out_of_range&) {
            cout << "Processed all packets!" << endl;
            break;
        }
    }
    return (0);
}
```

priority_queue

A *priority queue* is a queue that keeps its elements in sorted order. Instead of a strict FIFO ordering, the element at the head of queue at any given time is the one with the highest priority. This element could be the oldest on the queue or the most recent. If two elements have equal priority, their relative order in the queue is FIFO.

The STL `priority_queue` container adapter is also defined in <queue>. Its template definition looks something like this (slightly simplified) one:

```
template <typename T, typename Container = vector<T>, typename Compare =
    less<T> >;
```

It's not as complicated as it looks! You've seen the first two parameters before: T is the element type stored in the `priority_queue` and `Container` is the underlying container on which the `priority_queue` is adapted. The `priority_queue` uses `vector` as the default, but `deque` works as well. `list` does not work because the `priority_queue` requires random access to its elements for sorting them. The third parameter, `Compare`, is trickier. As you'll learn more about in Chapter 22, `less` is a class template that supports comparison of two objects of type T with `operator<`. What this means for you is that the priority of elements in the `queue` is determined according to `operator<`. You can customize the comparison used, but that's a topic for Chapter 22. For now, just make sure that you define `operator<` appropriately for the types stored in the `priority_queue`.

> **The head element of the priority queue is the one with the "highest" priority, by default determined according to `operator<` such that elements that are "less" than other elements have lower priority.**

Priority Queue Operations

The `priority_queue` provides even fewer operations than does the `queue`. `push()` and `pop()` allow you to insert and remove elements respectively, and `top()` returns a `const` reference to the head element.

> **`top()` returns a `const` reference even when called on a non-const object. The `priority_queue` provides no mechanism to obtain the tail element.**
>
> **`pop()` does not return the element popped. If you want to retain a copy, you must first retrieve it with `top()`.**

Like the queue, the priority_queue supports size() and empty(). However, it does not provide any comparison operators. The Standard Library Reference resource on the Web site for details.

This interface is obviously limited. In particular, the priority_queue provides no iterator support, and it is impossible to merge two priority_queues.

Priority Queue Example: An Error Correlator

Single failures on a system can often cause multiple errors to be generated from different components. A good error-handling system uses *error correlation* to avoid processing duplicate errors and to process the most important errors first. You can use a priority_queue to write a very simple error correlator. This class simply sorts events according to their priority, so that the highest-priority errors are always processed first. Here is the class definition:

```cpp
#include <ostream>
#include <string>
#include <queue>
#include <stdexcept>

// Sample Error class with just a priority and a string error description
class Error
{
    public:
        Error(int priority, std::string errMsg) :
            mPriority(priority), mError(errMsg) {}
        int getPriority() const {return mPriority; }
        std::string getErrorString() const {return mError; }

        friend bool operator<(const Error& lhs, const Error& rhs);
        friend std::ostream& operator<<(std::ostream& str, const Error& err);

    protected:
        int mPriority;
        std::string mError;
};

// Simple ErrorCorrelator class that returns highest priority errors first
class ErrorCorrelator
{
    public:
        ErrorCorrelator() {}

        //
        // Add an error to be correlated.
        //
        void addError(const Error& error);

        //
        // Retrieve the next error to be processed.
        //
        Error getError() throw (std::out_of_range);

    protected:
        std::priority_queue<Error> mErrors;
```

```
      private:
          // Prevent assignment and pass-by-reference.
          ErrorCorrelator(const ErrorCorrelator& src);
          ErrorCorrelator& operator=(const ErrorCorrelator& rhs);
};
```

Here are the definitions of the functions and methods.

```
#include "ErrorCorrelator.h"
using namespace std;

bool operator<(const Error& lhs, const Error& rhs)
{
    return (lhs.mPriority < rhs.mPriority);
}

ostream& operator<<(ostream& str, const Error& err)
{
    str << err.mError << " (priority " << err.mPriority << ")";
    return (str);
}

void ErrorCorrelator::addError(const Error& error)
{
    mErrors.push(error);
}

Error ErrorCorrelator::getError() throw (out_of_range)
{
    //
    // If there are no more errors, throw an exception.
    //
    if (mErrors.empty()) {
        throw (out_of_range("No elements!"));
    }

    // Save the top element.
    Error top = mErrors.top();
    // Remove the top element.
    mErrors.pop();
    // Return the saved element.
    return (top);
}
```

Here is a simple unit test showing how to use the `ErrorCorrelator`. Realistic use would require multiple threads so that one thread adds errors, while another processes them.

```
#include "ErrorCorrelator.h"
#include <iostream>
using namespace std;

int main(int argc, char** argv)
{
    ErrorCorrelator ec;
```

```
        ec.addError(Error(3, "Unable to read file"));
        ec.addError(Error(1, "Incorrect entry from user"));
        ec.addError(Error(10, "Unable to allocate memory!"));

        while (true) {
            try {
                Error e = ec.getError();
                cout << e << endl;
            } catch (out_of_range& ) {
                cout << "Finished processing errors\n";
                break;
            }
        }

        return (0);
}
```

stack

The stack is almost identical to the queue, except that it provides "last-in, first-out" (LIFO) semantics instead of FIFO. The template definition looks like this:

```
template <typename T, typename Container = deque<T> > class stack;
```

You can use any of the three standard sequential containers as the underlying model for the stack.

Stack Operations

Like the queue, the stack provides push() and pop(). The difference is that push() adds a new element to the top of the stack, "pushing down" all elements inserted earlier, and pop() removes the element from the top of the stack, which is the most recently inserted element. The top() method returns a const reference to the top element if called on a const object and a non-const reference if called on a non-const object.

> **pop() does not return the element popped. If you want to retain a copy, you must first retrieve it with top().**

The stack supports empty(), size(), and the standard comparison operators. See the Standard Library Reference resource on the Web site for details.

Stack Example: Revised Error Correlator

Suppose that you decide to rewrite the previous ErrorCorrelator class so that it gives out the most recent errors instead of those with the highest priority. You can simply substitute a stack for the priority_queue in the ErrorCorrelator class definition. Now, the Errors will be distributed from the class in LIFO instead of priority order. Nothing in the method definitions needs to change because the push(), pop(), top(), and empty() methods exist on both the priority_queue and stack.

```
#include <ostream>
#include <string>
```

```
#include <stack>
#include <stdexcept>

// Details of Error class omitted for brevity

//
// Simple ErrorCorrelator class that returns most recent errors first
//
class ErrorCorrelator
{
    public:
        ErrorCorrelator() {}

        //
        // Add an error to be correlated.
        //
        void addError(const Error& error);

        //
        // Retrieve the next error to be processed.
        //
        Error getError() throw (std::out_of_range);

    protected:
        std::stack<Error> mErrors;

    private:
        // Prevent assignment and pass-by-reference.
        ErrorCorrelator(const ErrorCorrelator& src);
        ErrorCorrelator& operator=(const ErrorCorrelator& rhs);
};
```

Associative Containers

Unlike the sequential containers, the associative containers do not store elements in a linear configuration. Instead, they provide a mapping of keys to values. They generally offer insertion, deletion, and lookup times that are equivalent to each other.

The four associative containers provided by the STL are map, multimap, set, and multiset. Each of these containers stores its elements in a sorted, treelike, data structure.

The pair Utility Class

Before learning about the associative containers, you must become familiar with the pair class, which is defined in the <utility> header file. pair is a class template that groups together two values of possibly different types. The values are accessible through the first and second public data members. operator== and operator< are defined for pairs to compare both the first and second elements. Here are some examples:

```
#include <utility>
#include <string>
#include <iostream>
```

```
using namespace std;

int main(int argc, char** argv)
{
    // Two-argument ctor and default ctor
    pair<string, int> myPair("hello", 5), myOtherPair;

    // Can assign directly to first and second
    myOtherPair.first = "hello";
    myOtherPair.second = 6;

    // Copy ctor.
    pair<string, int> myThirdPair(myOtherPair);

    // operator<
    if (myPair < myOtherPair) {
        cout << "myPair is less than myOtherPair\n";
    } else {
        cout << "myPair is greater than or equal to myOtherPair\n";
    }

    // operator==
    if (myOtherPair == myThirdPair) {
        cout << "myOtherPair is equal to myThirdPair\n";
    } else {
        cout << "myOtherPair is not equal to myThirdPair\n";
    }

    return (0);
}
```

The library also provides a utility function template, make_pair(), that constructs a pair from two variables. For example, you could use it like this:

```
pair<int, int> aPair = make_pair(5, 10);
```

Of course, in this case you could have just used the two-argument constructor. However, make_pair() is more useful when you want to pass a pair to a function. Unlike class templates, function templates can infer types from parameters, so you can use make_pair() to construct a pair without explicitly specifying the types.

> **Using pointer types in pairs is risky because the pair copy constructor and assignment operator perform only shallow copies and assignments of pointer types.**

map

The map is one of the most useful containers. It stores key/value pairs instead of just a single value. Insertion, lookup, and deletion are all based on the key; the value is just "along for the ride." The term "map" comes from the conceptual understanding that the container "maps" keys to values. You might be more familiar with the concept of a hash table. The map provides a similar interface; the differences are in the underlying data structure and the algorithmic complexity of the operations.

The map keeps elements in sorted order, based on the keys, so that insertion, deletion, and lookup all take logarithmic time. It is usually implemented as some form of balanced tree, such as a red-black tree. However, the tree structure is not exposed to the client.

You should use a map whenever you need to store and retrieve elements based on a "key" value.

Constructing Maps

The map template takes four types: the key type, the value type, the comparison type, and the allocator type. As usual, we ignore the allocator in this chapter; see Chapter 23 for details. The comparison type is similar to the comparison type for priority_queue described above. It allows you to specify a different comparison class than the default. You usually shouldn't need to change the sorting criteria. In this chapter, we use only the default less comparison. When using the default, make sure that your keys all respond to operator< appropriately.

If you're interested in further detail, Chapter 22 explains how to write your own comparison classes.

If you ignore the comparison and allocator parameters (which we urge you to do), constructing a map is just like constructing a vector or list, except that you specify the key and value types separately in the template. For example, the following code constructs a map that uses ints as the key and stores objects of the Data class (whose full definition is not shown):

```
#include <map>
using namespace std;

class Data
{
    public:
        Data(int val = 0) { mVal = val; }
        int getVal() const { return mVal; }
        void setVal(int val) {mVal = val; }
        // Remainder of definition omitted
    protected:
        int mVal;
};

int main(int argc, char** argv)
{
    map<int, Data> dataMap;
    return (0);
}
```

Inserting Elements

Inserting an element into the sequential containers such as vector and list always requires you to specify the position at which the element is to be added. The map, along with the other associative containers, is different. The map internal implementation determines the position in which to store the new element; you need only to supply the key and the value.

> map and the other associative containers do provide a version of insert() that takes an iterator position. However, that position is only a "hint" to the container as to the correct position. The container is not required to insert the element at that position.

When inserting elements, it is important to keep in mind that maps support so-called "unique keys:" every element in the map must have a different key. If you want to support multiple elements with the same key, you must use multimaps, which are described below.

There are two ways to insert an element into the map: one clumsy and one not so clumsy.

The insert() Method

The clumsy mechanism to add an element to a map is the insert() method. One problem is that you must specify the key/value pair as a pair object. The second problem is that the return value from the basic form of insert() is a pair of an iterator and a bool. The reason for the complicated return value is that insert() does not overwrite an element value if one already exists with the specified key. The bool element of the return pair specifies whether the insert() actually inserted the new key/ value pair. The iterator refers to the element in the map with the specified key (with a new or old value, depending on whether the insert succeeded or failed). Continuing the map example from the previous section, here is how to use insert():

```cpp
#include <map>
#include <iostream>
using namespace std;

class Data
{
    public:
        Data(int val = 0) { mVal = val; }
        int getVal() const { return mVal; }
        void setVal(int val) {mVal = val; }
        // Remainder of definition omitted
    protected:
        int mVal;
};

int main(int argc, char** argv)
{
    map<int, Data> dataMap;
    pair<map<int, Data>::iterator, bool> ret;

    ret = dataMap.insert(make_pair(1, Data(4)));
    if (ret.second) {
        cout << "Insert succeeded!\n";
    } else {
        cout << "Insert failed!\n";
    }

    ret = dataMap.insert(make_pair(1, Data(6)));
    if (ret.second) {
        cout << "Insert succeeded!\n";
    } else {
        cout << "Insert failed!\n";
    }
    return (0);
}
```

Note the use of `make_pair()` to construct the `pair` to pass to the `insert()` method. The output from the program is:

```
Insert succeeded!
Insert failed!
```

operator[]

The less clumsy way to insert an element into the `map` is through the overloaded `operator[]`. The difference is mainly in the syntax: you specify the key and value separately. Additionally, `operator[]` always succeeds. If no element value with the given key exists, it creates a new element with that key and value. If an element with the key exists already, `operator[]` replaces the element value with the newly specified value. Here is the previous example using `operator[]` instead of `insert()`:

```cpp
#include <map>
#include <iostream>
using namespace std;

class Data
{
    public:
        Data(int val = 0) { mVal = val; }
        int getVal() const { return mVal; }
        void setVal(int val) {mVal = val; }
        // Remainder of definition omitted
    protected:
        int mVal;
};

int main(int argc, char** argv)
{
    map<int, Data> dataMap;
    dataMap[1] = Data(4);
    dataMap[1] = Data(6); // Replaces the element with key 1
    return (0);
}
```

There is, however, one major caveat to `operator[]`: it always constructs a new value object, even if it doesn't need to use it. Thus, it requires a default constructor for your element values, and can be less efficient than `insert()`.

Map Iterators

`map` iterators work similarly to the iterators on the sequential containers. The major difference is that the iterators refer to key/value pairs instead of just the values. In order to access the value, you must retrieve the `second` field of the `pair` object. Here is how you can iterate through the `map` from the previous example:

```cpp
#include <map>
#include <iostream>
using namespace std;

class Data
{
```

```
        public:
            Data(int val = 0) { mVal = val; }
            int getVal() const { return mVal; }
            void setVal(int val) {mVal = val; }
            // Remainder of definition omitted
        protected:
            int mVal;
};

int main(int argc, char** argv)
{
    map<int, Data> dataMap;

    dataMap[1] = Data(4);
    dataMap[1] = Data(6); // Replaces the element with key 1

    for (map<int, Data>::iterator it = dataMap.begin();
        it != dataMap.end(); ++it) {
            cout << it->second.getVal() << endl;
    }
    return (0);
}
```

Take another look at the expression used to access the value:

```
it->second.getVal()
```

it refers to a key/value pair, so you can use the -> operator to access the second field of that pair, which is a Data object. You can then call the getVal() method on that data object.

Note that the following code is functionally equivalent:

```
(*it).second.getVal()
```

You still see a lot of code that like around because -> didn't used to be required for iterators.

> You can modify element values through non-const iterators, but you cannot modify the key of an element, even through a non-const iterator, because it would destroy the sorted order of the elements in the map.

map iterators are bidirectional.

Looking Up Elements

The map provides logarithmic lookup of elements based on a supplied key. If you already know that an element with a given key is in the map, the simplest way to look it up is through operator[]. The nice thing about operator[] is that it returns a reference to the element that you can use (or modify on a non-const map) directly, without worrying about pulling the value out of a pair object. Here is an extension to the preceding example to call the setVal() method on the Data object value at key 1:

```
#include <map>
#include <iostream>
using namespace std;

class Data
{
    public:
        Data(int val = 0) { mVal = val; }
        int getVal() const { return mVal; }
        void setVal(int val) {mVal = val; }
        // Remainder of definition omitted
    protected:
        int mVal;
};

int main(int argc, char** argv)
{
    map<int, Data> dataMap;
    dataMap[1] = Data(4);
    dataMap[1] = Data(6);
    dataMap[1].setVal(100);

    return (0);
}
```

However, if you don't know whether the element exists, you may not want to use operator[], because it will insert a new element with that key if it doesn't find one already. As an alternative, the map provides a find() method that returns an iterator referring to the element with the specified key, if it exists, or the end() iterator if its not in the map. Here is an example using find() to perform the same modification to the Data object with key 1:

```
#include <map>
#include <iostream>
using namespace std;

class Data
{
    public:
        Data(int val = 0) { mVal = val; }
        int getVal() const { return mVal; }
        void setVal(int val) {mVal = val; }

        // Remainder of definition omitted
    protected:
        int mVal;
};

int main(int argc, char** argv)
{
    map<int, Data> dataMap;
    dataMap[1] = Data(4);
    dataMap[1] = Data(6);
```

```
    map<int, Data>::iterator it = dataMap.find(1);
    if (it != dataMap.end()) {
        it->second.setVal(100);
    }

    return (0);
}
```

As you can see, using `find()` is a bit clumsier, but it's sometimes necessary.

If you only want to know whether or not an element with a certain key is in the map, you can use the `count()` member function. It returns the number of elements in the map with a given key. For maps, the result will always be 0 or 1 because there can be no elements with duplicate keys. The following section shows an example using `count()`.

Removing Elements

The map allows you to remove an element at a specific iterator position or to remove all elements in a given iterator range, in amortized constant and logarithmic time, respectively. From the client perspective, these two `erase()` methods are equivalent to those in the sequential containers. A great feature of the map, however, is that it also provides a version of `erase()` to remove an element matching a key. Here is an example:

```
// #includes, Data class definition, and beginning of main function omitted.
// See previous examples for details.
map<int, Data> dataMap;
dataMap[1] = Data(4);
cout << "There are " << dataMap.count(1) << " elements with key 1\n";
dataMap.erase(1);
cout << "There are " << dataMap.count(1) << " elements with key 1\n";
```

Map Example: Bank Account

You can implement a simple bank account database using a map. A common pattern is for the key to be one field of a `class` or `struct` that is stored in the map. In this case, the key is the account number. Here are simple `BankAccount` and `BankDB` classes:

```
#include <map>
#include <string>
#include <stdexcept>
using std::map;
using std::string;
using std::out_of_range;

class BankAccount
{
    public:
        BankAccount(int acctNum, const string& name) :
            mAcctNum(acctNum), mClientName(name) {}
        void setAcctNum(int acctNum) { mAcctNum = acctNum; }
        int getAcctNum() const {return (mAcctNum); }
        void setClientName(const string& name) { mClientName = name; }
        string getClientName() const { return mClientName; }
```

```
            // Other public methods omitted

    protected:
        int mAcctNum;
        string mClientName;
        // Other data members omitted
};

class BankDB
{
    public:
        BankDB() {}

        // Adds acct to the bank database. If an account
        // exists already with that number, the new account is
        // not added. Returns true if the account is added, false
        // if it's not.
        bool addAccount(const BankAccount& acct);

        // Removes the account acctNum from the database
        void deleteAccount(int acctNum);

        // Returns a reference to the account represented
        // by its number or the client name.
        // Throws out_of_range if the account is not found
        BankAccount& findAccount(int acctNum) throw(out_of_range);
        BankAccount& findAccount(const string& name) throw(out_of_range);

        // Adds all the accounts from db to this database.
        // Deletes all the accounts in db.
        void mergeDatabase(BankDB& db);

    protected:
        map<int, BankAccount> mAccounts;
};
```

Here are implementations of the BankDB methods:

```
#include "BankDB.h"
#include <utility>
using namespace std;

bool BankDB::addAccount(const BankAccount& acct)
{
    // Declare a variable to store the return from insert().
    pair<map<int, BankAccount>::iterator, bool> res;
    // Do the actual insert, using the account number as the key.
    res = mAccounts.insert(make_pair(acct.getAcctNum(), acct));

    // Return the bool field of the pair specifying success or failure.
    return (res.second);
}

void BankDB::deleteAccount(int acctNum)
{
```

```
        mAccounts.erase(acctNum);
}

BankAccount& BankDB::findAccount(int acctNum) throw(out_of_range)
{
    // Finding an element via its key can be done with find().
    map<int, BankAccount>::iterator it = mAccounts.find(acctNum);
    if (it == mAccounts.end()) {
        throw (out_of_range("No account with that number."));
    }
    // Remember that iterators into maps refer to pairs of key/value.
    return (it->second);
}

BankAccount& BankDB::findAccount(const string& name) throw(out_of_range)
{
    //
    // Finding an element by a non-key attribute requires a linear
    // search through the elements.
    //
    for (map<int, BankAccount>::iterator it = mAccounts.begin();
         it != mAccounts.end(); ++it) {
        if (it->second.getClientName() == name) {
            // Found it!
            return (it->second);
        }
    }
    throw (out_of_range("No account with that name."));
}

void BankDB::mergeDatabase(BankDB& db)
{
    // Just insert copies of all the accounts in the old db
    // into the new one.
    mAccounts.insert(db.mAccounts.begin(), db.mAccounts.end());

    // Now delete all the accounts in the old one.
    db.mAccounts.clear();
}
```

multimap

The multimap is a map that allows multiple elements with the same key. The interface is almost identical to the map interface, with the following changes:

❏   multimaps do not provide operator[]. The semantics of this operator do not make sense if there can be multiple elements with a single key.

❏   Inserts on multimaps always succeed. Thus, the multimap insert() that adds a single element doesn't need to return the pair of the iterator and bool. It returns only the iterator.

> multimaps allow you to insert identical key/value pairs. If you want to avoid this redundancy, you must check explicitly before inserting a new element.

The trickiest aspect of `multimaps` is looking up elements. You can't use `operator[]`, because it is not provided. `find()` isn't very useful because it returns an `iterator` referring to any one of the elements with a given key (not necessarily the first element with that key).

Luckily, `multimaps` store all elements with the same key together and provide methods to obtain `iterators` for this subrange of elements with the same key in the container. `lower_bound()` and `upper_bound()` each return a single `iterator` referring to the first and one-past-the-last elements matching a given key. If there are no elements matching that key, the `iterators` returned by `lower_bound()` and `upper_bound()` will be equal to each other.

In case you don't want to call two separate methods to obtain the `iterators` bounding the elements with a given key, `multimaps` also provide `equal_range()`, which returns a `pair` of the two `iterators` that would be returned by `lower_bound()` and `upper_bound()`.

The example in the next section illustrates the use of these methods.

> **The** `lower_bound()`, `upper_bound()`, **and** `equal_range()` **methods exist for** maps **as well, but their usefulness is limited.**

multimap Example: Buddy Lists

Most of the numerous online chat programs allow users to have a "buddy list" or list of friends. The chat program confers special privileges on users in the buddy list, such as allowing them to send unsolicited messages to the user.

One way to implement the buddy lists for an online chat program is to store the information in a `multimap`. One `multimap` could store the buddy lists for every user. Each entry in the container stores one buddy for a user. The key is the user and the value is the buddy. For example, if the two authors of this book had each other on their individual buddy lists, there would be two entries of the form "Nicholas Solter" maps to "Scott Kleper" and "Scott Kleper" maps to "Nicholas Solter." The `multimap` allows multiple values for the same key, so the same user is allowed multiple buddies. Here the `BuddyList` class definition:

```
#include <map>
#include <string>
#include <list>

using std::multimap;
using std::string;
using std::list;

class BuddyList
{
    public:
        BuddyList();

        //
        // Adds buddy as a friend of name
        //
        void addBuddy(const string& name, const string& buddy);
```

```
        //
        // Removes buddy as a friend of name
        //
        void removeBuddy(const string& name, const string& buddy);

        //
        // Returns true if buddy is a friend of name.
        // Otherwise returns false.
        //
        bool isBuddy(const string& name, const string& buddy) const;

        //
        // Retrieves a list of all the friends of name
        //
        list<string> getBuddies(const string& name) const;

    protected:
        multimap<string, string> mBuddies;
    private:
        // Prevent assignment and pass-by-value.
        BuddyList(const BuddyList& src);
        BuddyList& operator=(const BuddyList& rhs);
};
```

Here is the implementation. It demonstrates the use of `lower_bound()`, `upper_bound()`, and `equal_range()`:

```
#include "BuddyList.h"
using namespace std;

BuddyList::BuddyList()
{
}

void BuddyList::addBuddy(const string& name, const string& buddy)
{
    // Make sure this buddy isn't already there.
    // We don't want to insert an identical copy of the
    // key/value pair.
    if (!isBuddy(name, buddy)) {
        mBuddies.insert(make_pair(name, buddy));
    }
}

void BuddyList::removeBuddy(const string& name, const string& buddy)
{
    // Declare two iterators into the map.
    multimap<string, string>::iterator start, end;

    // Obtain the beginning and end of the range of elements with
    // key name. Use both lower_bound() and upper_bound() to demonstrate
    // their use. Otherwise, could just call equal_range().
    start = mBuddies.lower_bound(name);
    end = mBuddies.upper_bound(name);
```

```
        // Iterate through the elements with key name looking
        // for a value buddy.
        for (start; start != end; ++start) {
            if (start->second == buddy) {
                // We found a match! Remove it from the map.
                mBuddies.erase(start);
                break;
            }
        }
    }
}

bool BuddyList::isBuddy(const string& name, const string& buddy) const
{
    // Declare two iterators into the map.
    multimap<string, string>::const_iterator start, end;
    // Obtain the beginning and end of the range of elements with
    // key name. Use both lower_bound() and upper_bound() to demonstrate
    // their use. Otherwise, could just call equal_range().
    start = mBuddies.lower_bound(name);
    end = mBuddies.upper_bound(name);

    // Iterate through the elements with key name looking
    // for a value buddy. If there are no elements with key name,
    // start equals end, so the loop body doesn't execute.
    for (start; start != end; ++start) {
        if (start->second == buddy) {
            // We found a match!
            return (true);
        }
    }
    // No matches
    return (false);
}

list<string> BuddyList::getBuddies(const string& name) const
{
    // Create a variable to store the pair of iterators.
    pair<multimap<string, string>::const_iterator,
        multimap<string, string>::const_iterator> its;

    // Obtain the pair of iterators marking the range containing
    // elements with key name.
    its = mBuddies.equal_range(name);

    // Create a list with all the names in the range
    // (all the buddies of name).
    list<string> buddies;
    for (its.first; its.first != its.second; ++its.first) {
        buddies.push_back((its.first)->second);
    }

    return (buddies);
}
```

Note that `removeBuddy()` can't simply use the version of `erase()` that erases all elements with a given key, because it should erase only one element with the key, not all of them. Note also that `getBuddies()` can't use `insert()` on the `list` to insert the elements in the range returned by `equal_range()`, because the elements referred to by the `multimap` iterators are key/value pairs, not `strings`. `getBuddies()` must iterate explicitly through the `list` extracting the `string` from each key/value pair and pushing it onto the new `list` to be returned.

Here is a simple test of the `BuddyList`:

```
#include "BuddyList.h"
#include <iostream>
using namespace std;

int main(int argc, char** argv)
{
    BuddyList buddies;

    buddies.addBuddy("Harry Potter", "Ron Weasley");
    buddies.addBuddy("Harry Potter", "Hermione Granger");
    buddies.addBuddy("Harry Potter", "Hagrid");
    buddies.addBuddy("Harry Potter", "Draco Malfoy");
    // That's not right! Remove Draco.
    buddies.removeBuddy("Harry Potter", "Draco Malfoy");

    buddies.addBuddy("Hagrid", "Harry Potter");
    buddies.addBuddy("Hagrid", "Ron Weasley");
    buddies.addBuddy("Hagrid", "Hermione Granger");

    list<string> harryBuds = buddies.getBuddies("Harry Potter");

    cout << "Harry's friends: \n";
    for (list<string>::const_iterator it = harryBuds.begin();
    it != harryBuds.end(); ++it) {
        cout << "\t" << *it << endl;
    }

    return (0);
}
```

set

The `set` container is very similar to the `map`. The difference is that instead of storing key/value pairs, in `sets` the value itself is the key. `sets` are useful for storing information in which there is no explicit key, but that you want sorted for quick insertion, lookup, and deletion.

The interface supplied by `set` is almost identical to that of the `map`. The main difference is that the `set` doesn't provide `operator[]`. Also, although the standard doesn't state it explicitly, most implementations make the `set` iterator identical to `const_iterator`, such that you can't modify the elements of the `set` through the `iterator`. Even if your version of the STL permits you to modify `set` elements through an `iterator`, you should avoid doing so because modifying elements of the `set` while they are in the container would destroy the sorted order.

set Example: Access Control List

One way to implement basic security on a computer system is through access control lists. Each entity on the system, such as a file or a device, has a list of users with permissions to access that entity. Users can generally be added to and removed from the permissions list for an entity only by users with special privileges. Internally, the set container provides a nice way to represent the access control list. You could use one set for each entity, containing all the usernames who are allowed to access the entity. Here is a class definition for a simple access control list:

```
#include <set>
#include <string>
#include <list>
using std::set;
using std::string;
using std::list;

class AccessList
{
    public:
        AccessList() {}

        //
        // Adds the user to the permissions list
        //
        void addUser(const string& user);

        //
        // Removes the user from the permissions list
        //
        void removeUser(const string& user);

        //
        // Returns true if user is in the permissions list
        //
        bool isAllowed(const string& user) const;

        //
        // Returns a list of all the users who have permissions
        //
        list<string> getAllUsers() const;

    protected:
        set<string> mAllowed;
};
```

Here are the method definitions.

```
#include "AccessList.h"
using namespace std;

void AccessList::addUser(const string& user)
{
    mAllowed.insert(user);
}
```

```
void AccessList::removeUser(const string& user)
{
    mAllowed.erase(user);
}

bool AccessList::isAllowed(const string& user) const
{
    return (mAllowed.count(user) == 1);
}

list<string> AccessList::getAllUsers() const
{
    list<string> users;
    users.insert(users.end(), mAllowed.begin(), mAllowed.end());
    return (users);
}
```

Finally, here is a simple test program:

```
#include "AccessList.h"
#include <iostream>
#include <iterator>
using namespace std;

int main(int argc, char** argv)
{
    AccessList fileX;

    fileX.addUser("nsolter");
    fileX.addUser("klep");
    fileX.addUser("baduser");
    fileX.removeUser("baduser");

    if (fileX.isAllowed("nsolter")) {
        cout << "nsolter has permissions\n";
    }

    if (fileX.isAllowed("baduser")) {
        cout << "baduser has permissions\n";
    }

    list<string> users = fileX.getAllUsers();
    for (list<string>::const_iterator it = users.begin();
    it != users.end(); ++it) {
        cout << *it << " ";
    }
    cout << endl;

    return (0);
}
```

multiset

The multiset is to the set what the multimap is to the map. The multiset supports all the operations of the set, but it allows multiple elements that are equal to each other to be stored in the container simultaneously. Note that it's possible for elements that are objects to be equal to each other with operator== even if they are not identical. We don't show an example of the multiset because it's so similar to set and multimap.

Other Containers

As mentioned earlier, there are several other parts of the C++ language that work with the STL to varying degrees, including arrays, strings, streams, and the bitset.

Arrays as STL Containers

Recall that "dumb" pointers are bona fide iterators because they support the required operators. This point is more than just a piece of trivia. It means that you can treat normal C++ arrays as STL containers by using pointers to their elements as iterators. Arrays, of course, don't provide methods like size(), empty(), insert(), and erase(), so they aren't true STL containers. Nevertheless, because they do support iterators through pointers, you can use them in the algorithms described in Chapter 22 and in some of the methods described in this chapter.

For example, you could copy all the elements of an array into a vector using the vector insert() method that takes an iterator range from any container. The insert() method prototype looks like this:

```
template <typename InputIterator> void insert(iterator position,
    InputIterator first, InputIterator last);
```

If you want to use an int array as the source, then the templatized type of InputIterator becomes int*. Here is the full example:

```
#include <vector>
#include <iostream>

using namespace std;

int main(int argc, char** argv)
{
    int arr[10]; // normal C++ array
    vector<int> vec; // STL vector

    //
    // Initialize each element of the array to the value of
    // its index.
    //
    for (int i = 0; i < 10; i++) {
        arr[i] = i;
    }

    //
    // Insert the contents of the array into the
    // end of the vector.
    //
    vec.insert(vec.end(), arr, arr + 10);
```

```
        // Print the contents of the vector.
        for (i = 0; i < 10; i++) {
            cout << vec[i] << " ";
        }

        return (0);
    }
```

Note that the iterator referring to the first element of the array is simply the address of the first element. Recall from Chapter 13 that the name of an array alone is interpreted as the address of the first element. The iterator referring to the end must be one past the last element, so it's the address of the first element plus 10.

Strings as STL Containers

You can think of a `string` as a sequential container of characters. Thus, it shouldn't be surprising to learn that the C++ `string` is a full-fledged sequential container. It contains `begin()` and `end()` methods that return iterators into the `string`, `insert()` and `erase()` methods, `size()`, `empty()`, and all the rest of the sequential container basics. It resembles a `vector` quite closely, even providing methods `reserve()` and `capacity()`. However, unlike `vectors`, `strings` are not required to store their elements contiguously in memory. They also fail to provide a few methods that `vectors` support, such as `push_back()`.

> The C++ string is actually a **typedef** of a **char** instantiation of the **basic_string** template class. However, we refer to **string** for simplicity. The discussion here applies equally to **wstring** and other instantiations of the **basic_string** template.

You can use `string` as an STL container just as you would use `vector`. Here is an example:

```
#include <string>
#include <iostream>
using namespace std;

int main(int argc, char** argv)
{
    string str1;

    str1.insert(str1.end(), 'h');
    str1.insert(str1.end(), 'e');
    str1.insert(str1.end(), 'l');
    str1.insert(str1.end(), 'l');
    str1.insert(str1.end(), 'o');

    for (string::const_iterator it = str1.begin(); it != str1.end(); ++it) {
        cout << *it;
    }
    cout << endl;

    return (0);
}
```

In addition to the STL sequential container methods, `strings` provide a whole host of useful methods and `friend` functions. The `string` interface is actually quite a good example of a cluttered interface, one of the design pitfalls discussed in Chapter 5. The full `string` interface is summarized in the Standard Library Reference resource on the Web site; this section merely showed you how `strings` can be used as STL containers.

Streams as STL Containers

Input and output streams are not containers in the traditional sense: they do not store elements. However, they can be considered sequences of elements, and as such share some characteristics with the STL containers. C++ streams do not provide any STL-related methods directly, but the STL supplies special iterators called `istream_iterator` and `ostream_iterator` that allow you to "iterate" through input and output streams. Chapter 23 explains how to use them.

bitset

The `bitset` is a fixed-length abstraction of a sequence of bits. Recall that a bit can represent two values, often referred to as 1 and 0, on and off, or true and false. The `bitset` also uses the terminology *set* and *unset*. You can *toggle* or *flip* a bit from one value to the other.

The `bitset` is not a true STL container: it's of fixed size, it's not templatized on an element type, and it doesn't support iteration. However, it's a useful utility, which is often lumped with the containers, so we provide a brief introduction here. The Standard Library Reference resource on the Web site contains a thorough summary of the `bitset` operations.

bitset Basics

The `bitset`, defined in the `<bitset>` header file, is templatized on the number of bits it stores. The default constructor initializes all fields of the `bitset` to 0. An alternative constructor creates the `bitset` from a `string` of 0s and 1s.

You can adjust the values of the individual bits with the `set()`, `reset()`, and `flip()` methods, and you can access and set individual fields with an overloaded `operator[]`. Note that `operator[]` on a non-const object returns a proxy object to which you can assign a Boolean value, call `flip()`, or negate with ~. You can also access individual fields with the `test()` method.

Additionally, you can stream `bitsets` with the normal insertion and extraction operators. The `bitset` is streamed as a string of 0s and 1s.

Here is a small example:

```
#include <bitset>
#include <iostream>
using namespace std;

int main(int argc, char** argv)
{
    bitset<10> myBitset;

    myBitset.set(3);
    myBitset.set(6);
```

```
        myBitset[8] = true;
        myBitset[9] = myBitset[3];

        if (myBitset.test(3)) {
            cout << "Bit 3 is set!\n";
        }
        cout << myBitset << endl;

        return (0);
}
```

The output is:

```
Bit 3 is set!
1101001000
```

Note that the leftmost character in the output string is the highest numbered bit.

Bitwise Operators

In addition to basic bit manipulation routines, the bitset provides implementations of all the bitwise operators: &, |, ^, ~, <<, >>, &=, |=, ^=, <<=, and >>=. They behave just as they would on a "real" sequence of bits. Here is an example:

```
#include <bitset>
#include <iostream>
using namespace std;

int main(int argc, char** argv)
{
    string str1 = "0011001100";
    string str2 = "0000111100";
    bitset<10> bitsOne(str1), bitsTwo(str2);

    bitset<10> bitsThree = bitsOne & bitsTwo;
    cout << bitsThree << endl;
    bitsThree <<= 4;
    cout << bitsThree << endl;

    return (0);
}
```

The output of the program is:

```
0000001100
0011000000
```

bitset Example: Representing Cable Channels

One possible use of bitsets is tracking channels of cable subscribers. Each subscriber could have a bitset of channels associated with his or her subscription, with set bits representing the channels to which he or she actually subscribes. This system could also support "packages" of channels, also represented as bitsets, which represent commonly subscribed combinations of channels.

The following `CableCompany` class is a simple example of this model. It uses two `map`s, each of `string/`
`bitset`, storing the cable packages as well as the subscriber information.

```cpp
#include <bitset>
#include <map>
#include <string>
#include <stdexcept>
using std::map;
using std::bitset;
using std::string;
using std::out_of_range;

const int kNumChannels = 10;

class CableCompany
{
    public:
        CableCompany() {}

        // Adds the package with the specified channels to the databse
        void addPackage(const string& packageName,
            const bitset<kNumChannels>& channels);

        // Removes the specified package from the database
        void removePackage(const string& packageName);

        // Adds the customer to the database with initial channels found in package
        // Throws out_of_range if the package name is invalid.
        void newCustomer(const string& name, const string& package)
            throw (out_of_range);

        // Adds the customer to the database with initial channels specified
        // in channels
        void newCustomer(const string& name, const bitset<kNumChannels>& channels);

        // Adds the channel to the customers profile
        void addChannel(const string& name, int channel);

        // Removes the channel from the customers profile
        void removeChannel(const string& name, int channel);

        // Adds the specified package to the customers profile
        void addPackageToCustomer(const string& name, const string& package);

        // Removes the specified customer from the database
        void deleteCustomer(const string& name);

        // Retrieves the channels to which this customer subscribes
        // Throws out_of_range if name is not a valid customer
        bitset<kNumChannels>& getCustomerChannels(const string& name)
            throw (out_of_range);

    protected:
        typedef map<string, bitset<kNumChannels> > MapType;
        MapType mPackages, mCustomers;
};
```

Here are the implementations of the preceding methods:

```cpp
#include "CableCompany.h"
using namespace std;

void CableCompany::addPackage(const string& packageName,
    const bitset<kNumChannels>& channels)
{
    // Just make a key/value pair and insert it into the packages map.
    mPackages.insert(make_pair(packageName, channels));
}

void CableCompany::removePackage(const string& packageName)
{
    // Just erase the package from the package map.
    mPackages.erase(packageName);
}

void CableCompany::newCustomer(const string& name, const string& package)
    throw (out_of_range)
{
    // Get a reference to the specified package.
    MapType::const_iterator it = mPackages.find(package);
    if (it == mPackages.end()) {
        // That package doesn't exist. Throw an exception.
        throw (out_of_range("Invalid package"));
    } else {
        // Create the account with the bitset representing that package.
        // Note that it refers to a name/bitset pair. The bitset is the
        // second field.
        mCustomers.insert(make_pair(name, it->second));
    }
}

void CableCompany::newCustomer(const string& name,
    const bitset<kNumChannels>& channels)
{
    // Just add the customer/channels pair to the customers map.
    mCustomers.insert(make_pair(name, channels));
}

void CableCompany::addChannel(const string& name, int channel)
{
    // Find a reference to the customers.
    MapType::iterator it = mCustomers.find(name);
    if (it != mCustomers.end()) {
        // We found this customer; set the channel.
        // Note that it is a reference to a name/bitset pair.
        // The bitset is the second field.
        it->second.set(channel);
    }
}

void CableCompany::removeChannel(const string& name, int channel)
{
```

```
        // Find a reference to the customers.
        MapType::iterator it = mCustomers.find(name);
        if (it != mCustomers.end()) {
            // We found this customer; remove the channel.
            // Note that it is a refernce to a name/bitset pair.
            // The bitset is the second field.
            it->second.reset(channel);
        }
    }

    void CableCompany::addPackageToCustomer(const string& name, const string& package)
    {
        // Find the package.
        MapType::iterator itPack = mPackages.find(package);
        // Find the customer.
        MapType::iterator itCust = mCustomers.find(name);
        if (itCust != mCustomers.end() && itPack != mPackages.end()) {
            // Only if both package and customer are found, can we do the update.
            // Or-in the package to the customers existing channels.
            // Note that it is a reference to a name/bitset pair.
            // The bitset is the second field.
            itCust->second |= itPack->second;
        }
    }

    void CableCompany::deleteCustomer(const string& name)
    {
        // Remove the customer with this name.
        mCustomers.erase(name);
    }

    bitset<kNumChannels>& CableCompany::getCustomerChannels(const string& name)
        throw (out_of_range)
    {
        // Find the customer.
        MapType::iterator it = mCustomers.find(name);
        if (it != mCustomers.end()) {
            // Found it!
            // Note that it is a reference to a name/bitset pair.
            // The bitset is the second field.
            return (it->second);
        }
        // Didn't find it. Throw an exception.
        throw (out_of_range("No customer of that name"));
    }
```

Finally, here is a simple program demonstrating how to use the CableCompany class:

```
#include "CableCompany.h"
#include <iostream>
using namespace std;

int main(int argc, char** argv)
{
    CableCompany myCC;
```

```
string basic_pkg = "1111000000";
string premium_pkg = "1111111111";
string sports_pkg = "0000100111";

myCC.addPackage("basic", bitset<kNumChannels>(basic_pkg));
myCC.addPackage("premium", bitset<kNumChannels>(premium_pkg));
myCC.addPackage("sports", bitset<kNumChannels>(sports_pkg));

myCC.newCustomer("Nicholas Solter", "basic");
myCC.addPackageToCustomer("Nicholas Solter", "sports");
cout << myCC.getCustomerChannels("Nicholas Solter") << endl;

return (0);
}
```

Summary

This chapter introduced the standard template library containers. It also presented sample code illustrating a variety of uses to which you can put these containers. Hopefully you appreciate the power of the vector, deque, list, stack, queue, priority_queue, map, multimap, set, multiset, string, and bitset. Even if you don't incorporate them into your programs immediately, at least keep them in the back of your mind for future projects.

Now that you are familiar with the containers, the next chapter can illustrate the true beauty of the STL by discussing the generic algorithms. Chapter 23, the third, and final, STL chapter, closes with a discussion of the more advanced features and provides a sample container and iterator implementation.

22

Mastering STL Algorithms and Function Objects

As you read in Chapter 21, the STL provides an impressive collection of generic data structures. Most libraries stop there. The STL, however, contains an additional assortment of generic algorithms that can, with some exceptions, be applied to elements from any container. Using these algorithms, you can find elements in containers, sort elements in containers, process elements in containers, and perform a whole host of other operations. The beauty of the algorithms is that they are independent not only of the types of the underlying elements, but of the types of the containers on which they operate. Algorithms perform their work using only the iterator interfaces.

Many of the algorithms accept *callbacks*: a function pointer or something that behaves like a function pointer, such as an object with an overloaded operator(). Conveniently, the STL provides a set of classes that can be used to create callback objects for the algorithms. These callback objects are called function objects, or just *functors*.

This chapter includes:

❑   An overview of the algorithms and three sample algorithms: find(), find_if(), and accumulate()

❑   A detailed look at function objects

    ❑   Predefined function object classes: arithmetic function objects, comparison function objects, and logical function objects

    ❑   Function object adapters

    ❑   How to write your own function objects

❑ The details of the STL algorithms

    ❑ The utility algorithms

    ❑ The nonmodifying algorithms: search, numerical processing, comparison, and operational

    ❑ The modifying algorithms

    ❑ Sorting algorithms

    ❑ Set algorithms

❑ A large example: auditing voter registrations

Overview of Algorithms

The "magic" behind the algorithms is that they work on iterator intermediaries instead of on the containers themselves. In that way, they are not tied to specific container implementations. All the STL algorithms are implemented as function templates, where the template type parameters are usually iterator types. The iterators themselves are specified as arguments to the function. Recall from Chapter 11 that templatized functions can usually deduce the template types from the function arguments, so you can generally call the algorithms as if they were normal functions, not templates.

The iterator arguments are usually iterator ranges. As explained in Chapter 21, iterator ranges are half-open such that they include the first element in the range, but exclude the last. The last iterator is really a "past-the-end" marker.

Some algorithms require additional template type parameters and arguments, which are sometimes function callbacks. These callbacks can be function pointers or function objects. Function objects are discussed in more detail in the next section. First, it's time to take a detailed look at a few algorithms.

The best way to understand the algorithms is to look at some examples. After you've seen how a few of them work, it's easy to pick up the others. This section describes the `find()`, `find_if()`, and `accumulate()` algorithms in detail. The next section presents the function objects, and the final section discusses each of the classes of algorithms with representative samples.

The find() and find_if() Algorithms

`find()` looks for a specific element in an iterator range. You can use it on elements in any container type. It returns an iterator referring to the element found, or the end iterator of the range. Note that the range specified in the call to `find()` need not be the entire range of elements in a container; it could be a subset.

> If `find()` fails to find an element, it returns an iterator equal to the end iterator specified in the function call, not the end iterator of the underlying container.

Here is an example of `find()`:

```cpp
#include <algorithm>
#include <vector>
#include <iostream>
using namespace std;

int main(int argc, char** argv)
{
    int num;

    vector<int> myVector;
    while (true) {
        cout << "Enter a number to add (0 to stop): ";
        cin >> num;
        if (num == 0) {
            break;
        }
        myVector.push_back(num);
    }

    while (true) {
        cout << "Enter a number to lookup (0 to stop): ";
        cin >> num;
        if (num == 0) {
            break;
        }
        vector<int>::iterator it = find(myVector.begin(), myVector.end(), num);
        if (it == myVector.end()) {
            cout << "Could not find " << num << endl;
        } else {
            cout << "Found " << *it << endl;
        }
    }

    return (0);
}
```

The call to `find()` is made with `myVector.begin()` and `myVector.end()` as arguments, in order to search all the elements of the `vector`.

Here is a sample run of the program:

```
Enter a number to add (0 to stop): 3
Enter a number to add (0 to stop): 4
Enter a number to add (0 to stop): 5
Enter a number to add (0 to stop): 6
Enter a number to add (0 to stop): 0
Enter a number to lookup (0 to stop): 5
Found 5
Enter a number to lookup (0 to stop): 8
Could not find 8
Enter a number to lookup (0 to stop): 4
Found 4
```

```
Enter a number to lookup (0 to stop): 2
Could not find 2
Enter a number to lookup (0 to stop): 0
```

Some containers, such as map and set, provide their own versions of find() as class methods.

> If a container provides a method with the same functionality as a generic algorithm, you should use the method instead, because it's faster. For example, the generic find() algorithm runs in linear time, even on a map iterator, while the find() method on a map runs in logarithmic time.

find_if() is similar to find(), except that it accepts a *predicate function callback* instead of a simple element to match. A predicate returns true or false. find_if() calls the predicate on each element in the range until the predicate returns true. find_if() then returns an iterator referring to that element. The following program reads test scores from the user, then checks if any of the scores are "perfect." A perfect score is a score of 100 or higher. The program is similar to the previous example. Only the differences are highlighted.

```cpp
#include <algorithm>
#include <vector>
#include <iostream>
using namespace std;

bool perfectScore(int num)
{
    return (num >= 100);
}

int main(int argc, char** argv)
{
    int num;

    vector<int> myVector;
    while (true) {
        cout << "Enter a test score to add (0 to stop): ";
        cin >> num;
        if (num == 0) {
            break;
        }
        myVector.push_back(num);
    }

    vector<int>::iterator it = find_if(myVector.begin(), myVector.end(),
        perfectScore);
    if (it == myVector.end()) {
        cout << "No perfect scores\n";
    } else {
        cout << "Found a \"perfect\" score of " << *it << endl;
    }
    return (0);
}
```

This program passed a pointer to the `perfectScore()` function, which the `find_if()` algorithm then called on each element until it returned `true`.

Unfortunately, the STL provides no `find_all()` or equivalent algorithm that returns all instances matching a predicate. Chapter 23 shows you how to write your own `find_all()` algorithm.

The accumulate() Algorithms

It's often useful to calculate the sum, or some other arithmetic quantity, of all the elements in a container. The `accumulate()` function does just that. In its most basic form, it calculates the sum of the elements in a specified range. For example, the following function calculates the arithmetic mean of a sequence of integers in a `vector`. The arithmetic mean is simply the sum of all the elements divided by the number of elements.

```
#include <numeric>
#include <vector>
using namespace std;

double arithmeticMean(const vector<int>& nums)
{
    double sum = accumulate(nums.begin(), nums.end(), 0);
    return (sum / nums.size());
}
```

Note that `accumulate()` is declared in `<numeric>`, not in `<algorithm>`. Note also that `accumulate()` takes as its third parameter an initial value for the sum, which in this case should be `0` (the identity for addition) to start a fresh sum.

The second form of `accumulate()` allows the caller to specify an operation to perform instead of addition. This operation takes the form of a binary callback. Suppose that you want to calculate the geometric mean, which is the product of all the numbers in the sequence to the power of the inverse of the size. In that case, you would want to use `accumulate()` to calculate the product instead of the sum. You *could* write it like this:

```
#include <numeric>
#include <vector>
#include <cmath>
using namespace std;

int product(int num1, int num2)
{
    return (num1 * num2);
}

double geometricMean(const vector<int>& nums)
{
    double mult = accumulate(nums.begin(), nums.end(), 1, product);
    return (pow(mult, 1.0 / nums.size()));
}
```

Note that the `product()` function is passed as a callback to `accumulate()` and that the initial value for the accumulation is 1 (the identity for multiplication) instead of 0. The next section shows you how to use `accumulate()` in the `geometricMean()` function without writing a function callback.

Function Objects

Now that you've seen a few STL algorithms, you are able to appreciate function objects. Recall from Chapter 16 that you can overload the function call operator in a class such that objects of the class can be used in place of function pointers. These objects are called function objects, or just functors.

Many of the STL algorithms, such as `find_if()` and the second form of `accumulate()`, require a function pointer as one of the parameters. When you use these functions, you can pass a functor instead of a function pointer. That fact, in and of itself, is not necessarily cause for jumping up and down with joy. While you can certainly write your own functor classes, the real attraction is that C++ provides several predefined functor classes that perform the most commonly used callback operations. This section describes these predefined classes and shows you how to use them.

> All the predefined function object classes are located in the `<functional>` header file.

Arithmetic Function Objects

C++ provides functor class templates for the five binary arithmetic operators: `plus`, `minus`, `multiplies`, `divides`, and `modulus`. Additionally, unary `negate` is supplied. These classes are templatized on the type of the operands and are wrappers for the actual operators. They take one or two parameters of the template type, perform the operation, and return the result. Here is an example using the `plus` class template:

```
#include <functional>
#include <iostream>
using namespace std;

int main(int argc, char** argv)
{
    plus<int> myPlus;

    int res = myPlus(4, 5);
    cout << res << endl;

    return (0);
}
```

This example is silly, because there's no reason to use the `plus` class template when you could just use `operator+` directly. The benefit of the arithmetic function objects is that you can pass them as callbacks to algorithms, which you cannot do directly with the arithmetic operators.

For example, the implementation of the `geometricMean()` function earlier in this chapter used the `accumulate()` function with a function pointer callback to multiply two integers. You could rewrite it to use the `multiplies` function object:

```
#include <numeric>
#include <vector>
#include <cmath>
#include <functional>
using namespace std;

double geometricMean(const vector<int>& nums)
{
    double mult = accumulate(nums.begin(), nums.end(), 1,
        multiplies<int>());
    return (pow(mult, 1.0 / nums.size()));
}
```

The expression `multiplies<int>()` creates a new object of the `multiplies` class, instantiating it with the `int` type.

The other arithmetic function objects behave similarly.

> **The arithmetic function objects are just wrappers around the arithmetic operators. If you use the function objects as callbacks in algorithms, make sure that the objects in your container implement the appropriate operation, such as `operator*` or `operator+`.**

Comparison Function Objects

In addition to the arithmetic function object classes, the C++ language provides all the standard comparisons: `equal_to`, `not_equal_to`, `less`, `greater`, `less_equal`, and `greater_equal`. You've already seen `less` in Chapter 21 as the default comparison for elements in the `priority_queue` and the associative containers. Now you can learn how to change that criterion. Here's an example of a `priority_queue` using the default comparison operator: `less`.

```
#include <queue>
#include <iostream>
using namespace std;

int main(int argc, char** argv)
{
    priority_queue<int> myQueue;

    myQueue.push(3);
    myQueue.push(4);
    myQueue.push(2);
    myQueue.push(1);

    while (!myQueue.empty()) {
        cout << myQueue.top() << endl;
        myQueue.pop();
    }

    return (0);
}
```

The output from the program looks like this:

```
4
3
2
1
```

As you can see, the elements of the queue are removed in descending order, according to the less comparison. You can change the comparison to greater by specifying it as the comparison template argument. Recall from chapter 21 that the priority_queue template definition looks like this:

```
template <typename T, typename Container = vector<T>, typename Compare =
    less<T> >;
```

Unfortunately, the Compare type parameter is last, which means that in order to specify the comparison you must also specify the container. Here is an example of the above program modified so that the priotity_queue sorts elements in ascending order using greater:

```
#include <queue>
#include <functional>
#include <iostream>
using namespace std;

int main(int argc, char** argv)
{
    priority_queue<int, vector<int>, greater<int> > myQueue;

    myQueue.push(3);
    myQueue.push(4);
    myQueue.push(2);
    myQueue.push(1);

    while (!myQueue.empty()) {
        cout << myQueue.top() << endl;
        myQueue.pop();
    }

    return (0);
}
```

The output now looks like this:

```
1
2
3
4
```

Several algorithms that you will learn about later in this chapter require comparison callbacks, for which the predefined comparators come in handy.

Logical Function Objects

C++ also provides function object classes for the three logical operations: logical_not, logical_and, and logical_or. However, they are not typically useful with the standard STL.

Function Object Adapters

When you try to use the basic function objects provided by the standard, it often feels as if you're trying to put a square peg into a round hole. For example, you can't use the basic comparison function objects with find_if() because find_if() passes only one argument to its callback each time instead of two. The *function adapters* attempt to rectify this problem and others. They provide a modicum of support for *functional composition*, or combining functions together to create the exact behavior you need.

Binders

Suppose that you want to use the find_if() algorithm to find the first element in a sequence that is greater than or equal to 100. To solve this problem earlier in the chapter, we wrote a function perfectScore() and passed a function pointer to it to find_if(). Now that you know about the comparison functors, it seems as if you should be able to implement a solution using the greater_equal class template.

The problem with greater_equal is that it takes two parameters, whereas find_if() passes only one parameter to its callback predicate each time. You need the ability to specify that find_if() should use greater_equal, but should pass 100 as the second argument each time. That way, each element of the sequence will be compared against 100. Luckily, C++ gives you a way to say exactly that:

```cpp
#include <algorithm>
#include <vector>
#include <iostream>
#include <functional>
using namespace std;

int main(int argc, char** argv)
{
    int num;

    vector<int> myVector;
    while (true) {
        cout << "Enter a test score to add (0 to stop): ";
        cin >> num;
        if (num == 0) {
            break;
        }
        myVector.push_back(num);
    }

    vector<int>::iterator it = find_if(myVector.begin(), myVector.end(),
        bind2nd(greater_equal<int>(), 100));
```

```
    if (it == myVector.end()) {
        cout << "No perfect scores\n";
    } else {
        cout << "Found a \"perfect\" score of " << *it << endl;
    }
    return (0);
}
```

The `bind2nd()` function is called a *binder* because it "binds" the value 100 as the second parameter to `greater_equal`. The result is that `find_if()` compares each element against 100 with `greater_equal`.

You can use `bind2nd()` with any binary function. There is also an equivalent `bind1st()` function that binds an argument to the first parameter of a binary function.

Negators

The *negators* are functions similar to the binders that simply negate the result of a predicate. For example, if you wanted to find the first element in a sequence of test scores less than 100, you could apply a negator adapter to the result of `greater_equal` like this:

```
int main(int argc, char** argv)
{
    int num;

    vector<int> myVector;
    while (true) {
        cout << "Enter a test score to add (0 to stop): ";
        cin >> num;
        if (num == 0) {
            break;
        }
        myVector.push_back(num);
    }

    vector<int>::iterator it = find_if(myVector.begin(), myVector.end(),
        not1(bind2nd(greater_equal<int>(), 100)));
    if (it == myVector.end()) {
        cout << "All perfect scores\n";
    } else {
        cout << "Found a \"less-than-perfect\" score of " << *it << endl;
    }
    return (0);
}
```

The function `not1()` negates the result of every call to the predicate it takes as an argument. Of course, you could also just use `less` instead of `greater_equal`. There are cases, often when using nonstandard functors, that `not1()` comes in handy. The "1" in `not1()` refers to the fact that its operand must be a unary function (one that takes a single argument). If its operand is a binary function (takes two arguments), you must use `not2()` instead. Note that you use `not1()` in this case because, even though `greater_equal` is a binary function, `bind2nd()` has already converted it to a unary function, by binding the second argument always to 100.

As you can see, using functors and adapters can quickly become complicated. Our advice is to limit their use to simple cases where the intention is clearly understandable, and to write your own functors or employ explicit loops for more complicated situations.

Calling Member Functions

If you have a container of objects, you sometimes want to pass a pointer to a class method as the callback to an algorithm. For example, you might want to find the first empty `string` in a `vector` of `strings` by calling `empty()` on each `string` in the sequence. However, if you just pass a pointer to `string::empty()` to `find_if()`, the algorithm has no way to know that it received a pointer to a method instead of a normal function pointer or functor. As explained in Chapter 9, the code to call a method pointer is different from that to call a normal function pointer, because the former must be called in the context of an object. Thus, C++ provides a conversion function called `mem_fun_ref()` that you can call on a method pointer before passing it to an algorithm (the "fun" in `mem_fun_ref()` refers to "function" and in no way implies that using it is fun). You can use it like this:

```
#include <functional>
#include <algorithm>
#include <string>
#include <vector>
#include <iostream>
using namespace std;

void findEmptyString(const vector<string>& strings)
{
    vector<string>::const_iterator it = find_if(strings.begin(), strings.end(),
        mem_fun_ref(&string::empty));

    if (it == strings.end()) {
        cout << "No empty strings!\n";
    } else {
        cout << "Empty string at position: " << it - strings.begin() << endl;
    }
}
```

`mem_fun_ref()` generates a function object that serves as the callback for `find_if()`. Each time it is called back, it calls the `empty()` method on its argument.

> **`mem_fun_ref()` works for both 0-argument and unary methods. The result can be used as the callback where a unary or binary function is expected, respectively.**

If you have a container of pointers to objects instead of objects themselves, you must use a different function adapter, `mem_fun()`, to call member functions. For example:

```
#include <functional>
#include <algorithm>
#include <string>
#include <vector>
#include <iostream>
using namespace std;
```

```
    void findEmptyString(const vector<string*>& strings)
    {
        vector<string*>::const_iterator it = find_if(strings.begin(), strings.end(),
            mem_fun(&string::empty));

        if (it == strings.end()) {
            cout << "No empty strings!\n";
        } else {
            cout << "Empty string at position: " << it - strings.begin() << endl;
        }
    }
```

Adapting Real Functions

You can't use normal function pointers directly with the function adapters bind1st(), bind2nd(), not1(), or not2(), because these adapters require specific typedefs in the function objects they adapt. Thus, one last function adapter provided by the C++ standard library, ptr_fun(), allows you to wrap regular function pointers in a way that they can be used with the adapters. It is useful primarily for using legacy C functions, such as those in the C Standard Library. If you write your own callbacks, we encourage you to write function object classes, as described in the next section.

For example, suppose that you want to write a function isNumber() that returns true if every character in a string is a digit. As explained in Chapter 21, the C++ string provides an iterator. Thus, you can use the find_if() algorithm to search for the first nondigit in the string. If you find one, the string is not a number. The <cctype> header file provides a legacy C function called isdigit(), which returns true if a character is a digit, false otherwise. The problem is that you want to find the first character that is not a digit, which requires the not1() adapter. However, because isdigit() is a C function, not a function object, you need to use the ptr_fun() adapter to generate a function object that can be used with not1(). The code looks like this:

```
#include <functional>
#include <algorithm>
#include <cctype>
#include <string>
using namespace std;

bool isNumber(const string& str)
{
    string::const_iterator it = find_if(str.begin(), str.end(),
        not1(ptr_fun(::isdigit)));
    return (it == str.end());
}
```

Note the use of the :: scope resolution operator to specify that isdigit() should be found in the global scope.

Writing Your Own Function Objects

You can, of course, write your own function objects to perform more specific tasks than those provided by the predefined functors. If you want to be able to use the function adapters with these functors, you must supply certain typedefs. The easiest way to do that is to subclass your function object classes from either `unary_function` or `binary_function`, depending on whether they take one or two arguments. These two classes, both defined in `<functional>`, are templatized on the parameter and return types of the "function" they provide. For example, instead of using `ptr_fun()` to convert `isdigit()`, you could write a wrapper function object like this:

```
#include <functional>
#include <algorithm>
#include <cctype>
#include <string>
using namespace std;
```

```
class myIsDigit : public unary_function<char, bool>
{
    public:
        bool operator() (char c) const { return (::isdigit(c)); }
};
```

```
bool isNumber(const string& str)
{
    string::const_iterator it = find_if(str.begin(), str.end(),
        not1(myIsDigit()));
    return (it == str.end());
}
```

Note that the overloaded function call operator of the `myIsDigit` class must be `const` in order to pass objects to `find_if()`.

> **The algorithms are allowed to make multiple copies of function object predicates and call different ones for different elements. Thus, you shouldn't write them such that they count on any internal state to the object being consistent between calls.**

Algorithm Details

This chapter describes the general categories of algorithms, with examples of each. The Standard Library Reference resource on the Web site contains a summary of *all* the algorithms, but for nitty-gritty details, you should consult one of the books on the STL listed in Appendix B.

Recall from Chapter 21 that there are five types of iterators: input, output, forward, bidirectional, and random-access. There is no formal class hierarchy of these iterators, because the implementations for each container are not part of the standard hierarchy. However, one can deduce a hierarchy based on the functionality they are required to provide. Specifically, every random access iterator is also bidirectional, every bidirectional iterator is also forward, and every forward iterator is also input and output.

The standard way for the algorithms to specify what kind of iterators they need is to use the following names for the iterator template arguments: `InputIterator`, `OutputIterator`, `ForwardIterator`, `BidirectionalIterator`, and `RandomAccessIterator`. These names are just names: they don't provide binding type checking. Therefore, you could, for example, try to call an algorithm expecting a

RandomAccessIterator by passing a bidirectional iterator. The template doesn't do type checking, so it would allow this instantiation. However, the code in the function that uses the random access iterator capabilities would fail to compile on the bidirectional iterator. Thus, the requirement is enforced, just not where you would expect. The error message can therefore be somewhat confusing. For example, attempting to use the generic sort() algorithm, which requires a random access iterator, on a list, which provides only a bidirectional iterator, gives this error in g++:

```
/usr/include/c++/3.2.2/bits/stl_algo.h: In function `void
    std::sort(_RandomAccessIter, _RandomAccessIter) [with _RandomAccessIter =
    std::_List_iterator<int, int&, int*>]':
Sorting.cpp:38:    instantiated from here
/usr/include/c++/3.2.2/bits/stl_algo.h:2178: no match for `
    std::_List_iterator<int, int&, int*>& - std::_List_iterator<int, int&,
    int*>&' operator
```

Don't worry if you don't understand this error yet. The sort() algorithm is covered later in this chapter.

Most of the algorithms are defined in the <algorithm> header file, but a few algorithms are located in <numeric>. They are all in the std namespace. See the Standard Library Reference resource on the Web site for details.

Utility Algorithms

The STL provides three utility algorithms implemented as function templates: min(), max(), and swap(). min() and max() compare two elements of any type with operator< or a user-supplied binary predicate, returning a reference to the smaller or larger element, respectively. swap() takes two elements of any type by reference and switches their values.

These utilities do not work on sequences of elements, so they do not take iterator parameters.

The following program demonstrates the three functions:

```cpp
#include <algorithm>
#include <iostream>
using namespace std;

int main(int argc, char** argv)
{
    int x = 4, y = 5;
    cout << "x is " << x << " and y is " << y << endl;
    cout << "Max is " << max(x, y) << endl;
    cout << "Min is " << min(x, y) << endl;
    swap(x, y);
    cout << "x is " << x << " and y is " << y << endl;
    cout << "Max is " << max(x, y) << endl;
    cout << "Min is " << min(x, y) << endl;

    return (0);
}
```

Here is the program output:

```
x is 4 and y is 5
Max is 5
Min is 4
x is 5 and y is 4
Max is 5
Min is 4
```

Nonmodifying Algorithms

The nonmodifying algorithms include functions for searching elements in a range, generating numerical information about elements in a range, comparing two ranges to each other, and processing each element in a range.

Search Algorithms

You've already seen two examples of search algorithms: `find()` and `find_if()`. The STL provides several other variations of the basic `find()` algorithm that work on unsorted sequences of elements. `adjacent_find()` finds the first instance of two consecutive elements that are equal to each other. `find_first_of()` searches for one of several values simultaneously. `search()` and `find_end()` search for subsequences matching a specified sequence of elements, starting from either the beginning or end of the supplied range. `search_n()` can be thought of as a special case of `search()` or a general case of `adjacent_find()`: it finds the first sequence of n consecutive elements matching a supplied value. Finally, `min_element()` and `max_element()` find the minimum or maximum element in a sequence.

> **find_end()** is the equivalent of **search()** that starts from the end of the sequence instead of the beginning. It is not the reverse equivalent of **find()**. There is no reverse equivalent of **find()**, **find_if()**, or other algorithms that search for a single element, because you can use a **reverse_iterator** to achieve the same effect. **reverse_iterators** are described in Chapter 23.

`find()`, `adjacent_find()`, `min_element()`, and `max_element()` run in linear time. The others run in quadratic time. All the algorithms use default comparisons of `operator==` or `operator<`, but also provide overloaded versions that allow the client to specify a comparison callback.

Here are examples of the preceding search algorithms:

```
#include <algorithm>
#include <iostream>
#include <vector>
using namespace std;

int main(int argc, char** argv)
{
    // The list of elements to be searched
    int elems[] = {5, 6, 9, 8, 8, 3};
```

```
    // Construct a vector from the list, exploiting the
    // fact that pointers are iterators too.
    vector<int> myVector(elems, elems + 6);
    vector<int>::const_iterator it, it2;

    // Find the min and max elements in the vector.
    it = min_element(myVector.begin(), myVector.end());
    it2 = max_element(myVector.begin(), myVector.end());
    cout << "The min is " << *it << " and the max is " << *it2 << endl;

    // Find the first pair of matching consecutive elements.
    it = adjacent_find(myVector.begin(), myVector.end());
    if (it != myVector.end()) {
        cout << "Found two consecutive equal elements of value "
            << *it << endl;
    }

    // Find the first of two values.
    int targets[] = {8, 9};
    it = find_first_of(myVector.begin(), myVector.end(), targets,
        targets + 2);

    if (it != myVector.end()) {
        cout << "Found one of 8 or 9: " << *it << endl;
    }

    // Find the first subsequence.
    int sub[] = {8, 3};
    it = search(myVector.begin(), myVector.end(), sub, sub + 2);
    if (it != myVector.end()) {
        cout << "Found subsequence 8, 3 at position " << it - myVector.begin()
            << endl;
    }

    // Find the last subsequence (which should be the same as the first).
    it2 = find_end(myVector.begin(), myVector.end(), sub, sub + 2);
    if (it != it2) {
        cout << "Error: search and find_end found different subsequences "
            << " even though there is only one match.\n";
    }

    // Find the first subsequence of two consecutive 8s.
    it = search_n(myVector.begin(), myVector.end(), 2, 8);
    if (it != myVector.end()) {
        cout << "Found two consecutive 8s starting at position "
            << it - myVector.begin() << endl;
    }

    return (0);
}
```

```
The min is 3 and the max is 9
Found two consecutive equal elements of value 8
Found one of 8 or 9: 9
Found subsequence 8, 3 at position 4
Found two consecutive 8s starting at position 3
```

There are also several search algorithms that work only on sorted sequences: `binary_search()`, `lower_bound()`, `upper_bound()`, and `equal_range()`. `binary_search()` finds a matching element in logarithmic time. The other three are similar to their method equivalents on the `map` and `set` containers. See Chapter 21 and the Standard Library Reference resource on the Web site.

> Remember to use equivalent container methods when available instead of the algorithms, because the methods are more efficient.

Numerical Processing Algorithms

You've seen an example of one numerical processing algorithm already: `accumulate()`. In addition, the `count()` and `count_if()` algorithms are useful for counting the number of elements of a given value in a container. They function similarly to the `count()` method on the `map` and `set` containers.

The other numerical processing algorithms are less useful, so they are not discussed here. See the Standard Library Reference resource on the Web site for details if you are interested.

Comparison Algorithms

You can compare entire ranges of elements in three different ways: `equal()`, `mismatch()`, and `lexicographical_compare()`. Each of the algorithms compares elements at parallel positions in the two ranges to each other in order. `equal()` returns `true` if all parallel elements are equal. `mismatch()` returns iterators referring into each range at the first point where parallel elements are unequal. `lexicographical_compare()` returns `true` if all the elements in the first range are less than their parallel elements in the second range, or if the first range is shorter than the second, and all elements up to that point are less than the parallel elements in the second range. You can think of this function as a generalization of alphabetization to noncharacter elements.

> If you want to compare the elements of two containers of the same type, you can use `operator==` or `operator<` instead of `equal()` or `lexicographical_compare()`. The algorithms are useful primarily for comparing sequences of elements from different container types.

Here are some examples of `equal()`, `mismatch()`, and `lexicographical_compare()`:

```cpp
#include <algorithm>
#include <vector>
#include <list>
#include <iostream>
using namespace std;

// Function template to populate a container of ints.
// The container must support push_back().
template<typename Container>
void populateContainer(Container& cont)
{
    int num;

    while (true) {
        cout << "Enter a number (0 to quit): ";
        cin >> num;
        if (num == 0) {
            break;
        }
        cont.push_back(num);
    }
}

int main(int argc, char** argv)
{
    vector<int> myVector;
    list<int> myList;

    cout << "Populate the vector:\n";
    populateContainer(myVector);
    cout << "Populate the list:\n";
    populateContainer(myList);
    if (myList.size() < myVector.size()) {
        cout << "Sorry, the list is not long enough.\n";
        return (0);
    }

    // Compare the two containers.
    if (equal(myVector.begin(), myVector.end(), myList.begin())) {
        cout << "The two containers have equal elements\n";
    } else {
        // If the containers were not equal, find out why not.
        pair<vector<int>::iterator, list<int>::iterator> miss =
            mismatch(myVector.begin(), myVector.end(), myList.begin());
        cout << "The first mismatch is at position "
            << miss.first - myVector.begin() << ". The vector has value "
            << *(miss.first) << " and the list has value " << *(miss.second)
            << endl;
    }

// Now order them.
    if (lexicographical_compare(myVector.begin(), myVector.end(), myList.begin(),
        myList.end())) {
```

```
            cout << "The vector is lexicographically first.\n";
        } else {
            cout << "The list is lexicographically first.\n";
        }

        return (0);
    }
```

Here is a sample run of the program:

```
Populate the vector:
Enter a number (0 to quit): 5
Enter a number (0 to quit): 6
Enter a number (0 to quit): 7
Enter a number (0 to quit): 8
Enter a number (0 to quit): 0
Populate the list:
Enter a number (0 to quit): 5
Enter a number (0 to quit): 6
Enter a number (0 to quit): 7
Enter a number (0 to quit): 9
Enter a number (0 to quit): 0
The first mismatch is at position 3. The vector has value 8 and the list has value 9
The vector is lexicographically first.
```

Operational Algorithms

There is only one algorithm in this category: for_each(). However, it is one of the most useful algorithms in the STL. It executes a callback on each element of the range. You can use it with simple function callbacks for things like printing every element in a container. For example:

```cpp
#include <algorithm>
#include <map>
#include <iostream>
using namespace std;

void printPair(const pair<int, int>& elem)
{
    cout << elem.first << "->" << elem.second << endl;
}

int main(int argc, char** argv)
{
    map<int, int> myMap;
    myMap.insert(make_pair(4, 40));
    myMap.insert(make_pair(5, 50));
    myMap.insert(make_pair(6, 60));
    myMap.insert(make_pair(7, 70));
    myMap.insert(make_pair(8, 80));

    for_each(myMap.begin(), myMap.end(), &printPair);

    return (0);
}
```

You can also perform much fancier tasks by using a functor to retain information between elements. `for_each()` returns a copy of the callback object, so you can accumulate information in your functor that you can retrieve after `for_each()` has finished processing each element. For example, you could calculate both the `min` and `max` elements in one pass by writing a functor that tracks both the minimum and maximum elements found so far. The `MinAndMax` functor shown in the following example assumes that the range on which it is called contains at least one element. It uses a Boolean `first` variable to initialize `min` and `max` to the first element, after which it compares each subsequent element to the currently stored `min` and `max` values.

```cpp
#include <algorithm>
#include <functional>
#include <vector>
#include <iostream>
using namespace std;

// The populateContainer() function is identical to the one shown above for
// comparison alglorithms, so is omitted here.

class MinAndMax : public unary_function<int, void>
{
    public:
        MinAndMax();
        void operator()(int elem);

        // Make min and max public for easy access.
        int min, max;

    protected:
        bool first;
};

MinAndMax::MinAndMax() : min(-1), max(-1), first(true)
{
}

void MinAndMax::operator()(int elem)
{
    if (first) {
        min = max = elem;
    } else if (elem < min) {
        min = elem;
    } else if (elem > max) {
        max = elem;
    }
    first = false;
}

int main(int argc, char** argv)
{
    vector<int> myVector;
    populateContainer(myVector);
```

```
    MinAndMax func;
    func = for_each(myVector.begin(), myVector.end(), func);
    cout << "The max is " << func.max << endl;
    cout << "The min is " << func.min << endl;

    return (0);
}
```

You might be tempted to ignore the return value of `for_each()`, yet still try to read information from `func` after the call. However, that doesn't work because `func` is not necessarily passed-by-reference into `for_each()`. You must capture the return value in order to ensure correct behavior.

A final point about `for_each()` is that your callback is allowed to take its argument by reference and modify it. That has the effect of changing values in the actual iterator range. The voter registration example later in this chapter shows a use of this capability.

Modifying Algorithms

The STL provides a variety of modifying algorithms that perform tasks such as copying elements from one range to another, removing elements, or reversing the order of elements in a range.

The modifying algorithms all have the concept of *source* and *destination* ranges. The elements are read from the source range and added to or modified in the destination range. The source and destination ranges can often be the same, in which case the algorithm is said to operate *in place*.

> **Ranges from `maps` and `multimaps` cannot be used as destinations of modifying algorithms. These algorithms overwrite entire elements, which in a `map` consist of key/value pairs. However, `maps` and `multimaps` mark the key `const`, so it cannot be assigned to. Similarly, many implementations of `set` and `multiset` provide only `const` iteration over the elements, so you cannot generally use ranges from these containers as destinations of modifying algorithms either. Your alternative is to use an *insert iterator*, described in Chapter 23.**

Transform

The `transform()` algorithm is similar to `for_each()`, in that it applies a callback to each element in a range. The difference is that `transform()` expects the callback to generate a new element for each call, which it stores in the destination range specified. The source and destination ranges can be the same if you want transform to replace each element in a range with the result from the call to the callback. For example, you could add 100 to each element in a `vector` like this:

```
#include <algorithm>
#include <functional>
#include <iostream>
#include <vector>
using namespace std;
```

```
// The populateContainer() function is identical to the one shown above for
// comparison alglorithms, so is omitted here.

void print(int elem)
{
    cout << elem << " ";
}

int main(int argc, char** argv)
{
    vector<int> myVector;
    populateContainer(myVector);
    cout << "The vector contents are:\n";
    for_each(myVector.begin(), myVector.end(), &print);
    cout << endl;
    transform(myVector.begin(), myVector.end(), myVector.begin(),
        bind2nd(plus<int>(), 100));
    cout << "The vector contents are:\n";
    for_each(myVector.begin(), myVector.end(), &print);
    cout << endl;
    return (0);
}
```

Another form of `transform()` calls a binary function on pairs of elements in the range. See the Standrad Library Reference resource on the Web site. Interestingly, by writing the right functors for `transform()`, you could use it to achieve the functionality of many of the other modifying algorithms, such as `copy()` and `replace()`. However, it is usually more convenient to use the simpler algorithms when possible.

> `transform()` **and the other modifying algorithms often return an iterator referring to the past-the-end value of the destination range. The examples in this book usually ignore that return value. Consult the Standard Library Reference resource on the Web site for the specifics.**

Copy

The `copy()` algorithm allows you to copy elements from one range to another. The source and destination ranges must be different, but they can overlap. Note that `copy()` doesn't insert elements into the destination range. It just overwrites whatever elements were there already. Thus, you can't use `copy()` directly to insert elements into a container, only to overwrite elements that were previously in a container.

> **Chapter 23 describes how to use** *iterator adapters* **to insert elements into a container or stream with `copy()`.**

Here is a simple example of `copy()` that exploits the `resize()` method on `vectors` to ensure that there is enough space in the destination container:

```
#include <algorithm>
#include <vector>
#include <iostream>
using namespace std;

// The populateContainer() and print() functions are identical to those
// in the previous example, so are omitted here.

int main(int argc, char** argv)
{
    vector<int> vectOne, vectTwo;

    populateContainer(vectOne);

    vectTwo.resize(vectOne.size());
    copy(vectOne.begin(), vectOne.end(), vectTwo.begin());
    for_each(vectTwo.begin(), vectTwo.end(), &print);

    return (0);
}
```

Replace

The `replace()` and `replace_if()` algorithms replace elements in a range matching a value or predicate, respectively, with a new value. For example, you could force all elements in an integer range to be between 0 and 100 by replacing all values less than 0 with 0 and replacing all values greater than 100 with 100:

```
#include <algorithm>
#include <functional>
#include <vector>
#include <iostream>
using namespace std;

// The populateContainer() and print() functions are identical to those
// in the previous example, so are omitted here.

int main(int argc, char** argv)
{
    vector<int> myVector;
    populateContainer(myVector);
    replace_if(myVector.begin(), myVector.end(), bind2nd(less<int>(), 0), 0);
    replace_if(myVector.begin(), myVector.end(), bind2nd(greater<int>(), 100),
        100);
    for_each(myVector.begin(), myVector.end(), &print);
    cout << endl;

    return (0);
}
```

There are also variants of `replace()` called `replace_copy()` and `replace_copy_if()` that copy the results to a different destination range.

Remove

The `remove()` and `remove_if()` algorithms remove certain elements from a range. The elements to remove can be specified by either a specific value or with a predicate. It is important to remember that these elements are not removed from the underlying container, because the algorithms have access only to the iterator abstraction, not to the container. Instead, the removed elements are copied to the end of the range, and the new end of the (shorter) range is returned. If you want to actually erase the removed elements from the container, you must use the `remove()` algorithm, then call `erase()` on the container. Here is an example of a function that removes empty `strings` from a `vector` of `strings`. It is similar to the function `findEmptyString()` shown earlier in the chapter.

```
#include <functional>
#include <algorithm>
#include <string>
#include <vector>
#include <iostream>
using namespace std;

void removeEmptyStrings(vector<string>& strings)
{
    vector<string>::iterator it = remove_if(strings.begin(), strings.end(),
        mem_fun_ref(&string::empty));
    // Erase the removed elements.
    strings.erase(it, strings.end());
}

void printString(const string& str)
{
    cout << str << " ";
}

int main(int argc, char** argv)
{
    vector<string> myVector;
    myVector.push_back("");
    myVector.push_back("stringone");
    myVector.push_back("");
    myVector.push_back("stringtwo");
    myVector.push_back("stringthree");
    myVector.push_back("stringfour");

    removeEmptyStrings(myVector);
    cout << "Size is " << myVector.size() << endl;
    for_each(myVector.begin(), myVector.end(), &printString);
    cout << endl;
    return (0);
}
```

The `remove_copy()` and `remove_copy_if()` variations of `remove()` do not change the source range. Instead they copy all unremoved elements to a different destination range. They are similar to `copy()`, in that the destination range must already be large enough to hold the new elements.

> The `remove()` family of functions is *stable* in that it maintains the order of elements remaining in the container even while moving the removed elements to the end.

Unique

The `unique()` algorithm is a special case of `remove()` that removes all duplicate contiguous elements. You may recall from Chapter 21 that the `list` container provides a `unique()` method that implements the same semantics. You should generally use `unique()` on sorted sequences, but nothing prevents you from running it on unsorted sequences.

The basic form of `unique()` runs in place, but there is also a version of the algorithm called `unique_copy()` that copies its results to a new destination range.

Chapter 21 showed an example of the `list unique()` algorithm, so we omit an example of the general form here.

Reverse

The `reverse()` algorithms simply reverses the order of the elements in a range. The first element in the range is swapped with the last, the second with the second-to-last, and so on.

The basic form of `reverse()` runs in place, but there is also a version of the algorithm called `reverse_copy()` that copies its results to a new destination range.

Other Modifying Algorithms

There are several other modifying algorithms described in the Standard Library Reference resource on the Web site, including `iter_swap()`, `swap_ranges()`, `fill()`, `generate()`, `rotate()`, `next_permutation()`, and `prev_permutation()`. We have found these algorithms to be less useful on a day-to-day basis than those shown earlier. However, if you ever need to use them, the Standard Library Reference resource on the Web site contains all the details.

Sorting Algorithms

The STL provides several variations of sorting algorithms. These algorithms don't apply to associative containers, which always sort their elements internally. Additionally, the `list` container supplies its own version of `sort()`, which is more efficient than the general algorithm. Thus, most of these sorting algorithms are useful only for `vectors` and `deques`.

Basic Sorting and Merging

The `sort()` function uses a quicksort-like algorithm to sort a range of elements in $O(N \log N)$ time in the general case. Following the application of `sort()` to a range, the elements in the range are in nondecreasing order (lowest to highest), according to `operator<`. If you don't like that order, you can specify a different comparison callback such as `greater`.

A variant of `sort()`, called `stable_sort()`, maintains the relative order of equal elements in the range. `stable_sort()` uses a mergesort-like algorithm.

Once you have sorted the elements in a range, you can apply the `binary_search()` algorithm to find elements in logarithmic instead of linear time.

The `merge()` function allows you to merge two sorted ranges together, while maintaining the sorted order. The result is a sorted range containing all the elements of the two source ranges. `merge()` works in linear time. Without `merge()`, you could still achieve the same effect by concatenating the two ranges and applying `sort()` to the result, but that would be less efficient ($O(N \log N)$ instead of linear).

> **Always ensure that you supply a big enough range to store the result of the merge!**

Here is an example of sorting and merging:

```cpp
#include <algorithm>
#include <vector>
#include <iostream>
using namespace std;

// The populateContainer() and print() functions are identical to those
// in the example above, so they are omitted here.

int main(int argc, char** argv)
{
    vector<int> vectorOne, vectorTwo, vectorMerged;
    cout << "Enter values for first vector:\n";
    populateContainer(vectorOne);
    cout << "Enter values for second vector:\n";
    populateContainer(vectorTwo);

    sort(vectorOne.begin(), vectorOne.end());
    sort(vectorTwo.begin(), vectorTwo.end());
    // Make sure the vector is large enough to hold the values
    // from both source vectors.
    vectorMerged.resize(vectorOne.size() + vectorTwo.size());
    merge(vectorOne.begin(), vectorOne.end(), vectorTwo.begin(),
        vectorTwo.end(), vectorMerged.begin());

    cout << "Merged vector: ";
    for_each(vectorMerged.begin(), vectorMerged.end(), &print);
    cout << endl;

    while (true) {
        int num;
        cout << "Enter a number to find (0 to quit): ";
        cin >> num;
        if (num == 0) {
            break;
        }
        if (binary_search(vectorMerged.begin(), vectorMerged.end(), num)) {
            cout << "That number is in the vector.\n";
        } else {
            cout << "That number is not in the vector\n";
```

```
        }
    }

    return (0);
}
```

Heapsort

A heap structure stores elements in a semi-sorted order so that finding the highest element is a constant time operation. Removing the highest element and adding a new element both take logarithmic time. For general information on heap data structures, consult one of the data structures books listed in Appendix B.

The STL provides four algorithms for manipulating a heap structure.

❏   `make_heap()` turns a range of elements into a heap in linear time. The highest element is the first element in the range.

❏   `push_heap()` adds a new element to the heap by incorporating the element in the previous end position of the range. That is, `push_heap()` takes an iterator range [first,last) and expects that [first,last-1) is a valid heap and that the element at position last – 1 is a new element to be added to the heap. In terms of containers, if you have a heap in a `deque` container, you can use `push_back()` to add a new element to the `deque`, then call `push_heap()` on the `deque` beginning and end iterators. `push_heap()` runs in logarithmic time.

❏   `pop_heap()` removes the highest element from the heap and reorders the remaining elements to keep the heap structure. It reduces the range representing the heap by one element. If the range before the call was [first,last), the new range is [first,last-1). As usual, the algorithm can't actually remove the element from the container. If you want to remove it you must call `erase()` or `pop_back()` after calling `pop_heap()`. `pop_heap()` runs in logarithmic time.

❏   `sort_heap()` turns a heap range into a fully sorted range in $O(N \log N)$ time.

Heaps are useful for implementing priority queues. In fact, the `priority_queue` container presented in Chapter 21 is implemented with these heap algorithms. If you are ever tempted to use the heap algorithms directly, you should first make sure that the `priority_queue` interface does not meet with your satisfaction. We don't show an example of the heap functions here, but the Standard Library Reference resource on the Web site contains the details in case you ever need to use them.

Other Sorting Routines

There are several other sorting routines, including `partition()`, `partial_sort()`, and `nth_element()`. They are mostly useful as building blocks for a quicksort-like algorithm. Given that `sort()` already provides a quicksort-like algorithm, you usually shouldn't need to use these other sorting routines. However, the Standard Library Reference resource on the Web site contains the details in case the need arises.

random_shuffle()

The final "sorting" algorithm is technically more of an "anti-sorting" algorithm. `random_shuffle()` rearranges the elements of a range in a random order. It's useful for implementing tasks like sorting a deck of cards.

Set Algorithms

The final class of algorithms in the STL is five functions for performing set operations. Although these algorithms work on any sorted iterator range, they are obviously aimed at ranges from the set container.

The `includes()` function implements standard subset determination, checking if all the elements of one sorted range are included in another sorted range, in any order.

The `set_union()`, `set_intersection()`, `set_difference()`, and `set_symmetric_difference()` functions implement the standard semantics of those operations. In case you haven't studied set theory recently, here's a rundown. The result of union is all the elements in either set. The result of intersection is all the elements in both sets. The result of difference is all the elements in the first set but not the second. The result of symmetric difference is the "exclusive or" of sets: all the elements in one, but not both, sets.

> As usual, make sure that your result range is large enough to hold the result of the operations. For `set_union()` and `set_symmetric_difference()`, the result is at most the sum of the sizes of the two input ranges. For `set_intersection()` and `set_difference()` it's at most the maximum of the two sizes.
>
> Remember that you can't use iterator ranges from associative containers, including sets, to store the results.

Here is an example of these algorithms:

```
#include <algorithm>
#include <iostream>
#include <vector>
using namespace std;

// The populateContainer() and print() functions are identical to those
// in the example above, so are omitted here.

int main(int argc, char** argv)
{
    vector<int> setOne, setTwo, setThree;
    cout << "Enter set one:\n";
    populateContainer(setOne);
    cout << "Enter set two:\n";
    populateContainer(setTwo);

    // set algorithms work on sorted ranges
    sort(setOne.begin(), setOne.end());
    sort(setTwo.begin(), setTwo.end());

    if (includes(setOne.begin(), setOne.end(), setTwo.begin(), setTwo.end())) {
        cout << "The second set is a subset of the first\n";
```

```
    }
    if (includes(setTwo.begin(), setTwo.end(), setOne.begin(), setOne.end())) {
        cout << "The first set is a subset of the second\n";
    }

    setThree.resize(setOne.size() + setTwo.size());
    vector<int>::iterator newEnd;
    newEnd = set_union(setOne.begin(), setOne.end(), setTwo.begin(),
        setTwo.end(), setThree.begin());
    cout << "The union is: ";
    for_each(setThree.begin(), newEnd, &print);
    cout << endl;

    newEnd = set_intersection(setOne.begin(), setOne.end(), setTwo.begin(),
        setTwo.end(), setThree.begin());
    cout << "The intersection is: ";
    for_each(setThree.begin(), newEnd, &print);
    cout << endl;

    newEnd = set_difference(setOne.begin(), setOne.end(), setTwo.begin(),
        setTwo.end(), setThree.begin());
    cout << "The difference between set one and set two is: ";
    for_each(setThree.begin(), newEnd, &print);
    cout << endl;

    newEnd = set_symmetric_difference(setOne.begin(), setOne.end(), setTwo.begin(),
        setTwo.end(), setThree.begin());
    cout << "The symmetric difference is: ";
    for_each(setThree.begin(), newEnd, &print);
    cout << endl;

    return (0);
}
```

Here is a sample run of the program:

```
Enter set one:
Enter a number (0 to quit): 5
Enter a number (0 to quit): 6
Enter a number (0 to quit): 7
Enter a number (0 to quit): 8
Enter a number (0 to quit): 0
Enter set two:
Enter a number (0 to quit): 8
Enter a number (0 to quit): 9
Enter a number (0 to quit): 10
Enter a number (0 to quit): 0
The union is: 5 6 7 8 9 10
The intersection is: 8
The difference between set one and set two is: 5 6 7
The symmetric difference is: 5 6 7 9 10
```

Algorithms and Function Objects Example: Auditing Voter Registrations

Voter fraud can be a problem in the United States. People sometimes attempt to register and vote in two or more different counties. Additionally, convicted felons, who are ineligible to vote in some states, occasionally attempt to register and vote anyway. Using your newfound algorithm and function object skills, you could write a simple voter registration auditing function that checks the voter rolls for certain anomalies.

The Voter Registration Audit Problem Statement

The voter registration audit function should audit the information for a single state. Assume that voter registrations are stored by county in a map that maps county names to a list of voters. Your audit function should take this map and a list of convicted felons as parameters, and should remove all convicted felons from the lists of voters. Additionally, the function should find all voters who are registered in more than one county and should remove those names from all counties. For simplicity, assume that the list of voters is simply a list of string names. A real application would obviously require more data, such as address and party affiliation.

The auditVoterRolls() Function

This example takes a *top-down* approach, starting from the highest-level function and making calls to functions and functors that are not yet written. As the example progresses, the missing implementations will be filled in.

The top-level function, auditVoterRolls(), works in three steps:

1. Find all the duplicate names in all the registration lists by making a call to getDuplicates().

2. Combine the list of duplicates and the list of convicted felons, and remove duplicates in the combined list.

3. Remove from every voter list all the names found in the combined list of duplicates and convicted felons. The approach taken here is to use for_each() to process each list in the map, applying a user-defined functor RemoveNames to remove the offending names from each list.

Here's the implementation of auditVoterRolls():

```
//
// auditVoterRolls
//
// Expects a map of string/list<string> pairs keyed on county names
// and containing lists of all the registered voters in those counties
//
// Removes from each list any name on the convictedFelons list and
// any name that is found on any other list
//
void auditVoterRolls(map<string, list<string> >& votersByCounty,
```

```
                const list<string>& convictedFelons)
{
    // Get all the duplicate names.
    list<string> duplicates = getDuplicates(votersByCounty);

    // Combine the duplicates and convicted felons--we want
    // to remove names on both lists from all voter rolls.
    duplicates.insert(duplicates.end(), convictedFelons.begin(),
        convictedFelons.end());

    // If there were any duplicates, remove them.
    // Use the list versions of sort and unique instead of the generic
    // algorithms, because the list versions are more efficient.
    duplicates.sort();
    duplicates.unique();

    // Now remove all the names we need to remove.
    for_each(votersByCounty.begin(), votersByCounty.end(),
        RemoveNames(duplicates));
}
```

The getDuplicates() Function

The `getDuplicates()` function must find any name that is on more than one voter registration list. There are several different approaches one could use to solve this problem. This implementation simply combines the `lists` from each county into one big `list` and sorts it. At that point, any duplicate names between the different `lists` will be next to each other in the big `list`. Now `getDuplicates()` can use the `adjacent_find()` algorithm on the big, sorted, `list` to find all consecutive duplicates. Here is the implementation:

```
//
// getDuplicates()
//
// Returns a list of all names that appear in more than one list in
// the map
//
// The implementation generates one large list of all the names from
// all the lists in the map, sorts it, then finds all duplicates
// in the sorted list with adjacent_find().
//
list<string> getDuplicates(const map<string, list<string> >& voters)
{
    list<string> allNames, duplicates;

    // Collect all the names from all the lists into one big list.
    map<string, list<string> >::const_iterator it;
    for(it = voters.begin(); it != voters.end(); ++it) {
        allNames.insert(allNames.end(), it->second.begin(), it->second.end());
    }

    // Sort the list--use the list version, not the general algorithm,
    // because the list version is faster.
    allNames.sort();
```

```
    //
    // Now that it's sorted, all duplicate names will be next to each other.
    // Use adjacent_find() to find instances of two or more identical names
    // next to each other.
    //
    // Loop until adjacent_find returns the end iterator.
    //
    list<string>::iterator lit;
    for (lit = allNames.begin(); lit != allNames.end(); ++lit) {
        lit = adjacent_find(lit, allNames.end());
        if (lit == allNames.end()) {
            break;
        }
        duplicates.push_back(*lit);
    }


    //
    // If someone was on more than two voter lists, he or she will
    // show up more than once in the duplicates list. Sort the list
    // and remove duplicates with unique.
    //
    // Use the list versions because they are faster than the generic versions.
    //
    duplicates.sort();
    duplicates.unique();

    return (duplicates);
}
```

The RemoveNames Functor

The `auditVoterRolls()` function uses the following line to remove all the offending (duplicate and felon) names from each `list` in the voter registration `map`:

```
for_each(votersByCounty.begin(), votersByCounty.end(),
    RemoveNames(duplicates));
```

The `for_each()` algorithm calls the `RemoveNames` functor on each `string/list<string>` pair in the map. The definition of the `RemoveNames` functor class looks like this:

```
//
// RemoveNames
//
// Functor class that takes a string/list<string> pair and removes
// any strings from the list that are found in a list of names
// (supplied in the constructor)
//
class RemoveNames : public unary_function<pair<const string, list<string> >,
    void>
{
public:
        RemoveNames(const list<string>& names) : mNames(names) {}
        void operator() (pair<const string, list<string> >& val);
```

```
        protected:
            const list<string>& mNames;
    };
```

Note that `RemoveNames` subclasses `unary_function`, a technique described earlier in this chapter. The constructor takes a reference to a `list` of names, which it stores for use in its function-call operator. Recall that the parameter to the functor callback is an element of the `map`, which is a `string/list<string>` pair. The function call operator's job is to remove any names from the `string list` that are found in the `mNames list`. The implementation uses the `remove_if()` algorithm with a special predicate `NameInList`.

```
//
// Function-call operator for RemoveNames functor.
//
// Uses remove_if() followed by erase to actually delete the names
// from the list
//
// Names are removed if they are in our list of mNames. Use the NameInList
// functor to check if the name is in the list.
//
void RemoveNames::operator() (pair<const string, list<string> >& val)
{
    list<string>::iterator it = remove_if(val.second.begin(), val.second.end(),
        NameInList(mNames));
    val.second.erase(it, val.second.end());
}
```

Remember that the `remove()` family of algorithms don't really remove elements; they only move them to the end of the range. You must call `erase()` on the container to actually remove the elements.

The NameInList Functor

The `RemoveNames` functor calls `remove_if()` with a predicate functor of the `NameInList` class. The `NameInList` functor returns `true` if the `string` given to it as an argument is in the `list mNames`. The class definition looks like this:

```
//
// NameInList
//
// Functor to check if a string is in a list of strings (supplied
// at construction time).
//
class NameInList : public unary_function<string, bool>
{
    public:
        NameInList(const list<string>& names) : mNames(names) {}
        bool operator() (const string& val);

    protected:
        const list<string>& mNames;
};
```

The implementation of the function-call operator simply uses `find()` to search for the name parameter in the `mNames` list of strings, returning `true` if `find()` returns a valid iterator, and `false` if it returns the end iterator.

```
//
// function-call operator for NameInList functor
//
// Returns true if it can find name in mNames, false otherwise.
// Uses find() algorithm.
//
bool NameInList::operator() (const string& name)
{
    return (find(mNames.begin(), mNames.end(), name) != mNames.end());
}
```

Testing the auditVoterRolls() Function

That's the complete implementation of the voter roll audit functionality. Here is a small test program:

```
#include <algorithm>
#include <functional>
#include <map>
#include <list>
#include <iostream>
#include <utility>
#include <string>
using namespace std;

void printString(const string& str)
{
    cout << " {" << str << "}";
}

void printCounty(const pair<const string, list<string> >& county)
{
    cout << county.first << ":";
    for_each(county.second.begin(), county.second.end(), &printString);
    cout << endl;
}

int main(int argc, char** argv)
{
    map<string, list<string> > voters;
    list<string> nameList, felons;
    nameList.push_back("Amy Aardvark");
    nameList.push_back("Bob Buffalo");
    nameList.push_back("Charles Cat");
    nameList.push_back("Dwayne Dog");

    voters.insert(make_pair("Orange", nameList));

    nameList.clear();
    nameList.push_back("Elizabeth Elephant");
```

```
        nameList.push_back("Fred Flamingo");
        nameList.push_back("Amy Aardvark");

        voters.insert(make_pair("Los Angeles", nameList));

        nameList.clear();
        nameList.push_back("George Goose");
        nameList.push_back("Heidi Hen");
        nameList.push_back("Fred Flamingo");

        voters.insert(make_pair("San Diego", nameList));

        felons.push_back("Bob Buffalo");
        felons.push_back("Charles Cat");

        for_each(voters.begin(), voters.end(), &printCounty);
        cout << endl;
        auditVoterRolls(voters, felons);
        for_each(voters.begin(), voters.end(), &printCounty);

        return (0);
    }
```

The output of the program is:

```
Los Angeles: {Elizabeth Elephant} {Fred Flamingo} {Amy Aardvark}
Orange: {Amy Aardvark} {Bob Buffalo} {Charles Cat} {Dwayne Dog}
San Diego: {George Goose} {Heidi Hen} {Fred Flamingo}

Los Angeles: {Elizabeth Elephant}
Orange: {Dwayne Dog}
San Diego: {George Goose} {Heidi Hen}
```

Summary

This chapter concludes the basic STL functionality. It provided an overview of the various algorithms and function objects available for your use, and showed you how to write your own function objects. We hope that you have gained an appreciation for the usefulness of the STL containers, algorithms, and function objects. If not, think for a moment about rewriting the voter registration audit example without the STL. You would need to write your own linked-list and map classes, and your own searching, removing, finding, iterating, and other algorithms. The program would be much longer, harder to debug, and more difficult to maintain.

If you aren't impressed by the algorithms and function objects, or find them too complex, you obviously don't have to use them. Feel free to pick and choose as well: if the find() algorithm fits perfectly in your program, don't eschew it just because you aren't using the other algorithms. Also, don't take the STL as an all-or-nothing proposition. If you want to use only the vector container and nothing else, that's fine too.

Chapter 23 continues the STL topic with some advanced features, including allocators, iterator adapters, and writing your own algorithms, containers, and iterators.

23

Customizing and Extending the STL

The previous two chapters have shown that the STL is a powerful general-purpose collection of containers and algorithms. The information covered so far should be sufficient for most applications. The STL, however, is much more flexible and extensible than the previous chapters have demonstrated. For example, you can apply iterators to input and output streams; write your own containers, algorithms, and iterators; and even specify your own memory allocation schemes for containers to use. This chapter provides a taste of these advanced features, primarily through the development of a new STL container: the `hashmap`. The specific contents of the chapter include:

❑   A closer look at allocators

❑   Iterator adapters

❑   Extending the STL

  ❑   Writing algorithms

  ❑   Writing containers: a hash map implementation

  ❑   Writing Writing iterators: a hash map iterator implementation

This chapter is not for the faint of heart! The contents delve into some of the most complicated and syntactically confusing areas of the C++ language. If you're happy with the basic STL containers and algorithms from the previous two chapters, you can skip this one. However, if you really want to understand the STL, not just use it, give this chapter a chance. Make sure that you're comfortable with the template material in Chapter 11 before reading this chapter.

Allocators

Recall from Chapter 21 that every STL container takes an `Allocator` type as a template parameter, for which the default will usually suffice. For example, the `vector` template definition looks like this:

```
template <typename T, typename Allocator = allocator<T> > class vector;
```

The container constructors then allow you to specify an object of type `Allocator`. These extra parameters permit you to customize the way the containers allocate memory. Every memory allocation performed by a container is made with a call to the `allocate()` method of the `Allocator` object. Conversely, every deallocation is performed with a call to the `deallocate()` method of the `Allocator` object. The standard library provides a default `Allocator` class called `allocator`, which implements these methods simply as wrappers for `operator new` and `operator delete`.

If you want containers in your program to use a custom memory allocation and deallocation scheme, such as a memory pool, you can write your own `Allocator` class. Any class that provides `allocate()`, `deallocate()`, and several other required methods and `typedefs` can be used in place of the default `allocator` class. However, in our experience, this feature is rarely used, so we have omitted the details from this book. For more details, consult one of the books on the C++ Standard Library listed in Appendix B.

Iterator Adapters

The Standard Library provides three *iterator adapters*: special iterators that are built on top of other iterators. You'll learn more about the adapter design pattern in Chapter 26. For now, just appreciate what these iterators can do for you. All three iterator adapters are declared in the `<iterator>` header.

> *You can also write your own iterator adapters. Consult one of the books on the Standard Library listed in Appendix B for details.*

Reverse Iterators

The STL provides a `reverse_iterator` class that iterates through a bidirectional or random access iterator in reverse direction. Applying `operator++` to a `reverse_iterator` calls `operator--` on the underlying container iterator, and vice versa. Every *reversible container* in the STL, which happens to be every container that's part of the standard, supplies a `typedef reverse_iterator` and methods called `rbegin()` and `rend()`. `rbegin()` returns a `reverse_iterator` starting at the last element of the container, and `rend()` returns a `reverse_iterator` starting at the first element of the container.

The `reverse_iterator` is useful mostly with algorithms in the STL that have no equivalents that work in reverse order. For example, the basic `find()` algorithm searches for the first element in a sequence. If you want to find the last element in the sequence, you can use a `reverse_iterator` instead. Note that when you call an algorithm like `find()` with a `reverse_iterator`, it returns a `reverse_iterator` as well. You can always obtain a normal `iterator` from a `reverse_iterator` by calling the `base()` method on the `reverse_iterator`. However, due to the implementation details of `reverse_iterator`, the `iterator` returned from `base()` always refers to one element past the element referred to by the `reverse_iterator` on which it's called.

Here is an example of `find()` with a `reverse_iterator`:

```cpp
#include <algorithm>
#include <vector>
#include <iostream>
#include <iterator>
using namespace std;

// The implementation of populateContainer() is identical to that shown in
// Chapter 22, so it is omitted here.

int main(int argc, char** argv)
{
    vector<int> myVector;
    populateContainer(myVector);

    int num;
    cout << "Enter a number to find: ";
    cin >> num;

    vector<int>::iterator it1;
    vector<int>::reverse_iterator it2;
    it1 = find(myVector.begin(), myVector.end(), num);
    it2 = find(myVector.rbegin(), myVector.rend(), num);

    if (it1 != myVector.end()) {
        cout << "Found " << num << " at position " << it1 - myVector.begin()
            << " going forward.\n";
        cout << "Found " << num << " at position "
            << it2.base() - 1 - myVector.begin() << " going backward.\n";
    } else {
        cout << "Failed to find " << num << endl;
    }

    return (0);
}
```

One line in this program needs further explanation. The code to print out the position found by the reverse iterator looks like this:

```cpp
cout << "Found " << num << " at position "
    << it2.base() - 1 - myVector.begin() << " going backward.\n";
```

As noted earlier, `base()` returns an `iterator` referring to one past the element referred to by the `reverse_iterator`. In order to get to the same element, you must subtract one.

Stream Iterators

As mentioned in Chapter 21, the STL provides adapters that allow you to treat input and output streams as input and output iterators. Using these iterators you can adapt input and output streams so that they can serve as sources and destinations, respectively, in the various STL algorithms. For example, you can use the `ostream_iterator` with the `copy()` algorithm to print the elements of a container with only one line of code:

```
#include <algorithm>
#include <iostream>
#include <iterator>
#include <vector>
using namespace std;

int main(int argc, char** argv)
{
    vector<int> myVector;
    for (int i = 0; i < 10; i++) {
        myVector.push_back(i);
    }

    // Print the contents of the vector.
    copy(myVector.begin(), myVector.end(), ostream_iterator<int>(cout, " "));
    cout << endl;
}
```

`ostream_iterator` is a template class that takes the element type as a type parameter. Its constructor takes an output stream and a `string` to write to the stream following each element.

Similarly, you can use the `istream_iterator` to read values from an input stream using the iterator abstraction. An `istream_iterator` can be used as sources in the algorithms and container methods. It's usage is less common than that of the `ostream_iterator`, so we don't show an example here. Consult one of the references in Appendix B for details.

Insert Iterators

As mentioned in Chapter 22, algorithms like `copy()` don't insert elements into a container; they simply replace old elements in a range with new ones. In order to make algorithms like `copy()` more useful, the STL provides three insert iterator adapters that actually insert elements into a container. They are templatized on a container type, and take the actual container reference in their constructor. By supplying the necessary iterator interfaces, these adapters can be used as the destination iterators of algorithms like `copy()`. However, instead of replacing elements in the container, they make calls on their container to actually insert new elements.

The basic `insert_iterator` calls `insert(position, element)` on the container, the `back_insert_iterator` calls `push_back(element)`, and the `front_insert_iterator` calls `push_front(element)`.

For example, you can use the `back_insert_iterator` with the `remove_copy_if()` algorithm to populate a new `vector` with all elements from an old `vector` that are not equal to 100:

```
#include <algorithm>
#include <functional>
#include <iterator>
#include <vector>
#include <iostream>

using namespace std;

// The implementation of populateContainer() is identical to that shown in
// Chapter 22, so it is omitted here.
```

```
    int main(int argc, char** argv)
{
    vector<int> vectorOne, vectorTwo;
    populateContainer(vectorOne);

    back_insert_iterator<vector<int> > inserter(vectorTwo);
    remove_copy_if(vectorOne.begin(), vectorOne.end(), inserter,
        bind2nd(equal_to<int>(), 100));

    copy(vectorTwo.begin(), vectorTwo.end(), ostream_iterator<int>(cout, " "));
    cout << endl;

    return (0);
}
```

As you can see, when you use insert iterators, you don't need to size the destination containers ahead of time.

The insert_iterator and front_insert_iterator function similarly, except that the insert_iterator also takes an initial iterator position in its constructor, which it passes to the first call to insert(position, element). Subsequent iterator position hints are generated based on the return value from each insert() call.

One huge benefit of insert_iterator is that it allows you to use associative containers as destinations of the modifying algorithms. Recall from Chapter 22 that the problem with associative containers is that you are not allowed to modify the elements over which you iterate. By using an insert_iterator, you can instead insert elements, allowing the container to sort them properly internally. Recall from Chapter 21 that associative containers actually support a form of insert() that takes an iterator position, and are supposed to use the position as a "hint," which they can ignore. When you use an insert_iterator on an associative container, you can simply pass the begin or end iterator of the container to use as the hint. Here is the previous example modified so that the destination container is a set instead of a vector:

```
#include <algorithm>
#include <functional>
#include <iterator>
#include <vector>
#include <iostream>
#include <set>

using namespace std;

// The implementation of populateContainer() is identical to that shown in
// Chapter 22, so it is omitted here.

int main(int argc, char** argv)
{
    vector<int> vectorOne;
    set<int> setOne;
    populateContainer(vectorOne);

    insert_iterator<set<int> > inserter(setOne, setOne.begin());
    remove_copy_if(vectorOne.begin(), vectorOne.end(), inserter,
```

```
                    bind2nd(equal_to<int>(), 100));

        copy(setOne.begin(), setOne.end(), ostream_iterator<int>(cout, " "));
        cout << endl;

        return (0);
}
```

Note that the `insert_iterator` modifies the iterator position hint that it passes to `insert()` after each call to `insert()`, such that the position is one past the just-inserted element.

Extending the STL

The STL includes many useful containers, algorithms, and iterators that you can use in your applications. It is impossible, however, for any library to include all possible utilities that all potential clients might need. Thus, the best libraries are extensible: they allow clients to adapt and add to the basic capabilities to obtain exactly the functionality they require. The STL is inherently extensible because of its fundamental structure of separating data from the algorithms that operate on them. You can write your own container that can work with the STL algorithms simply by providing an iterator that conforms to the STL standard. Similarly, you can write a function that works with iterators from the standard containers. This section explains the rules for extending the STL and provides sample implementations of extensions.

Why Extend the STL?

If you sit down to write an algorithm or container in C++, you can either make it adhere to the STL conventions or not. For simple containers and algorithms, it might not be worth the extra effort to follow the STL guidelines. However, for substantial code that you plan to reuse, the effort pays off. First, the code will be easier for other C++ programmers to understand, because you follow well-established interface guidelines. Second, you will be able to utilize your container or algorithm on the other parts of the STL (algorithms or containers), without needing to provide special hacks or adapters. Finally, it will force you to employ the necessary rigor required to develop solid code.

Writing an STL Algorithm

The algorithms described in Chapter 22 are useful, but you will inevitably encounter situations in your programs for which you need new algorithms. When that happens, it is usually not difficult to write your own algorithm that works with STL iterators just like the standard algorithms.

find_all()

Suppose that you wanted to find all the elements matching a predicate in a given range. `find()` and `find_if()` are the most likely candidate algorithms, but each return an iterator referring to only one element. In fact, there is no standard algorithm to find all the elements matching a predicate. Luckily, you can write your own version of this functionality called `find_all()`.

The first task is to define the function prototype. You can model `find_all()` after `find_if()`. It will be a templatized function on two type parameters: the iterator and the predicate. Its arguments will be start and end iterators and the predicate object. Only its return value differs from find_if(): instead of returning a single iterator referring to the matching element, find_all() returns a vector of iterators referring to all the matching elements. Here is the prototype:

```
template <typename InputIterator, typename Predicate>
vector<InputIterator>
find_all(InputIterator first, InputIterator last, Predicate pred);
```

Another option would be to return an iterator that iterates over all the matching elements in the container, but that would require you to write your own iterator class.

The next task is to write the implementation. find_all() can be layered on top of find_if() by calling find_if() repeatedly. The first call to find_if() uses the whole supplied range from first to last. The second call uses a smaller range, from the element found from the previous call to last. The loop continues until find_if() fails to find a match. Here is the implementation:

```
template <typename InputIterator, typename Predicate>
vector<InputIterator>
find_all(InputIterator first, InputIterator last, Predicate pred)
{
    vector<InputIterator> res;

    while (true) {
        // Find the next match in the current range.
        first = find_if(first, last, pred);
        // check if find_if failed to find a match
        if (first == last) {
            break;
        }
        // Store this match.
        res.push_back(first);
        // Shorten the range to start at one past the current match
        ++first;
    }
    return (res);
}
```

Here is some code that tests the function:

```
int main(int argc, char** argv)
{
    int arr[] = {3, 4, 5, 4, 5, 6, 5, 8};
    vector<int*> all = find_all(arr, arr + 8, bind2nd(equal_to<int>(), 5));

    cout << "Found " << all.size() << " matching elements: ";

    for (vector<int*>::iterator it = all.begin(); it != all.end(); ++it) {
        cout << **it << " ";
    }
    cout << endl;

    return (0);
}
```

This test code is somewhat cryptic, so here's a bit of explanation. The test uses an array of `int`s as an STL container. Recall from Chapter 21 that C-style arrays are legitimate containers, with pointers serving as the iterators. The begin iterator of an array is simply a pointer to the first element. The end iterator is a pointer to one-past the last element.

After finding iterators to all the elements, the test code counts the number of elements found, which is simply the number of iterators in the `all` vector. Then, it iterates through the `all` vector, printing each element. Note the double dereference of `it`: the first dereference gets to the `int*` and the second gets to the actual `int`.

Iterator Traits

Some algorithm implementations need additional information about their iterators. For example, they might need to know the type of the elements referred to by the iterator in order to store temporary values, or perhaps they want to know whether the iterator is bidirectional or random access.

C++ provides a class template called `iterator_traits` that allows you to find this info. You instantiate the `iterator_traits` class template with the iterator type of interest, and access one of five `typedefs`: `value_type`, `difference_type`, `iterator_category`, `pointer`, and `reference`. For example, the following template function declares a temporary variable of the type to which an iterator of type `IteratorType` refers:

```
#include <iterator>

template <typename IteratorType>
void iteratorTraitsTest(IteratorType it)
{
    typename std::iterator_traits<IteratorType>::value_type temp;
    temp = *it;
    cout << temp << endl;
}
```

Note the use of the `typename` keyword in front of the `iterator_traits` line. As explained in Chapter 21, you must specify `typename` explicitly whenever you access a type based on one or more template parameters. In this case, the template parameter `IteratorType` is used to access the `value_type` type.

Writing an STL Container

The C++ standard contains a list of requirements that any container must fulfill in order to qualify as an STL container. Additionally, if you want your container to be sequential (like a `vector`) or associative (like a `map`), it must conform to supplementary requirements.

Our suggestion when writing a new container is to write the basic container first following the general STL rules such as making it a class template, but without worrying too much about the specific details of STL conformity. After you've developed the implementation, you can add the iterator and methods so that it can work with the STL framework. This section takes that approach to develop a *hashmap*.

A Basic Hashmap

The most glaring omission from the STL is a hash table container. Unlike the STL `map` and `set`, which provide logarithmic insertion, lookup, and deletion times, a hash table provides constant time insertion, deletion, and lookup in the average case. Instead of storing elements in sorted order, it *hashes*, or maps, each element to a particular *bucket*. As long as the number of elements stored isn't significantly greater than the number of buckets, and the *hash function* evenly distributes elements between the buckets, the insertion, deletion, and lookup operations all run in constant time.

> *This section assumes that you are familiar with hashed data structures. If you are not, consult one of the standard data structure texts listed in Appendix B.*

Many specific implementations of the STL provide a nonstandard hash table. As you can guess, however, due to the lack of standardization, each implementation is slightly different. This section provides an implementation of a simple, but fully functional, `hashmap` that you can take with you between platforms. Like a `map`, a `hashmap` stores key/value pairs. In fact, the operations it provides are almost identical to those provided by the `map`.

This `hashmap` implementation uses chained hashing (also called open hashing) and does not attempt to provide advanced features like rehashing.

The Hash Function

The first choice when writing a `hashmap` is how to handle hash functions. Recalling the adage that a good abstraction makes the easy case easy and the hard case possible, a good `hashmap` interface allows clients to specify their own hash function and number of buckets in order to customize the hashing behavior for their particular workload. On the other hand, clients that do not have the desire, or ability, to write a good hash function and choose a number of buckets should be able to use the container without doing so. One solution is to allow clients to provide a hash function and number of buckets in the `hashmap` constructor, but also to provide defaults values. It also makes sense to package the hash function and the number of buckets into a hashing class. Our default hash class definition looks like this:

```cpp
// Any Hash Class must provide two methods: hash() and numBuckets().
template <typename T>
class DefaultHash
{
    public:
        // Throws invalid_argument if numBuckets is nonpositive
        DefaultHash(int numBuckets = 101) throw (invalid_argument);
        int hash(const T& key) const;
        int numBuckets() const { return mNumBuckets; }

    protected:
        int mNumBuckets;
};
```

Note that the `DefaultHash` class is templatized on the key type that it hashes, in order to support a templatized `hashmap` container. The implementation of the constructor is trivial:

```cpp
// Throws invalid_argument if numBuckets is nonpositive
template <typename T>
DefaultHash<T>::DefaultHash(int numBuckets) throw (invalid_argument)
{
    if (numBuckets <= 0) {
        throw (invalid_argument("numBuckets must be > 0"));
    }
```

```
        mNumBuckets = numBuckets;
}
```

The implementation of hash() is trickier, partially because it must apply to keys of any type. It is supposed to map the key to one of the mNumBuckets buckets. It uses the *division method* for hashing, in which the bucket is an integer value of the key modulo the number of buckets.

```
// Uses the division method for hashing.
// Treats the key as a sequence of bytes, sums the ASCII
// values of the bytes, and mods the total by the number
// of buckets.
template <typename T>
int DefaultHash<T>::hash(const T& key) const
{
    int bytes = sizeof(key);
    unsigned long res = 0;
    for (int i = 0; i < bytes; ++i) {
        res += *((char*)&key + i);
    }
    return (res % mNumBuckets);
}
```

Unfortunately, the preceding method doesn't work on strings because different string objects can contain the same string value. Thus, the same string value could hash to different buckets. Therefore, it's also a good idea to provide a partial specialization of the DefaultHash class for strings:

```
// Specialization for strings
template <>
class DefaultHash<string>
{
    public:
        // Throws invalid_argument if numBuckets is nonpositive
        DefaultHash(int numBuckets = 101) throw (invalid_argument);
        int hash(const string& key) const;
        int numBuckets() const { return mNumBuckets; }

    protected:
        int mNumBuckets;
};

// Throws invalid_argument if numBuckets is nonpositive
DefaultHash<string>::DefaultHash(int numBuckets) throw (invalid_argument)
{
    if (numBuckets <= 0) {
        throw (invalid_argument("numBuckets must be > 0"));
    }
    mNumBuckets = numBuckets;
}

// Uses the division method for hashing after summing the
// ASCII values of all the characters in key.
int DefaultHash<string>::hash(const string& key) const
{
```

```
        int sum = 0;

        for (size_t i = 0; i < key.size(); i++) {
            sum += key[i];
        }
        return (sum % mNumBuckets);
}
```

If the client wants to use other pointer types or objects as the key, she should write her own hash class for those types.

> **The hash functions shown in this section are simple examples for the basic** hashmap
> **implementation. They do not guarantee uniform hashing for all key universes.**
> **If you need more mathematically rigorous hash functions (or don't know what**
> **"uniform hashing" is), consult an algorithms reference.**

The Hashmap Interface

A hashmap supports three basic operations: insertion, deletion, and lookup. Of course, it provides a constructor, destructor, copy constructor, and assignment operator as well. Here is the public portion of the hashmap class template:

```
template <typename Key, typename T, typename Compare = std::equal_to<Key>,
    typename Hash = DefaultHash<Key> >
class hashmap
{
    public:
        typedef Key key_type;
        typedef T mapped_type;
        typedef pair<const Key, T> value_type;

        // Constructors
        // Throws invalid_argument if the hash object specifies a nonpositive
        // number of buckets
        explicit hashmap(const Compare& comp = Compare(),
            const Hash& hash = Hash()) throw(invalid_argument);

        // destructor, copy constructor, assignment operator
        ~hashmap();
        hashmap(const hashmap<Key, T, Compare, Hash>& src);
        hashmap<Key, T, Compare, Hash>& operator=(
            const hashmap<Key, T, Compare, Hash>& rhs);

        // Element insert
        // Inserts the key/value pair x
        void insert(const value_type& x);

        // Element delete
        // Removes the element with key x, if it exists
        void erase(const key_type& x);
```

```
        // Element lookup
        // find returns a pointer to the element with key x.
        // Returns NULL if no element with that key exists.
        value_type* find(const key_type& x);

        // operator[] finds the element with key x or inserts an
        // element with that key if none exists yet. Returns a reference to the
        // value corresponding to that key.
        T& operator[] (const key_type& x);

    protected:
        // Implementation details not shown yet
};
```

As you can see, the key and value types are both template arguments like in the STL map. The hashmap stores pair<const Key, T> as the actual elements in the container. The insert(), erase(), find(), and operator[] methods are straightforward. However, a few aspects of this interface require further explanation.

The Compare Template Argument

Like the map, set, and other standard containers, the hashmap allows the client to specify the comparison type as a template parameter and to pass a specific comparison object of that type in the constructor. Unlike the map and set, the hashmap does not sort elements by key, but must still compare keys for equality. Thus, instead of using less as the default comparison, it uses equal_to. The comparison object is used only to detect attempts to insert duplicate keys into the container.

The Hash Template Argument

When you allow clients to define their own classes, from which they construct objects to pass in the constructor, you must figure out how to specify the type of that parameter in the constructor. There are several ways to do it. The STL way, which is on the complicated end of the spectrum, takes the class type as a template parameter and uses that templatized type as the type in the constructor. We follow that approach for the hash class, as you can see above. Thus, the hashmap template takes four template parameters: the key type, the value type, the comparison type, and the hash type.

The typedefs

The hashmap class template defines three typedefs:

```
        typedef Key key_type;
        typedef T mapped_type;
        typedef pair<const Key, T> value_type;
```

The value_type, in particular, is useful for referring to the more cumbersome pair<const Key, T>. As you will see, these typedefs are also required of STL containers by the standard.

The Implementation

After finalizing the hashmap interface, it's time to choose the implementation model. The basic hash table structure generally consists of a fixed number of buckets, each of which can store one or more elements. The buckets should be accessible in constant time based on a bucket-id (the result of hashing a key). Thus, a vector is the most appropriate container for the buckets. Each bucket must store a list of elements, so the STL list can be used as the bucket type. Thus, the final structure is a vector of lists of pair<const Key, T> elements. Here are the protected members of the hashmap class:

```
protected:
    typedef list<value_type> ListType;

    // In this first implementation, it would be easier to use a vector
    // instead of a pointer to a vector, which requires dynamic allocation.
    // However, we use a ptr to a vector so that, in the final
    // implementation, swap() can be implemented in constant time.
    vector<ListType>* mElems;
    int mSize;
    Compare mComp;
    Hash mHash;
```

Without the typedefs for value_type and ListType, the line declaring mElems would look like this:

```
vector<list<pair<const Key, T> > >* mElems;
```

The mComp and mHash members store the comparison and hashing objects, respectively, and mSize stores the number of elements currently in the container.

The Constructor

The constructor initializes all the fields and allocates a new vector. Unfortunately, the template syntax is somewhat dense. Consult Chapter 11 for details on writing class templates if the syntax confuses you.

```
// Construct mElems with the number of buckets.
template <typename Key, typename T, typename Compare, typename Hash>
hashmap<Key, T, Compare, Hash>::hashmap(
    const Compare& comp, const Hash& hash) throw(invalid_argument) :
    mSize(0), mComp(comp), mHash(hash)
{
    if (mHash.numBuckets() <= 0) {
        throw (invalid_argument("Number of buckets must be positive"));
    }
    mElems = new vector<list<value_type> >(mHash.numBuckets());
}
```

The implementation requires at least one bucket, so the constructor enforces that restriction.

Destructor, Copy Constructor, and Assignment Operator

Only the mElems data member needs destroying, copying, and assigning. Here are the implementations of the destructor, copy constructor, and assignment operator:

```
template <typename Key, typename T, typename Compare, typename Hash>
hashmap<Key, T, Compare, Hash>::~hashmap()
{
    delete mElems;
}
```

```
template <typename Key, typename T, typename Compare, typename Hash>
hashmap<Key, T, Compare, Hash>::hashmap(
    const hashmap<Key, T, Compare, Hash>& src) :
    mSize(src.mSize), mComp(src.mComp), mHash(src.mHash)
{
    // Don't need to bother checking if numBuckets is positive, because
    // we know src checked

    // Use the vector copy constructor.
    mElems = new vector<list<value_type> >(*(src.mElems));
}

template <typename Key, typename T, typename Compare, typename Hash>
hashmap<Key, T, Compare, Hash>& hashmap<Key, T, Compare, Hash>::operator=(
    const hashmap<Key, T, Compare, Hash>& rhs)
{
    // Check for self-assignment.
    if (this != &rhs) {
        delete mElems;
        mSize = rhs.mSize;
        mComp = rhs.mComp;
        mHash = rhs.mHash;
        // Don't need to bother checking if numBuckets is positive, because
        // we know rhs checked

        // Use the vector copy constructor.
        mElems = new vector<list<value_type> >(*(rhs.mElems));
    }
    return (*this);
}
```

Note that the copy constructor and assignment operator both construct the new vector using its copy constructor with the vector from the source hashmap as the source.

Element Lookup

Each of the three major operations (lookup, insertion, and deletion) requires code to find an element with a given key. Thus, it is helpful to have a protected helper method that performs that task. findElement() first uses the hash object to hash the key to a specific bucket. Then, it looks in that bucket for an element with a key matching the given key. The elements stored are key/value pairs, so the actual comparison must be done on the first field of the element. The comparison function object specified in the constructor is used to perform the comparison. lists require linear search to find matching elements, but you could use the find() algorithm instead of an explicit for loop.

```
template <typename Key, typename T, typename Compare, typename Hash>
typename list<pair<const Key, T> >::iterator
hashmap<Key, T, Compare, Hash>::findElement(const key_type& x, int& bucket) const
{
    // Hash the key to get the bucket.
    bucket = mHash.hash(x);

    // Look for the key in the bucket.
    for (typename ListType::iterator it = (*mElems)[bucket].begin();
```

```
            it != (*mElems)[bucket].end(); ++it) {
            if (mComp(it->first, x)) {
                return (it);
            }
        }
        return ((*mElems)[bucket].end());
    }
```

Note that `findElement()` returns an iterator referring to an element in the `list` representing the bucket to which the key hashed. If the element is found, the iterator refers to that element; otherwise, it is the end iterator for that `list`. The bucket is returned by reference in the bucket argument.

The syntax in this method is somewhat confusing, particularly the use of the `typename` keyword. As explained in Chapter 21, you must use the `typename` keyword whenever you are using a type that is dependent on a template parameter. Specifically, the `type list<pair<const Key, T> >::iterator` type is dependent on both the `Key` and `T` template parameters.

Another note on the syntax: `mElems` is a pointer, so it must be dereferenced before you can apply `operator[]` to it to obtain a specific element. Hence the somewhat ugly: `(*mElems)[bucket]`.

You can implement the `find()` method as a simple wrapper for `findElement()`:

```
template <typename Key, typename T, typename Compare, typename Hash>
typename hashmap<Key, T, Compare, Hash>::value_type*
hashmap<Key, T, Compare, Hash>::find(const key_type& x)
{
    int bucket;
    // Use the findElement() helper.
    typename ListType::iterator it = findElement(x, bucket);
    if (it == (*mElems)[bucket].end()) {
        // We didn't find the element--return NULL.
        return (NULL);
    }
    // We found the element. Return a pointer to it.
    return (&(*it));
}
```

The `operator[]` method is similar, except that if it can't find the element it inserts it:

```
template <typename Key, typename T, typename Compare, typename Hash>
T& hashmap<Key, T, Compare, Hash>::operator[] (const key_type& x)
{
    // Try to find the element.
    // If it doesn't exist, add a new element.
    value_type* found = find(x);
    if (found == NULL) {
        insert(make_pair(x, T()));
        found = find(x);
    }
    return (found->second);
}
```

This method is somewhat inefficient, because in the worst case it calls `find()` twice and `insert()` once. However, each of these operations runs in constant time with respect to the number of elements in the `hashmap`, so the overhead is not too significant.

Element Insert

`insert()` must first check if an element with that key is already in the `hashmap`. If not, it can add the element to the `list` in the appropriate bucket. Note that `findElement()` returns by reference the bucket to which the key hashes, even if the element with that key is not found.

```
template <typename Key, typename T, typename Compare, typename Hash>
void hashmap<Key, T, Compare, Hash>::insert(const value_type& x)
{
    int bucket;
    // Try to find the element.
    typename ListType::iterator it = findElement(x.first, bucket);

    if (it != (*mElems)[bucket].end()) {
        // The element already exists.
        return;
    } else {
        // We didn't find the element, so insert a new one.
        mSize++;
        (*mElems)[bucket].insert((*mElems)[bucket].end(), x);
    }
}
```

Element Delete

`erase()` follows the same pattern as `insert()`: it first attempts to find the element by calling `findElement()`. If the element exists, it erases it from the list in the appropriate bucket. Otherwise, it does nothing.

```
template <typename Key, typename T, typename Compare, typename Hash>
void
hashmap<Key, T, Compare, Hash>::erase(const key_type& x)
{
    int bucket;

    // First, try to find the element.
    typename ListType::iterator it = findElement(x, bucket);

    if (it != (*mElems)[bucket].end()) {
        // The element already exists--erase it.
        (*mElems)[bucket].erase(it);
        mSize--;
    }
}
```

Using the Basic Hashmap

Here is a small test program demonstrating the basic `hashmap` class template.

```
#include "hashmap.h"

int main(int argc, char** argv)
{
    hashmap<int, int> myHash;
    myHash.insert(make_pair(4, 40));
    myHash.insert(make_pair(6, 60));

    hashmap<int, int>::value_type* x = myHash.find(4);
    if (x != NULL) {
        cout << "4 maps to " << x->second << endl;
    } else {
        cout << "cannot find 4 in map\n";
    }

    myHash.erase(4);

    hashmap<int, int>::value_type* x2 = myHash.find(4);
    if (x2 != NULL) {
        cout << "4 maps to " << x2->second << endl;
    } else {
        cout << "cannot find 4 in map\n";
    }

    myHash[4] = 35;

    return (0);
}
```

The output is:

```
4 maps to 40
cannot find 4 in map
```

Making the Hashmap an STL Container

The basic hashmap shown in the previous section follows the spirit, but not the letter, of the STL. For most purposes, the preceding implementation is good enough. However, if you want to use the STL algorithms on your hashmap, you must do a bit more work. The C++ standard specifies specific methods and typedefs that a data structure must provide in order to qualify as a container.

Typedef Container Requirements

The typedefs include:

Type Name	Description
value_type	The element type stored in the container
reference	A reference to the element type stored in the container
const_reference	A reference to a const element type stored in the container

Table continued on following page

Type Name	Description
`iterator`	The type of the "smart pointer" for iterating over elements of the container
`const_iterator`	A version of `iterator` for iterating over `const` elements of the container
`size_type`	Type that can represent the number of elements in the container; usually just `size_t` (from `<cstddef>`)
`difference_type`	Type that can represent the difference of two `iterators` for the container; usually just `ptrdiff_t` (from `<cstddef>`)

Here are the definitions in the `hashmap` class of all these `typedefs` except `iterator` and `const_iterator`. Writing an iterator is covered in detail in a subsequent section. Note that `value_type` (plus `key_type` and `mapped_type`, which are discussed later) was already defined in our previous version of the `hashmap`.

```
template <typename Key, typename T, typename Compare = std::equal_to<Key>,
    typename Hash = DefaultHash<Key> >
class hashmap
{
    public:
        typedef Key key_type;
        typedef T mapped_type;
        typedef pair<const Key, T> value_type;
        typedef pair<const Key, T>& reference;
        typedef const pair<const Key, T>& const_reference;
        typedef size_t size_type;
        typedef ptrdiff_t difference_type;
        // Remainder of class definition omitted for brevity
};
```

Method Container Requirements

In addition to the `typedefs`, every container must provide the following methods:

Method	Description	Complexity
Default Constructor	Constructs an empty container	Constant
Copy constructor	Performs a deep copy	Linear
Assignment operator	Performs a deep copy	Linear
Destructor	Destroys dynamically allocated memory; calls destructor on all elements left in container	Linear
`iterator begin();` `const_iterator begin() const;`	Returns an iterator referring to the first element in the container	Constant

Method	Description	Complexity
`iterator end();` `const_iterator end() end;`	Returns an iterator referring to the last element in the container	Constant

`operator==`
`operator!=`
`operator<`
`operator>`
`operator<=`
`operator>=`
	Comparison operators that compare two containers, element by element	Linear

`void swap(Container&);`	Swaps the contents of the container passed to the method with the object on which the method is called	Constant (though technically the standard says only "should")
`size_type size() const;`	Returns the number of elements in the container	Constant (though technically the standard says only "should")
`size_type max_size() const;`	Returns the maximum number of elements the container can hold	Constant (though technically the standard says only "should")
`bool empty() const;`	Specifies whether the container has any elements	Constant

In this `hashmap` example, we omit the comparison operators. Implementing them would be a good exercise for the reader!

Here are the declarations and definitions of all the remaining methods except for `begin()` and `end()`. Those are covered in the next section:

```
template <typename Key, typename T, typename Compare = std::equal_to<Key>,
    typename Hash = DefaultHash<Key> >
class hashmap
{
    public:
        // typedefs omitted for brevity
        // Constructors
        explicit hashmap(const Compare& comp = Compare(),
            const Hash& hash = Hash()) throw(invalid_argument);
        // destructor, copy constructor, assignment operator
        ~hashmap();
        hashmap(const hashmap<Key, T, Compare, Hash>& src);
        hashmap<Key, T, Compare, Hash>& operator=(
            const hashmap<Key, T, Compare, Hash>& rhs);
```

```
        // Size methods
        bool empty() const;
        size_type size() const;
        size_type max_size() const;
        // Other modifying utilities
        void swap(hashmap<Key, T, Compare, Hash>& hashIn);

        // Other methods omitted for brevity
};
```

The implementations of the constructor, destructor, copy constructor, and assignment operator are identical to those shown above in the "Basic Hashmap Implementation" section.

The implementations of `size()` and `empty()` are easy because the `hashmap` implementation tracks its size in the `mSize` data member. Note that the `size()` method returns a `size_type`, which, as a return type, must be qualified with the explicit `hashmap<Key, T, Compare, Hash>` type name.

```
template <typename Key, typename T, typename Compare, typename Hash>
bool hashmap<Key, T, Compare, Hash>::empty() const
{
    return (mSize == 0);
}

template <typename Key, typename T, typename Compare, typename Hash>
typename hashmap<Key, T, Compare, Hash>::size_type
    hashmap<Key, T, Compare, Hash>::size() const
{
    return (mSize);
}
```

`max_size()` is a little trickier. At first, you might think the maximum size of the `hashmap` container is the sum of the maximum size of all the `lists`. However, the worst-case scenario is that all the elements hash to the same bucket. Thus, the maximum size it can claim to support is the maximum size of a single `list`.

```
template <typename Key, typename T, typename Compare, typename Hash>
typename hashmap<Key, T, Compare, Hash>::size_type
    hashmap<Key, T, Compare, Hash>::max_size() const
{
    // In the worst case, all the elements hash to the
    // same list, so the max_size is the max_size of a single
    // list. This code assumes that all the lists have the same
    // max_size.
    return ((*mElems)[0].max_size());
}
```

Finally, the implementation of `swap()` simply uses the `swap()` utility function to swap each of the four data members. Note that the `vector` pointers are swapped, which is a constant-time operation.

```
// Just swap the four data members.
// Use the generic swap template.
template <typename Key, typename T, typename Compare, typename Hash>
void hashmap<Key, T, Compare, Hash>::swap(
    hashmap<Key, T, Compare, Hash>& hashIn)
{
    // Explicitly qualify with std:: so the compiler doesn't think
    // it's a recursive call.
    std::swap(*this, hashIn);
}
```

Writing an Iterator

The most important container requirement is the iterator. In order to work with the generic algorithms, every container must provide an iterator for accessing the elements in the container. Your iterator should generally be a class that looks like a smart pointer: it provides overloaded `operator*` and `operator->`, plus some other operations depending on its specific behavior. As long as your iterator provides the basic iteration operations, everything should be fine.

The first decision to make about your iterator is what kind it will be: forward, bidirectional, or random access. Random access iterators don't make much sense for associative containers, so bidirectional seems like the logical choice for the `hashmap` iterator. That means you must provide the additional operations described in Chapter 21, including `operator++`, `operator--`, `operator==`, and `operator!=`.

The second decision is how to order the elements of your container. The `hashmap` is unsorted, so iterating in a sorted order is probably too difficult. Instead, your iterator can just step through the buckets, starting with the elements in the first bucket and progressing to those in the last bucket. This order will appear random to the client, but will be consistent and repeatable.

The third decision is how to represent your iterator internally. The implementation is usually quite dependent on the internal implementation of the container. The first purpose of an iterator is to refer to a single element in the container. In the case of the `hashmap`, each element is in an STL list, so perhaps the `hashmap` iterator can be a wrapper around a `list` iterator referring to the element in question. However, the second purpose of a bidirectional iterator is to allow the client to progress to the next or previous element from the current. In order to progress from one bucket to the next, you need to track also the current bucket and the `hashmap` object to which the iterator refers.

Once you've chosen your implementation, you must decide on a consistent representation for the end iterator. Recall that the end iterator should really be the "past-the-end" marker: the iterator that's reached by applying `++` to an iterator referring to the final element in the container. The `hashmap` iterator can simply use as its end iterator the end iterator of the `list` of the final bucket in the `hashmap`.

The HashIterator Class

Given the decisions made in the previous section, it's time to define the `HashIterator` class. The first thing to note is that each `HashIterator` object is an iterator for a specific instantiation of the `hashmap` class. In order to provide this one-to-one mapping, the `HashIterator` must also be a class template on the same parameters as the `hashmap` class.

The main question in the class definition is how to conform to the bidirectional iterator requirements. Recall that anything that behaves like an iterator is an iterator. Your class is not required to subclass another class in order to qualify as a bidirectional iterator. However, if you want your iterator to be usable in the generic algorithms functions, you must specify its traits. Recall from the discussion of writing STL algorithms earlier that `iterator_traits` is a class template that defines five `typedef`s for each iterator type. It can be partially specialized for your new iterator type if you want. Alternatively, the default implementation of the `iterator_traits` class template just grabs the five `typedef`s out of the iterator class itself. Thus, you can define those `typedef`s directly in your iterator class. In fact, C++ makes it even easier than that. Instead of defining them yourself, you can just subclass the `iterator` class template, which provides the `typedef`s for you. That way you only need to specify the iterator type and the element type as template arguments to the `iterator` class template. The `HashIterator` is a bidirectional iterator, so you can specify `bidirectional_iterator_tag` as the iterator type. Other legal iterator types are `input_iterator_tag`, `output_iterator_tag`, `forward_iterator_tag`, and `random_access_iterator_tag`. The element type is simply `pair<const Key, T>`.

Basically, it all boils down to the fact that you should subclass your iterator classes from the generic `iterator` class template.

Here is the basic `HashIterator` class definition:

```cpp
// HashIterator class definition
template<typename Key, typename T, typename Compare, typename Hash>
class HashIterator : public std::iterator<std::bidirectional_iterator_tag,
    pair<const Key, T> >
{
    public:
        HashIterator(); // Bidirectional iterators must supply default ctors.
        HashIterator(int bucket,
            typename list<pair<const Key, T> >::iterator listIt,
            const hashmap<Key, T, Compare, Hash>* inHashmap);

        pair<const Key, T>& operator*() const;

        // Return type must be something to which -> can be applied.
        // Return a pointer to a pair<const Key, T>, to which the compiler will
        // apply -> again.
        pair<const Key, T>* operator->() const;
        HashIterator<Key, T, Compare, Hash>& operator++();
        const HashIterator<Key, T, Compare, Hash> operator++(int);

        HashIterator<Key, T, Compare, Hash>& operator--();
        const HashIterator<Key, T, Compare, Hash> operator--(int);

        // Don't need to define a copy constructor or operator= because the
        // default behavior is what we want

        // Don't need destructor because the default behavior is what we want.
        // (not deleting mHashmap) is what we want.

        // These are ok as member functions because we don't support
        // comparisons of different types to this one.
        bool operator==(const HashIterator& rhs) const;
        bool operator!=(const HashIterator& rhs) const;
```

```
    protected:
        int mBucket;
        typename list<pair<const Key, T> >::iterator mIt;
        const hashmap<Key, T, Compare, Hash>* mHashmap;

        // Helper methods for operator++ and operator--
        void increment();
        void decrement();
};
```

If the definitions and implementations (shown in the next section) of the overloaded operators confuse you, consult Chapter 16 for details on operator overloading.

The HashIterator Method Implementations

The `HashIterator` constructors initialize the three member variables. The default constructor exists only so that clients can declare `HashIterator` variables without initializing them. An iterator constructed with the default constructor does not need to refer to any value, and attempting any operations on it is allowed to have undefined results.

```
// Dereferencing or incrementing an iterator constructed with the
// default ctor is undefined, so it doesn't matter what values we give
// here.
template<typename Key, typename T, typename Compare, typename Hash>
HashIterator<Key, T, Compare, Hash>::HashIterator()
{
    mBucket = -1;
    mIt = list<pair<const Key, T> >::iterator();
    mHashmap = NULL;
}

template<typename Key, typename T, typename Compare, typename Hash>
HashIterator<Key, T, Compare, Hash>::HashIterator(
    int bucket, typename list<pair<const Key, T> >::iterator listIt,
    const hashmap<Key, T, Compare, Hash>* inHashmap) :
    mBucket(bucket), mIt(listIt), mHashmap(inHashmap)
{
}
```

The implementations of the dereferencing operators are concise, but can be tricky. Recall from Chapter 16 that `operator*` and `operator->` are asymmetric. `operator*` returns the actual underlying value, which in this case is the element to which the iterator refers. `operator->`, on the other hand, must return something to which the arrow operator can be applied again. Thus, it returns a pointer to the element. The compiler then applies `->` to the pointer, which will result in accessing a field of the element.

```
// Return the actual element
template<typename Key, typename T, typename Compare, typename Hash>
pair<const Key, T>& HashIterator<Key, T, Compare, Hash>::operator*() const
{
    return (*mIt);
}
```

```
// Return the iterator, so the compiler can apply -> to it to access
// the actual desired field.
template<typename Key, typename T, typename Compare, typename Hash>
pair<const Key, T>*
    HashIterator<Key, T, Compare, Hash>::operator->() const
{
    return (&(*mIt));
}
```

The increment and decrement operators are implemented as described in Chapter 16, except that the actual incrementing and decrementing procedures are performed in the increment() and decrement() helper methods.

```
// Defer the details to the increment() helper.
template<typename Key, typename T, typename Compare, typename Hash>
HashIterator<Key, T, Compare, Hash>&
    HashIterator<Key, T, Compare, Hash>::operator++()
{
    increment();
    return (*this);
}

// Defer the details to the increment() helper.
template<typename Key, typename T, typename Compare, typename Hash>
const HashIterator<Key, T, Compare, Hash>
    HashIterator<Key, T, Compare, Hash>::operator++(int)
{
    HashIterator<Key, T, Compare, Hash> oldIt = *this;
    increment();
    return (oldIt);
}

// Defer the details to the decrement() helper.
template<typename Key, typename T, typename Compare, typename Hash>
HashIterator<Key, T, Compare, Hash>&
    HashIterator<Key, T, Compare, Hash>::operator--()
{
    decrement();
    return (*this);
}

// Defer the details to the decrement() helper.
template<typename Key, typename T, typename Compare, typename Hash>
const HashIterator<Key, T, Compare, Hash>
    HashIterator<Key, T, Compare, Hash>::operator--(int)
{
    HashIterator<Key, T, Compare, Hash> newIt = *this;
    decrement();
    return (newIt);
}
```

Incrementing a HashIterator tells it to refer to the "next" element in the container. This method first increments the list iterator, then checks if it's reached the end of its bucket. If so, it finds the next empty bucket in the hashmap and sets the list iterator equal to the start element in the bucket. Note that it can't simply move to the next bucket, because there might not be any elements in it. If there are no more empty buckets, mIt is set to the end iterator of the last bucket in the hashmap, which is the special "end" position of the HashIterator. Recall that iterators are not required to be any safer than dumb pointers, so error checking for things like incrementing an iterator already at the end is not required.

```cpp
// Behavior is undefined if mIt already refers to the past-the-end
// element in the table, or is otherwise invalid.
template<typename Key, typename T, typename Compare, typename Hash>
void HashIterator<Key, T, Compare, Hash>::increment()
{
    // mIt is an iterator into a single bucket.
    // Increment it.
    ++mIt;

    // If we're at the end of the current bucket,
    // find the next bucket with elements.
    if (mIt == (*mHashmap->mElems)[mBucket].end()) {
        for (int i = mBucket + 1; i < (*mHashmap->mElems).size(); i++) {
            if (!((*mHashmap->mElems)[i].empty())) {
                // We found a nonempty bucket.
                // Make mIt refer to the first element in it.
                mIt = (*mHashmap->mElems)[i].begin();
                mBucket = i;
                return;
            }
        }
        // No more empty buckets. Assign mIt to refer to the end
        // iterator of the last list.
        mBucket = (*mHashmap->mElems).size() - 1;
        mIt = (*mHashmap->mElems)[mBucket].end();
    }
}
```

Decrement is the inverse of increment: it makes the iterator refer to the "previous" element in the container. However, there is an asymmetry because of the asymmetry between the way the start and end positions are represented: start is the first element, but end is "one past" the last element. The algorithm for decrement checks first if the underlying list iterator is at the start of its current bucket. If not, it can just be decremented. Otherwise, the code needs to check for the first nonempty bucket before the current one. If one is found, the list iterator must be set to refer to the last element in the bucket, which is the end iterator decremented by one. If no nonempty buckets are found, the decrement is invalid, so the code can do anything it wants (behavior is undefined).

```cpp
// Behavior is undefined if mIt already refers to the first element
// in the table, or is otherwise invalid.
template<typename Key, typename T, typename Compare, typename Hash>
void HashIterator<Key, T, Compare, Hash>::decrement()
{
    // mIt is an iterator into a single bucket.
    // If it's at the beginning of the current bucket, don't decrement it.
    // Instead, try to find a nonempty bucket ahead of the current one.
    if (mIt == (*mHashmap->mElems)[mBucket].begin()) {
        for (int i = mBucket - 1; i >= 0; --i) {
            if (!((*mHashmap->mElems)[i].empty())) {
```

```
                    mIt = (*mHashmap->mElems)[i].end();
                    --mIt;
                    mBucket = i;
                    return;
                }
            }
            // No more nonempty buckets. This is an invalid decrement.
            // Assign mIt to refer to one before the start element of the first
            // list (an invalid position).
            mIt = (*mHashmap->mElems)[0].begin();
            --mIt;
            mBucket = 0;
        } else {
            // We're not at the beginning of the bucket, so
            // just move down.
            --mIt;
        }
    }
}
```

Note that both `increment()` and `decrement()` access `protected` members of the hashmap class. Thus, the hashmap class must declare `HashIterator` to be a `friend` class.

After `increment()` and `decrement()`, `operator==` and `operator!=` are positively simple. They just compare each of the three data members of the objects.

```
template<typename Key, typename T, typename Compare, typename Hash>
bool HashIterator<Key, T, Compare, Hash>::operator==(
    const HashIterator& rhs) const
{
    // All fields, including the hashmap to which the iterators refer,
    // must be equal.
    return (mHashmap == rhs.mHashmap && mBucket == rhs.mBucket &&
        mIt == rhs.mIt);
}

template<typename Key, typename T, typename Compare, typename Hash>
bool HashIterator<Key, T, Compare, Hash>::operator!=(
    const HashIterator& rhs) const
{
    return (!operator==(rhs));
}
```

Const Iterators

Technically, you should provide both an iterator and a `const` iterator for your hashmap class. The const iterator should function like the iterator, but should provide read-only access to the elements. The iterator should always be convertible to a `const` iterator. We omit the details of the `const` iterator and leave its implementation as an exercise for the reader.

Iterator Typedefs and Access Methods

The final piece involved in providing iterator support for the hashmap is to supply the necessary `typedefs` in the hashmap class definition and to write the `begin()` and `end()` methods on the hashmap. The `typedefs` and method prototypes look like this:

```
template <typename Key, typename T, typename Compare = std::equal_to<Key>,
    typename Hash = DefaultHash<Key> >
class hashmap
{
    public:
        // Other typedefs omitted for brevity
        typedef HashIterator<Key, T, Compare, Hash> iterator;
        typedef HashIterator<Key, T, Compare, Hash> const_iterator;

        // Iterator methods
        iterator begin();
        iterator end();
        const_iterator begin() const;
        const_iterator end() const;
        // Remainder of class definition omitted for brevity
};
```

The trickiest aspect of begin() is to remember to return the end iterator if there are no elements in the table.

```
template <typename Key, typename T, typename Compare, typename Hash>
typename hashmap<Key, T, Compare, Hash>::iterator
    hashmap<Key, T, Compare, Hash>::begin()
{
    if (mSize == 0) {
        // Special case: there are no elements, so return the end iterator
        return (end());
    }

    // We know there is at least one element. Find the first element.
    for (size_t i = 0; i < mElems->size(); ++i) {
        if (!((*mElems)[i].empty())) {
            return (HashIterator<Key, T, Compare, Hash>(i,
                (*mElems)[i].begin(), this));
        }
    }
    // Should never reach here, but if we do, return the end iterator
    return (end());
}
```

end() creates a HashIterator referring to the end iterator of the last bucket.

```
template <typename Key, typename T, typename Compare, typename Hash>
typename hashmap<Key, T, Compare, Hash>::iterator
    hashmap<Key, T, Compare, Hash>::end()
{
    // The end iterator is just the end iterator of the list in last bucket.
    return (HashIterator<Key, T, Compare, Hash>(mElems->size() - 1,
        (*mElems)[mElems->size() - 1].end(), this));
}
```

Because we don't provide a const_iterator, the implementations of the const versions of begin() and end() are identical to the non-const begin() and end().

Using the HashIterator

Now that the `hashmap` supports iteration, you can iterate over its elements just as you would on any STL container, and you can pass the iterators to methods and functions.

```cpp
#include "hashmap.h"
#include <iostream>
#include <map>
using namespace std;

int main(int argc, char** argv)
{
    hashmap<string, int> myHash;
    myHash.insert(make_pair("KeyOne", 100));
    myHash.insert(make_pair("KeyTwo", 200));
    myHash.insert(make_pair("KeyThree", 300));

    for (hashmap<string, int>::iterator it = myHash.begin();
        it != myHash.end(); ++it) {
        // Use both -> and * to test the operations.
        cout << it->first << " maps to " << (*it).second << endl;
    }

    // Create a map with all the elements in the hashmap.
    map<string, int> myMap(myHash.begin(), myHash.end());
    for (map<string, int>::iterator it = myMap.begin();
        it != myMap.end(); ++it) {
        // Use both -> and * to test the operations.
        cout << it->first << " maps to " << (*it).second << endl;
    }

    return (0);
}
```

Note on Allocators

As described earlier in this chapter, all the STL containers allow you to specify a custom memory allocator. A "good citizen" `hashmap` implementation should do the same. However, we omit those details because they obscure the main points of this implementation.

Note on Reversible Containers

If your container supplies a bidirectional or random access iterator, it is considered *reversible*. Reversible containers are supposed to supply two additional `typedef`s:

Type Name	Description
`reverse_iterator`	The type of the "smart pointer" for iterating over elements of the container in reverse order
`const_reverse_iterator`	A version of `reverse_iterator` for iterating over const elements of the container in reverse order

Additionally, the container should provide `rbegin()` and `rend()` which are symmetric with `begin()` and `end()`. The usual implementations just use the `reverse_iterator` adapter described earlier in this chapter. We leave them as an exercise for the reader.

Making the Hashmap an Associative Container

In addition to the basic container requirements shown already, you can also make your container adhere to additional requirements for either associative or sequential containers. The `hashmap`, like the `map`, is obviously an associative container, so it should conform to the following `typedefs` and methods.

Associative Container Typedef Requirements

Associative containers require three additional `typedefs`:

Type Name	Description
key_type	The key type with which the container is instantiated
key_compare	The comparison class or function pointer type with which the container is instantiated
value_compare	Class for comparing two `value_type` elements

Our implementation also throws in a `mapped_type typedef`, because that's what the `map` does. The `value_compare` is implemented not as a `typedef`, but as a nested class definition. Alternatively, the class could be a `friend` class of the `hashmap`, but this definition follows the `map` definition found in the standard. The purpose of the `value_compare` class is to call the comparison function on the keys of two elements.

```cpp
template <typename Key, typename T, typename Compare = std::equal_to<Key>,
    typename Hash = DefaultHash<Key> >
class hashmap
{
    public:
        typedef Key key_type;
        typedef T mapped_type;
        typedef pair<const Key, T> value_type;
        typedef Compare key_compare;
        typedef pair<const Key, T>& reference;
        typedef const pair<const Key, T>& const_reference;
        typedef HashIterator<Key, T, Compare, Hash> iterator;
        typedef HashIterator<Key, T, Compare, Hash> const_iterator;
        typedef size_t size_type;
        typedef ptrdiff_t difference_type;

    // Required class definition for associative containers
        class value_compare :
            public std::binary_function<value_type, value_type, bool>
        {
            friend class hashmap<Key, T, Compare, Hash>;
            public:
```

```
                    bool operator() (const value_type& x, const value_type& y) const
                    {
                        return comp(x.first, y.first);
                    }
            protected:
                Compare comp;
                value_compare(Compare c) : comp(c) {}
        };
        // Remainder of hashmap class definition omitted for brevity
    };
```

Associative Container Method Requirements

The standard prescribes quite a few additional method requirements for associative containers:

Method	Description	Complexity
Constructor taking an iterator range.	Constructs the container and inserts elements in the iterator range. The iterator range need not refer into another container of the same type. **Note that all constructors of associative containers must take a comparison object of type** `value_compare`. **The constructors should provide a default constructed object as the default value.**	NlogN

`key_compare key_comp() const;`
 	
`value_compare value_comp() const;`
	Returns the comparison objects for comparing just keys or entire values.	Constant

`pair<iterator, bool> insert(value_type&);`
 	
`iterator insert(iterator, value_type&);`
 	
`void insert(InputIterator start, InputIterator end);`
	Three different forms of insert. The `iterator` position in the second is a hint, which can be ignored. The range in the third need not be from a container of the same type. Containers that allow duplicate keys return just `iterator` from the first form, because `insert()` always succeeds.	Logarithmic

`size_type erase(key_type&);`
`void erase(iterator);`
 	
`void erase(iterator start, iterator end);`
	Three different forms of erase. The first form returns the number of values erased (0 or 1, in containers that do not allow duplicate keys). The second and third forms erase the elements at `iterator` position, or in the range start to end.	Logarithmic, except for the second form, which should be amortized constant.

`void clear();`	Erases all elements	Linear

Method	Description	Complexity

`iterator find(key_type&);`
 	
`const_iterator`
`find(key_type&) const;`
	Finds the element with the specified key.	Logarithmic

`size_type count(key_type&)` `const;`	Returns the number of elements with the specified key (0 or 1 in containers that do not allow duplicate keys).	Logarithmic

`iterator`
`lower_bound(key_type&);`
 	
`iterator`
`upper_bound(key_type&);`
 	
`pair<iterator, iterator>`
`equal_range(key_type&);`
 	
`const_iterator`
`lower_bound(key_type&)`
`const;`
 	
`const_iterator`
`upper_bound(key_type&)`
`const;`
 	
`pair<const_iterator,`
`const_iterator>`
`equal_range(key_type&)`
`const;`
	Returns iterators referring to the first element of specified key, one past the last element of specified key, or both.	Logarithmic

Note that `lower_bound()`, `upper_bound()`, and `equal_range()` make sense only on sorted containers. Thus, the hashmap does not provide them.

Here is the complete hashmap class definition. Note that the prototype for `insert()`, `erase()`, and `find()` need to change slightly from the previous versions shown.

```
template <typename Key, typename T, typename Compare = std::equal_to<Key>,
    typename Hash = DefaultHash<Key> >
class hashmap
{
    public:
        typedef Key key_type;
        typedef T mapped_type;
        typedef pair<const Key, T> value_type;
        typedef Compare key_compare;
        typedef pair<const Key, T>& reference;
        typedef const pair<const Key, T>& const_reference;
        typedef HashIterator<Key, T, Compare, Hash> iterator;
        typedef HashIterator<Key, T, Compare, Hash> const_iterator;
        typedef size_t size_type;
        typedef ptrdiff_t difference_type;
```

685

```
// Required class definition for associative containers
class value_compare :
    public std::binary_function<value_type, value_type, bool>
{
    friend class hashmap<Key, T, Compare, Hash>;
    public:
        bool operator() (const value_type& x, const value_type& y) const
        {
            return comp(x.first, y.first);
        }
    protected:
        Compare comp;
        value_compare(Compare c) : comp(c) {}
};

// The iterator class needs access to protected members of the hashmap.
friend class HashIterator<Key, T, Compare, Hash>;

// Constructors
explicit hashmap(const Compare& comp = Compare(),
    const Hash& hash =  Hash()) throw(invalid_argument);

template <class InputIterator>
hashmap(InputIterator first, InputIterator last,
    const Compare& comp = Compare(), const Hash& hash = Hash())
    throw(invalid_argument);

// destructor, copy constructor, assignment operator
~hashmap();
hashmap(const hashmap<Key, T, Compare, Hash>& src);
hashmap<Key, T, Compare, Hash>& operator=(
    const hashmap<Key, T, Compare, Hash>& rhs);

// Iterator methods
iterator begin();
iterator end();
const_iterator begin() const;
const_iterator end() const;

// Size methods
bool empty() const;
size_type size() const;
size_type max_size() const;

// Element insert methods
T& operator[] (const key_type& x);
pair<iterator, bool> insert(const value_type& x);
iterator insert(iterator position, const value_type& x);
template <class InputIterator>
void insert(InputIterator first, InputIterator last);

// Element delete methods
void erase(iterator position);
size_type erase(const key_type& x);
void erase(iterator first, iterator last);

// Other modifying utilities
```

```
        void swap(hashmap<Key, T, Compare, Hash>& hashIn);
        void clear();

        // Access methods for STL conformity
        key_compare key_comp() const;
        value_compare value_comp() const;

        // Lookup methods
        iterator find(const key_type& x);
        const_iterator find(const key_type& x) const;
        size_type count(const key_type& x) const;

    protected:
        typedef list<value_type> ListType;

        typename ListType::iterator findElement(
            const key_type& x, int& bucket) const;
        vector<ListType>* mElems;
        size_type mSize;
        Compare mComp;
        Hash mHash;
};
```

hashmap Constructors

The implementation of the default constructor was shown earlier. The second constructor is a method template so that it can take an iterator range from any container, not just other hashmaps. If it were not a method template, it would need to specify the InputIterator type explicitly as HashIterator, limiting it to iterators from hashmaps. Despite the syntax, the implementation is uncomplicated: it initializes all the data members, then calls insert() to actually insert all the elements in the specified range.

```
// Make a call to insert() to actually insert the elements.
template <typename Key, typename T, typename Compare, typename Hash>
template <class InputIterator>
hashmap<Key, T, Compare, Hash>::hashmap(
    InputIterator first, InputIterator last, const Compare& comp,
    const Hash& hash) throw(invalid_argument) : mSize(0), mComp(comp), mHash(hash)
{
    if (mHash.numBuckets() <= 0) {
        throw (invalid_argument("Number of buckets must be positive"));
    }
    mElems = new vector<list<value_type> >(mHash.numBuckets());
    insert(first, last);
}
```

hashmap Insertion Operations

The first version of insert() adds a key/value pair to the hashmap. It is identical to the version shown earlier in the "A Basic Hashmap" section, except that it returns an iterator/bool pair. The iterator must be a HashIterator, constructed to refer to the element that was just inserted, or the element with the specified key, if it already exists.

```
template <typename Key, typename T, typename Compare, typename Hash>
pair<typename hashmap<Key, T, Compare, Hash>::iterator, bool>
    hashmap<Key, T, Compare, Hash>::insert(const value_type& x)
{
    int bucket;
    // Try to find the element.
    typename ListType::iterator it = findElement(x.first, bucket);

    if (it != (*mElems)[bucket].end()) {
        // The element already exists.
        // Convert the list iterator into a HashIterator, which
        // also requires the bucket and a pointer to the hashmap.
        HashIterator<Key, T, Compare, Hash> newIt(bucket, it, this);

        // Some compilers don't like make_pair here.
        pair<HashIterator<Key, T, Compare, Hash>, bool> p(newIt, false);
        return (p);
    } else {
        // We didn't find the element, so insert a new one.
        mSize++;
        typename ListType::iterator endIt =
            (*mElems)[bucket].insert((*mElems)[bucket].end(), x);
        pair<HashIterator<Key, T, Compare, Hash>, bool> p(
            HashIterator<Key, T, Compare, Hash>(bucket, endIt, this), true);
        return (p);
    }
}
```

The version of insert() that takes a position is useless for hashmaps. The implementation completely ignores position, and defers to the first version of insert().

```
template <typename Key, typename T, typename Compare, typename Hash>
typename hashmap<Key, T, Compare, Hash>::iterator
    hashmap<Key, T, Compare, Hash>::insert(typename hashmap<Key, T, Compare,
    Hash>::iterator position, const value_type& x)
{
    // Completely ignore position
    return (insert(x).first);
}
```

The third form of insert() is a method template for the same reason as the constructor shown earlier: it should be able to insert elements using iterators from containers of any type. The actual implementation uses an insert_iterator, which was described earlier in this chapter.

```
template <typename Key, typename T, typename Compare, typename Hash>
template <class InputIterator>
void hashmap<Key, T, Compare, Hash>::insert(InputIterator first,
    InputIterator last)
{
    // Copy each element in the range by using an insert_iterator
    // adapter. Give begin() as a dummy position--insert ignores it
    // anyway.
    insert_iterator<hashmap<Key, T, Compare, Hash> > inserter(*this, begin());
    copy(first, last, inserter);
}
```

hashmap Erase Operations

The first version of `erase()` is identical to the version shown earlier in the "A Basic Hashmap" section, except that it returns the number of elements erased (either 0 or 1).

```
template <typename Key, typename T, typename Compare, typename Hash>
typename hashmap<Key, T, Compare, Hash>::size_type
hashmap<Key, T, Compare, Hash>::erase(const key_type& x)
{
    int bucket;

    // First, try to find the element.
    typename ListType::iterator it = findElement(x, bucket);

    if (it != (*mElems)[bucket].end()) {
        // The element already exists--erase it.
        (*mElems)[bucket].erase(it);
        mSize--;
        return (1);
    } else {
        return (0);
    }
}
```

The second form of `erase()` must remove the element at a specific iterator position. The iterator given is, of course, a `HashIterator`. Thus, the `hashmap` must have some ability to obtain the underlying bucket and `list` iterator from the `HashIterator`. The approach we take is to make the `hashmap` class a friend of the `HashIterator` (not shown in the class definition above).

```
template <typename Key, typename T, typename Compare, typename Hash>
void hashmap<Key, T, Compare, Hash>::erase(
    hashmap<Key, T, Compare, Hash>::iterator position)
{
    // Erase the element from its bucket.
    (*mElems)[position.mBucket].erase(position.mIt);
    mSize--;
}
```

The final version of `erase()` removes a range of elements. It simply iterates from `first` to `last`, calling `erase()` on each element, thus letting the previous version of `erase()` do all the work.

```
template <typename Key, typename T, typename Compare, typename Hash>
void hashmap<Key, T, Compare, Hash>::erase(
    hashmap<Key, T, Compare, Hash>::iterator first,
    hashmap<Key, T, Compare, Hash>::iterator last)
{
    typename hashmap<Key, T, Compare, Hash>::iterator cur, next;

    // Erase all the elements in the range.
    for (next = first; next != last; ) {
        cur = next++;
        erase(cur);
    }
}
```

`clear()` uses the `for_each()` algorithm to call `clear()` on the `list` representing each bucket.

```
template <typename Key, typename T, typename Compare, typename Hash>
void hashmap<Key, T, Compare, Hash>::clear()
{
    // Call clear on each list.
    for_each(mElems->begin(), mElems->end(), mem_fun_ref(&ListType::clear));
    mSize = 0;
}
```

hashmap Accessor Operations

The standard requires accessors for the key comparison and value comparison objects.

```
template <typename Key, typename T, typename Compare, typename Hash>
typename hashmap<Key, T, Compare, Hash>::key_compare
    hashmap<Key, T, Compare, Hash>::key_comp() const
{
    return (mComp);
}

template <typename Key, typename T, typename Compare, typename Hash>
typename hashmap<Key, T, Compare, Hash>::value_compare
    hashmap<Key, T, Compare, Hash>::value_comp() const
{
    return (value_compare(mComp));
}
```

The `find()` method is identical to the version shown earlier for the basic `hashamp`, except for the return code. Instead of returning a pointer to the element, it constructs a `HashIterator` referring to it. The `const` version is identical, so its implementation is not shown here.

```
template <typename Key, typename T, typename Compare, typename Hash>
typename hashmap<Key, T, Compare, Hash>::iterator
    hashmap<Key, T, Compare, Hash>::find(const key_type& x)
{
    int bucket;
    // Use the findElement() helper.
    typename ListType::iterator it = findElement(x, bucket);
    if (it == (*mElems)[bucket].end()) {
        // We didn't find the element--return the end iterator.
        return (end());
    }
    // We found the element--convert the bucket/iterator to a HashIterator.
    return (HashIterator<Key, T, Compare, Hash>(bucket, it, this));
}
```

The implementation of `count()` is a wrapper for `find()`, returning 1 if it finds the element, 0 if it doesn't. Recall that `find()` returns the end iterator if it can't find the element. `count()` retrieves an end iterator by calling `end()` in order to compare it.

```
template <typename Key, typename T, typename Compare, typename Hash>
typename hashmap<Key, T, Compare, Hash>::size_type
    hashmap<Key, T, Compare, Hash>::count(const key_type& x) const
{
    // There are either 1 or 0 elements matching key x.
    // If we can find a match, return 1, otherwise return 0.
    if (find(x) == end()) {
        return (0);
    } else {
        return (1);
    }
}
```

The final method is not required by the standard, but is provided for ease of use. The prototype and implementations are identical to those of the operator[] in the STL map. The comments explain the potentially confusing one-line implementation.

```
template <typename Key, typename T, typename Compare, typename Hash>
T& hashmap<Key, T, Compare, Hash>::operator[] (const key_type& x)
{
    // This definition is the same as that used by map, according to
    // the standard.
    // It's a bit cryptic, but it basically attempts to insert
    // a new key/value pair of x and a new value. Regardless of whether
    // the insert succeeds or fails, insert() returns a pair of an
    // iterator/bool. The iterator refers to a key/value pair, the
    // second element of which is the value we want to return.
    return (((insert(make_pair(x, T()))).first)->second);
}
```

Note on Sequential Containers

The hashmap developed in the preceding sections is an associative container. However, you could also write a sequential container, in which case you would need to follow a different set of requirements. Instead of listing them here, it's easier to point out that the deque container follows the prescribed sequential container requirements almost exactly. The only difference is that it provides an extra resize() method (not required by the standard). Consult the Standard Library Reference resource on the Web site for details on the deque capabilities.

Summary

The final example in this chapter showed almost complete development of a hashmap associative container and its iterator. This hashmap implementation is available for downloading with the rest of the examples, as described in the Introduction. Feel free to incorporate it into your programs. In the process of reading this chapter, you also hopefully gained an appreciation for the steps to develop containers. Even if you never write another STL algorithm or container, you understand better the STL's mentality and capabilities, and you can put it to better use.

This chapter concluded the three-chapter tour of the STL. Even with three chapters, there are still features that we omitted. If this material excited you, consult some of the resources in Appendix B for more information. On the other hand, we realize that the syntax and material in these chapters was dense. As described in Chapters 21 and 22, don't feel compelled to use all the features discussed here. Forcing them into your programs without a true need will just complicate them. However, we encourage you to consider incorporating aspects of the STL into your programs where they make sense. Start with the containers, maybe throw in an algorithm or two, and before you know it, you'll be a convert!

24

Exploring Distributed Objects

Distributed computing is simply the idea that a program's operation can be spread across multiple computers on a network. As networks grow faster and more common, an increasing number of applications leverage other computers on the network during their processing.

In this chapter, you will learn about *distributed objects*: the application of object-oriented technologies to distributed computing. This chapter begins by defining distributed computing and distributed objects in more detail, including sample use cases. Next, you will be introduced to CORBA, a powerful architecture for programming distributed objects. Finally, you'll read about XML technologies and their role in distributed computing.

The Appeal of Distributed Computing

Distributed computing has received much attention in the last decade as the Internet has risen to prominence. Yet it is more than a buzzword — a distributed program is an ideal fit for certain types of applications. For example, try to imagine writing a program that contains all of the information available on the Web. It would be nearly impossible. The Web is only able to contain its massive amount of data and dynamic content because it is distributed across many different machines.

Distribution for Scalability

In an average day, your desktop computer probably spends most of its time doing nothing. Even when you are actively using your computer, modern processors are so fast that they are idle much of the time, waiting for us human beings to catch up. The reality is that the world contains many computers, most of which aren't exactly overworked. They are, however, ready to be put to use.

Most computer users have more than enough power on their desktop PC's. If you use a monitoring tool to examine the utilization of your processor, you'll see that it rarely hits 100 percent for any length of time. Some applications, however, are extremely processor-intensive. It might take hours to run a program full of complex calculations on your desktop computer. If you were able to harness the power of the unused processors on your network, that time could be greatly reduced. This technique is referred to as *grid computing*.

One of the classic real-world examples of an application that uses distribution for speed is image rendering. The generation of just one still frame of movie-quality computer animation requires an enormous amount of computation. 3-D rendering applications have taken advantage of distributed computing for many years. So-called *rendering farms* can be assembled with high-speed network connections. One machine might serve as the central "brain" and hand out small chunks of computation to each machine in the farm. The brain machine would gather the results to assemble the final image or movie.

The SETI@home project is another example of using distributed computing to increase computational performance. The program aids in the Search for Extra-Terrestrial Intelligence (SETI) by spreading the analysis of signals from space among all participating computers. It would be impractical to attempt to analyze such an enormous amount of data on a single computer. The SETI@home project gives users a program they can run on their home PC's that processes chunks of data when the computer isn't being used. Of course, we can't call it a success quite yet (no little green men have been found), but as an early widespread distributed Internet application, it helped popularize the technology.

Distribution for Reliability

Distributed computing can be seen as a solution to Murphy's Law — *whatever can go wrong, will go wrong*. Certain applications, such as Web sites and databases, need to be available and working at all times. These applications can be written so that they are running on multiple computers on the network. If one machine goes down, another can immediately take over. In cases like this, distribution becomes mainly an issue of synchronization. All instances of the application need to communicate enough so that when a failover occurs, the user doesn't experience any change.

When you access a large-scale Web site, you are really connecting to one of many servers, all of which contain mirror images of the same data. A device known as a *load balancer* is often used to route incoming requests to an available machine. If one machine fails, the load balancer ceases to send it any requests until it is repaired.

Distribution for Centrality

It is often useful to have one system on a network that controls or monitors the behavior of other applications. For example, Sassafras Software's KeyServer is an application that allows network administrators to ensure that software being used on their network doesn't violate licensing terms. When a user on the network launches an application, the application contacts the KeyServer to request permission to run. The KeyServer keeps track of how many copies are currently running. If additional licenses are available, the requested application starts up normally. Incidentally, KeyServer also makes use of distribution for reliability — administrators can install multiple "shadow" KeyServers in case one goes down.

Distributed Content

Peer-to-peer applications have exploded in popularity recently. The basic idea is that users on a network all run an application that lets them communicate on a one-to-one basis. In a file-sharing application, each user makes files stored on his or her local computers available on the network. Users seeking that file can connect to the user who has it and begin a transfer. By distributing the file-sharing application across all of its users, the application is able to offer a larger quantity of content than could be housed on a single server. It also distributes the communications load, so there is no central server that becomes a bottleneck for all requests.

Distributed versus Networked

You should keep in mind that not all applications that take advantage of networking are necessarily distributed applications. A networked application communicates with other machines to request or transfer data. The term *distributed* implies a much richer interaction.

The distinction is sometimes difficult to see. For example, consider a video game. If the game communicates with a central server to check for updates, it would be a networked application because the game itself isn't running on multiple applications — it simply talks to another machine in the course of its operation. However, if the game allowed multiple players to participate on different machines, it could be implemented as a distributed application.

The best approach to labeling an application as distributed or networked (other than deciding it's an entirely academic distinction and doesn't really matter) is to take the position of one machine and determine whether computation is happening on another machine. In the networked game case, the individual copies of the game are most likely operating on their own machines. They use the network only for status updates, as shown in Figure 24-1. As the figure shows, when the player on Machine A shoots his or her gun, the information about the shot is transmitted to Machine B. Both machines take appropriate action based on the same event. This style of networked game isn't generally considered a distributed application.

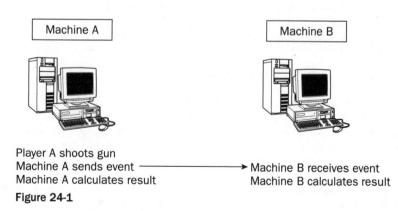

Player A shoots gun
Machine A sends event ⟶ Machine B receives event
Machine A calculates result Machine B calculates result

Figure 24-1

You could imagine such a game that actually was implemented in a distributed manner. Instead of one machine sending an event to the other machine and processing the result independently, the processing could be performed once, spread across the two machines. As shown in Figure 24-2, Machine A might send the event and let Machine B determine what the outcome is. From the point of view of Machine A, some of the data processing occurs externally, which is a good indication that it is running a distributed application.

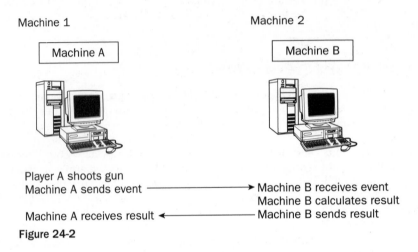

Figure 24-2

Distributed Objects

Distributed computing existed before object-oriented programming (OOP) became popular, so the two ideas are definitely distinct. However, the application of OOP concepts to distributed computing yields powerful new abstractions. If you imagine calling a method on an object that actually exists on a computer thousands of miles away, or passing an object between hosts on a network, you start to see how nicely OOP meshes with distributed computing.

Serialization and Marshalling

Fundamentally, transmitting raw data is all that a network knows how to do. Networks don't know anything about C++, objects, or code execution. They simply move data from one place to another. This simplicity is one of the greatest features of networks. A heterogeneous collection of computers, with various architectures and operating systems, can participate on the same network because the network makes few assumptions about the environments of its participants.

For distributed applications, the simplicity of networking presents a slight problem. It would be nice if you could send an object from one machine to another simply by calling a function that puts that object on the network, but it's more complicated than that because the network doesn't know about objects. Instead, you need to convert the object into raw bytes. Instead of sending the actual object, you must send data that describes the object. The recipient needs to interpret the raw bytes to reconstruct what will hopefully be a duplicate of the original.

The process of converting an in-memory object to a flattened raw representation is known as *serialization* or *marshalling*. The process of reconstructing the object is called *deserialization* or *unmarshalling*. You may be familiar with marshalling from Chapter 14, which showed an example of using a string to represent an object. Marshalling is useful for more than just networking. If you want to save an object to disk, you will most likely marshal it into a flattened format first.

Serialization in Action

Consider the following function declarations, which provide the ability to send data to another computer over the network and receive data from another computer. As explained in Chapter 18, networking isn't a built-in capability of C++, so the actual networking library provided by your operating system will certainly be different from that in this extremely simple version.

```
/**
 * Sends data to another host on the network
 *
 * @param inHostName  the name of the other machine
 * @param inData      the data you want to send
 */
void send(const string& inHostName, const string& inData);

/**
 * Receives incoming data from the network
 *
 * @return            the data that was received
 */
string read();
```

Imagine that you are writing an inventory control application for a company that has warehouses throughout the United States. Each warehouse location will run a copy of the program, but the program needs to be able to fulfill orders for any location. In other words, you can use the program running in Pittsford, New York to order an item at the warehouse in Onion Creek, Washington.

Because all of the programs at all of the locations use the same Order class to represent an order, what you really want to do is send orders over the network from Pittsford to Onion Creek. Here is a class definition for the Order class:

```
// Order.h

class Order
{
    public:
        Order();

        int getItemNumber() const;
        void setItemNumber(int inItemNumber);

        int getQuantity() const;
        void setQuantity(int inQuantity);

        int getCustomerNumber() const;
        void setCustomerNumber(int inCustomerNumber);
```

```
    protected:
        int mItemNumber;
        int mQuantity;
        int mCustomerNumber;
};
```

At this point, there is a mismatch between the data you want to send (an object) and the capabilities of the network functions, which only process `strings`. The solution is to add serialization and deserialization capabilities to the `Order` class. The new class definition is shown here:

```
// Order.h
```

```
#include <string>
```

```
class Order
{
    public:
        Order();

        int getItemNumber() const;
        void setItemNumber(int inItemNumber);

        int getQuantity() const;
        void setQuantity(int inQuantity);

        int getCustomerNumber() const;
        void setCustomerNumber(int inCustomerNumber);

        /**
         * Converts the object into raw data that can be sent over the
         * network
         *
         * @return          a string representing this object
         */
        std::string serialize();

        /**
         * Adjusts this object to represent the data in inData
         *
         * @param inData     a string representing Order data
         */
        void deserialize(const std::string& inData);

    protected:
        int mItemNumber;
        int mQuantity;
        int mCustomerNumber;
};
```

The implementation of the `Order` class follows. Only the serialization methods are highlighted because the rest of the class implementation is remarkably uninteresting.

```
// Order.cpp

#include "Order.h"
#include <iostream>
#include <sstream>
#include <string>

using namespace std;

Order::Order() : mItemNumber(-1), mQuantity(-1), mCustomerNumber(-1)
{
}

int Order::getItemNumber()
{
    return mItemNumber;
}

void Order::setItemNumber(int inItemNumber)
{
    mItemNumber = inItemNumber;
}

int Order::getQuantity()
{
    return mQuantity;
}

void Order::setQuantity(int inQuantity)
{
    mQuantity = inQuantity;
}

int Order::getCustomerNumber()
{
    return mCustomerNumber;
}

void Order::setCustomerNumber(int inCustomerNumber)
{
    mCustomerNumber = inCustomerNumber;
}
```

```
string serialize()
{
    // Use a stream to output all the values, separated by tabs.
    ostringstream outStream;

    outStream << getItemNumber() << "\t" <<
                 getQuantity() << "\t" <<
                 getCustomerNumber();

    return outStream.str();
}
```

```
void deserialize(const string& inData)
{
    // Use an input stream to read the values back in the same order.
    istringstream inStream(inData);

    if (!inStream.good()) {
        cerr << "Error deserializing!" << endl;
    } else {
        inStream >> mItemNumber;
        inStream >> mQuantity;
        inStream >> mCustomerNumber;
    }
}
```

Simply by providing a way to convert an object to and from a string, you can transmit a representation of the object through a network. If your program makes heavy use of serialization, you may decide to include `operator<<` and `operator>>` in every class to provide serialization.

Remote Procedure Calls

A *remote procedure call* (RPC) refers to the conceptual behavior of calling a method or function that executes on another machine. In C++, this behavior is *conceptual* in nature because the language doesn't provide any actual mechanism to call a function that isn't in some way linked into the actual program binary. Rather, RPC in C++ generally involves calling a *stub method* locally that is actually hiding some networking code that obtains the result from a remote host.

By using the networking capabilities of your operating system and the serialization techniques shown earlier, it is possible to write your own RPC mechanism. You might define a class that represents a remote host, containing a number of stub methods that are actually executed on the remote host but return the result to the local caller. Such a class definition follows, containing stub methods that can be used to obtain information about the status of the remote machine or perform a restart.

```
class RemoteHost
{
    public:
        /**
         * Creates a remote host, which is available at the
         * given address
         */
        RemoteHost(const string& inAddress);

        int getNumConnectedUsers() const;
        int getAvailableMemory() const ;
        int getAvailableDiskSpace() const ;

        void restartNow();

    protected:
        string mAddress;
};
```

The implementations of these methods would still be defined normally, but would make use of the networking library to obtain the actual result from the remote machine. The actual code would vary depending on the networking library, but here is some pseudocode that makes use of the networking functions defined in the previous section:

```
int RemoteHost::getAvailableMemory() const
{
    // Send the string "getAvailableMemory()" to the remote host, instructing
    // it to send back its available memory.
    send(mAddress, "getAvailableMemory()");

    // Get the result from the remote host.
    string result = read();

    // Convert result into an int.
    // Return the int result.
}
```

The implementation on the remote host would need to parse and interpret the messages it receives in order to respond with the correct result. Here is some pseudocode for the remote host implementation.

```
void respondToRPC(const string& inRequestHost, const string& inMessage)
{
    string response = "";

    // Look at the message to determine which operation is requested.
    if (inMessage == "getAvailableMemory()") {
        // Use a local function to get the available memory on this machine.
        int memAvail = getAvailMem();
        // Convert the result into a string and put it in the response variable.
    } else if (...) {
        // Handle other messages.
    }

    // Send the response back to the requestor.
    send(inRequestHost, response);
}
```

The preceding pseudocode examples look simple, but a number of complications would quickly arise if you tried to turn it into actual production code. Some of the issues you would encounter are:

❑ How do you deal with different data types, including complex types such as objects?

❑ How do you deal with RPC calls that aren't recognized by the remote machine?

❑ How do you deal with versioning? What if some remote machines are upgraded and no longer respond in the same way as others?

❑ How do you deal with network errors, missing hosts, overloaded networks, and so on?

❑ How do you deal with platform issues, such as byte order differences?

For these reasons, as well as for the usual avoidance of reinventing the wheel, programmers typically use an existing RPC package that facilitates this type of interaction. The rest of this chapter covers CORBA and XML, two very different technologies that can both aid in RPC communication.

CORBA

The *Common Object Request Broker Architecture*, or *CORBA*, is a standardized language-independent and platform-independent architecture for defining, implementing, and using distributed objects. The main goal of CORBA is to provide a programming environment that hides all the details of serialization and remote procedure calls discussed in the previous section. CORBA also supports *location transparency*: you can write code that uses objects without knowing whether those objects are really local or remote.

The CORBA architecture itself is not an implementation, and actually includes several standards. The two most important standards are the *Interface Definition Language* (*IDL*), which defines the syntax for writing distributed object definitions, and the *Internet Inter-ORB Protocol* (*IIOP*) for making remote method invocations. Additionally, CORBA defines many optional accompanying services, including a name service, an event service, a time service, and numerous others.

> There are a number of open-source implementations of the CORBA standards available for use at no cost. The examples in this chapter use the "omniORB" framework, which is available at **http://omniorb.sourceforge.net/**.

Using CORBA requires several steps, including defining your object interfaces, "compiling" the interfaces to generate the networking and serialization code, defining the class method implementation, writing a server process, and writing clients. This section examines each of those steps in the context of developing an extremely simple distributed database, in which clients can access a database server that resides in a different process or even on a different node. The discussion here barely scratches the surface of this powerful, but complicated, architecture. If you are interested in using it for your distributed object framework, you should consult some of the references in Appendix B.

Interface Definition Language

CORBA does an excellent job of separating object interfaces from their implementations. You write a distributed CORBA class by first defining its interface in the Interface Definition Language (IDL). This language looks a lot like C++, but isn't identical. In fact, the IDL is implementation language independent. You could theoretically write an implementation for the class in C++ and a client that uses it in Java.

Writing the Interface

In this step, you specify the prototypes for methods that the object implements. However, unlike in C++ class definitions, you don't show member variables or other implementation details.

For example, suppose that you want your simple distributed database to store key/value records where the key and value are both `strings`. Here is the IDL file for a database that supports two methods:

```
// database.idl

interface database {
    void addRecord(in string key, in string record);
    string lookupRecord(in string key);
};
```

The word "in" before the parameters specifies value parameters instead of reference parameters.

Generating Stubs and Skeletons

After writing your object interface, you compile the IDL file with an IDL compiler, which generates the remote procedure call and networking layers for you. There are IDL compilers available for a variety of languages, including Java, Python, C, and, of course, C++. This step generates two sets of files: the *stubs* and the *skeletons*.

Stubs

As described in the previous section on RPC, the stubs are the client side of the object methods, which hide the networking and serialization code required to make the actual remote call to another machine. The omniORB IDL compiler puts stub code from the IDL file name.idl in the header file name.hh and the source file nameSK.cc. Here is a small sample of the stub code in database.hh, which is generated from the database.idl file:

```
// This file is generated by omniidl (C++ backend)- omniORB_4_0. Do not edit.

// <There's a lot more code than we show here.>

class _objref_database :
  public virtual CORBA::Object, public virtual omniObjRef
{
public:
  void addRecord(const char* key, const char* record);
  char* lookupRecord(const char* key);

  inline _objref_database()  { _PR_setobj(0); }  // nil
  _objref_database(omniIOR*, omniIdentity*);

protected:
  virtual ~_objref_database();


private:
  virtual void* _ptrToObjRef(const char*);

  _objref_database(const _objref_database&);
  _objref_database& operator = (const _objref_database&);
  // not implemented

  friend class database;
};
```

Here is one of the method implementations from databaseSK.cc:

```
// This file is generated by omniidl (C++ backend)- omniORB_4_0. Do not edit.

// <There's a lot more code than we show here.>

void _objref_database::addRecord(const char* key, const char* record)
{
  _0RL_cd_D115D31DB8E47435_00000000 _call_desc(_0RL_lcfn_D115D31DB8E47435_10000\
000, "addRecord", 10);
```

```
      _call_desc.arg_0 = key;
      _call_desc.arg_1 = record;

      _invoke(_call_desc);
   }
```

Don't worry about understanding this code! We just want to give you an example of the work that goes on "behind the scenes."

Skeletons

The skeletons are the basis for your class implementation and are usually abstract base classes generated from the IDL interface. omniORB places the skeletons in the same `database.hh` and `databaseSK.cc` files in which it puts the stub code. Here is some of the skeleton code from `database.hh`:

```
class _impl_database :
   public virtual omniServant
{
public:
   virtual ~_impl_database();

   virtual void addRecord(const char* key, const char* record) = 0;
   virtual char* lookupRecord(const char* key) = 0;

public:  // Really protected, workaround for xlC
   virtual _CORBA_Boolean _dispatch(omniCallHandle&);

private:
   virtual void* _ptrToInterface(const char*);
   virtual const char* _mostDerivedRepoId();
};

class POA_database :
   public virtual _impl_database,
   public virtual PortableServer::ServantBase
{
public:
   virtual ~POA_database();

   inline ::database_ptr _this() {
      return (::database_ptr) _do_this(::database::_PD_repoId);
   }
};
```

Note that an `in string` parameter in the IDL file is translated as a `const char*` in the generated C++ code. POA stands for *Portable Object Adapter*, a CORBA component that manages object references on the server side.

Implementing the Class

Now that you've defined your interface and generated the stubs and skeletons, the next step is to write a class that provides actual implementations of the methods in the IDL file. You write this class by subclassing the abstract skeleton class and filling in the data members and method implementations. You don't need to worry about serialization or networking code when you implement the methods. You just write them as if they were normal methods. The skeleton code handles all the gory RPC details for you. Here is a definition of the DatabaseServer class based on the previous omniORB skeleton code:

```
// DatabaseServer.h
#include "database.hh"
#include <map>
#include <string>

class DatabaseServer : public POA_database,
                       public PortableServer::RefCountServantBase
{
    public:
        DatabaseServer();
        virtual ~DatabaseServer();
        virtual void addRecord(const char* key, const char* record);
        virtual char* lookupRecord(const char* key);

    protected:
        std::map<std::string, std::string> mDb;
};
```

Note that this class subclasses the previous POA_database skeleton abstract class, as well as a reference counting mix-in class supplied by the framework. It adds a protected map data member for storing the key/value pairs.

Here are the method implementations:

```
#include "DatabaseServer.h"
using namespace std;

DatabaseServer::DatabaseServer()
{
}

DatabaseServer::~DatabaseServer()
{
}

void DatabaseServer::addRecord(const char* key, const char* record)
{
    mDb[key] = record;
}

char* DatabaseServer::lookupRecord(const char* key)
{
    return (CORBA::string_dup(mDb[key].c_str()));
}
```

The only tricky thing about these implementations is to remember to copy the string you return from lookupRecord() using the CORBA::string_dup() method.

Using the Objects

You're now ready to use your distributed objects. Using the objects requires two steps. One piece of code must create an object and register it with the *Object Request Broker (ORB)* framework via the Portable Object Adapter. It must also provide a way for client code to lookup references to the object. One technique is to use a *nameserver*. This nameserver must be available from all the machines on which the distributed program runs. As a nameserver, it maps names to object references and tracks the actual physical location of all the distributed objects on the system. If you don't have a nameserver available, you can use other ad hoc methods to register and lookup object references. Although the CORBA standard includes a nameserver, and omniORB supplies one, for simplicity our database example just writes the object reference key to a file.

The code that wants to use an object looks it up in the nameserver, or, in our case, the file, to retrieve a reference to it. When this client code calls a method on the reference, the request is sent to the ORB layer, which is either a layer in each process, or its own process on each node, depending on the implementation. At this point, there are two options. If the underlying object is in the same process as the caller, the method is executed locally as a normal C++ method call. However, if the underlying object is in a different process on the same machine, or on a remote machine, the ORB sends the method request over the network to the server process. All this work occurs under the surface: the code that makes the method call on the object reference doesn't need to worry about whether the actual object is local or remote.

Figure 24-3 shows the basic CORBA architecture.

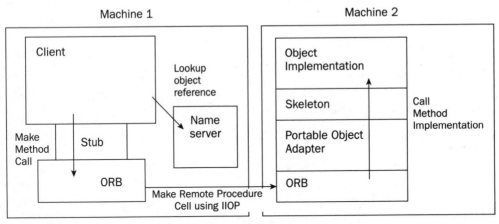

Figure 24-3

> CORBA works for interprocess communication on the same machine as well as intermachine communication. You can use CORBA as a mechanism for "sharing" objects between processes on the same machine.

The rest of this section continues the database example by showing a sample implementation of a server and client. We don't expect you to understand all the code details; we merely want to give you a sample so you get a general feeling for CORBA programming and a taste of how powerful the technology can be. If you want to become an expert CORBA programmer, you should consult the references listed in Appendix B.

The Server Process

The server process must initialize the ORB, create a new `DatabaseServer` object, register the object, and save a key to its reference in a file for clients to find. This example assumes that clients will have access to the directory from which this server process is started, either through a network file system, or because they are running on the same node. The comments explain the steps taken. Note that you don't use a special compiler to compile this code; you can use a standard C++ compiler, such as g++, as long as you link to the appropriate omniORB libraries.

```cpp
#include "DatabaseServer.h"
#include <iostream>
#include <fstream>
using namespace std;

const char* objRefFile = "OBJ_REF_FILE.dat";

int main(int argc, char** argv)
{
    // Try to initialize the orb.
    CORBA::ORB_var orb;
    try {
        orb = CORBA::ORB_init(argc, argv);
    } catch(CORBA::SystemException&) {
        cerr << "Unable to initialize the ORB\n";
        exit(1);
    }

    // Obtain a reference to the "Portable Object Adapter" and downcast
    // it to the appropriate type.
    CORBA::Object_var obj = orb->resolve_initial_references("RootPOA");
    PortableServer::POA_var poa = PortableServer::POA::_narrow(obj);

    // Create the DatabaseServer object and register/activate it
    // with the portable object adapter.
    DatabaseServer* myDb = new DatabaseServer();
    PortableServer::ObjectId_var dbid = poa->activate_object(myDb);

    // Write a string version of the object reference to a
    // file so clients can find us.
    CORBA::Object_var dbobj = myDb->_this();
    CORBA::String_var sior(orb->object_to_string(dbobj));

    ofstream ostr(objRefFile);
    if (ostr.fail()) {
        cerr << "Unable to open object reference file for writing.\n";
        exit(1);
    }
    ostr << (char*)sior;
    ostr.close();
```

```
    // Tell the reference counter that we're done with the object.
    // Now only the POA has a reference to it.
    myDb->_remove_ref();

    // Move the POA from holding to active state, so that it will process
    // incoming requests.
    PortableServer::POAManager_var pman = poa->the_POAManager();
    pman->activate();

    // Wait for incoming requests.
    orb->run();

    // Shouldn't return from the run call, but if we do, we need to clean up
    orb->destroy();
    return (0);
}
```

The Client Process

The final step is to write a client process. Here is a basic client that reads the object reference key from a file, creates an object reference from the key, and calls two methods on the object reference. These calls are translated by the ORB layer into calls to the `DatabaseServer` object in the server process.

```
#include "database.hh"
#include <iostream>
#include <fstream>
using namespace std;

const char* objRefFile = "OBJ_REF_FILE.dat";

int main(int argc, char** argv)
{
    // Try to initialize the orb.
    CORBA::ORB_var orb;
    try {
        orb = CORBA::ORB_init(argc, argv);
    } catch(CORBA::SystemException&) {
        cerr << "Unable to initialize the ORB\n";
        exit(1);
    }

    // Read the server object reference from the file.
    ifstream istr(objRefFile);
    if (istr.fail()) {
        cerr << "No object reference file!\n";
        exit(1);
    }
    char objRef[1024];
    istr.getline(objRef, 1024);

    // Construct an object reference from the string.
    database_var dbref;
    try {
        CORBA::Object_var obj = orb->string_to_object(objRef);
```

```
                dbref = database::_narrow(obj);
                if(CORBA::is_nil(dbref) ) {
                    cerr << "Can't narrow reference to type database\n";
                    exit (1);
                }
        } catch(CORBA::SystemException&) {
            cerr << "Unable to find the object reference\n";
        }

        // Make calls on the object reference, which are translated to
        // calls on the server object in the server process.
        try {
            dbref->addRecord("key1", "value1");
            const char* lookup = dbref->lookupRecord("key1");
            if (strcmp(lookup, "value1") == 0) {
                cout << "Success!\n";
            } else {
                cout << "strings don't match\n";
            }
        } catch(CORBA::COMM_FAILURE&) {
            cerr << "Communication error\n";
            exit(1);
        } catch(CORBA::SystemException&) {
            cerr << "Communication error (SystemException)\n";
            exit(1);
        }

        // We're done.
        orb->destroy();

        return (0);
}
```

As you can see, the CORBA framework is certainly complicated and has a steep learning curve. However, it can be invaluable for industrial-strength distributed programming.

XML

Extensible Markup Language (XML) is a simple and general markup language. Fundamentally, XML can be used to represent just about anything. You could use XML as the file format for storing an MP3 music playlist or as the internal representation of a complex purchase order. Because XML is easy to work with and has cross-platform support, it has quickly become popular as a format for network communication, remote procedure calls, and distributed objects.

A Crash Course in XML

One of the greatest aspects of XML, and surely one of the reasons for its rapid adoption, is that it has a very friendly learning curve. Getting started with XML is easy. Within minutes, you'll know the terminology and be able to read and write valid XML. From there, an XML developer can proceed down any number of more complex roads, such as XML transformations, or Simple Object Access Protocol (SOAP), a distributed object technology built upon XML.

What Is XML?

XML is merely a *syntax* for describing data. Outside of a specific application, XML data has no meaning. For example, you could write a home inventory program that produces a perfectly valid XML document describing all of your worldly possessions. If you gave that document to somebody else, they might be able to look at it and figure it out, but the XML-based home inventory program that they wrote wouldn't necessarily be able to interpret it. The reason is that XML defines the structure of the document but not its meaning. Another application may represent the same information in a different structure.

XML is written in a plain text format, which makes it easy for human beings to grok. Even if you've never seen XML before, you can probably understand the following snippet of XML data:

```
<inventory>
    <office>
        <desk type="wood"/>
        <computer type="Macintosh"/>
        <chair type="leather"/>
    </office>
    <kitchen>
        <mixer type="chrome"/>
        <stove type="electric"/>
    </kitchen>
</inventory>
```

In addition to readability, the text format also means that XML is easy to work with in software. You don't need to learn a complicated framework or purchase an expensive toolset to parse text. Because even the most obscure operating systems understand plain text, it's easy to send XML between systems without worrying about binary compatibility issues.

To be fair, textual representation has some downsides. Readability quickly becomes verbosity. An XML representation of data is usually larger than its equivalent binary representation. When the data set is large, the XML representation can grow to be enormous. Text also takes time to parse, unlike a binary format, which doesn't require any parsing at all.

The other important characteristic about XML, implied by the indentation of the previous example, is that it is hierarchical. As you'll see, XML is often parsed into a tree structure that you can walk through to process the data.

XML Structure and Terminology

XML documents begin with a *document prolog*, which specifies the character encoding and other metadata about the document. Many programmers omit the prolog, but some stricter XML parsers will fail to recognize the document as XML if the prolog is not found on the first line. The details of information that can be specified in the prolog are beyond the scope of this book. The following prolog is sufficient for most uses:

```
<?xml version="1.0"?>
```

The document prolog is a special type of *tag*, a piece of syntax that XML recognizes as having some sort of meaning. If you have written HTML files, you're already familiar with tags. The body of an XML document is made up of *element tags*. They are simply markers that identify the start and end of a logical piece of the structure. In XML, every starting element tag has a corresponding ending element tag. For example, the following line of XML uses the tag `sentence` to mark the start and end of a sentence element.

```
<sentence>Let's go get some ice cream.</sentence>
```

In XML, the end tag is written as a slash followed by the name of the element. Element tags don't always have to contain data as the previous example does. In XML, you can have an *empty tag*, which simply exists on its own. One way of doing this is to follow a start tag immediately with an end tag:

```
<empty></empty>
```

XML also provides a shorthand for empty element tags. If you end a tag with a slash, it serves as both the start tag and the end of the element:

```
<empty />
```

The topmost element, which contains all other elements in the document, is known as the *root element*.

In addition to its name, an element tag can contain key/value pairs called *attributes*. There are no set-in-stone rules about what can be written as an attribute (remember: XML is just a syntax) but in general, attributes provide metainformation about the element. For example, the sentence element could have an attribute that gives the speaker of the sentence:

```
<sentence speaker="Marni">Let's go get some ice cream.</sentence>
```

Elements can have multiple attributes, though they must have unique keys:

```
<sentence speaker="Marni" tone="pleading">Let's go get some ice cream.</sentence>
```

When you see an XML element whose name has a colon in it, such as `<a:sentence>`, the string prior to the colon, is its *namespace*. Just like namespaces in C++, namespaces in XML allow you to segment the use of names.

In the previous examples, the content of an element was either empty or textual data, commonly referred to as a *text node*. In XML, elements can also contain other elements, which gives XML its hierarchical structure. In the following example, the dialogue element is made up of two sentence elements. Note that the indentation exists only for readability — XML ignores white space between tags.

```
<dialogue>
    <sentence speaker="Marni">Let's go get some ice cream.</sentence>
    <sentence speaker="Scott">After I'm done writing this C++ book.</sentence>
</dialogue>
```

Those are the basics! Elements, attributes, and text nodes are the building blocks of XML. For more advanced syntax, such as special character escaping, consult one of the XML reference books listed in Appendix B.

XML as a Distributed Object Technology

Since XML is simple and easy to work with, it has become popular as a mechanism for serialization. XML serialized objects can be sent across a network, and the sender can be confident that the recipient will be able to parse them, regardless of their platform. For example, consider the simple class shown here:

```
class Simple
{
    public:
        std::string mName;
        int     mPriority;

        std::string mData;
};
```

An object of type `Simple` could be serialized to the following XML:

```
<Simple name="some name" priority="7">this is the data</Simple>
```

Of course, since XML doesn't specify how individual nodes should be used, you could just as easily serialize it as follows:

```
<Simple name="some name" priority="7" data="this is the data" />
```

As long as the recipient of the serialized XML is aware of the rules you are using to serialize the object, they should be able to deserialize it.

XML serialization has increased in popularity as a simpler alternative to heavyweight distributed object technologies such as CORBA. XML has a much more gradual learning curve than CORBA and offers many of the same benefits, such as platform and language independence.

Generating and Parsing XML in C++

Because XML is merely a file format, and not an object description language, the task of converting data to and from XML is left to the programmer. In general, writing XML is the easy part. Reading XML is usually aided by a third-party XML library.

Generating XML

To use XML as a serialization technology, your objects will need to be able to convert themselves into XML. In many cases, building a stream of XML on the fly is the easiest way to output XML. In fact, the notion that XML elements are "wrapped" in other elements makes things even easier. You can build new XML documents as amalgams of existing ones. If that sounds a bit complicated, consider the following example. Assume that you have a function called `getNextSentenceXML()`, which asks the user for a sentence and returns it as an XML representation of the sentence. Because that function returns the sentence as a valid XML element, you could create a dialogue of sentences by wrapping the results of multiple calls to `getNextSentenceXML()` in a dialogue element tag:

```
string getDialogueXML()
{
    sstringstream outStream;

    // Begin the dialogue element.
    outStream << "<dialogue>";

    while (true) {
        // Get the next sentence.
        string sentenceXML = getNextSentenceXML();
        if (sentenceXML == "") break;

        // Add the sentence element.
        outStream << sentenceXML;
    }

    // End the dialogue element.
    outStream << "</dialogue>";

    return outStream.toString();
}
```

If subsequent calls to getNextSentenceXML() returned the sentences from the preceding example, the result of this function would be:

```
<dialogue><sentence speaker="Marni">Let's go get some ice
cream.</sentence><sentence speaker="Scott">After I'm done writing this C++
book.</sentence></dialogue>
```

The output is a bit strange because it wasn't formatted with line breaks and tabs. It is, however, valid XML. If you wanted to beautify the output a bit, you have a few options:

❑   You could use a third-party tool after the fact. For example, the open-source command-line program tidy (http://tidy.sourceforge.net) has an XML pretty-print feature among its many useful tools.

❑   You could include carriage returns and spaces manually in your code. This quickly gets complicated because inside of getNextSentenceXML(), the code has no idea how many tabs to use.

❑   You could use (or write) a simple XML generation class library that is aware of nested elements and formats them appropriately.

An XML Output Class

Even though outputting XML is straightforward, there are several good reasons to factor XML output code into a separate class or set of classes. In addition to the formatting issue seen previously, separating out the code for XML generation provides the following benefits:

❑   Cleaner code. Who wants < all over the place?!

❑   A central location to implement escaping of special characters.

713

❑   A more object-oriented approach. XML elements could be objects, which can then be stored, passed to methods, and organized.

❑   Reduction of the possibility of XML syntax errors by centralizing output.

Writing an XML generation class is also temptingly simple. The class definition of a simple XML `Element` class is shown here:

```
// XMLElement.h

#include <string>
#include <vector>
#include <map>
#include <iostream>

class XMLElement
{
    public:
        XMLElement();

        void setElementName(const std::string& inName);

        void setAttribute(const std::string& inAttributeName,
                          const std::string& inAttributeValue);

        void addSubElement(const XMLElement* inElement);

        // Setting a text node will override any nested elements.
        void setTextNode(const std::string& inValue);

        friend std::ostream& operator<<(std::ostream& outStream,
                                        const XMLElement& inElem);

    protected:
        void writeToStream(std::ostream& outStream, int inIndentLevel = 0) const;


        void indentStream(std::ostream& outStream, int inIndentLevel) const;

    private:
        std::string                          mElementName;
        std::map<std::string, std::string>   mAttributes;
        std::vector<const XMLElement*>       mSubElements;
        std::string                          mTextNode;
};
```

Using this class, a user could easily create `XMLElement` objects, set their attributes, and set text nodes or subelements. At any time, the client can call `operator<<` to get the XML representation of the current state of the element.

A sample implementation is shown next. Because it uses C++ syntax, which you're a pro at by now, we won't explain every single line. Take a look at the inline comments if it doesn't make sense at first glance.

```cpp
#include "XMLElement.h"

using namespace std;

XMLElement::XMLElement() : mElementName("unnamed")
{
}

void XMLElement::setElementName(const string& inName)
{
    mElementName = inName;
}

void XMLElement::setAttribute(const string& inAttributeName,
                             const string& inAttributeValue)
{
    // Set the key/value pair, replacing the existing one if it exists.
    mAttributes[inAttributeName] = inAttributeValue;
}

void XMLElement::addSubElement(const XMLElement* inElement)
{
    // Add the new element to the vector of subelements.
    mSubElements.push_back(inElement);
}

void XMLElement::setTextNode(const string& inValue)
{
    mTextNode = inValue;
}

ostream& operator<<(ostream& outStream, const XMLElement& inElem)
{
    inElem.writeToStream(outStream);
    return (outStream);
}

void XMLElement::writeToStream(ostream& outStream, int inIndentLevel) const
{
    indentStream(outStream, inIndentLevel);
    outStream << "<" << mElementName;  // open the start tag

    // Output any attributes.
    for (map<string, string>::const_iterator it = mAttributes.begin();
            it != mAttributes.end(); ++it) {
        outStream << " " << it->first << "=\"" << it->second << "\"";
    }

    // Close the start tag.
    outStream << ">";

    if (mTextNode != "") {
        // If there's a text node, output it.
```

```
                outStream << mTextNode;
        } else {
            outStream << endl;
            // Call writeToStream at inIndentLevel+1 for any subelements.
            for (vector<const XMLElement*>::const_iterator it = mSubElements.begin();
                    it != mSubElements.end(); ++it) {
                (*it)->writeToStream(outStream, inIndentLevel + 1);
            }
            indentStream(outStream, inIndentLevel);
        }

        // Write the close tag.
        outStream << "</" << mElementName << ">" << endl;
}

void XMLElement::indentStream(ostream& outStream, int inIndentLevel) const
{
    for (int i = 0; i < inIndentLevel; i++) {
        outStream << "\t";
    }
}
```

The preceding implementation is a great starting point and is perfect for simple XML applications. One of the features that is missing is the escaping of special characters. For example, the character & needs to be escaped as & inside of an XML document. Here is a sample program that shows the use of the XMLElement class to build the document that was output manually in the previous example:

```
int main(int argc, char** argv)
{
    XMLElement dialogueElement;
    dialogueElement.setElementName("dialogue");

    XMLElement sentenceElement1;
    sentenceElement1.setElementName("sentence");
    sentenceElement1.setAttribute("speaker", "Marni");
    sentenceElement1.setTextNode("Let's go get some ice cream.");

    XMLElement sentenceElement2;
    sentenceElement2.setElementName("sentence");
    sentenceElement2.setAttribute("speaker", "Scott");
    sentenceElement2.setTextNode("After I'm done writing this C++ book.");

    // Add the sentence elements as subelements of the dialogue element.
    dialogueElement.addSubElement(&sentenceElement1);
    dialogueElement.addSubElement(&sentenceElement2);

    // Output the dialogue element to stdout.
    cout << dialogeElement;

    return 0;
}
```

The output of this program is:

```
<dialogue>
        <sentence speaker="Marni">Let's go get some ice cream.</sentence>
        <sentence speaker="Scott">After I'm done writing this C++ book.</sentence>
</dialogue>
```

> **Many XML Parsing libraries also include XML output facilities. If you are using an XML parser for input (described next), check into its output capabilities before writing your own.**

Parsing XML

To deserialize XML objects, you'll need to interpret, or *parse*, the document. Unless the XML you are reading is extremely simple and rigidly defined, you will most likely want to use a third-party XML parsing library. XML parsing libraries typically come in two flavors, SAX and DOM.

A *SAX (Simple API for XML)* parser uses an event-based parsing model. To use a SAX parser, you register callback functions or an object that implements certain methods. As the document is parsed, the appropriate functions or methods are called, giving you a chance to perform an action. For example, if you wanted to look for duplicate XML element names in a document, you could register a callback that is triggered upon reaching an element start tag. Internally, you would keep a list of elements that had already been encountered. Using that list, you could detect the duplicates.

A *DOM (Document Object Model)* parser converts an XML document into a treelike structure that you can easily walk through in code. To programmers accustomed to object-oriented hierarchies and tree data structures, the DOM approach may seem more natural. The disadvantage of the DOM approach is performance. Because it parses the entire document and builds a structure, it is generally slower and more memory-intensive than SAX. Though the rest of this section deals only with DOM parsers, you will find that most XML parsers support both SAX and DOM.

The Xerces XML Library

One of the most popular XML parsers is Xerces, which is part of the Apache XML project. Xerces is an open-source parser and is available for several languages, including C++. You can download the Xerces-C++ library from `http://xml.apache.org/`.

Once you have Xerces installed and added to your C++ project, you can offload the work of parsing XML. Xerces is easy to get started with even though it has a wealth of functionality — a sign of a well-designed library!

The most important class in the Xerces DOM parser is DOMNode. A DOMNode is a single unit of XML data, possibly including other nodes. The subclasses of DOMNode include DOMDocument, DOMElement, DOMAttr, DOMText, an so on. Working with an Xerces DOM generally involves starting with the root node (a DOMDocument) and walking through the tree of nodes to find the desired data. Figure 24-4 shows a slightly simplified version of the node tree for the <dialogue> XML document. It is simplified in that it only shows nodes that actually contain data.

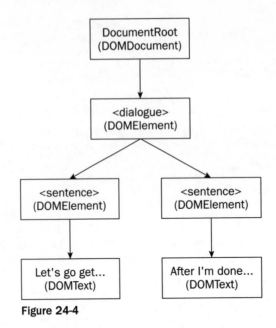

Figure 24-4

The XML attributes are not shown in Figure 24-4 because they are properties of an element, not children of the element.

Using Xerces

The one tricky aspect that you will face first is the way that Xerces represents strings. Because XML can be encoded in various ways, the library has its own character type: XMLch. It also has a utility class called XMLString that makes it easy to work with XMLch strings and convert them to more familiar chars. For example, if a Xerces method returns data as an XMLch* string, you can output it by using XMLString::transcode() to get a C-style string:

```
void outputXercesString(XMLch* inXercesString)
{
    char* familiarString = XMLString::transcode(inXercesString);
    cout << familiarString << endl;
}
```

Because transcode() allocates memory for the C-style string, you must also release it with XMLString::release(), which (in a somewhat bizarre design choice) takes a pointer to the C-style string. The modified version below avoids a memory leak:

```
void outputXercesString(XMLch* inXercesString)
{
    char* familiarString = XMLString::transcode(inXercesString);
    cout << familiarString << endl;
    XMLString::release(&familiarString);
}
```

With that bit of oddness out of the way, it's time to parse some XML. This example parses a file named test.xml into a DOM tree, and then loops through all of the nodes, printing out the names of all elements that are encountered, any attributes contained within those elements, and the contents of any text nodes.

The program begins by including the necessary standard headers and Xerces headers. It also declares XERCES_CPP_NAMESPACE_USE, which is a #define in Xerces that gives the correct namespace to the file.

```
#include <xercesc/util/PlatformUtils.hpp>

#include <xercesc/dom/DOM.hpp>
#include <xercesc/parsers/XercesDOMParser.hpp>
#include <xercesc/util/XMLString.hpp>


#include <iostream>

XERCES_CPP_NAMESPACE_USE
using namespace std;

void printNode(const DOMNode* inNode);
```

The program's main() is fairly straightforward, even though this is where the actual parsing is taking place. It begins by initializing the Xerces library. Next, it creates a new DOM parser and tells it to parse the file. The result of this operation is a DOMNode that represents the document as a whole. To obtain the root element, getDocumentElement() is called. This value is passed to printNode(), which walks through the tree, printing out the data. Finally, the program cleans up the XML library before exiting.

```
int main(int argc, char** argv)
{
    XMLPlatformUtils::Initialize();

    XercesDOMParser* parser = new XercesDOMParser();
    parser->parse("test.xml");

    DOMNode* node = parser->getDocument();
    DOMDocument* document = dynamic_cast<DOMDocument*>(node);
    if (document != NULL) {
        printNode(document->getDocumentElement());
    }

    delete parser;
    XMLPlatformUtils::Terminate();

    return 0;
}
```

The printNode() function is where things get interesting. Because the parameter inNode can be any type of XML node, the function tries its two known node types in sequence. It first attempts to dynamically cast the node into a text node, catching the cast error in case the node is a different type:

```
void printNode(const DOMNode* inNode)
{
    try {
      const DOMText& textNode = dynamic_cast<const DOMText&>(*inNode);
      char* text = XMLString::transcode(textNode.getData());
      cout << "Found text data: " << text << endl;
      XMLString::release(&text);
    } catch (bad_cast) {
      // Not a text node . . .
    }
```

Next, it tries to cast to an element node. If this cast is successful, the element's name and any attributes are printed out.

```
    try {
        const DOMElement& elementNode = dynamic_cast<const DOMElement&>(*inNode);
        char* tagName = XMLString::transcode(elementNode.getTagName());
        cout << "Found tag named: " << tagName << endl;
        XMLString::release(&tagName);

        // Look at the attribute list.
        DOMNamedNodeMap* attributes = elementNode.getAttributes();
        for (int i = 0; i < attributes->getLength(); i++) {
            try {
                const DOMAttr& attrNode =
                    dynamic_cast<const DOMAttr&>(*attributes->item(i));
                char* name = XMLString::transcode(attrNode.getName());
                char* value = XMLString::transcode(attrNode.getValue());
                cout << "Found attribute pair: (" << name << "=" << value << ")"
                    << endl;
                XMLString::release(&name);
                XMLString::release(&value);
            } catch (bad_cast) {
                cerr << "Error converting attribute!" << endl;
            }
        }
    } catch (bad_cast) {
      // Not an element node . . .
    }
```

Finally, the function calls `printNode()` recursively on children nodes. In practice, children nodes will only exist on element nodes.

```
        // Print any subelements.
        DOMNodeList* children = inNode->getChildNodes();
        for (int i = 0; i < children->getLength(); i++) {
            printNode(children->item(i));
        }
    }
}
```

If the `<dialogue>` document is provided as input, this program will produce the following output:

```
Found tag named: dialogue
Found text data:

Found tag named: sentence
Found attribute pair: (speaker=Marni)
Found text data: Let's go get some ice cream.
Found text data:

Found tag named: sentence
Found attribute pair: (speaker=Scott)
Found text data: After I'm done writing this C++ book.
Found text data:
```

Note that the white space between tags is being read as a text node.

> The Xerces library is exception-savvy. The previous example will abort in the face of an exception other than **bad_cast**, but a production-quality application would catch and handle Xerces exceptions.

XML Validation

XML is a general-purpose syntax with no predefined tags or semantics of its own. However, that doesn't mean that any XML application can interpret any XML input. When you write an application that deals with XML, you need to specify the specific type of XML that you can interpret. XML validation allows you to define the specific format of XML that your application allows, including the element names, their organization, and their attributes.

DTD (Document Type Definition)

Document Type Definitions are the original technique for specifying the type of an XML document. The structure of a DTD initially looks like XML itself, but it's not. Instead of a hierarchical format, DTDs are written as a series of declarations about the document type. The details of DTD creation are beyond the scope of this book. To give you an idea of what a DTD looks like, however, here is the DTD corresponding to the `<dialogue>` document:

```
<?xml version="1.0" encoding="UTF-8"?>
<!ELEMENT dialogue (sentence+)>
<!ELEMENT sentence (#PCDATA)>
<!ATTLIST sentence
  speaker (Marni | Scott) #REQUIRED
>
```

Inside of an XML document, you can specify the DTD to which it conforms by including a DOCTYPE assertion at the top of the file:

```
<?xml version="1.0"?>
<!DOCTYPE dialogue SYSTEM "dialogue.dtd">
<dialogue>
    <sentence speaker="Marni">Let's go get some ice cream.</sentence>
    <sentence speaker="Scott">After I'm done writing this C++ book.</sentence>
</dialogue>
```

The DOCTYPE assertion requires two parameters. The first is the root element of the document and the second is the location of the DTD file. In this case, the DTD resides on the local system in a file named dialogue.dtd.

Most XML parsing libraries, including Xerces, can validate an XML file against its DTD. That way, you can guarantee that your program will only operate on data that it can interpret.

XML Schema

Validation of XML documents is a great idea, but the DTD format leaves much to be desired. On complex documents, DTDs quickly become unwieldy. They also don't provide facilities for defining complex types, ordering, or data content. Not to mention the fact that DTDs aren't even written in XML!

XML Schema is an attempt to provide a more functional way of defining the type of an XML document. XML Schema definitions are vastly more flexible than DTDs, but that added flexibility brings added complexity. There are several excellent books about XML Schema (see Appendix B), so we will again provide only a very simple example:

```
<?xml version="1.0" encoding="UTF-8"?>
<xs:schema xmlns:xs="http://www.w3.org/2001/XMLSchema">
    <xs:element name="dialogue">
        <xs:complexType>
            <xs:sequence>
                <xs:element ref="sentence" maxOccurs="unbounded"/>
            </xs:sequence>
        </xs:complexType>
    </xs:element>
    <xs:element name="sentence">
        <xs:complexType>
            <xs:simpleContent>
                <xs:extension base="xs:string">
                    <xs:attribute name="speaker" use="required">
                        <xs:simpleType>
                            <xs:restriction base="xs:NMTOKEN">
                                <xs:enumeration value="Marni"/>
                                <xs:enumeration value="Scott"/>
                            </xs:restriction>
                        </xs:simpleType>
                    </xs:attribute>
                </xs:extension>
            </xs:simpleContent>
        </xs:complexType>
    </xs:element>
</xs:schema>
```

Just as with a DTD, you can correlate an XML schema with an XML document. Instead of using a DOC-TYPE declaration, you specify the location of the schema within an attribute of the root element:

```
<?xml version="1.0"?>
<dialogue xmlns:xsi="http://www.w3.org/2001/XMLSchema-instance"
        xsi:noNamespaceSchemaLocation="dialogue.xsd">
    <sentence speaker="Marni">Let's go get some ice cream.</sentence>
    <sentence speaker="Scott">After I'm done writing this C++ book.</sentence>
</dialogue>
```

Note that the xmlns:xsi attribute specifies that the document is an instance of the XML Schema located at the xsi:noNamespaceSchemaLocation attribute.

> Software packages such as xmlspy from Altova Software (www.xmlspy.com) can greatly ease the process of generating and interpreting XML, XML schemas, and DTDs.

Building a Distributed Object with XML

An XML distributed object is simply an object that knows how to output itself as XML and populate itself from XML. In this section, you will turn the Simple class defined earlier into a distributed object using XML serialization.

The XMLSerializable Mix-in Class

In an application that deals with many distributed objects, it is often convenient to have a common parent class for all such objects. The XMLSerializable class, defined in the following example, requires that subclasses implement methods to read themselves from XML and write themselves to XML. This is an example of a mix-in class (see Chapter 25 for further details).

```
class XMLSerializable
{
    public:
        virtual std::string toXML() = 0;
        virtual void fromXML(const std::string& inXML) = 0;
};
```

Here is the new Simple class, modified to inherit from XMLSerializable:

```
class Simple : public XMLSerializable
{
    public:
        std::string mName;
        int     mPriority;

        std::string mData;
```

```
        virtual std::string toXML();
        virtual void fromXML(const std::string& inXML);
};
```

Implementing XML Serialization

The actual serialization code is aided greatly by the XMLElement class implemented earlier and the use of the Xerces library:

```
string Simple::toXML()
{
    XMLElement simpleElement;
    simpleElement.setElementName("simple");

    simpleElement.setAttribute("name", mName);

    // Convert the int into a string.
    ostringstream tempStream;
    tempStream << mPriority;
    simpleElement.setAttribute("priority", tempStream.str());

    // Add the data as a text node.
    simpleElement.setTextNode(mData);

    // Convert the XMLElement into a string.
    ostringstream resultStream;
    resultStream << simpleElement;

    return resultStream.str();
}

void Simple::fromXML(const string& inString)
{
    static const char* bufID = "simple buffer";


    // Use MemBufInputSource to read the XML content from a string.
    MemBufInputSource src((const XMLByte*)inString.c_str(),
                          inString.length(), bufID);
    XercesDOMParser* parser = new XercesDOMParser();
    parser->parse(src);

    DOMNode* node = parser->getDocument();
    DOMDocument* document = dynamic_cast<DOMDocument*>(node);
    if (document == NULL) {
        delete parser;
        return;
    }

    // Document should be the <simple> element.
    try {
        const DOMElement& elementNode =
          dynamic_cast<const DOMElement&>(*document->getDocumentElement());
```

```
        // Get the name attribute.
        XMLCh* nameKey = XMLString::transcode("name");
        char* name = XMLString::transcode(elementNode.getAttribute(nameKey));
        XMLString::release(&nameKey);
        mName = name;
        XMLString::release(&name);

        // Get the priority attribute.
        XMLCh* priorityKey = XMLString::transcode("priority");
        char* priorityStr =
            XMLString::transcode(elementNode.getAttribute(priorityKey));
        XMLString::release(&priorityKey);
        // Parse the priority number.

        istringstream tmpStream(priorityStr);
        tmpStream >> mPriority;

        XMLString::release(&priorityStr);

        // Get the data as a text node.
        const XMLCh* textData = elementNode.getTextContent();
        char* data = XMLString::transcode(textData);
        mData = data;
        XMLString::release(&data);

    } catch (bad_cast) {
        cerr << "cast exception while parsing Simple object from XML" << endl;
    } catch (...) {
      cerr << "an unknown error occurred while parsing a Simple object from XML"
          << endl;
    }

    delete parser;
}
```

Following is a `main()` that tests the serialization functionality by creating a `Simple` object, writing it to XML, then reading that same XML output into a new `Simple` object. When finished, both objects should be equivalent.

```
int main(ing argc, char** argv)
{
    XMLPlatformUtils::Initialize();

    Simple test;
    test.mName = "myname";
    test.mPriority = 7;
    test.mData = "my data";

    string xmlData = test.toXML();

    Simple test2;
    test2.fromXML(xmlData);
```

```
        if (test.mName == test2.mName) {
            cout << "Names are equivalent!" << endl;
        } else {
            cout << "ERROR: Names are not equivalent!" << endl;
        }

        if (test.mPriority == test2.mPriority) {
            cout << "Priorities are equivalent!" << endl;
        } else {
            cout << "ERROR: Priorities are not equivalent!" << endl;
        }

        if (test.mData == test2.mData) {
            cout << "Data is equivalent!" << endl;
        } else {
            cout << "ERROR: Data is not equivalent!" << endl;
        }

        XMLPlatformUtils::Terminate();

        return 0;
    }
```

Using the Distributed Object

Now that `Simple` objects can read themselves from XML and write themselves to XML, they are fully XML serializable. XML serialization is the foundation for using XML as a distributed object technology. The other piece to the puzzle is the transmission of XML serialized objects between different machine and applications.

Just as with the traditional serialization schemes described earlier in this chapter, you can use XML serialization with any network or data interchange technology that you wish. You can write a program that emails serialized objects around, or compresses them and sends them as binary data over a network. Because XML is merely a syntax, the programmer is left to decide on the exact semantics of the XML content and the mechanism of its transmission.

SOAP (Simple Object Access Protocol)

One of the "killer apps" for XML is the exchange of data over a network. As you already know, XML is perfect for such applications because it is easy to work with and recognized by all platforms. The major downside is that applications that are exchanging data via XML need to be in agreement on the particular semantics of the XML data being exchanged. With only XML at your disposal, you couldn't write an application that made RPC-style calls to somebody else's application without obtaining the format of the XML they are expecting.

SOAP is an XML-based standard for exchanging data. It provides a standard way to make RPC-style requests, provide metadata about XML, represent simple and complex data types in XML (using XML schemas), and handle errors. By using SOAP-based XML as a data exchange format, applications can communicate without reinventing the wheel.

An Introduction to SOAP

This section introduces some of the terminology used in SOAP without getting into the nitty-gritty details of the syntax. The details of implementing SOAP applications are best left to SOAP-specific texts. Additionally, a number of emerging SOAP frameworks and hardware appliances spare programmers the details of the SOAP syntax by wrapping it in a programmatic or graphical interface. So, while you may have to look at raw SOAP data for debugging purposes, it's becoming less likely that you'll have to write it by hand.

All of the data in a SOAP message is contained in a *SOAP Envelope*. The envelope is divided into two parts — the *SOAP Header* and the *SOAP Body*. As you may have guessed, the SOAP `Header` contains metainformation about the message. For example, because XML is a plain text–readable format, it is highly susceptible to malicious changes as it moves through the network. The header can contain digital signatures that are used to verify the integrity of a SOAP message.

The contents of the SOAP `Body` vary depending on the style of SOAP being used. *Document-style SOAP* messages simply provide an XML payload in the SOAP `Body`. An application that wants to move XML-serialized data from one machine to another using the SOAP standard would most likely take advantage of Document-style SOAP. Here is an example of a Document-style SOAP message:

```
<soap:Envelope xmlns:soap="http://schemas.xmlsoap.org/soap/envelope/ ">
    <soap:Body>
        <dialogue>
            <sentence speaker="Marni">Let's go get some ice cream.</sentence>
            <sentence speaker="Scott">After I'm done writing this C++
book.</sentence>
        </dialogue>
    </soap:Body>
</soap:Envelope>
```

RPC-style SOAP is a more structured type of SOAP message that is used to make requests to remote machines and receive responses. In an RPC-style request, the SOAP `Body` contains a description of the request being made on the remote machine, including parameters to the request. Here is a simple RPC request to a method that adds two numbers:

```
<soap:Envelope xmlns:soap="http://schemas.xmlsoap.org/soap/envelope/ ">
    <soap:Body>
        <myNS:AddNumbers xmlns:myNS="mynamespace">
            <myNS:arg1>7</myNS:arg1>
            <myNS:arg2>4</myNS:arg2>
        </myNS:AddNumbers>
    </soap:Body>
</soap:Envelope>
```

The SOAP `Body` of the response to an RPC-style request contains an XML element containing the results of the RPC call:

```
<soap:Envelope xmlns:soap="http://schemas.xmlsoap.org/soap/envelope/ ">
    <soap:Body>
        <myNS:AddNumbersResponse xmlns:myNS="mynamespace">
            <myNS:result>11</myNS:result>
        </myNS:AddNumbersResponse>
    </soap:Body>
</soap:Envelope>
```

While some of the syntax may still be a mystery, hopefully you have a good idea of what is contained in a SOAP message. You should also begin to see the power of using SOAP for distributed applications — using only simple XML, you can issue requests and receive responses from any application that speaks SOAP. No elaborate, expensive, or platform-specific technologies are required. SOAP also has an advantage over non-SOAP serialized XML because the semantics are specified. If two people were to write applications that communicated via serialized XML, they would have to agree on the names of attributes and elements. If they used SOAP, they could focus on the specifics of their application.

SOAP is quickly gaining popularity as a data exchange mechanism for businesses and for Web services. Many of the existing SOAP frameworks are written for Java (with the notable exception of Microsoft's .NET which tends to have C# in mind). However, there is nothing platform specific about SOAP. In fact, SOAP may be the perfect way to expose your C++ applications to a wider audience using other languages.

Summary

In this chapter, you've seen how you can write new types of applications by using network technologies. You've learned about the mechanisms for distributed communication — serialization and remote procedure calls. You've also been exposed to several ways to implement these technologies, including custom serialization, CORBA, XML, and SOAP.

Distributed computing truly opens up a new world of possibilities for your applications. Now that you know the concepts and the different technologies, you have the basic requirements for the next distributed killer app.

25

Incorporating Techniques and Frameworks

One of the major themes of this book has been the adoption of reusable techniques and patterns. As a programmer, you tend to face similar problems repeatedly. With an arsenal of diverse approaches, you can save yourself time by applying the proper technique to a given problem.

This chapter focuses on design techniques — C++ idioms that aren't necessarily built-in parts of the language, but are nonetheless frequently used. The first part of this chapter covers the language features in C++ that are common but involve easy-to-forget syntax. Most of this material is a review, but it is a useful reference tool when the syntax escapes you. The topics covered include:

- ❏ Starting a class from scratch
- ❏ Extending a class with a subclass
- ❏ Throwing and catching exceptions
- ❏ Reading from a file
- ❏ Writing to a file
- ❏ Defining a template class

The second part of this chapter focuses on higher-level techniques that build upon C++ language features. These techniques offer a better way to accomplish everyday programming tasks. Topics include:

- ❏ Smart pointers with reference counting
- ❏ The double-dispatch technique
- ❏ Mix-in classes

Many of the previous chapters referred to these concepts without providing detailed code examples. In this chapter, you will see concrete examples of these concepts with code that you can use in your programs.

This chapter concludes with an introduction to frameworks, a coding technique that greatly eases the development of large applications.

"I Can Never Remember How to . . ."

Chapter 1 compared the size of the C standard to the size of the C++ standard. It is possible, and somewhat common, for a C programmer to memorize the entire C language. The keywords are few, the language features are minimal, and the behaviors are well defined. This is not the case with C++. Even the authors of this book, who are self-proclaimed geniuses, need to look things up. With that in mind, we present the following examples of coding techniques that are used in almost all C++ programs. When you remember the concept but forget the syntax, turn to these pages for a refresher.

. . . Write a Class

Don't remember how to get started? No problem — here is the definition of a simple class:

```cpp
/**
 * Simple.h
 *
 * A simple class that illustrates class definition syntax.
 *
 */
#ifndef _simple_h_
#define _simple_h_

class Simple {

    public:
        Simple();                   // Constructor
        virtual ~Simple();          // Destructor

        virtual void publicMethod();    // Public method

        int mPublicInteger;         // Public data member

    protected:
        int mProtectedInteger;      // Protected data member

    private:
        int mPrivateInteger;        // Private data member

        static const int mConstant = 2; // Private constant

        static int sStaticInt;      // Private static data member

        // Disallow assignment and pass-by-value
```

```
        Simple(const Simple& src);
        Simple& operator=(const Simple& rhs);
};
#endif
```

Next, here is the implementation, including the initialization of the static data member:

```
/**
 * Simple.cpp
 *
 * Implementation of a simple class
 *
 */

#include "Simple.h"

int Simple::sStaticInt = 0;    // Initialize static data member.

Simple::Simple()
{
    // Implementation of constructor
}

Simple::~Simple()
{
    // Implementation of destructor
}

void Simple::publicMethod()
{
    // Implementation of public method
}
```

. . . Subclass an Existing Class

To subclass, you declare a new class that is a *public* extension of another class. Here is the definition for a sample subclass called SubSimple:

```
/**
 * SubSimple.h
 *
 * A subclass of the Simple class
 *
 */

#ifndef _subsimple_h_
#define _subsimple_h_

#include "Simple.h"

class SubSimple : public Simple
{
```

```
    public:
        SubSimple();                // Constructor
        virtual ~SubSimple();       // Destructor

        virtual void publicMethod();  // Overridden method

        virtual void anotherMethod(); // Added method
};

#endif
```

The implementation:

```
/**
 * SubSimple.cpp
 *
 * Implementation of a simple subclass
 *
 */

#include "SubSimple.h"

SubSimple::SubSimple() : Simple()
{
    // Implementation of constructor
}

SubSimple::~SubSimple()
{
    // Implementation of destructor
}

void SubSimple::publicMethod()
{
    // Implementation of overridden method
}

void SubSimple::anotherMethod()
{
    // Implementation of added method
}
```

. . . Throw and Catch Exceptions

If you've been working on a team that doesn't use exceptions (for shame!) or if you've gotten used to Java-style exceptions, the C++ syntax may escape you. Here's a simple refresher, which uses the built-in exception class std::runtime_error. In most large programs, you will write your own exception classes.

```
#include <stdexcept>
#include <iostream>
```

```
void throwIf(bool inShouldThrow) throw (std::runtime_error)
{
    if (inShouldThrow) {
        throw std::runtime_error("Here's my exception");
    }
}

int main(int argc, char** argv)
{
    try {
        throwIf(false); // doesn't throw
        throwIf(true);  // throws!
    } catch (const std::runtime_error& e) {
        std::cerr << "Caught exception: " << e.what() << std::endl;
    }
}
```

. . . Read from a File

Complete details for file input are included in Chapter 14. Below is a quick sample program for file reading basics. This program reads its own source code and outputs it one token at a time.

```
/**
 * readfile.cpp
 */

#include <iostream>
#include <fstream>
#include <string>

using namespace std;

int main()
{
    ifstream inFile("readfile.cpp");

    if (inFile.fail()) {
        cerr << "Unable to open file for reading." << endl;
        exit(1);
    }

    string nextToken;
    while (inFile >> nextToken) {
        cout << "Token: " << nextToken << endl;
    }

    inFile.close();

    return 0;
}
```

... *Write to a File*

The following program outputs a message to a file, then reopens the file and appends another message. Additional details can be found in Chapter 14.

```cpp
/**
 * writefile.cpp
 */
#include <iostream>
#include <fstream>

using namespace std;

int main()
{
    ofstream outFile("writefile.out");

    if (outFile.fail()) {
        cerr << "Unable to open file for writing." << endl;
        exit(1);
    }

    outFile << "Hello!" << endl;

    outFile.close();

    ofstream appendFile("writefile.out", ios_base::app);

    if (appendFile.fail()) {
        cerr << "Unable to open file for writing." << endl;
        exit(1);
    }

    appendFile << "Append!" << endl;

    appendFile.close();
}
```

... *Write a Template Class*

Template syntax is one of the messiest parts of the C++ language. The most-forgotten piece of the template puzzle is that code that uses the template needs to be able to see the method implementations as well as the class template definition. The usual technique to accomplish this is to #include the source file in the header file so that clients can simply #include the header file as they normally do. The following program shows a class template that simply wraps an object and adds *get* and *set* semantics to it.

```cpp
/**
 * SimpleTemplate.h
 */

template <typename T>
class SimpleTemplate
{
```

```
    public:
        SimpleTemplate(T& inObject);

        const T& get();
        void set(T& inObject);

    protected:
        T& mObject;
};

#include "SimpleTemplate.cpp" // Include the implementation!
```

```
/**
 * SimpleTemplate.cpp
 */

template<typename T>
SimpleTemplate<T>::SimpleTemplate(T& inObject) : mObject(inObject)
{
}

template<typename T>
const T& SimpleTemplate<T>::get()
{
    return mObject;
}

template<typename T>
void SimpleTemplate<T>::set(T& inObject)
{
    mObject = inObject;
}
```

```
/**
 * TemplateTest.cpp
 */

#include <iostream>
#include <string>

#include "SimpleTemplate.h"

using namespace std;

int main(int argc, char** argv)
{
    // Try wrapping an integer.
    int i = 7;
    SimpleTemplate<int> intWrapper(i);
    i = 2;
    cout << "wrapper value is " << intWrapper.get() << endl;

    // Try wrapping a string.
    string str = "test";
```

```
        SimpleTemplate<string> stringWrapper(str);
        str += "!";
        cout << "wrapper value is " << stringWrapper.get() << endl;
}
```

There Must Be a Better Way

As you read this paragraph, thousands of C++ programmers throughout the world are solving problems that have already been solved. Someone in a cubicle in San Jose is writing a smart pointer implementation from scratch that uses reference counting. A young programmer on a Mediterranean island is designing a class hierarchy that could benefit immensely from the use of mix-in classes.

As a Professional C++ programmer, you need to spend less of your time reinventing the wheel, and more of your time adapting reusable concepts in new ways. The following techniques are general-purpose approaches that you can apply directly to your own programs or customize for your needs.

Smart Pointers with Reference Counting

Chapters 4 and 13 introduced the notion of a *smart pointer*: a method for wrapping dynamically allocated memory in a safe stack-based variable. Chapter 16 showed an implementation of a smart pointer using a template class. The following technique enhances the example from Chapter 16 by including reference counting.

The Need for Reference Counting

As a general concept, *reference counting* is the technique for keeping track of the number of instances of a class or particular object that are in use. A reference-counting smart pointer is one that keeps track of how many smart pointers have been built to refer to a single real pointer. This way, smart pointers can avoid double deletion.

The double deletion problem is easy to provoke with non-reference-counting smart pointers. Consider the following class, Nothing, which simply prints out messages when an object is created or destroyed.

```
class Nothing
{
    public:
        Nothing() { cout << "Nothing::Nothing()" << endl; }
        ~Nothing() { cout << "Nothing::~Nothing()" << endl; }
};
```

If you were to create two standard C++ auto_ptrs and have them both refer to the same Nothing object, both smart pointers would attempt to delete the same object when they go out of scope:

```
void doubleDelete()
{
    Nothing* myNothing = new Nothing();

    auto_ptr<Nothing*> autoPtr1(myNothing);
    auto_ptr<Nothing*> autoPtr2(myNothing);
}
```

The output of the previous function would be:

```
Nothing::Nothing()
Nothing::~Nothing()
Nothing::~Nothing()
```

Yikes! One call to the constructor and two calls to the destructor? And this from a class that's supposed to make pointers safe?

If you only use smart pointers for simple cases, such as allocating memory that is only used within a function, this issue will not be a problem. However, if your program stores several smart pointers in a data structure or otherwise complicates the use of smart pointers by copying them, assigning them, or passing them as arguments to functions, adding another level of safety is essential.

> A reference-counting smart pointer is safer than the built-in `auto_ptr` because it keeps track of the number of references to a pointer and deletes the memory only when it is no longer in use.

The SuperSmartPointer

The approach for `SuperSmartPointer`, a reference-counting smart pointer implementation is to keep a static `map` for reference counts. Each key in the `map` is the memory address of a traditional pointer that is referred to by one or more `SuperSmartPointers`. The corresponding value is the number of `SuperSmartPointers` that refer to that object.

The implementation of `SuperSmartPointer` that follows is based on the smart pointer code shown in Chapter 16. You may want to review that code before continuing. The major changes occur when a new pointer is set (through the single argument constructor, the copy constructor, or `operator=`) and when a `SuperSmartPointer` is finished with an underlying pointer (upon destruction or reassignment with `operator=`).

On initialization of a new pointer, the `initPointer()` method checks the static `map` to see if the pointer is already contained by an existing `SuperSmartPointer`. If it is not, the count is initialized to 1. If it is already in the `map`, the count is bumped up. When the pointer is reassigned or the containing `SuperSmartPointer` is destroyed, the `finalizePointer()` method is called. The method begins by printing an error if the pointer is not found in the `map`. If the pointer is found, its count is decremented by one. If this brings the count down to zero, the underlying pointer can be safely released. At this time, the key/value pair is explicitly removed from the `map` to keep the map size down.

```cpp
#include <map>
#include <iostream>

template <typename T>
class SuperSmartPointer
{
    public:
        explicit SuperSmartPointer(T* inPtr);
        ~SuperSmartPointer();

        SuperSmartPointer(const SuperSmartPointer<T>& src);
        SuperSmartPointer<T>& operator=(const SuperSmartPointer<T>& rhs);
```

```
        const T& operator*() const;
        const T* operator->() const;
        T& operator*();
        T* operator->();

        operator void*() const { return mPtr; }

    protected:
        T* mPtr;
        static std::map<T*, int> sRefCountMap;

        void finalizePointer();
        void initPointer(T* inPtr);
};

template <typename T>
std::map<T*, int>SuperSmartPointer<T>::sRefCountMap;

template <typename T>
SuperSmartPointer<T>::SuperSmartPointer(T* inPtr)
{
    initPointer(inPtr);
}

template <typename T>
SuperSmartPointer<T>::SuperSmartPointer(const SuperSmartPointer<T>& src)
{
    initPointer(src.mPtr);
}

template <typename T>
SuperSmartPointer<T>&
SuperSmartPointer<T>::operator=(const SuperSmartPointer<T>& rhs)
{
    if (this == &rhs) {
        return (*this);
    }
    finalizePointer();
    initPointer(rhs.mPtr);

    return (*this);
}

template <typename T>
SuperSmartPointer<T>::~SuperSmartPointer()
{
    finalizePointer();
}

template<typename T>
void SuperSmartPointer<T>::initPointer(T* inPtr)
{
    mPtr = inPtr;
    if (sRefCountMap.find(mPtr) == sRefCountMap.end()) {
```

```
            sRefCountMap[mPtr] = 1;
    } else {
            sRefCountMap[mPtr]++;
    }
}

template<typename T>
void SuperSmartPointer<T>::finalizePointer()
{
    if (sRefCountMap.find(mPtr) == sRefCountMap.end()) {
        std::cerr << "ERROR: Missing entry in map!" << std::endl;
        return;
    }
    sRefCountMap[mPtr]--;
    if (sRefCountMap[mPtr] == 0) {
        // No more references to this object--delete it and remove from map
        sRefCountMap.erase(mPtr);
        delete mPtr;
    }
}

template <typename T>
const T* SuperSmartPointer<T>::operator->() const
{
    return (mPtr);
}

template <typename T>
const T& SuperSmartPointer<T>::operator*() const
{
    return (*mPtr);
}

template <typename T>
T* SuperSmartPointer<T>::operator->()
{
    return (mPtr);
}

template <typename T>
T& SuperSmartPointer<T>::operator*()
{
    return (*mPtr);
}
```

Unit Testing the SuperSmartPointer

The Nothing class defined above can be employed for a simple unit test for SuperSmartPointer. One modification is needed to determine if the test passed or failed. Two static members are added to the Nothing class, which track the number of allocations and the number of deletions. The constructor and destructor modify these values instead of printing a message. If the SuperSmartPointer works, the numbers should always be equivalent when the program terminates.

```
class Nothing
{
    public:
        Nothing() { sNumAllocations++; }
        ~Nothing() { sNumDeletions++; }

        static int sNumAllocations;
        static int sNumDeletions;
};

int Nothing::sNumAllocations = 0;
int Nothing::sNumDeletions = 0;
```

Following is the actual test. Note that an extra set of curly braces is used to keep the SuperSmartPointers in their own scope so that they are both allocated and destroyed inside of the function.

```
void testSuperSmartPointer()
{
    Nothing* myNothing = new Nothing();

    {
        SuperSmartPointer<Nothing> ptr1(myNothing);
        SuperSmartPointer<Nothing> ptr2(myNothing);
    }

    if (Nothing::sNumAllocations != Nothing::sNumDeletions) {
        std::cout << "TEST FAILED: " << Nothing::sNumAllocations <<
                    " allocations and " << Nothing::sNumDeletions <<
                    " deletions" << std::endl;
    } else {
        std::cout << "TEST PASSED" << std::endl;
    }
}
```

A successful execution of this test program will result in the following output:

```
TEST PASSED
```

You should also write additional tests for the SuperSmartPointer class. For example, you should test the copy construction and operator= functionality.

Enhancing This Implementation

The static reference count map provides the SuperSmartPointer with an additional layer of safety over built-in C++ smart pointers. However, the new implementation is not completely free of problems.

Recall that templates exist on a per-type basis. In other words, if you have some SuperSmartPointers that store pointers to integers and others that store pointers to characters, there are actually two classes generated at compile time: SuperSmartPointer<int> and SuperSmartPointer<char>. Because the reference count map is stored statically within the class, two maps will be generated. In most cases, this won't cause a problem, but you *could* cast a char* to an int* resulting in two SuperSmartPointers of two different template classes that refer to the same variable. Because the table data is separate, double deletion would occur, as demonstrated by the following code:

```
char* ch = new char;

SuperSmartPointer<char> ptr1(ch);
SuperSmartPointer<int> ptr2((int*)ch);  // BUG! Double deletion will occur!
```

One solution to this problem is to make the reference map a global variable, though globals are often frowned upon. Another solution would be to wrap the map in a nontemplate class, perhaps called `MapManager`, which is referenced by the `SuperSmartPointer` template classes.

The other issue with this implementation is that it is not thread safe. As you have read previously, threads are not a feature of the C++ language. However, threads are so common in modern programming that you should be aware of this omission. Access to the static map should be protected by a lock so that concurrent additions and deletions do not conflict with each other.

If you use the `SuperSmartPointer` in production code, you should consider whether the code given above is appropriate for your application or if you should add thread safety and a global map.

Double Dispatch

Double dispatch is a technique that adds an extra dimension to the concept of polymorphism. As described in Chapter 3, polymorphism lets the program determine behavior based on run-time types. For example, you could have an `Animal` class with a `move()` method. All `Animals` move, but they differ in terms of *how* they move. The `move()` method is defined for every subclass of `Animal` so that the appropriate method can be called, or dispatched, for the appropriate animal at run time without knowing the type of the animal at compile time. Chapter 10 explained how to use virtual methods to implement this run-time polymorphism.

Sometimes, however, you need a method to behave according to the run-time type of two objects, instead of just one. For example, suppose that you want to add a method to the `Animal` class that returns `true` if the animal eats another animal and `false` otherwise. The decision is based on two factors — the type of the animal doing the eating, and the type of the animal being eaten. Unfortunately, C++ provides no language mechanism to choose a behavior based on the run-time type of more than one object. Virtual methods alone are insufficient for modeling this scenario because they determine a method, or behavior, depending on the run-time type of only the receiving object.

Some object-oriented languages provide the ability to choose a method at run-time based on the run-time types of two or more methods. They call this feature *multi-methods*. In C++, however, there is no core language feature to support multi-methods. Fortunately, the *double dispatch* technique provides a technique to make functions virtual for more than one object.

> **Double dispatch is really a special case of *multiple dispatch*, in which a behavior is chosen depending on the run-time types of two or more objects. In practice, double dispatch, which chooses a behavior based on the run-time types of exactly two objects, is usually sufficient.**

Attempt #1: Brute Force

The most straightforward way to implement a method whose behavior depends on the run-time types of two different objects is to take the perspective of one of the objects and use a series of if/else constructs to check the type of the other. For example, you could implement a method called eats() on each Animal subclass that takes the other animal as an argument. The method would be declared pure virtual in the base class as follows:

```
class Animal
{
    public:
        virtual bool eats(const Animal& inPrey) const = 0;
};
```

Each subclass would implement the eats() method and return the appropriate value based on the type of the argument. The implementation of eats() for several subclasses follows. Note that the Dinosaur subclass avoids the series of if/else constructs because (according to the authors) dinosaurs eat anything.

```
bool Bear::eats(const Animal& inPrey) const
{
    if (typeid(inPrey) == typeid(Bear&)) {
        return false;
    } else if (typeid(inPrey) == typeid(Fish&)) {
        return true;
    } else if (typeid(inPrey) == typeid(Dinosaur&)) {
        return false;
    }
    return false;
}

bool Fish::eats(const Animal& inPrey) const
{
    if (typeid(inPrey) == typeid(Bear&)) {
        return false;
    } else if (typeid(inPrey) == typeid(Fish&)) {
        return true;
    } else if (typeid(inPrey) == typeid(Dinosaur&)) {
        return false;
    }
    return false;
}

bool Dinosaur::eats(const Animal& inPrey) const
{
    return true;
}
```

The brute force approach works, and it's probably the most straightforward technique for a small number of classes. However, there are several reasons why you might want to avoid such an approach:

❑ OOP purists often frown upon explicitly querying the type of an object because it implies a design that is lacking in proper object-oriented structure.

❑ Because all types are checked inside a single method, a subclass would have to override all cases or none. For example, if you wanted to implement a CannibalisticBear class, which ate other Bears, you would have to reimplement all the existing Bear eating behavior in the subclass.

❑ As the number of types grows, such code can grow messy and repetitive.

❑ This approach does not force subclasses to consider new types. For example, if you added a Donkey subclass, the Bear class would continue to compile, but would return false when told to eat a Donkey, even though everybody knows that bears eat donkeys.

Attempt #2: Single Polymorphism with Overloading

You could attempt to use polymorphism with overloading to circumvent all of the cascading if/else constructs. Instead of giving each class a single eats() method that takes an Animal reference, why not overload the method for each Animal subclass? The base class definition would look like this:

```
class Animal
{
    public:
        virtual bool eats(const Bear& inPrey) const = 0;
        virtual bool eats(const Fish& inPrey) const = 0;
        virtual bool eats(const Dinosaur& inPrey) const = 0;
};
```

Because the methods are pure virtual in the superclass, each subclass would be forced to implement the behavior for every other type of Animal. For example, the Bear class would contain the following methods:

```
class Bear : public Animal
{
    public:
        virtual bool eats(const Bear& inBear) const { return false; }
        virtual bool eats(const Fish& inFish) const { return true; }
        virtual bool eats(const Dinosaur& inDinosaur) const { return false; }
};
```

This approach initially appears to work, but it really solves only half of the problem. In order to call the proper eats() method on an Animal, the compiler needs to know the compile-time type of the animal being eaten. A call such as the following will be successful because the compile-time types of both the eater and the eaten animals are known:

```
Bear myBear;
Fish myFish;

cout << myBear.eats(myFish) << endl;
```

The missing piece is that the solution is only polymorphic in one direction. You could access `myBear` in the context of an `Animal` and the correct method would be called:

```
Bear myBear;
Fish myFish;
Animal& animalRef = myBear;

cout << animalRef.eats(myFish) << endl;
```

The reverse is not true. If you accessed `myFish` in the context of the `Animal` class and passed that to the eats method, you would get a compile error because there is no eats method that takes an `Animal`. The compiler cannot determine, at compile time, which version to call. The following example will not compile:

```
Bear myBear;
Fish myFish;
Animal& animalRef = myFish;

cout << myBear.eats(animalRef) << endl;  // BUG! No such method Bear::eats(Animal&)
```

Because the compiler needs to know which overloaded version of the `eats()` method is going to be called at compile time, this solution is not truly polymorphic. It would not work, for example, if you were iterating over an array of `Animal` references and passing each one to a call to `eats()`.

Attempt #3: Double Dispatch

The double dispatch technique is a truly polymorphic solution to the multiple type problem. In C++, polymorphism is achieved by overriding methods in subclasses. At run time, methods are called based on the actual type of the object. The single polymorphic attempt above didn't work because it attempted to use polymorphism to determine which overloaded version of a method to call instead of using it to determine on which class to call the method.

To begin, focus on a single subclass, perhaps the `Bear` class. The class needs a method with the following declaration:

```
virtual bool eats(const Animal& inPrey) const;
```

The key to double dispatch is to determine the result based on a method call on the argument. Suppose that the `Animal` class had a method called `eatenBy()`, which took an `Animal` reference as a parameter. This method would return `true` if the current `Animal` gets eaten by the one passed in. With such a method, the definition of `eats()` becomes very simple:

```
bool Bear::eats(const Animal& inPrey) const
{
    return inPrey.eatenBy(*this);
}
```

At first, it looks like this solution simply adds another layer of method calls to the single polymorphic method. After all, each subclass will still have to implement a version of `eatenBy()` for every subclass of `Animal`. However, there is a key difference. Polymorphism is occurring twice! When you call the eats method on an `Animal`, polymorphism determines whether you are calling `Bear::eats`, `Fish::eats`, or one of the others. When you call eatenBy(), polymorphism again determines which class's version of the method to call. It calls eatenBy() on the run-time type of the inPrey object. Note that the run-time type of *this is always the same as the compile-time type so that the compiler can call the correctly overloaded version of eatenBy() for the argument (in this case Bear).

Following are the class definitions for the Animal hierarchy using double dispatch. Note that forward class declarations are necessary because the base class uses references to the subclasses.

```cpp
// forward references
class Fish;
class Bear;
class Dinosaur;

class Animal
{
    public:
        virtual bool eats(const Animal& inPrey) const = 0;

        virtual bool eatenBy(const Bear& inBear) const = 0;
        virtual bool eatenBy(const Fish& inFish) const = 0;
        virtual bool eatenBy(const Dinosaur& inDinosaur) const = 0;
};

class Bear : public Animal
{
    public:
        virtual bool eats(const Animal& inPrey) const;

        virtual bool eatenBy(const Bear& inBear) const;
        virtual bool eatenBy(const Fish& inFish) const;
        virtual bool eatenBy(const Dinosaur& inDinosaur) const;
};

class Fish : public Animal
{
    public:
        virtual bool eats(const Animal& inPrey) const;

        virtual bool eatenBy(const Bear& inBear) const;
        virtual bool eatenBy(const Fish& inFish) const;
        virtual bool eatenBy(const Dinosaur& inDinosaur) const;
};

class Dinosaur : public Animal
{
    public:
        virtual bool eats(const Animal& inPrey) const;

        virtual bool eatenBy(const Bear& inBear) const;
        virtual bool eatenBy(const Fish& inFish) const;
        virtual bool eatenBy(const Dinosaur& inDinosaur) const;
};
```

The implementations follow. Note that each `Animal` subclass implements the `eats()` method in the same way, but it cannot be factored up into the parent class. The reason is that if you attempt to do so, the compiler won't know which overloaded version of the `eatenBy()` method to call because `*this` would be an `Animal`, not a particular subclass. Recall that method overload resolution is determined according the compile-time type of the object, not its run-time type.

```cpp
bool Bear::eats(const Animal& inPrey) const
{
    return inPrey.eatenBy(*this);
}

bool Bear::eatenBy(const Bear& inBear) const
{
    return false;
}

bool Bear::eatenBy(const Fish& inFish) const
{
    return false;
}

bool Bear::eatenBy(const Dinosaur& inDinosaur) const
{
    return true;
}


bool Fish::eats(const Animal& inPrey) const
{
    return inPrey.eatenBy(*this);
}

bool Fish::eatenBy(const Bear& inBear) const
{
    return true;
}

bool Fish::eatenBy(const Fish& inFish) const
{
    return true;
}

bool Fish::eatenBy(const Dinosaur& inDinosaur) const
{
    return true;
}


bool Dinosaur::eats(const Animal& inPrey) const
{
    return inPrey.eatenBy(*this);
}

bool Dinosaur::eatenBy(const Bear& inBear) const
```

```
    {
        return false;
    }

    bool Dinosaur::eatenBy(const Fish& inFish) const
    {
        return false;
    }

    bool Dinosaur::eatenBy(const Dinosaur& inDinosaur) const
    {
        return true;
    }
```

Double dispatch is a concept that takes a bit of getting used to. We suggest playing with this code to adapt to the concept and its implementation.

Mix-In Classes

Chapters 3 and 10 introduced the technique of using multiple inheritance to build *mix-in classes*. As you may recall, mix-in classes add a small piece of extra behavior to a class in an existing hierarchy. You can usually spot a mix-in class by its name, such as `Clickable`, `Drawable`, `Printable`, or `Lovable`.

Designing a Mix-In Class

Mix-in classes come in several forms. Because mix-in classes are not a formal language feature, you can write them however you want without breaking any rules. Some mix-in classes simply indicate that a class supports a certain behavior, such as a hypothetical `Drawable` mix-in class. Any class that mixes in the `Drawable` class must implement the method `draw()`. The mix-in class itself contains no functionality — it simply marks an object as supporting the `draw()` behavior. This usage is similar to Java's notion of an interface — a list of prescribed behaviors without their implementation.

Other mix-in classes contain actual code. You might have a mix-in class called `Playable` that is mixed into certain types of media objects. The mix-in class could contain most of the code to communicate with the computer's sound drivers. By mixing in the class, the media object would get that functionality for free.

When designing a mix-in class, you need to consider what behavior you are adding and whether it belongs in the object hierarchy or in a separate class. Using the previous example, if all media classes are playable, the base class should descend from `Playable` instead of mixing the `Playable` class into all of the subclasses. If only certain media classes are playable and they are scattered throughout the hierarchy, a mix-in class makes sense.

One of the cases where mix-in classes are particularly useful is when you have classes organized into a hierarchy on one axis, but they also contain similarity on another axis. For example, consider a war simulation game played on a grid. Each grid location can contain an `Item` with attack and defense capabilities and other characteristics. Some items, such as a `Castle`, are stationary. Others, such as a `Knight` or `FloatingCastle`, can move throughout the grid. When initially designing the object hierarchy, you might end up with something like Figure 25-1, which organizes the classes according to their attack and defense capabilities.

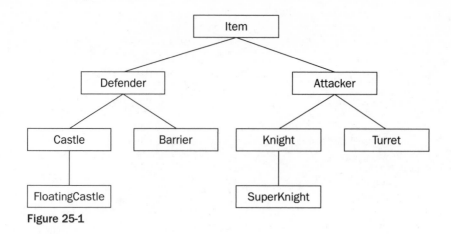

Figure 25-1

The hierarchy in Figure 25-1 ignores the movement functionality that certain classes contain. Building your hierarchy around movement would result in a structure similar to Figure 25-2.

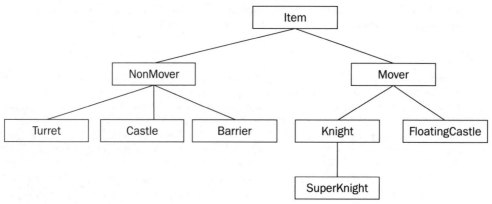

Figure 25-2

Of course, the design of Figure 25-2 throws away all the organization of Figure 25-1. What's a good object-oriented programmer to do?

There are two common solutions for this problem. Assuming that you go with the first hierarchy, organized around attackers and defenders, you need some way to work movement into the equation. One possibility is that, even though only a portion of the subclasses support movement, you *could* add a move() method to the Item base class. The default implementation would do nothing. Certain subclasses would override move() to actually change their location on the grid.

The other approach is to write a Movable mix-in class. The elegant hierarchy from Figure 25-1 could be preserved, but certain classes in the hierarchy would subclass Movable in addition to their parent in the diagram. Figure 25-3 shows this design.

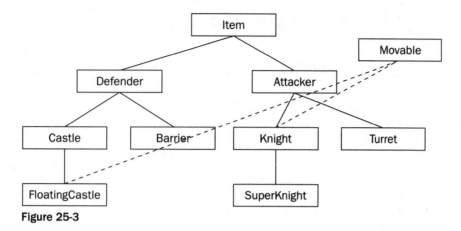

Figure 25-3

Implementing a Mix-In Class

Writing a mix-in class is no different from writing a normal class. In fact, it's usually much simpler. Using the earlier war simulation, the `Movable` mix-in class might look as follows:

```
class Movable
{
    public:
        virtual void move() = 0;
};
```

The `Movable` mix-in class, as defined earlier, doesn't contain any actual functionality. However, it does two very important things. First, it provides a type for `Items` that can be moved. This allows you to create, for example, an array of all movable items without knowing or caring what actual subclass of `Item` they belong to. The `Movable` class also declares that all movable items must implement a method called `move()`. This way, you could iterate over all of the `Movable` objects and tell each of them to move.

Using a Mix-In Class

The code for a mix-in class is syntactically equivalent to multiple inheritance. In addition to subclassing your parent class in the main hierarchy, you also subclass the mix-in class:

```
class FloatingCastle : public Castle, public Movable
{
    public:
        virtual void move();
// Other methods and members not shown here
}
```

The only remaining task is to provide a definition of the `move()` method for `FloatingCastle`. Once that is done, you'll have a class that exists in the most logical place in the hierarchy but still shares commonality with objects elsewhere in the hierarchy.

Object-Oriented Frameworks

When graphical operating systems first came on the scene in the 1980s, procedural programming was the norm. At the time, writing a GUI application usually involved manipulating complex data structures and passing them to OS-provided functions. For example, to draw a rectangle in a window, you might populate a `Window` struct with the appropriate information and pass it to a `drawRect()` function.

As object-oriented programming grew in popularity, programmers looked for a way to apply the OO paradigm to GUI development. The result is known as an *Object-Oriented Framework*. In general, a framework is a set of classes that are used collectively to provide an object-oriented interface to some underlying functionality. When talking about frameworks, programmers are usually referring to large class libraries that are used for general application development. However, a framework can really represent functionality of any size. If you write a suite of classes that provides database functionality for your application, those classes could be considered a framework.

Working with Frameworks

The defining characteristic of a framework is that it provides its own set of techniques and patterns. Frameworks usually require a bit of learning to get started with because they have their own mental model. Before you can work with a large application framework, such as the Microsoft Foundation Classes (MFC), you need to understand its view of the world.

Frameworks vary greatly in their abstract ideas and in their actual implementation. Many frameworks are built on top of legacy procedural APIs, which may affect various aspects of their design. Other frameworks are written from the ground up with object-oriented design in mind. Some frameworks might ideologically oppose certain aspects of the C++ language, such as the BeOS framework, which consciously shunned the notion of multiple inheritance.

When you start working with a new framework, your first task is to find out what makes it tick. To what design principles does it subscribe? What mental model were its developers trying to convey? What aspects of the language does it use extensively? These are all vital questions, even though they may sound like things that you'll pick up along the way. If you fail to understand the design, model, or language features of the framework, you will quickly get into situations where you overstep the bounds of the framework. For example, if the framework uses a custom `String` class and you start coding with C-style strings, you will be stuck with conversion work that could have been easily avoided.

An understanding of the framework's design will also make it possible for you to extend it. For example, if the framework omits a feature, such as support for printing, you could write your own printing classes using the same model as the framework. By doing so, you retain a consistent model for your application, and you have code that can be reused by other applications.

The Model-View-Controller Paradigm

As mentioned, frameworks vary in their approaches to object-oriented design. One common paradigm is known as *model-view-controller*, or MVC. This paradigm models the notion that many applications commonly deal with a set of data, one or more views on that data, and manipulation of the data.

In MVC, a set of data is called the *model*. In a race car simulator, the model would keep track of various statistics, such as the current speed of the car and the amount of damage it has sustained damage. In practice, the model often takes the form of a class with many getters and setters. The class definition for the model of the race car might look like this:

```
class RaceCar
{
    public:
        RaceCar();

        int getSpeed();
        void setSpeed(int inValue);

        int getDamageLevel();
        void setDamageLevel(int inValue);

    protected:
        int mSpeed;
        int mDamageLevel;
};
```

A *view* is a particular visualization of the model. For example, there could be two views on a `RaceCar`. The first view could be a graphical view of the car, and the second could be a graph that shows the level of damage over time. The important point is that both views are operating on the same data — they are simply different ways of looking at the same information. This is one of the main advantages of the MVC paradigm — by keeping data separated from its display, you can keep your code more organized and easily create additional views.

The final piece to the MVC paradigm is the *controller*. The controller is the piece of code that changes the model in response to some event. For example, when the driver of the race car simulator runs into a concrete barrier, the controller would instruct the model to bump up the car's damage level and reduce its speed.

The three components of MVC interact in a feedback loop. Actions are handled by the controller, which adjusts the model, resulting in a change to the view(s). This interaction is shown in Figure 25-4.

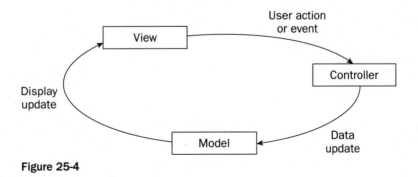

Figure 25-4

The model-view-controller paradigm has gained widespread support within many popular frameworks. Even nontraditional applications, such as Web applications, are starting to move in the direction of MVC because it enforces a clear separation between data, the manipulation of data, and the displaying of data.

Summary

In this chapter, you have read about some of the common techniques that Professional C++ programmers use consistently in their projects. As you advance as a software developer, you will undoubtedly form your own collection of reusable classes and libraries. Discovering design techniques opens the door to developing and using *patterns*, which are higher-level reusable constructs. You will experience the many applications of patterns next in Chapter 26.

26

Applying Design Patterns

The design pattern concept is a simple, but powerful, idea. Once you are able to recognize the recurring object-oriented interactions that occur in a program, finding an elegant solution becomes a matter of merely selecting the appropriate pattern to apply. You have already learned about one pattern in depth — the Iterator pattern, which is used heavily in the STL. This chapter describes several additional design patterns in detail and presents sample implementations.

Recall from Chapter 4 that design patterns are an emerging concept. Certain patterns go by different names or are subject to different interpretations. Any aspect of design is likely to provoke debate among programmers, and the authors believe that is a good thing. Don't simply accept these patterns as the only way to accomplish a task — draw on their approaches and ideas to refine them and form new patterns.

The patterns discussed in this chapter are:

- ❑ Singleton
- ❑ Factory
- ❑ Proxy
- ❑ Adapter
- ❑ Decorator
- ❑ Chain of Responsibility
- ❑ Observer/Listener

The Singleton Pattern

The *singleton* is one of the simplest design patterns. In English the word "singleton" means "one of a kind" or "individual." It has a similar meaning in programming. The singleton pattern is a strategy for enforcing the existence of exactly one instance of a class in a program. Applying the singleton pattern to a class guarantees that only one object of that class will ever be created. The singleton pattern also specifies that the one object is globally accessible from anywhere in the program. Programmers usually refer to a class following the singleton pattern as a *singleton class*.

The singleton pattern is especially helpful when you design a program with a general *application class* that handles the startup, shutdown, and flow control of the application. It would be inappropriate to have two application objects in a single program. In fact, it could prove disastrous to have two application objects that both think they are controlling the flow of the application. By using the singleton pattern, you can ensure that there is exactly one application object accessible from anywhere in the program.

You should use the singleton pattern whenever you want to create exactly one object of a class in a program. If your program relies on the assumption that there will be exactly one instance of a class, you should enforce that assumption with the singleton pattern.

Example: A Logging Mechanism

Singletons are particularly useful for utility classes. Many applications have a notion of a logger — a class that is responsible for writing status information, debugging data, and errors to a central location. The ideal logging class has the following characteristics:

❑   It is available at all times.

❑   It is easy to use.

❑   It provides a set of useful features.

The singleton pattern is a good match for a logger because, even though the logger could be used in many different contexts and for many different purposes, it is conceptually a single instance. Implementing the logger class as a singleton also makes it easier to use because you never have to worry about *which* logger is the current one or how to get a hold of the current logger. Because there's only one, it's a moot point!

Implementation of a Singleton

There are two basic ways to implement a singleton in C++. The first approach uses static methods to form a class that needs no instantiation. The second uses access control levels to regulate the creation and access of one single instance.

Both approaches are shown here, using a simple Logger class as an example. This Logger class provides the following features:

❑   It can log a single string or a vector of strings.

❑   Each log message has an associated *log level*, which is prefixed to the log message.

❑   Every log message is flushed to disk so that it will appear in the file immediately.

Static Class Singleton

Technically, a class that uses all static methods isn't really a singleton: it's a *nothington*, to coin a new term. The term *singleton* implies that there is exactly one instance of the class. If all of the methods are static and the class is never instantiated at all, can you call it a singleton? The authors claim that, because design patterns exist to help you build a mental model of object-oriented structures, you can call a static class a singleton if you please. However, you should recognize that a static class as a singleton lacks polymorphism and a built-in mechanism for construction and destruction. For cases like the `Logger` class, these may be acceptable losses.

The public interface to the `Logger` static class follows. Note that it uses all static methods for access, so there is no need ever to instantiate a `Logger` object. In fact, the constructor has been made private to enforce this behavior.

```
/**
 * Logger.h
 *
 * Definition of a singleton logger class, implemented with static methods
 */

#include <iostream>
#include <fstream>
#include <vector>
class Logger
{
    public:
        static const std::string kLogLevelDebug;
        static const std::string kLogLevelInfo;
        static const std::string kLogLevelError;

        // Logs a single message at the given log level
        static void log(const std::string& inMessage,
                        const std::string& inLogLevel);

        // Logs a vector of messages at the given log level
        static void log(const std::vector<std::string>& inMessages,
                        const std::string& inLogLevel);

        // Closes the log file
        static void teardown();

    protected:
        static void init();

        static const char* const kLogFileName;

        static bool sInitialized;
        static std::ofstream sOutputStream;

    private:
        Logger() {}

};
```

The implementation of the `Logger` class is fairly straightforward. The `sInitialized` static member is checked within each logging call to make sure that the `init()` method has been called to open the log file. Once the log file has been opened, each log message is written to it with the log level prepended.

```cpp
/**
 * Logger.cpp
 *
 * Implementation of a singleton logger class
 */
#include <string>
#include "Logger.h"

using namespace std;

const string Logger::kLogLevelDebug = "DEBUG";
const string Logger::kLogLevelInfo = "INFO";
const string Logger::kLogLevelError = "ERROR";

const char* const Logger::kLogFileName = "log.out";

bool Logger::sInitialized = false;
ofstream Logger::sOutputStream;

void Logger::log(const string& inMessage, const string& inLogLevel)
{
    if (!sInitialized) {
        init();
    }
    // Print the message and flush the stream with endl.
    sOutputStream << inLogLevel << ": " << inMessage << endl;

}

void Logger::log(const vector<string>& inMessages, const string& inLogLevel)
{
    for (size_t i = 0; i < inMessages.size(); i++) {

        log(inMessages[i], inLogLevel);
    }
}

void Logger::teardown()
{
    if (sInitialized) {
        sOutputStream.close();
        sInitialized = false;
    }
}

void Logger::init()
{
  if (!sInitialized) {
      sOutputStream.open(kLogFileName, ios_base::app);
      if (!sOutputStream.good()) {
```

```
            cerr << "Unable to initialize the Logger!" << endl;
            return;
        }
        sInitialized = true;
    }
}
```

Access-Controlled Singleton

Object-oriented purists (Warning: they are out there, and they may work at your company!) might scoff at the static class solution to the singleton problem. Since you can't instantiate a `Logger` object, you can't build a hierarchy of loggers and make use of polymorphism. Such a hierarchy is rarely employed in the singleton case, but it is a valid drawback. Perhaps more significantly, as a result of using entirely static methods, there is no object orientation at all. The class built in the previous example is essentially a collection of C-style functions, not a cohesive class.

To build a true singleton in C++, you can use the access control mechanisms as well as the `static` keyword. With this approach, an actual `Logger` object exists at run time, and the class enforces that exactly one exists. Clients can always get a hold of that object through a static method called `instance()`. The class definition looks like this:

```
/**
 * Logger.h
 *
 * Definition of a true singleton logger class
 */
#include <iostream>
#include <fstream>
#include <vector>

class Logger
{
    public:
        static const std::string kLogLevelDebug;
        static const std::string kLogLevelInfo;
        static const std::string kLogLevelError;

        // Returns a reference to the singleton Logger object
        static Logger& instance();

        // Logs a single message at the given log level
        void log(const std::string& inMessage,
                const std::string& inLogLevel);

        // Logs a vector of messages at the given log level
        void log(const std::vector<std::string>& inMessages,
                const std::string& inLogLevel);

    protected:
        // Static variable for the one-and-only instance
        static Logger sInstance;

        // Constant for the filename
```

```
        static const char* const kLogFileName;

        // Data member for the output stream
        std::ofstream mOutputStream;

    private:
        Logger();
        ~Logger();

};
```

One advantage of this approach is already apparent. Because an actual object will exist, the init() and teardown() methods present in the static solution can be omitted in favor of a constructor and destructor. This is a big win, because the previous solution required the client to explicitly call teardown() to close the file. Now that the logger is an object, the file can be closed when the object is destructed, which will happen when the program ends.

The implementation follows. Notice that the actual log() methods remain unchanged, except for the fact that they are no longer static. The constructor and destructor are called automatically because the class contains an instance of itself as a static member. Because they are private, no external code can create or delete a Logger.

```
/**
 * Logger.cpp
 *
 * Implementation of a singleton logger class
 */
#include <string>
#include "Logger.h"

using namespace std;

const string Logger::kLogLevelDebug = "DEBUG";
const string Logger::kLogLevelInfo = "INFO";
const string Logger::kLogLevelError = "ERROR";

const char* const Logger::kLogFileName = "log.out";

// The static instance will be constructed when the program starts and
// destructed when it ends.
Logger Logger::sInstance;

Logger& Logger::instance()
{
    return sInstance;
}

Logger::~Logger()
{
    mOutputStream.close();
}

Logger::Logger()
```

```
{
    mOutputStream.open(kLogFileName, ios_base::app);
    if (!mOutputStream.good()) {
        cerr << "Unable to initialize the Logger!" << endl;
    }
}

void Logger::log(const string& inMessage, const string& inLogLevel)
{
    mOutputStream << inLogLevel << ": " << inMessage << endl;
}

void Logger::log(const vector<string>& inMessages, const string& inLogLevel)
{
    for (size_t i = 0; i < inMessages.size(); i++) {
        log(inMessages[i], inLogLevel);
    }
}
```

Using a Singleton

The two programs below display the usage of the two different versions of the Logger class.

```
// TestStaticLogger.cpp

#include "Logger.h"
#include <vector>
#include <string>

int main(int argc, char** argv)
{
    Logger::log("test message", Logger::kLogLevelDebug);

    vector<string> items;
    items.push_back("item1");
    items.push_back("item2");

    Logger::log(items, Logger::kLogLevelError);

    Logger::teardown();
}
```

```
// TestTrueSingletonLogger.cpp

#include "Logger.h"
#include <vector>
#include <string>

int main(int argc, char** argv)
{
    Logger::instance().log("test message", Logger::kLogLevelDebug);

    vector<string> items;
```

```
        items.push_back("item1");
        items.push_back("item2");

        Logger::instance().log(items, Logger::kLogLevelError);
}
```

Both programs have the same functionality. After executing, the file log.out should contain the following lines:

```
DEBUG: test message
ERROR: item1
ERROR: item2
```

The Factory Pattern

A factory in real life constructs tangible objects, such as tables or cars. Similarly, a *factory* in object-oriented programming constructs objects. When you use factories in your program, portions of code that want to create a particular object ask the factory for an instance of the object instead of calling the object constructor themselves. For example, an interior decorating program might have a FurnitureFactory object. When part of the code needs a piece of furniture such as a table, it would call the createTable() method of the FurnitureFactory object, which would return a new table.

At first glance, factories seem to lead to complicated designs without clear benefits. It appears that you're only adding another layer of complexity to the program. Instead of calling createTable() on a FurnitureFactory, you could simply create a new Table object directly. However, factories can actually be quite useful. Instead of creating various objects all over the program, you centralize the object creation for a particular domain. This localization is often a better model of real-world creation of objects.

Another benefit of factories is that you can use them alongside class hierarchies to construct objects without knowing their exact class. As you'll see in the following example, factories can run parallel to class hierarchies.

Example: A Car Factory Simulation

In the real world, when you talk about driving a car, you can do so without referring to the specific type of car. You could be discussing a Toyota or a Ford. It doesn't matter, because both Toyotas and Fords are drivable. Now, suppose that you want a new car. You would then need to specify whether you wanted a Toyota or a Ford, right? Not always. You could just say "I want a car," and depending on where you were, you would get a specific car. If you said, "I want a car" in a Toyota factory, chances are you'd get a Toyota. (Or you'd get arrested, depending on how you asked). If you said, "I want a car" in a Ford factory, you'd get a Ford.

The same concepts apply to C++ programming. The first concept, of a generic car that's drivable, is nothing new: it's standard polymorphism, which you learned about in Chapter 3. You could write an abstract Car class that defines a drive() method. Both Toyota and Ford could be subclasses of the Car class, as shown in Figure 26-1.

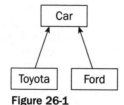

Figure 26-1

Your program could drive `Cars` without knowing whether they were really `Toyotas` or `Fords`. However, with standard object-oriented programming, the one place that you'd need to specify `Toyota` or `Ford` is when you create the car. Here, you would need to call the constructor for one or the other. You can't just say, "I want a car." However, suppose that you also had a parallel class hierarchy of car factories. The `CarFactory` superclass could define a virtual `buildCar()` method. The `ToyotaFactory` and `FordFactory` subclasses would override the `buildCar()` method to build a `Toyota` or a `Ford`. Figure 26-2 shows the `CarFactory` hierarchy.

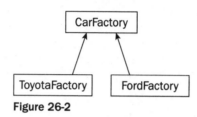

Figure 26-2

Now, suppose that there is one `CarFactory` object in a program. When code in the program, such as a car dealer, wants a new car, it calls `buildCar()` on the `CarFactory` object. Depending on whether that car factory was really a `ToyotaFactory` or a `FordFactory`, the code would get either a `Toyota` or a `Ford`. Figure 26-3 shows the objects in a car dealer program using a `ToyotaFactory`:

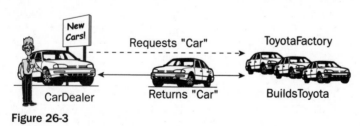

Figure 26-3

Figure 26-4 shows the same program, but with a `FordFactory` instead of a `ToyotaFactory`. Note that the `CarDealer` object and its relationship with the factory stay the same:

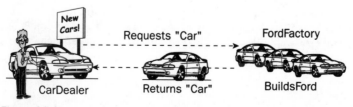

Figure 26-4

The main benefit of this approach is that factories abstract the object creation process: you can easily substitute a different factory in your program. Just as you can use polymorphism with the created objects, you can use polymorphism with factories: when you ask the car factory for a car, you might not know whether it's a Toyota factory or a Ford factory, but either way it will give you a Car that you can drive. This approach leads to easily extensible programs: simply changing the factory instance can allow the program to work on a completely different set of objects and classes.

Implementation of a Factory

One reason for using factories is if the type of the object you want to create depends on some condition. For example, if you are a dealer who needs a car right away, you might want to put your order into the factory that has the fewest requests, regardless of whether the car you eventually get is a Toyota or a Ford. The following implementation will show how to write such factories in C++.

The first thing you'll need is the hierarchy of cars. To keep this example simple, the Car class simply has an abstract method that returns a description of the car. Both Car subclasses are also defined in the following example, using inline methods to return their descriptions.

```
/**
 * Car.h
 *
 */

#include <iostream>

class Car
{
    public:
        virtual void info() = 0;
};

class Ford : public Car
{
    public:
        virtual void info() { std::cout << "Ford" << std::endl; }
};

class Toyota : public Car
{
    public:
        virtual void info() { std::cout << "Toyota" << std::endl; }
};
```

The CarFactory base class is a bit more interesting. Each factory keeps track of the number of cars in production. When the public requestCar() method is called, the number of cars in production at the factory is increased by one, and calling the pure virtual createCar() method returns a new car. The idea is that individual factories will override createCar() to return the appropriate type of car. The factory itself implements requestCar(), which takes care of updating the number of cars in production. CarFactory also provides a public method to query the number of cars being produced at each factory.

The class definitions for the `CarFactory` subclass are shown here:

```
/**
 * CarFactory.h
 */

// For this example, the Car class is assumed to already exist.
#include "Car.h"

class CarFactory
{
    public:
        CarFactory();

        Car* requestCar();

        int getNumCarsInProduction() const;

    protected:
        virtual Car* createCar() = 0;

    private:
        int mNumCarsInProduction;
};

class FordFactory : public CarFactory
{
    protected:
        virtual Car* createCar();
};

class ToyotaFactory : public CarFactory
{
    protected:
        virtual Car* createCar();
};
```

As you can see, the subclasses simply override `createCar()` to return the specific type of car that they produce. The implementation of the `CarFactory` hierarchy is shown here:

```
/**
 * CarFactory.cpp
 */

#include "CarFactory.h"

// Initialize the count to zero when the factory is created.
CarFactory::CarFactory() : mNumCarsInProduction(0) {}

// Increment the number of cars in production and return the
// new car.
Car* CarFactory::requestCar()
{
```

```
        mNumCarsInProduction++;
        return createCar();
    }

    int CarFactory::getNumCarsInProduction() const
    {
        return mNumCarsInProduction;
    }

    Car* FordFactory::createCar()
    {
        return new Ford();
    }

    Car* ToyotaFactory::createCar()
    {
        return new Toyota();
    }
```

The implementation approach used in this example is called an *abstract factory* because the type of the object that is created depends on which *concrete* subclass of the factory class is being used. A similar pattern can be implemented in a single class instead of a class hierarchy. In that case, a single `create()` method takes a type or string parameter from which it decides which object to create. For example, a `CarFactory` object would provide a `buildCar()` method that takes a string representing the type of car and constructs the appropriate type. However, that technique is less interesting and less flexible than the factory hierarchy described previously.

> **Factory methods are one way to implement *virtual constructors*: methods that create objects of different types. For example, the `buildCar()` method creates both `Toyotas` and `Fords`, depending on the concrete factory object on which it is called.**

Using a Factory

The simplest way to use a factory is simply to instantiate it and to call the appropriate method, as in the following piece of code:

```
    ToyotaFactory myFactory;

    Car* myCar = myFactory.requestCar();
```

A more interesting example makes use of the virtual constructor idea to build a car in the factory that has the fewest cars in production. To do this, you will need a function that looks at several factories and chooses the least busy one, such as the following function:

```
    CarFactory* getLeastBusyFactory(const vector<CarFactory*>& inFactories)
    {
        if (inFactories.size() == 0) return NULL;

        CarFactory* bestSoFar = inFactories[0];
```

```
        for (size_t i = 1; i < inFactories.size(); i++)
        {
            if (inFactories[i]->getNumCarsInProduction() <
                    bestSoFar->getNumCarsInProduction()) {
                bestSoFar = inFactories[i];
            }
        }

        return bestSoFar;
}
```

The following sample program makes use of this function to build 10 cars, whatever brand they might be, from the currently least busy factory.

```
int main(int argc, char** argv)
{
    vector<CarFactory*> factories;

    // Create 3 Ford factories and 1 Toyota factory.
    FordFactory* factory1 = new FordFactory();
    FordFactory* factory2 = new FordFactory();
    FordFactory* factory3 = new FordFactory();
    ToyotaFactory* factory4 = new ToyotaFactory();

    // To get more interesting results, preorder some cars.
    factory1->requestCar();
    factory1->requestCar();
    factory2->requestCar();
    factory4->requestCar();

    // Add the factories to a vector.
    factories.push_back(factory1);
    factories.push_back(factory2);
    factories.push_back(factory3);
    factories.push_back(factory4);

    // Build 10 cars from the least busy factory.
    for (int i = 0; i < 10; i++) {
        CarFactory* currentFactory = getLeastBusyFactory(factories);
        Car* theCar = currentFactory->requestCar();
        theCar->info();
    }
}
```

When executed, the program will print out the make of each car produced:

```
Ford
Ford
Ford
Toyota
Ford
Ford
Ford
```

```
Toyota
Ford
Ford
```

The results are rather predictable because the loop effectively iterates through the factories in a round-robin fashion. However, one could imagine a scenario where multiple dealers are requesting cars, and the current status of each factory isn't quite so predictable.

Other Uses of Factories

You can also use the factory pattern for more than just modeling real-world factories. For example, consider a word processor in which you want to support documents in different languages so that each document uses a single language. There are many aspects of the word processor in which the choice of document language requires different support: the character set used in the document (whether or not accented characters are needed), the spellchecker, the thesaurus, and the way the document is displayed to name a few. You could use factories to design a clean word processor by writing an abstract `LanguageFactory` superclass and concrete factories for each language of interest, such as `EnglishLanguageFactory` and `FrenchLangugaeFactory`. When the user specifies a language for a document, the program instantiates the appropriate language factory and attaches it to the document. From then on, the program doesn't need to know which language is supported in the document. When it needs a language-specific piece of functionality, it can just ask the `LanguageFactory`. For example, when it needs a spellchecker, it can call the `createSpellchecker()` method on the factory, which will return a spellchecker in the appropriate language.

The Proxy Pattern

The *proxy* pattern is one of several patterns that divorce the abstraction of a class from its underlying representation. A proxy object serves as a stand-in for a real object. Such objects are generally used when using the real object would be time-consuming or impossible.

You may have already used the proxy pattern without formally recognizing it as such. Proxies are very handy in unit testing. Instead of using live stock price data to test a stock prediction tool, you could write a proxy class that mimics the behavior of a stock feed but uses fixed data.

Example: Hiding Network Connectivity Issues

Consider a networked game with a `Player` class that represents a person on the Internet who has joined the game. The `Player` class would include functionality that requires network connectivity, such as an instant messaging feature. In the event that a player's connection becomes slow or unresponsive, the `Player` object representing that person can no longer receive instant messages.

Because you don't want to expose network problems to the user, it may be desirable to have a separate class that hides the networked parts of a `Player`. This `PlayerProxy` object would substitute for the actual `Player` object. Clients of the class would either use the `PlayerProxy` class at all times as a gatekeeper to the real `Player` class, or the system would substitute a `PlayerProxy` when a `Player` became unavailable. During a network failure, the `PlayerProxy` object could still display the player's name and last-known state, and could continue to function when the original `Player` object cannot. Thus, the proxy class hides some undesirable semantics of the underlying `Player` class.

Implementation of a Proxy

The public interface for a `Player` class follows. The `sendInstantMessage()` method requires network connectivity to properly function.

```
class Player
{
    public:
        virtual string getName();

        // Sends an instant message to the player over the network
        // and returns the reply as a string. Network connectivity
        // is required.
        virtual string sendInstantMessage(const string& inMessage) const;
};
```

Proxy classes often evoke the is-a versus has-a debate. You *could* implement `PlayerProxy` as a completely separate class that contains a `Player` object. This design would make most sense if the `PlayerProxy` is always used by the program when it wants to talk to a `Player` object. Alternatively, you could implement `PlayerProxy` as a subclass that overrides functionality that requires network connectivity. This design makes it easy to swap out a `Player` for a `PlayerProxy` when network connectivity ceases. This example uses the latter approach by subclassing `Player`, as shown here:

```
class PlayerProxy : public Player
{
    public:
        virtual string sendInstantMessage(const string& inMessage) const;
};
```

The implementation of the `PlayerProxy`'s `sendInstantMessage()` method simply cuts out the network functionality and returns a string indicating that the player has gone offline.

```
string PlayerProxy::sendInstantMessage(const string& inMessage)
{
    return "The player could not be contacted.";
}
```

Using a Proxy

If a proxy is well written, using it should be no different from using any other object. For the `PlayerProxy` example, the code that uses the proxy could be completely unaware of its existence. The following function, designed to be called when the `Player` has won, could be dealing with an actual `Player` or a `PlayerProxy`. The code is able to handle both cases in the same way because the proxy ensures a valid result.

```
bool informWinner(const Player* inPlayer)
{
    string result;

    result = inPlayer->sendInstantMessage("You have won! Want to play again?");

    if (result == "yes") {
```

```
            cout << inPlayer->getName() << " wants to play again" << endl;
            return true;
    } else {
            // The player said no, or is offline.
            cout << inPlayer->getName() << " does not want to play again" << endl;
            return false;
    }
}
```

The Adapter Pattern

The motivation for changing the abstraction given by a class is not always driven by a desire to hide functionality or protect against performance concerns. Sometimes, the underlying abstraction cannot be changed but it doesn't suit the current design. In this case, you can build an *adapter* or *wrapper* class. The adapter provides the abstraction that the rest of the code uses and serves as the bridge between the desired abstraction and the actual underlying code. You've already seen adapters in use by the STL. Recall that the STL provides container adapters, such as the stack and queue, which are wrappers around other containers like deque and list.

Example: Adapting an XML Library

In Chapter 24, you read about the Xerces XML parsing library. Xerces is a great general-purpose tool — it implements many obscure XML standards and provides much flexibility. However, there are several reasons why you might want a wrapper around Xerces. Your use case might be simple enough that you require only a subset of Xerces' functionality. By writing a wrapper, you can maximize ease of use for the features that are relevant to you. Also, putting a wrapper around Xerces gives you the freedom to switch between different XML libraries. Perhaps you foresee a move to custom XML code down the road, or wish to allow users to write their own XML parsing code. As long as their code supports the same interface as your wrapper, it will work.

Implementation of an Adapter

The first step in writing an adapter is reading and understanding the class or library that you're going to adapt. If you are unfamiliar with Xerces, you should review Chapter 24 before continuing.

The next step is to define the new interface to the underlying functionality. For this example, we will assume that users only need the Xerces features that were discussed in Chapter 24 — the ability to read XML elements, attributes, and text nodes. A single class, ParsedXMLElement, serves as an adapter to Xerces. The client creates a ParsedXMLElement from a file, which represents the root node. All subelements of that element are also represented as ParsedXMLElements. The following class definition shows the public functionality of ParsedXMLElement:

```
// ParsedXMLElement.h

#include <string>
#include <vector>

class ParsedXMLElement
{
```

```
    public:
        ParsedXMLElement(const std::string& inFilename);
        ~ParsedXMLElement();

        std::string getName() const;
        std::string getTextData() const;
        std::string getAttributeValue(const std::string& inKey) const;
        std::vector<ParsedXMLElement*> getSubElements() const;
};
```

Because the adapter will be using Xerces behind the scenes, some additions are needed to this class definition. The `ParsedXMLElement` will be responsible for initializing the Xerces library when the first `ParsedXMLElement` root object is created and terminating the library when the last root object is deleted. In order to implement this functionality, the `ParsedXMLElement` needs to keep a static count of the number of root element objects in existence. Additionally, each `ParsedXMLElement` will contain a pointer to a Xerces `DOMElement`, which is used to actually obtain the parsed data. The `XercesDOMParser` object will need to remain in existence as long as associated `DOMElements` exist. The parser will live in the root object, so a comment warns clients that subelements are invalid once the root element is destroyed. Here is the modified definition of `ParsedXMLElement`:

```
// ParsedXMLElement.h

#include <string>
#include <vector>

#include <xercesc/util/PlatformUtils.hpp>
#include <xercesc/parsers/XercesDOMParser.hpp>
#include <xercesc/dom/DOM.hpp>

XERCES_CPP_NAMESPACE_USE

/**
 * Note: If the root element is deleted, subelements become
 * invalid.
 */
class ParsedXMLElement
{
    public:
        ParsedXMLElement(const std::string& inFilename);
        ~ParsedXMLElement();

        std::string getName() const;
        std::string getTextData() const;
        std::string getAttributeValue(const std::string& inKey) const;
        // The caller is responsible for freeing the ParsedXMLElements
        // pointed to by the elements of the vector.
        std::vector<ParsedXMLElement*> getSubElements() const;

    protected:
        // This constructor is used internally to create subelements.
        ParsedXMLElement(DOMElement* inElement);

        XercesDOMParser* mParser;
        DOMElement*      mElement;
```

```
        static int        sReferences;

    private:
        // Disallow copy construction and op=.
        ParsedXMLElement(const ParsedXMLElement&);
        ParsedXMLElement& operator=(const ParsedXMLElement& rhs);
};
```

The implementation of the wrapper is very similar to the examples in Chapter 24, so we won't go into too much detail here: the code below should speak for itself. The important point is that every public method of `ParsedXMLElement` is really fronting calls to Xerces. We hope you agree that `ParsedXMLElement` provides a friendlier interface to this subset of Xerces functionality:

```cpp
#include "ParsedXMLElement.h"

#include <xercesc/util/XMLString.hpp>

#include <iostream>

XERCES_CPP_NAMESPACE_USE
using namespace std;

// No references by default
int ParsedXMLElement::sReferences = 0;

ParsedXMLElement::ParsedXMLElement(const std::string& inFilename)
{
    if (sReferences == 0) {
        // First element--initialize the library
        XMLPlatformUtils::Initialize();
    }
    sReferences++;

    mParser = new XercesDOMParser();
    mParser->parse(inFilename.c_str());

    DOMNode* node = mParser->getDocument();
    DOMDocument* document = dynamic_cast<DOMDocument*>(node);
    if (document == NULL) {
        cerr << "WARNING: No XML document!" << endl;
        return;
    }

    mElement = dynamic_cast<const DOMElement*>(document->getDocumentElement());
    if (mElement == NULL) {
        cerr << "WARNING: XML Document had no root element!" << endl;
    }
}

ParsedXMLElement::~ParsedXMLElement()
{
    if (mParser != NULL) {
        // This is the root element.
```

```
        delete mParser;

        sReferences--;
        if (sReferences == 0) {
            // Last element destroyed
            XMLPlatformUtils::Terminate();
        }
    }
}

string ParsedXMLElement::getName() const
{
    char* tagName = XMLString::transcode(mElement->getTagName());
    string result(tagName);
    XMLString::release(&tagName);

    return result;
}

string ParsedXMLElement::getTextData() const
{
    // We assume that the first text node we reach is the one we want.
    DOMNodeList* children = mElement->getChildNodes();
    for (int i = 0; i < children->getLength(); i++) {
        DOMText* textNode = dynamic_cast<DOMText*>(children->item(i));
        if (textNode != NULL) {
            char* textData = XMLString::transcode(textNode->getData());
            string result(textData);
            XMLString::release(&textData);
            return result;
        }
    }

    // No text nodes were found.
    return "";
}

string ParsedXMLElement::getAttributeValue(const std::string& inKey) const
{
    XMLCh* key = XMLString::transcode(inKey.c_str());

    const XMLCh* value = mElement->getAttribute(key);
    XMLString::release(&key);

    char* valueString = XMLString::transcode(value);
    string result(valueString);
    XMLString::release(&valueString);

    return result;
}

vector<ParsedXMLElement*> ParsedXMLElement::getSubElements() const
{
```

```
        vector<ParsedXMLElement*> result;

        DOMNodeList* children = mElement->getChildNodes();
        for (int i = 0; i < children->getLength(); i++) {
            DOMElement* elNode = dynamic_cast<DOMElement*>(children->item(i));
            if (elNode != NULL) {
                result.push_back(new ParsedXMLElement(elNode));
            }
        }

        return result;
    }

ParsedXMLElement::ParsedXMLElement(DOMElement* inElement)
{
    mParser = NULL; // No parser for a subelement
    mElement = inElement;
}
```

Using an Adapter

Since adapters exist to provide a more appropriate interface for underlying functionality, their use should be straightforward and specific to the particular case. Given the previous example, the following program outputs selected information about an XML file:

```
int main(int argc, char** argv)
{
    ParsedXMLElement e("test.xml");
    cout << "root name: " << e.getName() << endl;

    vector<ParsedXMLElement*> subelements = e.getSubElements();
    for (vector<ParsedXMLElement*>::iterator it = subelements.begin();
         it != subelements.end(); ++it) {
        cout << "subelement name: " << (*it)->getName() << endl;
        cout << "subelement speaker: " << (*it)->getAttributeValue("speaker")
            << endl;
        cout << "subelement text data: " << (*it)->getTextData() << endl;
    }

    for (vector<ParsedXMLElement*>::iterator it = subelements.begin();
         it != subelements.end(); ++it) {
        delete *it;
    }

    return 0;
}
```

When used with the example file from Chapter 24, the output will be:

```
root name: dialogue
subelement name: sentence
subelement speaker: Marni
subelement text data: Let's go get some ice cream.
subelement name: sentence
subelement speaker: Scott
subelement text data: After I'm done writing this C++ book.
```

The Decorator Pattern

The *decorator* pattern is exactly what it sounds like — a "decoration" on an object. The pattern is used to change the behavior of an object at runtime. Decorators are a lot like subclasses, but their effects can be temporary. For example, if you have a stream of data that you are parsing and you reach data that represents an image, you could temporarily decorate the stream object with an `ImageStream` object. The `ImageStream` constructor would take the stream object as a parameter and would have built-in knowledge of image parsing. Once the image was parsed, you could continue using the original object to parse the remainder of the stream. The `ImageStream` acts as a decorator because it adds new functionality (image parsing) to an existing object (a stream).

Example: Defining Styles in Web Pages

As you may already know, Web pages are written in a simple text-based structure called Hypertext Markup Language (HTML). In HTML, you can apply styles to a text by using style tags, such as `<B>` and `</B>` for bold and `<I>` and `</I>` for italic. The following line of HTML will display the message in bold:

```
<B>A party? For me? Thanks!</B>
```

The following line will display the message in bold italic:

```
<I><B>A party? For me? Thanks!</B></I>
```

Assume that you are writing an HTML editing application. Your users will be able to type in paragraphs of text and apply one or more styles to them. You *could* make each type of paragraph a new subclass, as shown in Figure 26-5, but that design could be cumbersome and would grow exponentially as new styles were added.

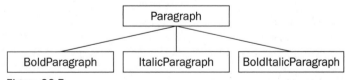

Figure 26-5

The alternative is to consider styled paragraphs not as *types* of paragraphs, but as *decorated* paragraphs. This leads to situations like the one shown in Figure 26-6, where an `ItalicParagraph` operates on a `BoldParagraph`, which in turn operates on a `Paragraph`. The recursive decoration of objects nests the styles in code just as they are nested in HTML.

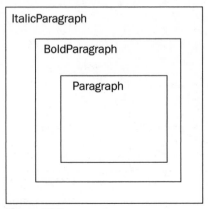

Figure 26-6

Implementation of a Decorator

To decorate the `Paragraph` class with zero or more styles, you will need a hierarchy of styled `Paragraph` classes. Each of the styled `Paragraph` classes will be able to be constructed from an existing `Paragraph`. This way, they can all decorate a `Paragraph` or a styled `Paragraph`. The most convenient way to implement the styled classes is as subclasses of `Paragraph`. Here is the `Paragraph` base class, with inlined method implementations:

```
class Paragraph
{
    public:
        Paragraph(const string& inInitialText) : mText(inInitialText) {}

        virtual string getHTML() const { return mText; }

    protected:
        string mText;
};
```

The `BoldParagraph` class will be a subclass of `Paragraph` so that it can override `getHTML()`. However, vecause we intend to use it as a decorator, its only public noncopy constructor takes a `const` reference to a `Paragraph`. Note that it passes an empty string to the `Paragraph` constructor because `BoldParagraph` doesn't make use of the `mText` data member — its only purpose in subclassing `Paragraph` is to override `getHTML()`.

```
class BoldParagraph : public Paragraph
{
    public:
        BoldParagraph(const Paragraph& inParagraph) :
                Paragraph(""), mWrapped(inParagraph) {}

        virtual string getHTML() const {
            return "<B>" + mWrapped.getHTML() + "</B>";
        }

    protected:
        const Paragraph& mWrapped;
};
```

The `ItalicParagraph` class is almost identical:

```
class ItalicParagraph : public Paragraph
{
    public:
        ItalicParagraph(const Paragraph& inParagraph) :
                Paragraph(""), mWrapped(inParagraph) {}

        virtual string getHTML() const {
            return "<I>" + mWrapped.getHTML() + "</I>";
        }

    protected:
        const Paragraph& mWrapped;
};
```

Again, remember that `BoldParagraph` and `ItalicParagraph` only subclass `Paragraph` so that they can override `getHTML()`. The content of the paragraph comes from the wrapped object, not from the `mText` data member.

Using a Decorator

From the user's point of view, the decorator pattern is appealing because it is very easy to apply, and is transparent once applied. The client doesn't need to know that a decorator has been employed at all. A `BoldParagraph` behaves just like a `Paragraph`.

Here is a quick program that creates and outputs a paragraph, first in bold, then in bold and italic:

```
int main(int argc, char** argv)
{
    Paragraph p("A party? For me? Thanks!");

    // Bold
    cout << BoldParagraph(p).getHTML() << endl;

    // Bold and Italic
    cout << ItalicParagraph(BoldParagraph(p)).getHTML() << endl;
}
```

The output of this program will be:

```
<B>A party? For me? Thanks!</B>
<I><B>A party? For me? Thanks!</B></I>
```

There is an interesting side effect of this implementation that just happens to work correctly for HTML. If you applied the same style twice in a row, the effect would only occur once:

```
cout << BoldParagraph(BoldParagraph(p)) .getHTML() << endl;
```

The result of this line is:

```
<B>A party? For me? Thanks!</B>
```

If you can see the reason why, you've mastered C++! What's happening here is that instead of using the `BoldParagraph` constructor that takes a `const Paragraph` reference, the compiler is using the built-in copy constructor for `BoldParagraph`! In HTML, that's fine — there's no such thing as double-bold. However, other decorators built using a similar framework may need to implement the copy constructor to properly set the reference.

The Chain of Responsibility Pattern

A *chain of responsibility* is used when you want each class in an object-oriented hierarchy to get a crack at performing a particular action. The technique generally employs polymorphism so that the most specific class gets called first and can either handle the call or pass it up to its parent. The parent then makes the same decision — it can handle the call or pass it up to its parent. A chain of responsibility does not necessarily have to follow a class hierarchy, but it typically does.

Chains of responsibility are perhaps most commonly used for event handling. Many modern applications, particularly those with graphical user interfaces, are designed as a series of events and responses. For example, when a user clicks on the *File* menu and selects *Open*, an open event has occurred. When the user clicks the mouse on the drawable area of a paint program, a mouse down event occurs. As the shape is drawn, mouse move events continually occur until the eventual mouse up event. Each operating system has its own way of naming and using these events, but the overall idea is the same. When an event occurs, it is somehow communicated to the program, which takes appropriate action.

As you know, C++ does not have any built-in facilities for graphical programming. It also has no notion of events, event transmission, or event handling. A chain of responsibility is a reasonable approach to event handling because in an object-oriented hierarchy, the processing of events often maps to the class/subclass structure.

Example: Event Handling

Consider a drawing program, which has a hierarchy of `Shape` classes, as in Figure 26-7.

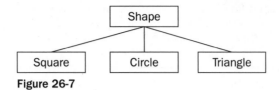

Figure 26-7

The leaf nodes handle certain events. For example, `Square` or `Circle` can receive mouse down events that will select the chosen shape. The parent class handles events that have the same effect regardless of the particular shape. For example, a delete event is handled the same way, regardless of the type of shape being deleted. The ideal algorithm for handling a particular event is to start at the leaf nodes and walk up the hierarchy until the message is handled. In other words, if a mouse down event occurs on a `Square` object, first the `Square` will get a chance to handle the event. If it doesn't recognize the event, the `Shape` class gets a chance. This approach is an example of a chain of responsibility because each subclass may pass the message up to the next class in the chain.

Implementation of a Chain of Responsibility

The code for a chained messaging approach will vary based on how the operating system handles events, but it tends to resemble the following code, which uses integers to represent types of events.

```cpp
void Square::handleMessage(int inMessage)
{
    switch (inMessage) {
        case kMessageMouseDown:
            handleMouseDown();
            break;

        case kMessageInvert:
            handleInvert();
            break;

        default:
            // Message not recognized--chain to superclass
            Shape::handleMessage(inMessage);
    }
}
```

```cpp
void Shape::handleMessage(int inMessage)
{
    switch (inMessage) {
        case kMessageDelete:
            handleDelete();
            break;

        default:
            cerr << "Unrecognized message received: " << inMessage << endl;
            break;
    }
}
```

When the event-handling portion of the program or framework receives a message, it finds the corresponding shape and calls `handleMessage()`. Through polymorphism, the subclass's version of `handleMessage()` is called. This gives the leaf node first crack at handling the message. If it doesn't know how to handle it, it passes it up to its superclass, which gets the next chance. In this example, the final recipient of the message simply prints an error if it is unable to handle the event. You could also throw an exception or have your `handleMessage()` method return a boolean indicating success or failure.

Note that while event chains usually correlate with the class hierarchy, they do not have to. In the preceding example, the `Square` class could have just as easily passed the message to an entirely different object. The chained approach is flexible and has a very appealing structure for object-oriented hierarchies. The downside is that it requires diligence on the part of the programmer. If you forget to chain up to the superclass from a subclass, events will effectively get lost. Worse, if you chain to the wrong class, you could end up in an infinite loop!

Using a Chain of Responsibility

For a chain of responsibility to respond to events, there must be another class that *dispatches* the events to the correct object. Because this task varies so greatly by framework or platform, pseudocode for handling a mouse down event is presented below in lieu of platform-specific C++ code.

```
MouseLocation loc = getClickLocation();

Shape* clickedShape = findShapeAtLocation(loc);

clickedShape->handleMessage(kMessageMouseDown);
```

The Observer Pattern

The other common model for event handling is known as *observer, listener messaging,* or *publish and subscribe.* This is a more prescriptive model that is often less error-prone than message chains. With the publish and subscribe technique, individual objects *register* the events they are able to understand with a central event handling registry. When an event is received, it is transmitted to the list of subscribed objects.

Example: Event Handling

Just as with the earlier chain of responsibility pattern, observers are often used to handle events. The main difference between the two patterns is that the chain of responsibility works best for logical hierarchies where you need to find the correct class to handle the event. Observers work best when events can be handled by multiple objects or are unrelated to a hierarchy.

Implementation of an Observer

The definition of a simple event registry class is shown in the following example. It allows any object that extends the mix-in class `Listener` to subscribe to one or more events. It also contains a method for

the program to call when an event is received, which will dispense the event to all subscribed
`Listeners`.

```
/**
 * Listener.h
 *
 * Mix-in class for objects that are able to respond to events
 */

class Listener
{
    public:
        virtual void handleMessage(int inMessage) const = 0;
};
```

```
/**
 * EventRegistry.h
 *
 * Maintains a directory of Listeners and their corresponding events. Also
 * handles transmission of an event to the appropriate Listener.
 */

#include "Listener.h"
#include <vector>
#include <map>

class EventRegistry
{
    public:
        static void registerListener(int inMessage, const Listener* inListener);

        static void handleMessage(int inMessage);

    protected:
        static std::map<int, std::vector<const Listener*> > sListenerMap;
};
```

The implementation of the `EventRegistry` class follows. When a new `Listener` is registered, it is
added to the vector of `Listener` references stored in the listener map for the given event. When an
event is received, the registry simply retrieves the vector and passes the event to each `Listener`.

```
/**
 * EventRegistry.cpp
 *
 * Implements the EventRegistry class
 */

#include "EventRegistry.h"
#include <iostream>

using namespace std;
```

```
    // Define the static map.
    map<int, vector<const Listener*> > EventRegistry::sListenerMap;

    void EventRegistry::registerListener(int inMessage, const Listener* inListener)
    {
        // Recall from Chapter 21 that indexing into a map adds the element
        // with the specified key if it does not already exist.
        sListenerMap[inMessage].push_back(inListener);
    }

    void EventRegistry::handleMessage(int inMessage)
    {
        // Check to see if the message has *any* listeners.
        if (sListenerMap.find(inMessage) == sListenerMap.end()) return;

        for (int i = 0; i < sListenerMap[inMessage].size(); i++) {
            sListenerMap[inMessage].at(i)->handleMessage(inMessage);
        }
    }
```

Using an Observer

Following is a very simple unit test that demonstrates how to use the *publish and subscribe* technique. The class `TestListener` subscribes to message 0 in its constructor. Subscribing to a message in a constructor is a common pattern for objects that are `Listeners`. The class contains two flags that keep track of whether message 0 was successfully received and whether any unknown messages were received. If message 0 was received and no unknowns were received, the test passes.

```
class TestListener : public Listener
{
    public:
        TestListener();

        void handleMessage(int inMessage);

        bool fMessage0Received;
        bool fUnknownMessageReceived;
};

TestListener::TestListener()
{
    fMessage0Received = false;
    fUnknownMessageReceived = false;

    // Subscribe to event 0.
    EventRegistry::registerListener(0, this);
}

void TestListener::handleMessage(int inMessage)
{
    switch (inMessage) {
        case 0:
            fMessage0Received = true;
```

```
                    break;

            default:
                    fUnknownMessageReceived = true;
                    break;
        }
}

int main(int argc, char** argv)
{
    TestListener tl;

    EventRegistry::handleMessage(0);
    EventRegistry::handleMessage(1);
    EventRegistry::handleMessage(2);

    if (!tl.fMessage0Received) {
        cout << "TEST FAILED: Message 0 was not received" << endl;
    } else if (tl.fUnknownMessageReceived) {
        cout << "TEST FAILED: TestListener received unknown message" << endl;
    } else {
        cout << "TEST PASSED" << endl;
    }
}
```

An actual implementation in your program would vary from the implementation shown based on the services provided by the environment and your individual needs. As you may have noticed, this implementation does not provide a way to unregister a Listener. Unless all objects are guaranteed to stick around forever, they should be unregistered on deletion to avoid bugs. This implementation also allows objects to register twice, which may be undesirable depending on your use case.

Summary

This chapter has given you just a taste of how patterns can help you organize object-oriented concepts into high-level designs. There is a seemingly infinite supply of design patterns cataloged and discussed on the Portland Pattern Repository Wiki at www.c2.com. It's easy to get carried away and spend all your time trying to find the specific pattern that applies to your task. We recommend that you focus on a few patterns that interest you and focus your learning on how patterns are developed, not just the small differences between similar ones. After all, to paraphrase the old saying, "Teach me a design pattern, and I'll code for a day. Teach me how to *create* design patterns, and I'll code for a lifetime."

Design patterns are a terrific way to end your journey through *Professional C++ Programming* because they are a perfect example of how good C++ programmers can become great C++ programmers. By thinking through your designs, experimenting with different approaches in object-oriented programming, and selectively adding new techniques to your coding repertoire, you'll be able to take your C++ skills to the Professional level.

C++ Interviews

Reading this book will surely give your C++ career a kick-start, but employers will want you to prove yourself before they offer the big bucks. Interview methodologies vary from company to company, but many aspects of technical interviews are predictable. A thorough interviewer will want to test your basic coding skills, your debugging skills, your design and style skills, and your problem solving skills. The set of questions you might be asked is quite large. In this appendix, you'll read about some of the different types of questions you may encounter and the best tactics for landing that high-paying C++ programming job you're after.

This appendix iterates through the chapters of the book, discussing the aspects of each chapter that are likely to come up in an interview situation. Each section also includes a discussion of the types of questions that could be designed to test those skills and the best ways to deal with the questions.

Chapter 1: A Crash Course in C++

A technical interview will often include some basic C++ questions to weed out the candidates who put C++ on their resume simply because they've heard of the language. These questions might be asked during a *phone screen*, when a developer or recruiter calls you before bringing you in for an in-person interview. They could also be asked via email or in person. When answering these questions, remember that the interviewer is just trying to establish that you've actually learned and used C++. You generally don't need to get every detail right to earn high marks.

Things to Remember

- ❑ `main()` and its parameters
- ❑ Header file syntax, including the omission of ".h" for standard library headers
- ❑ Basic use of namespaces
- ❑ Language basics, such as loop syntax, the ternary operator, and variables
- ❑ The difference between the stack and the heap
- ❑ Dynamically allocated arrays
- ❑ Use of `const`

Types of Questions

Basic C++ questions will often come in the form of a vocabulary test. The interviewer may ask you to define C++ terms, such as `const` or `static`. He or she may simply be looking for the textbook answer, but you can often score extra points by giving sample usage or extra detail. For example, in addition to saying that one of the uses of `const` is to specify that a reference argument cannot be changed, you can also say that a `const` reference is more efficient than a copy when passing an object into a function or method.

The other form that basic C++ competency questions can take is a short program that you write in front of the interviewer. An interviewer may give you a warm-up question, such as, "Write *Hello, World* in C++." When you get a seemingly simple question like this, make sure that you score all the extra points you can by showing that you are namespace-savvy, you use streams instead of `printf()`, and you know which standard headers to include.

Chapter 2: Designing Professional C++ Programs

Your interviewer will want to make sure that in addition to knowing the C++ language, you are skilled at applying it. You may not be asked a design question explicitly, but good interviewers have a variety of techniques to sneak design into other questions, as you'll see.

Things to Remember

- ❑ Design is subjective — be prepared to defend design decisions you make during the interview.
- ❑ Recall the details of a design you've done in the past prior to the interview in case you are asked for an example.
- ❑ Be prepared to define *abstraction* and give an example.
- ❑ Be prepared to tout the benefits of code reuse.
- ❑ Be prepared to sketch out a design visually, including class hierarchies.

Types of Questions

Design questions are hard for an interviewer to come up with — any program that you could design in an interview setting is probably too simple to demonstrate real-world design skills. Design questions may come in a more fuzzy form, such as, "Tell me the steps in designing a good program" or "Explain the principle of abstraction." They can also be less explicit. When discussing your previous job, the interviewer can say, "Can you explain the design of that project to me?"

Chapter 3: Designing with Objects

Object-oriented design questions are used to weed out C programmers who merely know what a reference is from C++ programmers who actually use the object-oriented features of the language. Interviewers don't take anything for granted; even if you've been using object-oriented languages for years, they may still want to see evidence that you understand the methodology.

Things to Remember

- ❑   The difference between the procedural and object-oriented paradigms
- ❑   The difference between a class and an object
- ❑   Expressing classes in terms of components, properties, and behaviors
- ❑   Is-a and has-a relationships
- ❑   The tradeoffs involved in multiple inheritance

Types of Questions

There are typically two ways to ask object-oriented design questions. You can be asked to define an object-oriented concept, or you can be asked to sketch out an object-oriented hierarchy. The former is pretty straight-forward. Remember that examples might earn you extra credit.

If you're asked to sketch out an OO hierarchy, the interviewer will usually provide a simple application, such as a card game, for which you should design a class hierarchy. Interviewers often ask design questions about games because they are applications with which most people are already familiar. They also help lighten the mood a bit when compared to questions about things like database implementation. The hierarchy you generate will, of course, vary based on the game or application they are asking you to design. Here are some points to consider:

- ❑   The interviewer wants to see your thought process. Think aloud, brainstorm, engage the interviewer in a discussion, and don't be afraid to erase and go in a different direction.

- ❑   The interviewer may assume that you are familiar with the application. If you've never heard of blackjack and you get a question about it, ask the interviewer to clarify or change the question.

❑ Unless the interviewer gives you a specific format to use when describing the hierarchy, we recommend that your class diagram take the form of an inheritance tree with a rough list of methods and data members for each class.

❑ You may have to defend your design or revise it to take added requirements into consideration. Try to gauge whether the interviewer sees actual flaws in your design or whether she just wants to put you on the defensive to see your skills of persuasion.

Chapter 4: Designing with Libraries and Patterns

A potential employer will want to know that you're able to work with code that you didn't write. If you've listed specific libraries on your resume, you should be prepared to answer questions on those. If not, a general understanding of the importance of libraries will probably suffice.

Things to Remember

❑ The tradeoffs between building from scratch and reusing existing code

❑ The basics of big-O notation (or at least remember that $O(n \log n)$ is better than $O(n2)$)

❑ The functionality that is included in the C++ Standard Library

❑ The high-level definition of design patterns

Types of Questions

If the interviewer is asking you about a specific library, he or she will probably focus on the high-level aspects of the library as opposed to technical specifics. For example, one of the authors often asks candidates what the strengths and weaknesses of the STL are from a library design point of view. The best candidates talk about the STL's breadth and standardization as strengths and its steep learning curve as the major drawback.

You may also be asked a design question that initially doesn't sound as if it's related to libraries. For example, the interviewer could ask how you would go about creating an application that downloads MP3 music off the Web and plays it on the local computer. This question isn't explicitly related to libraries, but that's what it's getting at: the question is really asking about process. You should begin by talking about how you would gather requirements and do initial prototypes. Because the question mentions two specific technologies, the interviewer would like to know how you would deal with them. This is where libraries come into play. If you tell the interviewer that you would write your own Web classes and MP3 playing code, you won't fail the test, but you will be challenged to justify the time and expense of reinventing these tools. A better answer would be to say that you would survey existing libraries that perform Web and MP3 functionality to see if one exists that suits the project. You might want to name some technologies that you would start with, such as libcurl for Web retrieval in Linux or the Windows Media library for music playback in Windows.

Chapter 5: Designing for Reuse

Interviewers rarely ask questions about designing reusable code. This omission is unfortunate because having programmers on staff who can only write single-purpose code can be detrimental to a programming organization. Occasionally, you'll find a company that is savvy on code reuse and asks about it in their interviews. Such a question is an indication that it might be a good company to work for!

Things to Remember

- ❑ The principle of abstraction
- ❑ The creation of subsystems and class hierarchies
- ❑ The general rules for good interface design
- ❑ When to use templates and when to use inheritance

Types of Questions

Questions about reuse will almost certainly be about previous projects on which you have worked. For example, if you worked at a company that produced both consumer and professional video-editing applications, the interviewer may ask how code was shared between the two applications. Even if you aren't explicitly asked about code reuse, you might be able to sneak it in. When you're describing some of your past work, tell the interviewer if the modules you wrote were used in other projects. Even when answering apparently straight coding questions, make sure to consider and mention the interfaces involved.

Chapter 6: Maximizing Software Engineering Methods

You should be suspicious if you go through the complete interview process with a company, and the interviewers do *not* ask any process questions — it may mean that they don't have any process or that they don't care about it. Alternatively, they might not want to scare you away with their process behemoth. Most of the time, you'll get a chance to ask questions of the company. We suggest you consider asking about engineering processes as one of your standard questions.

Things to Remember

- ❑ Traditional life-cycle models
- ❑ The tradeoffs of formal models, such as the Rational Unified Process
- ❑ The main principles of Extreme Programming
- ❑ Other processes you have used

Types of Questions

The most common question you'll be asked is to describe the process that your previous employer used. When answering, you should mention what worked well and what failed, but try not to denounce any particular methodology. The methodology you criticize could be the one that your interviewer uses. If you loathe Extreme Programming, keep it to yourself for now!

The authors spend a dizzying amount of their time reading resumes and one trend is clear — everybody is listing Extreme Programming as a skill these days. While there's little hard data on the subject, it certainly seems unlikely that strict adherence to XP is commonplace in programming environments. What we've found is that many organizations have started to look into XP and have adopted some of its principles without subscribing to it in any formal way.

If the interviewer asks you about XP, he or she probably doesn't want you simply to recite the textbook definition — the interviewer knows that you can read the table of contents of an XP book. Instead, pick a few ideas from XP that you find appealing. Explain each to the interviewer along with your thoughts on them. Try to engage the interviewer in a conversation, proceeding in a direction in which he or she is interested based on the cues that person gives.

> **The more time you spend chatting about high-level concepts such as XP, the less time the interviewer will have to grill you on details like template syntax. You can't avoid technical questions entirely, but you can minimize them!**

Chapter 7: Coding with Style

Anybody who's coded in the professional world has had a coworker who codes as if they learned C++ from the back of a cereal box. Nobody wants to work with someone who writes messy code, so interviewers sometimes attempt to determine a candidate's style skills.

Things to Remember

❑ Style matters, even during interview questions that aren't explicitly style related!

❑ Well-written code doesn't need extensive comments.

❑ Comments can be used to convey metainformation.

❑ The principle of decomposition

❑ The principle of refactoring

❑ Naming techniques

Types of Questions

Style questions can come in a few different forms. One of the authors was once asked to write the code for a relatively complex algorithm on a whiteboard. As soon as he wrote the first variable name, the interviewer stopped him and told him he passed. The question wasn't about the algorithm; it was just a red herring to see how well he named his variables. More commonly, you may be asked to submit code that you've written or simply to give your opinions on style.

You need to be careful when a potential employer asks you to submit code. You probably cannot legally submit code that you wrote for a previous employer. You also have to find a piece of code that shows off your skills without requiring too much background knowledge. For example, you wouldn't want to submit your master's thesis on high-speed image rendering to a company that is interviewing you for a database administration position.

If the company gives you a specific program to write, that's a perfect opportunity to show off what you've learned in this book. How many other candidates will include unit tests with their program or extensive comments? Even if the potential employer doesn't specify the program, you should consider writing a small program specifically to submit to the company. Instead of selecting some code you've already written, start from scratch to produce code that is relevant to the job and highlights good style.

Chapters 8 and 9: Classes and Objects

There are no bounds to the types of questions you can be asked about classes and objects. Some interviewers are syntax-fixated and might throw some complicated code at you. Others are less concerned with the implementation and more interested in your design skills.

Things to Remember

- ❑ Basic class definition syntax
- ❑ Access specifiers for methods and data members
- ❑ The use of the "this" pointer
- ❑ Object creation and destruction
- ❑ Cases when the compiler generates a constructor for you
- ❑ Initializer lists
- ❑ Copy constructor and assignment operator
- ❑ The `mutable` keyword
- ❑ Method overloading and default parameters
- ❑ Friend classes

Types of Questions

Questions such as, "What does the keyword mutable mean?" make great phone screening questions. A recruiter may have a list of C++ terms and will move candidates to the next stage of the process based on the number that they get right. You may not know all of the terms that are thrown at you, but keep in mind that other candidates are facing the same questions and it's one of the few metrics available to a recruiter.

The *find the bug* style of question is popular among interviewers and course instructors alike. You will be presented with some nonsense code and asked to point out its flaws. Interviewers struggle to find quantitative ways to analyze candidates, and this is one of the few ways to do it. In general, your approach should be to read each line of code and voice your concerns, brainstorming aloud. The types of bugs can fall into these categories:

❑ **Syntax errors.** These are rare — interviewers know you can find compile-time bugs with a compiler.

❑ **Memory problems.** These include problems such as leaks and double deletion.

❑ **"You wouldn't do that" problems.** This category includes things that are technically correct but have an undesirable outcome.

❑ **Style errors.** Even if the interviewer doesn't count it as a bug, point out poor comments or variable names.

Here's a find the bug problem that demonstrates each of these areas:

```cpp
class Buggy
{
    Buggy(int param);
    ~Buggy();

    double fjord(double inVal);
    int fjord(double inVal);

protected:
    void turtle(int i = 7, int j);
    int param;
    double* graphicDimension;
};

Buggy::Buggy(int param)
{
    param = param;
    graphicDimension = new double;
}

Buggy::~Buggy()
{
}

double Buggy::fjord(double inVal)
{
    return inVal * param;
}

int Buggy::fjord(double inVal)
{
    return (int)fjord(inVal);
}

void Buggy::turtle(int i, int j)
```

```
{
    cout << "i is " << i << ", j is " << j << endl;
}
```

Take a careful look at the code, and then consult the following corrected version for the answers:

```
#include <iostream> // Streams are used in the implementation.

class Buggy
{
public: // These should probably be public or else the class is pretty useless.
    Buggy(int inParam);  // Parameter naming
    ~Buggy();

    Buggy(const Buggy& src);                // Provide copy ctor and operator=
    Buggy& operator=(const Buggy& rhs);  // when the class has dynamically
                                         // allocated memory.

    double fjord(double inVal); // int version won't compile
                                // (overloaded methods differ only
                                // in return type). It's also useless
                                // because it just returns the argument
                                // it's given.

protected:
    void turtle(int i, int j);  // Only last arguments can have defaults.
    int mParam;                 // Data member naming
    double* graphicDimension;
};

Buggy::Buggy(int inParam) : mParam(inParam) // Avoid name ambiguity.
{
    graphicDimension = new double;
}

Buggy::~Buggy()
{
    delete graphicDimension;   // Avoid memory leak.
}

Buggy::Buggy(const Buggy& src)
{
    graphicDimension = new double;
    *graphicDimension = *(src.graphicDimension);
}

Buggy& Buggy::operator=(const Buggy& rhs)
{
    if (this == &rhs) {
        return (*this);
    }
    delete graphicDimension;
    graphicDimension = new double;
```

```
        *graphicDimension = *(rhs.graphicDimension);
        return (*this);
}

double Buggy::fjord(double inVal)
{
        return inVal * mParam;      // Changed data member name
}

void Buggy::turtle(int i, int j)
{
        std::cout << "i is " << i << ", j is " << j << std::endl; // Namespaces
}
```

Chapter 10: Discovering Inheritance Techniques

Questions about inheritance usually come in the same forms as questions about classes. The interviewer might also ask you to implement a class hierarchy to show that you have worked with C++ enough to subclass without looking it up in a book.

Things to Remember

❑   The syntax for subclassing a class

❑   The difference between private and protected from a subclass point of view

❑   Method overriding and virtual

❑   Chained constructors

❑   The ins and outs of upcasting and downcasting

❑   The principle of polymorphism

❑   Pure virtual methods and abstract base classes

❑   Multiple inheritance

❑   Runtime Type Identification (RTTI)

Types of Questions

Many of the pitfalls in inheritance questions are related to getting the details right. When you are writing a base class, don't forget to make the methods virtual. If you mark all methods virtual, be prepared to justify that decision. You should be able to explain what virtual means and how it works. Similarly, don't forget the public keyword before the name of the parent class in the subclass definition (e.g., class Foo : public Bar). It's unlikely that you'll be asked to perform nonpublic inheritance during an interview.

More challenging inheritance questions have to do with the relationship between a superclass and a subclass. Be sure you know how the different access levels work, and the difference between private and protected. Remind yourself of the phenomenon known as *slicing*, when certain types of casts cause a class to lose its subclass information.

Chapter 11: Writing Generic Code with Templates

As one of the most arcane parts of C++, templates are a good way for interviewers to separate the C++ novices from the pros. While most interviewers will forgive you for not remembering some of the advanced template syntax, you should go into the interview knowing the basics.

Things to Remember

- ❑ How to write a basic templatized class
- ❑ The two main disadvantages of templates — ugly syntax and code bloat
- ❑ How to use a templatized class

Types of Questions

Many interview questions start out with a simple problem and gradually add complexity. Often, interviewers have an endless amount of complexity that they are prepared to add and they simply want to see how far you get. For example, an interviewer might begin a problem by asking you to create a class that provides sequential access to a fixed number of `int`s. Next, the class will need to grow to accommodate an arbitrary sized array. Then, it will need arbitrary data types, which is where templates come in. From there, the interviewer could take the problem in a number of directions, asking you to use operator overloading to provide array-like syntax or continuing down the template path by asking you to provide a default type.

Templates are more likely to be employed in the solution of another coding problem than to be asked about explicitly. You should brush up on the basics in case the subject comes up. However, most interviewers understand that the template syntax is difficult, and asking someone to write complex template code in an interview is rather cruel.

Chapter 12: Understanding C++ Quirks and Oddities

Many interviews tend to focus on the more obscure cases because that way experienced C++ programmers can demonstrate that they have conquered the unusual parts of C++. Sometimes interviewers have difficulty coming up with interesting questions and end up asking the most obscure question they can think of.

Things to Remember

❑ References must be bound to a variable when they are declared and the binding cannot be changed.

❑ The advantages of pass-by-reference over pass-by-value

❑ The many uses of `const`

❑ The many uses of `static`

❑ The different types of casts in C++

Types of Questions

Asking a candidate to define `const` and `static` is a classic C++ interview question. Both keywords provide a sliding scale with which an interviewer can assess an answer. For example, a fair candidate will talk about `static` methods and `static` data members. A good candidate will give good examples of `static` methods and `static` data members. A great candidate will also know about `static` linkage and `static` variables in functions.

The edge cases described in this chapter also come in find-the-bug type problems. Be on the lookout for misuse of references. For example, imagine a class that contains a reference as a data member:

```
class Gwenyth
{
    public:
        int& mCaversham;
};
```

Because `mCaversham` is a reference, it needs to be bound to a variable when the class is constructed. To do that, you'll need to use an initializer list. The class could take the variable to be referenced as a parameter to the constructor:

```
class Gwenyth
{
    public:
        Gwenyth(int i);
        int& mCaversham;
};

Gwenyth::Gwenyth(int i) : mCaversham(i)
{
}
```

Chapter 13: Effective Memory Management

Memory-related questions tend to be asked by low-level programmers or C++ programmers who have a background in C. The goal is to determine whether the object-oriented aspects of C++ have distanced you too much from the underlying implementation details. Memory management questions will give you a chance to prove that you know what's really going on.

Things to Remember

❑   Drawing the stack and the heap can help you understand what's going on.

❑   Use new and delete instead of malloc() and free().

❑   Use new[] and delete[] for arrays.

❑   If you have an array of pointers to objects, you still need to allocate memory for each individual pointer and delete the memory — the array allocation syntax doesn't take care of pointers!

❑   In a pinch, you can always say, "Of course in real life, I would run this through valgrind to expose the problem."

Types of Questions

Find-the-bug questions often contain memory issues, such as double-deletion, new/new[] mixup, and memory leaks. When you are tracing through code that makes heavy use of pointers and arrays, you should draw and update the state of memory as you process each line of code. Even if you see the answer right away, it will let the interviewer know that you're able to draw the state of memory.

Another good way to find out if a candidate understands memory is to ask how pointers and arrays differ. At this point, the differences may be so tacit in your mind that the question catches you off-guard for a moment. If that's the case, skim Chapter 13 again for the discussion.

Chapter 14: Demystifying C++ I/O

If you're interviewing for a job writing GUI applications, you probably won't get too many questions about I/O streams because GUI apps tend to use other mechanisms for I/O. However, streams can come up in other problems and, as a standard part of C++, they are fair game as far as the interviewer is concerned.

Things to Remember

❑   The definition of a stream

❑   Basic input and output using streams

❑   The concept of manipulators

❑   Types of streams (console, file, string, etc.)

❑   Error-handling techniques

❑   The importance of internationalization

Types of Questions

I/O may come up in the context of any question. For example, the interviewer could ask you to read in a file containing test scores and put them in a vector. This question tests basic C++ skills, basic STL, and basic I/O. Even if I/O is only a small part of the problem you're working on, be sure to check for errors.

If you don't, you're giving the interviewer an opportunity to say something negative about your otherwise perfect program.

Your interviewer may not ask specifically about internationalization, but you can show your worldwide appeal by using `wchar_t` instead of `char` during the interview. If you do receive a question about your experience with internationalization, be sure to mention the importance of considering worldwide use from the beginning and show that you know about the locale facilities of C++.

Chapter 15: Handling Errors

Managers sometimes shy away from hiring recent graduates or novice programmers for vital (and high-paying) jobs because it is assumed that they don't write production-quality code. You can prove to an interviewer that your code won't keel over randomly by demonstrating your error-handling skills during an interview.

Things to Remember

❏ Catch exceptions as `const` references.

❏ For production code, hierarchies of exceptions are preferable to a few generic ones.

❏ Throw lists in C++ aren't like throw lists in Java!

❏ Smart pointers help avoid memory leaks when exceptions are thrown.

Types of Questions

You're unlikely to get a question directly about exceptions, unless it's something cruelly specific, such as asking you to describe how the stack unwinds. However, interviewers will be on the lookout to see how you report and handle errors.

Of course, not all programmers understand or appreciate exceptions. Some may even have a bias against them for performance reasons. If the interviewer asks you to do something without exceptions, you'll have to revert to traditional `NULL` checks and error codes. That would be a good time to demonstrate your knowledge of `nothrow new`!

Chapter 16: Overloading C++ Operators

It's possible, though somewhat unlikely, that you would have to perform something more difficult than a simple operator overload during an interview. Some interviewers like to have an advanced question on hand that they don't really expect anybody to answer correctly. The intricacies of operator overloading make great nearly impossible questions because few programmers get the syntax right without looking it up. That means it's a great area to review before an interview.

Things to Remember

- ❑ Overloading stream operators, because they are the most commonly overloaded operators, and are conceptually unique

- ❑ What a functor is and how to create one

- ❑ Choosing between a method operator or a global friend function

- ❑ Some operators can be expressed in terms of others (i.e., `operator<=` can be written by negating the result of `operator >`).

Types of Questions

Let's face it — operator overloading questions (other than the simple ones) are cruel. Anybody who is asking such questions knows this and is going to be impressed when you get it right. It's impossible to predict the exact question that you'll get, but the number of operators is finite. As long as you've seen an example of overloading each operator that it makes sense to overload, you'll do fine!

Besides asking you to implement an overloaded operator, you could be asked high-level questions about overloaded operators. A find-the-bug question could contain an operator that is overloaded to do something that is conceptually wrong for the particular operator. In addition to syntax, keep the use cases and theory of operator overloading in mind.

Chapter 17: Writing Efficient C++

Efficiency questions are quite common in interviews because many organizations are facing scalability issues with their code and need programmers who are savvy about performance.

Things to Remember

- ❑ Language level efficiency is important, but it can only go so far. Design-level choices are ultimately more significant.

- ❑ Reference parameters are more efficient because they avoid copying.

- ❑ Object pools can help avoid the overhead of creating and destroying objects.

- ❑ Profiling is vital to determine which operations are really consuming the most running time.

Types of Questions

Often, the interviewer will use his own product as an example to drive efficiency questions. Sometimes the interviewer will describe an older design and some performance-related symptoms he experienced. The candidate is supposed to come up with a new design that alleviates the problem. Unfortunately, there is a major problem with questions like this — what are the odds that you're going to come up with the same solution that the interviewer did when the problem was actually solved? Because the odds are slim, you need to be extra careful to justify your designs. You may not come up with the actual solution, but you can still have an answer that is correct or even better than the company's newer design.

Other types of efficiency questions may ask you to tweak some C++ code for performance or iterate on an algorithm. For example, the interviewer could show you code that contains extraneous copies or inefficient loops.

Chapter 18: Developing Cross-Platform and Cross-Language Applications

Few programmers submit resumes that list only a single language or technology, and few large applications rely on only a single language or technology. Even if you're only interviewing for a C++ position, the interviewer can still ask questions about other languages, especially as they relate to C++.

Things to Remember

❑   The ways in which platforms can differ (architecture, sizes, etc.)

❑   The fine line between programming and scripting

❑   The interactions between C++ and other languages

Types of Questions

The most popular cross-language question is to compare and contrast two different languages. You should avoid saying just positive or just negative things about a particular language, even if you really hate Java. The interviewer wants to know that you are able to see tradeoffs and make decisions based on them.

Cross-platform questions are more likely to be asked while discussing previous work. If your resume indicates that you once wrote C++ applications that ran on a custom hardware platform, you should be prepared to talk about the compiler you used and the challenges of that platform.

Chapter 19: Becoming Adept at Testing

Potential employers value strong testing abilities. Because your resume probably doesn't indicate your testing skills, unless you have explicit QA experience, you might face interview questions about testing.

Things to Remember

❑   The difference between black box and white box testing

❑   The concept of unit testing and writing tests along with code

❑   Techniques for higher-level tests

❑   Testing and QA environments in which you've worked before: what worked and what didn't?

Types of Questions

An interviewer could ask you to write some tests during the interview, but it's unlikely that a program presented during an interview would contain the depth necessary for interesting tests. It's more likely that you will be asked high-level testing questions. Be prepared to describe how testing was done at your last job and what you liked and didn't like about it. After you answer, this is a good question for you to ask the interviewer. Hopefully, it will start a conversation about testing and give you a better idea of the environment at your potential job.

Chapter 20: Conquering Debugging

Engineering organizations look for candidates who are able to debug both their own code as well as code that they've never seen before. Technical interviews often attempt to size up your debugging muscles.

Things to Remember

- ❑ Debugging doesn't start when bugs appear; you should instrument your code ahead of time so you're prepared for the bugs when they arrive

- ❑ Logs and debuggers are your best tools

- ❑ The symptom that a bug exhibits may appear to be unrelated to the actual cause

- ❑ Memory diagrams can be helpful in debugging, especially during an interview

Types of Questions

During an interview, you might be challenged with an obscure debugging problem. Remember that the process is the most important thing, and the interviewer probably knows that. Even if you don't find the bug during the interview, make sure that the interviewer knows what steps you would go through to track it down. If the interviewer hands you a function and tells you that it crashes when run, he or she should award just as many points to a candidate who properly discusses the sequence of steps to find the bug as to a candidate who finds it right away.

Chapters 21, 22, and 23: The Standard Template Library

As you've seen, the STL can be difficult to work with. Few interviewers would expect you to recite the details of STL classes unless you claim to be an STL expert. If you know that the job you're interviewing for makes heavy use of the STL, you might want to write some STL code the day before to refresh your memory. Otherwise, recalling the high-level design of the STL should suffice.

Things to Remember

❑   The different types of containers and their relationships with iterators

❑   Basic usage of `vector`, which is probably the most frequently used STL class

❑   Usage of associative containers, such as `map`

❑   The purpose of STL algorithms and some of the built-in algorithms

❑   The ways in which you can extend the STL (details are most likely unnecessary)

❑   Your own opinions about the STL

Types of Questions

If interviewers are dead set on asking detailed STL questions, there really are no bounds to the types of questions they could ask. If you're feeling uncertain about syntax though, you should state the obvious during the interview — "In real life, of course, I'd look that up in *Professional C++*, but I'm pretty sure it works like this . . ." At least that way the interviewer is reminded that he or she should forgive the details as long as you get the basic idea right.

High-level questions about the STL are often used to gauge how much you've used the STL without making you recall all the details. For example, casual users of the STL are familiar with associative and nonassociative containers. A slightly more advanced user would be able to define an iterator and describe how iterators work with containers. Other high-level questions could ask you about your experience with STL algorithms or whether you've customized the STL.

Chapter 24: Exploring Distributed Objects

Because distributed applications are quite common, you might be asked to design a distributed system or answer questions about a particular distributed technology.

Things to Remember

❑   The reasons why distributed computing is used

❑   The difference between distributed and networked computing

❑   The concepts of serialization and RPC

❑   The details of CORBA or XML if you are claiming competence in these technologies

Types of Questions

Many technical resumes are a sea of acronyms and buzzwords. If you list a technology like XML on your resume, a potential employer has no way of knowing your level of expertise. Unless you specifically say "Basic XML skills" or "XML expert," you can expect questions that are designed to determine where you stand on that continuum. For XML in particular, questions may involve defining terms like *schema* or hands-on exercises such as writing a schema that applies to a given XML document.

Since XML has become such a popular buzzword, one of the authors has started bringing a simple XML document to interviews. The candidate is asked to point out all of the attributes, all of the elements, and all of the text nodes. It puts the candidate on the spot, but effectively proves whether that person has worked with XML or simply understands that it's an HTML-like syntax.

Chapter 25: Incorporating Techniques and Frameworks

Each of the techniques presented in Chapter 25 would make a fine interview question. Rather than repeat what you already read in the chapter, we suggest that you skim back over Chapter 25 prior to an interview to make sure that you are able to understand each of the techniques.

Chapter 26: Applying Design Patterns

Because design patterns are becoming very popular in the professional world (many candidates even list them as skills), it's likely that you'll encounter an interviewer who wants you to explain a pattern, give a use case for a pattern, or implement a pattern.

Things to Remember

❑   The basic idea of a pattern as a reusable object-oriented design concept

❑   The patterns you have read about in this book as well as others that you've used in your work

❑   The fact that there are hundreds of patterns with often-conflicting names, so you and your interviewer may use different words for the same thing

Types of Questions

Answering questions about design patterns is usually a walk in the park, unless the interviewer expects you to know the details of every single pattern known to humankind. Luckily, most programmers who appreciate design patterns will simply want to chat about them with you and get your opinions. After all, looking concepts up in a book or online instead of memorizing them is a good pattern itself!

B

Annotated Bibliography

This appendix contains a list of books and online resources on various C++-related topics that we either consulted while writing this book or recommend for further or background reading.

C++

Beginning C++

- ❑ Harvey M. Deitel and Paul J. Deitel, *C++ How to Program (Fourth Edition)*, Prentice Hall, 2002, ISBN: 0-130-38474-7

Known as simply the "Deitel" book, this text assumes no prior programming experience.

- ❑ Bruce Eckel, *Thinking in C++, Volume 1: Introduction to Standard C++ (Second Edition)*, Prentice Hall, 2000, ISBN: 0-139-79809-9.

An excellent introduction to C++ programming that expects the reader to know C already. Available at no cost online at www.bruceeckel.com.

- ❑ Stanley B. Lippman and Josée Lajoie, *C++ Primer (Third Edition)*, Addison Wesley, 1998, ISBN: 0-201-82470-1.

This book requires no knowledge of C++, but experience with high-level object-oriented languages is assumed.

- ❑ Steve Oualline, *Practical C++ Programming (Second Edition)*, O'Reilly, 2003, ISBN: 0-596-00419-2.

An introductory C++ text that assumes no prior programming experience.

- ❑ Walter Savitch, *Problem Solving with C++: The Object of Programming (Fourth Edition)*, Addison Wesley Longman, 2002, ISBN: 0-321-11347-0.

This book assumes no prior programming experience. It is often used as a textbook in introductory programming courses.

General C++

- ❏ Marshall Cline, *C++ FAQ LITE*, www.parashift.com/c++-faq-lite.

- ❏ Marshall Cline, Greg Lomow, and Mike Giru, *C++ FAQs (Second Edition)*, Addison Wesley, 1998, ISBN: 0-201-30983-1.

This compilation of frequently asked questions from the comp.lang.c++ newsgroup is useful for quickly looking up a specific point about C++. The printed version contains more information than the online version, but the material available online should be sufficient for most professional C++ programmers.

- ❏ Stephen C. Dewhurst, *C++ Gotchas*, Addison Wesley, 2003, ISBN: 0-321-12518-5.

Provides 99 specific tips for C++ programming.

- ❏ Bruce Eckel and Chuck Allison, *Thinking in C++, Volume 2: Practical Programming (Second Edition)*, Prentice Hall, 2003, ISBN: 0-130-35313-2.

The second volume of Eckel's book covers more advanced C++ topics. It's also available at no cost online at www.bruceeckel.com.

- ❏ Ray Lischner, *C++ in a Nutshell*, O'Reilly, 2003, ISBN: 0-596-00298-X.

A C++ reference, covering everything from the basics to more advanced material.

- ❏ Scott Meyers, *Effective C++ (Second Edition): 50 Specific Ways to Improve Your Programs and Designs*, Addison Wesley, 1998, ISBN: 0-201-92488-9.

- ❏ Scott Meyers, *More Effective C++: 35 New Ways to Improve Your Programs and Designs*, Addison Wesley, 1996, ISBN: 0-201-63371-X.

These two books provide excellent tips-and-tricks on commonly misused and misunderstood features of C++.

- ❏ Stephen Prata, *C++ Primer Plus*, Sams Publishing, 2001, ISBN: 0-672-32223-4.

One of the most comprehensive C++ books available.

- ❏ Bjarne Stroustrup, *The C++ Programming Language (Special Third Edition)*, Addison Wesley, 2000, ISBN: 0-201-70073-5.

The "Bible" of C++ books, written by the designer of C++ himself. Every C++ programmer should own a copy of this book, but it can be a bit obscure in places for the C++ novice.

- ❏ *The C++ Standard: Incorporating Technical Corrigendum No. 1*, John Wiley & Sons, 2003, ISBN: 0-470-84674-7.

This book is almost 800 pages of dense standard-eze. It doesn't explain how to use C++, only what the formal rules are. We don't recommend this book unless you really want to understand every detail of C++.

- ❏ Newsgroups at http://groups.google.com, including comp.lang.c++.moderated and comp.std.c++.

The newsgroups contain a lot of useful information if you're willing to wade through the flame wars, insults, and misinformation that appear as well.

❏   *The C++ Resources Network* at `www.cplusplus.com/`.

This Web page isn't as useful as it sounds. As of this writing, the C++ reference section is still under construction.

I/O Streams

❏   Cameron Hughes and Tracey Hughes, *Mastering the Standard C++ Classes: An Essential Reference*, Wiley, 1999, ISBN: 0-471-328-936.

A good book for learning how to write custom `istream` and `ostream` classes.

❏   Cameron Hughes and Tracey Hughes, *Stream Manipulators and Iterators in C++*, Professional Technical Reference, Prentice Hall, `http://phptr.com/articles/article.asp?p=171014&seqNum=2`.

This well-written article by the authors of *Mastering the Standard C++ Classes* takes the mystery out of defining custom `stream` manipulators in C++.

❏   Philip Romanik and Amy Muntz, *Applied C++: Practical Techniques for Building Better Software*, Addison Wesley, 2003, ISBN: 0-321-10894-9.

In addition to a unique blend of software development advice and C++ specifics, this book provides one of the best explanations we've read of locale and Unicode support in C++.

❏   Joel Spolsky, *The Absolute Minimum Every Software Developer Absolutely, Positively Must Know About Unicode and Character Sets (No Excuses!)*, `www.joelonsoftware.com/articles/Unicode.html`.

After reading Joel's treatise on the importance of internationalization, you'll want to check out his other entries on *Joel on Software*.

❏   Unicode, Inc., *Where is my Character?*, `www.unicode.org/standard/where`.

The best resource for finding Unicode characters, charts, and tables.

The C++ Standard Library

❏   Nicolai M. Josuttis, *The C++ Standard Library: A Tutorial and Reference*, Addison Wesley, 1999, ISBN: 0-201-37926-0.

This book covers the entire standard library, including I/O `streams` and `strings` as well as the containers and algorithms. It's an excellent reference.

❏   Scott Meyers, *Effective STL: 50 Specific Ways to Improve Your Use of the Standard Template Library*, Addison Wesley, 2001, 0-201-74962-9.

Meyers wrote this book in the same spirit as his "Effective C++" books. It provides targeted tips for using the STL, but is not a reference or tutorial.

❏   David R. Musser, Gillmer J. Derge, and Atul Saini, *STL Tutorial and Reference Guide (Second Edition)*, Addison Wesley, 2001, ISBN: 0-201-37923-6.

This book is similar to the Josuttis text, but covers only the STL part of the standard library.

C++ *Templates*

- ❏ Herb Sutter, *Sutter's Mill: Befriending Templates*, C/C++ User's Journal, `www.cuj.com/documents/s=8244/cujcexp2101sutter/sutter.htm`.

The best explanation we could find about making function templates friends of classes.

- ❏ David Vandevoorde and Nicolai M. Josuttis, *C++ Templates: The Complete Guide*, Addison Wesley, 2002, ISBN: 0-201-73484-2.

Everything you ever wanted to know (or didn't want to know) about C++ templates. It assumes significant background in general C++.

C

- ❏ Brian W. Kernighan and Dennis M. Ritchie, *The C Programming Language (second edition)*, Prentice Hall, 1998, ISBN: 0-13-110362-8.

"K and R," as this book is known, is an excellent reference on the C language. It's not as useful for learning it the first time.

- ❏ Peter Prinz, Tony Crawford (Translator), Ulla Kirch-Prinz, *C Pocket Reference*, O'Reilly, 2002, ISBN: 0-596-00436-2.

A concise reference to all things C.

- ❏ Eric S. Roberts, *The Art and Science of C: A Library Based Introduction to Computer Science*, Addison Wesley, 1994, ISBN: 0-201-54322-2.
- ❏ Eric S. Roberts, *Programming Abstractions in C: A Second Course in Computer Science*, Addison Wesley, 1997, ISBN: 0-201-54541-1.

These two books provide a great introduction to programming in C with good style. They are often used as textbooks in introductory programming courses.

- ❏ Peter Van Der Linden, *Expert C Programming: Deep C Secrets*, Pearson Education, 1994, ISBN: 0-131-77429-8.

An enlightening and often hysterical look at the C language, its evolution, and its inner workings.

Integrating C++ and Other Languages

- ❏ Ian F. Darwin, *Java Cookbook*, O'Reilly, 2001, ISBN: 0-596-00170-3.

This book provides step-by-step instructions for using JNI to integrate Java with other languages, including C++.

Algorithms and Data Structures

❑ Thomas H. Cormen, Charles E. Leiserson, Ronald L. Rivest, and Clifford Stein, *Introduction to Algorithms (Second Edition)*, The MIT Press, 2001, ISBN: 0-262-03293-7.

This text is one of the most popular introductory algorithms books, covering all the common data structures and algorithms. The authors learned algorithms and data structures as an undergraduate from the first edition of this book.

❑ Donald E. Knuth, *The Art of Computer Programming Volume 1: Fundamental Algorithms (Third Edition)*, Addison Wesley, 1997, ISBN: 0-201-89683-4.

❑ Donald E. Knuth, *The Art of Computer Programming Volume 2: Seminumerical Algorithms (Third Edition)*, Addison Wesley, 1997, ISBN: 0-201-89684-2.

❑ Donald E. Knuth, *The Art of Computer Programming Volume 3: Sorting and Searching (Third Edition)*, Addison Wesley, 1998, ISBN: 0-201-89685-0.

For those of you who enjoy mathematical rigor, there is no better algorithms and data structures text than Knuth's three-volume tome. It is probably inaccessible without undergraduate knowledge of mathematics or theoretical computer science.

❑ Kyle Loudon, *Mastering Algorithms with C*, O'Reilly, 1999, ISBN: 1-565-92453-3.

An approachable reference to data structures and algorithms.

Open-Source Software

❑ The Open Source Initiative at www.opensource.org.

❑ The GNU Operating System — Free Software Foundation at www.gnu.org.

These Web pages for the two main open-source movements explain their philosophies and provide information about obtaining open-source software and contributing to its development.

❑ sourceforge.net at www.sourceforge.net.

This Web site hosts many open-source projects. It's a great resource for finding useful open-source software.

Software-Engineering Methodology

❑ Barry W. Boehm, TRW Defense Systems Group, *A Spiral Model of Software Development and Enhancement*, IEEE Computer, 21(5):61-72, 1988.

This landmark paper described the state of software development at the time and proposed the Spiral Model.

❑ Kent Beck, *Extreme Programming Explained: Embrace Change*, Pearson Education, 1999, ISBN: 0-201-61641-6.

One of several books in a series that promote Extreme Programming as a new approach to software development.

❑ Robert T. Futrell, Donald F. Shafer, and Linda Isabell Shafer, *Quality Software Project Management*, Pearson Education, 2003, ISBN: 0-130-91297-2.

A guidebook for anybody who is responsible for the management of the software development process.

❑ Robert L. Glass, *Facts and Fallacies of Software Engineering*, Pearson Education, 2002, ISBN: 0-321-11742-5.

This book discusses various aspects of the software development process and exposes hidden truisms along the way.

❑ Philippe Kruchten, *Rational Unified Process: An Introduction (Second Edition)*, Addison Wesley, 2000, ISBN: 0-201-70710-1.

Provides an overview of RUP, including its mission and processes.

❑ Edward Yourdon, *Death March (Second Edition)*, Prentice Hall, 2003, ISBN: 0-131-43635-X.

A wonderfully enlightening book about the politics and realities of software development.

❑ Rational Unified Process from IBM, www3.software.ibm.com/ibmdl/pub/software/rational/web/demos/viewlets/rup/runtime/index.html

The IBM Web site contains a wealth of information about RUP, including the interactive presentation at the above URL.

Programming Style

❑ Martin Fowler, Kent Beck, John Brant, William Opdyke, Don Roberts, *Refactoring: Improving the Design of Existing Code*, Addison Wesley, 1999, ISBN: 0-201-48567-2.

This classic book espouses the practice of recognizing and improving bad code.

❑ James Foxall, *Practical Standards for Microsoft Visual Basic .NET*, Microsoft Press, 2002, ISBN: 0-7356-1356-7.

Exhibits the tenets of Microsoft Windows coding style, using Visual Basic

❑ Diomidis Spinellis, *Code Reading: The Open Source Perspective*, Addison Wesley, 2003, ISBN: 0-201-79940-5.

This unique book turns the issue of programming style upside down by challenging the reader to learn to read code properly in order to become a better programmer.

❑ Dimitri van Heesch, *Doxygen*, http://www.stack.nl/~dimitri/doxygen/index.html.

A highly configurable program that generates documentation from source code and comments.

Computer Architecture

❏ David A. Patterson and John L. Hennessy, *Computer Organization & Design: The Hardware/Software Interface (Second Edition)*, Morgan Kaufman, 1997, ISBN: 1-558-60428-6.

❏ John L. Hennessy and David A. Patterson, *Computer Architecture: A Quantitative Approach (Third Edition)*, Morgan Kaufman, 2002, ISBN: 1-558-60596-7.

These two books provide all the information most software engineers ever need to know about computer architecture.

Efficiency

❏ Dov Bulka and David Mayhew, *Efficient C++: Performance Programming Techniques*, Addison Wesley, 1999, ISBN: 0-201-37950-3.

One of the few books to focus exclusively on efficient C++ programming, it covers both language-level and design-level efficiency.

❏ GNU gprof, `www.gnu.org/software/binutils/manual/gprof-2.9.1/gprof.html`.

Information about the gprof profiling tool.

❏ Rational Software from IBM, `www-306.ibm.com/software/rational`.

Rational Quantify is an excellent (but not free) profiling tool.

Testing

❏ Elfriede Dustin, *Effective Software Testing: 50 Specific Ways to Improve Your Testing*, Addison Wesley, 2002, ISBN: 0-201-79429-2.

While this book is aimed at quality assurance professionals, any software engineer will benefit from its discussion of the software-testing process.

Debugging

❏ The Gnu DeBugger (GDB), at `www.gnu.org/software/gdb/gdb.html`.

GDB is an excellent symbolic debugger.

❏ Rational Software from IBM, `www-306.ibm.com/software/rational`.

Rational Purify is an excellent (but not free) memory error–debugging tool.

❏ Valgrind, at `http://valgrind.kde.org`.

An open-source memory-debugging tool for Linux.

Distributed Objects

- ❏ Jim Farley, *Java Distributed Computing*, O'Reilly, 1998, ISBN: 1-56592-206-9.

Provides a Java-centric view of distributed computing technologies.

- ❏ Ron Hipschman, *How SETI@home Works*, `http://setiathome.ssl.berkeley.edu/about_seti/about_seti_at_home_1.html`.

Interesting background on the SETI@home project, which uses distributed computing to analyze data from space.

- ❏ Sassafras Software, *General KeyServer Questions*, `http://www.sassafras.com/faq/general.html`

Information about KeyServer, an application that uses distributed computing to control software licenses.

CORBA

- ❏ The Object Management Group's CORBA site at `http://www.corba.org`

CORBA is a "product" of the Object Management Group (OMG). This Web site contains basic background information and links to the actual standards involved.

- ❏ Michi Henning and Steve Vinoski, *Advanced CORBA Programming with* C++, Addison Wesley, 1999, ISBN: 0-201-379270-9.

There are a lot more books out there on CORBA with Java than with C++. This book focuses on C++, and, despite the title, is accessible to a CORBA beginner.

XML and SOAP

- ❏ Ethan Cerami, *Web Services Essentials*, O'Reilly, 2002, ISBN: 0-596-00224-6.

This book explains the emerging concept of Web services and the use of SOAP for distributed computing. Examples are provided in Java.

- ❏ Erik T. Ray, *Learning XML (Second Edition)*, O'Reilly, 2003, ISBN: 0-596-00420-6.

The de-facto XML reference. Includes discussions of associated technologies like XML schema, XPath, and XHTML.

- ❏ James Snell, Doug Tidwell, Pavel Kulchenko, *Programming Web Services with SOAP*, O'Reilly, 2001, ISBN: 0-596-00095-2.

This book discusses SOAP and related technologies, such as UDDI and WSDL. Examples are provided in Java, Perl, C#, and Visual Basic.

- ❏ Eric van der Vlist, *XML Schema*, O'Reilly, 2002, ISBN: 0-596-00252-1.

This book tackles the difficult topic of XML Schema and discusses the nuances of the language.

- ❏ Altova Software xmlspy, `www.xmlspy.com`.

Information about the xmlspy software package from Altova Software.

Design Patterns

- ❏ Andrei Alexandrescu, *Modern C++ Design: Generic Programming and Design Patterns Applied*, Addison Wesley, 2001, ISBN: 0-201-70431-5.

Offers an approach to C++ programming employing highly reusable code and patterns.

- ❏ Cunningham and Cunningham, *The Portland Pattern Repository*, www.c2.com/cgi/wiki?WelcomeVisitors.

You could spend all day browsing through this community-edited Web site about design patterns.

- ❏ Erich Gamma, Richard Helm, Ralph Johnson, and John Vlissides, *Design Patterns: Elements of Reusable Object-Oriented Software*, Addison Wesley, 1995, ISBN: 0-201-63361-2.

Called the "Gang of Four" book (because of its four authors), this text is the seminal work in design patterns.

Index

P